Lissack and Horlick
on Bribery

Lissack and Horlick on Bribery

Richard Lissack
QC of the Outer Temple, Barrister and

Fiona Horlick
of the Outer Temple, Barrister

Members of the LexisNexis Group worldwide

United Kingdom	LexisNexis, a Division of Reed Elsevier (UK) Ltd, Halsbury House, 35 Chancery Lane, London WC2A 1EL, and London House, 20–22 East London Street, Edinburgh EH7 4BQ
Australia	LexisNexis Butterworths, Chatswood, New South Wales
Austria	LexisNexis Verlag ARD Orac GmbH & Co KG, Vienna
Benelux	LexisNexis Benelux, Amsterdam
Canada	LexisNexis Canada, Markham, Ontario
China	LexisNexis China, Beijing and Shanghai
France	LexisNexis SA, Paris
Germany	LexisNexis Deutschland GmbH, Munster
Hong Kong	LexisNexis Hong Kong, Hong Kong
India	LexisNexis India, New Delhi
Italy	Giuffrè Editore, Milan
Japan	LexisNexis Japan, Tokyo
Malaysia	Malayan Law Journal Sdn Bhd, Kuala Lumpur
New Zealand	LexisNexis NZ Ltd, Wellington
Poland	Wydawnictwo Prawnicze LexisNexis Sp, Warsaw
Singapore	LexisNexis Singapore, Singapore
South Africa	LexisNexis Butterworths, Durban
USA	LexisNexis, Dayton, Ohio

© Reed Elsevier (UK) Ltd 2011
Published by LexisNexis

ISBN 978-1-4057-6457-5

9 781405 764575

ISBN 13: 9781405764575
Printed and bound in Great Britain by CPI William Clowes Limited, Beccles, Suffolk NR34 7TL
Visit LexisNexis at www.lexisnexis.co.uk

Preface

The Bribery Act 2010 marks a step change in the UK's approach to bribery and corruption. The aim of this book is to provide a complete guide to the Act in a practical and accessible way.

Aspects of the Act are highly controversial. Whilst much of the previous law relating to individual culpability derived from statutes of some antiquity, and the common law developments along side, remain relevant, the Act changes forever the legal landscape in other respects. The concept of corporate liability for both the primary offences of bribery and the secondary offence created by section 7 is entirely new. The single statutory corporate defence of having adequate procedures in place is again fresh in formulation and application. That it is a burden placed on the defence to discharge may in due course raise again the interaction between the reverse burden of proof in a criminal statute and fair trail rights. Furthermore, the introduction of the concept of fixing senior officers of corporations with criminal liability for its bribery through the portal of consent or connivance is entirely novel in this area of law, borrowing from principles well-established in other areas of regulatory crime. The reach of the statute is novel too: it applies not just to commercial entities—it goes far wider than that. More extensive still is its jurisdictional reach, which appears to be worldwide and certainly makes this Act a long-arm statute that stretches far beyond the US Foreign Corrupt Practices Act, for example.

Covering all aspects of the statute, this book embraces international comparative standards, compares our law with that of the United States—helpful we hope to the many organisations whose activities may attract the attention of the authorities in both countries. It covers sport, specific high risk areas of commerce, as well as viewing the Act through the prism of employment law rights and responsibilities too. Its analysis of the adequate procedures measures should provide a very useful working guide to proportionate compliance.

We hope that this book provides to practitioners and others alike a useful guide to the law as it now is and how it should be complied with.

The authors are a distinguished team of practitioners in the UK and the US with experience and authority in their chosen subjects. Our colleagues from Outer Temple Chambers have a collective breadth of proven expertise, which they have brought to bear very effectively on this book. Jonathan Cotton from Slaughter and May brought a particular perspective to Chapter 6 which is both illuminating, thoughtful and practical, and the work of the distinguished team of FCPA practitioners from Hughes Hubbard Reed LLP provides an excellent synthesis of the Bribery Act's closest cousin. Many thanks to them for their excellent work.

We would all like to thank the team at LexisNexis for inviting us to write this book, and for their expertise in editing and publishing it. Special thanks are due to our editor, without whom the book would never have been completed.

The law stated is correct as at the date of publication.

The book is dedicated to Holly, Lucy and Emily Lissack and to Alexander, Jack and Hugo Horlick.

Richard Lissack QC

Fiona Horlick

Outer Temple Chambers, London

May 2011

Contributors

Chapter 1
Robert Rhodes QC and
Robert Dickason
Outer Temple Chambers

Chapter 2
Fiona Horlick
Outer Temple Chambers

Chapter 3
Brendan Finucane QC and
Anthony Haycroft
Outer Temple Chambers

Chapter 4
Robert-Jan Temmink and
Kate Edwards
Outer Temple Chambers

Chapter 5
Fiona Horlick
Outer Temple Chambers

Chapter 6
Jonathan Cotton
Partner, Slaughter and May and
Richard Lissack QC
Outer Temple Chambers

Chapter 7
Kevin T Abikoff,
Edward JM Little and
John F Wood,
Partners at Hughes Hubbard and Reed, New York

Chapter 8
Michael Bowes QC,
Eleanor Davison and
Nicholas Medcroft
Outer Temple Chambers

Chapter 9
Nicholas Medcroft and
Clare Baker
Outer Temple Chambers

Chapter 10
Andrew Short QC,
Keith Bryant,
Robert-Jan Temmink,
James Leonard and
Michael Uberoi
Outer Temple Chambers

Contents

References are to paragraph numbers.

Contents

Contents

Contents

7 The international perspective: lessons from US authorities' enforcement of the Foreign Corrupt Practices Act

Contents

Table of Statutes

References in **bold** type indicate that the section of the Act is set out in part or in full.

Table of Statutory Instruments

Paragraph references printed in **bold** type indicate where the Statutory Instrument is set out in part or in full.

Table of Cases

Table of Cases

D

E

F

G

Table of Cases

Table of Cases

S

Table of Cases

W

Chapter 1

HISTORY AND CONTEXT

A INTRODUCTION

1.1 Corruption is sometimes excused as a necessary way of doing business ('everyone is doing it') or obtaining political favours. That is a misconception. At conferences held in Valletta in 1994 and Prague in 1997, European Ministers of Justice pointed out that corruption represents a major threat to the rule of law, democracy, human rights, fairness and social justice. It hinders economic development and endangers the moral foundations of society.

Corruption has extensive links with organised crime. Notorious examples of corruption in Third World countries have deprived starving people of money and supplies sent to them, the benefit going mainly to dishonest politicians.

1.2 Public concern in Europe about corruption resulted in the Criminal Law Convention on Corruption of January 1999, closely followed by the Civil Law Convention on Corruption of November 1999.

In the UK, the widespread concern about the necessity to reduce, if not eliminate, corruption has led eventually to the Bribery Act 2010[1], which comes into force in April 2011 and is expected to revolutionise UK law and practice regarding corruption.

[1] See para **1.83** ff.

B THE DEVELOPMENT OF THE LAW ON CORRUPTION IN ENGLAND AND WALES

1.3 Corruption is a protean beast. It can take innumerable forms and pervade all walks of life at all levels. It is not easy to identify, even if one is looking for it. The many guises in which corrupt conduct may be clothed go some way to explaining why a general offence of 'corruption' would inevitably be either too narrow to catch all its forms or too wide to retain any coherent sense or meaning. It is therefore not surprising that anti-corruption laws in England and Wales have developed over the centuries in a patchwork way, with specific offences and provisions targeting specific manifestations of corruption.

Corruption at common law

1.4 The best known corruption offence at common law was bribery. *Russell on Crime*[1] provides the following general statement of the offence:

'[B]ribery is the receiving or offering [of] any undue reward by or to any person whatsoever, in a public office, in order to influence his behaviour in office, and incline him to act contrary to the known rules of honesty and integrity'.

[1]   12th edn, 1964.

1.5 There is a debate as to whether bribery at common law was to be regarded as a single offence or a collection of discrete bribery offences distinguished by the office or function involved. Historically, misdemeanours against the common law in the form of bribery were charged in a variety of situations. The common law offence caught bribery of privy councillors[1], of justices[2], of corporators[3] and of coroners[4]. It also covered bribery of jurors[5], despite the existence of the specific common law offence of embracery, considered at para **1.9**; and the sale and purchase of public offices[6], despite the Sales of Offices Acts dating back to 1551.

[1]   *R v Vaughan* (1769) 4 Burr 2494.
[2]   *R v Gurney* (1867) 31 JP 584.
[3]   *R v Plympton* (1724) 2 Ld Raym 1377.
[4]   *R v Harrison* (1800) 1 East PC 382.
[5]   *R v Young* (1801) 2 East 14, 16.
[6]   *R v Pollman* (1809) 2 Camp 229.

1.6 A telling example of the breadth of the common law offence came in the case of *R v Beale*[1], in which the clerk of an officer in charge of French prisoners held captive at Porchester Castle took bribes to secure their release out of turn. This was held to have constituted a misdemeanour against the common law. It was observed by Lawrence J in the later case of *R v Whitaker*[2] that this was so even though the other prisoners injured as a result of the bribery were not British subjects: '[O]nly of its magnanimity our common law threw its protection round them and treated them as though they were'. It is clear from this that the courts were willing to adopt a broad approach which would catch the kinds of opprobrious conduct the offence was there to deter.

[1]   (1798) 1 East 183.
[2]   [1914] 3 KB 1283 at 1298, 10 Cr App Rep 245.

1.7 In *R v Whitaker*, the Court of Appeal was called upon to determine precisely who should be counted as a 'public officer' for the purposes of common law bribery. The defendant colonel had been indicted for taking bribes from a catering company with an interest in providing services to the army. It was argued on his behalf that he could not properly be convicted because the common law offence was restricted to bribery of those in judicial and ministerial offices. The Court of Appeal was not persuaded. It held (at 1296) that a public officer was 'an officer who discharges any duty in the discharge of which the public are interested, more clearly so if he is paid out of a fund provided by the public'. In other words, every officer who was not a judicial officer was a ministerial officer. That definition was wide enough to include those who are discharging ad hoc public duties, dealing with voters at elections, whether parliamentary[1] or local government[2].

[1]   *R v Pitt and Mead* (1762) 3 Burr 1335.
[2]   *R v Lancaster and Worrall* (1890) 16 Cox CC 737.

1.8 The breadth of the common law offence was again apparent from its mens rea element, namely an intention to incline a public officer to act 'contrary to the known rules of honesty and integrity'. As long as the briber's intention had been to produce any effect at all on the officer's decision, de minimis or not, that would be enough (*Gurney*, above).

1.9 Corruption of course goes far beyond bribery, and the common law developed other anti-corruption offences to tackle other forms of corrupt behaviour. The specific criminality of jury tampering was caught by the offence of embracery, which *Russell on Crime* records as comprising:

> '[a]ny attempt whatsoever to corrupt or influence or instruct a jury . . . or in any way to incline them to be more favourable to the one side than to the other, by money, promises, letters, threats, or persuasions, except only by the strength of the evidence and the arguments of counsel in open court . . . '.

1.10 This particular offence was overtaken by other arms of the common law. It was apparent by the mid-twentieth century that charges of embracery were few and far between. When the Court of Appeal came to hear *R v Owen*[1], in which the defendant had approached a juror over the short adjournment and attempted to persuade her of the guilt of the accused, Lawton LJ described the embracery charge as very rare and commented that, in modern times, the conduct in question was much more likely to be charged as contempt of court or, if multiple persons were involved, a conspiracy to pervert the course of justice. This observation is supported by *A-G v Judd*[2], in which a recently convicted defendant who had asked a juror to write to the judge to say that she was mistaken about his guilt found himself in contempt. Nevertheless, regardless of their individual prosecutorial uses, the trio of embracery, contempt of court and conspiracy to pervert did between them make an effective means of remedying corruption in the courtroom.

[1]   [1976] 3 All ER 239, [1976] 1 WLR 840 at 841.
[2]   [1995] COD 15, DC.

1.11 Other spheres of public life particularly vulnerable to corruption could also call upon the common law. In terms of prejudicing elections, the matters of treating, undue influence and personation were corrupt electoral practices, albeit superseded by the provisions of the Representation of the People Act 1983. A more generalised offence capable of catching corrupt behaviour is that of misconduct in public office, which continues to cause difficulties of definition (see most recently *A-G's Reference (No 3 of 2004)*[1] and *R v W*[2]) but remains very much in use where the impropriety amounts to wilful misconduct. Mention should also be made of extortion, which addressed its own particular form of corruption until statute intervened in the form of the Theft Act 1968; and of conspiracy to defraud, although guidance from the Attorney-General following the Fraud Act 2006 now greatly restricts the circumstances in which it may be charged[3]. It may be a reflection of the efficacy of the common law offences that it was not until the second half of the nineteenth century, with its boom in commerce and associated corruption, that Parliament felt the need to introduce specific anti-corruption provisions to supplement them[4].

[1]   [2004] EWCA Crim 868, [2005] QB 73.
[2]   [2010] EWCA Crim 372, [2010] 3 WLR 165.

Corruption under statute

1.12 The dramatic increase in trade and industry in the Victorian era paved the way for corruption on a grander scale. One legal writer observed that[1]:

> 'As competition grew keener, business was sought for by devious and crooked ways . . . in course of time, bribes became so usual an accompaniment of certain professions and trades as almost to partake of a custom. *Così fan tutti* (so do they all) was not an uncommon defence'.

1 Albert Crew, *Secret Commissions and Bribes: the Prevention of Corruption Act 1906*, p 57.

1.13 As honest tradesmen increasingly found themselves being pushed out of business by the corrupt tendencies of their competitors, public disquiet grew. *The Times* began to report more and more instances of bribery and corruption. In *Coe v Southern*[1], a theatre stage manager was shown to have been receiving half the fees paid by actors to agents for securing engagements. The courts had little sympathy for corrupt commercial practices. In 1877, Sir George Jessel MR tried an action brought by a firm of merchants complaining that their shipping agent in Lancashire had been routinely issuing two invoices for each transaction[2]. Counsel for the shipping agent submitted that he had 'a mass of evidence . . . There are a large number of most respectable people in court to give evidence in proof that the practice is universal'. The riposte from the Master of the Rolls was immediate: 'You can send those respectable people home; they have come to prove an iniquitous practice, and the sooner they leave the court the better'.

1 (1876) Times, December.
2 Albert Crew, *Secret Commissions and Bribes: the Prevention of Corruption Act 1906*, p 58.

1.14 The defendants in *Oetzmann v Long*[1] received a similar reception in the High Court. The plaintiffs had sought damages on the basis that the defendants, who procured contracts on their behalf for the supply of ivory, had been bribed to procure contracts in excess of market prices. Lord Russell CJ called for statutory intervention:

> 'The business of corrupt bargains was a malignant canker; it was affecting dishonesty in all or in many details of the relations of life and was not confined to commercial relations. It was dishonest to fair dealing; it was dishonest to the fair employer; it broke down that principle of morality which ought to be preserved among men who desire to cultivate and deserve honesty. The legislature had made it a crime to make corrupt bargains with persons holding public positions—surveyors, architects, clerks of public bodies and the like, and if the evil which constantly cropped up in courts of justice continued the legislature must attempt the task of cutting out this canker and so far as the matter rested with juries, they must not flinch from their duty'.

1 (1896) Draper's Record, 11 July.

1.15 The dicta of the Lord Chief Justice were brought to the attention of the Attorney-General, Sir Richard Webster, but his view remained that the law as it stood was 'sufficiently strong to prevent and, if necessary, punish' the guilty parties[1]. In terms of legislation, the main anti-corruption statute at the time was the Public Bodies Corrupt Practices Act 1889. The Act was passed in direct response to revelations of malpractice within the Metropolitan Board of Works, the local government body for London. The result of the Act being reactive legislation was that it was specifically restricted to bribery of employees within local government and select other public bodies. It was not until the Prevention of Corruption Act 1916 that the definition of public body within the 1889 Act was extended to 'local and public authorities of all descriptions' (except the Crown or government departments). The limited ambit of the 1889 Act meant that it could do nothing to address the rapidly expanding influence of corruption in the private sector.

[1]   43 Official Report (4th series) cols 1267–8, 31 July 1896.

1.16 Public unrest and reports of corruption continued throughout the 1890s, and eventually led to the appointment of the Special Committee of Secret Commissions of the London Chamber of Commerce. The Committee reported in 1899 as follows:

> 'Your Committee conclude from the evidence before them that secret commissions in various forms are prevalent in almost all trades and professions to a great extent, and that in some trades the practice has increased, and is increasing, and they are of the opinion that the practice is producing a great evil, alike to the morals of the commercial community and to the profits of honest traders'.

1.17 Crediting the Committee's work, Lord Russell introduced a Secret Commissions Bill in 1899 which was intended, as stated in the memorandum to the Bill, 'to check, by making them criminal, a large number of inequitable and illegal secret payments, all of which are dishonest, and tend to stifle confidence between man and man and to discourage honest trade and enterprise'. The Bill had been drafted in conjunction with Sir Edward Fry, a former Lord Justice of Appeal and great anti-corruption advocate, but its passage was protracted. Lord Russell's death in August 1900 meant waiting for Lord Alverstone, the then Lord Chief Justice, to reintroduce the Bill in 1901. Much debate ensued, focusing on the (now familiar) issues of the Attorney-General's consent to prosecution and use of the nebulous adverb 'corruptly'. The Commons rejected the Bill twice before it received Royal Assent as the Prevention of Corruption Act 1906 and finally came into force on 1 January 1907.

1.18 Notwithstanding its delayed entry onto the statute books, the Prevention of Corruption Act 1906 soon became an effective prosecutorial tool. By 1913, it was reported that 'prosecutions under the Act have been numerous and have generally resulted in conviction and drastic sentences or heavy penalties'[1]. The mercantile community of its own volition established the Secret Commissions and Bribery Prevention League for the chief purpose of ensuring that the 1906 Act was effectively enforced. Perhaps it was the enthusiasm of the honest trader—and juryman—for this particular piece of legislation that contributed to the substantial number of convictions. Only ten months after it had come into force, at the Gloucester Diocesan Conference on 12 October 1907, Kennedy LJ was praising the work of the 1906 Act:

> '[Corruption] is obviously a dangerous and seductive form of immorality: it is difficult to detect, for it is in the interest alike of the giver and the receiver of the corrupt gift to keep the thing secret; its ugliness can easily be disguised under the mask of generosity or gratitude; and it had become at the time of the passing of this Act so notoriously common practice that I verily believe that not infrequently both the guilty parties had persuaded themselves, or almost persuaded themselves, that they were not doing anything which was really deserving of serious reproach.'

1   Albert Crew, *Secret Commissions and Bribes: the Prevention of Corruption Act 1906*, p 100.

1.19 One might have thought as a result of the apparent success of the Prevention of Corruption Act 1906 that the problems of domestic corruption would improve. Indeed, they may well have done, but the public scandals that would soon erupt across the press gave the opposite impression. The 'Marconi Scandal 1911–1913' is the foremost example. Several senior government officials—including the future Prime Minister, David Lloyd George—purchased shares in American Marconi before they went on sale to the public. They did so in the knowledge that the British government had just signed a lucrative contract with Marconi, which resulted in a predictable doubling of share value. Nevertheless, the first Nolan Report (referred to at para **1.25**) observed at p 104 that, although the ministers at first attempted to conceal what they had done, 'they suffered no adverse political consequences (apart from embarrassment)'.

1.20 The Marconi Scandal was not the only cause for concern in the wartime era. There were considerable doubts and questions over the awarding of contracts by the War Office, and regarding the sale of honours by the coalition government to support dwindling party funds. Ministers repeatedly denied in Parliament that honours had been sold, but the falsity of their statements was stark. The King himself, George V, was outraged, describing the offer of a peerage to a businessman recently convicted of fraud as 'little less than an insult to the Crown and the House of Lords'. Only following a report by a Royal Commission set up in 1922 to investigate the honours system was the Honours (Prevention of Abuses) Act 1925 passed, requiring the vetting of political candidates for honours by three non-governmental Privy Councillors.

1.21 In the interim, the Prevention of Corruption Act 1916 was enacted. Its primary purpose was 'to allow prosecution for an offence under the Prevention of Corruption Act, 1906, to be instituted without the necessity of first obtaining the consent in England of the Attorney-General or Solicitor-General . . . '. It was implemented as an emergency measure following the above-mentioned contracts scandals involving the War Office. That is the context in which it amended the 1889 and 1906 Acts to expand the scope of public sector criminal liability. The most profound change wrought by the 1916 Act was the introduction of the presumption of corruption in cases where payments were made to employees of public bodies responsible for the awarding of contracts.

1.22 The clamour of public scandal lessened over the decades that followed. The only significant outcry came after the Second World War in the form of the Belcher scandal. John Belcher, a junior Board of Trade Minister, was found by a Tribunal chaired by Mr Justice Lysnkey to have accepted gifts in exchange for 'improper official favours'. Mr Belcher wasted no time in submitting his resignation. The relative quiet, however, was not to last much longer. By the 1970s, the infamous 'Poulson Affair' had exploded.

1.23 John Poulson was an extraordinarily successful architect who reached the pinnacle of his career in the 1960s. He is said to have owned the largest architectural firm in Europe, and many of his projects related to local authority building of various types. In 1961, he met T Dan Smith, leader of the Labour majority and chairman of the planning and housing committees on Newcastle City Council. During the 1960s, Smith was responsible for the appointment of councillors on various local authorities as consultants who were expected to exercise their influence in Poulson's favour. Ultimately, Poulson's empire collapsed and he was forced to file for bankruptcy in 1972, in light of which his corrupt scheme was exposed and investigated by the Fraud Squad. A large number of civil servants across diverse government departments were discovered to have been involved. The Home Secretary, Mr Maudling, resigned as a result of the affair. Poulson was eventually sentenced to seven years' imprisonment.

1.24 To calm public unrest while the Poulson investigation was ongoing, the Prime Minister, Mr Heath, appointed Lord Redcliffe-Maud to examine potential conflicts of interest within local government. The Redcliffe-Maud Committee reported in 1974 and recommended that the presumption of corruption under the Prevention of Corruption Act 1916 should be expanded beyond contract cases to other exercises of discretion, such as planning and housing, and beyond local authority employees to elected members. It also recommended the disqualification of those convicted of corruption from standing for election to a public body. Disqualification would be for five years for a first offence and life for a second. The Committee also produced in draft form a National Code of Local Government Conduct, which went on to form the basis of the now familiar codes of conduct to be found in all sorts of employment, public and private.

1.25 In the event, the recommendations of the Redcliffe-Maud Committee were not acted upon. This was in no small part due to the imminent publication of the Report of the Royal Commission on Standards of Conduct in Public Life, 1974–1976, known as the Salmon Report. By the time of the Salmon Report, the details of the Poulson Affair had been exposed, and Lord Salmon stated expressly that he hoped the recommendations of his Report would 'make it much more difficult for anything resembling the Poulson affair to occur in the future'. The Salmon Commission, although restricted in its terms of reference to the public sector, conducted a careful and thorough analysis of the Prevention of Corruption Acts 1889 to 1916. It highlighted inconsistencies and potential areas of exploitation, and sought to ensure protection for 'whistleblowers'. However, the Salmon Report, along with its Redcliffe-Maud predecessor, was destined to go no further than a shelf in Westminster. No discussion was had in the Commons; it received an ambivalent response in the Lords; and no further attention was paid to standards in public life until the first report of the Committee of Standards in Public Life, chaired by Lord Nolan ('the Nolan Committee'), in May 1995. That is not to say that no action had been taken over the 1960s and 1970s to tackle corruption in some ways: one need only look at the statute book. But such action as had been taken was restricted largely to regulatory control[1].

[1]   The following Acts all contained prohibitions against corrupt conduct within their particular
      spheres: Licensing Act 1964, s 178; Criminal Law Act 1967, s 5; Local Government Act 1972,
      s 117(2); Customs and Excise Management Act 1979, s 15 (abolished by the Commissioners
      for Revenue and Customs Act 2005, s 52(1)(a)(ii), leaving such instances to be governed by the
      general law on corruption).

1.26 Lord Nolan's remit was much wider than that which had been afforded
to Lords Redcliffe-Maud and Salmon. His terms of reference required him to
look again at corruption 'to examine current concerns about standards of
conduct of all holders of public office'. The Nolan Committee went on to
produce no fewer than seven Reports addressing different areas of public life.
The conclusion of its first Report, and most important for the development of
the law on corruption, was that:

> 'while it was not possible to say conclusively that standards of behaviour in public
> life had declined, it was the case that conduct in public life was more rigorously
> scrutinised than in the past, that the standards demanded by the public remained
> high, and that the great majority of people in public life met those standards. The
> Report noted, however, weaknesses in the procedures for maintaining and
> enforcing those standards, which meant people in public life were not always as
> clear as they should have been about where the boundaries of acceptable conduct
> lay'[1].

[1]   First Report of the Committee on Standards in Public Life Volume 1: Report (Cm 2850-I).

1.27 The Committee recommended that public bodies devise codes of conduct
conforming to the 'seven principles of public life' (selflessness, objectivity,
integrity, accountability, openness, honesty and leadership) and that the
Law Commission should be invited to consider how the law on corruption
might be clarified and consolidated. The Law Commission took up that flag:
see paras **1.84** and **1.94–1.96**. Any proposals for reform, however, could no
longer be restricted to a consideration of domestic law. By this time, bribery
and corruption had become a global issue and the UK's obligations did not lie
solely at home.

C   INTERNATIONAL DEVELOPMENTS

1.28 It is apparent from domestic experience over the last 150 years that the
rise in corruption directly correlates to growth in trade and industry. Thus it
comes as no surprise that, with the increasingly transnational nature of
commerce in modern times, the fight against corruption has been elevated to
the international plane. Since the 1960s and 1970s, several international
bodies have turned their attention to this issue, and there are in place now a
vast number of instruments of varying obligation and territorial scope. This
section examines the main instruments. Not all elements of these instruments
are legally binding, and there is a significant margin of appreciation afforded
to contracting states in their implementation. It should be borne in mind,
however, that while the focus of this text rests primarily upon the criminalisation of bribery and corruption, this remains just one element of the larger
anti-corruption picture. Considerable emphasis must also be placed upon the
importance of international cooperation, awareness, deterrence, effective
monitoring, and appropriate civil sanctions.

Organisation for Economic Cooperation and Development ('OECD')

1.29 The Convention on the Organisation for Economic Cooperation and Development was originally signed by 20 states on 14 December 1960. It was ratified by the UK on 2 May 1961, and its membership now stands at 34 states[1]. Article 1 of the founding Convention states that the aim of the OECD is to promote policies designed:

(1)   to achieve the highest sustainable economic growth and employment and a rising standard of living in member countries, while maintaining financial stability, and thus to contribute to the development of the world economy;

(2)   to contribute to sound economic expansion in member as well as non-member countries in the process of economic development; and

(3)   to contribute to the expansion of world trade on a multilateral, non-discriminatory basis in accordance with international obligations.

[1]   Australia, Austria, Belgium, Canada, Chile, Czech Republic, Denmark, Estonia, Finland, France, Germany, Greece, Hungary, Iceland, Ireland, Israel, Italy, Japan, Korea, Luxembourg, Mexico, Netherlands, New Zealand, Norway, Poland, Portugal, Slovak Republic, Slovenia, Spain, Sweden, Switzerland, Turkey, UK, United States.

1.30 After an unsuccessful attempt in the late 1970s by the United Nations to implement an anti-corruption Convention, it was the OECD which made the first real progress at an international level. In 1989, it established an informal working group to explore comparative approaches to tackling corruption. The result of the working group's review was that, although some member states had in place provisions targeting the bribery of foreign public officials, some did not, and in any event their application was inconsistent. Only the United States' Foreign Corrupt Practices Act 1977 imposed criminal sanctions for individual and corporate bribery abroad[1].

[1]   For the sake of comparison, in 2009 the UK, representing 3.9% of the world's exports, secured only two convictions for bribery of a foreign public official; the United States, representing 10%, secured 60 (including plea bargains): www.oecd.org/dataoecd/23/20/45460981.pdf, p 4.

1.31 In 1994, the OECD adopted the Recommendation of the Council on Bribery in International Business Transactions, which encouraged but did not compel the taking of 'effective measures to detect, prevent and combat bribery of foreign public officials in international business'. The Recommendation operated in effect as a halfway house while the Working Group on Bribery was formalised and further work was carried out to address the most effective and efficient ways of harmonising anti-corruption measures. A Revised Recommendation was adopted in 1997, followed by the important OECD Convention on Combating Bribery of Foreign Public Officials in International Business Transactions ('the OECD Convention'), signed on 17 December 1997 and entering into force on 15 February 1999. In addition to the 34 members[1], Argentina, Brazil, Bulgaria and South Africa have also adopted the OECD Convention and have introduced implementing legislation.

[1]   See para **1.29** fn 1.

1.32 The terms of the OECD Convention focus on what is known as 'active bribery' (ie the supply of bribery: the recipient of the bribe is not targeted). Its scope is expressly restricted to the bribery of foreign public officials, and articles 1 and 2 require states to take necessary measures to establish the same as a criminal offence, whether committed by individuals or legal persons. Article 3 requires 'effective, proportionate and dissuasive' criminal penalties, as well as the consideration of additional civil sanctions. Article 4 requires states to establish jurisdiction where the offences are committed wholly or partly within their territory, or where committed abroad by their nationals. Articles 5–8 relate to enforcement, limitation, parity with money laundering, and accounting requirements. Articles 9–11 seek to ensure international cooperation in terms of mutual legal assistance, extradition, and effective communication via the OECD. Article 12 mandates states' cooperation with the Working Group on Bribery when monitoring compliance. The remaining articles deal with the formalities of the Convention.

1.33 The OECD has, in addition to the core anti-bribery Convention and related materials, adopted a number of Recommendations targeting particular risk areas for corruption. On 7 May 1996, the Development Assistance Committee of the OECD adopted anti-corruption proposals for bilateral aid procurement, recommending that members introduce or require anti-corruption provisions governing bilateral aid-funded procurement[1]. On 18 December 2006, the OECD Council adopted its Recommendation on Bribery and Officially Supported Export Credits[2]. This built upon a more general Action Statement in 2000 and provides specific steps for members to take in order to level the playing field among providers of export credits. On 25 May 2009, the OECD Council adopted its Recommendation on Tax Measures for Further Combating Bribery of Foreign Public Officials in International Business Transactions, which urges the disallowance of tax deductibility in respect of bribes paid to foreign public officials, and encourages the sharing of information by tax authorities[3].

[1] www.oecd.org/dataoecd/56/29/28321276.pdf.
[2] www.oecd.org/officialdocuments/displaydocumentpdf/?cote=td/ecg(2006)24&doclanguage=en.
[3] www.oecd.org/dataoecd/18/15/43188874.pdf.

1.34 Most recently, on 9 December 2009, marking the tenth anniversary of the entry into force of the OECD Convention, the OECD Council released its Recommendation for Further Combating Bribery of Foreign Public Officials in International Business Transactions[1]. This instrument supplements the provisions of the OECD Convention and is aimed at enhancing the ability of member states to prevent, detect and investigate foreign bribery. With the OECD's Good Practice Guide on Internal Controls, Ethics and Compliance set out in Annex II, the Recommendation calls on member states to ensure effective corporate liability, to formulate and review policies for dealing with facilitation payments, to provide channels for internal reporting, to work with the private sector to ensure best practice, and to cooperate with other member states to investigate, prosecute and recover the proceeds of corruption. Because the Recommendation forms part of the overall OECD Convention framework, compliance with its provisions will be monitored as part of the Working Group on Bribery's periodical review of implementation.

[1] www.oecd.org/dataoecd/11/40/44176910.pdf.

UK compliance with the OECD Convention

1.35 The Working Group's periodical reviews, established by article 12 of the OECD Convention, merits a special mention in terms of the development of anti-corruption law in the UK. The monitoring system consists of a two-phase peer review and subsequent 'follow ups' to ensure the implementation of the Working Group's recommendations. Phase 1 examines states' current anti-corruption laws in order to highlight potential deficiencies in complying with the requirements of the Convention. Phase 2 involves a week-long visit by the Working Group to each state in order to conduct meetings with the relevant public bodies and stakeholder organisations, and to conduct a detailed analysis of the state of implementation. The political aspect of these phases ought not to be underestimated. They have the potential to become a source of embarrassment within the international community.

1.36 The UK sought to implement the OECD Convention by enacting Part 12 of the Anti-terrorism, Crime and Security Act 2001, which came into force on 14 February 2002. Section 108 of the 2001 Act extended the existing law of bribery (both at common law and under statute) to bribery of foreign public officials. Section 109 of the Act extended the jurisdiction of domestic courts by providing that acts which would constitute bribery or corruption if committed in the UK would thenceforth constitute bribery or corruption if committed outside the UK by its nationals or bodies incorporated under its law. Under s 110 of the Act, the presumption of corruption does not apply to offences committed as a result of ss 108 and 109.

1.37 The Anti-terrorism, Crime and Security Act 2001 had been passed in response to the tragic events of 11 September 2001. Lord Rooker said in the House of Lords, on behalf of the government, that 'corruption engenders the conditions that cause terrorism and allow it to flourish'[1]. The provisions of Part 12, however, were only intended to be temporary. The Privy Counsellor Review Committee stated in its 2003 review of the Act that[2]:

> 'It is welcome that these measures, which have little direct bearing on terrorism, but are in themselves largely uncontroversial, are going to be repealed and replaced in their proper context, the Corruption Bill, which is currently subject to consultation'.

The problems which dogged the Corruption Bill, and ultimately prevented its enactment, meant the continued governance of Part 12 until the enactment of the Bribery Act 2010.

[1]   629 HL Official Report (5th series) col 152, 27 November 2001.
[2]   Anti-terrorism, Crime and Security Act 2001 Review: Report (2003) HC 100, para 415.

1.38 The Working Group assessed the amendments made by the Anti-terrorism, Crime and Security Act 2001 as part of its Phase 1 bis review, published on 3 March 2003. It concluded that, while some 'very significant steps' had been taken, there remained 'areas of uncertainty'[1]. The conclusion of the Phase 1 Report was therefore to recommend that the UK 'enact a comprehensive anti-corruption statute' in order to clarify the inconsistencies and uncertainties of the current law[2].

[1]   www.oecd.org/dataoecd/12/50/2498215.pdf, at E(a) para 3.

[2] At E(b) para 1.

1.39 On 17 March 2005, the Working Group published its Phase 2 review, which examined what steps had been taken to implement the recommendations made in the Phase 1 Report. It found none, and its response was somewhat acidic[1]:

> '[S]ince the Phase 1 bis the United Kingdom has not enacted any new foreign bribery offence. The Working Group therefore recommends that the United Kingdom enact at the earliest possible date comprehensive legislation whose scope includes the bribery of a foreign public official'.

[1] www.oecd.org/dataoecd/62/32/34599062.pdf, para 248.

1.40 The steps which the UK had in fact been taking over that two year period are considered below. From an international perspective, however, no effective progress had been made to implement the Working Group's recommendations, or otherwise to remedy the deficiencies of, and gaps in, the current law. Vociferous criticism, both domestic and international, put the government under increasing pressure to expedite reform. A press release from the OECD on 16 October 2008 stated[1]:

> 'Current UK legislation makes it very difficult for prosecutors to bring an effective case against a company for alleged bribery offences. Although the UK ratified the OECD Anti-Bribery Convention 10 years ago, it has so far failed to successfully prosecute any bribery case against a company'.

[1] www.oecd.org/document/8/0,3343,en_2649_34855_41515464_1_1_1_37447,00.html.

1.41 The prospect of an imminent further visit by the Working Group in January 2009 compounded the sense of urgency. The government's concern to emphasise the steps being taken was implicit in the Working Group's 2009 Annual Report[1]:

> 'In January 2009, a delegation from the Working Group visited London at the United Kingdom's invitation as a follow-up to the UK's Phase 2 bis report in October 2008. The delegation discussed with UK officials proposals by the UK Law Commission for reforming the bribery law in that country. The UK provided written reports on legislative progress relevant to foreign bribery in each Working Group meeting in 2009. In December 2009, the UK also presented an oral follow-up report on the implementation of all Phase 2 bis recommendations, confirming that a new Bribery Act had been introduced to the United Kingdom Parliament with the intention of approval before June 2010'.

[1] www.oecd.org/dataoecd/23/20/45460981.pdf, p 22.

1.42 The article 12 compliance monitoring provisions of the OECD Convention have thus played their part in developing the anti-corruption law of the UK.

The United Nations

1.43 The United Nations was responsible for taking the early initiative in the fight against corruption. In 1974, the Commission on Transnational Corporations was created, tasked with the drafting of a Code of Conduct on

Transnational Corporations. In 1975, General Assembly Resolution 3514 was passed, condemning all forms of corrupt practice and urging member states to take the necessary steps to prosecute instances of corruption and bribery within their jurisdiction. In 1976, the Ad Hoc Intergovernmental Working Group on the Problem of Corrupt Practices was established, only to be replaced two years later by the Committee on an International Agreement on Illicit Payments. The Committee produced a draft text on illicit payments to be included within the Code of Conduct on Transnational Corporations, but this was in fact never adopted.

1.44 Nearly 20 years elapsed before the next major UN development. In 1996, the General Assembly adopted a Declaration against Corruption and Bribery in International Commercial Transactions. Although this was a non-binding measure, it led to the drafting of the UN Convention against Transnational Organised Crime. The Convention came into force on 29 September 2003 and was ratified by the UK on 9 February 2006. Articles 8 and 9 require member states to criminalise bribery of public officials, at home or abroad, but it was soon acknowledged by the General Assembly (Resolution 55/61) that a discrete anti-corruption Convention would be needed.

1.45 In December 2000, the Ad Hoc Committee for the Negotiation of the Convention against Corruption was established. After more than 18 months of consultation, the Convention was finally approved and adopted by the General Assembly by Resolution 58/4 on 31 October 2003. It was signed by the UK on 9 December 2003 and ratified on 9 February 2006. The purposes of the Convention are stated to be:

(1)   to promote and strengthen measures to prevent and combat corruption more efficiently and effectively;

(2)   to promote, facilitate and support international cooperation and technical assistance in the prevention of and fight against corruption, including in asset recovery;

(3)   to promote integrity, accountability and proper management of public affairs and public property.

1.46 The UN Convention against Corruption has been heralded by Transparency International as 'unique . . . not only in its global coverage but also in the extensiveness and detail of its provisions'. The Convention has eight parts:

(1)   Chapter I contains the statement of purpose above, together with interpretative provisions and articles on the scope of application and the protection of member state sovereignty;

(2)   Chapter II requires member states to develop, implement and maintain effective preventative measures, including developing and maintaining anti-corruption policies and procedures; establishing anti-corruption bodies and systems to ensure the fairness of public sector employment, procurement and finance management; drafting public sector codes of conduct; promoting transparency; combating the risk of corruption in the judicial and prosecutorial services; raising awareness; preventing money laundering; and taking measures to prevent corruption in the private sector. Chapter II also requires member states to disallow the tax deductibility of bribes;

(3)   Chapter III contains the crucial provisions on criminalisation and law enforcement, considered in greater detail below;
(4)   Chapter IV contains detailed provisions for ensuring international cooperation, including extradition;
(5)   Chapter V governs asset recovery;
(6)   Chapter VI requires that anti-corruption technical assistance and training be provided;
(7)   Chapters VII and VIII relate to implementation and other formalities.

1.47 The articles in Chapter III are the most relevant for present purposes. They comprise a cocktail of mandatory obligations and obligations for consideration. In terms of the mandatory obligations, bribery is defined in articles 15 and 16 but is limited to bribery of national public officials, foreign public officials and public officials of international organisations (each of which is further defined by article 2). Nevertheless, member states are obliged to 'adopt such legislative and other measures as may be necessary to establish [the relevant forms of bribery] as criminal offences'. Also to be criminalised, pursuant to articles 17, 23 and 25 are embezzlement, misappropriation and other diversion of property by a public official, the laundering of proceeds of crime, and the obstruction of justice in relation to offences established by the Convention. Corporate liability is compulsory (article 26), as are inchoate and accessorial modes of liability (article 27).

1.48 Among the non-mandatory provisions, member states must consider criminalising the following:

(1)   trading in influence (defined at length by article 18, but essentially the bribery of one person in order that he exercise his influence over another person or body);
(2)   intentional abuse of function by a public official for the purpose of obtaining an undue advantage for himself or another (article 19);
(3)   intentional illicit enrichment by a public official (article 20);
(4)   bribery and embezzlement in the private sector (articles 21 and 22);
(5)   intentional concealment or continued retention of property in the knowledge that such property is the result of a Convention offence (article 24); and
(6)   the attempt or preparation to commit a Convention offence (article 27).

1.49 The UN's contribution to the anti-corruption fight has not been limited to its resolutions, declarations and conventions. The Global Programme against Corruption was launched in 1999 for the purpose of assisting member states to strengthen and coordinate their anti-corruption measures. The United Nations Office on Drugs and Crime continues to produce guidance materials for effective implementation and has also published a series of 'case studies' reporting on corruption at various levels within particular countries, including Iran, Iraq, Nigeria, Romania and South Africa.

Council of Europe

1.50 The Council of Europe was founded in 1949 and currently has 47 member states. The UK has been a member state since 1949. In 1994, the Council established the Multidisciplinary Group on Corruption with the aim, amongst others, of drafting one or more international conventions to combat corruption. These came in the form of the Criminal Law Convention on Corruption, the Additional Protocol to that Convention, and the Civil Law Convention on Corruption. In parallel with these instruments came the Twenty Guiding Principles for the Fight against Corruption, which were adopted on 6 November 1997 and set out broad aspirational targets for the establishment of an effective anti-corruption regime.

1.51 The Criminal Law Convention on Corruption was signed by the UK on 27 January 1999 and ratified on 9 December 2003, with a reservation. The provisions of the Convention became binding on their entry into force on 1 April 2004. Paragraph 21 of the Explanatory Notes to the Convention makes clear the overarching aim of harmonisation and cooperation between member states in order to establish an effective anti-corruption network. This lofty goal informs the relatively broad drafting of the Convention provisions. Member states are required to criminalise both active and passive bribery—that is to say the payer and recipient of the bribe. The net of potential recipients is then cast widely, to include:

(1)   domestic and foreign public officials (articles 1, 2 and 5);
(2)   members of any domestic or foreign public assembly exercising legislative or administrative powers (articles 4 and 6);
(3)   any persons who direct or work for, in any capacity, private sector entities (articles 7 and 8)[1];
(4)   officials of international organisations (article 9);
(5)   members of international parliamentary assemblies (article 10); and
(6)   judges and officials of international courts (article 11).

[1]   It is worth noting that private sector bribery must be committed 'in the course of business' and must involve a breach of duty.

1.52 Furthermore, the Convention requires the criminalisation of:

(1)   trading in influence, whether active or passive (article 12);
(2)   the laundering of the proceeds of Convention offences (article 13);
(3)   the concealment or disguise of Convention offences by false accounting (article 14); and
(4)   participation in Convention offences (article 15).

1.53 As regards corporate liability, article 18 requires that member states ensure that legal persons may be convicted of active bribery, trading in influence and money laundering where those offences were committed by a individual in a 'leading position' within the company and for the company's benefit. Member states must establish jurisdiction over offences which occur wholly or partly within their territory, or are committed by—or involve—their nationals. As with many comparable instruments, the Convention requires 'effective, proportionate and dissuasive sanctions' (article 19), the establishment of specialist anti-corruption bodies (article 20) and the pursuit of effective international cooperation (article 21).

1.54 The reservation adopted by the UK, pursuant to article 37 of the Convention, relates to active bribery in the private sector, trading in influence and jurisdiction[1]. As regards active bribery, the UK acknowledged that its current law did not extend to cases of undue advantages being given to third parties rather than agents, and expressed its intention to amend via the Corruption

Bill. Equally as regards trading in influence, the government reserved the right not to establish the entirety of the conduct canvassed by article 12 as criminal. Under article 17 jurisdiction, it also reserved the right not to criminalise:

(1)   acts of corruption by its public officials or members of its domestic public assemblies except where those persons are also UK nationals; and

(2)   cases of mere involvement of its public officials or members of its domestic public assemblies.

[1]   conventions.coe.int/treaty/Commun/ListeDeclarations.asp?NT=173&CM=&DF=&CL=ENG &VL=1.

1.55 The Convention was supplemented by the Additional Protocol to the Criminal Law Convention with effect from 1 February 2005. The UK signed the Additional Protocol on 15 May 2003 and ratified it on 9 December 2003. This extended the ambit of criminalisation to include offences for bribery (active or passive) of domestic or foreign jurors and arbitrators.

1.56 The Civil Law Convention on Corruption was adopted on 4 November 1999 and came into force on 1 November 2003. It requires member states to enable victims of corruption to sue for compensation. Damages can be recovered in respect of 'material damage, loss of profits and non-pecuniary loss' where somebody has committed a corrupt act, authorised another to do so, or failed to take reasonable steps to prevent such an act. Notably, member states themselves may be liable for the latter where damage is suffered as a result of an act of corruption by the state's public officials. The UK signed the Convention on 8 June 2000 but has yet to ratify it.

1.57 Monitoring of compliance with both the Criminal Law and Civil Law Conventions on Corruption is the task of Group of States against Corruption (GRECO). The aim of GRECO is to 'improve the capacity of its members to fight corruption by monitoring their compliance with Council of Europe anti-corruption standards through a dynamic process of mutual evaluation and peer pressure'. For that reason, full membership of GRECO is restricted to those states willing to engage fully with the evaluation process. To date, three rounds of evaluation have been launched and it is the third of these which addresses, amongst other things, implementation of the Criminal Law Convention on Corruption.

The European Union

1.58 Article 29 of the EU Treaty states that combating corruption and fraud is part of its objective to create an area of security, freedom and justice. It was recognised in the Explanatory Report on the Convention on the fight against corruption involving officials of the European Communities or officials of member states of the European Union, approved by the Council in 3 December 1998[1], that:

'From an international rather than the national perspective . . . the principal weakness in the fight against corruption with transnational features has been the fact that criminal law in the member states has often failed to address the issue of the corruption of foreign officials and officials employed by international organisations'.

There are now a host of instruments which have been produced by the EU in pursuit of its article 29 objective. The main texts are outlined here.

¹ OJ 1998 C 391.

1.59 The First Protocol to the Convention on the Protection of the European Communities' Financial Interests entered force on 17 October 2002. It was created in response to the Council's Resolution of 6 December 1994, which determined at point 7(h) that 'Member states should take effective measures to punish bribery involving officials of the European Communities in relation to the financial interests of the Communities'. The date of notification for both the First Protocol and the main Convention in the UK was 11 October 1999, and both instruments are binding. The provisions of the First Protocol distinguish between active and passive bribery but are restricted to bribery of 'officials', both national and Community. Member states must take necessary measures to ensure that bribery of officials is criminal and punished by effective, proportionate and dissuasive criminal penalties. The UK did not pass any additional legislation in response to the entry into force of the First Protocol and was criticised as a result because it was not clear whether EU officials fell within the scope of the old law[1].

¹ ec.europa.eu/dgs/olaf/mission/legal/annex709final_en.pdf, pp 38–39.

1.60 The Second Protocol, adopted on 19 June 1997, extended the scope of member states' anti-corruption obligations but has not yet entered into force. It requires the criminalisation of money laundering and accessorial roles in corruption offences. It expands the scope of liability to include legal persons 'when committed for their benefit by any person, acting either individually or as part of an organ of the legal person, who has a leading position within the legal person . . . ' Measures must be taken where a 'lack of supervision or control' (article 3(2)) has made possible the commission of a corruption offence. Member states are also required to enable the confiscation of the proceeds of corruption and to cooperate with the Commission.

1.61 The Convention on the Fight against Corruption involving Officials of the European Communities or Officials of Member States of the European Union entered force on 26 September 2005, having been signed by the UK on 25 June 1997 and ratified on 11 October 1999. It represented a widening of the earlier EU-centric provisions so that bribery need no longer have damaged or have been likely to damage the EU's financial interests. It also ensured that member states' criminal law covered bribery of other states' officials. Familiar provisions on international cooperation, and in particular on extradition, were included. One noteworthy inclusion is the requirement for member states to found criminal liability for 'heads of businesses' where active corruption has been committed by a person under their authority acting on behalf of the business (article 6).

1.62 A final but important EU instrument relates to private sector bribery. This ought not be surprising given the Community's role in protecting free trade. Thus when a Joint Action adopted on 22 December 1998[1] did not result in the anticipated criminalisation of private sector corruption within two years, the Council adopted the Framework Decision of 22 July 2003. The Preamble recites that:

> 'Member states attach particular importance to combating corruption in both the public and private sector, in the belief that in both those sectors it poses a threat to a law-abiding society as well as distorting competition in relation to the purchase of goods or commercial services and impeding sound economic development . . . '

The Framework Decision was addressed to all member states and is thus binding upon them from the date of publication, 31 July 2003.

[1]   98/742/JHA.

1.63 Article 2 of the Framework Decision requires criminalisation of active and passive corruption in the private sector, but is limited to intentional conduct carried out in the course of business activities, whether or not for profit. The litmus test is whether the bribee is to act in breach of duty, which should include 'as a minimum any disloyal behaviour constituting a breach of a statutory duty or . . . of professional regulations or instructions . . . ' (article 1). Instigating, aiding or abetting corruption must also constitute an offence (article 3). As regards the liability of legal persons, article 6 of the Framework Decision is similar in its terms to article 3 of the Second Protocol above, which is not yet in force. Thus there must be liability for active or passive corruption committed by someone in a leading position within the legal person for its benefit. There are a number of ways in which someone may be held to be in a leading position (article 5(1)) and, as with the Second Protocol, liability can be founded upon a lack of supervision or control (article 5(2)).

1.64 Following debate in the House of Lords, it was considered that the requirements of the Framework Decision were met by existing law[1]. The Commission did not agree. Its report on implementation by member states concluded that, while the UK had successfully implemented certain provisions, it had only partially transposed others[2]. The Staff Working Paper annexed to the report provides the more detailed analysis underpinning it[3]. From these documents it is apparent that the Commission felt that it was not clear whether the concept of breach of duty had been successfully transposed. It was also unclear whether the Company Directors Disqualification Act 1986 was alone sufficient to satisfy article 4. Of particular interest is the Commission's conclusion that existing UK law on the liability of legal persons, and consequent sanctions, was deficient. The UK had relied, in order to comply with the 'lack of supervision or control' element, upon the Prevention of Corruption Act 1906, the Interpretation Act 1978, the Proceeds of Crime Act 2002 and the civil law of negligence. However:

> 'The Commission's view here is that the liability is a criminal liability, which must be matched by a criminal sanction and that such a criminal sanction may be supplemented by other measures which are administrative or civil in nature. The Commission does not consider that administrative or civil sanctions alone are sufficient.'

[1]   691 HL Official Report (5th series) cols WA194–WA196, 1 May 2007.

2   Report from the Commission to the Council based on article 9 of the Council Framework Decision 2003/568/JHA of 22 July 2003 on combating corruption in the private sector, COM (2007) 328 final, 18 June 2007.
3   eur-lex.europa.eu/LexUriServ/LexUriServ.do?uri=SEC:2007:0808:FIN:EN:HTML.

Further international efforts

1.65 Alongside the major initiatives outlined above, anti-corruption efforts have continued apace across a number of other countries and international organisations. In terms of the development of the law on corruption in the UK, the impact of the work of these bodies is inevitably more limited because their instruments are not binding. They are nonetheless helpful comparators when considering domestic law and its reform, as acknowledged by the Law Commission when it came to formulating its proposals[1]. Particularly noteworthy contributions include:

(1)   the African Union Convention on Preventing and Combating Corruption: The African Union was created in 2002, and aims to promote democracy, human rights and development across Africa. Its Convention entered force on 5 August 2006. It targets public and private sector corruption, trading in influence, illicit enrichment, the diversion of public funds and—of particular contextual importance—the corrupt financing of political parties. Familiar provisions on awareness and international cooperation are included, as well as the creation of an Advisory Board on Corruption within the African Union, comprising 11 elected members, to monitor and promote the anti-corruption process;

(2)   South African Development Community Protocol against Corruption: The South African Development Community was established in 1992 and, in August 2000, decided upon a number of initiatives to fight local corruption. Within a year, the Protocol was drafted and signed. It is broken down into standard sections addressing preventative measures, criminalisation, cooperation, proceeds of crime and monitoring. The criminalisation provisions include quite a wide range of corrupt conduct and are notably supplemented by the power of member states to agree between themselves additional forms of corruption above and beyond the minimum established by the Protocol;

(3)   the Economic Community of West African States Protocol on the Fight against Corruption: This tracks closely the terms of the South African Development Community Protocol above;

(4)   the Inter-American Convention against Corruption: This entered force in March 1997 as the product of the Organization of American States. It was the first binding instrument to tackle corruption on a regional level. Criminalisation of bribery of governmental and foreign public officials is mandatory. Further provisions targeting other forms of corrupt behaviour by public officials (including the improper use of confidential or classified information, the improper use of state property and the procuring of a public authority decision for illicit gain) must be considered;

(5)   Commonwealth initiatives: The Commonwealth is a voluntary association of 54 countries that support each other and work together towards shared goals in democracy and development. In November 1999, the Commonwealth Heads of government endorsed the proposals of the Expert Group on Good Governance in the form of a Framework for Commonwealth Principles on Promoting Good Governance and Combating Corruption. The Framework Principles highlight as the core areas for action: (1) ethics and integrity in the public and private sectors; (2) economic and fiscal policies; (3) management of services provided in the public interest; (4) the judiciary and legal system; and (5) civil society. In pursuance of these Principles, the Commonwealth offers its member states a number of forms of assistance. Expert Groups examine individual states and identify key areas for action. Mutual legal assistance is provided for in the Harare Scheme on Mutual Assistance in Criminal Matters, and the London Scheme for Extradition within the Commonwealth. The efforts of the Commonwealth Working Group on Asset Repatriation are of particular importance in supporting the smaller and more poorly resourced member states. It is this feature of bilateral support which makes the work of the Commonwealth particularly significant in terms of its contribution to the global anti-corruption agenda;

(6)   Anti-Corruption Action Plan for Asia and the Pacific: The Action Plan is the product of collaboration between countries of the Asia-Pacific region and the OECD. Its terms are non-binding and based upon three pillars: effective and transparent systems of public service; anti-corruption law and integrity in business; and public participation. To date, it has been endorsed by 28 countries, which are at differing stages of implementation;

(7)   International Chamber of Commerce ('ICC'): In 1977, the ICC published its Report on Extortion and Bribery in Business Transactions, which included Rules of Conduct for combating extortion and bribery, updated in 1994 and 2005. The Rules are non-binding but state in their Introduction that voluntary adherence will both promote business integrity and act as a defence for those businesses endangered by corruption;

(8)   the World Bank and International Monetary Fund ('IMF'): The World Bank is required to ensure that its loans are put to the purpose for which they are given. To this end, a policy targeting fraud and corruption was included in its Procurement Guidelines, issued in 1996. The Guidelines warn of the action the World Bank will take if corrupt, fraudulent, collusive or coercive practices are identified. This includes rejecting proposals, cancelling loans, barring the award of Bank-financed contracts, and requiring the inspection of accounts. Alongside these Guidelines sit the IMF's two codes of practice. The first, the Code of Good Practices on Fiscal Transparency, was adopted in 1998, and sets out a framework for best practice in the conduct of fiscal policy. The second, the Code of Good Practices on Transparency in Monetary and Financial Policies: Declaration of Principles, was adopted in 1999. It gives instruction on the accountability, management and supervision

of fiscal authorities. The clarity of structure and management encouraged by the IMF's Codes of Good Practices act to reduce the opportunities for corruption and concealment;

(9)   other anti-corruption organisations: The array of bodies, organisations and associations playing their part in the fight against corruption is too numerous to list here[2]. Suffice it to say that they play a key role in raising awareness and providing support and training. The work of Transparency International and its 2002 Business Principles for Countering Bribery is particularly important in this regard. So too is that of The Corner House in the field of advocacy, and of the considerable research work of UNICORN. The materials provided on the websites of these organisations and many others constitute invaluable resources for businesses facing the real problems of corruption.

[1]   Reforming Bribery: A Consultation Paper (Law Commission Consultation Paper No 185), Apps A–C.
[2]   For more detailed discussion of some of the NGOs, see Chapter 2.

D   THE NEED FOR NEW LEGISLATION

1.66 The state of domestic law prior to the advent of the Bribery Act 2010 was one of abject disarray. Calls for reform were virtually universal. As the OECD observed, it was 'widely recognised that the current substantive law governing bribery in the UK is characterised by complexity and uncertainty'[1]. The government described the law as 'fragmented and out of date'[2]. The statistics are telling. From 2001 to 2005, there were only 43 convictions under the Prevention of Corruption Act 1906 and just three under the Public Bodies Corrupt Practices Act 1889[3]. It took until 2009 to secure a single conviction of a British company for bribery. This section explores some of the key deficiencies fuelling the calls for reform.

[1]   Phase 2 report, para 194.
[2]   Bribery: Reform of the Prevention of Corruption Acts and SFO Powers in Cases of Bribery of Foreign Officials: a Consultation Paper (Dec 2005) p 3.
[3]   Reforming Bribery: A Consultation Paper (Law Commission Consultation Paper No 185), p 19.

Inconsistency between the Prevention of Corruption Acts

1.67 The fragmentation of the old law across the three main statutes was both unnecessarily complicated and gave rise to marked inconsistency. The terminology used to describe the bribe varied, with the common law requiring an undue reward, the Public Bodies Corrupt Practices Act 1889 specifying a 'gift, loan, fee, reward or advantage' and the Prevention of Corruption Act 1906 providing for some 'gift or consideration'. The scope of potential bribees varied also. At common law, the recipient had to be a public officer, but under the 1889 Act, he could be a 'member, officer, or servant of a public body'. Whilst undoubtedly the two modes of expression would overlap in most instances, one had to wonder what else might be captured by the broader definition of the 1889 Act. One would be forgiven for thinking that Parliament must have used those words for a reason when legislating against the common law background. In addition was the distinct concept of bribery of an agent under the 1906 Act. This applied across both public and private sectors, but it was not always clear who might count as an agent. Police officers caused particular difficulty, with the English courts holding that they were agents of the state[1] and the Scottish courts considering them to be agents of the Chief Constable[2]. Judicial officers and local councillors were other unclear cases.

1 *Fisher v Oldham Corpn* [1930] 2 KB 364, 28 LGR 293.
2 *Graham v Hart* [1908] SC (J) 26.

1.68 Assuming that the recipient of the bribe was not in question, the manner of bribery proscribed by the Acts differed. The Public Bodies Corrupt Practices Act 1889 could apply where the bribee was no longer, or not yet, in office at the time of the bribe. The language of the Prevention of Corruption Act 1906, however, appeared to require the agent to receive the bribe, or agree to receive it, during the currency of the agency. Furthermore, under the 1889 Act, the recipient need not have been the public officer intended to be influenced by the bribe, thereby catching cases where it was the officer's wife who took the bribe. There was no such latitude under the 1906 Act—an increasingly glaring omission given that modern day corruption commonly involves several intermediaries. At the same time, the 1889 Act was narrower than the 1906 Act in that the bribe had to be connected to a particular 'matter or transaction' and so did not include general sweeteners designed to secure more favourable treatment in the future.

1.69 These inconsistencies were more than simply a matter of form. The OECD criticised the lack of an autonomous definition of 'foreign public official'. Its concern was that, simply tacking the 'foreign' element onto the front of 'public official' (under the Anti-terrorism, Crime and Security Act 2001, Pt 12) was artificial, and might fail to catch instances of bribery contrary to the OECD Convention[1]. In a similar vein, the Working Group expressed discomfort at having to assume that the different formulations of the bribe and modes of commission under the Acts would always catch the OECD's proscribed offers, promises or gifts of any undue pecuniary or other advantage[2]. Of greater significance was the response of the Serious Fraud Office to the Law Commission's consultation paper on bribery. In its experience, payments made through intermediaries were frequent and difficult to prosecute, and it should make no difference that the beneficiary of the bribe might be, and commonly was, a third party.

1 Phase 1 bis report, pp 13–14; Phase 2 report, para 183.
2 Phase 1 bis report, p 14; Phase 2 report, para 181.

'Corruptly'

1.70 The one area of absolute consistency between the Prevention of Corruption Acts was the difficulty of interpreting the nebulous word 'corruptly'. This adverb was the hallmark of wrongdoing which made the offence one of corruption rather than simple dishonesty, sharp practice or otherwise immoral behaviour. Both the 1889 and 1906 Acts incorporated 'corruptly' as an element of their offences, but neither provided a definition. Professor Lanham described the authorities on the interpretation of this word as in 'impressive disarray'[1].

1   'Bribery and Corruption', *Essays in Honour of JC Smith* (1987) pp 92, 104.

1.71 The House of Lords had taken the view in *Cooper v Slade*[1] that 'corruptly' did not mean 'dishonestly', but rather 'purposely doing an act which the law forbids as tending to corrupt'. The Act for interpretation in that case had been the Corrupt Practices Act 1854. *Cooper v Slade* was the prevailing appellate authority at the time the Prevention of Corruption Acts were enacted, although it is not known whether any account was taken of the decision at the drafting stage.

1   (1858) 22 JP 511.

1.72 Almost a century later, in *R v Lindley*[1], Pearce J threw the law into confusion by interpreting 'corruptly' under the Prevention of Corruption Act 1906 as a dishonest intention to weaken the loyalty of servants to their masters. This was then followed in *R v Calland*[2], in which an inspector of a life insurance company was charged under the 1906 Act for rewarding an agent of the Ministry of Social Security for keeping him informed of the names and addresses of parents of newborn children. Veale J held that 'corruptly' meant 'dishonestly trying to wheedle an agent away from his loyalty to his employer' and, unless dishonesty could be shown on the part of the defendant, the offence of corruption was not made out.

1   [1957] Crim LR 321.
2   [1967] Crim LR 236.

1.73 In the meantime, the Court of Appeal had given judgment in *R v Smith*[1]. The defendant had been charged under the Public Bodies Corrupt Practices Act 1889 for offering a gift to the Mayor of Castleford in order to use his mayoral influence on the borough council. The Court of Appeal expressly approved the definition given in *Cooper v Slade*, and went on to state that 'corruptly' in that case 'denotes that the person making the offer does so deliberately and with the intention that the person to whom it is addressed should enter into a corrupt bargain'[2]. In response to the suggestion that such an approach would be circular and render 'corruptly' devoid of meaning, the Lord Chief Justice observed that it might retain an independent function in cases of inducements rather than rewards[3].

1   [1960] 2 QB 423, [1960] 1 All ER 256.
2   At 428 per Lord Parker CJ.
3   At 429.

1.74 The most recent authorities have rejected the approach in *Lindley* and *Calland*, considering that dishonesty was a different concept from corruption, not a necessary element to make out the 1906 Act offence[1]. The Court of Appeal in *Wellburn* took the view that 'corruptly' was an 'ordinary word' which should cause a jury little difficulty[2]. Although it is undoubtedly true that corruption is much easier to know than to describe (hence the difficulties of devising an appropriate model for reform), that was of little comfort to lawyers who were attempting to advise whether a jury might classify a particular form of business activity as corruption rather than hopeful generosity or something else. The division of senior appellate authority on the interpretation of 'corruptly' in fact reflected well the lack of clarity afflicting the old law.

[1]   *R v Wellburn* (1979) 69 Cr App Rep 254; *R v Harvey* [1999] Crim LR 70, CA; *R v Godden-Wood* [2001] EWCA Crim 1586, [2001] Crim LR 810.

[2]   (1979) 69 Cr App Rep 254 at 265 per Lawton LJ.

Public/private distinction

1.75 An obvious target for reform was the imperfect and increasingly untenable distinction between bribery and corruption in the public sector and that in the private sector. The 1889 Act was confined to bribery of members, officers and servants of public bodies, whereas the 1906 Act targeted bribery of 'agents' regardless of sector. This led to confusion and charging errors, with the conviction in *R v Natji (Naci Vedat)*[1] being quashed because the defendant employee of the Immigration and Nationality Department of the Home Office, as an employee of the Crown, was held not to fall within the 1889 Act. Moreover, despite the key concept of 'corruptly' remaining the same in both public and private sectors, the operation of the presumption of corruption under the Prevention of Corruption Act 1916 shifted the burden of proof in certain public sector cases involving contracts.

[1]   [2002] EWCA Crim 271, [2002] 1 WLR 2337.

1.76 Although historically explicable, support for retaining a public/private distinction had dwindled. Whereas instances of public sector corruption are all the worse because of the higher standards of integrity expected and the level of trust reposed by society as a whole, this is not of itself a compelling justification for maintaining the distinction at law. On the contrary, the increase of public and quasi-public functions being carried out by private contractors, and the growing frequency of public/private joint ventures, made the distinction ever more difficult to apply with any certainty. The risk of inconsistent application undermined the efficacy and authority of the law. Human rights lawyers could vouch for the volume of litigation generated over the phrase 'public body' in the Human Rights Act 1998, s 6. Thus when the government resurrected the public/private distinction in its 2005 consultation paper, the majority of consultees were in favour of abolition.

Corporate liability

1.77 The problem of corporate liability, which is central to tackling modern day corruption, was not one that would have presented itself to the draftsmen of the Prevention of Corruption Acts 1889 to 1906. The Interpretation Act 1978 extended the ambit of the Acts so that references to 'persons' included both natural and legal persons, incorporated or unincorporated. To the extent that the old law embraced bribery by unincorporated bodies, English law went beyond any of its international obligations. In terms of the effectiveness of

English corporate liability, however, vociferous criticism continued. The familiar but critical hindrance of the identification doctrine under *Tesco Supermarkets Ltd v Nattrass*[1] frustrated domestic and international bodies alike. The onus upon the prosecution to show corruption on the part of a directing mind of the company was a formidable one, and operated as an effective bar to prosecuting corporate bribery[2]. The OECD concluded after its follow-up visit in 2008 that[3]:

> 'The Working Group is particularly concerned that the UK's continued failure to address deficiencies in its laws on bribery of foreign public officials and on corporate liability for foreign bribery has hindered investigations. The Working Group reiterates its previous 2003, 2005 and 2007 recommendations that the UK enact new foreign bribery legislation at the earliest possible date. The Group also strongly regrets the uncertainty about the UK's commitment to establish an effective corporate liability regime in accordance with the Convention, as recommended in 2005, and urges the UK to adopt appropriate legislation as a matter of high priority'.

[1] [1972] AC 153, [1971] 2 All ER 127, HL.
[2] It was not enough to show that the defendant employee was a 'responsible agent', 'high executive' or 'agent acting on behalf of a company': *R v Andrews Weatherfoil Ltd* [1972] 1 All ER 65, [1972] 1 WLR 118, CA.
[3] OECD Working Group Report, Executive Summary, p 4.

1.78 The general position under the old law was therefore that, although the threshold for successfully prosecuting corporate bribery was set so high that it undermined the purpose of the international conventions, the UK was nonetheless technically compliant. Its international obligations examined earlier in this chapter generally required only that the liability of legal persons be established. The OECD's mid-term study of Phase 2 Reports (2006, para 125), for example, stated that only Luxembourg and the Slovak Republic were non-compliant with the corporate liability requirements of article 2 of the OECD Convention. That was so despite the considerable criticism the OECD had levelled at English corporate liability in its Phase 2 (2005, paras 195–206) and follow-up (2007, p 21) Reports.

1.79 There were, however, two areas of disputed compliance. The first was that raised by the European Commission in its Explanatory Report to the Second Protocol to the Convention on the Protection of the European Communities' Financial Interests. Article 3(1) of the Second Protocol identifies three ways in which a person could occupy a 'leading position' within a company: 'a power of representation of the legal person, or an authority to take decisions on behalf of the legal person, or an authority to exercise control within the legal person'. The UK relied upon the common law's acceptance of the third, but para 3.2 of the Explanatory Report stated that member states would have to transpose all three elements. Nevertheless, at no point did the European Commission identify a breach of article 3(1) by the UK, which it did for other member states; nor did it require a follow-up investigation.

1.80 The second potential gap in compliance, highlighted at para **1.58**, is the requirement of article 5(2) of the European Union Framework Decision of 22 July 2003 to establish liability for failures of supervision or control[1]. The European Commission was of the view that failure to supervise needed to be established as a criminal offence, and therefore rejected the government's reliance upon the Proceeds of Crime Act 2002 and the tort of negligence. An analysis by the Law Commission, however, concluded that criminal liability was not mandatory, and opined that the European Commission's interpretation of article 5(2) was incorrect[2]. At the same time, it acknowledged the weakness of relying on laws as broad as the Proceeds of Crime Act 2002 and on negligence, which were far from designed to deal with failures to prevent bribery and might not do so adequately in all situations, particularly given that damages awarded in tortious claims for bribery would be restricted to purely economic loss. The aim of tortious compensation is to put the claimant back in his pre-tort position, which is markedly different in approach from the deterrent and penal provisions of the various international Conventions. It is therefore fair to say that, although the UK may in fact have been fully compliant with its international obligations prior to the enactment of the Bribery Act 2010, its regime for corporate liability was largely a toothless one in the fight against corruption.

[1] Similar requirements are incorporated by Article 3(2) of the Second Protocol of the Convention on the Protection of the European Communities' Financial Interests.
[2] Reforming Bribery: A Consultation Paper (Law Commission Consultation Paper No 185), pp 141–143.

A lacuna in jurisdiction

1.81 The extension of domestic courts' jurisdiction pursuant to the Anti-terrorism, Crime and Security Act 2001, Pt 12, whilst a step forward, left room for injustice. From 14 February 2002, nationals of the UK or bodies incorporated under its laws could be prosecuted for acts of corruption committed abroad. Foreign nationals or companies incorporated under foreign laws, however, could not be prosecuted for corruption committed abroad even if they were domiciled or habitually resident in England and Wales, or had their headquarters here. On one view, this amounted to an unfair distinction in the ambit of the criminal law between persons, natural and legal, who for all intents and purposes resided and conducted their business in the UK as equals.

1.82 Other extra-territorial weaknesses could be identified. A company incorporated under the law of a Crown Dependency or Overseas Territory could commit bribery abroad under English law. More significantly, because foreign persons could engage in bribery abroad without committing an offence known to English law, no secondary liability could attach to British nationals or companies incorporated here. Thus, if a German national committed bribery in Germany, he would not commit an offence under English law, and so a British national could not be guilty of assisting or encouraging the bribery, even if the assistance or encouragement were provided in Britain. Likewise, a British company could from London encourage and assist an Italian national to commit bribery in Rome with impunity (assuming the Italian national was not its employee). By the same principle, the London company would not be guilty of an offence even if the bribery in Rome were being committed by its own foreign subsidiary. Given the realities of corruption in the modern corporate era, this was an unsatisfactory state of affairs[1].

[1] The problems of inchoate liability were separately addressed by the Serious Crime Act 2007, Pt 2. The Bribery Act 2010, Sch 1 amends the Serious Crime Act 2007, Sch 1, so as to

incorporate the new bribery offences.

E   WHEELS OF REFORM

1.83 In December 1996, the government published a paper on bribery in relation to Parliamentary privilege[1], but it was not until June 1997 that it produced a consultation document specifically on corruption. At the same time, the Home Secretary announced plans to refer the matter to the Law Commission, as had been recommended by the Nolan Committee.

[1]   Clarification of the Law Relating to Bribery of Members of Parliament (December 1996).

Law Commission proposals—round one

1.84 The Law Commission published its first consultation paper with provisional proposals for reform on 15 January 1997[1]. Responses were invited by 30 June 1997 and the final Report was published on 2 March 1998[2]. It recommended that:

(1)   corruption should be codified within a single Bill;
(2)   the public/private distinction and presumption of corruption should be abolished;
(3)   it should be an offence to act corruptly in the 'hope' or 'expectation' of a bribe, even when no such bribe had been agreed;
(4)   bribery should be split into five offences: two for persons corruptly conferring or offering to confer an advantage; two for persons corruptly obtaining or soliciting or agreeing to obtain an advantage; and one for those who performed their functions as agents corruptly;
(5)   the Bill should list relevant agent/principal relationships;
(6)   acting corruptly should be defined as acting 'primarily in return for the conferring of an advantage';
(7)   cases of procuring a breach of duty through threats or deception should not be caught;
(8)   there should be a number of defences available, including acting in return for remuneration from the principal or with the principal's consent;
(9)   in order to preserve consistency with other offences and avoid human rights issues, there should be no extension of police powers; and
(10)   bribery should be added to the list of Group A offences in the Criminal Justice Act 1993, Pt 1, extending the domestic courts' jurisdiction to certain acts of bribery committed outside the UK.

[1]   Legislating the Criminal Code: Corruption (1997) Law Commission Consultation Paper No 145.
[2]   Legislating the Criminal Code: Corruption (1998) Law Com No 248. Both the consultation paper and the report are available at www.lawcom.gov.uk/closed_consultations.htm#1998.

The government's response

1.85 Two years after the Law Commission Report, in June 2000, the government published its White Paper, *Raising Standards and Upholding Integrity: the Prevention of Corruption*[1]. It accepted the majority of the Law Commission's proposals, and stated at para 4.1 that they fulfilled the UK's international obligations, even those arising from instruments ratified after the Report had been published. It approved:

(1)   the focus on the principal/agent relationship;
(2)   the provision of exceptions;
(3)   the removal of the public/private distinction and consequent abolition of the presumption of corruption;
(4)   the definition of relevant fiduciary relationships;
(5)   the extension of jurisdiction to bribery abroad; and
(6)   the proposal that corruption offences be triable either way.

[1]   (Cm 4759).

1.86 There were notable points of departure, however, including:

(1)   the extension of corruption to include trading in influence, as provided for by the then unratified Criminal Law Convention on Corruption;
(2)   the inclusion of corruption by Members of Parliament;
(3)   the extension of jurisdiction to cover UK nationals committing corruption abroad; and
(4)   the retention of consent by a law officer to every prosecution.

1.87 One immediate result of the government's broad agreement with the Law Commission proposals was the swift enactment of the Anti-terrorism, Crime and Security Act 2001, Pt 12, considered at para **1.36**.

1.88 In April 2001, the government published its response to comments made in consultation[1]. The responses it had received to the White Paper had not caused it to alter its position, but a number of points of clarification were made. First, it rejected a suggestion that abuse of the markets should be criminalised, on the basis that this function was performed by the Fair Trading Act 1973 and the Competition Act 1998. Second, although the Corruption Bill would not extend to Scotland (where the Prevention of Corruption Acts would continue to govern), the Scottish Executive was keen to take a consistent approach. Third, it was considered that no extension of the SFO's powers would be necessary for it to be able to prosecute under the new offences.

[1]   Raising Standards and Upholding Integrity: the Prevention of Corruption: Government Response to the Comments made in Consultations (Cm 4759).

The draft Corruption Bill

1.89 The draft Corruption Bill was published on 24 March 2003 in largely the same form as had been recommended by the Law Commission[1]. The government's initial proposal to introduce an offence of trading influence had been abandoned, but its insistence on requiring the consent of the Attorney-General remained. The passage of the Bill was not a smooth one. Some four months later, the Joint Committee on the draft Corruption Bill loosed a barrage of criticism in the form of its 31 July 2003 Report[2]. While not disputing the need for reform, the Joint Committee considered that:

(1)   the proposed offences did not cover principal to principal bribery or where an agent unreasonably believes that the principal has consented[3];

(2)   the definition of corruption was too vague, making it difficult for businesses to understand and comply with, and risking interpretations inconsistent with, the UK's international obligations[4];

(3)   the focus on the agent/principal relationship was too restrictive[5]; and

(4)   the waiver of Parliamentary privilege in corruption cases should be narrowed.

[1]   Cm 5777, available at www.archive2.official-documents.co.uk/document/cm57/5777/5777.pdf.

[2]   Joint Committee on the Draft Corruption Bill, Session 2002–2003, HL Paper 157, HC 705 (2003).

[3]   At paras 30–31.

[4]   At para 26. For example, there was a concern that foreign public official 'agents' might seek to raise as a defence the consent of the person conceived to be their 'principal'. Alternative definitions were proposed at para 92.

[5]   At para 81.

1.90 The Joint Committee's conclusion was that the agent/principal model upon which the draft Corruption Bill was based needed to be reassessed[1]. In particular, it was felt that 'principal' may not always be an accurate descriptor for the victim of bribery, such as where the person who suffers loss and whose trust is betrayed is different from the person legally characterised as the principal. Similarly, the agent/principal approach breaks down where there is no principal at all, for example, a public sector worker who does not owe any identifiable duty.

[1]   Joint Committee on the Draft Corruption Bill, Session 2002–2003, HL Paper 157, HC 705 (2003), para 89.

1.91 The government's reply to the Joint Committee report was published in December 2003[1]. It accepted a number of the Joint Committee's recommendations, including the narrowing of the waiver of Parliamentary privilege, possibly pending the creation of a separate Parliamentary Privilege Bill; the 'downgrading' of prosecutorial consent to the DPP or a nominated deputy; and the need for further consideration regarding whether the exemption for intelligence agencies might breach international obligations. On the core issues, however, the government remained supportive of the Bill. In particular, it felt that:

(1)   the agent/principal model should be retained, since it had been successfully adopted in general terms in Ireland, Canada and Australia, and to abandon it would be to 'cast the criminal net unacceptably wide'[2];

(2)   bribery between principals was already covered by other legislation, such as the cartel offence in the Enterprise Act 2002; and

(3)   the effect of the 'primary motivator'[3] qualification would prevent small gratuities being caught[4].

[1]   The government reply to the report from the Joint Committee on the Draft Corruption Bill, Session 2002–2003 HL Paper 157, HC 705 (2003) Cm 6086, available at www.archive2.off

29

icial-documents.co.uk/document/cm60/6086/6086.pdf.
2   At paras 2–16.
3   That is, the requirement that the bribee act 'primarily in return for the conferring of an advantage'.
4   Committee on the Draft Corruption Bill, Session 2002–2003, HL Paper 157, HC 705 (2003), para 9.

1.92 Notwithstanding the government's broad support for the draft Corruption Bill, its passage was effectively halted by the concerns of the Joint Committee. Two years later, on 8 December 2005, the Home Office sought to forge a new path by the publication of a further consultation paper: *Bribery: Reform of the Prevention of Corruption Acts and SFO Powers in Cases of Bribery of Foreign Officials*[1]. The response to consultation was published in March 2007, at which point the government announced that it would be inviting the Law Commission to re-examine the matter. This time, however, to take account of the Joint Committee's reservations on the draft Corruption Bill and the recent consultation feedback, the Commission's terms of reference would be adjusted to focus on bribery. The government's response to consultation indicated that:

(1)   the agent/principal model was not acceptable to Parliament, and a new basis for criminalising corruption needed to be found;
(2)   'corruptly' was the most suitable epithet to govern the mens rea, but the lessons of the old law mandated a more detailed definition;
(3)   despite the enormous volume of attention the mens rea issue had received by various bodies, no satisfactory definition had been identified, and this was therefore a primary issue for the Commission to attempt to resolve;
(4)   in particular, the threshold of 'primary' motivation might be lowered, despite its utility in excluding cases of proper corporate hospitality;
(5)   although there were arguments for retaining the public/private distinction, exculpatory defences could be formulated to protect the private sector, possibly to include the principal's consent, corporate hospitality and 'normal practice';
(6)   the presumption of corruption should in any event be abandoned;
(7)   it was inappropriate to make specific provision for corporate liability in advance of the Commission's general review of the law in this area; and
(8)   consent to prosecution could be provided by the DPP or nominated deputy.

1   www.homeoffice.gov.uk/documents/450272/2005-cons-bribery.

1.93 The government made it clear that it did not wish to pursue separate offences of bid-rigging and trading in influence. It also took the view that a number of quasi-corrupt areas should be left for separate review. These included:

—   the offence of misuse of public office;
—   Parliamentary privilege; and
—   political party donations.

Given the areas of significant debate already identified by the draft Corruption Bill, the best way forward would be to find a solution to the primary form of corruption: bribery.

Law Commission proposals—round two

1.94 The Law Commission's consultation paper *Reforming Bribery* was published on 31 October 2007, and its Report of the same name on 20 November 2008[1]. The review was wide-ranging and explored a number of models for the new bribery offences, including the agent/principal relationship and alternative focuses on the stages of improper conduct in bribery (ie improper payment, improper influence and improper conduct). Consideration was given to separate mens rea elements for the briber and the bribee. Contrary to the government's indication, the case was made for a separate offence of bribery of a foreign public official in order clearly to satisfy Convention requirements. Various modes of corporate accountability were discussed, covering both corporate and individual liability. Defences proposed in the consultation paper of a reasonable belief of imminent danger, or that the advantage was legally required, were jettisoned in the final Report. It was recommended that there should be a defence to the discrete offence of bribery of a foreign public official that the briber had a reasonable belief that the conferring of the advantage was legally required. The appendices to the consultation paper and Report provided comparative studies and consideration of the interrelationship between bribery and other forms of financial crime. The recommendations in the final Report were the product of a broad spectrum of responses from the judiciary, legal practitioners, government departments, enforcement agencies, NGOs and other international bodies with particular experience in anti-corruption measures[2].

[1] Both are available at www.lawcom.gov.uk/bribery.htm.
[2] See Appendix B to the report.

1.95 In terms of the offences, the Law Commission recommended that:

(1) two general offences of bribery be created, targeting the briber and bribee respectively;

(2) the briber would commit an offence by—directly or via a third party—giving, offering or promising an advantage to the bribee or another, intending that the bribee or another perform a relevant function improperly, or rewarding them for the same, and this would include cases where the mere acceptance of the advantage would be improper;

(3) the bribee would commit an offence by requesting, agreeing to receive or accepting an advantage for himself or another with the intention that a relevant function would be improperly performed by himself or another, or as a reward for or in anticipation of the same, and this would include cases where the mere acceptance of the advantage would be improper;

(4) 'improper performance' should mean performance in breach of an expectation of good faith or impartiality, or in breach of a position of trust;

(5) the relevant function must relate to the past or present performance of a public function, or one connected with trade, employment or business activities of persons corporate or incorporate;

(6) there should be a discrete offence of bribing a foreign public official;

(7)   there should be a corporate offence of negligently failing to prevent active bribery, subject to an adequate procedures defence;

(8)   there should be an offence of consent to, or connivance at, corporate bribery by directors, managers, secretaries or similar officers of a body corporate;

(9)   jurisdiction should be extended to include offences committed abroad by nationals of, or those ordinarily resident in, the UK, or by legal persons incorporated under its laws;

(10)   consent to prosecution could be provided by the DPP, the directors of the SFO or HMRC, or authorised deputies; and

(11)   the bribery offences would be triable either way, with the maximum penalty for conviction on indictment being raised to ten years and an unlimited fine (or the latter only for corporate convictions).

1.96 Appendix A to the Law Commission's final Report contained a draft Bribery Bill and Explanatory Notes in accordance with its recommendations, which were warmly received by Lord Woolf:

> 'I am delighted to learn of the proposals of the Law Commission as to proposed amendments of the Law of Bribery. Although the proposals still have to be reduced to their final form, it is already clear that these amendments would result in a much needed improvement to our law and would redress the criticisms that have been made of our existing law by commentators from home or abroad. The new law should be much easier to enforce and while requiring higher standards of conduct is still perfectly fair. Those who conduct their business ethically should not fall foul of the proposed law, while those who seek to hide their dishonest conduct by the use of third parties should not be able to do so'.

The White Paper and joint committee report

1.97 The government published its response to the Law Commission's Report on 25 March 2009 in the form of the White Paper *Bribery: Draft Legislation* (Cm 7570). In his foreword to the White Paper, Jack Straw, the government's 'Anti-Corruption Champion', expressed his gratitude to the Law Commission for its thorough examination, and stated his belief that:

> 'the draft Bribery Bill strikes the right balance between the need for clarity and legal certainty on the one hand, and the need to differentiate between bribery and the legitimate giving and receiving of advantages on the other. It will provide the basis for a modern, clear and consolidated law that complements and supports our international efforts and equips our courts and prosecutors to deal effectively with bribery of all kinds, wherever it occurs.'

1.98 The draft Bribery Bill set out in the White Paper largely adopted the provisions drafted in-house at the Law Commission. The proposed defence to bribery of a foreign public official, namely a reasonable belief that the advantage was legally required, was dropped. Pre-legislative scrutiny began in May 2009 and continued for two months. Those giving evidence to the Joint Committee included:

—   Law Commissioner Professor Jeremy Horder, who had primary responsibility for the Commission's bribery project;

—   distinguished practitioners and academics whose views had helped sculpt the Commission's proposals;

—   the heads of major business confederates;

— the directors of the primary enforcement agencies;
— Jack Straw, Secretary of State for Justice; and
— the Attorney-General, Baroness Scotland of Asthal QC[1].

Despite a number of amendments being proposed, support for the Bribery Bill was strong.

[1] The uncorrected transcripts of the evidence presented to the Joint Committee are available at www.publications.parliament.uk/pa/jt/jtbribe.htm.

1.99 The Joint Committee's Report was published on 28 July 2009[1]. The Committee supported the thrust of the Bribery Bill, but expressed its discontent over the speed with which its passage through Parliament was being propelled[2]:

'We strongly support the draft Bribery Bill. It represents an important, indeed overdue, step in reforming the United Kingdom's bribery laws, which have been a source of criticism at home and abroad for more than thirty years. We also welcome the draft Bill's publication for pre-legislative scrutiny, but we are disappointed that the government has given us so little time to carry out our task. Our dissatisfaction will be shared by many others if the government does not now find time promptly to introduce a Bribery Bill that reflects the changes that we have proposed'.

[1] www.publications.parliament.uk/pa/jt200809/jtselect/jtbribe/115/115i.pdf.
[2] At p 5.

1.100 It was the view of the Joint Committee that:

(1) the 'improper performance' model, restricted by the concepts of good faith, impartiality and trust, struck a careful balance between simplicity, certainty and effectiveness[1];

(2) no gaps in the criminal law were anticipated, but the government should consider carefully whether conduct properly to be characterised as a civil wrong might also be subsumed[2];

(3) the government should clarify its position on the extent to which cultural variations, for example in hospitality, could be taken into account[3];

(4) the Law Commission should be invited to consider whether the Honours (Prevention of Abuses) Act 1925 would remain necessary[4];

(5) the discrete offence of bribery of a foreign public official was an important step, and the defence of reasonable belief was on balance rightly rejected, but the requirement that the official be neither permitted nor required by 'law' to be influenced should be amended to 'written law', meaning statutes, regulations and case law[5];

(6) the requirement to prove negligence in corporate failures to prevent bribery should be removed (along with the disapplication of the defence by cl 5(5) where a 'senior officer' had been negligent)—although this would lead to strict liability, this would not be unfair, given that businesses are well placed to demonstrate the adequacy of their procedures[6];

(7) guidance on the 'adequate procedures' defence would be crucial, and must show that it would be interpreted in a flexible and proportionate manner[7];

(8)   prosecutorial discretion could be relied upon in instances of facilitation payments and corporate hospitality to avoid 'legitimising corruption at the thin end of the wedge'[8];

(9)   consent to prosecution could properly be given by the directors of the prosecuting authorities, especially given the pending reform of the Attorney-General's role[9];

(10)   the increase of the maximum sentence to ten years was supported for the Bill to have teeth, but the government would have to clarify how unlimited fines would be assessed, and would have to take action to prevent the automatic and perpetual debarring of companies following conviction[10];

(11)   the proposal to grant domestic intelligence agencies authority to commit bribery was entirely unsupported by evidence and might breach the UK's international obligations[11]; and

(12)   the clause relating to Parliamentary privilege should be removed so that an approach consistent with the Parliamentary Standards Bill could be taken[12].

[1]   www.publications.parliament.uk/pa/jt200809/jtselect/jtbribe/115/115i.pdf, para 35.
[2]   At para 36.
[3]   At para 41.
[4]   At para 50.
[5]   At paras 64, 71.
[6]   At paras 89, 103.
[7]   At paras 92, 117, 121.
[8]   At paras 138, 147.
[9]   At para 171.
[10] At para 192. The debarring regime is part of the Public Contracts Regulations 2006.
[11] At para 203.
[12] At paras 206–228.

House of Lords debate

1.101 The Bribery Bill was introduced to the House of Lords on 19 November 2009 and had its second reading on 9 December 2009. By this time, cl 15 on corruption by Members of Parliament had been removed in accordance with the recommendations of the Joint Committee. Central to the debate in the Lords were the key issues of:

—   facilitation payments;
—   strict corporate liability; and
—   the exemptions for the armed forces and intelligence services.

1.102 In relation to facilitation payments, Lord Lyell observed that the United States' Foreign Corrupt Practices Act had been amended 11 years after its entry into force to permit such payments[1]. Lord Goodhart repeated the concern of the Law Commission that decriminalising facilitation payments risked allowing corruption at the thin end of the wedge[2]. Lord Mackay of Clashfern gave an example of barge owners queuing to pass through a lock: 'barge people from the United States will give the pourboire and get through, while the people from other countries will get left behind'[3]. Lord Williamson of Horton spoke out in support of the 'bold approach' taken by the Bill[4]. An amendment proposed by Lord Henley to require 'corrupt intent' was met by a response from Lord Bach, for the government, who quoted the Law Commission's view that the 'lack of clarity surrounding this concept (of acting corruptly) weakened the effective application of the law'[5]. As a result, the amendment was withdrawn.

[1] 716 HL Official Report (5th series) col GC27, 7 January 2010.
[2] At col GC29.
[3] At col GC30.
[4] At col GC30.
[5] At col GC34.

1.103 Clause 7 dealt with the corporate offence of failing to prevent bribery. There was particular concern regarding the strict liability nature of the clause. Lord Henley raised the difficulties of consortia and contractors, through which much business in the petroleum, mineral, banking, financial and construction industries is conducted. The fact that these relationships are predominantly governed by contract raised the question whether cl 7 would be sensitive enough to cope with such situations[1]. Lord Tunnicliffe, for the government, responded that cl 7 would be sufficiently broad to cater for a variety of corporate structures[2]. There was marked agreement on the need for guidance to be issued in advance of the Bill becoming law, and Lord Tunnicliffe noted the work already being done by the Ministry of Justice in respect of this[3]. There was debate as to whether the requirement for guidance should form part of the Bill, and this resulted in the insertion by the government at the Report Stage of what is now the Bribery Act 2010, s 9.

[1] 716 HL Official Report (5th series) col GC57.
[2] At col GC58.
[3] At col GC51.

1.104 On the same issue of the corporate offence, it is noteworthy that, at the Report Stage, a further amendment proposed by Lord Henley was discussed which would shift the burden of proof to the prosecuting authorities to establish that the defendant had failed to take adequate steps to prevent bribery. Lord Goodhart, on behalf of the Liberal Democrats but echoed by Lord Tunnicliffe, described the amendment as a 'wrecking' one 'for the principal reason that if any prosecution has to identify a single individual . . . who [was] negligent in preventing bribery, it would make it almost impossible to obtain a conviction'[1]. The amendment was withdrawn.

[1] 717 HL Official Report (5th series) col 140, 2 February 2010.

1.105 The exemption which is now provided for the armed forces and intelligence services by s 13 of the Act, attracted considerable criticism. The version of the clause before the Lords was originally drafted more widely than its final form, extending the defence to actions of a 'law enforcement agency' investigating serious crime. There was considerable dispute as to whether law enforcement agencies should have the protection of such a broad defence, and this aspect of the clause was removed at Report Stage. The debate in the Lords went beyond this specific reference, however. Lord Goodhart for the Liberal Democrats stated that 'we would prefer to knock out Clause 12 altogether'[1]. The breadth of the drafting of 'proper exercise' and 'any function' was dangerously unlimited. So hotly contested was this clause that it merited its own Report by the Constitutional Committee, which repeated its recommendation which had been dropped by the government at the Draft Bill stage that 'the defences in respect of both the intelligence services and the armed forces should be accompanied by a system of prior ministerial authorisation'[2]. It was this recommendation that led to the compromise position of having the organisational and ministerial safeguards now contained in s 13(2), (3) and (4) of the Act.

1   716 HL Official Report (5th series) col GC96, 13 January 2010.
2   Clause 12 of the Bribery Bill: Further Report, Select Committee on the Constitution, HL 49 2009/10.

Reactions to the Bribery Act 2010

1.106 The Bribery Act received Royal Assent on 8 April 2010. Its entry into force, initially planned for April 2011, was postponed until 1 July 2011 to allow for publication of government guidance pursuant to s 9. The Act itself has been greeted with an admixture of enthusiasm, relief and trepidation. Enthusiasm came from those who strove hard for effective reform. Transparency International, for example, has described the Bribery Act as 'one of the toughest anti-bribery laws in the world, with several provisions that go further than the US Foreign Corrupt Practices Act'[1]. Enthusiasm also came from the prosecuting authorities, now fully equipped to tackle corruption head-on. Robert Amaee, former Head of Anti-Corruption at the SFO, confirmed on 23 September 2010 that firms paying 'significantly serious' facilitation payments would face prosecution[2]. In terms of the broader picture, the criminal law can now play an effective part in the fight against corruption alongside the regulatory and civil regimes[3].

1   www.transparency.org.uk/publications/113-2010-bribery-act-a-briefing-for-ngos/download.
2   www.telegraph.co.uk/finance/newsbysector/banksandfinance/8019024/SFO-to-prosecute-seri ous-overseas-bribes.html.
3   For example, in January 2009, the FSA imposed a significant regulatory penalty on Aon Limited for having inadequate anti-corruption procedures.

1.107 In terms of relief, Royal Assent must have been met with many a sigh and mopping of brows in the political arena. After over a decade of concerted effort from the Law Commission and the government, an unpalatable return to the drawing board and countless consultation papers, the UK now has in force a robust and extensive anti-corruption regime. Time will tell its effectiveness.

1.108 As for trepidation, lawyers and their clients are holding their breath in anticipation of the s 7 corporate offence and the defence of 'adequate procedures'. It will be an unhappy solicitor who finds his client the first in the dock. The MoJ final guidance, published on 30 March 2011, however, will have provided some reassurance[1]. Issued in conjunction with prosecutorial direction for the DPP and SFO[2], it sets out six principles, complete with commentary and case studies, aimed at guiding businesses of varying size and resources in the development, implementation and review of effective anti-bribery procedures. Katja Hall, CBI Chief Policy Director, welcomed the guidance:

'The Government has listened to concerns that honest companies could have been unwittingly caught out by poorly-drafted legislation and has clarified a number of important areas. These include the extent of liability through the supply chain, joint ventures, due diligence and corporate hospitality'[3].

Such sentiment is, however, not shared by all, with many criticising the government for bowing to pressure from UK business. One extreme view was expressed by Chandrashekhar Krishnan, Executive Director of Transparency International UK: 'Parts of it read more like a guide on how to evade the Act, than how to develop company procedures that will uphold it'[4]. One thing is sure: the early days of the Bribery Act will be replete with activity as companies seek to comply with the letter and spirit of the guidance. Busy clients upset about having to write or revamp their procedures will have to console themselves that the eradication of corruption will, in the long term, have a positive effect on their staff, trade and profit. As the Law Commission's Professor Horder in his evidence to the Joint Committee candidly observed[5]:

' . . . although I hesitate to say it, lawyers may be some element of a force for the good in this whole process, although they will make some money doing it, no doubt'.

[1] Available at www.justice.gov.uk/guidance/bribery.htm.
[2] Available at www.sfo.gov.uk.
[3] Press release, 30 March 2011, available at www.cbi.org.uk.
[4] Statement issued 30 March 2011, available at www.transparency.org.uk.
[5] Joint Committee on the Draft Bribery Bill, HL 115, HC 430, uncorrected oral evidence of 14 May 2009, question 38, available at www.publications.parliament.uk/pa/jt200809/jtselect/jtbribe/uc430-i/uc43002.htm.

KEY POINTS FROM CHAPTER 1

1.109 Key points from this chapter are:

- Historically, the law on bribery and corruption in England and Wales developed in a piecemeal fashion.
- In the modern era, bribery and corruption are a global phenomenon. There are now a considerable number of anti-corruption instruments in place designed to harmonise international measures in the fight against corruption.
- The old law in England and Wales was ill-equipped effectively to tackle corruption in its various forms. Compliance with the UK's international obligations was repeatedly called into question.
- Mounting domestic and international pressure led the government of the day to attempt reform. The Bribery Act 2010 represents the culmination of years of concerted effort and has been generally well received. Time will tell its effectiveness.

Chapter 2

NGOS AND OTHER NATIONAL AND INTERNATIONAL ORGANISATIONS

2.1 There are a plethora of NGOs and other types of organisations whose work is either primarily in the field of corruption, such as Transparency International, or whose work spans a number of fields of which bribery and corruption is one. Of the latter variety, some have sprung from a desire to promote a more equal world, particularly to ensure that the potential financial and social benefits in resource-rich countries are trickled down to the whole of society rather than being, through corruption, concentrated in the hands of an elite few or being funnelled abroad. Some of the organisations do valuable research and produce well-respected reports into particular countries or industry sectors. As such they are useful tools for risk assessment. Some also produce guidelines and 'toolkits' which can help inform policy and procedures for business enterprises.

A   TRANSPARENCY INTERNATIONAL

2.2 Transparency International (TI)[1] is 'the world's leading non-government anti-corruption organisation'. This is no idle claim, as it is the premier NGO in the anti-corruption field. Its international secretariat is in Berlin and it has over 90 autonomous 'chapters' worldwide. There are further countries in which either chapters are in the process of being formed or TI has a significant national contact. Its global objectives are reducing corruption in politics, curbing corruption in public contracting, enhancing private sector anti-corruption standards, advancing international conventions against corruption and promoting sustainable development by reducing corruption. It has unparalleled international influence and liaises, advises and consults with national governments and with international organisations.

[1]   www.transparency.org.

2.3 TI publishes a number of useful and well respected reports:

—   Annual Reports: setting out events and TI's work over the previous year;
—   Corruption Perceptions Index: an annual ranking of nearly 180 countries by perception of their corruption as determined by expert assessments and opinion surveys. The latest CPI was published in October 2010 and shows that nearly three quarters of the 178 countries in the

index score below five, on a scale from 10 (highly clean) to 0 (highly corrupt). Denmark, New Zealand and Singapore were tied at the top of the list with a score of 9.3, followed closely by Finland and Sweden at 9.2. Bringing up the rear was Somalia with a score of 1.1, slightly trailing Burma and Afghanistan at 1.4 and Iraq at 1.5. The CPI also tracks changes, for example an improvement in scores from 2009 to 2010 for Bhutan, Chile, Ecuador, FYR Macedonia, Gambia, Haiti, Jamaica, Kuwait, and Qatar and a decline in scores from 2009 to 2010 for the Czech Republic, Greece, Hungary, Italy, Madagascar, Niger and the United States;

— Bribe Payers Index: an assessment of the supply side of corruption, which ranks corruption by source country and industry sector. This was last published in 2008 and ranked 22 leading international and regional exporting countries by the tendency of their firms to bribe abroad based on the responses of 2,742 senior business executives. The Bribe Payers Survey, which served as the basis for the BPI, also looked at the likelihood of firms in 19 specific sectors to engage in bribery. Companies in public works contracts and construction; real estate and property development; oil and gas; heavy manufacturing, and mining were seen to bribe officials most frequently. The cleanest sectors, in terms of bribery of public officials, were identified as information technology, fisheries, and banking and finance. A second sectoral ranking evaluated the likelihood of companies from the 19 sectors to attempt to wield undue influence on government rules, regulations and decision-making through private payments to public officials. Public works contracts and construction; oil and gas; mining, and real estate and property development were seen as the sectors whose companies were most likely to use legal or illegal payments to influence the state. The banking and finance sector may exert considerable undue influence on regulators, a significant finding in light of the ongoing global financial crisis. The sectors where companies are seen as least likely to exert undue pressure on the public policy process are agriculture, fisheries and light manufacturing;

— Global Corruption Barometer: a biannual public opinion survey assessing general public attitudes towards, and experience of, corruption in various countries. The latest survey was published in December 2010 and captures the experiences and views of more than 91,500 people in 86 countries and territories, making it the only world-wide public opinion survey on corruption. It showed that corruption had increased over the last three years according to 60 per cent of those surveyed. In the past 12 months one in four people reported paying a bribe to one of nine institutions and services, from health to education to tax authorities. The police are cited as being the most frequent recipient of bribes, according to those surveyed. About 30 per cent of those who had contact with the police reported having paid a bribe. More than 20 countries have reported significant increases in petty bribery since 2006. The biggest increases were in Chile, Colombia, Kenya, FYR Macedonia, Nigeria, Poland, Russia, Senegal and Thailand. More than one in two people in sub-Saharan Africa reported paying a bribe, more than anywhere else in the world;

— Global Corruption Reports: a series of reports on an annual theme, together with country and regional reports. The 2009 Report, with a special focus on corruption and the private sector, documented the many corruption risks for businesses, ranging from small entrepreneurs in sub-Saharan Africa to multinationals from Europe and North America and examined the scale, scope and consequences of a wide range of corruption issues, including bribery and policy capture, corporate fraud, cartels, corruption in supply chains and transnational transactions, emerging challenges for carbon trading markets, sovereign wealth funds and growing economic centres, such as Brazil, China and India. The 2008 Report had a focus on corruption in the water sector. The next Report will be on corruption and climate change;

— National Integrity Systems Reports: The NIS country reports present the results of the NIS assessment in form of a comprehensive analysis of the anti-corruption provisions and capacities in a country, including recommendations for key areas of anti-corruption reform. They include an executive summary, country and corruption profiles and a review of recent anti-corruption activities. TI has conducted more than 70 NIS country assessments since 2001, as well as a number of related regional overviews;

— Progress Reports on the enforcement of the OECD Convention: This has identified that of 36 industrialised countries party to the OECD anti-bribery convention, which forbids bribery of foreign officials, as many as 20 show little or no enforcement of the rules;

— TRAC: Transparency in Reporting on Anti-Corruption: The first global survey of 500 companies' public reporting on anti-corruption was published in 2009 and found that, on average, leading companies still have a long way to go in demonstrating that they are embedding anti-corruption practices into their organisations. It was found that information about management systems lags behind companies' stated anti-corruption and anti-bribery policies. While companies may often report high-level strategic commitments to anti-corruption, they do not always report on the necessary support systems required to meet these requirements. Companies from Canada and the United States were found to be among the top performing group. Companies from Russia and Taiwan were among the weakest performers;

— Promoting Revenue Transparency: the latest Report, a joint project with the Revenue Watch Institute, was published in October 2010 and compared how much 41 governments disclose publicly about the money they receive for oil, gas and minerals exploitation, and about contracts and other basic data;

— Policy Position Papers: these set out TI's policies and the background research done on a number of topics.

2.4 The UK chapter is TI-UK[1]. It was set up in 1994 and is now registered as a charity with a board of trustees and an advisory council. The current chairman, John Drysdale, had a long career in banking. The executive director is Chandrashekhar Krishnan, who joined in 2004 having been Deputy Director for Strategic Planning at the Commonwealth Secretariat. The Director of External Affairs is Robert Barrington, who joined in 2008. He was previously Director of Governance and Sustainable Investment at F&C Asset

Management, and CEO (Europe) of the environmental research group Earth-watch Institute. TI-UK sees the UK as having a unique position as a world political and business centre with close links with developing countries. TI-UK's role is to raise awareness about corruption, advocate legal and regulatory reform at national and international level, to design practical tools for institutions, individuals and companies wishing to combat corruption and finally to act as the leading centre of anti-corruption expertise in the UK. Its aim is that the UK should no longer tolerate corruption nationally or contribute to it internationally though international financial, trade or other business relations. TI-UK has further specific objectives, such as preventing corruption in the defence sector: a success for TI-UK in this field was the launch of industry-wide anti-corruption codes in the UK and Europe in 2008[2]. Also, in the area of contraction projects, it helped found the UK Anti-Corruption Forum (see para **2.17**).

1   www.transparency.org.uk.
2   www.defenceagainstcorruption.org.

2.5 TI-UK has been particularly influential in the bringing into existence of the Bribery Act 2010. In 2006 it drafted a Private Members' Bill which was introduced in the House of Commons in May 2006 under the 10-minute rule. Following criticism by the OECD of the UK's record on anti-corruption, TI-UK's Bill was introduced in the House of Lords and was debated in a second reading in March 2007. The aim of introducing such a Bill was to demonstrate that it was possible to draft a simple and effective Bill (a government anti-corruption Bill having been roundly criticised by the Joint Parliamentary Committee in 2003). The Home Office recognised that TI has 'considerable authority' 'as a serious organisation with the combat of corruption as its sole focus'. Following that, TI-UK gave evidence to the Law Commission in the preparation of its report and to the Joint Committee during the passage of the Bribery Bill through Parliament.

2.6 In July 2010 TI-UK published its own adequate procedures guidance entitled 'The 2010 UK Bribery Act Adequate Procedures' which itself is based on the TI guidance 'Business principles for Countering Bribery'. This 95-page document is a detailed guide to some of the potential problems facing companies and to suggested procedures and solutions. It includes a short guide to the Bribery Act 2010, risk assessment, suggested policies and procedures and their means of implementation, monitoring and review and applying due diligence to business partners and a 231-point checklist.

B   TRACE INTERNATIONAL

2.7 TRACE is a US (based in Annapolis) non-profit membership association founded in 2001 by anti-bribery practitioners[1]. Its stated purpose is to 'promote transparency and anti-bribery compliance in international business transactions' and 'to set a common standard for two shared elements of anti-bribery compliance: due diligence reviews and anti-bribery training for business intermediaries and company employees based around the world' by pooling anti-bribery solutions and resources. TRACE has a number of 'partner' law firms around the world which provide pro bono information on each country's bribery and compliance issues. TRACE has an online resource service, which includes foreign law summaries and guidelines on topics such as gifts and hospitality. The TRACE Compendium is an extremely useful, albeit with a marked US bias, searchable database of bribery and corruption cases and enforcement actions. Non-members can also sign up for email updates when new cases are announced. TRACE also publishes annual reports and compliance guidance. 2010 saw the publication of the TRACE due diligence guidebook *Doing Business with Intermediaries Internationally* and the TRACE Global Enforcement Report 2010.

[1]   www.traceinternational.org.

C   GLOBAL WITNESS

2.8 Global Witness[1] was established in the UK 1993 by three men who worked at the Environmental Investigation Agency. Now it has over 40 staff and offices in London and the US. The focus of its original attention was on the role played by natural resources in fuelling corruption and conflict. After investigating the funding of the Khmer Rouge through the illegal timber trade, it tuned its attention to 'blood diamonds' reporting in 1998 on the use of diamonds in the civil war in Angola, then to corruption in the oil industry in Angola in a report published in 1998. Global Witness co-launched Publish What You Pay in 2002 (see para **2.20**) and in 2003 was nominated for the Nobel Peace Prize for work on conflict diamonds. Since then it has investigated the smuggling of natural resources in the Congo (DRC), the Burmese illegal timber trade and corruption in the cocoa trade. Its latest campaign centred on the role of banks in facilitating corruption; its report on this was published in October 2010 and concluded that 'British high street banks have accepted millions of pounds in deposits from corrupt Nigerian politicians, raising serious questions about their commitment to tackling financial crime'[2].

[1]   www.globalwitness.org.
[2]   www.globalwitness.org/library/british-banks-complicit-nigerian-corruption-court-documents-reveal.

2.9 Global Witness makes the financial link between the value of natural resources to that of aid: 'In 2008, exports of oil and minerals from Africa were worth roughly \$393 billion—over ten times the value of exported farm products (\$38 billion) and nearly nine times the value of international aid (\$44 billion)'[1]. Its 2009 Annual Review states that:

'Our work has revealed how, rather than benefiting a country's citizens, abundant timber, minerals, oil or other natural resources can incentivise corruption, destabilise governments and lead to war. Rather than using their wealth wisely as a building block for development, countries rich in natural resources frequently end up blighted by inequality and bad governance'.

In further statements Global Witness posits that:

'Countries relying on oil and mining revenues are often poor, badly run, corrupt and prone to violent instability. This is in large part because the political elite place their own vested interests above their responsibilities to their population'[2].

[1]   www.globalwitness.org/sites/default/files/pdfs/2009_annual_review.pdf..
[2]   www.globalwitness.org/our-campaigns.

2.10 Global Witness, as part of the BOND group (UK membership body for anti-poverty NGOs working in international development) lobbied for the introduction of the Bribery Act 2010.

D   THE CORNER HOUSE

2.11 The Corner House[1] was founded in 1997 and is a UK not-for-profit company. Its aim is to 'support democratic and community movements for environmental and social justice'. Part of its remit is corruption and bribery where it impacts upon its core aims. In 2005 it brought a claim for judicial review against the Department of Trade and Industry's decision to weaken anti-corruption procedures following lobbying by BAE Systems and other defence and aerospace companies. The Corner House claimed that the Export Credits Guarantee Department (ECGD) had, in November 2004, significantly weakened its rules aimed at reducing corruption without consulting The Corner House or other interested NGOs. The Corner House argued that the ECGD had, however, 'carried out extensive and detailed consultation with its corporate customers and their representatives', who had lobbied the ECGD intensively on these rules and that 'The one-sided nature of the consultation that did occur led to a result biased in favour of the ECGD's commercial customers'[2]. The government settled out of court and agreed to instigate a full public consultation on its changes to its anti-corruption rules. In 2006, The Corner House and Campaign against Arms Trade began a claim for judicial review of the decision of the SFO and the Attorney-General to drop the investigation into bribery allegations involving BAE Systems plc in Saudi Arabia on the ground that the UK had contravened its obligations under the OECD's Anti-Bribery Convention and that the SFO Director had not upheld 'the rule of law'. In April 2008 the High Court ruled that the decision was unlawful. In July 2008 the House of Lords overturned the High Court ruling, stating that the SFO Director was exercising his legal discretion.

[1]   www.thecornerhouse.org.uk.
[2]   www.thecornerhouse.org.uk/resource/corner-house-double-victory-uk-government-departments-anti-bribery-rules-and-public-intere-0.

2.12 The Corner House gave evidence to the Joint Committee during the Bribery Bill's passage through Parliament.

E   INTERNATIONAL CHAMBER OF COMMERCE

2.13 The International Chamber of Commerce ('ICC')[1] was founded in 1919 and acts on behalf of world business, traditionally by making representations to governments and international organisations such as the UN. Its aim is to 'serve world business by promoting trade and investment, open markets for goods and services, and the free flow of capital'. It has associations in 130 countries and its thousands of company members represent every business and industry sector. The ICC promotes self regulation. In the aftermath of international bribery scandals in the 1970s the ICC published a report in 1977 on 'Extortion and Bribery in International Business Transactions', which included 'Rules of Conduct to Combat Extortion and Bribery'. The rules, although voluntary, had the objective of eradicating bribery and extortion. The

ICC encouraged the UN to adopt an anti-corruption convention. Following further corruption cases in the 1990s, the ICC published a second report in 1996 and a revised version of its rules was a consequence of the adoption of the 1997 OECD Convention on Combating Bribery of Foreign Public Officials. The rules were revised in 2005. The ICC Commission on Anti-Corruption latest handbook is entitled *Fighting Corruption: A Corporate Practices Manual*[2].

1   www.iccwbo.org.
2   www.iccbooks.com/Product/ProductInfo.aspx?id=654.

2.14 The ICC has actively worked with the UN, the OECD, the EU and the Council of Europe to counter corruption in business transactions. The ICC emphasised the need to combat corruption between private business enterprises. The ICC business perspective is that private business corruption distorts competition and that the distinction between public and private corruption cannot be maintained in the modern business world where there is a greater intersection between the private and public sectors. Together with TI, the UN Global Compact and PACI, the ICC jointly published *Clean Business is Good Business—The Business Case against Corruption*[1]. As that publication makes clear, corruption is expensive for businesses, with estimates of over $1 trillion paid annually in bribes adding up to 10 per cent to the total cost of doing business globally and up to 25 per cent to the cost of procurement contracts in developing countries.

1   www.unglobalcompact.org/docs/issues_doc/Anti-Corruption/clean_business_is_good_business.pdf.

F   BUSINESS ANTI-CORRUPTION PORTAL

2.15 The Business Anti-Corruption Portal is a website[1] managed by Global Advice Network, which aims to provide a 'comprehensive and practical business tool' for small and medium enterprises doing business in developing and emerging markets, to support such enterprises in fighting corruption. It is supported by the Department for Business Innovation and Skills, and other agencies and government ministries. The website or 'portal' contains a number of 'tools' including:

—   definitions and references to national and international legislation;
—   60 country profiles with key business and corruption-related information to enable corruption risk assessment to be carried out;
—   a model code of conduct;
—   due diligence tools;
—   anti-corruption initiatives;
—   training.

1   www.business-anti-corruption.com.

2.16 As far as the country profiles are concerned, they are designed to offer general guidance on types of corruption, such as bribes and facilitation payments, existing in each country and focus on the judicial system, the police, licences, public utilities, tax and custom administrations, public procurement and contracting, and natural resources and the extractive industries. The 'portal' has four different versions: English, German, Russian and Chinese.

G   UK ANTI-CORRUPTION FORUM

2.17 The UK Anti-Corruption Forum[1] is, in fact, an alliance, first formed in 2004, of UK business associates, professional institutions, civil society organisations and companies with interests in the domestic and international infrastructure, construction and engineering sectors. Its objective is 'to help create a business environment that is free from corruption'. It has a number of working groups:

— the Business Practices Working Group develops best practice anti-corruption guidelines;
— the External Liaison Working Group liaises with the UK government and international and national organisations to promote the interests and ideas of the Forum;
— the Law and Enforcement Working Group looks at anti-corruption laws and enforcement and recommends improvements.

The Forum contributed to the evidence before the Joint Committee as the Bribery Bill passed through Parliament. The Forum also holds meetings and produces publications on anti-corruption measures.

[1]   www.anticorruptionforum.org.uk.

H   THE PARTNERSHIP AGAINST CORRUPTION INITIATIVE OF WORLD ECONOMIC FORUM

2.18 The Partnership Against Corruption Initiative ('PACI')[1] is a partnership of CEOs from the engineering, construction, energy, metals and mining industries launched in 2004, but now multi-sectoral, with the aim of developing principles and practices based on integrity, fairness and ethical conduct to ensure a level playing field business-wise. It works with other organisations such as TI (see para **2.2**), the ICC (see para **2.13**), the UN Global Compact (see para **2.42**) and the OECD. It has developed the 'PACI Principles for Countering Bribery', which emphasise a top-down commitment to zero tolerance anti-corruption policies. PACI's publications include the RESIST (Resisting Extortion and Solicitation in International Transactions) anti-corruption toolkit.

[1]   www.weforum.org/issues/partnership-against-corruption-initiative.

I   U4 ANTI-CORRUPTION RESOURCE CENTRE

2.19 The U4 Resource Centre[1] is operated by an institute in Norway: a private social science research foundation working on issues of development and human rights. The Resource Centre was initially established in 2002 as a result of the so-called 'Utstein-partnership', which began in 1999 with an initiative taken by the ministers of international development from the Netherlands, Germany, Norway and the UK to formalise their cooperation. High on the priority list was anti-corruption. The U4 Anti-Corruption Resource Centre assists donor practitioners in more effectively addressing corruption challenges through their development support. U4 serves eight development agencies:

— DFID (UK);
— Norad (Norway);
— CIDA (Canada);
— GTZ (Germany);
— MinBuZa (the Netherlands);
— Sida (Sweden);
— BTC (Belgium); and
— AusAID (Australia),

by providing resources and services. Sweden (Sida) and Canada (CIDA) joined as U4 partners in 2005. BTC (Belgium) and AusAid (Australia) became funding U4 partners in 2008 and 2009 respectively. The subjects addressed on the website include political corruption, corruption in emergencies, public financial management, health, education, debarment and public expenditure racking surveys. TI (see para **2.2**) also provides a helpdesk for U4 members.

[1] www.u4.no.

J   PUBLISH WHAT YOU PAY

2.20 Publish What You Pay ('PWYP')[1] was launched in 2002 with the aim of promoting transparency in the extractive industry. Now it is a global network of civil society organisations that wish for oil, gas and mining revenues to form the basis for development and improve the lives of people in resource-rich countries. PWYP undertakes public campaigns and policy advocacy to achieve disclosure of information about extractive industry revenues and contracts. PWYP member organisations span nearly 70 countries. In 26 of these countries, there are organised national coalitions affiliated to PWYP.

[1] www.publishwhatyoupay.org.

2.21 PWYP's objective is for companies to 'publish what you pay' and for governments to 'publish what you earn' as a necessary first step towards a more accountable system for the management of natural resource revenues. Further, PWYP wants transparent and accountable management and expenditure of public funds in order to address poverty and corruption that often exist in resource rich countries. An additional aim of PWYP is for the public disclosure of extractive industry contracts and for licencing procedures to be carried out transparently in line with best international practice. It is the view of PWYP that the contracts between governments and oil, gas and mining companies are central to any effort to trace revenues and expenditures in the extractive industries. PWYP found that the recent commodities boom in oil, gas and mineral resources such as copper, tin and iron—driven in part by growth in middle-income countries such as China and India—had resulted in large profits for many extractive companies, but that in many countries where these resources are found high poverty levels persist.

2.22 In December 2010 PWYP won the Commitment to Development Award from the Centre for Global Development and Foreign Policy magazine in recognition of the US chapter of PWYP's role in the passage of a landmark provision in the Wall Street Reform and Consumer Protection Act, requiring energy and mining companies to make public their payments to governments. The provision requires energy and mining companies registered with the Securities and Exchange Commission to disclose payments made to the US and foreign governments for oil, gas or minerals.

K   TIRI

2.23 Tiri[1] is an independent non-profit organisation founded in 2003 with an aim of working towards practical ideas to make integrity work in society. Its rationale is that integrity offers the largest opportunity for improvements in sustainable and equitable development worldwide. Tiri's approach centres on facilitating and supporting collaborative, locally-focused interaction between different stakeholder constituencies to develop practical, effective and scalable solutions to identified challenges that promote greater integrity in public and private sector governance, particularly in relation to the management and allocation of public resources. Within its programmes it works with local organisations and reform leaders such as grassroots NGOs, universities, chief judges, African media groups, electoral commissioners, UN agencies and others. Tiri is currently piloting an initiative in China to promote ideas and solutions to problems in doing business in low governance environments and is working with senior executives, regulators, policymakers and academic experts.

[1]   www.tiri.org.

2.24 Most pertinently with regard to bribery, Tiri's programme in relation to Public Office corruption states that:

'Corruption and the lack of integrity cripple the delivery of basic government services and aid to citizens who not only need them but should have them as a matter of right. To counter this waste many countries have introduced anti-corruption legislation, whistleblower protection and accountability law. Yet governments are finding that whilst these negative sanctions and enforcements are necessary, they do not help to reinforce the positive values of public service. These central values which include service reliability, professionalism, merit and honesty have often been watered down or rendered meaningless in environments where abuse, nepotism and corruption are widespread. There is a lack of individual and institutional integrity'[1].

[1]   www.tiri.org/index.php?option=com_content&task=view&id=136&ItemID=.

2.25 Tiri further states that:

'a large percentage of public money—up to 60% in some sectors—is wasted through bribery, kleptocracy, issue of funds, procurement fraud and "ghost" payments. Further the justice and effectiveness of public service institutions is deformed by abuse of power, perversion of justice, election-tampering and nepotism'[1].

Tiri argues for the necessity of cultural and behavioural change and has started a leadership programme to 'professionalise' middle and senior government officials. The programme uses a combination of teaching methods, including case scenarios and case studies on DVD with country-specific elements and contextual training. There is online training and leadership encouragement to foster change within a country's public officials.

¹   www.tiri.org/index.php?option=com_content&task=view&id=136&Itemid=.

L   GLOBAL INTEGRITY

2.26 Global Integrity[1] is an independent non-profit organisation tracking governance and corruption trends around the world. Global Integrity uses local teams of researchers and journalists to monitor openness and accountability. It was formed in 1999 by an investigative-journalist turned government watchdog, Charles Lewis, who had recently begun a nationwide project assessing transparency and conflicts of interest in each of the 50 US state legislatures and South African political scientist Marianne Camerer, who was researching the successes and failures of anti-corruption efforts in Africa. Thus Global Integrity became the middle ground between political science and political journalism, rigorous data gathering and on-the-ground reporting. Global Integrity:

> 'works with in-country local experts around the world—journalists, researchers, and academics—to apply a unique methodology for qualitatively and quantitatively assessing anti-corruption mechanisms, openness, and government accountability. Our objective is to understand the public policies, institutions, and practices that deter, prevent, or punish corruption'[2].

This results in an action-oriented, diagnostic toolkit unique to each country's fight against corruption: the Global Integrity Report. This started in a small way in 2002 and by 2006 Global Integrity produced in-depth anti-corruption assessments for 43 countries on five continents. The Report includes countries which Global Integrity has put on a 'Grand Corruption Watchlist' which is explained in this way:

> 'Beginning in 2008, Global Integrity began looking for possible triggers of "grand corruption" in the countries assessed in the annual Global Integrity Report—countries where certain key anti-corruption safeguards were so weak that the risk of large-scale theft of public resources was greater than in most countries. We look in our data for three red flags: extremely poor conflicts of interest safeguards in government, weak oversight over large state-owned enterprises, and poor or non-existent controls over the flow of money into the political process'.

¹   www.globalintegrity.org.
²   www.globalintegrity.org/aboutus/story.cfm.

2.27 Working with a network of more than 650 in-country experts in 92 countries, more countries are covered each year in the annual Report. Global Integrity country assessments play an important role in shaping the World Bank's Country Policy and Institutional Assessments (CPIA) process. CPIA assessments are internal World Bank country reviews compiled on an annual basis for countries across multiple socio-economic dimensions. CPIA ratings significantly influence the World Bank's International Development Association loan allocations.

M   GROUP OF STATES AGAINST CORRUPTION (GRECO)

2.28 GRECO was established in 1999 by the Council of Europe to monitor states' compliance with the organisation's anti-corruption standards. Its objective is to improve the capacity of members to fight corruption by monitoring their compliance with the standards through mutual evaluation and peer pressure and by identifying deficiences in national anti-corruption policies and prompting reforms. It also provides a means of sharing best practice in the prevention and detection of corruption. Membership currently consist of 47 European states and the USA, and it is based in Strasbourg. GRECO has a number of meetings during the year, carries out evaluations and publishes reports. It works in cycles with thematic evaluation rounds. It is currently in its third evaluation round. It produces individual country compliance reports: in 2010 on Bulgaria, Latvia, Estonia, Monaco, Austria and Switzerland and other countries. In 2009 it published 'Corruption in Sport' and in 2010 'Political Financing' looking at the transparency of political funding, monitoring compliance with existing regulations and the penalties for breach of those regulations. A team of experts is appointed by GRECO for the evaluation of a particular member state, who then make an analysis based on a written questionnaire and meetings with public officials, civil society representatives and on-site visits to the particular country. A report is drafted for comment by the country and then submitted to GRECO either with recommendations for action that must be undertaken by the state or with observations. There is then a further compliance procedure.

N   UNCAC COALITION

2.29 The UNCAC Coalition[1] is a global network of approximately 240 civil society organisations in over 100 countries, committed to promoting the ratification, implementation and monitoring of the UN Convention against Corruption (UNCAC). Established in August 2006, it mobilises civil society action for UNCAC at international, regional and national levels. The Coalition includes international, regional and national groups working in the areas of human rights, labour rights, governance, economic development, environment and private sector accountability. The member groups include AccessInfoEurope, AfriCOG, Basel Institute on Governance, BRAC University Institute of Governance, Christian Aid, Commonwealth Human Rights Initiative, GAATW, Global Witness, Institute for Security Studies in Africa, PSI Link, Tax Justice Network, Tearfund, Transparency International, UNICORN and others. The secretariat for the Coalition is provided by Transparency International, one of its founding members.

[1]   www.uncaccoalition.org.

2.30 The Coalition engages in joint action around common positions on the UNCAC, facilitates the exchange of information among members, and supports national civil society efforts to promote the UNCAC. The Coalition's primary campaign objective during 2006–2009 was to secure an effective, transparent and participatory monitoring mechanism for the UNCAC. To this end, members engaged in joint advocacy ahead of and during key intergovernmental meetings. This phase ended with the adoption, in November 2009, of an UNCAC review mechanism that started operation in July

2010. The Coalition now seeks to ensure that civil society groups can contribute to the review process and to support them in making quality submissions. It also aims to gain government agreement to publish review reports for public scrutiny. The Coalition also sets advocacy targets in relation to specific UNCAC-related topics, such as access to information, asset recovery and protection of whistleblowers and anti-corruption activists.

O   ONE WORLD TRUST

2.31 The One World Trust[1] is an independent think tank: it conducts research, develops recommendations and advocates for reform to make policy and decision-making processes in global governance more accountable to the people they affect, now and in the future, and to ensure that international laws are strengthened and applied equally to all.

[1]   www.oneworldtrust.org.

2.32 It was established shortly after the Second World War by a group of UK Parliamentarians, who shared concerns about the rise of nuclear armament, the need to rebuild societies, and a still fragile framework of international law and institutions after the war. They founded, as one of the first of its kind, the All-Party Parliamentary Group for World Government (since 2007 APPG for World Governance) to promote the awareness and engagement of Parliamentarians in global governance, and to help the emerging United Nations and other global institutions to become democratic, accountable and transparent.

2.33 The One World Trust was soon after set up as a separate charity to promote research and educate the public about developments in relation to global institutions and policy. It promotes education, training and research into the changes required within global organisation in order to make them answerable to the people they affect and ensures that international laws are strengthened and applied equally to all. It also develops practical tools and recommendations in support of organisational reform, identifying gaps in the accountability of governance systems, and highlighting opportunities for cross-sector learning.

2.34 Its Global Accountability Report is an annual assessment of the capabilities of the world's most powerful global organisations from the intergovernmental, non-governmental and corporate sectors to be accountable. The aim of the Report is to broaden understanding of, and commitment to, common principles of accountability among global actors from all sectors. First published in 2003, the Report has assessed the accountability capabilities of 90 global organisations. The Trust believes that those most affected by the activities of global organisations have the least ability to influence them and that while there have been advances in extending principles of accountability to the global level, the results of the 2008 Report reveal that even the highest performers have only basic accountability policies and systems in place. The Global Accountability Report uses four dimensions—transparency, participation, evaluation, and complaints handling—to examine the capabilities of global actors to be accountable. Within each dimension, an organisation's accountability capabilities are measured by assessing the integration of key good practice principles in policies and procedures, and the existence of management systems to support their implementation. The Trust's website also contains some case studies showing the implementation of some organisations's policy in practice.

P GLOBAL ORGANIZATION OF PARLIAMENTARIANS AGAINST CORRUPTION

2.35 The Global Organization of Parliamentarians against Corruption (GOPAC)[1] is an international governance network comprised of some 500 current and ex-parliamentarian members in 60 countries who are dedicated to good governance and parliamentary oversight to prevent corruption. GOPAC programming is closely aligned with the United Nations Convention against Corruption (UNCAC). It has a number of national and regional chapters. Given the perceived level of corruption of politicians, one can only hope that such an organisation continues to grow.

1 www.gopacnetwork.org.

2.36 GOPAC has established Global Task Forces for each key policy position to assist parliamentarians identify specific actions they could take to combat corruption, namely anti-money laundering and parliamentary ethics. It has also produced a 'Toolkit' to provide a standard basis to identify strengths and weakness of the capacity and performance of their country's parliamentarians in preventing corruption, identify recent and any ongoing improvement initiatives and suggest further practical steps that might be taken[1].

1 www.gopacnetwork.org/Docs/kuwait/Declaration_and_new_resolutions_ENG.pdf.

Q INTERNATIONAL BUSINESS LEADERS FORUM

2.37 Founded in 1990, International Business Leaders Forum ('IBLF') is an independent, not-for-profit organisation working with leading global companies on responsible business solutions to sustainable development challenges. With 50 staff it has headquarters in London and offices in New York serving the USA, Canada and Latin America; Hong Kong serving Asia Pacific; Moscow serving Russia and an office in India. IBLF is supported by a network of over 100 multinational companies from Europe, America, Asia and the Middle East. It also works with government bodies and inter-governmental organisations such as the UN and the World Bank, NGOs and the public sector as well as having regional affiliates and networks across the world in key markets such as Latin America, Asia Pacific, Europe, Russia and the Commonwealth of Independent States (CIS).

2.38 One of its programmes is 'Business Standards', which is designed to reduce operating costs/reputation risks in markets where government regulation is inadequate or ineffective. Business standards and the counterpart, corruption, is a major area of IBLF's work with companies. IBLF stresses the business case for combating bribery and corruption. It produces a number of reports and guides which research and document examples of good corporate practice and which are practical tools and guidelines to help companies develop and implement anti-corruption policies. It has collaborated both with

TI and UN Global Compact in the development of tools for companies. EITI Business Guide, a joint publication of IBLF and the Extractive Industries Transparency Initiative ('EITI') in 2008, outlines how business can support the implementation of the EITI[1]. IBLF serves as the co-secretariat for the UN Global Compact in the UK and has advised corporate partners such as Unilever, BP, Shell, ABB, Diageo, Nestlé, and BMW on their engagement and communication in support of the Compact, including interpreting implications, internal communication and action programmes. Outside the UK it has held consultations, workshops and conferences on countering corruption in various countries including Russia, Poland, Indonesia, Turkey, Philippines, China, Czech Republic, Kenya and Hungary.

[1] For further details of the EITI see Chapter 10.

2.39 IBLF launched its anti-corruption work in Russia in 2007 with an initiative called 'Corporate Governance in Practice' which brought over 50 companies together to discuss how to improve business standards. In 2009, a series of round-tables called 'Reducing the Risk of Corruption in Russian Business' took place and in December 2009, IBLF co-organised a major conference for business leaders on improving the effectiveness of independent directors on Russian boards. Via the China Business Leaders Forum, and in collaboration with Renmin University of China, IBLF has been convening regular meetings since early-2005 for leaders of Chinese and foreign companies to come together to share good business practice. In May 2008 a new 'Integrity and Transparency in Business Relationships Initiative' was launched in partnership between IBLF, the Vietnam Chamber of Commerce & Industry (VCCI), TI and the Embassy of Sweden. This builds on a nine-year partnership between IBLF and VCCI that led to the creation of a Business for Sustainable Development Office in VCCI. IBLF has done similar work in other countries.

R   INTERNATIONAL CORPORATE GOVERNANCE NETWORK

2.40 The International Corporate Governance Network ('ICGN')[1] is a not-for-profit body founded in 1995. It now has a global membership organisation of over 500 leaders in corporate governance in 50 countries including institutional investors, business leaders, policy makers and professional advisers. Its aim is to raise standards of corporate governance worldwide by promoting best practice guidance, encourage leadership development and keeping its members informed on emerging issues in corporate governance through publications and the ICGN website. In addition, the ICGN actively promotes research in corporate governance by commissioning surveys on member opinion on key issues.

[1] www.icgn.org.

2.41 ICGN Best Practice Guidance includes: 'Anti-Corruption Practices' and the 'Statement and Guidance on Anti-corruption Practices (2009)'. The Statement provides initial guidance to investors in the form of questions to ask company representatives about anti-corruption policies and procedures, enforcement, transparency and voluntary initiatives. The ICGN recognised that 'investors have an important role to play in confronting bribery and corruption through open and constructive engagement with companies' and that:

'investors should engage with companies to ensure they demonstrate to their owners that they have appropriate systems in place to detect and corrupt payments, benefits or other actions and take appropriate preventative and enforcement measures to deal with corrupt activities'.

The ICGN made clear in this document that there was a high commercial price to pay for weak anti-corruption controls, for example deals being called off during pre-merger due diligence, difficulties accessing the capital markets of countries where anti-corruption enforcement extends extraterritorially and a greater risk of lack of control over financial fraud and theft of company assets.

S   UNITED NATIONS GLOBAL COMPACT

2.42 The United Nations Global Compact[1] is a voluntary initiative that seeks to advance universal principles on human rights, labour, environment and anti-corruption through the active engagement of the corporate community, in cooperation with civil society and representatives of organised labour. With over 8,700 corporate participants and other stakeholders from over 130 countries, it is the largest voluntary corporate responsibility initiative in the world.

[1]   www.unglobalcompact.org.

2.43 The UN Global Compact is a strategic policy initiative for businesses that are committed to aligning their operations and strategies with ten universally accepted principles in the areas of human rights, labour, environment and anti-corruption. It provides a practical framework for the development, implementation, and disclosure of sustainability policies and practices, offering participants a wide spectrum of management tools and resources designed to help advance sustainable business models and markets.

2.44 The UN Global Compact has shaped an initiative that provides collaborative solutions to the most fundamental challenges facing both business and society. The initiative seeks to combine the best properties of the UN, such as moral authority and convening power, with the private sector's solution-finding strengths, and the expertise and capacities of a range of key stakeholders. The Global Compact is global and local; private and public; voluntary yet accountable.

2.45 The UN Global Compact incorporates a transparency and accountability policy known as the Communication on Progress (COP). The annual posting of a COP is an important demonstration of a participant's commitment to the UN Global Compact and its principles. Participating companies are required to follow this policy. The UN Global Compact's policy on communicating progress asks participants to communicate annually to all stakeholders their progress in implementing the ten principles. Participants are also expected to submit a link to, or description of, their communication on progress to the Global Compact website and/or, Global Compact local network website. If a participant fails to communicate its progress by the deadline, it will be listed as 'non-communicating' on the Global Compact website. If a further year passes without the submission of a COP, the company will be de-listed. The UN Global Compact reserves the right to publish the names of companies that have been de-listed for failure to communicate their progress. The Global Compact website offers a comprehensive, searchable database of all Global Compact participants, including links to companies' annual COPs.

T   UNICORN AND TUAC

2.46 UNICORN[1] works with trade unions around the world to combat bribery and corruption by increasing awareness and use of anti-corruption instruments, campaigning for measures to protect whistleblowers and supporting trade union anti-corruption activities. It describes itself as making 'a unique contribution to the global fight against bribery and corruption by mobilising the strengths of the trade union movement'. Further:

> 'in the workplace, bribery and corruption threaten workers' rights, safety and jobs and create climates of fear. Winning the fight against bribery and corruption depends on the involvement of people on-the-ground: at work and in the community. Trade unions, as representatives of millions of public and private sector workers and members of civil society, have a crucial role to play'[2].

UNICORN is financed by grants from charitable trusts. It also receives in-kind support from trade unions.

[1]   www.againstcorruption.org.
[2]   www.againstcorruption.org/aboutus.asp.

2.47 The Trade Union Advisory Committee ('TUAC')[1] to the OECD is an interface to allow trade unions to consult with the OECD. It is an international trade union organisation which has consultative status with the OECD and its various committees. TUAC's role is to help ensure that global markets are balanced by an effective social dimension. Through regular consultations with various OECD committees, the secretariat and member governments, TUAC coordinates and represents the views of the trade union movement in the industrialised countries. It is also responsible for coordinating the trade union input to the annual G8 economic summits and employment conferences.

[1]   www.tuac.org.

U   INTERNATIONAL BANKS

2.48 It is worth noting that international banks such as the World Bank and the European Bank for Reconstruction and Development publish their own anti-corruption guidance. The World Bank in particular:

> 'views good governance and anti-corruption as important to its poverty alleviation mission. Many governance and anti-corruption initiatives are taking place throughout the World Bank Group. They focus on internal organisational integrity, minimising corruption on World Bank-funded projects, and assisting countries in improving governance and controlling corruption'[1].

The World Bank also publishes The Worldwide Governance Indicators which report aggregate and individual governance indicators for 213 economies over the period 1996–2009, for six dimensions of governance including control of corruption and rule of law. The individual data sources underlying the aggregate indicators are drawn from a diverse variety of survey institutes, think tanks, NGOs and international organisations.

[1] web.worldbank.org/WBSITE/EXTERNAL/WBI/EXTWBIGOVANTCOR/0,,menuPK
    :1740542~pagePK:64168427~piPK:64168435~theSitePK:1740530,00.html.

V   CONCLUSION

2.49 The above is not an exhaustive list of the multitude of organisations with some interest in and input into the topics of bribery and corruption. However, this chapter provides a body of information which will enable individuals and business enterprises to carry out further research into particular countries or business and industry sectors, to make risk assessments and to form policies, in particular using the many suggested guidelines and toolkits available, to counter bribery within their own business practices. Many of the organisations encourage contact with their experts and are more than willing to assist with information.

Chapter 3

UK LEGISLATION PRIOR TO THE BRIBERY ACT 2010

A   OVERVIEW

3.1 The Bribery Act 2010, although much wider in scope, has some of its roots in the previous law which sought to counter corruption in certain areas. An overview and knowledge of the past authorities and legislation is important for assessing the ways in which the new Act will be used. It is also a useful guide to sentencing.

3.2 Bribery has been unlawful since at least Magna Carta. The Great Charter declares: 'We will sell to no man . . . either justice or right'. As well as being an offence at common law various statutes outlaw bribery. The main statutes are the Public Bodies Corrupt Practices Act 1889 and the Prevention of Corruption Act 1906, both of which are supplemented by the Prevention of Corruption Act 1916. In addition the Anti-Terrorism, Crime and Security Act 2001 contains important provisions. Various other statutes also contain discrete offences involving bribery, namely: Sale of Offices Act 1551; Sale of Offices Act 1809; Honours (Prevention of Abuses) Act 1925; Licensing Act 1964; Criminal Law Act 1967; Local Government Act 1972; Customs and Excise Management Act 1979 and the Representation of the People Act 1983.

3.3 As we shall see, the common law offence and the statutory offences do not form a coherent pattern of offences but rather are a miscellany of different forms of bribery distinguished by a particular office held or function performed by the individual concerned. Even the mental element involved varies from offence to offence save where there is a requirement of acting 'corruptly' as in the Public Bodies Corrupt Practices Act 1889 and the Prevention of Corruption Act 1906. In practice, offences are tried under the relevant statutory provisions rather than at common law.

B   COMMON LAW OFFENCES

Bribery

3.4 According to *Russell on Crime*[1] bribery at common law is 'the receiving or offering [of] any undue reward by or to any person whatsoever, in a public office, in order to influence his behaviour in office, and incline him to act contrary to the known rules of honesty and integrity'. In other words, it is a crime to bribe the holder of a public office or for any office holder to accept a bribe. Both the maker of the bribe and its recipient commit the offence but if the public officer does not accept the bribe, the maker alone may be guilty of attempting to bribe.

¹   (12th edn, 1964), p 381.

The bribe itself: 'Any undue reward'

3.5 A reward that is in the nature of a treat only is no bribe at common law. Willes J in the *Bodmin Case*¹ stated he as a judge had to swear that he would not take any gift from a man who had a plea pending unless it was 'meat or drink, and that of small value'. When does entertainment become a bribe? Nicholas J in the South African authority of *S v Deal Enterprises (Pty) Ltd*² explained that there had to be an intention to bribe by the reward and that such intention could be inferred from all the circumstances. These circumstances include the nature and value of the entertainment, the relationship between the giver and recipient of the entertainment and their relative social and financial positions. The rationale for not prohibiting small value treats/entertainment is linked to the mental element, which is discussed in para **3.8**. Small value items are not regarded as having been given in order to influence a person, or incline him to act contrary to the known rules of honesty and integrity³. The purchase and sale of public offices is also bribery⁴.

¹   (1869) 1 O'M & H 121.
²   1978 (3) SA 302 at 311.
³   *Woodward v Maltby* [1959] VR 794.
⁴   *R v Pollman* (1809) 2 Camp 229.

The person being bribed: 'Public officer'

3.6 The following are examples of bribes of public officers at common law:

—   a privy councillor¹;
—   a coroner²;
—   a juror³;
—   a justice of the peace⁴.

¹   *R v Vaughan* (1769) 4 Burr 2494.
²   *R v Harrison* (1800) 1 East PC 382.
³   *R v Young* (1801) 2 East 14.
⁴   *R v Gurney* (1867) 31 JP 584.

3.7 Whilst all of the above examples relate to persons involved in the administration of justice, 'public office' is not restricted to this area. The Court of Appeal in *R v Whitaker*¹ stated that it covers any officer who discharges any duty in the discharge of which the public are interested, and especially so if he is paid out of a public fund. In that case it was held to apply to the colonel of a regiment who accepted from a firm of caterers sums of money paid to induce him to accept their representative as tenant of the regimental canteen. The offence also applies even if the duty involved is not a full-time post such as electors at:

— parliamentary elections[2];
— local government elections[3].

[1]   [1914] 3 KB 1283, 10 Cr App Rep 245.
[2]   *R v Pitt and Mead* (1762) 3 Burr 1335.
[3]   *R v Lancaster and Worrall* (1890) 16 Cox CC 737.

The mental element

3.8 As we have seen in the definition by Russell, vis-à-vis the public officer, the maker of the bribe must intend to 'influence his behaviour in office, and incline him to act contrary to the known rules of honesty and integrity'. Of course, this will include situations where the public officer is to act in breach of his duties of office, but this is not a necessary ingredient. In the case of attempting to bribe a justice of the peace in *Gurney* (see para **3.6**) it was held sufficient that the attempt was simply to have any effect at all on the justice's decision.

Territorial jurisdiction

3.9 The Anti-Terrorism, Crime and Security Act 2001 is considered in more detail at para **3.39** ff. For the purpose of the common law offence the public officer does not need to have a connection with the UK nor carry out his functions in the UK (Anti-Terrorism, Crime and Security Act 2001, s 108(1)).

Embracery

3.10 The offence of embracery is now considered obsolete as it was last charged in the nineteenth century. It involves any attempt to corrupt or influence or instruct any juror or incline them to favour one side rather than the other by money, promises, threats or persuasions. It is irrelevant whether the jurors actually deliver any verdict or if they do, whether the verdict be a true one or not[1].

[1]   Hawk PC c 27 tit 8; *R v Opie and Dodge* (1670) 1 Wms Saund 300; *R v Dunn* [1906] Vict LR 493.

3.11 The reason the offence is now regarded as obsolete and has not been used for over a century is that at common law the behaviour is more likely to be charged as either a conspiracy to pervert the course of justice or (if only a single person is involved) as a contempt of court[1]. In addition, by the Criminal Justice and Public Order Act 1994, s 51, it is now a statutory offence to intimidate a witness or juror.

[1]   *R v Owen* [1976] 3 All ER 239, [1976] 1 WLR 840, CA; *A-G v Judd* [1995] COD 15, DC.

Misconduct in public office

3.12 This common law offence overlaps with that of simple bribery. It is committed by the holder of a public office and, as with bribery, it will extend to persons holding judicial posts, central and local government, civil servants and police officers. The 'misconduct' may be an act or omission and so malfeasance, misfeasance and neglect of duty are all included. It was once thought that the culpability required dishonesty or corruption as the cases in the eighteenth and nineteenth centuries concerned these matters, but this was 'an accident of circumstance and not a necessary ingredient of the offence'[1]. What is required is 'wilful', ie deliberate, misconduct. According to *A-G's Reference (No 3 of 2004)*[2] the wilful conduct involves 'deliberately doing something which is wrong, knowing it to be wrong or with reckless indifference as to whether it is wrong or not'. The

> ' . . . element of culpability which is not restricted to corruption or dishonesty . . . must be of such a degree that the misconduct impugned is calculated to injure the public interest so as to call for condemnation and punishment'[3].

The degree of misconduct is high and so a serious mistake alone is insufficient[4].

[1] Widgery CJ in *R v Dytham* [1979] QB 722 at 726.
[2] [2004] EWCA Crim 868, [2005] 1 QB 73 at [28].
[3] *R v Dytham* [1979] 1 QB 722 at 727.
[4] *A-G's Reference (No 3 of 2004)*at [56].

3.13 Examples of the offence include:

— a constable neglecting to levy a penalty under a justice's warrant[1];
— a magistrate alleged for 'fear or favour' to have refused to take the examination of two persons[2];
— a county court registrar who ordered monies to be paid out of court in funds for claimants for his own personal advantage[3];
— a police officer ignoring a violent offence being committed in front of him[4];
— a local authority manager improperly getting his men to perform work at the house of his girlfriend[5];
— a police officer misusing the Police National Computer to supply confidential information to a criminal[6].

[1] *R v Wyat (or Wyatt)* (1705) Fortes Rep 127.
[2] *R v Borron* (1820) 3 B & Ald 432.
[3] *R v Llewellyn-Jones* [1968] 1 QB 429, [1967] 3 All ER 225, CA.
[4] *R v Dytham* [1979] 1 QB 722.
[5] *R v Bowden* [1995] 4 All ER 505, [1996] 1 WLR 98, CA.
[6] *R v Hardy, A-G's Reference (No 1 of 2007)* [2007] EWCA Crim 760, [2007] 2 Cr App Rep (S) 544.

Penalties for the common law offences

3.14 The offences above at common law are triable only on indictment and the penalty is imprisonment and/or an unlimited fine, both at the court's discretion. In effect, up to life imprisonment is available at common law as well as non-custodial sentences such as disqualification from company directorship.

C   PUBLIC BODIES CORRUPT PRACTICES ACT 1889

Definition of the offences

3.15 The Public Bodies Corrupt Practices Act 1889 ('the PBCPA 1889') relates to corruption in public office, as the title makes clear. It contains two offences in s 1 which are mirror images of each other. The first relates to the recipient of a bribe and the second to the maker of it. It provides:

'(1)   Every person who shall by himself or by or in conjunction with any other person, corruptly solicit or receive, or agree to receive, for himself, or for any other person, any gift, loan, fee, reward, or advantage whatever as an inducement to, or reward for, or otherwise on account of any member, officer, or servant of a public body as in this Act defined, doing or forbearing to do anything in respect of any matter or transaction whatsoever, actual or proposed, in which the said public body is concerned, shall be guilty of a misdemeanour.

(2)   Every person who shall by himself or by or in conjunction with any other person corruptly give, promise, or offer any gift, loan, fee, reward, or advantage whatsoever to any person, whether for the benefit of that person or of another person, as an inducement to or reward for or otherwise on account of any member, officer, or servant of any public body as in this Act defined, doing or forbearing to do anything in respect of any matter or transaction whatsoever, actual or proposed, in which such public body as aforesaid is concerned, shall be guilty of a misdemeanour'.

3.16 For the bribe to be corrupt there must be a causal link between it and an act or omission relating to the public office held. So the bribe must act as an inducement to, a reward for, or otherwise on account of the public officer doing or forbearing to do anything in respect of a matter concerning his office.

Definition of relevant terms (s 7)

3.17 The bribe can take many forms, namely 'gift, loan, fee, reward, or advantage'. The terms 'gift', 'loan', 'fee' and 'reward' are not defined, although 'advantage' is given a partial definition by s 7:

'Advantage includes any office or dignity, and any forbearance to demand any money or money's worth or valuable thing, and includes any aid, vote, consent, or influence, or pretended aid, vote, consent, or influence, and also includes any promise or procurement of or agreement or endeavour to procure, or the holding out of any expectation of any gift, loan, fee, reward, or advantage, as before defined'.

3.18 'Public body' is defined as:

'any council of a county or county of a city or town, any council of a municipal borough, also any board, commissioners, select vestry, or other body which has power to act under and for the purposes of any Act relating to local government, or the public health, or to poor law or otherwise to administer money raised by rates in pursuance of any public general Act, [and includes any body which exists in a country or territory outside the United Kingdom and is equivalent to any body described above]¹.

The definition is supplemented by the Prevention of Corruption Act 1916, s 4(2) by stating that 'public body' includes 'local and public authorities of all descriptions'.

₁ Words in square brackets substituted by the Anti-terrorism, Crime and Security Act 2001, s 108(3).

3.19 So the PBCPA 1889 is not confined to local government corruption, but includes any body which performs public or statutory duties unless run for private profit[1]. Some bodies are expressly declared in their relevant legislation as a 'public body'. Examples include the Civil Aviation Authority by the Civil Aviation Act 1982, s 19(1) and the National Assembly of Wales by the Government of Wales Act 2006. However, such express declaration is not essential. The Crown is not a public body nor is any central government department[2]. So any corruption concerning the Crown or central government must be dealt with under the Prevention of Corruption Act 1906: see para **3.27**.

₁ *DPP v Holly* [1978] AC 43, [1977] 1 All ER 316, HL.
₂ *R v Natji (Naci Vedat)* [2002] EWCA Crim 271, [2002] 1 WLR 2337.

3.20 'Public office' is defined as:

'any office or employment of a person as a member, officer or servant of such public body'.

3.21 'Person' is defined as including 'a body of persons, corporate or unincorporate'.

'Corruptly'

3.22 The offence in both the PBCPA 1889 and the Prevention of Corruption Act 1906 requires the bribe to be given and/or received 'corruptly'. This term is not defined by the Acts but has been interpreted by case law. It does not mean 'dishonestly'[1]. The definition given by the courts is circular as it means purposefully doing an act which the law forbids as tending to corrupt[2]. The courts have not defined 'corrupt'. A dictionary definition of 'corrupt' is 'rotten, depraved or wicked'. In *Harvey* (above) it was held that 'corruptly' was to be construed as meaning the deliberate offering of money or other favours, with the intention that it should operate on the mind of the person being bribed, to encourage him to enter into a corrupt bargain. So any improper and unauthorised gift or payment offered to a public officer is likely to be corrupt.

₁ *R v Harvey* [1999] Crim LR 70, CA.
₂ *Cooper v Slade* (1858) 22 JP 511; *R v Wellburn* (1979) 69 Cr App Rep 254.

3.23 The following points should be noted on the issue of acting corruptly:

— no bargain needs to be struck between the parties. As such a 'reward' can be a gift given after the fact for a past favour without an antecedent agreement[1];
— a failure to influence the public officer in the performance of his duties is no defence[2]; so also a bribe may be innocently received by the recipient but still corruptly given[3];
— there is no need to prove the public officer was aware of the bribe or the improper offer having been made, so long as the apparent purpose of the deed was to affect the conduct of that person corruptly[4]. In that case

the person soliciting money for a bribe had no intention at all of using it to bribe the public officer but intended to keep the money for himself. It was held this was a corrupt payment;

— offering a bribe to a mayor with a view to expose the mayor's alleged corruption was still made with intention to corrupt, since motive is irrelevant[5]. This case is not the same as the situation where a bribe is offered to a public officer who pretends to accept it to expose the giver as being corrupt[6];

— there is a presumption of corruption in certain cases: see the Prevention of Corruption Act 1916 at para **3.34**.

[1]   *R v Andrews Weatherfoil Ltd* [1972] 1 All ER 65, [1972] 1 WLR 118, a case of a prosecution of a limited company.
[2]   *R v Parker* (1985) 82 Cr App Rep 69, [1985] Crim LR 589, CA. This was a case of a chairman of a local district planning committee receiving sums of money from a building firm after they were granted planning permission.
[3]   *R v Millray v Window Cleaning Co Ltd* [1962] Crim LR 99.
[4]   *Singh (Jagdeo) v State of Trinidad and Tobago* [2005] UKPC 35, [2006] 1 WLR 146.
[5]   *R v Smith (John)* [1960] 2 QB 423, [1960] 1 All ER 256, CA.
[6]   *R v Mills* (1978) 68 Cr App Rep 154 at 159, CA.

Penalties

3.24 Section 2 of the PBCPA 1889 (as amended by the Representation of the People Act 1948) provides that on conviction a person shall be liable:

— on indictment to a term of imprisonment not exceeding seven years and/or an unlimited fine;

— on summary conviction to a term of imprisonment not exceeding six months (to be increased to 12 months from a date to be appointed by the Criminal Justice Act 2003, s 282(2), (3)) and a fine not exceeding the statutory maximum;

— in either case a requirement to pay to the public body the amount or value of any gift, loan, fee or reward received; forfeiture of public office; a five-year ban on being elected or appointed to any public office and if an officer if servant of a public body, the forfeiture of any compensation or pension he would otherwise be entitled to;

— in either case on a second like offence, the ban from holding public office is increased to a life ban, with a five-year ban on being registered as a voter or voting at an election;

— in either case a person convicted of this offence may also be made the subject of a financial reporting order (Serious Organised Crime and Police Act 2005, s 76).

3.25 It should be noted that the fact that the appointment or election of the holder of the public office may be shown to have been invalid for some reason is no defence by the PBCPA 1889, s 3.

Consent to prosecute

3.26 By the PBCPA 1889, s 4(1), no prosecution may be started under the Act except by or with the consent of the Attorney-General. In practice this function is delegated and may be exercised by senior Crown Prosecutors but it is a mandatory requirement. Failure to obtain such consent will render proceedings invalid[1].

[1]   *R v Pearce* (1980) 72 Cr App Rep 295, [1981] Crim LR 639, CA.

D   PREVENTION OF CORRUPTION ACT 1906

3.27 The PBCPA 1889 is confined to bribing persons holding a public office. The Prevention of Corruption Act 1906 ('the PCA 1906'), however, is very broadly worded as it applies to both the public and private sector. In essence it makes it a crime to bribe any agent.

Corrupt payments

3.28 Section 1(1) provides as follows:

'If any agent corruptly accepts or obtains, or agrees to accept or attempts to obtain, from any person, for himself or for any other person, any gift or consideration as an inducement or reward for doing or forbearing to do, or for having after the passing of this Act done or forborne to do, any act in relation to his principal's affairs or business, or for showing or forbearing to show favour or disfavour to any person in relation to his principal's affairs or business; or
If any person corruptly gives or agrees to give or offers any gift or consideration to any agent as an inducement or reward for doing or forbearing to do, or for having after the passing of this Act done or forborne to do, any act in relation to this principal's affairs or business, or for showing or forbearing to show favour or disfavour to any person in relation to his principal's affairs or business; . . . he shall be guilty of a misdemeanour'.

'Agent'

3.29 The following points should be noted on the issue of who is an 'agent':

—   an 'agent' includes 'any person employed by or acting for another' and a 'principal' includes an employer (s 1(2));

—   given that 'agent' includes 'any person', an agent may be in the public or private sectors;

—   'a person serving under the Crown or under any corporation or any . . . borough, county, or district council, or any board of guardians' is also an agent although he may not be an agent in the ordinary meaning of that term (s 1(3)). So a superintendent registrar of births, deaths and marriages is an agent serving under the Crown[1];

—   whilst 'agent' does include Crown servants, it appears not to include local government councillors, who would need to be dealt with under the PBCPA 1889;

—   it is immaterial if the agent's affairs or business have no UK connection but are conducted abroad (s 1(4)). The same applies to a 'principal';

—   the definition of an 'agent' is supplemented by s 4(3) of the 1916 Act. That provides that a person serving under any other public body (see para **3.18**) is also an agent for the purposes of the PCA 1906;

— in the private sector it is more likely that 'agent' carries its ordinary meaning in law, namely employees and agents acting on behalf of a principal. As such it is likely to be narrower than cases in the public sector;

— if a person uses his position to receive a corrupt payment it is immaterial that the work in respect of which he gets the payment does not relate to his duties[2].

1   *R v Barrett* [1976] 3 All ER 895, [1976] 1 WLR 946, CA.
2   *R v Dickinson and de Rable* (1948) 33 Cr App Rep 5, [1948] WN 320, CCA.

'Gift or consideration'

3.30 The PCA 1906 uses the expression 'gift or consideration'. 'Consideration' is defined as 'includes valuable consideration of any kind'. The word connotes a contract or bargain between the parties, unlike a 'gift'[1]. Although 'gift or consideration' is a different expression from that used in the PBCPA 1889, namely 'gift, loan, fee, reward or advantage', there seems to be no real difference between the phrases. This is especially so given the phrasing of the PCA 1916, s 2, which refers to both Acts and refers to 'money, gift or other consideration'.

1   *R v Braithwaite* [1983] 2 All ER 87, [1983] 1 WLR 385, CA.

Comparison with the PBCPA 1889

3.31 The PCA 1906 has much in common with the PBCPA 1889:

— the requisite mental element is 'corruptly' and the law and cases set out at paras **3.22–3.23** apply. The case of *R v Godden-Wood*[1] dismissed the argument that *Harvey* (see para **3.22**) only applied to public bodies. The test for corruption was the same in both the public and private sectors;
— there is also a presumption of corruption in certain cases[2];
— the penalty is the same as under the PBCPA 1889 (s 1(1) and see para **3.24**);
— a prosecution can also only be started with the consent of the Attorney-General (s 2 see para **3.26**).

1   [2001] EWCA Crim 1586, [2001] Crim LR 810.
2   See para **3.34** ff.

False statements

3.32 One feature of the PCA 1906 which is different from the PBCPA 1889 is that s 1(1) continues on to create another offence, namely knowingly giving to an agent, or knowing use by an agent, of documents which are false, erroneous or defective, and which are intended to mislead the agent's principal. The end of s 1(1) reads as follows:

'If any person knowingly gives to any agent, or if any agent knowingly uses with intent to deceive his principal, any receipt, account, or other document in respect of which the principal is interested, and which contains any statement which is false or erroneous or defective in any material particular, and which to his knowledge is intended to mislead the principal; he shall be guilty of a misdemeanour.'

3.33 The following points should be noted in relation to this offence:

— no bribery or corruption of the agent is necessary and indeed he may be misled[1];

— the document concerned must originate outside the business of the agent and principal[2];

— 'knowingly' means knowledge of both the falsity as well as of the giving. Wilful blindness is sufficient 'knowledge'[3].

[1] *Sage v Eicholz* [1919] 2 KB 171, 17 LGR 354.
[2] *R v Tweedie* [1984] QB 729, [1984] 2 All ER 136, CA. In that case an employee concealed his failure to sell precious metals by sending to his employer's accounts section a trading sheet which falsely showed that the sales had been made. As the document originated from inside the business it was not covered by the PCA 1906.
[3] *Westminster City Council v Croyalgrange Ltd* [1986] 2 All ER 353, [1986] 1 WLR 674, HL.

E   PREVENTION OF CORRUPTION ACT 1916

3.34 In 1916 the presumption of corruption was introduced. This means if a person gives a gift etc to any employee of the Crown, a government department or a public body, and that person or their principal holds or seeks to obtain a contract from the Crown, a government department, or a public body, that gift shall be presumed to be corrupt unless the accused person can prove otherwise. This represents a reversal of the burden of proof and applies to both the PBCPA 1889 and the PCA 1906.

3.35 Section 2 of the Prevention of Corruption Act 1916 ('the PCA 1916') is as follows:

'Where in any proceedings against a person for an offence under the Prevention of Corruption Act 1906, or the Public Bodies Corrupt Practices Act 1889, it is proved that any money, gift, or other consideration has been paid or given to or received by a person in the employment of His Majesty or any Government Department or a public body by or from a person, or agent of a person, holding or seeking to obtain a contract from His Majesty or any Government Department or public body, the money, gift, or consideration shall be deemed to have been paid or given and received corruptly as such inducement or reward as is mentioned in such Act unless the contrary is proved'.

3.36 The following points should be noted in relation to the presumption:

— the burden of proof is upon the defendant but it may be discharged by proof on a balance of probabilities rather than the higher standard upon the Crown[1];

— the presumption only applies to the two Acts and so is inapplicable on a charge of a statutory conspiracy as it is contrary to the Criminal Law Act 1977, s 1;

— the presumption does not apply to anything which is only an offence due to the provisions on overseas corruption within the Anti-terrorism,

Crime and Security Act 2001.

[1]   *R v Carr-Briant* [1943] KB 607, [1943] 2 All ER 156, CCA.

'Public body'

3.37 Section 4(2) of the PCA 1916 extends the meaning of 'public body' for both the PBCPA 1889 and the PCA 1906 (see para **3.18**). It provides:

> 'In this Act and in the Public Bodies Corrupt Practices Act 1889, the expression "public body" includes, in addition to the bodies mentioned in the last-mentioned Act, local and public authorities of all descriptions [(including authorities existing in a country or territory outside the United Kingdom)]'[1].

[1]   Set out as amended by the Anti-terrorism, Crime and Security Act 2001, s 108(4).

'Agent'

3.38 Section 4(3) of the PCA 1916 extends the meaning of 'agent' for the purposes of the PCA 1906. It provides:

> 'A person serving under any such public body is an agent within the meaning of the Prevention of Corruption Act 1906, and the expressions "agent" and "consideration" in this Act have the same meaning as in the Prevention of Corruption Act 1906, as amended by this Act'[1].

[1]   See para **3.29**.

F   ANTI-TERRORISM, CRIME AND SECURITY ACT 2001

3.39 By the Anti-terrorism, Crime and Security Act 2001, s 108, the existing offences of bribery at common law and the statutory offences under the PBCPA 1889 and the PCA 1906 are extended to bribery of foreign individuals (see paras **3.9**, **3.18** and **3.29**). So a British national can be tried and convicted in the UK of bribing foreign public office holders, including foreign MPs, judges, and ministers under the PBCPA 1889 and of bribing foreign agents in both the private and public sectors under the PCA 1906.

3.40 By the Anti-terrorism, Crime and Security Act 2001, s 109, any acts of bribery or corruption committed abroad by UK nationals and/or bodies incorporated under UK law, which would be offences if committed within the UK and whether at common law, under the PBCPA 1889 or under the first two offences of the PCA 1906, s 1, may be tried in the UK. As the 2001 Act applies to companies, it means that a company may be prosecuted for authorising, directing or conniving in a subsidiary to pay a bribe to a foreign national.

3.41 The Act is not retrospective and so only applies to acts occurring after its commencement, namely 14 February 2002.

G   OTHER RELEVANT UK STATUTES

3.42 The following statutes also contain indictable offences of bribery or offences akin to it.

Sale of Offices Act 1551 and Sale of Offices Act 1809

3.43 The combination of these two Acts makes it an offence to buy or sell or receive any money or reward for any Crown office and any military or naval commission or place under the control of any public department whether in the UK or in any 'dominions, colonies, or plantations' under British possession. The 1809 Act was extended to the Air Force by the Air Force (Application of Enactments) (No 2) Order 1918[1]. As well as an unlimited fine and imprisonment, the office is forfeit and there is an absolute disqualification from holding it again[2].

[1]   SR & O 1918 No 548.
[2]   *R v Earl of Macclesfield* (1725) 16 State Tr 767, HL.

Sheriffs Act 1887

3.44 It is an offence under the Sheriffs Act 1887, s 27 to buy or sell various offices, including those of under-sheriff, deputy sheriff and bailiff. The offence applies to holders and non-holders of the relevant office. The penalty set out in s 29 of the Act is up to one year's imprisonment and a fine (or up to three years' imprisonment if he does not have the ability to pay the fine).

Honours (Prevention of Abuses) Act 1925

3.45 The Honours (Prevention of Abuses) Act 1925 prohibits both the receiving and giving of 'cash for honours'. It is an offence by s 1(1):

'if any person accepts or obtains or agrees or attempt to obtain from any person, for himself or for any other person, or for any purpose, any gift, money or valuable consideration as an inducement or reward for procuring or assisting or endeavouring to procure the grant of a dignity or title of honour to any person, or otherwise in connection with such a grant'.

The mirror offence relating to the giver of the bribe is contained in s 1(2). There is no requirement to act 'corruptly'.

3.46 These offences are 'triable either way'. On indictment the penalty is a sentence of a maximum of two years' imprisonment and/or unlimited fine and forfeiture of the bribe. On summary conviction, as well as forfeiture and a fine not exceeding the prescribed sum (currently £5,000 under the Magistrates' Courts Act 1980, s 32), the term of imprisonment is currently three months but will increase to 12 months from a date to be appointed[1].

[1]   Criminal Justice Act 2003, s 282(2), (3).

Local Government Act 1972

3.47 The Local Government Act 1972, ss 94 and 95 provide that any member of a local authority who has a direct or indirect 'pecuniary' (financial) interest in an actual or proposed contract involving that local authority must both disclose the interest and refrain from participating in its consideration or voting. Failure to comply with the disclosure provision is an offence punishable on summary conviction by a fine, unless the person concerned can prove he did not know that the matter was the subject of consideration.

Customs and Excise Management Act 1979

3.48 By the Customs and Excise Management Act 1979, s 13, it was an offence to bribe customs commissioners or officers, but the offence was repealed by the Commissioners for Revenue and Customs Act 2005, s 52(1)(a)(ii). Of course the offences at common law and under the PBCPA 1889 and PCA 1906 would apply.

Representation of the People Act 1983

3.49 This Representation of the People Act 1983 creates certain offences concerning voting irregularities such as personation (s 60) and false declarations (s 62). In addition certain activities such as making false statements about candidates are deemed to be 'illegal practices' (ss 106–112). A person is guilty of a 'corrupt practice' if they are guilty of bribery, treating or undue influence (ss 113–115). Although an election shall not be liable to be avoided due to 'general corruption, bribery, treating or intimidation', a person's election may be void if they have committed 'corrupt or illegal practices' which are so extensive 'they may be reasonably supposed to have affected the result' (s 164(1)). A person is also incapable of being elected if they have employed a 'corrupt agent', namely a person previously convicted of a corruption offence (s 165(1)).

3.50 The penalty for a 'corrupt practice' on conviction on indictment is one or two years' imprisonment (depending upon the type of offence) and an unlimited fine, and on summary conviction is six months' imprisonment and a fine up to the statutory maximum (s 168). For an 'illegal practice' only summary proceedings are available with a penalty of a fine not exceeding level 5 on the standard scale (s 169).

H   APPLICABILITY OF PRIOR LEGISLATION, AUTHORITIES AND SENTENCING TO THE BRIBERY ACT 2010

Applicability

3.51 Chapters 4 and 5 below analyse the Bribery Act 2010 in detail. Some points about applicability of the prior legislation may tentatively be made here:

— the essence of a bribe in both the Bribery Act 2010, ss 1 and 2, refer to 'a financial or other advantage', which is not defined by the new Act. As such, the case law under the old law is likely to be of assistance in interpreting this term;

— the intention required in the new s 1 offence is to induce an improper performance or to reward an improper performance. As such, the authorities may be of some relevance albeit the word 'corruptly' is no longer an ingredient of the offences;

— it will be seen that the offences under the Bribery Act 2010 are not restricted to particular functions or roles like the PBCPA 1889 (public bodies) and likewise the PCA 1906 (agents). The functions and activities set out in the Bribery Act 2010, s 3 are much wider and so it is doubtful to what extent the old law will have much application. As such the courts are likely to seek to dissuade advocates from arguing other such concepts, as the words of the statute in this particular respect stand apart from the prior legislation.

Consent

3.52 Just as with the offences under the PBCPA 1889 and the PCA 1906, consent is needed to initiate proceedings under the Bribery Act 2010, though the person concerned is the DPP, the Director of the SFO or the Director of Revenue and Customs Prosecutions. In practice, there is little difference, as the power is usually delegated (see para **3.26**).

Sentencing

3.53 Undoubtedly older cases will be of use for sentencing under the Bribery Act 2010. However, it should be noted that some adjustment will be required, as the maximum term of imprisonment is now ten years, as opposed to the seven-year term under the PBCPA 1889 Act and PCA 1906 (see the Bribery Act 2010, s 11), and for the effects of inflation upon the sums involved in earlier reported cases. There are no Sentencing Council Guidelines for cases involving bribery and corruption, and no guideline cases. Most of the cases referred to hereafter can be found in *Current Sentencing Practice*[1] or in *Banks on Sentence*[2]. The courts have always drawn a distinction between the public and private sectors.

The following cases are offered by way of illustration.

[1]   Looseleaf, at B9-1.
[2]   (5th edn).

Private sector

3.54 *R v Anderson*[1]: the defendant, aged 38, a man of good character, was convicted of conspiracy to commit corruption and three counts of corruption, having received consideration of £2,500, either in cash or holidays, relating to his employment as a purchasing agent and chief buyer with a large manufacturer, in return for showing favour to a company supplying parts to his employer. An original sentence of three and a half years' imprisonment was reduced to 18 months on appeal as the appellant was a man broken by the effects of the conviction upon every area of his life.

[1]   (1982) 4 Cr App Rep (S) 33.

3.55 *R v Hopwood*[1]: the director of a company which required supplies of steel pleaded guilty to one count of corruption and was convicted of four others, relating to orders for steel of inferior quality in return for the rewiring of his house and later sums of money totalling more than £200,000, and also other gifts in return for not disclosing a fraud being carried out against his employers by a third party, which cost his employers about £1.75 million over several years. Maximum sentences at that time were two years' imprisonment in respect of each act of corruption. An appeal against a total of three and a half years' imprisonment was rejected on the basis that the appellant was lucky to have received a sentence of such a length.

1   (1985) 7 Cr App Rep (S) 402, CA.

3.56 *R v Wilcox*[1]: the appellant received £32,000 in relation to the renewal of contracts by the company for whom he worked with another company, in respect of which he had neither solicited the payments nor exercised any improper influence to secure the renewal of the contracts. The Court of Appeal said that immediate imprisonment was inevitable, but reduced the sentence from 12 months' imprisonment to 6 months.

1   (19954)16 Cr App Rep (S) 197, CA.

3.57 *R v Anderson*[1]: the defendant, aged 56 and of good character, with a favourable pre-sentence report, pleaded guilty late to corruption. He was employed as a strategic rail manager by Railfreight in charge of six inland terminals that hired additional road haulage from private contractors. His co-accused was the manager of a firm of hauliers who agreed to bribe the appellant £25,000, to be paid in regular but small instalments covered by false invoices in order to make them easier to hide, in return for £1 million worth of business. The appellant had received £8,500 from the account into which some £23,650 had been paid. On the basis of the decision in *R v Kefford*[2] the sentence was reduced on appeal from 12 months' imprisonment to 6 months.

1   [2002] EWCA Crim 2914, [2003] 2 Cr App Rep (S) 131.
2   [2002] EWCA Crim 519, [2002] 2 Cr App Rep (S) 495.

3.58 *R v Welcher*[1]: W was convicted of conspiracy to corrupt and conspiracy to defraud. He was employed as an engineering technician by Mars the confectionery company. He received bribes from his two co-defendants, S and H, who were the sole directors of a precision engineering company, in return for placing Mars work orders with them for the maintenance and repair of its machinery and authorising excessive bogus payments to their company. The corruption continued over more than a decade. Welcher had received cash payments in the region of £500,000 together with other benefits and the gain to S and H was accepted as being £3 million. The trial lasted two and a half months. S and H gave evidence. By the time of trial they were both in their sixties. There was considerable personal mitigation for both and having regard to the confiscation proceedings they would leave prison without assets and would lead the rest of their lives in poverty or in reduced circumstances. S was described as a broken man. Reports for both men were favourable, particularly for S. Welcher received four and a half years' imprisonment. S and H's appeals against six and a half years' imprisonment for conspiracy to defraud and shorter sentences on the other counts were dismissed, the court noting the serious corruption, the duration of the fraud and the sums involved.

[1]   [2007] EWCA Crim 480, [2007] 2 Cr App Rep (S) 519.

Local government

3.59 *R v Allday*[1]: the appellants pleaded guilty or were convicted of con-spiracy to contravene the PBCPA 1889, s 1(1) in relation to bribes paid by contractors to council employees operating a council tip to falsify the record of weight tipped, thereby reducing the amount charged to the contractor. Sentences were reduced on appeal from 21 months' imprisonment to 8 months, from 18 months' imprisonment to 6 months, and from 12 months' imprisonment to 4 months and 3 months respectively.

[1]   (1986) 8 Cr App Rep (S) 288, CA.

3.60 *R v Dearnley and Threapleton*[1]: the appellants were convicted of corruption. The first appellant was employed by a Metropolitan Council with responsibility for property management. The second appellant's companies provided security services to the council over a period of several years and received payments of almost £1m for their services. The second appellant provided the first appellant with a car valued at £5,445. The first appellant secured a loan from the council to pay for the car, and to clear debts. The Court of Appeal noted that there had been no suggestion of lack of value for the services provided and the car had been a modest one and reduced the sentence of each defendant from 18 months' imprisonment to 12 months.

[1]   [2001] 2 Cr App Rep (S) 42.

3.61 *R v Bush*[1]: the appellant was an officer in a local authority. He was convicted of soliciting and accepting payments of £100 per week and other services over a period of six years in return for putting the name of a company on the contracts list of the authority so that the company had the opportunity to tender for large contracts with the authority. The appellant had received about £40,000 in all. A sentence of four years' imprisonment following a trial was reduced to two and a half years on appeal.

[1]   [2002] EWCA Crim 1056, [2003] 2 Cr App Rep (S) 686.

3.62 *R v Speechley*[1]: the appellant was convicted of misconduct in a public office. He had been involved in local government for nearly 40 years and had become leader of the council in 1997. From 2000 he strongly supported a local by-pass scheme which became a council priority. He owned land affected by the line of the proposed by-pass but the way it was registered did not reveal where it was and he did not declare an interest in relation to the scheme despite advice and publicity in relation to his interest. After the police became involved he sold the land for £22,000 which was a reasonable price, more than it was worth as agricultural land but much less than its value as development land, which value was directly affected by the route of the proposed by-pass. He had not benefited financially from his conduct and resigned before his trial. The police investigation began in 2001 and his trial ended in 2004. The court held that many people, including the appellant himself, believed that if the by-pass had followed the proposed route that the land would have increased substantially in value, that he had chosen to conceal his interest, to ignore advice, and to press for the proposed route using the weight of his personality and office. A sentence of 18 months' imprisonment was upheld.

1   [2004] EWCA Crim 3067, [2005] 2 Cr App Rep (S) 75

Central government

3.63 *R v Patel*[1]: the appellant who was a civil servant in the immigration service pleaded guilty to corruption for accepting £500 to stamp a passport with the words 'Leave to remain'. A sentence of two years' imprisonment was upheld on appeal.

1   (1992) 13 Cr App Rep (S) 550, CA.

3.64 *R v Foxley*[1]: the appellant was convicted of 12 counts of corruption, contrary to the Prevention of Corruption Act 1906, s 1. He had been employed by the Ministry of Defence for 20 years, during 17 of which he had been concerned with ammunition procurement. In return for payments of over £2m to companies in which he had a beneficial interest, which he had taken meticulous care to conceal, he had shown favour to foreign companies in relation to the placing of substantial contracts. There was no evidence that the ammunition supplied was of inferior quality or that his actions had affected the Royal Ordnance factories. He did his best to frustrate investigations and destroyed documents. Application for leave to appeal against a sentence of four years' imprisonment and a confiscation order of just over £1.5m was refused.

1   [1995] 2 Cr App Rep 523, 16 Cr App Rep (S) 879, CA.

3.65 *R v Bennett and Wilson*[1]: the appellants were convicted of receiving and giving a bribe on two occasions respectively. The first appellant was employed in a government department with responsibility for the procurement of publicity material. The second appellant was the managing director of a group of companies involved in supplying printing work to the department. Over a period of about two years the second appellant made available to the first appellant two company cars at the expense of the second defendant's company. Sentences of nine months' imprisonment for each appellant were reduced to four months' imprisonment because of the unexplained delay of three years in instituting the proceedings.

1   [1996] 2 Cr App Rep (S) 162, CA.

3.66 *R v Ozakpinar*[1]: the appellant, who was the chief procurement officer of the CPS and was involved in the procurement of self-employed contractors, was convicted of false accounting and three counts of corruption. He engaged two personal friends to do work on behalf of the CPS. In one case he ensured that a friend received the contract to supply a computerised shopping system for stationery by selecting the friend as the sole candidate to be interviewed. The friend subsequently paid the appellant £12,000 on the completion of two phases of work carried out under the contract. In the second case the appellant ensured that the other friend was on the shortlist of candidates to be interviewed to complete a contract. The appellant then took part in the interviewing process and helped ensure that the friend obtained the contract. The friend then paid him £6,000 upon completion of the first phase of the contract. In relation to the false accounting the appellant subsequently obtained payment by means of his creation of a false invoice of almost £12,500, in excess of the true sum of £5,000, to be paid to a third person, whom he then asked to pay the excess of almost £7,500 into his bank account. Following his arrest this sum was repaid to the CPS. A total sentence of two and a half years' imprisonment was upheld on appeal.

[1]   [2008] EWCA Crim 875, [2009] 1 Cr App Rep (S) 35.

3.67 *R v John-Ayo*[1]: a civil servant was convicted of 14 counts of misconduct by issuing travel documents known as 'refugee passports' to 64 people, and granting a further 180 fraudulent applications for such documents, for gain, over a period of nine months. A sentence of nine years' imprisonment was upheld on appeal.

[1]   [2008] EWCA Crim 1651, [2009] 1 Cr App Rep (S) 416.

Prison officers

3.68 *R v Sanderson*[1]: the appellant pleaded guilty to 16 counts of corruption and three of theft. Whilst working as a civilian joiner at a prison where long term-prisoners were detained he began to supply tobacco and later spirits. Thereafter he joined the prison service and continued the same behaviour. Unlawful sentences in respect of some counts led to a reduction from three years' imprisonment to two years on appeal.

[1]   (1980) 2 Cr App Rep (S) 147, CA.

3.69 *R v Garner*[1]: the appellants pleaded guilty to conspiracy to corrupt for bribing a prison officer to take luxury food, alcohol and cigars to a serving prisoner. Sentences of 18 months', 12 months', and 12 months' imprisonment suspended were upheld on appeal.

[1]   (1988) 10 Cr App Rep (S) 445, CA.

Police officers as defendants

3.70 *R v Donald*[1]: the defendant was a detective constable who agreed to accept £50,000 and in fact accepted various sums totalling £18,500 from a man who was the subject of criminal proceedings in return for the disclosure of confidential information about the inquiry and to destroy surveillance logs. A sentence of 11 years' imprisonment was upheld on appeal.

[1]   [1997] 2 Cr App Rep (S) 272, CA.

3.71 *R v Nazir*[1]: a probationer police officer issued a fixed penalty notice to the driver of a car. The passenger told the probationer that she knew the defendant, a more senior police officer based at the same police station. The next day the defendant approached the probationer and persuaded him to give him the notice. The probationer reported the incident. When questioned, the defendant admitted that he had intended to destroy the notice. He pleaded guilty to misconduct in a public office. He lost his job and his accommodation. He expressed remorse. On appeal, a sentence of three months' imprisonment was reduced to one.

1 [2003] EWCA Crim 901, [2003] 2 Cr App Rep (S) 671.

3.72 *R v Pike-Williams*[1]: the defendant, aged 19, was employed at the front desk of a police station and for eight months she accessed confidential information on her friends and associates. A basis of plea that she had not disclosed the information to anyone and was motivated by curiosity was accepted. There were a number of references and a positive pre-sentence report. Sentenced to two months' imprisonment, the Court of Appeal held that on the basis of *Nazir* (above) the case did not pass the custody threshold and a significant community punishment order would have been appropriate, but as she had served most of her sentence a conditional discharge was imposed.

1 [2004] EWCA Crim 2400, 148 Sol Jo LB 1063.

3.73 *R v Burrows*[1]: the defendant was a probationary police officer who was persuaded by a more senior constable to make up notes relating to alleged violence by a person detained at a violent disturbance, and containing a false allegation of arrest of that person by the constable. CCTV showed that the probationer officer had not been present at the time of the events involving the constable, and in interview the defendant admitted that he had not been present, and at the first opportunity offered to give evidence for the prosecution, and in due course did so twice. The more senior constable was convicted of intending to pervert the course of justice and common assault on the person whom he had detained, and was sentenced to 18 months' imprisonment and six months' consecutive. In relation to the defendant there was over a year between his plea of guilty at the first opportunity to misconduct in a public office and sentence. There were character witnesses. On appeal the sentence of six months' imprisonment was reduced to three months because of his plea of guilty, having given evidence for the prosecution and the delay.

1 [2005] EWCA Crim 2805, [2006] 1 Cr App Rep (S) 542.

3.74 *R v Kassim*[1]: the defendant, aged 53, had come from the Yemen in 1976 and had joined the Metropolitan Police in 1988. Shortly before his trial he indicated pleas of guilty, and at his trial pleaded guilty, to three counts of misconduct in a public office and possession of a prohibited weapon. At the request of a diplomat at the Saudi Arabian Embassy he had used his position as a police officer to make enquiries into mainly Middle Eastern individuals for which he had been paid on an ad hoc basis. Upon search of his house on arrest a CS canister was found in his loft. The defendant admitted making the enquiries on behalf of the diplomat and receiving payment but denied that it was as much as the £14,000 alleged by the prosecution, and a basis of plea placed a more favourable complexion upon what he had done at the request of the diplomat. The pre-sentence report said that he was struggling financially to maintain a young family and had expressed genuine remorse. He had an exemplary record until these matters and two impressive service commendations. The CS canister had been left in his bag accidentally and he had forgotten about it. He had been dismissed from the police, lost much of his pension and had been ostracised by his local community. It was held that any abuse of the police information system about members of the public was a gross breach of trust and exacerbated by its use by foreign embassies which may have any number of unacceptable reasons to misuse it under the cloak of diplomatic immunity. The sentence of a total of two and a half years' imprisonment was upheld on appeal.

1   [2005] EWCA Crim 1020, [2006] 1 Cr App Rep (S) 12.

3.75 *R v Gellion*[1]: the defendant was an intelligence officer for the police aged 40 with 13 years' service. He came to know an active criminal M, and following an armed robbery of a Post Office, to which a car registered to M was connected, he warned M that surveillance was to be carried out on him. The car was later found burnt out and the defendant then made a PNC check on the car, purporting to do so on behalf of another officer. The police then carried out a sting on the defendant whereby an officer informed the defendant that there was an investigation into the anticipated sale of a credit card cloning machine to a member of M's family. The defendant phoned M's home soon afterwards and learning that M had been arrested then telephoned M's brother. When the defendant's home was searched 50 Winchester bullets and 50 Luger bullets were found, some of which were capable of discharge from a semi-automatic weapon. The defendant pleaded guilty to two counts of misconduct in a public office and two counts of possessing ammunition. There were glowing references and it was accepted that he had not received any reward. He expressed remorse. On appeal a sentence of four years' imprisonment for the misconduct and three months consecutive for the ammunition, although regarded as severe, was upheld.

1   [2006] EWCA Crim 281, [2006] 2 Cr App Rep 464.

3.76 *R v O'Leary*[1]: the defendant, a police constable in Liverpool, entered into an agreement with a former police officer M, who had criminal contacts, to supply him with confidential information. He did so over a period of almost two months. A covert camera at his police station showed him using a computer to obtain the confidential information using the passwords of other officers to do so. On some occasions he asked other officers to make the enquiries. In relation to one of the six counts of misconduct in a public office the information passed to M included information relating a possible underworld revenge shooting. The defendant maintained his innocence until shortly before trial, when a new indictment was preferred, and had made very extensive disclosure requests which had generated an immense amount of work to comply with them. A Newton hearing established that he had been paid £1,000 for the information and had expected to be paid further sums. He had performed charity work. It was held that his activities might encourage gang warfare in a city like Liverpool. He had not admitted his guilt until a very late stage; a Newton hearing had been necessary and it was idle for him to assert that he should be given a full discount for his plea. The sentence of three and a half years' imprisonment was upheld on appeal.

1   [2007] EWCA Crim 186, [2007] 2 Cr App Rep (S) 317.

3.77 *R v Ranson; R v Kerr*[1]: the defendants pleaded guilty to one count of misconduct in a public office. Both were police officers: R had 18 years' service and K five years. Investigations into R and K involving covert recordings revealed conversations which strongly implicated both in involvement in drugs, and both had phone numbers in their address books of people convicted of drugs offences. Both made no comment in interview. K pleaded guilty on the basis that he was aware that R was involved in drugs and that others known to them were involved in the supply and consumption of drugs and that by failing to report these matters he was guilty of the offence. R, who had been K's mentor in the police, had become involved with associates whom he knew had been involved in drugs and had himself used drugs and had failed to report matters to his superiors because he had been investigated before for unsuitable acquaintances. On appeal R's sentence of four years' imprisonment was reduced to three years, but a sentence of 18 months' imprisonment for K was upheld.

1   [2007] EWCA Crim 760, [2007] 2 Cr App R (S) 342.

3.78 *R v Hardy, A-G's Reference (No 1 of 2007)*[1]: the defendant was a serving police officer who was friendly with a criminal J, who had recent convictions for violence, and he had associated with others who had criminal convictions. He was suspended and disciplined for associating with criminals during which proceedings he admitted that he knew of J's convictions and having looked at intelligence relating to him on the PNC. He was reprimanded and warned to end his association with J. He did not do so and obtained confidential information to help J seek out two men who had allegedly stolen from J's partner, and another who had assaulted J, which the defendant had then got his partner to hand to J. The meeting between the partner and J was under surveillance and both were arrested. On arrest the defendant admitted most of the facts but sought to justify his actions saying that he believed that J would only talk to the men about whom he had provided information. The defendant pleaded guilty to misfeasance in a public office. His career was ended and he lost some part of his pension. It was accepted that he had not gained financially and that no harm had in fact resulted to anyone. At first instance he received 28 weeks' imprisonment suspended for two years and 300 hours unpaid work which he completed swiftly and in exemplary fashion. The Court of Appeal took the view that there was a serious risk that J would subject the men about whom the defendant provided information to serious harm and that an immediate custodial sentence with a deterrent element was required. The minimum sentence giving credit for the guilty plea was 18 months' immediate imprisonment but he had already completed the unpaid work and had served the equivalent of a 10-week sentence whilst awaiting trial and a four month curfew. He had also suffered further anxiety whilst awaiting the hearing of the reference. The Court of Appeal substituted a sentence of nine months' imprisonment suspended for two years in place of the 28 weeks and 300 hours' unpaid work.

1   [2007] EWCA Crim 760, [2007] 2 Cr App Rep (S) 544.

Trying to corrupt police officers

3.79 *R v Brown, Mahoney and King*[1]: King, who was a former police officer, pleaded guilty to various conspiracies to pervert the course of justice, conspiracies to corrupt a police officer and corruption. Brown was convicted of one conspiracy involving King, and Mahoney was convicted of two conspiracies involving King. The case involved three separate transactions involving King attempting to bribe a Detective Chief Inspector in respect of pending enquiries and prosecutions involving Brown and Mahoney and the return of a very valuable stolen property for which King received a substantial reward. The meetings with the Detective Chief Inspector were recorded by him. Substantial sums were paid or offered to the Detective Chief Inspector in return for bringing prosecutions to an end and to enable King to return the stolen property without anyone being arrested. King was 51, of good character, and he was in financial difficulties. Mahoney was 32 and had eight previous convictions for dishonesty. Brown was 25 and had no convictions and dealt sometimes in second-hand cars. He was regarded as gullible. King was the prime mover. It was held that deterrent sentences were appropriate. The starting point for King was taken as nine years' imprisonment but mitigating factors reduced the sentence to six years, with all sentences being made concurrent so that the total of nine years was reduced to six. Mahoney's sentence of five years' imprisonment was reduced to three and a half years and Brown's sentence of three years' imprisonment was reduced to 21 months.

[1]   [2000] 2 Cr App Rep (S) 284.

3.80 *R v Smith*[1]: the defendant, D, was a police sergeant in the CID and H was a drug dealer who was sentenced to eight years' imprisonment for drug trafficking offences, £130,000 having been found at his address. They pleaded guilty, shortly after a jury had been empanelled, to a conspiracy involving police corruption over a period of four years. H had supplied D with money and information about other criminals involved in drugs as D's unregistered informant, about which D had not told his superiors. H had suggested planting drugs on other criminals. D had provided H with information about police and customs operations against other drug dealers as a result of which five offenders escaped arrest when raids were planned on their addresses. H had recorded the conversations with D. D had assisted with the running of his father's hotel business and by 1995 it was in a poor financial state. H had invested £10,000 in the hotel business and then taken it over and used for storing and distributing drugs. The police started investigations and D ignored instructions to stop seeing H. H and D were arrested. D lied in interview. The prosecution could not be precise about the damage to the police or the profits made but it was clear that H and his associates were major players in the drugs world and the integrity of the police and its anti-drugs activities had been very seriously compromised. At first instance D was sentenced to seven years' imprisonment, the maximum, and H received five years' imprisonment consecutive to his sentence of eight years. On appeal D's sentence was reduced to six years to reflect some discount for the plea and H's sentence was reduced to four and a half years.

[1]   [2002] 1 Cr App Rep (S) 386.

KEY POINTS FROM CHAPTER 3

3.81 Key points from this chapter are:

- The common law offence of bribery and the various statutory offences do not form a coherent pattern of offences.
- The existing law in effect are a miscellany of different forms of bribery distinguished by a particular office held or function performed by the individual concerned.
- There is no uniformity in what mental element is required in the existing law in its various forms.
- At present prosecutions are brought under a relevant specific statutory offence rather than at common law.
- For practitioners the existing case law may be a useful guide in considering what 'a financial or other advantage' means in the Bribery Act 2010, ss 1 and 2.
- Likewise the existing case law may be a useful guide in considering the intention required in the new s 1 offence, namley to induce an improper performance or to reward an improper performance.
- The word 'corruptly' is no longer an ingredient of the offences.
- The courts are unlikely to want to consider the existing law in relation to concepts of particular functions and roles as the new law is wider in scope.
- Consent to prosecute is similar as under the old law (albeit now it will be from the DPP, the Director of the SFO or the Director of Revenue and Customs).
- Existing sentencing cases will be of some use and there are no guideline cases nor Sentencing Council Guidelines but some adjustment is needed for the change from a maximum term of 7 years to 10 years.

Chapter 4

THE BRIBERY ACT 2010

A   OVERVIEW OF THE ACT

4.1 The much-heralded Bribery Act 2010 received the Royal Assent on 8 April 2010. Previous anti-bribery law had been a hotch-potch mix of common law and statutory provisions from 1889 to 1916 which together were difficult to understand, hard to apply and even harder for prosecutors to use effectively[1]. The Bribery Act 2010 abolishes the common law offences and sweeps away the nineteenth and twentieth century Prevention of Corruption Acts.

[1]   See Chapter 3 for more detail on the provisions in force before the Bribery Act 2010.

4.2 Using a novel form of drafting (the introduction of 'cases' – samples of statutorily-restricted behaviour) the new offences created by the Act reach directors, managers and secretaries of companies as well as the corporate bodies and partnerships themselves. They have very broad jurisdictional reach which can affect any business, or part of a business in the UK, even if the underlying behaviour does not have any substantive connection with the UK.

4.3 Broadly, the Act creates four categories of offence:

—   bribing a person (s 1);
—   being bribed (s 2);
—   bribing foreign public officials (s 6); and
—   failure by a commercial organisation or partnership to prevent bribery (s 7).

The last offence is a strict liability offence for companies and extends to 'associated persons', which includes employees, agents or subsidiaries, subject to the defence that the company had in place 'adequate procedures' to prevent the bribery.

4.4 Following submissions at the review stage of the Bill, the Secretary of State had to publish guidance about procedures that relevant commercial organisations can put in place to avail themselves of the defence to the strict liability offence of failing to prevent bribery. The Ministry of Justice engaged in a consultation exercise with 'stakeholders' concerning that guidance, which was published on 30 March 2011. The guidance is dealt with more fully in Chapter 6.

4.5 Pursuant to s 18, the Act extends to England, Wales, Scotland and Northern Ireland. In England and Wales, no prosecutions under the Act may be instituted without the consent of the DPP, the Director of the SFO, or the Director of HMRC Prosecutions.

4.6 Penalties range from fines to imprisonment for up to 10 years, or both, and can extend not only to corporate bodies but also to the senior officers of the corporate bodies if the offences were committed with their consent or connivance.

4.7 There are defences available to members of the armed forces engaged on active service or members of the intelligence service for acts done by them which would otherwise constitute an offence under the Act. Those defences are set out in s 13 of the Act, which also defines the limits of 'armed forces' and 'intelligence service' together with what is meant by 'active service'. In all cases, the offensive act has to be 'necessary' in the proper exercise of their functions.

4.8 The Bribery Act's offences are widely drawn and several provisions of the Act are, arguably, difficult to define with any certainty. However, the Law Commission summarised the offences as follows:

> 'Do not make payments to someone (or favour them in any other way) if you know that this will involve someone in misuse of their position; do not misuse your position in connection with payments (or other favours) for yourself or others'.

That statement of principle underlies the Act and perhaps formulates the essence of what should, in reality, be nothing more than sound moral, ethical and legal ways of conducting business around the world.

4.9 'Standard' business practices such as facilitation payments, offset arrangements and even corporate hospitality, gifts and political donations either certainly will (in the case of facilitation or 'grease' payments) or may be caught by the Act. See Chapters 5 and 6 for further guidance. The SFO has stated that the decision about whether to prosecute is likely to be a matter of degree: the central component of the offences in ss 1, 2 and 6 is 'improper performance', either to induce someone to do something, or to reward someone for doing something. The concept of 'improper performance' is likely to be one of the touchstones for prosecuting authorities considering acts or omissions done or made by individuals and corporations, with a view to prosecution.

4.10 The Joint Parliamentary Committee on the Bribery Bill debated the dividing line between common business practice and illegal activity and acknowledged, for instance, that corporate hospitality is a 'legitimate part of doing business at home and abroad, provided that it remains within appropriate limits' and that 'most routine and inexpensive corporate hospitality would be unlikely to lead to a reasonable expectation of improper conduct'.

4.11 However, the notional dividing line between what is 'routine' and 'inexpensive' and what amounts to a bribe is unclear. For the moment individuals and companies will have to take a view on each situation, bearing in mind the Law Commission's summary, the final guidance issued by the Ministry of Justice (whether pursuant to the Bribery Act 2010, s 9, or otherwise) and the SFO or other prosecuting authorities, and guidance from the Department for Business, Innovation and Skills. As can be seen in further detail in Chapter 6, the MOJ final guidance also recommends adherence to guidance and principles issued by relevant trade bodies. The risk is that the general statements of principle found in the published guidance under s 9 are so nebulous, and so interpreted by prosecutors, commentators, and other interested parties, that companies are left in a situation where they simply cannot tell what behaviour is permissible, and what is not, together with unacceptable legal uncertainty about the procedures they ought to be adopting.

B   JURISDICTIONAL REACH

4.12 In summary, the offences of giving and receiving bribes and bribing foreign public officials will apply to UK companies, partnerships, citizens and individuals ordinarily resident in the UK, regardless of where the relevant act occurs. The offences will also be committed by non-UK nationals, companies, and partnerships if an act or omission forming part of the offence takes place within the UK. This means that all commercial organisations, whether companies or partnerships, that carry on business, or part of their business, within the UK will be subject to the provisions of the Act, regardless of the place of their incorporation, the place of their offices, or of where the conduct which forms part of the offences takes place.

4.13 Uncontroversially, the Bribery Act 2010, s 12(1) provides that the offences under ss 1, 2 and 6 are committed in the UK if any act or omission which forms part of those offences takes place in the UK.

4.14 Section 12(2) provides that an offence will be deemed to have been committed in the UK if a person with a 'close connection' to the UK does or makes an act or omission outside the UK which, if it had been done within the UK, would have formed part of an offence under ss 1, 2 or 6. Section 12(3) of the Act criminalises such behaviour in the UK even if done abroad.

4.15 'Close connection with the UK' is defined in s 12(4). A person has a close connection with the UK for the purposes of the Act if, at the time when the act or omission was done or made, he was:

— a British citizen;
— a British overseas territories citizen;
— a British National (Overseas);
— a British Overseas Citizen;
— a person who, under the British Nationality Act 1981, was a British subject;
— a British protected person within the meaning of the British Nationality Act 1981;
— an individual ordinarily resident in the UK;
— a body incorporated under the law of any part of the UK;
— a Scottish partnership.

4.16 An offence is committed under s 7 of the Act (the 'failure to prevent' offence) irrespective of where the constituent acts or omissions were made or done and regardless of where the body corporate carries on business, or whether there is any 'close connection'. This is because s 7(3) provides that a person associated with a relevant commercial organisation bribes another person if, and only if, he would be guilty of an offence under ss 1 or 6, or he would be guilty of such an offence if he were not a person with a close connection with the UK.

The concepts of 'relevant commercial organisation' and 'carrying on a business' are examined in further detail at para **4.98** ff.

4.17 There are three issues for non-UK-registered bodies corporate:

(1)   are they 'carrying on business'; and
(2)   is the business being carried on in the UK;
(3)   in circumstances where other anti-corruption legislation in other parts of the world (notably the FCPA in the US) have a different scope, different offences (and defences), and different territorial effect, bodies corporate will have to ensure that their global anti-corruption policies are sensitive to local laws, and take account of the stricter provisions of the Act to activities which are permissible under the FCPA.

4.18 The territorial effect of the corporate offence is that a commercial organisation may be found guilty of an offence based on the actions of an associated person or entity even though that person has no connection with the UK, has no formal contract with the organisation, has no degree of control over the organisation, and is no way controlled by the organisation. The only statutory defence is that set out below, that is, having in place adequate procedures to prevent bribery.

4.19 The term 'business' does not necessarily imply conducting activity with a view to profit or gain. Charitable activities could constitute 'carrying on business' for the purposes of the Act and the explicit reference to 'a trade or profession' being a business may indicate that mere membership of a professional body in the UK could constitute the carrying on a business, or at least part of a business, here.

4.20 Where no act or omission which forms part of the s 7 offence takes place in the UK, the prosecution of the offence may nonetheless take place in any part of the UK.

4.21 By ss 1, 2 and 6 the Bribery Act 2010 creates three primary offences and it expresses the conduct made criminal by the statute through the use of 'cases' or 'scenarios' to describe each type of activity caught by the section under consideration.

4.22 As to the primary offences:

—   s 1 deals with the conduct of the briber (see also para **4.32**); and
—   s 2 covers the conduct of the recipient of a bribe (see also para **4.41**); and
—   s 6 is concerned only with bribing a foreign official (see also para **4.45**).

What follows here is by way of introduction to the composition and scope of the offences.

4.23 Each primary or general bribery offence must be connected to a 'relevant' function or activity which must be performed 'improperly' and in a manner other than in accordance with the given 'relevant expectation'.

4.24 For the s 1 offence (bribing someone) it is necessary for the prosecution to prove only that a financial or other advantage was offered, promised or given either with the intention of inducing that person to perform a function or activity, or to reward them for improperly performing a function or activity (s 1(2)) or knowing or believing that the mere acceptance of the advantage would itself constitute the improper performance of the relevant function or activity (s 1(3)).

4.25 For the s 2 offence (being bribed) the prosecution must prove that a person or a body corporate requested, agreed to receive or accepted a financial or other advantage. Additionally, under Case 3 the prosecution has to prove knowledge or intention to bring about an improper performance. Under Cases 4, 5 and 6 knowledge or belief that the performance of a function or activity will amount to improper performance is irrelevant. Where a bribe is received by a third party acting on behalf of the true recipient of the bribe, there is no need for the prosecution to prove any subjective knowledge or belief, at all.

4.26 For the s 6 offence of bribing a foreign public official, intending to influence the official and obtain or retain business, or a business advantage, the prosecution is required to prove that there was an intention on the part of the briber to influence the official, that is, to obtain or retain business or an advantage in the conduct of business, but that intention need not be dishonest or improper.

4.27 The Bribery Act 2010 does not require the prosecution to prove an element of dishonesty or corruption in the commission of any of the offences, although it may be anticipated that as a body of decisions and case law grows under the Act, such aspects will be indicative of criminal conduct.

4.28 Where the prosecution has to prove an *objective* test of improper performance, the concept is defined by reference to a failure to perform the duties in line with relevant expectations; namely that the function:

(1)   will be performed in good faith;
(2)   will be performed impartially; or
(3)   imports a position of trust.

4.29 The expectations set out in the Bribery Act 2010 are to be judged by the standards expected of the reasonable person in the UK, not the standards of the location of the person accepting the bribe. This was much debated in Parliament during the passage of the Bill, and in the Bill's Committee stages. It was argued that influencing a person to perform their duties improperly (by behaving partially) is a low threshold which would potentially criminalise behaviour which, it was argued, should not be so characterised. The government's answer was that prosecutorial discretion would avoid non-criminal cases from reaching the courts. It is thought that the Attorney-General will publish guidance for prosecutors which should be made publicly available, but until that happens, the present tests for prosecutions will continue to apply, namely, whether the prosecution is likely to result in a conviction and whether prosecution is in the public interest.

4.30 Last, from the above it will be appreciated that the effect of the drafting of the Bribery Act 2010 means that the state of mind of the briber, or the person being bribed, is of limited effect, as exemplified further below. This is no accident. The Joint Parliamentary Committee Report on the Bill stated that:

' . . . we support the provisions in the draft Bill that enable a person to be convicted of being bribed . . . without proof of knowledge or intention, notwithstanding that subjective fault should ordinarily be required by the criminal law'[1].

The reasons for that view were those of public policy:

> 'this policy forms an important part of changing the culture in which taking a bribe is viewed as acceptable. In particular, we think that it should encourage anyone who is expected to act in good faith, impartially or under a position of trust, to think twice before accepting an advantage for their personal gain'.

It is hard to quarrel with the sentiment which, after all, was one of the aims of the Bribery Act 2010.

¹ (Cm 7748), November 2009.

C   STRICT LIABILITY

4.31 Perhaps recognising the difficulty in proving that the 'directing mind' of a corporation had the requisite intention, knowledge or belief necessary to commit the s 1, 2 or 6 offences, the Act provides a 'strict liability' offence in s 7, ie an offence where the prosecution does not have to prove mens rea, thus doing the act amounts to a crime regardless of the intention. The prosecution will not have to prove that the commercial organisation knew anything about the bribery; merely that it failed to prevent it.

There is just one defence available: that of having in place 'adequate procedures'. The adequate procedures are examined in further detail in Chapter 6.

D   SECTION 1 OFFENCE

4.32 The s 1 offence prohibits a person (which definition also includes a body corporate) from offering, promising, or giving a financial or other advantage:

— in order to induce a person improperly to perform a relevant function or duty;
— in order to reward a person for such improper activity; or
— where the person knows or believes that the acceptance of the advantage would itself constitute an improper performance of a function or duty.

It does not matter whether the advantage is offered, promised or given by a person directly, or through a third party.

The two cases

4.33 The Act provides two statutory 'cases' or examples of prohibited conduct: first, where a person offers, promises or gives a financial or other advantage to another person and intends the advantage either to induce a person (or another person) to perform a relevant function or activity improperly, or reward such behaviour (s 1(2)). Second, an offence is committed where a person offers, promises or gives a financial or other advantage to another person and knows or believes that the acceptance of the advantage would itself constitute the improper performance of a relevant function or activity (s 1(3)).

In either case, it does not matter whether the advantage is offered, promised or given directly, or indirectly through a third party.

Improper performance

4.34 'Improper performance' is defined in ss 3, 4 and 5 of the Act and again involves a two-stage process. The Act provides that a relevant function or activity is performed improperly if it is performed in breach of a 'relevant expectation', or the failure to perform a function or activity is itself a breach of the relevant expectation.

4.35 A relevant expectation means the expectation that a function or activity will be performed in good faith or impartially, or in the context of a function or activity performed as part of a position of trust, that it will be performed in a manner consistent with the duties required of the person in a position of trust. Although somewhat opaque, this latter provision probably means the relevant expectation that a person acting in a position of trust will not act in breach of his fiduciary or other duties which arise by virtue of his being in a position of trust.

4.36 The test is of what a reasonable person in the UK would expect in relation to the performance of the type of function or activity concerned. Where performance of a function or activity is not subject to UK law then any local custom or practice must be disregarded.

4.37 However, where a local custom or practice is permitted or required by the written law of the place where the bribe was made or accepted (ie law contained in any written constitution or provisions made by or under legislation in that place, or a judicial decision which is applicable and is evidenced in published, written sources), then it may be taken into account when considering whether a reasonable person in the UK would expect such behaviour in the performance of a relevant function or activity (s 5(2), (3)).

4.38 How that test is to be applied in practice has yet to be seen; it is likely to be developed in a number of test cases. The difficulty is that every individual in any business will have to make his own decision, and form a judgment, in respect of every transaction to determine whether it is likely to infringe the criminal law. This necessarily includes an assessment of what a reasonable person in the UK might or might not consider to be right or wrong, or at least reasonable to expect. The MOJ final guidance issued on 30 March 2011 gives an example:

> 'in order to proceed with a case under section 1 based on an allegation that hospitality was intended as a bribe, the prosecution would need to show that the hospitality was intended to induce conduct that amounts to a breach of an expectation that a person will act in good faith, impartially, or in accordance with a position of trust. This would be judged by what a reasonable person in the UK thought. So for example, an invitation to foreign clients to attend a Six Nations match at Twickenham as part of a public relations exercise designed to cement good relations or enhance knowledge in the organisation's field is extremely unlikely to engage section 1 as there is unlikely to be evidence of an intention to induce improper performance of a relevant function.'

Relevant function or activity

4.39 A 'relevant function or activity' is defined in s 3 of the Act. There are two sets of criteria which define a function or activity which, if influenced by the giving or receiving of a bribe, will give rise to criminal liability. To engage the provisions of the Act, the function or activity has to meet one or more of the conditions in each set of situations.

4.40 In order to come within the scope of the Act, the functions must be:

—   of a public nature; or
—   connected with a business; or
—   performed in the course of a person's employment; or
—   performed by or on behalf of a body of persons (whether corporate or unincorporated).

Additionally, the functions must meet one or more of the following conditions, namely that a person performing the function or activity is:

—   expected to perform it in good faith; or
—   expected to perform it impartially; or
—   in a position of trust by virtue of performing it.

It is irrelevant that the function or activity has no connection with the UK, nor that it is performed outside the UK.

E   SECTION 2 OFFENCE

4.41 The s 2 offence defines a further four scenarios which give rise to criminal liability. In summary, s 2 prohibits a person from requesting, agreeing to receive, or accepting a financial or other advantage ('a bribe') intending that a relevant function should then be performed improperly, either by that person, or by another person at the request of, or with the assent or acquiescence of, the first person.

4.42 The four examples of criminal conduct in relation to being bribed are:

(1)   where a person requests, agrees to receive or accepts a financial or other advantage ('a bribe') intending that a relevant function or activity should be performed improperly (s 2(2));
(2)   where that person requests, agrees to receive or accepts a bribe and that request, agreement or acceptance itself constitutes the improper performance of a relevant function or activity (s 2(3));
(3)   where that person requests, agrees to receive or accepts a bribe as a reward for improper performance of a relevant function or activity (s 2(4)); and
(4)   where a relevant function or activity is performed improperly (whether by that person or by someone else with that person's assent or acquiescence) in anticipation of requesting, agreeing to receive or accepting a bribe.

4.43 Again, it does not matter whether the bribe is requested, received (or agreed to be received) or accepted directly or through a third party; nor does it matter whether the bribe is, or will be, for the first person's benefit, or for the benefit of another person. Furthermore, it does not matter whether the person requesting or accepting the bribe knows or believes that the performance of the relevant function is improper.

4.44 The 'relevant function or activity' criteria and the 'improper performance' test are the same as those in respect of the s 1 offence (see para **4.32**).

F   SECTION 6 OFFENCE

4.45 Section 6 provides that it is an offence for a person (which definition also includes a body corporate) to offer, promise, or give any financial or other advantage to a foreign public official, either directly or through any third party, where the person's intention is to influence the official in his capacity as a foreign public official and the person intends to obtain or retain either business or an advantage in the conduct of the business.

4.46 'Foreign public official' is defined in the Bribery Act 2010, s 6(5) as an individual:

—   who holds a legislative, administrative or judicial position of any kind (whether appointed or elected);
—   who exercises a public function for or on behalf of a foreign country or for any public agency or public enterprise of that company; or
—   who is an official or agent of a public international organisation.

4.47 A 'public international organisation' is also defined, in s 6(6), as an organisation whose members are any of the following:

—   countries or territories;
—   governments of countries or territories;
—   other public international organisations;
—   a mixture of any of the above.

4.48 The offence is committed if a person bribes a foreign public official intending the bribe to influence the foreign public official in his official capacity. The person offering the bribe must also intend to obtain or retain business, or an advantage in the conduct of business and the act is not permitted by the local written law. The MOJ final guidance issued under s 9 draws attention to payments which some publicly-funded contracts require those tendering to offer in addition to the principal tender, for instance, an investment in the local economy, or a benefit to the local community. The guidance acknowledges that such additional payments could engage s 6 of the Act, but states that the prosecutors will consider what is in the public interest when deciding whether to prosecute. It is said that such considerations will 'provide an appropriate backstop in circumstances where the evidence suggests that the offer of additional investment is a legitimate part of a tender exercise'. Organisations bidding for such foreign work may be less sanguine about the 'appropriate backstop' when they come to assess the risks in becoming involved in such tenders. The best advice has to be that an organisation should look very carefully at every extra service purportedly required as part of the tender process, to assess whether it is a bona fide requirement of the tender process itself, or whether, in reality, it could be seen as a financial or other advantage for a foreign public official.

4.49 The s 6 offence does not require the intention that the foreign public official will perform his functions improperly, nor do they require that the payment should be made 'corruptly'—indeed that term is not to be found within the Act.

4.50 The offence is committed if a financial or other advantage is offered, or given or promised to a foreign public official where it is not legitimately due pursuant to the written law applicable to the official abroad. For instance, if the written law applicable to the foreign public official permits or requires him to accept an advantage then the financial or other advantage will be regarded as 'legitimately due'. The MOJ final guidance is keen to emphasise that 'bona fide hospitality and promotional, or other business expenditure which seeks to improve the image of a commercial organisation, better to present products and services, or establish cordial relations, is recognised as an established and important part of doing business and it not the intention of the Act to criminalise such behaviour', but no lines are drawn which would enable an organisation to be satisfy itself for sure that hospitality and promotional or other business expenditure could not be viewed by a prosecutor as a bribe.

4.51 'Advantage in the conduct of business' is not defined. It is notable that this phrase marks a departure from and expansion of the equivalent test in the US in the FCPA 1977.

4.52 However, the local written law applicable to this section is not exactly the same as that set out in s 5 in respect of the reasonable expectation test. In the case of the s 6 offence, the written law applicable to the foreign public official is:

—   the relevant laws of the UK, where the performance of the official's functions which the briber intends to influence would be subject to the laws of the UK;
—   where that provision does not apply, and the official is part of a public international organisation, the written rules of that organisation; and
—   where neither of those provisions apply, then the applicable written law is the same as that set out in s 5, namely, the law of the country or territory in relation to which the person is a foreign public official in so far as that law is contained in any written constitution or provisions made by or under legislation in the foreign country, or any judicial decision which is applicable and evidenced in published written sources.

4.53 In some respects it is difficult to see why the drafters of the Act considered it necessary to include this offence given the wide scope of the general offences, and the far-reaching territorial extent of the Act. However, the primary difference lies in the fact that, to secure a conviction in respect of a s 6 offence, bribery of a foreign public official does not include an intention that the official will perform his duties improperly.

G   SECTION 7 OFFENCE

4.54 Section 7 creates a strict liability offence for commercial organisations where a person associated with the commercial organisation bribes another person (where the associated person commits an offence under ss 1 or 6) intending to obtain or retain either business or an advantage in the conduct of business, save where the commercial organisation can prove that it had in place adequate procedures designed to prevent bribery.

4.55 Any commercial organisation, that is, a partnership or incorporated body (whether incorporated in the UK or elsewhere) which is formed, or carries on business, or even part of a business, in the UK, commits an offence if it allows anyone associated with it to bribe another person, intending to get or keep business or a business advantage for the organisation. The MOJ final guidance has sought to put a gloss on this definition, stating that 'The courts will be the final arbiter as to whether an organisation "carries on a business" in the UK taking into account the particular facts in individual cases'. The guidance then purports to set out the 'Government's intention' in relation to the statutory definition. The legal status of such an intention will now also fall to be determined by the courts. The guidance states that the Government expects that a 'common sense approach' will be adopted to determine whether a partnership is carrying on business in the UK. No further explanation is given, save that it continues 'it does not matter if [the partnership] pursues primarily charitable or educational aims or purely public functions. It will be caught if it engages in commercial activities, irrespective of the purpose for which profits are made'.

The same 'common sense approach' should be adopted in respect of bodies incorporated or partnerships formed outside the UK. The MOJ final guidance states that:

> 'the Government anticipates that applying a common sense approach would mean that organisations that do not have a demonstrable business presence in the United Kingdom would not be caught. The Government would not expect, for example, the mere fact that a company's securities have been admitted to the UK Listing Authority's Official List and therefore admitted to trading on the London Stock Exchange, in itself, to qualify that company as carrying on a business or part of a business in the UK'.

Such a position is, at first sight, surprising and has led Transparency International UK's Executive Director to state:

> 'It is deplorable that changes made to the draft Guidance since late last year, and now enshrined in the published version, depart from international good practice in several areas. The Ministry of Justice has exceeded its brief with this final Guidance which undermines the Act and will limit its effectiveness. There is now a significant risk that bribery will go unpunished. For instance, foreign companies could be listed on the London Stock Exchange, pay bribes and get away with it. This will disadvantage all honest companies and perversely turn on its head the Government's stated aim of creating a level playing field through the Act's extra-territorial reach'[1].

The MOJ final guidance also states that 'having a UK subsidiary will not, in itself, mean that a parent company is carrying on a business in the UK, since a subsidiary may act independently of its parent or other group companies'. Whilst that is plainly true, it is hard to see how a subsidiary, based in the UK and listed on the LSE should not, of itself, be regarded as carrying on business in the UK and why a company so incorporated should not be caught by the provisions of the Act.

[1] Chandrashekhar Krishnan, Executive Director of Transparency International UK, press release 30 March 2011.

4.56 The s 7 offence is a strict liability offence; the requirement in the Bill for a prosecutor to prove negligence on the part of the body corporate was removed prior to the Act being passed. The bribe has to be given with the intention of obtaining or retaining business, or a business advantage for the organisation.

4.57 The sole defence is that the organisation had in place adequate procedures 'designed to prevent persons associated with [it] from undertaking such conduct'. Section 9 requires the Ministry of Justice to publish guidance (which may be revised from time to time) about procedures that relevant commercial organisations can put in place to prevent associated persons from bribing.

The offence

4.58 A relevant commercial organisation is guilty of an offence under s 7 if a person associated with it bribes another person intending either:

— to obtain or retain business for the organisation; or
— to obtain or retain an advantage in the conduct of business for the organisation.

4.59 The company is liable for the actions of an associated person if that person is, or would be, guilty of an offence under s 1 (bribing a person) or s 6 (bribing foreign public officials). This is the case whether or not the person has been prosecuted for such an offence, or would be guilty of such an offence if s 12(2)(c) and (4) were omitted.

4.60 As stated above, under s 12 of the Act, the acts prohibited by s 1 (bribing a person) and s 6 (bribing foreign public officials) are only criminalised if they are either committed in the UK, or committed elsewhere but by individuals with a 'close connection' to the UK in circumstances where the acts or omissions would form part of the offences if they had been done or made in the UK.

4.61 In contrast, the corporate offence created by s 7 is committed irrespective of where in the world the constituent acts or omissions were carried out. The corporate offence is thus broader than the individual s 1 and s 6 offences and it is envisaged by legislators that companies will be prosecuted irrespective of whether an individual is also prosecuted.

4.62 There is no requirement that the company being prosecuted authorised, encouraged or was even aware of, the payment of the bribe. The organisation is strictly liable if a person associated with it pays a bribe (subject to the 'adequate procedures' defence).

The burden of proof

4.63 It will be for a company to prove that it has put 'adequate procedures' in place to prevent persons associated with it from undertaking prohibited conduct. This amounts to a reverse burden whereby the defendant company must prove its innocence. Such reverse burdens are controversial because prima facie they breach the fundamental principle that a criminal defendant is innocent until proven guilty.

The question of the legality of the reverse burden of proof is considered at para **4.76** ff.

4.64 How would a prosecution work under s 7? The prosecution must prove beyond reasonable doubt:

— that the entity was a relevant commercial organisation; and
— that an associated person would be convicted for an offence under ss 1 or 6; and
— that the offence was committed with the intention of retaining business or advantage in the conduct of business for the organisation.

In the event that any one or more of the above elements is not proven beyond reasonable doubt, the prosecution will fail. In the event that all three are made out beyond reasonable doubt, it is for the defendant company to prove on a balance of probabilities that adequate procedures were in place to prevent such activity taking place.

4.65 The associated person does not have to be convicted of any offence under the Act for the body corporate to become liable; it is enough that the associated person *would be* guilty of an offence under ss 1 or 6 of the Act if prosecuted.

4.66 The liability of a relevant commercial organisation under the Bribery Act 2010 generally is dealt at para **4.98** ff.

H MEANING OF 'ASSOCIATED PERSON'

4.67 The meaning of 'associated person' is set out in s 8. A person is associated with the company or partnership facing prosecution under s 7 if (disregarding any bribe under consideration) the person is a person who performs services for or on behalf of the organisation, his principal. The definition of 'performing services' is vague; the Act states that it will be determined by reference to all the relevant circumstances.

4.68 Section 8(3) sets out three examples of persons who might be 'associated persons' in practice: employees, agents and subsidiaries. However, it is clear that whether or not a person performs services for or on behalf of an organisation is a question of fact to be determined by reference to all the relevant circumstances and not just by reference to the nature of the relationship between the person and the organisation itself.

4.69 It follows that in any given situation, consideration will need to be given to whether it might be said that a person is not 'associated' with the organisation being prosecuted because it can be shown that they were not performing services for or on behalf of the organisation. This may amount to a complete defence to a charge under s 7.

4.70 The MOJ final guidance now devotes seven paragraphs to the definition of 'associated persons'. It remains to be seen whether the status of that guidance is challenged on the basis that it may appear that the primary legislation is now subject to interpretation, or even de facto amendment, by that which is written in the guidance issued by the MOJ. Clearly alive to that potential criticism, the guidance falls back on the provision in s 8(4) that the question as to whether a person is performing services for an organisation is to be determined by reference to all the circumstances, and not merely by reference to the nature of the relationship between that person and the organisation; through that back door the guidance then purports to define, within the 'broad scope of s 7' the meaning of 'associated persons'.

The first example is straightforward: a contractor could be an associated person to the extent that it is performing services for and on behalf of a commercial organisation. A supplier, performing services rather than acting as the seller of goods, may also be an associated person. However, the guidance now states that in a supply chain where there is a principal employer and a number of sub-contractors, an associated person is likely to be limited to the employer's contractual counterparty. That guidance runs contrary to all commentary on the Act and has greatly limited the scope of the concept of associated persons. It appears now to be enough for the employer to undertake necessary due diligence on its contractual counterparty, for instance, a sub-contractor, and merely to request that sub-contractor to adopt a similar approach to the next party in the chain.

Such an approach is certainly helpful for principal employers, particularly in the construction industry, but it is certainly not what was anticipated prior to publication of the guidance and it is, arguably, a narrower construction than the strict wording of the Act. The guidance also deals with joint ventures and it is suggested that the existence of a joint venture entity will not of itself mean that it is 'associate' with any of its members.

The guidance specifically states that 'a bribe paid on behalf of the joint venture entity by one of its employees or agents will not trigger liability for members of the joint venture simply by virtue of them benefiting indirectly from the bribe through their investment in or ownership of the joint venture'. It is hard to understand why such an example should not be caught by the provisions of the Act. In that example, the prosecution would have to prove that the entity was a relevant commercial organisation; that an associated person would be convicted of an offence under ss 1 or 6; and the offence was committed with the intention of obtaining or retaining a business advantage for the organisation. Why would the employee of a joint venture partner who has bribed someone for the benefit of the other joint venture partner not satisfy all of the ingredients of the offence?

The guidance states that the position will be different if the joint venture is conducted through a contractual agreement. It is suggested, in that case, that the degree of control one partner will have over the other is likely to be greater and will be one of the relevant considerations taken into account when determining whether the employee is acting for the organisation, or whether he is simply to be regarded as acting for his employer (who may be only one of several parties in a joint venture) and accordingly not 'associated' with another body in the joint venture. The same distinction is put forward in the case of agents. This appears to be a large step back from the position set out in the Act, and may act as a significant hurdle for prosecutors when attempting to determine whether a briber is an associated person with any particular entity.

The guidance ends with the Delphic statement that:

> 'The question of adequacy of bribery prevention procedures will depend in the final analysis on the facts of each case, including matters such as the level of control over the activities of the associated person and the degree of risk that requires mitigation. The scope of the definition at section 8 needs to be appreciated within this context'.

What this really appears to be is an exercise in statutory interpretation by the Legislature, or even the Executive, rather than the Judiciary. It will be interesting to see the approach the courts take to the language of the statute and the purported interpretation of it in the guidance.

4.71 The use of the example of 'subsidiary' in s 8(3) may also be problematic. There are a range of investment structures in companies varying from a position where an investor has the right to remove directors or has the majority of the voting rights to the opposite situation where an investor may only hold a single share. At what point do companies become associated? At what stage will the investor company, and its directors, become liable for the acts of the investee company. What degree of control will constitute association? This uncertainty has not been removed by any guidance which defines that essential degree of control.

4.72 There is a rebuttable presumption created by s 8(5) that an employee will be an associated person of his employer organisation. However, even where an employee is the associated person in question, it is possible, at least theoretically, for the organisation to produce evidence showing that the person was not, in fact, performing services for it. Such a position is now reiterated specifically in the MOJ final guidance (see paras 41 and 42).

4.73 Similarly, in unusual circumstances it may be possible to provide evidence showing that other categories of person outside employee, agent or subsidiary are performing services for or on behalf of an organisation. For example, with the right factual matrix it is conceivable that partners in a consortium, joint venture partners or non-employed volunteers could potentially be associated persons, and in the field of construction, it is possible that joint venture partners, sub-contractors or professional advisors would be associated persons over whom the organisation should be exercising supervision.

Conceivably, an associated person performing services for or on behalf of a company could include a supplier, distributor or licensee. However, as stated above, the MOJ's final guidance has sought significantly to reduce the reach of these provisions. The authors' view is that commercial organisations would be well-advised to assume that the provisions of the Act are as wide-ranging as originally envisaged—the scope of that range being set out above—without placing undue reliance on the guidance, the applicability of which has yet to be fully tested by the courts.

4.74 There is also a requirement for the prosecution to show that the intention behind the bribe was to benefit the organisation itself—it may be argued by organisations that a person who appears to be an 'associated person' has bribed someone not for the benefit of the organisation, but for the personal benefit of the person doing the bribing. However, it is more likely that the organisation will fall foul of the s 7 provisions since it is probable that the organisation will at least have retained business as a result of the bribe, if not obtained or retained an advantage in the conduct of its business.

4.75 However, an interesting area, which is highly sensitive to the particular facts in any given case, is the potential defence of a commercial organisation which may argue that, whilst a person other than an employee, agent or subsidiary, appears to be associated with the organisation and has been engaged in activity which would be caught by s 7, an offence has not been committed by the organisation because it is likely that the intention behind bribery will be to increase business or profits for the party giving the bribe and not for the organisation facing prosecution. This may be particularly pertinent when considering the position of joint venture partners where an organisation may argue that any bribe was not offered on behalf of the commercial organisation, but by and on behalf of the joint venture partner who would benefit from the business going ahead.

It remains to be seen whether such 'cut-throat' defences are run in the event of a prosecution of an 'associated person' and to what extent they may be successful.

I DEFENCES

4.76 The requisite elements of the offences have been examined above in the context of each offence. What follows is a consideration of some defences which may be open to individuals and commercial organisations, and a peculiarity of the drafting in respect of individual liability of senior officers in respect of the s 7 offence.

Adequate procedures

4.77 It will be a defence for a body corporate in a prosecution for failing to prevent bribery by its employees or other associated persons to prove that it had in place adequate procedures designed to prevent bribery.

The meaning of 'adequate procedures' is examined further in Chapter 6.

The European Convention on Human Rights

Certainty of law

4.78 The s 7 offence is undoubtedly the most broad and controversial of the new offences since it presents the possibility that a company may be prosecuted in respect of acts or omissions it neither knew about nor encouraged.

4.79 Criminal offences must be defined with sufficient precision to everyone subject to the criminal law, to determine, with a reasonable degree of certainty, the consequences of their actions.

4.80 The proposition finds further support in the European Convention on Human Rights ('ECHR'), to which effect is given in the Human Rights Act 1998 ('HRA 1998'). It is outside the scope of this Chapter to engage in a detailed analysis of the ECHR or the HRA 1998, but the requirement of legal certainty applies in respect of the right to liberty under article 5 (since any deprivation of liberty must be lawful, which includes the requirement that the law be sufficiently certain) and the principle in article 7 that there should be no punishment without law. The article 7 right is not confined to prohibiting the retrospective application of the criminal law to a defendant's disadvantage, but also requires an offence to be clearly defined in law.

4.81 The requirement is satisfied where the individual can know from the wording of the relevant provision and, if need be, with the assistance of the courts' interpretation of it, what acts and omissions will make him liable.

4.82 It is obviously essential for those engaged in commercial activities to be able to determine the law, and to draw a clear line between hard-edged business practices and serious criminal offences—a point which was made when the Law Commission were considering a general fraud offence in 2002.

4.83 Article 7 of the ECHR states:

'No one shall be held guilty of any criminal offence on account of any act or omission which did not constitute a criminal offence under national or international law at the time when it was committed. Nor shall a heavier penalty be imposed than the one that was applicable at the time the criminal offence was committed'.

4.84 There is a high threshold to be passed before the courts will find that a law is too uncertain so as to be found to be incompatible with the ECHR[1], and it remains to be seen whether the adequate procedures guidance and the Attorney-General's guidelines on prosecutorial discretion will provide enough certainty by the time the Act comes into force. As is discussed further in Chapter 6, the MOJ final guidance remains, as the draft guidance before it, open-ended, inconsistent in parts and arguably, no more than an iteration of common sense, without providing an adequate source of comfort for businesses wishing to implement procedures which ought to provide them with a statutory defence in the event of a prosecution under s 7 of the Act.

[1] See, for example, *Sunday Times v United Kingdom (Application 6538/74)* (1979) 2 EHRR 245; *SW and CR v United Kingdom (Applications 20166/92, 20190/92)* (1995) 21 EHRR 363; *Handyside v United Kingdom (Application 5493/72)* (1976) 1 EHRR 737; *Kokkinakis v Greece* (1993) 17 EHRR 397.

4.85 It is an unsatisfactory state of affairs to have to have recourse to a set of extra-statutory guidelines which, when currently considered, provide no more than a signpost to what ought to be best practice in any commercial organisation and which do not allow commercial organisations to determine *with certainty* whether proposed business activity will be judged to be legal or illegal.

The reverse burden of proof

4.86 In *Sheldrake v DPP, A-G's Reference (No 4 of 2002)*[1], Lord Bingham said:

'There can be no doubt that the underlying rationale of the presumption in domestic law and in the Convention is an essentially simple one: that it is repugnant to ordinary notions of fairness for a prosecutor to accuse a defendant of crime and for the defendant to be then required to disprove the accusation on pain of conviction and punishment if he fails to do so'.

[1] [2004] UKHL 43, [2005] 1 AC 264 at paras 3 and 9.

4.87 The European Court of Human Rights has held that a statutory provision which imposes a burden of proof on a defendant can only be justified if it is reasonable and proportionate and if the prosecution bears the overall burden of proof. For example, in the leading case of *Salabiaku v France (Application 10589/83)*[1] the provision at issue provided that the defendant had to prove that he did not know that a consignment of drugs was in his possession. The court held that this did not violate the ECHR, article 6(2), but only because the prosecution bore the burden of proving the actus reus of the offence.

[1]   (1988) 13 EHRR 379.

4.88 The House of Lords has adopted the same approach to reverse onus provisions given their prima facie violation of the presumption of innocence. The danger with reverse burdens is that the defendant is required to prove a fact on the balance of probabilities, which permits a conviction in spite of reasonable doubt as to his guilt. As Lord Steyn stated in *R v Lambert*[1]:

'The real concern is not whether the accused must disprove an element or prove an excuse, but that an accused may be convicted while a reasonable doubt exists. When that possibility exists, there is a breach of the presumption of innocence'.

[1]   [2001] UKHL 37, [2002] 2 AC 545 at 571.

4.89 Accordingly, reverse burdens will only be lawful where they are reasonable and proportionate. Proportionality involves the striking of a fair balance between the rights of the individual and the interests of the community.

4.90 The principal question in a proper analysis of such a provision is what the prosecution has to prove before the onus is transferred to the defendant[1]. The court will also ask whether the burden on the defendant relates to something which is likely to be difficult for him to prove, and the extent of the nature of the threat faced by society which the provision is designed to combat. The primary consideration, as expressed by Lord Woolf of Barnes sitting in the Privy Council is:

'whether it is primarily the responsibility of the prosecution to prove the guilt of the accused to the required standard ... If the prosecution retains responsibility for proving the essential ingredients of the offence, the less likely it is that an exception will be regarded as unacceptable'[2].

[1]   Lord Hope in *R v DPP, ex p Kebilene* [2000] 2 AC 326 at 386.
[2]   *A-G of Hong Kong v Kwong-kut (Lee)* [1993] AC 951 at 969C–970B, PC.

4.91 In *A-G's Reference (No 1 of 2004), R v Edwards*[1], the Court of Appeal heard four appeals concerning various different statutory defences where it was contended by the defendants that the cases raised a legal burden on them when raising the statutory defence, contrary to the ECHR, article 6. The Lord Chief Justice gave the decision of the court on the issue of the reverse burden of proof and held that:

—   the decision of the House of Lords in *R v Johnstone*[2] was the latest word on the subject and the courts should discourage the citation of any other authorities on the issue;
—   despite the existence of ECHR, article 6(2), it is possible in appropriate circumstances for the legal burden to be imposed on a defendant when raising a defence. This is likely to be the case where the overall burden

of proof rests on the prosecution but where there are significant reasons why it would be fair and reasonable to deny the defendant the protection of the general presumption of innocence;

— there should be a presumption that Parliament would not have made the exception to the presumption of innocence without good reason. However, the exception should go no further than is reasonably necessary;

— an evidential burden cannot contravene ECHR, article 6(2);

— the court must assess the realistic effects of the reverse burden of proof and the ultimate question is whether the exception/reverse burden would prevent a fair trial.

¹ [2004] EWCA Crim 1025, [2004] 4 All ER 457.
² [2003] UKHL 28, [2003] 3 All ER 884.

4.92 So, where a statute places merely an *evidential* burden upon a defendant, there will be no violation of ECHR, article 6(2)[1]. This requires the defendant to adduce evidence introducing reasonable doubt as to an issue or fact. In contrast, a *legal* burden upon the defendant requires him to disprove, on a balance of probabilities, one of the primary elements of the offence with which he is charged. Legal burdens (such as that created by the Bribery Act 2010, s 7) are much more problematic when considering compatibility with the ECHR.

¹ *R v DPP, ex p Kebilene* [2000] 2 AC 326, HL.

4.93 In *R v Davies (David Janway)*[1] the Court of Appeal held that the reverse burden created by the Health and Safety at Work Act 1974, s 40 created a legal and not merely an evidential burden. Nevertheless, it was held not to violate the ECHR, article 6(2). Fundamental to this finding was the fact that the prosecution still maintained the burden of showing various matters before the burden shifted to the defendant. Tuckey LJ stated[2]:

'Before any question of reverse onus arises the prosecution must prove that the defendant owes the duty . . . and that the safety standard . . . has been breached. Proof of these matters is not a formality. There may be real issues about whether the defendant owes the relevant duty or whether in fact the safety standard has been breached, for example where the cause of an accident is unknown or debatable. But once the prosecution have proved these matters the defence has to be raised and established by the defendant. The defence itself is flexible because it does not restrict the way in which the defendant can show that he has done what is reasonably practicable'.

¹ [2003] ICR 586.
² At para 26.

4.94 *R v Davies (David Janway)* was considered by the House of Lords in *R v Chargot (t/a Contract Services)*[1] where it was held that proceedings under the Health and Safety at Work Act 1974, ss 2 and/or 3 require the prosecution to prove only that the statutory objective set out in those sections (securing health, safety and welfare) has not been met; showing that an accident or death has occurred is sufficient. The burden then shifts to the defendant to show that all that was reasonably practicable was done to prevent the risk arising.

¹ [2008] UKHL 73, [2009] 2 All ER 645.

4.95 The decision to uphold the reverse burden in *Davies* and in *Chargot* was founded not least on the thesis that the court was satisfied that the reverse burden was not offensive due to the regulatory or quasi-criminal nature of the offences under consideration, in that they were not criminal offences in the conventional sense. That argument cannot be sustained for corporations when charged with an offence under the Bribery Act 2010, s 7, as the punishment is condine and the consequences of the utmost gravity. It will be interesting to see how the courts will approach the legality of the reverse burden in s 7.

Other defences

4.96 Section 13 of the Bribery Act 2010 provides a defence for a person charged with a bribery offence to prove that his conduct was necessary for the proper exercise of any function of an intelligence service, or the proper exercise of any function of the armed forces when engaged on active service. The reverse burden of proof in both cases is an evidential one, but even in this sensitive context, the Act still requires the intelligence services and defence counsel to have in place 'arrangements' designed to ensure that the conduct which would otherwise be criminal is necessary for the proper exercise of the person's function in his respective role.

4.97 It is unlikely that the 'arrangements' for the intelligence service and armed forces will be as extensive as the 'adequate procedures' required by commercial organisations and even more unlikely that the 'arrangements' will be published.

J   LIABILITY OF CORPORATE BODIES AND PARTNERSHIPS

4.98 A corporate entity can be prosecuted under the Bribery Act 2010 as a legal person under:

— s 1 (bribing a person);
— s 2 (being bribed);
— s 6 (bribing foreign public officials); and
— s 7 (failure by a commercial organisation or partnership to prevent bribery).

The s 7 offence may *only* be brought against a body corporate, whereas the offences under ss 1, 2 and 6 may be brought against individuals or corporate entities.

4.99 As stated above, the broad nature of the responsibility on commercial organisations to prevent bribery, acts or omissions which it did not know about, deprecated and deplored, taken together with a sole statutory defence which is currently nebulous and is principle-based rather than prescriptive, means that a company or partnership may be prosecuted for failing to prevent bribery by persons associated with it. A company may show by way of a defence that it had in place 'adequate procedures' to prevent associated persons from engaging in bribery.

Relevant commercial organisation

4.100 In order to fall within the ambit of s 7 the corporate body must be a 'relevant commercial organisation'. This means:

— a body incorporated under any part of the law of the UK and which carries on a business (whether there or elsewhere);
— any other body corporate (wherever incorporated) which carries on a business, or part of a business, in any part of the UK;
— a partnership which is formed under the law of any part of the UK and which carries on a business (whether there or elsewhere); and
— any other partnership (wherever formed) which carries on a business, or part of a business, in any part of the UK.

4.101 'Partnership' is defined by s 7(5) to include:

— partnerships within the Partnership Act 1890;
— limited liability partnerships; and
— firms or entities of 'a similar character' formed under the law of a country or territory outside the UK.

4.102 Thus, any company or partnership with a business connection to the UK, either because it was incorporated or formed in the UK or because its business is wholly or partly conducted from the UK, may be liable to prosecution if it fails to prevent associated persons bribing in order to obtain or retain business or an advantage in the conduct of business for the organisation.

Carrying on a business

4.103 Neither the Bribery Act 2010 itself, nor the Explanatory Notes to it, expand on what is considered to be 'carrying on a business or part of a business' in the UK. As set out above, the MOJ final guidance now seeks to limit the applicability of the Act somewhat, and specifically eschews the proposition that a mere listing on the London Stock Exchange will signify that an organisation is carrying on business in the UK. Furthermore, following publication of the guidance there is now some doubt about the extent to which a subsidiary can be said to be conducting business in the UK.

Notwithstanding the back-tracking and dilution of the statutory language in the guidance, the concept of 'carrying on a business or part of a business' would appear to be a familiar piece of statutory language borrowed from criminal statutes, an example being the Companies Act 2006, s 993, ie the offence of fraudulent trading, an element of which is the 'carrying on of a business'. In authorities under this provision a business may be 'carried on' even where a company has ceased trading save for the collection of debts and the payment of creditors[1] and a single large transaction may constitute the carrying on of a business[2]

It is also useful to look at the use of the phrase in other contexts.

[1]   *Re Sarflax Ltd* [1979] Ch 592, [1979] 1 All ER 529.
[2]   *Re Gerald Cooper Chemicals Ltd* [1978] Ch 262, [1978] 2 All ER 49.

4.104 In the employment context the phrase 'carry on business' has been held to have a wide-ranging meaning. In *Pervez v Macquarie Bank Ltd (London Branch) & Macquarie Group Ltd*[1] Mr Justice Underhill found (in a decision which the learned judge made clear was confined to its facts) that a company had carried on business in England merely by seconding the claimant to work in London.

[1]   (UKEAT/0246/10/CEA) (8 December 2010, unreported).

4.105 Regulation 19 of the Employment Tribunals (Constitution and Rules of Procedure) Regulations 2004[1], which are the regulations by which the tribunals are established, provides that

'(1)   An employment tribunal in England or Wales shall only have jurisdiction to deal with proceedings (referred to as "English and Welsh proceedings") where—

(a)   the respondents or one of the respondents resides or carries on business in England and Wales'.

It was argued that, since the claimant's employer's letterhead referred to it having an affiliated office in London, and the claimant's secondment being a business activity 'carried on' in London, and the claimant's dismissal letter coming from the 'UK branch' of the claimant's employer with the same London address as that at which the claimant was seconded, it followed that the respondent fell within the definition in reg 19.

[1]   SI 2004/1861.

4.106 For the respondent it was contended that none of those factors came close to establishing that the respondent carried on business in the UK since, on the evidence, it had no place of business in London and performed no transactions in the UK of any kind. It was not a case where the foreign company had overseas branches or offices and the word 'affiliated' did not connote such a connection. It was argued that a secondment in London constituted some part of the foreign company's business activities, but not every business-related activity performed within a country constituted the 'carrying on of business' there.

4.107 The judge accepted the respondent's submissions and found that the foreign company 'could not in any ordinary sense of the phrase be said to have been carrying on business in London'. However, the judge went on to find that 'if it followed that the Tribunal had no jurisdiction that would be a very surprising result' since:

'Parliament would have conferred rights on a group of employees but would in respect of one sub-set of that group have failed to provide a forum in which those rights could be enforced'.

4.108 On the one hand then, there was a finding that a secondment by a foreign company to a company in London constituted the carrying on of business in London, and on the other, the decision is one which the judge expressly stated turned on its facts. In the absence of any guidance in the Bribery Act 2010 about what constitutes 'carrying on of business' for the purposes of s 7(5) of the Act, commercial organisations would be wise to expect the courts to construe the term widely, at least as the jurisprudence develops.

4.109 There is analogous authority from tax law, which provides some guidance as to how the provision may be interpreted. In *American Leaf Blending Co Sdn Bhd v Director General of Inland Revenue* Lord Diplock said[1] the following:

' . . . in the case of a company incorporated for the purpose of making profits for its shareholders any gainful use to which it puts any of its assets prima facie amounts to the carrying on of a business . . . The carrying on of "business" no doubt, usually calls for some activity on the part of whoever carries it on, though, depending on the nature of the business, the activity may be intermittent with long intervals of quiescence in between'.

[1]   [1979] AC 676, [1978] 3 All ER 1185 at 1189, PC.

4.110 Whether a company or partnership is carrying on a business is a question of fact.

The receipt of income in many cases will probably lead to a finding that business is being carried on. However, as the following cases demonstrate, income is not a determinative factor and an examination of the *sources* of income, as well as the purpose for which the company was formed, should be carried out.

4.111 In *Salaried Persons Postal Loans Ltd v Revenue and Customs Comrs*[1] the High Court considered whether a company which had traded in money-lending until 1995 carried on a business thereafter. The company had relocated in 1966 and let out its former business premises thereafter for rental income. It continued to let out the premises after money-lending ceased, many years later, in 1995. The High Court held that, although there was a strong inference that a company was carrying on a business by letting out its property, the continued letting of the premises did not constitute carrying on a business because the retention of the property (and its letting) may have constituted an investment, but was not, in the circumstances of the case, a business. The rent received from the property was only a small part of the company's assets and the other facts did not support a finding that the company was trading or carrying on a business. The court also found that a company's objects could be used as a guide as to whether or not a company that was not trading was carrying on a business.

[1]   [2005] STC (SCD) 851.

4.112 The inference from the last finding of that court is that a commercial organisation may not be trading in the UK but, for the purposes of the Bribery Act 2010, and by analogy with tax and other authorities, may be carrying on a business, or at least part of a business.

4.113 In *IRC v Korean Syndicate Ltd*[1] in a Court of Appeal judgment Atkin LJ considered that if any emphasis were placed on the word 'active' it would unduly limit the meaning of the word 'business' stating:

'I am not sure that it was intended for a precise definition, but if it were so intended, I think the words [used by Rowlatt J in the *Marine Steam Turbine* case] would be too narrow . . . there is nothing in the Act which says that the business must be actively carried on'[2].

Lord Sterndale MR emphasised the purpose for which the company was set up stating that:

'a limited company comes into existence for some particular purpose, and if it comes into existence for the particular purpose of carrying out a transaction . . . and turning [it] to account, then that is a matter to be considered when you come to decide whether doing that is carrying on a business or not'.

[1]   [1921] 3 KB 258, 12 TC 181.
[2]   At 205.

4.114 In *Jowett (Inspector of Taxes) v O'Neill and Brennan Construction Ltd*[1] a company held money in an interest-bearing bank account as its sole asset in the year in question. The sums held were profits accumulated through previous years of trading, which had ceased during the period in question. The company later started trading again in a new and different trade. The High Court held that although the company had 'income' through the interest paid on the money in the year in question, it was not carrying on a business in that year.

[1]   [1998] STC 482, 70 TC 566.

4.115 In other fields of law it has been found that a company could not carry on business within the jurisdiction without some physical place of business in its own name, that of an agent being insufficient[1]. However, those authorities came from a time when international trade and commerce were less versed in electronic means of communication and trading and the prudent commercial organisation would be well-advised to consider *any* trading connection with the UK as a potential hook upon which liability under the Bribery Act 2010, s 7(5) could be hung.

[1]   See, for example *Dunlop Pneumatic Tyre Co Ltd v A-G für Motor und Motorfahrzeugbau vorm Cudell & Co* [1902] 1 KB 342, 71 LJKB 284, CA; *Davies v British Geon Ltd* [1957] 1 QB 1, [1956] 3 All ER 389, CA and *South India Shipping Corpn Ltd v Export-Import Bank of Korea* [1985] 2 All ER 219, [1985] 1 WLR 585.

4.116 A further instance of the construction and meaning of the phrase can be found in VAT regulations. Under the HMRC information and inspection power 'carrying on a business' is given what is described as 'its normal everyday meaning' and can include any trade, profession or undertaking by a person alone or in partnership, the letting of properties and any entity that is required to be or is registered for VAT under any schedule to the Value Added Tax Act 1994.

4.117 The guidance issued by HMRC as to when to register for VAT states that only persons 'in business' can register for VAT. Examples are given of earning an income through a trade, vocation or business, whether self-employed or not, charging admission to a premises, providing membership benefits in return for a subscription or similar, and others. These are qualified by the requirement that the activity has a degree of frequency, scale and temporal span. Activities that are essentially a recreation or hobby are not considered a business for VAT. In some instances those who supply goods or services *to* the UK from another country must register for VAT even if the business enterprise (or individual) does not have a place of business in the UK (or does not live in the UK in the case of an individual). Thus looking back at the 'normal everyday meaning' of 'carrying on a business', that definition includes being registered for VAT and thus could include a business without a place of business in the UK but is one that supplies goods or services to the UK.

4.118 Notwithstanding the MOJ final guidance, it may well be the case that the mere listing on the London Stock Exchange would be sufficient to satisfy the requirement of 'carrying on a business'. It remains to be seen how the courts will interpret the provision and the guidance which may well be seen to be at variance with each other. Alternatively, raising finance in the public markets of the UK, which is then used to meet or advance a company's business objectives, may be considered sufficient to satisfy the definition of 'carrying on business'. Looking to the FCPA 1977 in the US may be instructive. If a non-US company lists its shares on a US exchange it must register with the Securities and Exchange Commission ('SEC'). Alternatively, it may have to file periodic reports with the SEC. In either case the company becomes an 'issuer' and subject to all the US anti-bribery provisions without any further requirement.

4.119 In summary, a company or partnership must be 'carrying on a business' in order to be prosecuted under the Bribery Act 2010, s 7. Other than the fact that (by s 7(5)) 'business' includes a trade or profession, there is no definition within the Act of what 'carrying on a business' means.

4.120 Generally, examination of all the circumstances needs to be carried out, including:

— the purpose for which the business or partnership was formed or incorporated;
— the specific circumstances of the company or partnership in the period in question;
— the source of any income;
— according to the MOJ final guidance, it does not matter though for what purpose the business or partnership was generating its profits, so that charitable organisations will be considered to be carrying on a business;
— expenses incurred in the period in question.

4.121 Although any particular business needs to be considered in the context of the facts and circumstances at the time, the following seem likely:

— a non-trading holding company is unlikely to be carrying on a business, provided it has no assets other than shares in companies which are its subsidiaries, no entitlement to a deduction and no income other than dividends;
— an international corporation based in (for example) the US with a branch office in the UK would likely satisfy the 'carrying on a business' requirement because they are part of the same legal entity, though mere listing in the UK is not enough, and the degree of control the parent company has over the branch office is, according to the MOJ final guidance, likely to be examined carefully in the context of the factual investigation;

—   a parent company abroad with a UK subsidiary which is a separate legal entity will probably be considered to be 'carrying on a business' in the UK, although the precise connection between the companies will need to be examined.

K   LIABILITY OF COMPANY OFFICERS

4.122 Under the Bribery Act 2010, s 14, where an offence under ss 1, 2 or 6 is committed by a body corporate and it is proven that it is committed with the 'consent or connivance' of a senior officer[1] of that body corporate, the senior officer, as well as the body corporate, may be prosecuted. Penalties on indictment for individuals prosecuted in this way include an unlimited fine and imprisonment.

[1]   Which, in the case of a body corporate whose affairs are managed by its members (for instance, an LLP), means a member of the body corporate.

4.123 It is notable that, unlike similar provisions in other areas of law such as health and safety, it is not sufficient for a senior officer to have been *negligent* as to whether the body corporate was engaged in prohibited activity: there must be active knowledge in the sense of consent or connivance in the wrongdoing.

4.124 It is likely that the courts will consider carefully the role of the individual in question within the body corporate, their personal responsibilities and what, if anything, they could and should have done differently to prevent the prohibited conduct taking place, before making a decision as to the question of whether they consented or connived in the wrongdoing.

4.125 The burden of proving consent or connivance on the part of a senior officer rests on the prosecution[1]. In *Wotherspoon v HM Advocate* Lord Justice-General Emslie said[2] in relation to the similar provision contained in the HSWA 1974:

' . . . the functions of the office of a person charged with a contravention of section 37(1) will be a highly relevant consideration for any judge or jury and the question whether there was on his part, as the holder of his particular office, a failure to take a step which he could and should have taken will fall to be answered in light of the whole circumstances of the case including his state of knowledge of the need for action, or the existence of a state of fact requiring action to be taken of which he ought to have been aware'.

[1]   *R v P* [2007] EWCA Crim 1937, [2008] ICR 96 at 100.
[2]   1978 JC 74 at 78. Although Justice-General Emslie was considering the meaning of 'neglect' alongside 'consent' and 'connivance' and to this extent the case may not be applicable to the Bribery Act, it is likely that the functions of the senior officer will be examined in any event to determine whether he has connived or consented.

4.126 Section 14 provides that senior officers or persons purporting to act in such a capacity may face prosecution alongside the body corporate. Senior officer means a director, manager, secretary or other similar officer (s 14(4)). The phrase 'persons purporting to act in such a capacity' is less easy to define.

4.127 In *R v Boal*[1], a case under the similarly worded Fire Precautions Act 1971, the conviction of a bookshop manager was set aside on appeal on the basis that he was responsible only for the day-to-day running of the premises. The Court of Appeal held that:

> 'The intended scope of [section 23] is, we accept, to fix with criminal liability only those who are in a position of real authority, the decision-makers within the company who have both the power and responsibility to decide corporate policy and strategy. It is to catch those responsible for putting proper procedures in place: it is not intended to strike at underlings'[2].

[1] [1992] QB 591, [1992] 3 All ER 177.
[2] At 597.

4.128 It is assumed that s 14 of the Act will operate in a similar way so that, where a person is not one of the defined categories of person who could be individually liable for the corporate offence (director, manager, secretary) a close examination will need to be carried out as to their role, job responsibilities and position within the body corporate before they may be prosecuted as a person in a position of real authority.

The likely charge

4.129 Liability arises from proof of either 'consent' or 'connivance' in the prohibited activity (under ss 1, 2 or 6) by a senior officer. Only consent *or* connivance needs to be proven. However, relying on well-established principles of criminal law, an indictment containing both bases for conviction would be neither duplicitous nor improper. Where the prosecution puts its case on one basis, only then the indictment should reflect that[1].

[1] *R v Leighton and Town and Country Refuse Collections Ltd* [1997] Env LR 411, CA.

4.130 Providing guidance on the content of the indictment in such circumstances, in *R v Leighton and Town and Country Refuse Collections* Auld LJ stated[1]:

> 'The above statutory formula is to be found in many statutes creating offences which may be committed by corporate bodies. Where the prosecution case is that an accused must have committed the offence in one of the specified alternative ways, but cannot say which, it is commonly charged as one offence, stating the various ways in the alternative. That is well established . . . Accordingly, we are of the view that the indictment was not duplicitous in alleging the various alternatives in counts 2, 4, 6 and 8. However, we repeat the qualification that we have already expressed in relation to Ground 1, that the prosecution should only rely on alternatives if it needs to do so'.

[1] [1997] Env LR 411 at 419–420.

Consent

4.131 The meaning of 'consent' was considered in *A-G's Reference (No 1 of 1995) (B and F)*[1] in the context of the Banking Act 1987, s 96(1). It was held that a defendant has to be

'. . . proved to know the material facts which constitute the offence by the body corporate and to have agreed to its conduct of its business on the basis of those facts'.

1   [1996] 4 All ER 21, [1996] 1 WLR 970, CA.

4.132 Consent probably requires some agreement to the unlawful conduct to be actively communicated, either by words, in writing, or (if intention is absolutely clear) possibly by gesture[1]. Ignorance of the law is, as ever, no defence.

1   *Bell v Alfred Franks and Bartlett Co Ltd* [1980] 1 All ER 356 at 360.

Connivance

4.133 Connivance was defined in *Huckerby v Elliot*[1] as being a state of mind where a senior officer:

'. . . is well aware of what is going on but his agreement is tacit, not actively encouraging what happens but letting it continue and saying nothing about it'.

It has also been suggested that connivance is akin to 'wilful blindness'[2].

1   [1970] 1 All ER 189 at 194.
2   Per MacKay J in *R v Balfour Beatty Infrastructure Services Ltd* (1 September 2004, unreported) at 98.

4.134 It should also be remembered that the 'adequate procedures' defence available to a commercial organisation prosecuted under the Bribery Act 2010, s 7 does not apply to a senior officer of the organisation. Accordingly, any director who commits any act of bribery will have committed a criminal offence himself, as well as on behalf of the organisation.

4.135 There is one further consideration for senior officers in an organisation: the offence under the Bribery Act 2010, s 7 applies only to relevant commercial organisations, and not to individuals. The liability of senior officers in s 14 applies only in respect of ss 1, 2 and 6 of the Act. The effect of those sections is that it appears that senior officers of a commercial organisation cannot be held personally responsible for the failure of the organisation which they are managing to prevent bribery.

L   OTHER IMPORTANT PROVISIONS

4.136 As set out in further detail at para **10.141**, concerning the construction industry, under the EU Public Sector and Utilities Procurement Directives, implemented in the UK by the Public Contracts Regulations 2006[1] and the Utilities Contracts Regulations 2006[2], public authorities must exclude from public contracts a company, its directors or 'any other person who has powers of representation, decision or control' over the company that has been convicted of (amongst other things) a corruption offence. There is a real danger therefore that a conviction under the Bribery Act 2010, ss 1, 2 or 6, and a further danger that a conviction under s 7, may result in a commercial organisation being permanently excluded from government contracts across the whole EU.

1   SI 2006/5.
2   SI 2006/6.

4.137 The Bribery Act 2010 is made specifically applicable to individuals in the public service of the Crown so that civil servants, members of Parliament and other public service workers are rightly subject to the same rules as the rest of the population.

4.138 The issue of whether there should be exceptions for members of the armed and intelligence services was debated by the Law Commission and in the committee stages of the Bill. The result was that a defence was introduced for members of the intelligence services and members of the armed forces on active service (albeit that the defendant must prove that his actions were necessary for the proper exercise of his function with the relevant service). Further, the relevant organisations are required to have in place 'arrangements' designed to ensure that conduct which would otherwise be criminal, is necessary for the proper exercise of the functions of those organisations. This surely amounts to a secret 'adequate procedures' requirement, which we must hope, is rarely, if ever, tested by the courts.

Chapter 5

WHEN IS A BENEFIT A BRIBE?

A   DEFINITION OF A BRIBE UNDER THE BRIBERY ACT 2010

What is a bribe under the Bribery Act?

5.1 The answer to this crucial question will be a deciding factor in many an investigation and prosecution under the Bribery Act 2010. Whilst the detail of the legislation is dealt with in Chapter 4, this chapter explores in depth the likely approach of a UK criminal court to the definition of 'a bribe', there being no definition as such in the Bribery Act 2010.

5.2 The essential elements of three of the types of offences are set out below in so far as they relate to the specific question of the definition of a bribe under the Bribery Act 2010.

5.3 Bribing (s 1):

— offered, promised or given directly or indirectly;
— financial or other advantage;
— briber intends the advantage to induce or reward improper performance of a function of a public nature or any business (including trade or profession) activity or an activity performed in the course of employment or an activity performed by on behalf of a body of persons corporate or incorporate ('a relevant function or activity');
— performer of the function or activity is expected to perform it in good faith or impartially or is in a position of trust by performing it.

5.4 Being bribed (s 2):

— requested, agreed to receive or accepted;
— financial or other advantage;
— as a reward for, or in anticipation of, or as a consequence of the advantage, improperly performs a relevant function or the request, agreement or acceptance itself is the improper performance.

5.5 Bribing a foreign public official ('FPO') (s 6):

— offered, promised or given directly or indirectly;
— financial or other advantage;
— to the FPO or another at his request/assent/acquiescence;
— intend to influence the FPO in his capacity as an FPO;
— intended to obtain/retain business/business advantage.

5.6 *When is a benefit a bribe?*

5.6 From the analysis of ss 1, 2 and 6, the following working definition may be derived: in essence, a 'bribe' is a financial or other advantage used to induce or reward the improper performance of a function or activity, with the rider that as regards the s 6 offence, relating only to foreign public officials, what is required are the dual intents of influencing the FPO *and* of obtaining a business benefit of some kind. It will thus be evident that not every payment or benefit will fall into the definition of a bribe. A person can receive, for example, a gift and subsequently award a contract to the donor of the gift but that gift will not constitute a bribe unless the contract was awarded improperly by the recipient as a consequence of receiving the gift. There must be some reciprocity and direct connection between the giving or receipt of some 'advantage' and what is improperly obtained in exchange.

5.7 The remainder of this chapter will deal with the far more imprecise art of applying that working definition to specific, and often problematic, types of payments and other benefits. But in looking at specific areas, the general principle and character of a 'bribe' must always be at the forefront of any consideration of when a benefit is a bribe.

5.8 One litmus test for the legitimacy of a payment will be whether it passes the test of proportionality. Is the payment disproportionate to the pay-er's resources, the payee's resources or to the relationship, or all three? Whilst not likely to be dispositive of the question of whether or not any given payment is the right or the wrong side of the line, the proportionality of the payment will be a significant factor.

One man's once in a lifetime trip abroad is another's routine, weekly chore. One man's dream gift is another's trifle. There can be no set rules and limitation on what or would not in itself constitute a bribe. Every payment or benefit is relative. That relativity attaches to the donor, the recipient and the circumstances. A gift or dinner worth £100 will be insignificant to a multinational company but may represent a month's salary to the recipient. There will be variations according to the industry sector. Whilst many companies already subject to the provisions of the US Foreign Corrupt Practices Act of 1977 ('FCPA 1977') have internal compliance policies putting a financial cap, such as $100, on gifts, there are other business sectors, such as premiership football, where far more expensive gifts are a commonplace occurrence and not viewed as bribery. Is an exclusive and costly wristwatch given to a top player by a club hoping to sign him a bribe per se? He could easily afford it himself out of his very high weekly salary. Is it some improper inducement or merely a way of indicating that he is valued and will be cared for by his new club? At the opposite end of the scale, such a wristwatch given to a foreign public official who has the power to award a valuable contract in a high earning industry, but who could never hope to afford such a watch himself, must cross the line. It is not so much the value of the gift, albeit high, or the wealth (multi billion) of the donor but the relative poverty of the recipient that counts.

5.9 One might have hoped for detailed guidance from the prosecuting authorities but such guidance as exists has not been particularly helpful. For instance, an earlier statement by the SFO that a 'lavish' gift will be a corruption indicator is not constructive; what is meant by 'lavish'? By whose standards? Who sets the benchmark? Is it an ascertainable measure? Does it contain sufficient precision to enable an individual or company to regulate its conduct to avoid any breach of the Bribery Act 2010? Whilst it is recognised that discretion is necessary within the law to afford a necessary degree of flexibility, it is anticipated that a reliance on a wide ranging but poorly ascertainable prosecutorial discretion will lead to challenges in any future prosecution. The joint guidance for prosecutors issued by the SFO and DPP on 30 March 2011 states that:

'The more lavish the hospitality (beyond what may be reasonable standards in the particular circumstances) the greater the inference that it is intended to encourage or reward improper performance or influence an official. Lavishness is just one factor that may be taken into account in determining whether an offence has been committed. The full circumstances of each case would need to be considered. Other factors might include that the hospitality or expenditure was not clearly connected with legitimate business activity or was concealed'.

Although such a statement goes beyond the previous bald assertion, it does little to bring a greater degree of certainty.

5.10 As there are no decided cases under the Bribery Act 2010, it can be instructive to look at the US cases under the FCPA 1977, the US legislation covering bribery of FPOs. Although there can be no direct correlation between the Bribery Act 2010 and the FCPA 1977, some of the cases under the US Act provide examples of the factual matrix which led to investigations, prosecutions and civil settlements. Most US cases involving corporations are compromised with a plea agreement followed by fines and 'disgorgement'. Occasionally, individuals who face loss of liberty go to jury trial and are more likely to do so than corporations. Thus the 'facts' of the cases must be treated with a degree of caution, as there is no opening by the prosecution nor sentencing remarks by the judge which would give a detailed summary of the facts.

5.11 All of the following US cases involve gifts, travel and hospitality. However where, for example, improper gifts were given to government officials (the ambit of the FCPA 1977 being limited to foreign public officials), that was in the context of a wider scheme of bribery which almost always included improper payments in one form or another. But what is equally clear is that gifts, hospitality and other benefits will be treated as bribes if they are part of an endemic scheme and evidentially they can be of enormous value to the prosecution in proving the improper nature of other payments and in negativing an adequate procedures defence.

(a)   *United States v Vetco Gray UK Ltd*[1]: a UK and a US subsidiary of a Swiss parent company involved in deep-water oil drilling made payments totalling $1.1m over a five-year period to government officials in Nigeria, Angola and Kazakhstan to obtain and retain oil and gas contracts. Part of the payments to the Nigerian government officials included 'lavish' shopping trips to the US, the gift of a car, a generator, the payment of household expenses, medical appointments and beauty treatments. Part of the payments to engineers from the Angolan state-owned oil company included 'training trips' to the US, UK, Brazil and Norway. The company paid for all travel, hotels and meals plus per diem payments. For example, on one trip for five officials in 2001 each official received over $4,000 handed over in cash.

(b)   *SEC v Avery Dennison Corpn*[2]: Avery China sells reflective materials used in road signs and on emergency services vehicles. Although the case involved kickbacks to Chinese officials there was also evidence of sightseeing trips for the officials which were disguised as other expenses.

(c)   *United States v Metcalf & Eddy International, Inc*[3]: M&E was involved in a contract for maintaining wastewater and sewerage facilities in Egypt. During the bid process to obtain the contract, M&E paid for two trips to the US for an influential official. The first trip was ostensibly for the official to attend a water conference in Chicago. The trip did involve going to Chicago but it also included his wife and children and a visit to Orlando in Florida. The second trip, again including his family, was to Paris, Boston and San Diego. M&E paid for first class airfares, the majority of travel and entertainment costs and 150% of their estimated per diem expenses, paid in advance before he left Egypt.

(d)   *SEC v Syncor Int'l Corpn*[4]: Syncor was a US company that sold and operated medical imaging equipment in Taiwan, in Mexico and three European countries. The companies made improper cash payments to doctors in state-owned hospitals to obtain business. The improper payments in Europe not only included cash but also gifts such as computers and cameras as well as expensive wine and travel.

(e)   *SEC v Titan Corpn*[5]: the facts of this case are set out in full at para **5.162**. In addition to payments of $2m made to the President's re-election campaign, Titan also gave his wife an $1,800 pair of earrings. They also paid a large sum in travel expenses for a Beninese government official.

(f)   *United States v Ingersoll-Rand Italiana SpA*[6]: this case involved kickbacks to the Iraqi government under the UN Oil for Food programme. However, the Italian subsidiary also paid for eight Iraqi Ministry of Oil officials to ostensibly tour a manufacturing facility in Italy. In reality they spent the time in Florence, on holiday, paid for by the company and were given $8,000 in pocket money.

(g)   *Paradigm BV*[7]: a Dutch company providing software to extractive industries made improper payments to officials in Kazakhstan, China, Mexico, Nigeria and Indonesia. In China the company paid for 'training' trips for Chinese officials in connection with obtaining specific business. The expenses paid included airfares, hotels, meals, entertainment, sightseeing and gifts such as cash for shopping. A Mexican official was taken to California and entertained at dinners and in vineyards.

(h)   *Korean prosecution of Casa*[8]: a Spanish branch of a European aircraft manufacturer had a distributor in Korea who made improper payments to a senior Korean air force official and other officials. The company paid for the senior air force official and his wife to come to Spain for a product support review, including airfares and hotels.

(i)   *In the Matter of Schnitzer Steel Industries, Inc*[9]: a US company and its Korean subsidiary made improper payments to Chinese government officials in the form of kickbacks and rebates. However, gifts were given as well, including $10,000 worth of gift certificates and a $2,000 watch. Following an internal investigation, cash payments were changed to increased entertainment and effectively disguised in the process.

(j) *Lucent*[10]: the full details of this case are set out at para **5.79**. In brief it involved a US company which was in the communications systems industry. The company spent over $10m on trips for Chinese government officials, many of whom were senior officials or heads of state-owned telecommunications companies, over the period 2000–2003. The ostensible reason for the trips was for factory inspections by, or training for, Chinese officials. However, little or no time was involved in such activities and in fact the officials went to tourist destinations such as Las Vegas, the Grand Canyon, Disneyworld, Niagara Falls, New York and Hawaii. Lucent regarded these trips, especially those involving high ranking officials as a means of obtaining, retaining and enhancing business. Following factory relocations, customer trips included Australia and Europe even though neither country had factories. The appearance of legitimacy was created by a tour of the headquarters or some facility (not factory) but the visits were primarily sightseeing, entertainment and leisure which Lucent knew had little or no legitimate business purpose. 'Training' visits also included extensive and excessive sightseeing, entertainment and leisure elements.

(k) *SEC v The Dow Chemical Co*[11]: an Indian subsidiary made improper payments to Indian officials totalling $200,000 of which $37,000 consisted of gifts, travel and entertainment.

(l) *Universal Corporation*[12]: the company made improper payments through its subsidiaries of over $2.7m to government officials in Thailand, Mozambique and Malawi in connection with obtaining business for its tobacco operations. A small element of the payments was in the form of private trips on the company jet, bathroom renovations and airfares and 'pocket money' during purported inspection visits.

(m) *Veraz Networks*[13]: Veraz was a US company involved in communications systems. Veraz operated a 'gift scheme'. Veraz's consultant in China gave gifts amounting to $4,500 to officials in order to win business and further offered $35,000 in improper payments. Although Veraz, despite being the highest bidder, won the contract, they cancelled on discovery of the improper offer. There was also some suggestion of improper gifts and entertainment of Vietnamese officials including flowers for the wife of the CEO of a state-owned company.

(n) *Lindsey Manufacturing*[14]: a US company supplying emergency systems for electrical companies was allegedly involved in bribing Mexican officials. The payments included a $1.8m yacht, a Ferrari, very large American Express bills and cash payments to relatives of an official.

(o) *SEC v Siemens Aktiengesellschaft*[15]: this involved a German company with a number of subsidiaries which were involved in an extensive bribery scheme in 19 countries, including over 4,000 payments to government officials totalling $1.4billion between 2001 and 2007. Part of the allegation was that $14m was paid to Chinese officials including doctors in connection with medical equipment sales, and those payments included trips to holiday destinations such as Las Vegas.

(p) *UTStarcom*[16]: this case concerned a US company with a subsidiary in China involved in telecommunications. Between 2002 and 2007 the company provided 225 overseas 'training' trips for employees of the state-owned Chinese company who was UTStarcom's customer. In reality, the trips, costing a total of $7m, were entirely or primarily for sightseeing. The trips included visits to Hawaii, Las Vegas and New York where there were no company facilities and no training took place. UTStarcom also allegedly paid for Chinese officials to attend executive training at US universities and covered all expenses, totalling $4m and including travel, tuition, room and board, tourist trips and a cash allowance of $800–3,000 per person. The training covered general topics and was not specifically related to UTStarcom's business. The expenses were recorded as 'marketing expenses'. Further allegations include employing officials or their family members in the US and paying $23,000 in entertainment and gifts to a government official in Thailand including $10,000 worth of French wine, with some bottles costing $600.

(q) *United States v Carson*[17]: this case also involves trips to tourist destinations in the US to reward customers, retain business and obtain new business. The sightseeing trips were disguised as training or inspection trips. This was but one part of a much larger scheme of bribery involving large cash payments.

(r) *United States v Giffen*[18]: Giffen was the CEO of a New York merchant bank who advised the Republic of Kazakhstan in connection with the sale of its oil fields in the 1990s. It was alleged that Giffen paid $80m in bribes to the President of Kazakhstan and two other officials into Swiss bank accounts. These payments were sometimes disguised as loans or consultancy fees. Payments were made for the personal expenses of Kazakh officials and their families, including holidays, jewellery, and credit card bills. Giffen was also alleged to have provided senior officials with free luxury items such as speedboats, jewellery and fur coats.

(s) *United States v Bourke*[19]: this case involved a BVI company which attempted to gain control over the Azerbaijan state oil company through bribes. The allegations included $11m payments in cash/bank transfer as well as jewellery and other luxuries worth £600,000, and travel via private jet to the US for medical treatment and associated expenses such as hotels and meals.

(t) *ABB*[20]: a Swiss parent company had various subsidiaries, including a US company which was alleged to have made improper payments to Mexican officials as well as gifts of a yacht, a Ferrari and a Mediterranean cruise for officials and their wives.

(u) *Daimler*[21]: the German car manufacturer with subsidiaries in Russia and China was alleged to have made improper payments of tens of millions of dollars to officials in 20 countries between 1998 and 2008. Although the scheme involved cash/bank transfer payments there were also payments in the form of travel and gifts. For example, Daimler, in the belief it was necessary to provide gifts to secure a contract with the Turkmenistan government, gave a senior official an armoured Mercedes worth $300,000, a gold box and printed 10,000 copies of the official's personal manifesto both worth a further $250,000. An armoured

Mercedes worth much the same was given to a Liberian official to secure a contract. In order to secure contracts in Indonesia and reduce its tax liabilities, the company gave government officials golf outings, wedding presents for the children of a senior official and a discounted Mercedes to the child of another.

(v) *United States v Control Components, Inc*[22]: this case involved a US subsidiary of UK company which manufactures valves used in the energy industry. Employees of state-owned companies in China, South Korea, Malaysia and the UAE were rewarded for contracts with expensive holidays in tourist destinations under the guise of training and inspection trips, with gifts and in two cases by the payment of their children's college tuition.

[1] No 4:07-cr-00004–2 (SD Tex, Feb 6, 2007).
[2] No 1:09-CV-5493 (CD Cal, July 28, 2009).
[3] No 1:99-CV-12566 (D Mass, Dec 14, 1999).
[4] No 1:02-CV-2421 (DDC, 2002).
[5] No 05-CV-0411 (DDC, 2005).
[6] No 1:07-cr-00294 (DDC, 2007).
[7] Matter resolved through non-prosecution agreement (2007).
[8] Incheon District Court Decision (Criminal Division 12) 8 May 2008.
[9] SEC Administrative Proceeding No 3-12456 (Oct 16, 2006).
[10] Matter resolved through deferred-prosecution agreement (Dec 2007).
[11] No 1:07-CV-00336 (DDC, Feb 12, 2007).
[12] Settlement discussions ongoing.
[13] Ongoing investigation.
[14] Ongoing prosecution.
[15] No 08-CV-02167 (DDC 2008).
[16] Resolved through non-prosecution agreement (Dec 2009).
[17] No 8:09-cr-00077 (CD Ca, Apr 8,2009).
[18] 379 F Supp 2d 337 (SDNY, 2004).
[19] No 1:05-cr-00518-2, Second Superseding Indictment (SDNY, July 8, 2009).
[20] Ongoing investigation linked to cases of *United States v John Joseph O'Shea* No 09-00629 (SD Tex, 2009) and *United States v Ferdinand Maya Basurto* No 09-00325 (SD Tex, 2009).
[21] Settlement discussions ongoing.
[22] No 8:09-cr-00162 (CD Ca, July 27, 2009).

5.12 Certain themes can be extracted from the above cases. It would seem obvious that hugely valuable gifts, such as yachts and jewellery, would, almost without exception, be capable of being a bribe. Sightseeing tours are not permitted. Gifts and personal items for officials' family members could amount to bribes. However, there appears to be no guidance to be drawn from the cases as to the dividing line between what might potentially be caught by the Bribery Act 2010 and what would not. A £1,500 piece of jewellery may seem excessive, but what would be the situation be if it cost £100 or £500? Would it have to depend on the industry they work in, the country in which they live? An expensive watch in Premier League football is likely to be regarded as normal in an industry which pays its players £100,000 per week but would be abnormal for a struggling self-employed businessman trying to win a contract. £100 would not raise an eyebrow in a rich country but would do so in a country where it equated to a year's wages. Would a series of small gifts to the same person, the total worth of which is somewhat larger, be prosecuted?

B GIFTS AND BENEFITS

5.13 The difficulty with gifts is not new. As Euripides observed almost two and a half thousand years ago:

> 'The gods themselves, they say, are moved by gifts and gold speaks better than words with people'.
> 'There is no benefit in gifts from an evil man'.

It is therefore of assistance to applying our working definition in the context of gifts and benefits to look back both to previous statutory provisions and at contemporary sources that have, in one way or another, been fed into the process that has resulted in the Bribery Act 2010 as well as looking overseas for definition and application in parallel systems to our own.

Historical offences

5.14 For a full exposition of the old offences, see Chapter 3.

From the nineteenth century, the legislation has included the term 'gift' as can be seen below:

(a)   the Public Bodies Corrupt Practices Act 1889, s 1, provides:

> '(1) Every person who shall by himself or by or in conjunction with any other person, corruptly solicit or receive, or agree to receive, for himself, or for any other person, any gift, loan, fee, reward, or advantage whatever as an inducement to, or reward for, or otherwise on account of any member, officer, or servant of a public body as in this Act defined, doing or forbearing to do anything in respect of any matter or transaction whatsoever, actual or proposed, in which the said public body is concerned, shall be guilty of an offence'.

The terms 'gift', 'loan', 'fee' and 'reward' are not defined in the Act;

(b)   the Prevention of Corruption Act 1906, s 1(1), provides:

> 'If any agent corruptly accepts or obtains, or agrees to accept or attempts to obtain, from any person, for himself or for any other person, any gift or consideration as an inducement or reward for doing or forbearing to do, or for having after the passing of this Act done or forborne to do, any act in relation to his principal's affairs or business, or for showing or forbearing to show favour or disfavour to any person in relation to his principal's affairs or business; or

> If any person corruptly gives or agrees to give or offers any gift or consideration to any agent as an inducement or reward for doing or forbearing to do, or for having after the passing of this Act done or forborne to do, any act in relation to his principal's affairs or business, or for showing or forbearing to show favour or disfavour to any person in relation to his principal's affairs or business . . . he shall be guilty [of an offence]'.

The term 'consideration' is defined as including 'valuable consideration of any kind'. 'Gift' is not defined;

(c)   the Prevention of Corruption Act 1916, s 2, provides:

> 'Where in any proceedings against a person for an offence under the Prevention of Corruption Act 1906, or the Public Bodies Corrupt Practices Act 1889, it is proved that any money, gift, or other consideration has been paid or given to or received by a person in the employment of [Her] Majesty

or any Government Department or a public body by or from a person, or agent of a person, holding or seeking to obtain a contract from [Her] Majesty or any Government Department or public body, the money, gift, or consideration shall be deemed to have been paid or given and received corruptly as such inducement or reward as is mentioned in such Act unless the contrary is proved'.

Yet again the term 'gift' is not defined.

OECD Convention

5.15 Under the OECD Convention active bribery is defined as:

'intentionally promising, offering or giving, directly or indirectly, any undue advantage to a defined category of persons, for himself or herself or for a third party, for him or her to act or refrain from acting in the exercise of his or her functions'.

The term 'undue advantage' refers to something that the recipient is not lawfully entitled to accept or receive. It excludes, for example, minimum gifts or socially acceptable gifts.

OECD Working Paper: 'Business Approaches to Combating Corrupt Practices'

5.16 The Working Paper was published in June 2003, its purpose being to look at:

'anti-corruption material published on the websites of companies in UNCTAD's list of top 100 non-financial multinational enterprises. It seeks to understand these companies' views of corrupt business practices as well as their anti-corruption management and reporting practices'.

The paper noted that the public statements of the companies:

'show little evidence of a common model for describing acceptable or unacceptable gift giving and entertainment practices. Many of the websites contained language prohibiting employees (and sometimes also their family members) from accepting improper gifts and/or entertainment'.
'Most of these companies did not completely prohibit reception or giving of gifts or entertainment from or to business partners. Here, the line between acceptable business practice and bribery is, perhaps unavoidably, fuzzy . . . words such as appropriate, legitimate, reasonable, business-related, courtesy, token, modest and nominal were often used'.

The following examples were given of tests used by multinational enterprises:

— gifts or entertainment excessive in value and/or that exceed normal business customs;
— gifts or entertainment that are an inducement to business;
— gifts or entertainment that violate the law;
— gifts which give the appearance of impropriety.

Other Conventions and bodies

5.17 Other Conventions, such as the Inter-American Convention against Corruption and the African Union Convention on Preventing and Combating Corruption use the term 'gift' as part of the definition of a potential corrupt advantage. However, neither gives any further definition or guidance.

5.18 The International Chamber of Commerce's anti-corruption commission defines bribery as 'an offer or the receipt of any gift, loan, fee, reward or other advantage to or from any person as an inducement to do something which is dishonest or illegal'. Again, there is no guidance as to the ambit of a 'gift'.

Other countries

5.19 Other countries such as Germany, France, Japan and the US use the term 'gift' in their anti-corruption/bribery legislation and codes. 'Gift' tends not to be defined but there are statutory defences. For example in Japan 'mere gift' or 'gift in ordinary life' can provide a defence if the defendant can prove that the bribe was actually a gift and not made to gain an advantage.

5.20 All nine states which form the Commonwealth of Independent States ('CIS') have legislation under which gifts and other benefits can be considered a bribe if they are in exchange for an action or omission by the public official in favour of the donor. Minor gifts are permissible up to a varying value but generally one which is below $100. The exceptions are Armenia, where officials only have to transfer gifts to the state if they exceed five times their monthly salary, and Turkmenistan where there is no monetary upper limit.

5.21 In the US under the FCPA 1977 it is an offence to offer or give something of value to a foreign public official:

> 'with the intent to corruptly influence an official act or decision, induce an action in violation of a lawful duty, or secure an improper advantage, or induce any act that would assist the company in obtaining or retaining business'.

'Corruptly', although not defined in the legislation, is:

> 'the offer, payment, promise or gift, must be intended to induce the recipient to misuse his official position in order to wrongfully direct business to the payor or his client, or to obtain preferential legislative or a favourable regulation. The word "corruptly" connotes an evil motive or purpose, an intent to wrongfully influence the recipient'[1].

There is an 'affirmative' defence whereby the payment, gift, offer or promise of anything of value to a foreign official is made 'in accordance with the written laws and regulations' of that country. The term 'gift' is not, as such, defined but an analysis of the relevant US case law is set out at para **5.11**.

[1]   1977 Senate Report for the FCPA.

Law Commission

5.22 The Law Commission's Consultation Paper on reforming bribery[1] observed that:

'Corporate hospitality or gift-giving arguably bears some of the hallmarks of corrupt activity: an "advantage" is conferred and such conferment may be motivated by the hope of influencing a business relationship. However, it is also generally considered an acceptable part of business activity'.

[1]   Reforming Bribery: A Consultation Paper (Law Commission Consultation Paper No 185).

5.23 The Law Commission examined guidance from various bodies and corporations. Such guidance stressed that gifts should not be used as or seen as an inducement, that it should be proportionate and should be recorded. But monetary limits were rare and 'proportionate' not defined. 'Small gifts on formal occasions', as in the code for civil servants, is not a helpful definition. Certain organisation propose a 'blush' test—would it be embarrassing or reputationally damaging to disclose a gift or have its fact published in the media?

TRACE International

5.24 TRACE has produced guidelines on gifts and hospitality for public officials. It states that all benefits provided to foreign officials should:

— be reasonable and customary under the circumstances;
— not be motivated by a desire to influence the foreign official inappropriately;
— be tasteful and commensurate with generally accepted standards for professional courtesy in the country where the company has its headquarters;
— be provided openly and transparently;
— be given in good faith and without expectation of reciprocity;
— be provided in connection with a recognised gift-giving holiday or event in the case of gifts;
— be provided in connection with a bona fide and legitimate business purpose in the case of hospitality and travel;
— not be provided to any foreign official or group of foreign officials with such regularity or frequency as to create an appearance of impropriety or undermine the purpose of this policy; and
— comply with the local laws and regulations that apply to public officials.

The Serious Fraud Office position

5.25 The SFO has published a list of 'corruption indicators'[1]. Two of those are:

— 'lavish gifts being received';
— 'the payment of, or making funds available for high value expenses or school fees etc on behalf of others'.

The term 'lavish' is not defined and there is no guidance.

[1]   These appear on the SFO website, www.sfo.gov.uk/bribery—corruption.aspx.

5.26 *When is a benefit a bribe?*

MOJ guidance

5.26 The draft MOJ guidance was confined to stating that organisations could have a policy that covered, inter alia, gifts which ensured they were 'ethically sound and transparent'. The 'illustrative scenarios' did not deal with gifts. The final guidance does not specifically deal with gifts at all.

Drawing the line between a bribe and an acceptable gift

5.27 This brings us back to the central issue: how and where is the line drawn? As can readily be seen from above, there is no clear guidance, legislation or case law which would enable one to see where the line should be drawn, particularly with regard to monetary or other indicators of value. However, eleven principles can be set down with some confidence as amounting to the relevant indicia that a court may use in determining whether or not a payment is a bribe.

Motive

5.28 The gift should be made or received without placing the recipient under any obligation and without creating expectations.

The difference between a bribe and an acceptable gift is described in Professor Green's analysis as set out in his book *Lying, Cheating and Stealing: A Moral Theory of White-Collar Crime*[1]. He considers the difference as being the bilateral nature of a bribe:

> '[bribery] involves an agreement to exchange something of value in return for influence, whereas gifts . . . involve no such agreement'.

Thus the decision-making process, the business advantage, has been corrupted by the gift which acts as an inducement or reward for the improper performance of some public or business activity.

It should also be recognised that gifts carry a potential for grooming. Even small gifts, from the donor's point of view, if given with frequency can set up obligations or expectations.

[1]   (OUP USA, 2006).

Transparency

5.29 An openly given and received gift is much less likely to be called into question than one given or received in circumstances of secrecy or obfuscation.

Documentation

5.30 An unrecorded gift, or one which is incorrectly recorded or whose value or nature is disguised, will give rise to a presumption that it was acting as an improper inducement or reward.

Frequency

5.31 It is not just the value, monetary or otherwise, of a gift which may give rise to the suggestion of a bribe, but the frequency with which gifts are given to the same person, division, business enterprise or public department. There is an obvious difference between a bottle of wine at Christmas given to Mr X and a bottle every week to the same person. Small, but frequent, gifts set up a pattern and may amount to very much more in monetary terms.

Not contrary to local law

5.32 The gift must not be contrary to the local law of the state in which it was given or received either in terms of as a fact in itself or in terms of value. For example, the CIS countries tend to place monetary limits on gifts to public officials.

Recipient

5.33 Where the recipient is the spouse, child, parent or friend of the business associate of the donor of the gift, questions are likely to arise as to ts true nature.

Type of gift

5.34 Cash or cash equivalent such as vouchers and sexual or similarly inappropriate activities as a gift will give rise to a presumption of bribery.

Solicitation of gifts

5.35 Solicitation of a gift or any suggestion of its nature or value by the person in a position to give an advantage should be a red flag indicator of bribery. For example, the exchange of gifts such as pens at a signing ceremony for a contract can be part of normal business courtesies but where the other party suggests a particular pen and it is of high value compared to his salary, then the gift of the particular pen will have the hallmarks of bribery.

Normal business courtesies

5.36 The giving and receiving of gifts can be part of normal business courtesies.

Proportionality

5.37 The question of proportionality is explored at para **5.8**. Allowance must be made, within reason, for industry variants. However, there should be a strong evidential basis for asserting that a gift of more than 'modest' value is the norm within a particular business type. The ability to show that other companies within the same industry have similar guidelines and policies would be essential. It must be recognised that any individual or business enterprise making or receiving what could potentially be described as 'lavish' gift, especially if it formed part of a pattern of such gifts, is running the risk both of prosecution and of conviction by a jury who may well be drawn from a variety of backgrounds and could well be averse to a defence based on industry variant.

Cultural/country variants

5.38 The introduction of the FCPA 1977 in the US led to anxieties of cultural imperialism. The same disquiet was expressed during the various consultations and evidence-gathering prior to the passing of the Bribery Act 2010. In essence, there are those who argue that the UK is imposing Western values and culture onto other countries which have different cultural values and that criminalising behaviour which would be culturally normal in another country, is to set up the UK as an unappointed and unwelcome moral arbiter.

5.39 It is recognised that there is country variation but there is unwillingness, voiced by the SFO during evidence to the Joint Committee during the passage of the Bill through Parliament, to accept that cultural variation could be a defence, the justification for such reluctance being that the UK had to keep to a set of objective tests.

5.40 In some countries, gifts are given at certain times or seasons. But to be acceptable and not open to interpretation as a bribe, such a gift must be part of the local custom, given or received on the correct occasion and customary in type and value.

5.41 Cultural norms have, of course, been exploited. For instance, in South Korea the culture of rice cakes expenses, ttokkap, has been subverted. It was used as means of channelling large bribes by businesses to two, now former, presidents. In Nigeria, there have been accusations by a former president, General Obasanjo, that the local culture was one of giving token monetary gifts given as 'appreciation and hospitality' and foreign companies had used that local gift-giving culture as a subterfuge for bribery.

5.42 In some cultures the exchange of gifts between senior executives has a high symbolic value. There is an understandable concern on the part of businesses working in such cultures that a failure to give or accept a gift appropriate to status could be viewed as an insult and be detrimental to ongoing and future business relations.

With that abstract analysis in mind it is useful to stand back and consider how applying those principles may be less than easy in practice.

THE CHINESE PERSPECTIVE: A CASE STUDY

5.43 Westerners tend to keep a rigid divide between personal friends and business contacts. There is no such distinction in China. In fact, in an ideal world the Chinese will not do business with someone whom they have not first befriended. It is a question of trust. Much mystique surrounds 'guanxi'—the art of relationships in China—but despite being recognised in China for millennia, it is not unique to China and is akin to business networking in many other parts of the world. However, in China guanxi is part of the everyday language and is much used. Questions such as 'Do you know anyone with guanxi in X Ministry?' or answers such as 'He has guanxi in Y place. Mention my name as he owes me some guanxi' are commonplace. It has been described as a currency; the more favours you do, the more you are owed and thus the more guanxi you have in hand. Thus it makes good sense to give favours and help people even if there is no immediate or even prospective return. But you may well get something in return, be it cash or a favour for yourself or someone close to you. It developed in a society traditionally without transparency or rule of law, where people have to rely on their own networks. Something like a 'guanxi system' was bound to develop and over time become part of the psyche and the culture. It is part and parcel of China's much-lauded pragmatism, so well described in former leader Deng Xiaoping's axiom 'it does not matter if it is a black cat or a white cat, if it catches the mouse it is a good cat' (now sometimes transformed in street argot to 'it does not matter if it is a black mouse or a white mouse, if it avoids the cat it is a good mouse'). Its many forms range from what Westerners would call business connections (eg company A wants to buy a particular commodity so person B introduces them to company C who supplies that commodity) to facilitation payments to save time, through to nepotism, insider deals, bribery and corruption. Westerners, not knowing the system, recoil when suddenly asked a favour, especially a business favour, by a person they considered to be a friend. But the Chinese would not make that distinction.

5.44 Gifts in China are a mark of respect and a mutual recognition of prestige. Again, they are part of everyday life: everyone gives mooncakes at the Mid-Autumn Festival and Hong Bao, money in red envelopes, at Chinese New Year. The value of the gift is not in its monetary worth. But gifts must be exchanged on formal occasions. Sometimes the gifts may be very expensive but they are a reflection of status: the higher the status, the more expensive the gift. It is possible for Western companies, with policies on not accepting gifts above a token value, to cause great offence by returning them to their Chinese counterparts and indeed by not giving gifts themselves.

This case study illustrates that the balance to be struck can be subtle and that business enterprises must be alive to cultural issues in the countries in which they do business.

C   CORPORATE HOSPITALITY

5.45 This section examines corporate hospitality, including entertainment, travel, hotels and meals.

The distinction to be drawn between legitimate entertainment and bribery was neatly encapsulated in the South African case of *S v Deal Enterprises*[1] (a case involving bribes disguised as Christmas gifts) in which Nicholas J, dealing with entertainment, stated that the distinction lies in the intention with which the entertainment is provided, and that is something to be inferred from all the circumstances, including the relationship between giver and recipient, their respective financial and social positions and the nature and value of the entertainment.

[1]   1978 (3) SA 302.

5.46 Corporate hospitality is considered to be an almost essential part of business life. Nonetheless, it carries a potential to either be or be perceived to be, bribery. Many of the US cases show that legitimate corporate hospitality can easily be subverted and form an inducement to do business with those providing it. This has now been recognised by the MOJ final guidance which states that 'It is . . . clear that hospitality and promotional or other similar business expenditure can be employed as bribes'.

5.47 As with the definition of 'a bribe', when trying to distinguish between good and bad corporate hospitality and therefore making Nicholls J's crisp definition work in practice, it is necessary to search far outside the four corners of the Bribery Act 2010 itself.

Law Commission Consultation

5.48 The Law Commission Consultation[1] found that:

> 'Corporate hospitality or gift-giving arguably bears some of the hallmarks of corrupt activity: an "advantage" is conferred and such conferment may be motivated by the hope of influencing a business relationship . . . However, it is also generally considered an acceptable part of business activity'.

Consultees reported that it was seen as a vital marketing tool and that there were many legitimate and beneficial reasons for fostering good business and social relations through hospitality.

[1] Reforming Bribery: A Consultation Paper (Law Commission Consultation Paper No 185).

5.49 The consultation found almost no backing for a complete prohibition on corporate hospitality, but that there should be a proscription on hospitality that crossed the line from legitimate entertainment to conduct that was illegitimate, unacceptable or improper.

5.50 The difficulty that the Law Commission encountered, and which persists today, was to frame a test or define principles to determine where the line should be drawn between lawful and unlawful conduct. Government recognised the problem, saying that it 'lies in defining the point where corporate hospitality . . . become(s) improper'[1].

[1] Reforming Bribery: A Consultation Paper (Law Commission Consultation Paper No 185).

5.51 It was considered to be particularly important to identify the 'borderline between what is, and what is not, acceptable' as the reputational damage attached to bribery was seen to be particularly detrimental to any corporation. It would appear that the Law Commission anticipated, and hoped, that the government would provide some detailed guidance.

Law Commission Report on Reforming Bribery

5.52 In Appendix D to its Report on Reforming Bribery[1], the Law Commission identified the following:

— 'Many trade and similar organisations have expressed concerns about the potential for the provision of corporate hospitality to fall within the scope of bribery. These concerns fall into two categories: ensuring that conventional corporate hospitality practices should not fall into the ambit of bribery, and providing guidance on what kind and degree of corporate hospitality is or is not acceptable';

— 'Where a supplier provides corporate entertainment to regular customers, the purpose is normally to cement existing links with the customers, provide information, and keep the existence of the supplier at the forefront of the customers' minds when it comes to the placing of orders. In that sense it is obviously designed to assist in the acquisition and retention of business, and would be a pointless exercise if it were not. Where those entertained are employees of potential customers, and have responsibility for choosing among possible suppliers, the potentiality for bribery is present';

— in proposing a test of whether the recipient of hospitality (an advantage) was influenced by it in a way that breached an expectation that he would act in good faith or impartially, or in accordance with a position of trust, the Law Commission drew a distinction between hospitality extended between private companies and where the recipient was either a public official or a trustee;

— the primary reason for the recipient of hospitality in providing business to the donor was seen to be the test. If hospitality was merely one of a number of factors which influenced a business decision and was not the primary reason, then hospitality would fall outside the scope of bribery;

— ordinary hospitality in the private sector was seen as unlikely to be caught by the legislation, as there would be no breach of expectation as to how the recipient should behave. However, there were some situations, such as the provision of hospitality at a lap dancing club, which had the potential for influence if the recipient did not want his employers or anyone else to know about it;

— in contrast, in a public sector or trust situation, there was concern that even the mere provision of hospitality or hospitality of a 'special kind' (not specified), would be a breach of the expectation of the position of trust held by the recipient.

[1] Law Com No 313 (2008).

5.53 The main body of the report anticipated that the requirement that the giver of hospitality *intended* that the advantage conferred by such hospitality to lead to the recipient to behave improperly, as opposed to a *realisation* on the part of the giver that there was a *serious risk* that it would motivate the recipient to so behave, would provide the

'required degree of certainty and robust clarity in the law that people engaged in competing for business, as well as those performing public functions, are entitled to expect'[1].

[1] At para 3.68.

5.54 In addressing cultural differences in hospitality, The Law Commission did not wish to set up a defence that hid bribery under the guise of entertainment, but acknowledged that:

'[if] one country traditionally entertains all visiting business executives far more lavishly then is customary in other countries, that fact will still have a relevance to liability under our scheme. It would be evidence tending to show that, in spite of the fact that the hospitality was accepted, it did not mean that the executives departed from the standards of good faith or of impartiality that would be observed by a person of moral integrity'[1].

[1] At para 3.116.

Passage of the Bribery Bill through Parliament

(a) SFO position

5.55 The SFO submitted a memorandum to the Joint Committee on the draft Bribery Bill[1] in the following terms:

'Hospitality is different in that most routine and inexpensive hospitality would be unlikely to lead to a reasonable expectation of improper conduct. This would therefore not trigger the general offences.

For the offence we must still prove that the payer's intent is to influence the foreign public official in his/her capacity as a foreign public official. The provision of routine and inexpensive hospitality to a large group may not have that specific intent.

It becomes more difficult when more than routine hospitality is offered to targeted individuals. In circumstances like these, the SFO would advise the corporate to check the local laws about what foreign public officials can legitimately accept. This should not be too onerous for the corporate as it ought to be part of their due diligence in doing business there.

One would expect government and industry wide standards or codes of behaviour to cover such conduct in any event.

The SFO considers that prosecutorial discretion, backed by appropriate guidance, is the proper way forward on small facilitation payments and hospitality. If a case were to pass our threshold for acceptance however, we would rarely exercise the discretion and would look to prosecute.'

[1] www.publications.parliament.uk/pa/jt200809/jtselect/jtbribe/memo/430/ucm1402.htm.

5.56 During the course of evidence to the Joint Committee Richard Alderman, Director of the SFO[1], stated:

'In connection with hospitality, I think there is a quite clear distinction that I am sure juries will be able to make between inexpensive, modest hospitality offered to many and lavish hospitality that might be offered to a very small number of people in the hope of getting a contract'.

Further, and in answer to questions on whether there should be country variants in custom on entertaining:

'We are concerned to make sure that the argument that this is done in such and such a country is not one that we ought to permit. The focus is on eradicating bribery. It relates to big payments and small payments and the focus is on how we can make sure that corporates and individuals within the jurisdiction of our courts live up to the expectations that society and others have of them in order to eradicate bribery. That is why I think that it is right that we have some objective tests here about what is acceptable'.

He predicted that both sides, prosecution and defence, would call evidence as to what were the cultural norms.

1   On 10 June 2009. www.publications.parliament.uk/pa/jt200809/jtselect/jtbribe/uc430-v/uc 43002.htm.

(b) *Other prosecutorial positions*

5.57 The DPP too submitted a memorandum to the Joint Committee[1] in these terms:

'Corporate hospitality raises other issues from the types of facilitation payments described above. The primary one for prosecutors will be deciding whether there is evidence in any particular case that the hospitality provided contravenes clauses 1 and 2 of the Bill. The Bill does not provide guidance as to when corporate hospitality would be unlawful, that is to say improper, but it is not reasonable to expect that primary legislation could cover every situation.

Corporate hospitality may not be, and in many cases probably is not, provided with a view to inducing someone to perform a relevant function improperly. Culturally, corporate hospitality is generally accepted, though different standards may be expected and required of public officials or others working within or for the public sector. In many, if not most, cases it will simply be regarded as legitimate relationship-building and networking, with a view to obtaining a contract or maintaining a client relationship and would not be indicative of improper conduct. In some cases it may go beyond that; while it is dependent on the circumstances of the case, the greater the advantage conferred, the more likely it is that this is evidence that the advantage was promised or given to induce the recipient to perform his function improperly.

However, this is a matter of degree and there will inevitably be a grey area around the boundary of what is considered acceptable. To an extent, it may be possible to resolve some of the issues as to what is acceptable, legitimate, hospitality, and what is not, through the adoption and implementation of codes of practice in industries, professions and the public sector (though with self-regulation, there is obviously a risk of inconsistency of practice between industries). Codes of practice do provide clarity and assist in prevention and enforcement; when considering whether hospitality was improper, investigators and prosecutors would consider codes of practice as part of the investigation and review process'.

1   www.publications.parliament.uk/pa/jt200809/jtselect/jtbribe/memo/430/ucm1602.htm.

5.58 Detective Chief Superintendent Head, head of the Economic Crime directorate of the City of London Police (which includes investigations of bribery overseas), also gave evidence to the Joint Committee. On the question of the view that there may be country to country variation of custom with regard to the lavishness of entertaining and its effect on the bona fides of a company's hospitality:

'From our own perspective this is an issue of context around each individual case . . . The question is reasonableness . . . In the course of an investigation, I would anticipate that persons who are spoken to in relation to this would come forward with their defence of the fact that it is reasonable in X or in Y. In terms of the investigation, a large number of those questions will be asked as part of whether we go forward from here and how we go forward from here. Local context will be put into each investigation'[1].

1   www.publications.parliament.uk/pa/jt200809/jtselect/jtbribe/uc430-v/uc43002.htm.

(c)   *Law Commission: Professor Horder*

5.59 Professor Horder gave oral evidence to the Joint Committee, during the course of which he said:

> ' . . . the provision of hospitality of a very extravagant kind can amount to bribery . . . in our Bill there will be a clear line in the sand . . . when you lay on your corporate hospitality, it actually has to be your intention to produce an improper influence on the people there and it is not enough that you realise that it might have that effect in some speculative way . . . I think, so I am actually quite bullish about this, about the certainty that it provides for businesses and the provision of entertainment because, as I say, it is only in the case where you intended to have that corrupting effect, to use the broad term'.

Further:

> 'it is much easier for you to secure contracts if you are doing it on the basis of which people know who you are and you are not just a set of proposals on a piece of paper, and that seems to me perfectly normal and acceptable actually because it will still be the case that what matters to the contractor is the merits of putting the contract your way, but it is just that now they know more about you, the nature of your business, what you do, they have talked to your partners, your employees and so on and they are in a better position to assess those matters'.
> 'I think that the element of impropriety there is in awarding the contract other than on the merits, it is awarding the contract because you so much enjoyed being taken to Monte Carlo or wherever it may be. That is the improper element and it would be for the jury, I think, to determine whether that actually was really the point of the whole thing or whether actually this was, as I have just indicated, and this is the general purpose of corporate hospitality generally, a "getting to know you" session, which of course yes, does, or may have, an influence further down the line, but only in terms of persuading you of the merits of that company, its plausibility, its integrity and the way it does things. It is perfectly possible that a corporate hospitality session would be a disaster and they will end up thinking, "They're just a bunch of flashy people whom we don't want to do business with"; that is always possible'.

Professor Horder stated that he did not envisage prosecutions based purely on hospitality and that hospitality would evidentially be only part of a wider case of providing benefits. He saw the focus not being so much on the hospitably itself but on the individuals it was provided to. He further stated:

> 'What I am talking about is just the general run of lavish parties, meetings in hotels, flying people to expensive conferences and so on, those kinds of things which go on all the time, and I just do not really see the prosecution as having any prospect of establishing that there was an intention to influence people improperly; I do not see that'.

(d)   *Lord Tunnicliffe*

5.60 As government spokesperson for the MOJ, Lord Tunnicliffe wrote a letter to the House of Lords on 14 January 2010[1] 'to provide further clarification of corporate hospitality under the Bill following the debate . . . on 7 January'. In this letter he stated that:

> 'We recognise that corporate hospitality is an accepted part of modern business practice and the government is not seeking to penalise expenditure on corporate hospitality for legitimate commercial purposes. But lavish corporate hospitality

can be used as a bribe to secure advantages and the offence in the Bill must therefore be capable of penalising those who use it for such purposes'.

He further stated that ' . . . it is sufficient to rely on prosecutors to differentiate between legitimate and illegitimate corporate hospitality and to decide whether or not it would be in the public interest to bring a prosecution'.

[1] www.justice.gov.uk/publications/docs/letter-lord-henley-corporate-hospitality.pdf.

(e) *Joint Committee Report*

5.61 The conclusion in the Joint Committee Report[1] is as follows:

> 'Corporate hospitality is a legitimate part of doing business at home and abroad, provided it remains within appropriate limits. The general offences impose an appropriate limit on this activity under the "improper" performance test. However, the main limit under clause 4 [now the Bribery Act 2010, s 6] is based on prosecutorial discretion. We are content with this and call on the government to reassure the business community that it does not risk facing prosecution for providing proportionate levels of hospitality as part of competing fairly in the international arena'.

However, the Report highlighted that there was a wide prosecutorial discretion and although there may not be any public interest in prosecuting a company for providing hospitality to a public official which 'perfectly properly' influenced the official, the offence in relation to foreign officials was 'influence' based, not 'impropriety' based and thus even legitimate hospitality could potentially be caught by the legislation. The Report quoted the SFO's unhelpful comment that modest hospitality might fall outside the offence, as there might be no intention to influence a foreign official in those circumstances.

[1] www.publications.parliament.uk/pa/jt200809/jtselect/jtbribe/115/11510.htm#a26.

MOJ Guidance

5.62 The issuance of the final guidance was delayed from early January 2011 to 30 March 2011. It is understood that the delay was partly due to the Government coming under intense lobbying to issue clear guidance with regard to corporate hospitality. The final guidance does specifically address the issue of hospitality and promotional expenses. However, in the opinion of the author, goes no further than a definition that could be gleaned from an analysis of the Act together with previous statements as set out in the preceding paragraphs.

The foreword by Kenneth Clarke, Secretary of State for Justice, reassures business with the words ' . . . Rest assured—no one wants to stop firms getting to know their clients by taking them to events like Wimbledon or the Grand Prix'. It might be thought, however, that such reassurance does not deal with the more problematic scenarios, such as those identified in para **5.69**. Paragraph 20 of the final guidance states:

> 'By way of illustration, in order to proceed with a case under section 1 based on an allegation that hospitality was intended as a bribe, the prosecution would need to show that the hospitality was intended to induce conduct that amounts to a breach of an expectation that a person will act in good faith, impartially, or in

131

accordance with a position of trust. This would be judged by what a reasonable person in the UK thought. So, for example, an invitation to foreign clients to attend a Six Nations match at Twickenham as part of a public relations exercise designed to cement good relations or enhance knowledge in the organisation's field is extremely unlikely to engage section 1 as there is unlikely to be evidence of an intention to induce improper performance of a relevant function'.

This is no more than a restatement of s 1 itself and a recognition, as set out in para **5.6,** that there must be some reciprocity and direct connection between the giving or receipt of an 'advantage' and what is improperly obtained in exchange.

Paragraph 28 specifically states the same issue with regard to s 6:

'Where the prosecution is able to establish a financial or other advantage has been offered, promised or given, it must then show that there is a sufficient connection between the advantage and the intention to influence and secure business or a business advantage. Where the prosecution cannot prove this to the requisite standard then no offence under section 6 will be committed'.

In dealing with 'levels of expenditure', the final guidance addresses this issue only with regard to s 6 (and not ss 1 and 2) by stating:

' . . . the existence of this connection and such evidence may indeed relate to relatively modest expenditure. In many cases, however, the question as to whether such a connection can be established will depend on the totality of the evidence which takes into account all of the surrounding circumstances. It would include matters such as the type and level of advantage offered, the manner and form in which the advantage is provided, and the level of influence the particular foreign public official has over awarding the business. In this circumstantial context, the more lavish the hospitality or the higher the expenditure in relation to travel, accommodation or other similar business expenditure provided to a foreign public official, then, generally, the greater the inference that it is intended to influence the official to grant business or a business advantage in return. The standards or norms applying in a particular sector may also be relevant here. However, simply providing hospitality or promotional, or other similar business expenditure which is commensurate with such norms is not, of itself, evidence that no bribe was paid if there is other evidence to the contrary; particularly if the norms in question are extravagant. Levels of expenditure will not, therefore, be the only consideration in determining whether a section 6 offence has been committed. But in the absence of any further evidence demonstrating the required connection, it is unlikely, for example, that incidental provision of a routine business courtesy will raise the inference that it was intended to have a direct impact on decision making, particularly where such hospitality is commensurate with the reasonable and proportionate norms for the particular industry; eg the provision of airport to hotel transfer services to facilitate an on-site visit, or dining and tickets to an event'.

The final guidance goes on to give two illustrations with regard to s 6, both of which appear to have been informed by the FCPA cases, some of which are set out at para **5.11.**

5.63 So much for corporate hospitality generally: we now turn to specific areas of hospitality likely to be of practical concern: travel and hotels, meals and functions, sightseeing, sporting and cultural events, sexual entertainment and promotional expenses, and the issues each raises.

Travel and hotels

5.64 Travel expenses may be part of what are known as 'promotional expenses' for which see para **5.74**.

5.65 An analysis of the US cases gives some guidance on the type of travel expenses which benefit a customer and may fall within the ambit of bribery. Under the FCPA 1977 prosecutions, settlements and opinion procedures, a pattern of conduct which has led to investigations emerges. The factors to be considered are:

— the purpose of the travel. Travel for non-business reasons such as for medical appointments, shopping, holidays or sightseeing is likely to be a payment with an improper intent. The MOJ final guidance at paragraph 31 reiterates this point in the two illustrations given;

— the grade of travel. First class travel is unlikely to be seen as acceptable. However, there may well be industry and status variants. For a multi-million pound company dealing with another of similar wealth, first class travel may be the only way in which their executives ever travel. In those circumstances, an economy ticket might be perceived as an insult. At the other end of the scale, first class travel given to a foreign public official who has never before left his own country may well act as an improper influence;

— persona other than the customer or client. Payment for spouses, children and others closely connected with the customer or client is likely to be seen as unacceptable. Except in exceptional circumstances (for example a client has a disability which requires a travelling companion) there can be no legitimate business reason to pay the travel expenses of anyone else. However, it must be noted that the MOJ final guidance at paragraph 31 gives an example of potentially permissible hospitality as 'reasonable hospitality for the individual and his or her partner, such as fine dining and attendance at a baseball match'. This permissible expenditure does not, it seem, extend to travel and hotel expenses.

— the method of payment. Direct payment or reimbursement will cause difficulties. The payment should be made to the airline, train company, hotel or travel agent.

The MOJ final guidance adds a final complication by raising the question of whether hospitality or promotional expenditure in the form of travel and accommodation costs for a foreign public official could even amount to an advantage, as they would not be costs otherwise borne by the official but rather by his government. That does not, of course, address the more subtle questions of scale and 'lavishness' of the expenditure, or indeed whether that official would have otherwise have been sent on such a trip at his government's expense.

Meals and functions

5.66 Meals may be part of what are known as 'promotional expenses', for which see para **5.74**.

5.67 Corporate hospitality also encompasses paying for client meals either in a restaurant or hotel or as part of a function. Whilst it is extremely unlikely that a prosecution would be brought solely based on the provision of meals, they may form part of a wider pattern of payments and benefits. Again, it is a matter of weighing up a number of factors. Is the cost of the meal at the top end of the scale for meals in that location (there is an infinite regional/city/country variation of price)? Does it include very expensive single items, such as highly-priced bottles of wine? Is it typical for the business? In relative terms, how costly was it for the payer in terms of annual business-running costs? What is the relative status of the guests? Would the guest be able to afford to pay his own share? Are they chief executives of multi-national companies or relatively poor FPOs? How does the cost of the meal equate to the guest's monthly salary?

Sightseeing

5.68 This is covered in promotional expenses at para **5.74**.

Sporting and cultural events

5.69 Sporting and cultural events are frequently used for corporate client entertaining. They are said to provide a neutral and relaxed venue at which people can build business relationships in a social setting. Those who pay for such events are obviously not doing so for altruistic reasons and ultimately they intend to obtain and retain business. However, unless the donor intends to induce or reward improper conduct or they know or believe that mere acceptance would itself constitute improper conduct or, in the case of a FPO, they intend to influence him in his capacity as a FPO to obtain or retain business or a business advantage, such entertaining would not constitute an offence under the Bribery Act 2010. As it is put in the MOJ final guidance, 'an invitation to foreign clients to attend a Six Nations match at Twickenham as part of a public relations exercise designed to cement good relations or enhance knowledge in the organisation's field is extremely unlikely to engage section 1 as there is unlikely to be evidence of an intention to induce improper performance of a relevant function'. A large industry has grown up around this kind of entertaining. The industry has been fuelled in part by sporting authorities offering and encouraging the block booking purchase of tickets to premier events and the provision of special facilities. There are many companies which specialise in corporate hospitality and who market either pre-arranged or tailored packages. Typical one-day events are trips to watch a rugby international or a Formula 1 race. Even standard packages to these events are relatively expensive and thus it is likely that invitations will be targeted to individuals who the inviter believes will be, or have been, influential and beneficial to their business. Business enterprises will have to look carefully to the circumstances of the hospitality. Will the hospitality be close in time to an important business decision to be taken by the recipient, such as the award or renewal of a valuable contract? How important to the recipient is the particular hospitality? A recipient who is not especially keen on rugby is less likely to be improperly influenced by a day at Twickenham than a situation where the inviter company discovers that an influential client is an avid tennis fan but he cannot get tickets to the men's final at Wimbledon and then specifically arranges a day at those very finals. The second scenario sets up an obligation.

5.70 How generous is the entertainment? Does it involve more than a day out of the office? Does it take place abroad? Does it involve the payment of other associated expenses such as travel? The more generous, the longer it takes, the more added benefits there are, the more likely that a presumption of bribery will be established. Whilst it is not likely that a day out at an event in the UK for a UK-based client (or even a foreign client according to the MOJ final guidance: see para **5.69**) would lead to prosecution, corporate hospitality packages currently on offer can be far more extensive. For example, a trip to Las Vegas to watch a boxing match including business class travel, limousine transfers and luxury hotels or a similar jaunt to watch the football World Cup in another country with tickets to the final. Such a package is likely to cost the donor company several thousand pounds per person. Again, the recipient is overwhelmingly likely to have been chosen with great business care. Again, it will set up an obligation.

5.71 The frequency that the entertainment is given to a particular individual or organisation will be another factor to be weighed in the balance. A business enterprise might have a number of clients but a particular emphasis on one will call into question whether there is an intention to exert an improper influence.

5.72 Again, like many of the considerations of where an advantage or benefit conferred may cross the line and become a bribe, industry variation must be a factor. Is the type of invitation extended typical or otherwise of the business sector? Is it commonplace or unique and out of line with other companies? Can the inviter afford it? Does it constitute a significant percentage of annual costs?

Sexual entertainment

5.73 Any form of sexual or quasi-sexual entertainment, even if legal, such as a visit to a lap dancing club, may well be or be perceived to be exerting an improper influence.

Promotional expenses

5.74 Those involved in business or a trade or profession have many means available to them to promote their business, their products and their services. The term 'promotional expenses' has a particular legislative meaning in the FCPA 1977 in which it forms one of only two 'affirmative' defences. The FCPA permits payments to foreign officials if

> 'the payment, gift, offer or promise of anything of value that was made was a reasonable and bona fide expenditure, such as travel and lodging expenses, incurred by or on behalf of a foreign official . . . .directly related to . . . .the promotion, demonstration, or explanation of products or services'.

This defence has engendered a certain amount of academic discussion in the US: 'reasonable and bona fide expenditure' would not engage the FCPA because it would not be a corrupt payment and thus it is argued that promotional expenses do not need to come within a special affirmative defence.

5.75 Promotional expenses as such were not explicitly explored during the passage of the Bribery Bill though Parliament, either in written or oral evidence, where the focus was on corporate hospitality. Nor were they mentioned in the Law Commission's report on Reforming Bribery. There were two mentions in the Law Commission's Consultation Paper on Reforming Bribery, both in relation to corporate hospitality.

The MOJ final guidance states in one of the case studies that promotional expenses 'should seek to improve the image of (the company/firm/etc) as a commercial organisation, to better present its products or services, or establish cordial relations'. The use for establishing 'cordial relations' relaxes the definition as might have been understood from the FCPA model and blurs the distinction between hospitality and promotional expenses.

5.76 This section will use the FCPA 1977 definition of promotional expenses but widen its ambit to cover payments and other benefits to persons other than foreign officials so that these expenses can be seen within the context of the Bribery Act 2010.

5.77 'Promotional expenses' covers a wide range of factual situations, from the distribution of free samples of products, to conferences and seminars to promote and publicise a product or service, to taking potential customers to view a factory or an already installed and working product, to training customers to operate a product once it has been delivered. In the world of international business this might entail paying for the travel, hotel and food bills for persons from other countries.

5.78 The critical phrases in the FCPA definition are 'reasonable and bona fide' and 'directly related to'. The US cases provide examples of so-called promotional expenses that were neither directly related to promotion, demonstration or explanation, nor reasonable and bona fide. In general, training or inspection trips were used as a disguise for sightseeing and entertainment. Expenses which relate to items with little or no business validity are likely to fall within the ambit of the Bribery Act 2010.

5.79 The case of *Lucent* affords a graphic illustration: Lucent was a US company involved in communication systems. Much of their business was in China where they dealt with Chinese government officials. Many of the officials were senior, including heads of state-owned telecommunications companies. In the three years between 2000 and 2003, Lucent spent over $10m on trips for these officials from China to the US and other countries. The ostensible reasons for the trips were factory inspections or training. Sometimes the contractual terms stipulated that Lucent must invite representatives 'from the Buyer to the United States for the Factory Inspection for a period of two weeks' and that Lucent was 'responsible for the expenses of international airfare, US domestic travel, lodging and boarding and a reasonable allowance'. In reality, little or no time was spent on such business activities and the trips consisted of sightseeing and entertainment in tourist destinations such as Las Vegas, the Grand Canyon, Disneyworld, Niagara Falls, New York and Hawaii. For example, one or two days would be spent on legitimate business, followed by two weeks of entertainment and sightseeing paid for by Lucent. The payments included airfares, hotels, meals, sightseeing and per diems. The company had a 'customer visit request form' which included questions such as whether the customer was a 'decision maker' and whether sightseeing was 'required'. Internal documentation made clear that Lucent regarded these trips, especially those involving high-ranking officials as a means of obtaining, retaining and enhancing business. For example, a trip involving six officials who visited three Lucent facilities and then spent nine days sightseeing and being entertained to a total cost of $73,000, was expected to generate more than $500m in potential revenue. In 2002 two delegations totalling 19 officials spent just one day of the two-week trip at a factory and the rest of the trip in tourist destinations all over the US at a cost to Lucent of $130,000. The trips were designated in the accounts as 'factory inspections' but were used as a sales opportunity. Following factory relocations, customer trips included Australia and Europe even though neither had factories. The appearance of legitimacy was created by a tour of the headquarters or some facility (not factory) but the visits were primarily sightseeing, entertainment and leisure which Lucent knew had little or no legitimate business purpose. Lucent was also aware that specific sightseeing requests had to be acceded to as the Chinese officials made clear that they were being approached by Lucent's competitors. 'Training' visits also included extensive and excessive sightseeing, entertainment and leisure elements. For example, 21 days of a 'training trip' for six engineers known to be 'influencers' with regard to a potential $6m business opportunity, had five days of training followed by 16 days of all-expenses sightseeing and entertainment again at tourist destinations all over the US at a total cost of $46,000.

5.80 *Lucent* provides an extreme example. The dividing line is much less easy to discern if a legitimate trip for an overseas customer involves elements of benefits or advantages which are not strictly speaking related to the business element of the trip. For example, a UK company involved in green energy wants to promote its wind turbines to an Asian company. To do so it is necessary to bring the senior executives of the Asian company to the UK to see the turbines installed and working, and to visit the factory. The UK company pays the economy airfares of the Asian company representatives and the hotel bills. The trip is split between a visit to turbines in northern England and to the factory in the south west. For reasons of flight logistics, the total trip spans a weekend. In order to be hospitable, the UK company pays for some sightseeing during the weekend and modest expenses for meals taken out of the hotel. The UK company does not feel it would enhance business relations to ask the Asian company representatives for receipts for any cash payments they incurred during the weekend and gave them the spending money in advance. In theory, both the spending money and the sightseeing expenses could come within the Bribery Act 2010. However, unless the per diem payments were very large and the sightseeing was extensive and took up the majority of the trip, this is most unlikely to give rise to a prosecution.

5.81 A more difficult problem may arise with the scenario where a UK company arranges a legitimate trip for a FPO to view its facilities and factory. The expenses are modest, the travel economy and the hotel is not 5 star. The trip involves visiting a facility in Northern Scotland. Before the trip is arranged, the UK company's representative visits the FPO, who awards contracts, in his office in his home country with a view to promoting the company business. The FPO says that he has never been abroad and that it his life ambition to visit the Highlands of Scotland. The UK company has facilities all over the UK and indeed several close to Heathrow Airport, into which the FPO will fly. The FPO will need to inspect a facility in order to make a proper decision as to whether to award a contract to the company. Is the use of an otherwise legitimate trip, but which is specifically angled towards realising the FPO's 'life ambition', capable of being an offence under the Bribery Act 2010? The answer must be yes. Yet again, it is an illustration that there are a number of factors to be considered.

The pharmaceutical industry: a case study

5.82 The pharmaceutical industry has long been associated with the use and abuse of promotional expenses. It is notable that in Transparency UK's Adequate Procedures Guidance that two of the hypothetical (although based on real life examples) scenarios in relation to promotional expenses involve pharmaceutical companies.

5.83 The recent UK case of *R v Dougall*[1] is illustrative of a case of corrupt payments to secure contracts in the healthcare industry. Robert Dougall worked for a large UK manufacturer of orthopaedic products, whose parent company was Johnson and Johnson, based in the US. In order to maintain very substantial sales of their orthopaedic products, for use by Greek surgeons in the Greek Health Service, corrupt payments totalling £4.5 million over just under four years, were made to a distributor of the products in Greece, who passed on the incentives to the surgeons in the form of 'professional education' which was in fact no more than a euphemism for the corrupt payments. The payments ensured that the company maintained its very substantial share of the market in Greece, and were in effect funded by the Greek taxpayer. Without the payments the company would have lost its share of the market entirely. Dougall neither sought nor gained personal benefit from the corrupt payments which were simply company policy to ensure sales. The investigation was begun by the US Department of Justice, who then referred the case to the SFO. Dougall became a whistleblower and the SFO's first co-operating defendant. He pleaded guilty on 14 April 2010 to conspiring to make corrupt payments and give inducements contrary to the Prevention of Corruption Act 1906, s 1.

[1]   [2010] EWCA Crim 1048, [2010] Crim LR 661.

5.84 Healthcare fraud in itself is big business. According to the European Healthcare Fraud and Corruptions Network Annual Report for 2009/2010 the price tag for the EU alone is €56 billion a year[1]. Aside from fraud, in the US, a number of major US and UK pharmaceutical companies are under investigation. There were investigations and actions in relation to the Iraqi Oil for Food scandal. Now the focus of investigation is on the sales promotional activities of pharmaceutical companies.

[1]   The Annual Report is available on the EHFCN website, www.ehfcn.org.

5.85 There have been suggestions that large pharmaceutical companies spend a considerable proportion of their budget on promotion and advertising of their products, principally to health professionals, hospitals and state health departments. International and national symposia and scientific meetings of health professionals were an opportunity for hospitality and promotional on a grand scale. Health professionals and others in a position of influence were treated to international air travel, top class accommodation, meals, leisure activities and gifts all at the expense of the pharmaceutical companies. The need for ethical promotion of medicines and medicinal products was recognised as long ago as 1988 when the World Health Organisation published their own guidelines which included principles covering promotion, advertising, scientific meetings, hospitality and gifts. It stated that 'Scientific and educational activities should not be deliberately used for promotional purposes' and that:

'The fact of sponsorship by a pharmaceutical manufacturer or distributor should be clearly stated in advance, at the meeting and in any proceedings. The latter should accurately reflect the presentations and discussions. Entertainment or other hospitality, and any gifts offered to members of the medical and allied professions, should be secondary to the main purpose of the meeting and should be kept to a modest level'.

5.86 Such guidelines did nothing to quieten widespread public perception that continuing medical education was being used as a guise for influencing therapeutic decisions and that in reality health professionals were being 'bribed' through hospitality to use specific drugs or devices. There have been many studies on the link between self-interest and the loss of objectivity and altruism, as acknowledged in a US report by the Industry Funding of Medical Education taskforce published in April 2008[1]. The report identified the problem as follows:

'Some patterns of interaction that have evolved are, and others may be, inappropriate from the standpoints of medical professionalism and the best interests of patients. These include providing gifts to individuals (even when these gifts have educational or practice-related utility); distributing samples directly to practitioners; providing food, meals; or travel expenses; establishing speakers' bureaus; and ghost-writing. These commonplace patterns of interaction can create conflicts for the affected physicians, and therefore for their institutions, between their duty to exercise independent medical decision making in the best interest of their patients and the biasing influence of personal gifts and other favors on their decisions . . . what were originally experienced as simple gifts come to be seen as privileges, and these privileges evolve further into reliance and a sense of entitlement'.

[1] services.aamc.org/publications/index.cfm?fuseaction=Product.displayForm&prd_id=232& pr v_id=281.

5.87 In 2008 Pharmaceutical Research and Manufacturers of America published revised guidelines[1]. They included a ban on companies providing any travel or hotel expenses (unless there is a consulting arrangement between the doctor and the company or the doctor is a speaker at a conference), entertainment or recreational items, such as tickets to the theatre or sporting events, sporting equipment, or leisure or vacation trips to any healthcare professional. Speaker fees paid to individual doctors by some of the big companies are now published on an annual basis. The total sums paid to doctors for speaking, consultation and other associated costs such as travel can be at least $35m per annum per company.

5.87 When is a benefit a bribe?

The *Siemens* and *Syncor* cases as set out in para **5.11** are further examples of bribes masquerading as 'promotional expenses'.

[1] Code on Interaction with Healthcare Professionals (PhRMA, 2008), available at www.phrma. org/sites/default/files/369/phrma_marketing_code_2008-1.pdf .

5.88 In the UK, the Association of the British Pharmaceutical Industry ('ABPI'), has had guidelines since 1958, with a major review in 1992 and another in 2005. These guidelines were industry-written and voluntary only. The latest Code of Practice is from 2008. The 2005 Code restricted the payment of travel to meetings to economy airfares and venues which were not 'lavish'. In 2004, and before ABPI announced it would be revising its Code of Practice, the Health Committee of the House of Commons investigated the influence of the pharmaceutical industry. Its report was published in April 2005[1]. During the course of gathering evidence, concerns were expressed that the industry was using educational meetings as a mask for promotional hospitality by providing conferences and meeting in exclusive hotels and abroad whilst paying for travel and accommodation and that industry-paid speakers at conferences could not go 'off-message' for fear of being dropped by the company paying for their time and expenses. The Report noted that:

> 'During our inquiry some witnesses blamed the pharmaceutical companies for giving hospitality to prescribers and for paying what are sometimes significant sums to "key opinion leaders"; less attention was paid to the fact that the beneficiaries of the hospitality and payments willingly accepted it. Prescribers' evaluation of the merits of drugs may be influenced by the hospitality they receive from pharmaceutical companies'[2].

The Report recommended that:

> 'a register of interests be maintained by the relevant professional body (General Medical Council, Royal College of Nursing, Royal Pharmaceutical Society of Great Britain etc), detailing all substantial gifts, hospitality and honoraria received by members. The register should be made available for public inspection. Individual practitioners should be responsible for maintaining their entry on the register. Professional bodies should provide advice to their members about the levels of hospitality and payments that are acceptable'[3].

[1] The Influence of the Pharmaceutical Industry (Fourth Report of Session 2004–2005), HC 42-l.
[2] At para 381.
[3] At para 39.

5.89 The ABPI Code of Practice for the Pharmaceutical Industry[1], published in 2008, limited the provision of hospitality to meals and drinks, accommodation, genuine registration fees for meetings and reasonable travel costs. The costs should not exceed the level that the recipients would normally adopt when paying for themselves. Delegates are allowed to fund the difference themselves between economy and business or first class travel. This section of the Code provides an interesting example of the relationship between acceptable levels of hospitality being linked the recipients' ability to pay the same costs themselves.

[1] The Code is available online at www.pmcpa.org.uk/files/sitecontent/ABPI_Code_of_Practice _2008.pdf.

5.90 The European Federation of Pharmaceutical Industries and Associations describes itself as representing the pharmaceutical industry operating in Europe. It has a direct membership of 31 national associations and 40 leading pharmaceutical companies which overall encompasses 2,200 companies. Its Code of Practice adopted in October 2007[1], has similar provisions. For instance that:

> 'all promotional, scientific or professional meetings, congresses, conferences, symposia, and other similar events (including, but not limited to, advisory board meetings, visits to research or manufacturing facilities, and planning, training or investigator meetings for clinical trials and non-interventional studies) organised or sponsored by or on behalf of a company must be held in an "appropriate" venue that is conducive to the main purpose of the event and may only offer hospitality when such hospitality is appropriate'.

The Code further stipulates that events can not take place outside the company's home country unless there is some compelling geographical reason. Hospitality extended in connection with events is limited to travel, meals, accommodation and genuine registration fees. There appears to be no limit on the grade of travel. Gifts such as entertainment, to the personal benefit of the recipient, are not permitted. There are further provisions relating to the use and payment of healthcare professionals as consultants and advisors.

[1] The EFPIA Code on the promotion of prescription-only medicines to, and interactions with, healthcare professionals is available online at www.efpia.eu/Content/Default.asp?PageID= 559&DocID=3483.

5.91 A more direct difficulty arises with the sheer scale of potential profits to be made in the sales of medicines and medicinal products to state run health systems, as illustrated in the Department of Justice pronouncement that:

> 'The depth of government involvement in foreign health systems, combined with fierce industry competition and the closed nature of many public formularies, creates, in our view, a significant risk that corrupt payments will infect the process'[1].

The potential for prosecutions under the Bribery Act 2010, ss 1, 2, 6 and 7 remains a real possibility in this high-yield industry.

[1] www.justice.gov/criminal/pr/speeches-testimony/documents/11-12-09breuer-pharmaspeech. pdf.

D   FACILITATION PAYMENTS

5.92 In the formative stages of the Bribery Act 2010 the proposed treatment of facilitation payments was controversial. The final shape of the Bribery Act is not likely to diminish the debate.

What is a facilitation payment?

5.93 A facilitation payment is generally accepted to be a small payment or payment in kind generally made to a low level public official in order to expedite actions which that official would ordinarily perform as part of his job. They are also known as 'grease' payments, greasing the wheels of business and life in some countries.

5.94 The following are characteristics of a facilitation payment:

— of a minor nature;
— for the sole or dominant purpose of securing or expediting the performance of a routine government action;
— generally only applies to non-discretionary actions by a foreign official;
— only intended to influence the timing of an action as opposed to its outcome.

5.95 Common examples of facilitation payments:

— granting a permit or visa;
— providing utility services;
— loading or unloading cargo;
— protecting perishable commodities from deterioration;
— mail services.

What is not a facilitation payment?

5.96 A payment will not be a facilitation payment when it is provided with the intention of influencing a public official and is provided to obtain or retain a business advantage.

With this distinction in mind, it is useful to consider the issue of facilitation payments through the prism of the domestic debate that informed the final terms of the Bribery Act 2010 and also from an international perspective.

The OECD position

5.97 Under the OECD Convention, article 1, each party should take steps to make it a criminal offence for any person:

> 'intentionally to offer, promise or give any undue pecuniary or other advantage, whether directly or through intermediaries, to a foreign public official, for that official or for a third party, in order that the official act or refrain from acting in relation to the performance of official duties, in order to obtain or retain business or other improper advantage in the conduct of international business'.

5.98 The commentaries made clear that despite the 'corrosive' effects of such payments, facilitation payments could not be criminalised:

> 'Small "facilitation" payments do not constitute payments made "to obtain or retain business or other improper advantage" within the meaning of paragraph 1 and, accordingly, are also not an offence. Such payments, which, in some countries, are made to induce public officials to perform their functions, such as issuing licenses or permits, are generally illegal in the foreign country concerned. Other countries can and should address this corrosive phenomenon by such means as support for programmes of good governance. However, criminalisation by other countries does not seem a practical or effective complementary action'[1].

As a result a number of parties to the Convention have not prohibited payments to expedite, ensure or secure performance of routine government actions, specifically Australia, Canada, Korea, New Zealand and the United States.

[1] www.oecd.org/dataoecd/4/18/38028044.pdf.

The Australian position

5.99 Under the Australian criminal code it is a criminal offence to bribe a foreign official either in Australia itself or elsewhere in the world. Under Australian tax legislation and guidance a facilitation payment is not regarded as a bribe and may be tax deductible. The guidance defines a facilitation payment as a payment to a foreign public official, the value of which is of a minor nature, for the sole or dominant purpose of expediting or securing the performance of a routine government action of a minor nature, such as granting a permit or licence, processing government papers such as a visa, providing utility services, or loading or unloading cargo or protecting perishable commodities from deterioration. The action must be ordinarily and commonly performed by the official. A facilitation payment may be tax detectible. In contrast a 'bribe' would not be tax deductible and is defined as a benefit provided to another person that is not legitimately due to that person, provided with the intention of influencing a public official (who may or may not be the direct recipient of the benefit), provided to obtain or retain a business advantage. For example, a payment to a foreign trade official to secure or maintain foreign trade.

The Canadian position

5.100 The Canadian Corruption of Foreign Public Officials Act, s 3(4), which came into force on 14 February 1999, allows facilitation payments:

'Facilitation payments
(4) For the purpose of subsection (1), a payment is not a loan, reward, advantage or benefit to obtain or retain an advantage in the course of business, if it is made to expedite or secure the performance by a foreign public official of any act of a routine nature that is part of the foreign public official's duties or functions, including:
(a)   the issuance of a permit, licence or other document to qualify a person to do business;
(b)   the processing of official documents, such as visas and work permits;
(c)   the provision of services normally offered to the public, such as mail pick-up and delivery, telecommunication services and power and water supply; and
(d)   the provision of services normally provided as required, such as police protection, loading and unloading of cargo, the protection of perishable products or commodities from deterioration or the scheduling of inspections related to contract performance or transit of goods'.

The US position

5.101 Under the FCPA of 1977, it is a crime 'corruptly' to offer any kind of payment to a foreign official 'in order to assist . . . in obtaining or retaining business'. The statute provides an exception, however, for

'any facilitating or expediting payment . . . the purpose of which is to expedite or to secure the performance of a routine governmental action'.

A 'routine governmental action', in turn, is only an action which is ordinarily and commonly performed by a foreign official in:

— obtaining permits, licenses, or other official documents to qualify a person to do business in a foreign country;
— processing governmental papers, such as visas and work orders;
— providing police protection, mail pick-up and delivery, or scheduling inspections associated with contract performance or inspections related to transit of goods across country;
— providing phone service, power and water supply, loading and unloading cargo, or protecting perishable products or commodities from deterioration; or
— actions of a similar nature.

A company must properly account for any facilitating payments in its books and records.

5.102 The FCPA 1977 is now a relatively old piece of legislation and the decision of Congress to permit (but not condone) facilitation payments in the Act was a reflection of the perceived reality at the time—that they were a common occurrence in some countries and were culturally permitted, an outright ban would be unenforceable and would put US companies at a competitive disadvantage. Further it would raise questions of moral imperialism whilst not contributing substantiality to the reduction of corruption. But the experience is that they have proved difficult to define and impossible to place a monetary cap on.

Other countries

5.103 Of the signatories to the OECD only five countries make any provision for facilitation payments. It is unclear whether there is any country that permits by law its own public officials to receive payments over and above their salary. Indeed, the Chief of Crimes Convention Section of the UN, giving evidence on the Bribery Bill to the Joint Committee of the House of Parliament stated:

> 'I have never come across any country that has any legislation or any other regulation that allows public officials of any sort to receive payments above their normal salaries'[1].

Thus, in effect, those countries which make an exception for facilitation payments are doing so in the face of their own legislation which would criminalise such payments if they were made to their own officials. The exception is reserved for 'foreign' public officials.

[1]   www.publications.parliament.uk/pa/jt200809/jtselect/jtbribe/uc430-vi/uc43002.htm.

Facilitation payment and the Bribery Act 2010

5.104 There is no provision or exception for facilitation payments in the Bribery Act 2010. Facilitation payments are most likely to fall within the s 6 offence of bribing a foreign public official. However, they may also fall within s 1, which would then bring liability under s 7 by a potential failure to prevent bribery.

5.105 The question of facilitation payments was explored in some depth during both the Law Commission's consultation on reforming bribery and the passage of the Bribery Bill through Parliament. In essence it was felt that facilitation payments bring particular problems as the issues presented by them are often faced by more junior employees working in difficult and remote conditions. The failure to secure a service may result in very severe consequences for a business, for example perishable goods rotting on a ship which will not be unloaded without the payment of an unofficial fee, which are out of proportion to the fee demanded. The commercial pressure on an employee to pay the fee out of economic or other necessity may be hard to resist.

5.106 The counter argument is that a facilitation payment is a bribe by any other name and that it is the start of a slippery slope towards the payment of larger and more major bribes. In addition, it has been contended that in reality they do not make business sense, as once a company is known to be willing and able to make payments they are likely to be pressed for further payments. Officials who have obtained facilitation payments will habitually slow down procedures in order to have the excuse to ask for payments. The advantage is unenforceable and amounts to a hidden tax on business; even if each payment is small, the totality may be large, as illustrated by the case of Wabtec's Indian subsidiary who paid small individual fees to facilitate inspections, obtain compliance certificates and prevent excessive tax audits but where the annual total was over $40,000[1]. In addition, a distinction between permissible and illegal payments weakens a business enterprise's ability to put forward a consistent message on bribery and makes it confusing and difficult for employees to administer. It might also necessitate different compliance programmes, depending under which jurisdiction the company or subsidiary is operating. There will be a further difficulty in tax accounting, self-reporting and plea bargaining. A positive reason for outlawing all payments is that countries and companies may have a far greater confidence in doing business with UK companies precisely because there is a zero-tolerance approach.

[1] Resolved through a non-prosecution agreement.

5.107 There is a tendency to consider that facilitation payments only affect businesses. In fact, they are also applied to people, often poor people, living in the countries in which such payments are common. A graphic illustration is the Bangalore based not-for-profit organisation and website www.ipaidabribe.com which provides a forum for people in India to tell their stories of everyday 'facilitation payments' and to lobby for change.

The Law Commission

5.108 The Law Commission in its Consultation Paper said:

> 'It is generally accepted that a facilitation (or "speed" or "grease") payment is a payment made with the purpose of expediting or facilitating the provision of services or routine government action which an official is normally obliged to perform'[1].

In its final report[2], the Law Commission, having collated diverse representations from bodies ranging from the Council of HM Circuit Judges to the UK Anti-Corruption Forum, concluded as follows:

'5.108 We believe that facilitation payments are best handled through sensible use of the discretion not to prosecute.

5.109 Whilst it will clearly be a matter for the prosecution authorities, we suggest that it will rarely be in the public interest to prosecute individuals or organisations for the payment of small sums to secure the performance of routine tasks.

5.110 In summary, we believe that it is not necessary to make special provision or exception for facilitation payments. Sensible use of prosecutorial discretion should ensure that, where no public purpose would be served by securing a conviction in respect of a facilitation payment, a prosecution is not undertaken at all.

5.111 The discrete offence should create no special exception for "facilitation payments", howsoever defined'.

[1]   Reforming Bribery: A Consultation Paper (Law Commission Consultation Paper No 185).
[2]   Law Com No 313 (2008).

Passage of the Bribery Bill through Parliament

5.109 During the Bill's passage though both Houses, the Joint Committee received representations both oral and written from a wide range of bodies from the OECD, the Law Commission, the DPP, the SFO, the MOJ, representatives of industry and UK business, lawyers in private practice and NGOs and pressure groups. Businesses will wish to focus on the stated position of the prosecuting authorities in those submissions.

The SFO's written submission

5.110 The main points made by the SFO were:

— facilitation payments will be unlawful. In some cases the mere offer (and/or acceptance) of the advantage itself may amount to improper conduct;
— because of our acceptance threshold, small facilitation payments are unlikely to concern the SFO unless they are part of a larger pattern (when, by definition, they would no longer be small facilitation payments) where their nature and scale has to be evaluated;
— prosecutorial discretion, backed by appropriate guidance, is the proper way forward on small facilitation payments. If a case were to pass the threshold for acceptance the discretion would rarely be exercised and there would be prosecution;
— facilitation payments cut across transparency and openness;
— they also render a corporate more vulnerable to demands for larger bribes;
— they are a major contributor to the belief that bribery is a necessary part of business culture.

The DPP's submissions

5.111 The main points made by the DPP were:

— facilitation payments will be unlawful, however small and irrespective of the degree to which such payments were 'extorted' from the payer;

— it will normally be in the public interest to prosecute cases involving corruption, including the making of facilitation payments;
— where payments are small, prosecutors can use their discretion and reach decisions applying the public interest factors set out in the Code for Crown Prosecutors;
— if the law of any country permitted an official to require 'facilitation payments' (perhaps using the term 'commission') such activity would not be an offence because it was lawful in the country in question and not therefore improper.

Other representations

5.112 Transparency International (UK) restated its long-standing policy to oppose the use of facilitation payments. It further stated that it expected prosecutors to develop sensible criteria for assessing when prosecution was justified and that companies' internal codes of conduct would help inform prosecutors 'where lines should be drawn'.

5.113 The UK Anti-Corruption Forum, an alliance of UK business associations, professional institutions, civil society organisations and companies with interests in the domestic and international infrastructure, construction and engineering sectors made the following submissions:

— the payer of a facilitation payment is normally considerably less culpable than the recipient. This is because the payer is the victim of extortion and it is often unjust to make a payer guilty of an offence which it may be difficult to avoid committing. In many cases, a company may be forced to make such payments in order to obtain import or work permits to enable it to fulfil contractual obligations, failing which it would incur heavy penalties;
— minor facilitation payments are endemic in many jurisdictions. In addition, many payers of minor facilitation payments are junior employees travelling or working overseas who may be compelled to make these payments in difficult circumstances involving traffic police or immigration officials;
— there is also considerable confusion and uncertainty as to liability for facilitation payments and whether or not they constitute bribery;
— there should be a clear distinction between bribery and facilitation payments;
— there needs to be certainty as to the circumstances in which a facilitation payment will be prosecuted, and the circumstances in which it will not;
— there also needs to be certainty as to how facilitation payments should be accounted for in a company's books and records;
— if facilitation payments are to be outlawed, detailed guidance should be published on these issues;
— if facilitation payments are treated as criminal offences, the penalty for making a facilitation payment should be lower than that of a bribe, to reflect the fact that the payment is normally extorted or made under urgent necessity to meet commercial or personal obligations;
— the payer of a facilitation payment should not face mandatory exclusion (debarment) from public procurement contracts.

5.114 *When is a benefit a bribe?*

Other views

5.114–5.119 There were concerns expressed on the following lines:

— if facilitation payments were subject to prosecutorial discretion, such an approach would have the effect of criminalising conduct which the Law Commission says it would very rarely be in the public interest to prosecute. Further it would put ethical companies at an unfair disadvantage to those other companies who committed offences but who took comfort in the fact that risk of prosecution was minimal;
— organisations would also have difficulty in complying with their Proceeds of Crime Act 2002 obligations. The Proceeds of Crime Act 2002, and the associated reporting obligations attached to it, comes into play when an organisation is in receipt of, or is otherwise dealing in, the proceeds of crime. It does not matter that the crime connected with the person's receipt or dealing is not one which, ordinarily, the authorities will seek to prosecute.

Professor Horder from the Law Commission

5.120 In oral evidence to the Joint Committee Professor Horder said:

' . . . it seems like something readymade for litigation up and down the courts . . . we thought it best to leave the matter really to prosecutorial discretion, not least because, in some instances in another context, payments made by way of facilitation and so on will have to show up in a company's accounts somewhere and they must be in a position, at least, to say what those payments were. I think that that will, in the nature of things, keep so-called "facilitation payments" in check in terms of their nature and degree, but the reality is that, for example, a firm that, I do not know, has got a lot of aircraft or ships coming in and out of countries all over the globe, it may very well be that they have to give a bottle of whisky to the harbourmaster or someone each time they go through, and really it is not realistic, I think, to expect prosecutions to be undertaken in those cases, but it is a case where I think it is better that the law stays silent and we just carry on as we always have, only prosecuting where the public interest demands that you prosecute, and that would not be the case in such an example, I hope'.

The Joint Committee Report

5.121 The Report[1] made the following points:

— a 'facilitation payment' refers to the practice of paying a small sum of money to a public official (or other person) as a way of ensuring that they perform their duty, either more promptly or at all. This type of payment is illegal under the current law, but there is a general understanding that a prosecution is unlikely for an offence involving such small amounts of money. The position is different in the US and several other OECD member states where anti-corruption legislation includes a specific exception or defence for small facilitation payments;
— under the provisions of the draft Bill, facilitation payments will usually continue to be illegal. This is because a facilitation payment is likely to be "improper" under the general offences, while not being "legitimately due" under the foreign official offence, at least in the absence of authorisation under a local written law;

— a defence for facilitation payments would dilute the message of the Bill that bribery is wrong and it would be inconceivable that a Bill modernising and reforming the UK law on bribery should step backwards on this point;

— there were practical difficulties that have been encountered in those states that operate a defence for facilitation payments, rather than relying on prosecutorial discretion;

— it recognised that there remained undoubtedly difficult and unanswered dilemmas facing business, as Lord Robertson illustrated: 'stevedores on the docks of a country say they will not unload your ship unless a payment is made to their union or to their corporate organisation, what do you do? You say, "No. We will just let our ships lie there"?'[2].

[1] www.publications.parliament.uk/pa/jt200809/jtselect/jtbribe/115/11504.htm.
[2] At para 134 of the report.

5.122 The Report concluded:

'We agree with the government that facilitation payments should continue to be criminalised. A specific defence risks legitimising corruption at the thin end of the wedge. At the same time we recognise that business needs clarity about the circumstances in which facilitation payments will be prosecuted, particularly given the difficult situations that can arise. Therefore the basic principles of prosecution policy, which we would expect to adhere firmly to the concept of proportionality, must be made clear. But we would not welcome guidance that was so detailed that it effectively introduced a defence into the law'[1].

[1] At para 138 of the report.

The MOJ Guidance

5.123 The MOJ draft guidance was silent on facilitation payments except for a section in Annex B giving an 'Illustrative Scenario'. Annex B was not part of the guidance but was intended to be 'hypothetical circumstances that may be encountered by commercial organisations doing business in foreign markets' to assist companies in formulating procedures to prevent bribery. The scenario failed to make clear if the payments made fell into the generally accepted definition of facilitation payments and further, and unhelpfully, appeared to contain an element of political donation.

The MOJ final guidance firmly states that the Bribery Act 2010 does not provide exemption for such payments. However, the guidance does recognise that the eradication of facilitation payments 'is recognised at the national and international level as a long term objective that will require economic and social progress and sustained commitment to the rule of law in those parts of the world where the problem is most prevalent'. The guidance contains a case study addressing facilitation payments which relates to adequate procedures which are dealt with in detail in Chapter 6. One is then directed to the SFO/DPP guidance for issues relating to potential prosecutions.

The SFO/DPP guidance also states that there is no exemption for facilitation payments and that they remain illegal. The guidance then sets out factors in favour of or tending against prosecution whilst stating that prosecution will usually take place unless the prosecutor is sure that there are public interest factors tending against prosecution which outweigh those tending in favour. The factors are as follows:

Factors tending in favour of prosecution:

— large or repeated payments are more likely to attract a significant sentence;
— facilitation payments that are planned for or accepted as part of a standard way of conducting business may indicate the offence was premeditated;
— payments may indicate an element of active corruption of the official in the way the offence was committed;
— where a commercial organisation has a clear and appropriate policy setting out procedures an individual should follow if facilitation payments are requested and these have not been correctly followed;

Factors tending against prosecution:

— a single small payment likely to result in only a nominal penalty;
— the payment(s) came to light as a result of a genuinely proactive approach involving self-reporting and remedial action;
— where a commercial organisation has a clear and appropriate policy setting out procedures an individual should follow if facilitation payments are requested and these have been correctly followed;
— the payer was in a vulnerable position arising from the circumstances in which the payment was demanded.

Lessons to be learnt from the US

5.124 As set out in para **5.101**, under US law neither criminal nor civil liability attaches to payments to a foreign government official to secure the performance of, or to expedite, routine government action. The list of such routine action is provided for in the FCPA 1977 with a catch-all of 'actions of a similar nature'. Such a clause expands the potential ambit without indicating the limits. Nor does the FCPA set any monetary or other limitations on the magnitude of the payment. What is apparent is that four factors will influence whether such a payment is regarded as outside the defence because it was made for the purpose of obtaining or retaining business:

(1)   the decision to be made by the official is discretionary and the payment was made to alter the decision so as to increase the payer's business;
(2)   the payment was unusually large compared to the action performed;
(3)   the payment directly affects competitiveness and the official has control over future government business with the payer;
(4)   payment was for a service to which the payer is not entitled.

5.125 However, where the FCPA differs significantly from the Bribery Act 2010, s 6 (dealing with 'Bribery of foreign public officials') is that whereas the FCPA only criminalises payments made for the purposes of obtaining or retaining business, s 6(2) has, in addition, the criminalisation of a payment made with an intention to obtain or retain 'an advantage in the conduct of business'. This difference may well catch US-style facilitation payments, an example being that the speeding up of the unloading of perishable goods so that they can be delivered or sold whilst still fresh may well be regarded as a business advantage. Nonetheless, each factual situation would require an analysis of whether an 'advantage in the conduct of business' was intended to be obtained. It is arguable that the avoidance of a disadvantage, for example not being able to sell rotten goods, merely places a business in the position they would have been in had the goods been unloaded in a normal, timely manner.

5.126 A facilitation-type payment made to a person other than a foreign public official might fall within the Bribery Act 2010, s 1, but to be a bribe the payer would have to intend the *improper* performance of a 'relevant function or activity'. Arguably, by paying someone to do something that they were in any event duty bound to do, the payer is not intending anything improper.

5.127 Three US cases illustrate a range of factual situations and the attitude of the US courts:

(a) *United States v Kay*[1]: this company sold rice to Haiti. Imports of rice were taxed on their tonnage. In order to regain a competitive advantage lost through competitors using smugglers and corrupting customs officials, American Rice agreed with Haitian customs officials to falsely record a reduced rice tonnage shipped into Haiti which thus reduced the amount of tax paid by American Rice. The payments in return to the customs officials were recorded in American Rice's accounts as 'costs of sale'. The charges were dismissed in the lower court on the basis that bribes made to reduce taxes were not payments made for the purpose of 'obtaining or retaining business'. That ruling was overturned on appeal with the court emphasising that the exception was narrow and the circumstances of the case satisfied the requirement of a business nexus. What was required was that the prosecution establish a link between a reduction in taxes and obtaining or retaining business from someone. That 'someone' was not necessarily the government. This case has to be viewed against the appeal in the case of *Mattson and Harris* where, in withdrawing from the appeal, the SEC implied that bribes to the Indonesian tax authorities to reduce taxes could not be linked to assisting in obtaining or retaining business;

(b) *United States v Vitusa Corpn*[2]: the Dominican Republic owed Vitusa $1m for an order of milk powder which had been delivered in 1989. There was no dispute that the debt was legitimate. Despite attempts through legitimate avenues such as the US Ambassador and the American Chamber of Commerce, the debt was not honoured. In the middle of 1992 the company learnt that for a $50,000 'service fee' a senior Dominican Republic official would use his influence to obtain payment of the debt. Despite being told by an official at the US Embassy that such a payment was likely to fall foul of the FCPA, the company paid and shortly afterwards the debt was paid. Vitusa was prosecuted despite the DOJ acknowledging that payment was made to obtain 'a lawful and legitimate obligation owed by the Government of the Dominican Republic'. There appears to be some suggestion that the size of the payment (even though it was only 5% of the debt owed) and a notion (expressed by a representative of the DOJ at an FCPA conference) that expediting payments of an undisputed sum was discretionary because the official had to decide in which order to process applications and thus not a routine government action may have had a bearing on the decision to prosecute. Such a narrowing of the exception by suggesting that expediting government action automatically entails a discretionary reordering of priorities is likely to criminalise every facilitation payment. This has not been tested in the US courts;

(c) *In the Matter of BJ Services Company*[3]: the Argentinian subsidiary of a US company in the oilfield industry made payments to Argentinian customs official to overlook a customs ban on permanently, rather than temporarily, importing used components. There were some other payments made at other times for other violations. However, there was one payment to an official in the department of Industry and Commerce to expedite approval of the importation of some equipment. That payment appears to have been treated as a facilitation payment by the SEC.

[1] No 4:01-cr-914 (SD Tex, 2002).
[2] No 2:94-cr-00253 (DNJ, Apr 13, 1994).
[3] No 94-cr-253 (DNJ 1994).

5.128 The spectrum of the three cases referred to above would suggest that the exercise of prosecutorial discretion is inconsistently applied and this is compounded by the fact that no guidelines have been laid down by any US court. The consequent need for US corporations to exercise great caution in making facilitation payments, even in a legislative regime which provides an exception from criminal and civil penalty liability, strongly suggests that individual and businesses within the scope of the Bribery Act 2010 which has no such exception should be very careful indeed.

5.129 Examples of typical facilitation payment demands:

— International Co is running an operation in Transania. Approval is needed from a local government agency with regard to equipment being used by the company. An official from the local government agency makes a visit and makes it clear that approval will not be forthcoming without a cash 'fee' paid directly to him;

— International Co is about to start an engineering project in Transania. Work permits will be required for its entire staff. The official from the Labour Department says that a 'surcharge' is payable on each permit or there will be an indefinite delay on their issue. Lack of permits will have a serious effect on the ability of International Co to fulfil the contract and it will be subject to penalty payments;

— Transania previously required foreign workers to have permits to travel internally within the country. A foreign worker is stopped by a police officer who on examining his identification document says that the special stamp allowing internal travel is missing and he will have to confiscate the passport. He then offers to sort out the problem in return for a cash payment;

— International Co's new facility requires a connection to the electricity grid. The government-owned Transanian Electricity Board has outsourced connections to a private company whose engineer, on visiting the site, says that he has too much work on to effect the connection for many months. He leaves his private telephone number and says for a special payment he could move International Co to the top of the list. In such a case, the engineer is not a foreign public official but any payment to him is open to prosecution under the Bribery Act 2010;

— International Co's equipment is stuck in customs coming into Transania. On enquiry it would appear that the paperwork for importation is 'incomplete'. However, the customs officer says that payment direct to him of a special 'fee' will ensure completion within a short space of time;

— International Co's goods are waiting to be offloaded at Transania's main port. The port worker's union official tells the representative of International Co that worker's conditions are so bad that can only permit his members to unload the ship if International Co makes a monthly payment to the Workers Welfare Fund.

Avoiding the need to make facilitation payments

5.130 Adequate measures are addressed in Chapter 6. In essence, individuals and business enterprises need to start with a zero-tolerance policy. Most instances of demands or more subtle pressures to pay facilitation payments arise in a number of predictable situations. Identification of high-risk countries and regions, together with the likely problems encountered, will enable the drafting of tailored guidance. That will need to be accompanied by specific training both to resist demands and action to be taken afterwards. Pre-emptive planning will give the greatest assistance and support to those employees at the coal face.

Extortion and duress

5.131 It is recognised that there are some situations in which the demand for a facilitation payment is made in which refusal would put a person in danger either for themselves or a person to whom they are closely connected. The spectrum of situations may range from the extreme of a threat of death or grievous bodily harm which may well amount to a defence of duress, to more minor but none the less potentially dangerous situations where duress would not be available as a defence. Obvious examples are demand for a payment for providing medical services to a seriously ill person or a threat of being injured or tortured. More difficult situations arise when someone is falsely detained in custody in a country where the rule of law is weak and/or detention is a physical or mental danger in itself. In such a situation, there is no immediate threat to health and it is entirely possible that diplomatic or legal pressures would secure the person's release within a short period of time.

The MOJ final guidance specifically addresses this issue (all previous government pronouncements and the draft guidance having been silent) by stating that:

'It is recognised that there are circumstances in which individuals are left with no alternative but to make payments in order to protect against loss of life, limb or liberty. The common law defence of duress is very likely to be available in such circumstances'.

5.131 *When is a benefit a bribe?*

It remains to be seen as to how a court will approach the question of a defence of economic duress when dealing with a commercial organisation and a potential offence under s 7 of the Act.

5.132 Duress, being a defence to all crimes except murder and attempted murder, is potentially a defence to offences under the Bribery Act 2010. There is no definitive definition of the scope of the defence. Lord Simon in *DPP for Northern Ireland v Lynch*[1] attempted a working definition stating 'this at least seems to be established: that the type of threat which affords a defence must be one of human physical harm (including, possibly, imprisonment), so that threat of injury to property is not enough'. The threat may relate to a person for whose safety the defendant would reasonably regard himself as responsible[2]. From the cases of *Lynch, R v Howe*[3] and *R v Graham*[4] it is possible to formulate a test: was the threat of physical harm to the person (including possibly of imprisonment) made, which was of such gravity that it might well have caused a sober person of reasonable firmness sharing the defendant's characteristics and placed in the same situation to act in the same way as the defendant acted? The threat must be operative at the time the crime was committed and the failure of the defendant to avail himself of opportunities to render the threat ineffective is relevant evidence for the prosecution. It is relevant that the defendant belonged to a category of people less able to resist pressure[5]. In addition the defence of 'necessity' may be available if the commission of the crime was necessary or reasonably believed to have been so for the purpose of avoiding or preventing death or serious injury to himself or another, that necessity was the reason for the offence and the offence was reasonable and proportionate having regard to the evil to be avoided or prevented[6].

[1] [1975] AC 653, [1975] 2 WLR 641, HL.
[2] *R v Wright* [2000] Crim LR 510, CA.
[3] [1987] AC 417, [1987] 1 All ER 771, HL.
[4] [1982] 1 All ER 801, [1982] 1 WLR 294, CA.
[5] For a full exploration of the law on duress see *Archbold: Criminal Pleading, Evidence and Practice 2011* at 17-119ff.
[6] For a full exploration of the law on 'necessity' see *Archbold: Criminal Pleading, Evidence and Practice 2011* at 17-127ff.

5.133 Other situations which may amount to extortion are examples of providers of services refusing to carry out an urgent action. This is sometimes known as the '$10,000 fire' scenario, and is as follows: your office is burning down. It contains invaluable records, but as it is night time no employee is trapped in the building. The fire brigade turns up and contemplates the raging fire. Instead of rolling out the hoses, the fireman turns to you and says 'That looks like a $10,000 fire'. Do you agree to pay the money, or watch the building burn to the ground?

5.134 Alternatively, tax inspectors arrive on Monday morning for an unannounced audit of your company's books. You protest and say everything is up to date and all tax has been paid. The inspectors make clear that they will go through all records with a fine toothcomb and that there will be a large surcharge payable at the end for tax violations. They add that a small cash payment to each of them will make the problem go away. You know that there have been no violations and that it may be possible to prove your position after protracted litigation. However, the business would be unable to function in the meantime if it had to pay out a large sum in surcharges. Do you agree to pay or not?

5.135 The draft adequate procedures guidance issued by the MOJ is silent on extortion type situations. Transparency International's guidance states that a company's anti-bribery programme should recognise that there may be 'exceptional emergencies where an employee is under threat of violence or personal harm'. The United Nations Global Compact Office guidance also recognises that in clear extortion cases personal safety 'must be the paramount consideration'.

US cases

5.136 The decision in *United States v Viktor Kozeny*[1] may be of interest. This case concerned Azerbaijan. Payments were made to Azeri officials for participation in a proposed privatisation. The defendants pleaded the defence, citing an Azeri law which, while forbidding bribery, relieved from criminal responsibility the bribe-giver if he reported the matter to the authorities and/or if the payment was the result of extortion. The payments had been reported. The case turned on another matter and the question of extortion was left open although the corrupt intent requirement under the FCPA was also cited, 'The corrupt-intent requirement also can operate to exclude instances of true extortion, that is, instances in which a payment is made in response to a threat to life or property'. Thus the case has provided little guidance of the type of facts under US law that would establish a viable defence and appears to have raised more questions than it has answered.

[1] 493 F Supp 2d 693 (SDNY June 21 2007).

E   CHARITABLE DONATIONS AND SPONSORSHIP; SOCIAL RESPONSIBILITY PROGRAMMES

5.137 Charitable donations, sponsorship and social responsibility programmes can be used as a subterfuge for bribery. The obvious example is that as part of a business deal a business enterprise is asked to make a contribution to a charity. The charity is either only a front for what is, in effect, a straight bribe to obtain the business, or is run by a close associate of the person asking for the donation. This section of the chapter identifies some of the factors which are applicable.

The MOJ final guidance deals with 'Community benefits and charitable donations' in a case study. However, rather than actually providing guidance, this is treated as an aspect of adequate procedure and an application of some of the principles. For further details, see Chapter 6.

5.138 There must be no potential conflict of interest that could affect a transaction either by influencing a current business situation or being given retrospectively as a reward, for example the awarding of a contract.

5.139 The request or the perceived need to donate money or resources to social programmes or charities may be particularly difficult to resist where a business enterprise operates in a country which suffers from acute economic or social deprivation. For example an extractive industries company operating in a sub Saharan country may be asked by the official in charge of licences whether, as a rich Western company, they would like to build a school or a health clinic in the area of the country which the licences will cover. It is made clear that such a donation will make the issuing of the necessary licence a certainty. The representative of the company has been to the area and knows that the local villagers have no access to educational or health facilities. He believes that such a contribution with enhance the company's reputation both with the locals and in the country as a whole. Further he can see potential for positive publicity for the company via the company website and in media articles. The official in charge of licences tells the company representative that the school or clinic should be built through a particular charity and the company can donate through that charity. The company agrees. A year later the school is not up and running and indeed building works have not even started. The locals, having been promised this facility by the company, are angry. Some of the local workers are threatening to strike. When the company representative asks the official what has happened, he is told that unfortunately the charity had to fold and all the money has been lost. In fact, the money is now sitting in the foreign bank account of the official and his family members.

5.140 The financial abuse of charities can take a number of forms:

— the charity is merely a front to receive and launder illegal or illicit payments;
— the charity was actually established to provide cover for channelling funds;
— the recipients of charitable funds may misuse the money for non-charitable purposes;
— the charity's funds may be diverted when being moved, particularly if through international currencies or cash transfers.

5.141 Regions and countries which are identified as having significant levels of corruption require particular care. The political environment, cultural factors, the economic structure including the reliability of financial institutions, and the legal infrastructure are all risk factors which must be examined before making any kind of charitable donation.

5.142 The governance and persons involved in any charity or social responsibility programme must be carefully scrutinised to ensure that it is not associated with any relevant public official in the case of business transactions involving public officials. The same level of care will also need to be exercised in private business dealings, again to ensure that charitable donations are not made to the associates of anyone in a position to further the business interests of the persons involved. The fact that a charity is registered, for example, with the Charity Commissioner in the UK, can be of assistance in ascertaining the bona fides of a charity, as can a clear, published governance structure and a list of persons associated with or working for the charity. A charity run by one person without a verifiable board of directors is a bribery risk. Donors should be able to view clear financial statements with regard to past activities and confirmable sources of income. Charities with donations from opaque sources, or where the sources are very limited in number, also pose an obvious risk.

5.143 The form of charitable donation can vary. Aside from a straight financial contribution, it may be donation of equipment, materials or other company resources. Any donation which is solicited or at the behest of either a government official or someone in the position of influencing or enhancing business for the donor will be classified as a bribe.

5.144 There can also be a close association with political contributions in that such contributions can be disguised as charitable donations when made to a politician or political party's charity. These charitable donations can either be a method of gaining access to an official or a means of obtaining favour.

5.145 Sponsorship carries similar risks. Common examples of sponsorship are sporting and educational, from low level support for running a marathon to larger sums contributed to sports team training and trips or private educational support through a foundation, scholarship or third-party funding. Care must be taken to avoid any conflict of interest.

5.146 Cases:

(a)   *SEC v Schering-Plough Corpn*[1]: in 2004 Schering-Plough settled an SEC enforcement action that alleged violations of the FCPA's accounting provisions, agreeing, without admitting wrongdoing, to pay a fine of $500,000. The complaint alleged that Schering-Plough's subsidiary in Poland made charitable contributions to a Polish historic preservation organisation, the President of which was the director of a government program that financed the acquisition of medical supplies in the Polish region of Silesia. The first donation was made shortly after the director assumed his position. The donations were on documents as fighting viral hepatitis, preventing infectious liver diseases, preventing lung cancer and screening for skin cancer. In fact, the charity restored castles and historic sites and had no connection to medicine. There was then a significant increase in sales by the company to the Silesian government's healthcare network, increased disproportionately compared with sales of those products in other regions of Poland. Thus, even though the payments in fact were made to a bona fide charity, they were made to influence the director with respect to the purchase of Schering-Plough's products;

(b)   *Argo-Tech Corpn v Yamada Corpn and Upsilon International Corpn*[2]: in 2008 Argo-Tech, a US company which manufactures high-performance commercial and military aerospace equipment, filed a complaint against Yamada, a Japanese defence equipment trading company, and its indirect subsidiary, Upsilon International Corporation, with regard to an alleged breach of a distributorship agreement between Argo-Tech and Yamada in which Upsilon was distributor and sales agent of Argo-Tech products. The complaint alleged that that Upsilon and its parent company funnelled approximately $900,000 in corrupt payments through a charitable organisation to help secure a Japanese military hazardous clean-up project. At the time of publication of this book, the case was ongoing;

(c)   an older case, *Lamb v Phillip Morris*[3] involved an allegation by some US tobacco growers that Phillip Morris's subsidiaries made donations to a charity in Venezuela headed by the wife of the President of Venezuela, and in exchange obtained price controls on Venezuelan tobacco and stable taxes on tobacco which benefited Phillip Morris but artificially depressed prices in the US tobacco market.

[1]   No 1:04-cv-00945 (DDC, June 10, 2004).
[2]   No 08-cv-0721 (ND Ohio, 2008).
[3]   915 F 2d 1024 (6th Cir, 1990).

5.147 There are three examples of charitable donations/social projects that have been subject to the FCPA Opinion Review Procedures:

(a)   Opinion Review Procedure Release 09-10 (2009): an unnamed major global company that designs and manufactures a particular type of medical device wanted to start selling its products to the government of an unnamed foreign country where it already sold privately but its competitors sell to the state. In early 2009 representatives of the company visited the foreign country to meet with a senior government official. The senior official informed the company that all major manufacturers would be allowed to participate in tenders for government purchases of the medical devices, but not all products would be endorsed by the government. The senior official explained that the government would only endorse products that it had technically evaluated with favourable results. Because the foreign government was not familiar with the performance of the company's devices, the senior official advised the company that in order for its devices to be endorsed by the government, they would need to be evaluated by the government and the company provide sample devices to government health centres for evaluation following the use of the devices in patients. It was jointly decided that the optimal sample size for such a study was 100 units distributed among ten experienced health centres in the country. The company would provide accessories for the medical devices free of charge, as well as standard support. The approximate value of the devices and related items and services to be provided was \$19,000 per device, or \$1.9 million for all 100 units. The 100 recipients would be selected from a list of candidates who met objective medical criteria provided by the participating medical centres. They would also have to meet economic criteria and show that they could not themselves afford the cost of such a device. No one connected with the government agency responsible or closely connected with its employees would be eligible (unless they were of such low level as to be incapable of exerting influence). The company had no reason to believe that the senior official who suggested providing the devices would personally benefit from the donation of the devices and related items and services. It was determined that the proposed provision of 100 medical devices and related items and services fell outside the scope of the FCPA in that the donated products will be provided to the foreign government, as opposed to individual government officials, for ultimate use by patient recipients selected in accordance with specific objective guidelines;

(b)   Opinion Review Procedure Release 97-02 (1997): a US utility company was constructing a plant in a country in Asia that lacked adequate primary-level educational facilities in the region where the plant was under construction. A primary school construction project had been proposed near the location of the company's plant. Construction and supply costs of the elementary school would exceed $100,000. The company wished to donate $100,000 to this proposed school construction project. The donation would be made by the company directly to the government entity responsible for the construction and supply of the proposed elementary school. The company represented that, before releasing any funds, it would require a written agreement from the government entity that the funds would be used solely to construct and supply the elementary school. The written agreement would set forth other conditions to be met by the government entity, including guaranteeing the availability of land, teachers, and administrative personnel for the school; guaranteeing timely additional funding of the school project in the event of any financial shortfall; and guaranteeing provision of all funds necessary for the daily operation of the school. As the company's donation would be made directly to a government entity and not to any foreign government official the provisions of the FCPA did not appear to apply to this prospective donation;

(c)   Opinion Review Procedure Release 95-01 (1995): an unnamed US energy company wished to donate $10m to help fund a modern medical complex presently under construction near the company's future plant in an unnamed Asian country. The donation was to be made through a US charitable organisation and through a public liability company located in the foreign country. The facility was to be open to the public. The US company was anxious to ensure that its employees had access to modern medical facilities. This donation did not fall foul of the FCPA as none of the persons at the charity or involved in the foreign public liability company were connected to the foreign government; they would provide certification that none of the funds would be used in violation of the FCPA and would provide audited accounts showing the use of the donated funds.

F   POLITICAL CONTRIBUTIONS

5.148 A financial contribution to a political party or to an individual candidate may well be the personal choice of an individual residing in the country in which the contribution is made according to his or her political beliefs. Most countries have legislation governing the maximum amount that can be given and who can contribute. But what is the situation when a business enterprise makes a donation? Or employs a lobbyist to influence politicians who could have some bearing on the business enterprise's activities? Or makes contributions in a country far from that enterprise's home base but where it has significant business interests?

5.149 Transparency International's Global Corruption Barometer for 2009[1] asked more than 73,000 individuals around the world the extent to which they perceived six key sectors and institutions to be corrupt. The highest score was that of political parties which were perceived to be corrupt by 68 per cent of respondents, followed closely by the civil service (public officials/civil servants) and parliament at 63 and 60 per cent respectively.

¹ Available as a PDF on Transparency International's website: www.transparency.org.

Political lobbying within the UK

5.150 In February 2010 David Cameron, the soon-to-be Prime Minister, made a speech in which he promised that a Conservative-led government would stop the political lobbying industry from attempting to influence policy through former ministers. He was going to 'shine the light of transparency' so that politics 'comes clean about who is buying power and influence'¹. Mr Cameron went on to say that 'It is the next big scandal waiting to happen. It is an issue that crosses party lines, an issue that exposes the far too cosy relationships between politics, government, business and money'. Such wording makes clear that even within British politics there is more than a perception that it is possible for businesses to influence government policy and legislation to the benefit of those businesses. This was made graphically clear when two peers were suspended from the House of Lords in 2009, having been found willing to change legislation in exchange for cash in breach of parliamentary rules barring influence on legislation in return for financial inducement. The Code of Conduct² makes clear that any conflict between personal and public interest must be resolved in favour of the public interest. Public business, such as decisions taken and contracts awarded, cannot be done for personal gain.

¹ www.telegraph.co.uk/news/election-2010/7189466/David-Cameron-warns-lobbying-is-next-political-scandal.html.
² www.publications.parliament.uk/pa/ld/ldcond/ldcond.htm.

5.151 The lobbying industry in the UK is worth £2 billion. Many former ministers are paid large annual retainers either as consultants or directors by business to lobby on their behalf and almost always in the areas in which they formerly had direct influence. The very fact that, at present, ex-ministers are not permitted to begin to lobby government until 12 months have elapsed since they left office indicates that indeed lobbying is an effective tool. There are concerns as well within the business community that a minister will gain information from or about a number of competing businesses or have information about proposed developments in government policy which then will be used to the sole advantage of the particular business enterprise who buy that minister's services on leaving office.

5.152 Politicians need to be informed in order to formulate effective policy and thus need to speak to businesses and other interested parties in order to assimilate and understand the relevant issues. That type of approach envisages a balanced and wide-ranging enquiry. However, the difficulty arises when the politician is, in fact, closely financially allied to just one interested party. All members of the House of Commons and House of Lords, by virtue of the Political Parties, Elections and Referendums Act 2000 (as amended), have to register all financial interests over a small amount including remuneration, other benefits including gifts and hospitality and sponsorship. The full text of the accompanying Code of Conduct makes clear exactly what must be registered and the amounts involved[1].

[1] www.publications.parliament.uk/pa/cm200809/cmcode/735/73501.htm.

5.153 The Register of Member's Interests is a public document and as such is accessible and open. In contrast, lobbying may well be done in secret and in unrecorded meetings. The House of Commons Public Administration Committee, during the course of 2008–09, investigated the problems associated with the lobbying industry which they saw in the following terms:

> 'In fact, the concerns about party funding are precisely concerns about lobbying: the belief that those who have given money to the political party in power are likely to have privileged access to decision-makers and greater influence over government decisions as a result of their donations. A survey conducted by the Committee on Standards in Public Life (CSPL) showed that "people's perceptions of the behaviour of government ministers have become less positive over the past two years". The most prominent recent case of concern was the exemption for Formula One from the ban on tobacco advertising. Bernie Ecclestone, the head of Formula One, donated £1 million to the Labour party before the general election in May 1997. Almost immediately after a meeting in October 1997 between Rt Hon Tony Blair, the then Labour Prime Minister, and Mr Ecclestone, instructions were issued to the Department of Health to seek an exemption for Formula One from the EU's proposed ban on tobacco advertising. There has been long-standing concern about major business donors to parties receiving peerages and becoming part of the legislature, sometimes as Ministers. Political donations to election and pre-election campaigns in individual parliamentary constituencies are a further area of concern: the role of Lord Ashcroft, the Deputy Chairman of and the largest donor to the Conservative Party, has been prominently cited in this respect, often in connection with uncertainty about his tax and residency status. There has also been widespread public concern that some areas of government policy have effectively been captured at an early stage by interest groups, usually within industry, and that public consultations have been unbalanced in the favour of these interests. Two prominent recent cases have concerned nuclear power and Heathrow airport'[1].

In giving evidence to the Committee, witnesses expressed concerns as to privileged access leading to an uneven playing field, dubious practices involving setting up fake grass roots action groups, biased third-party endorsements presented as being independent, the likely limits to lobbyists commitment to transparency and the power of personal contacts. The committee expressed concern that ' . . . because secret lobbying by its very nature leaves no evidence trail, there could still be a significant problem even with little concrete evidence of one'. Actual evidence of a clear link between influence and outcome was difficult to show but examples were given of regular monthly meetings between a government department and a powerful lobbying group. Government policy was then formulated which was very close to the position advocated by that particular group. The House of Commons Public Administration Committee recommended a much greater degree of transparency.

[1] www.publications.parliament.uk/pa/cm200809/cmselect/cmpubadm/36/36i.pdf.

5.154 A full analysis of this subject is beyond the scope of this book. However, lobbying, payments and directorships given to politicians and civil servants

5.154 *When is a benefit a bribe?*

(the so-called 'revolving doors' situation), gifts, hospitality and meetings with government officials are likely to come under much greater scrutiny once the Bribery Act 2010 is in force.

Political contributions outside the UK

5.155 There can be little doubt that any business enterprise making a political contribution to an individual politician or to a political party in a country outside the UK and in which it has business interests is doing so in order to gain a business advantage. It has been argued that it may be permissible to make a contribution to a number of different parties in a country in order to promote democracy but even such an argument implies that democracy will probably be better for the donor than an alternative form of government.

5.156 Outside the UK, political parties are widely perceived to be the single most corrupt institution, followed by the civil service[1]. Some countries have single party government. Contributions by corporations are perceived as being prone to corruption. The risk is obvious: the business enterprise is either tendering for work which is publicly funded or requires the issuing of permission by government departments. Government is made up of politicians. Payments to those politicians in a position of influence within the government may well be corrupt.

[1]   According to Transparency International's Global Corruption Barometer (2009).

5.157 Scenario: Company A is in the extractive industry with a head office in the UK. Much of its operations for a number of years have been in country X, which is rich in oil. Company A enjoys a good relationship with the government minister in charge of oil licences, Mr O (who for the purposes of the Bribery Act 2010 is a foreign public official). Company A cannot operate without the oil licences and they must be renewed every two years. Elections are coming up within the next year in country A and there are several candidates for Mr O's seat. In addition, a number of other companies within the extractive industry are looking to move into country X. If Mr O fails to retain his seat, his ministerial job will be allocated to another person, who has much stronger links with Company A's rivals. Company A makes regular financial contributions to Mr O's political campaign and in addition provides him with printed electoral material for distribution in his constituency. Mr O is very grateful to Company A. Company A's ultimate intention is to retain business or an advantage in the conduct of its business. They have provided Mr O with a financial or other advantage. There can be no ideological reason for Company A to be supporting Mr O's political campaign and their only interest in such a campaign would be because of the position that Mr O holds within government.

5.158 In such a scenario, the link between political contributions and bribery is very clear, as are the risks that such contributions are used as a subterfuge for bribery. Transparency International has identified political contributions as one of the high risk areas for bribery in a company's operations. Not only is there the high risk that a political donation will be a financial advantage used to gain a business advantage, but also that any 'donation' merely masquerades as a political donation but is not actually used for any legitimate political purpose but is purely used for the personal gain or enrichment of the recipient business. Any enterprise wishing to make a political contribution should ask itself if there is, in reality, any legitimate reason to interfere in the politics of a country in which it operates.

5.159 Business enterprises also need to be very careful not to contravene the local legislation of the country in which they are making the contribution. Some countries have outright bans on contributions by companies or by foreign businesses, many have financial limits, as well as requirements for disclosure of finances including the origin of the donation and any consequent expenditure.

5.160 The UNCAC Coalition calls on countries to 'enhance transparency in the funding of candidates for elected public office and, where applicable, the funding of political parties'[1]. The African Union Convention and the Council of Europe have also encouraged greater transparency and issued disclosure guidelines.

[1]   www.uncaccoalition.org/en/learn-more/about-the-uncac.html.

5.161 Defining 'political contribution' and 'political cause' may be problematic. Financial contributions can include both donations and loans, including loans of property such as campaign premises or vehicles, loaning employees, contributing to research organisations with a strong political link, gifts to and tickets for fundraising events and advertising or promotional activity. All such contributions should be accounted for and transparent to avoid the risk of being characterised as bribery by virtue of their covert nature.

5.162 The *Titan Corporation* case[1] is illustrative. The company was involved in developing wireless telephone systems for developing countries. One of those countries was Benin. The Benin project was subject to government approval in Benin and that approval had to be authorised by the President of Benin. Titan acquired rights to develop the system from a company called Afronetwork which had a prior agreement with the Benin ministry for telecommunications, OPT. Due to a prior agreement between Afronetwork and OPT, Titan, on assignment of the contract, was obligated to pay part of its profits as 'subsidies for development' in Benin such as health, education and agriculture. These were referred to as 'social payments'. Four months before the election, demands were made to Titan by OPT and an agent for the President that Titan expedite the social payments (which were not yet due). $2m was paid in exchange for an increase in fees for Titan. The $2m was disguised in invoices for other services. In reality the money was provided to pay for the President's re-election campaign, for example to buy T-shirts with the President's picture and instructions to vote for him which were distributed to the electorate together with voting instructions just prior to the election. The use to which the 'social payments' were being put was known to Titan. The President was duly re-elected following which OPT and Titan signed an agreement which falsely stated that Titan had made substantial contributions to social programmes in Benin and confirmed the increase in fees to Titan.

[1]   *SEC v Titan Corp* No 05-CV-0411 (DDC 2005).

5.163 *When is a benefit a bribe?*

5.163 Professor Horder of the Law Commission gave evidence on the subject of political contributions overseas to the Joint Committee during the passage of the Bill through Parliament as follows:

> 'I think the example we give is that you are not a foreign public official if you are standing for office as a foreign public official, but we heard during consultation that it is not unheard-of for a company to make a payment to every single person standing for an election to public office because, very often, there will be a limited number of candidates, qualified persons, who can take the post and, therefore, it is actually possible to get them all in your pocket'[1].

Business enterprises should look to Chapter 6 for further guidance.

[1] www.publications.parliament.uk/pa/jt200809/jtselect/jtbribe/uc430-i/uc43002.htm.

KEY POINTS FROM CHAPTER 5

5.164 Key points from this chapter are:

- The definition of a bribe does not cover the donation or receipt of every benefit. There must be reciprocity and a direct connect between the benefit or advantage and what is improperly obtained in exchange.
- Proportionality is a useful litmus test for the legitimacy of a benefit.
- The cases decided under the FCPA are illustrative of factual scenarios of benefits which could be regards are bribes.
- There are indicia which assist in drawing the line between gifts and bribes.
- Ordinary corporate hospitality to cement business relations is very unlikely to be prosecuted.
- Levels of permissible expenditure are still not defined by the guidance issued by the MOJ, DPP and SFO.
- Promotional expenses should only be used to improve a commercial enterprise's image or present its products and services or to establish good business relations.
- Facilitation payments remain illegal and will be prosecuted if certain factual factors are present.
- Duress may be available as a defence to facilitation payments.
- Charitable donations, social responsibility programmes and political donations are vulnerable to subversion for illegal purposes.

Chapter 6

'ADEQUATE PROCEDURES' IN PRACTICE

A   GENERAL

6.1 The structure of the Bribery Act 2010 is considered in detail in Chapter 4. However, some brief repetition is useful in order to provide the statutory context for the practical real-world advice that this chapter offers.

6.2 First, it is worth reprising the essential features of both the offence and the defence to it, on which this chapter focuses. As to the offence, and perhaps recognising the difficulty in proving that the 'directing mind' of a corporation had the requisite intention, knowledge or belief necessary to commit the s 1, 2 or 6 offences, the Bribery Act 2010 provides a 'strict liability' offence in s 7, ie an offence where the prosecution does not have to prove mens rea and thus *doing* the act amounts to a crime regardless of the intention. To make out its case the prosecution will not have to prove that the commercial organisation knew anything about the bribery; merely that it failed to prevent it.

As to the defence available, there is just one: that of having in place 'adequate procedures'.

6.3 Thus, once the act of bribery is established by the prosecution, the burden shifts to the commercial organisation being accused to prove that it was more probable than not that it had in place 'adequate procedures'. If it fails to discharge that burden, it will be convicted and face serious financial and reputational damage and even ruin.

6.4 Second, while the creation of the s 7 offence is new in the field of the UK's bribery and corruption laws, the philosophy behind it, its structure, and in particular the introduction of a reverse burden of proof requiring a defendant to discharge an evidential and legal burden, are all in and of themselves not unprecedented.

6.5 In the field of regulatory and quasi-criminal offences, as is discussed in detail in Chapter 4, this approach is increasingly commonplace. There is therefore a significant body of law that is building up which illustrates the approach the courts are likely to take to the problematic issues of strict corporate liability and defences akin to the principles that underpin the 'adequate procedures' defence. Equally, the prospect of a UK jury in a criminal case examining issues such as whether in any given company there was a true and manifest top-level cultural commitment to stamp out or prevent bribery in the organisation's name, is illustrative of Parliament's increasing willingness to bring the boardroom within the reach of the criminal courts. See, for example the statutory test for gross negligence in the Corporate Manslaughter and Corporate Homicide Act 2007, s 8(3), which expressly permits a jury to examine the prevailing culture of the corporate defendant in the context of compliance with health and safety legislation and regulation.

6.6 One issue that comes into sharp relief when one considers application of the six Principles analysed below, is whether the European Convention on Human Rights (the 'ECHR'), articles 6 (right to a fair trial) and 7 (no punishment without law), are infringed both as to fair trial principles and certainty of laws.

6.7 The fair trial position in reverse burden cases sanctioned in *R v Davies (David Janway)*[1] and by the House of Lords in *R v Chargot Ltd (t/a Contract Services)*[2] will inevitably come in for early review when proceedings for an infringement of s 7 are brought. The holding that the reverse burden created by the Health and Safety at Work Act 1974, s 40, did not violate the ECHR, article 6(2), not least because of the nature of the offences created under ss 2 and 3 of that Act will certainly come in for scrutiny under the Bribery Act 2010.

[1]   [2003] ICR 586.
[2]   [2008] UKHL 73, [2009] 2 All ER 645, [2009] 1 WLR 1.

6.8 Equally, while it is settled law following *Sunday Times v United Kingdom (Application 6538/74)*[1], *Kokkinakis v Greece*[2], *SW and CR v United Kingdom (Applications 20166/92, 20190/92)*[3] and *Handyside v United Kingdom (Application 5493/72)*[4] that a high threshold must be passed before the courts will find that a law is too uncertain so as to be found to be incompatible with the ECHR, it remains to be seen whether sufficient clarity can be derived from the 'adequate procedures' guidance published by the Ministry of Justice with which this chapter is primarily concerned and the Serious Fraud Office's and Director of Public Prosecutions' Joint Prosecution Guidance (the 'SFO and DPP Joint Prosecution Guidance'), to allow commercial organisations to regulate their affairs with the requisite certainty for s 7 to be compatible and therefore lawful.

[1]   (1979) 2 EHRR 245, [1979] ECHR 6538/74.
[2]   (1993) 17 EHRR 397, [1993] ECHR 14307/88.
[3]   (1995) 21 EHRR 363.
[4]   (1976) 1 EHRR 737, [1976] ECHR 5493/72.

B   INTRODUCTION TO 'ADEQUATE PROCEDURES'

The practical challenge of the 'adequate procedures' defence

6.9 Questions about the s 7 offence and its 'adequate procedures' defence routinely asked by directors and managers of commercial organisations include 'Are we now required to have an anti-bribery compliance programme?', 'How far do we have to go with a compliance programme?' and, most importantly, 'Is our compliance programme "adequate" for the purposes of the defence?'.

As a result of the uncertain ambit of both the offence and its defence, the answers to these questions are not always clear-cut. Nevertheless, anti-bribery compliance programmes of the type contemplated by the statutory defence are not unprecedented and there is a body of material and experience available to guide a commercial organisation through the process of answering these questions. Although there will always remain some uncertainty as to whether an anti-bribery compliance programme will amount to 'adequate procedures' and thus provide a real prospect of a defence, provided a commercial organisation follows a sensible and proportionate approach, and adopts procedures which are clearly aimed at creating a culture of compliance within the organisation, that is implemented and operated at all levels within that organisation, it can take comfort that it will be in a considerably better position than a commercial organisation which either ignores anti-bribery compliance altogether or which pays mere lip-service to the concept of 'adequate procedures'. The Foreword to the official MOJ guidance (as described below) states that the offences in the Bribery Act 2010 are 'directed at making life difficult for the mavericks responsible for corruption, not unduly burdening the vast majority of decent, law-abiding firms'. Nothing in the Act, however, supports a distinction being made between what will be considered as adequate procedures for 'mavericks' and what will be considered adequate procedures for 'decent' firms.

Anti-bribery compliance programmes generally

6.10 Many commercial organisations are now subject to considerable regulation, some of it criminal, some of it quasi-criminal and some of it purely regulatory. This regulation extends beyond those business sectors, such as financial services and pharmaceuticals, which have long been subject to extensive regulation. Health and safety, data protection and anti-cartel laws are examples of laws and regulation of wide application across all business sectors, breaches of which can lead to the imposition of very significant corporate, and even personal, criminal or civil penalties. Listed companies are also subject to rules governing announcement obligations of material information to the market, the control of inside information and the like. Given the multi-national nature of many businesses, the regulatory and legal obligations imposed by a number of different jurisdictions will be relevant. In response to the challenges presented by these kinds of regulation, commercial organisations, particularly larger multi-national ones, have developed sophisticated compliance programmes designed to reduce the risk of being in breach.

6.11 As part of this increase in generally applicable compliance-type obligations there has, over recent years, been increased international enforcement of bribery laws. This is particularly true of the Foreign Corrupt Practices Act of 1977 (the 'FCPA') but, latterly, also of the English bribery laws in place before the Bribery Act 2010. In response, many businesses have increased their focus on the steps they take to comply with the local bribery laws which apply to their operations around the world. This has led to the development of detailed anti-bribery compliance programmes by many leading multi-national companies, particularly where there has been an incident of corruption in the past (whether or not leading to enforcement action) or among those who are participants in business sectors or markets perceived as high risk, perhaps as a result of prior enforcement action against a participant in that sector or market.

6.12 In many companies, anti-bribery compliance efforts often sit alongside, and are given similar importance to, other compliance obligations. They are combined into wider compliance programmes as part of broader codes of conduct or business ethics. Many such companies now publish details of their anti-bribery compliance programme on their websites: see for example the websites of BAE Systems plc, Siemens AG, GSK plc and BP plc, all of which contain examples of anti-bribery compliance forming part of broader codes of conduct or business ethics. Although, given the high profile and extent of their operations around the world, the larger multi-national companies have tended to lead the way on the development of codes of business ethics, it is not their exclusive preserve and other companies of varying sizes have also established their own codes of conduct.

6.13 A further development is the creation of industry standards in a particular business sector, such as the 'Common Industry Standards', an anti-bribery code of conduct for the Aerospace and Defence Industries Association of Europe, and the trans-Atlantic 'Global Principles of Business Ethics' in the same industry.

6.14 In tandem, or as a spur, to the development of anti-bribery compliance programmes by multi-national businesses and industry bodies, a considerable number of governmental and international agencies and non-governmental organisations have provided their own guidance or commentary on the design and possible content of an anti-bribery compliance programme. Examples of these can be found in:

—   Transparency International's publications such as its 'Business Principles for Countering Bribery' and accompanying guidance and its 'Six Step Process' for designing an anti-bribery compliance programme. This has been supplemented by a specific publication on 'adequate procedures', as noted below;

—   the OECD's 'Guidelines for Multi-national Enterprises', which includes suggestions for an anti-bribery compliance programme alongside other matters such as the environment, industrial relations and competition;

—   the anti-bribery element (Principle 10) of the United Nations Global Compact;

—   the 'Business Anti-Corruption Portal'[1], supported by a number of governments including the UK, Germany and the Netherlands;

—   the 'Woolf Committee Report' into the high ethical standards to which a global company should adhere, produced in May 2008 for BAE Systems plc by the retired senior English judge Lord Woolf;

—   the United States Federal Sentencing Guidelines Manual, Chapter 8B2.1; and

—   the Serious Fraud Office's 'Approach to Dealing with Overseas Corruption', para 22, published on 21 July 2009.

[1]   www.business-anti-corruption.com.

6.15 Before the Bribery Act 2010 was enacted, creating for the first time statutory offences of both primary and secondary corporate offending—the latter with its 'adequate procedures' defence, these practical precedents and other guidance documents already provided a wealth of material for any company around the world wishing to establish a new anti-bribery compliance programme or merely to review its existing anti-bribery compliance programme against emerging standards. For the purposes of the Bribery Act 2010, however, specific statutory guidance was required as a result of s 9. That section requires the Secretary of State to publish guidance about anti-bribery procedures, as discussed further below. That obligation was fulfilled at the end of March 2011 when the Ministry of Justice published its own guidance (the 'MOJ final guidance'). The challenge presented by these resources, including the MOJ final guidance itself, is their application to the specific circumstances of a particular company

Are all commercial organisations now required to have an anti-bribery compliance programme?

6.16 Nothing in the Bribery Act 2010 obliges a commercial organisation to adopt any, or any particular, anti-bribery compliance programme. Neither the Bribery Act 2010 nor the MOJ final guidance create an offence simply of not having 'adequate procedures'. The MOJ final guidance expressly acknowledges, however, that the 'adequate procedures' defence is intended to encourage commercial organisations to have anti-bribery compliance programmes.

6.17 Some industries are, however, subject to separate regulation which may have the effect of positively requiring commercial organisations in that sector to have anti-bribery compliance programmes. An example is the financial services sector where, in the UK, the Financial Services Authority (the 'FSA') principles require regulated entities to conduct themselves with integrity and take reasonable care to organise and control their affairs responsibly and effectively, with 'adequate' risk management systems. In January 2009, a large insurance broker was subject to a penalty from the FSA of £5.25 m for having failed to take reasonable care to organise and control its affairs responsibly and effectively because it did not have effective systems and controls for countering the risk of bribery[1]. The FSA has subsequently identified how some commercial insurance broker firms have serious weaknesses in systems and controls which mean that there is a significant risk of illicit payments being made to win business[2]. Moreover, in October 2010 a custodial sentence of 21 months was imposed on an insurance broker who had engaged in bribery[3].

---

[1]   See the FSA's Final Notice of 6 January 2009.
[2]   See FSA May 2010 publication 'Anti-bribery and corruption in commercial insurance broking'.
[3]   *R v Messent* [2011] EWCA Crim 644, [2011] All ER (D) 22 (Mar).

6.18 Subject to any such positive obligations, it is open to commercial organisations to decide how far they wish to go in putting in place an anti-bribery compliance programme, if at all. It is likely that in making this decision they will take into account the perceived risk of an offence being committed by the organisation (including under the wide provisions of s 7) and the damage that could cause to its business both in terms of criminal or civil penalties and to its reputation. Set against these risks are the costs of an anti-bribery compliance programme. It is conceivable that a commercial organisation might conclude, having weighed up these competing pressures, that it should not implement any procedures at all, particularly if it assesses the risk of bribery as low.

6.19 The MOJ's Quick Start Guide (discussed below) recognises the possibility that '... you do not need to put bribery prevention procedures in place if there is no risk of bribery on your behalf' (ie by an 'associated person' within s 7). This focuses on the risk of a s 7 offence being committed and concludes that if there is no risk of such an offence then there is no need to put in place 'adequate procedures'. However, it is not only the potential availability of a statutory defence to one specific offence in the Bribery Act 2010 that might lead a commercial organisation to put an anti-bribery compliance programme in place. In addition to reducing the risk of a s 7 offence and potentially being able to rely on the defence, other reasons for putting in place a programme are:

— to reduce the initial risk that it might commit a primary bribery offence itself under ss 1, 2 or 6, even though having 'adequate procedures' in place provides no direct defence to such offences;
— to increase the chances that any incident of bribery would be identified and thus self-reported to the Serious Fraud Office (the 'SFO'). The SFO has sought to encourage such reporting[1] and the SFO and DPP Joint Prosecution Guidance identifies pro-active self-reporting as one of the factors tending against prosecution;
— the general development of an enhanced reputation as a 'good corporate citizen' with potential business benefits; and
— the fact that potential customers or business partners are increasingly likely to expect a commercial organisation to be able to demonstrate its own ethical standards, including an anti-bribery compliance programme, before entering a business relationship with it. There is a risk that unless a commercial organisation has its own programme, it will be avoided as a business partner.

[1] SFO: 'Approach Of The Serious Fraud Office To Dealing With Overseas Corruption', 21 July 2009 (www.sfo.gov.uk/bribery--corruption/the-sfo's-response/self-reporting-corruption.aspx).

6.20 Given the above considerations, in commercial organisations of any size or diverse ownership and where managers are charged with protecting the organisation's assets or promoting its success (as is the case for companies incorporated in England and Wales), it seems unlikely that an organisation would conclude that it made sense not to put in place at least some procedures, no matter how basic. It is possible that the particular circumstances of one commercial organisation mean that it could come to such a conclusion, but it is likely to do so only after careful consideration.

C   THE MINISTRY OF JUSTICE FINAL GUIDANCE

Introduction

6.21 Section 9 of the Bribery Act 2010 requires the Secretary of State for Justice to publish 'guidance about procedures that relevant commercial organisations can put in place to prevent ['associated persons'] from bribing as mentioned in section 7(1)'. The MOJ final guidance published pursuant to that obligation is not definitive, does not address to any extent the question of 'adequacy', provides no safe harbour or checklists and is not binding on a court or a prosecutor. Beyond being mandated by statute, it has no particular status in law, although is likely to be the primary reference point for many businesses and prosecutors will be expected to consult it, as described further below.

The MOJ guidance was published for consultation in draft on 14 September 2010 with a consultation period through to November 2010 (the 'MOJ draft guidance'). It had been expected that the MOJ final guidance would then be published early in January 2011. However, the government received a considerable response to the consultation, alongside general lobbying from businesses concerned about the lack of clarity in the Act itself, both as to what would constitute 'adequate procedures' for the purposes of the defence and as to the intended scope of the substantive offences. As a result of the response to the consultation and the lobbying, the MOJ final guidance was not published in January 2011. In early February 2011 the Ministry of Justice said that it was ' . . . working on the guidance to make it practical and comprehensive for business, taking the time to ensure it is both accessible and effective for all sectors'.

6.22 The MOJ final guidance was published on 30 March 2011[1]. No doubt as a result of the consultation responses and lobbying, the MOJ final guidance is markedly different from the draft of six months earlier. Both the MOJ draft guidance and the MOJ final guidance set out six specific principles (the 'Principles') that it is said should inform an anti-bribery compliance programme. Although there were some changes to the Principles and substantial changes to their accompanying, relatively concise, commentary between the MOJ draft guidance and MOJ final guidance, the biggest change was in the overall structure. The MOJ draft guidance had, after setting out the Principles, provided 'Further Information About the Act'. This provided some clarification on the scope of the Bribery Act 2010. The MOJ final guidance, however, leads with long sections discussing Government policy and the scope of ss 1, 6 and 7, all with the apparent aim of clarifying what kinds of behaviour the Act criminalises rather than providing guidance about anti-bribery procedures. More of the MOJ final guidance is therefore devoted to the scope of the Act than to the Principles, although the scope of the offences must inform the scope of 'adequate procedures', at least for the purposes of the defence. Whereas the MOJ draft guidance had provided five 'illustrative scenarios' which were intended to look at the application of the Principles to some problem situations which commercial organisations might face, these were replaced by 11 'Case Studies' which are of greater practical use.

[1] The guidance is set out in Appendix 2.

6.23 The MOJ draft guidance suggested that it would not be the last word in the factors that go into designing an anti-bribery compliance programme. It expressly stated that it was 'designed to complement, not replace or supersede other forms of bribery prevention guidance'. However, this qualification has been removed, presumably so as to make the MOJ final guidance more definitive. By referring to other resources, the MOJ draft guidance created the risk that some organisations may have felt obliged to review those resources extensively in designing their programme, thus leading to an increased implementation burden. Although the MOJ final guidance does not make express reference to the other resources discussed at para **6.14**, these remain relevant and can be looked at in order to assist in seeking to establish 'adequate procedures'. As noted at para **6.17**, specific regulatory requirements may also apply in certain sectors and these should be identified and factored into the design of an anti-bribery compliance programme where applicable.

6.24 Whether, in assessing the adequacy of any particular anti-bribery compliance programme, a court will take into account suggestions and guidance offered in materials other than the MOJ final guidance remains to be seen. The SFO and DPP Joint Prosecution Guidance, published on the same day as the MOJ final guidance, makes it clear that prosecutors must take the MOJ final guidance into account when considering the adequacy of procedures in the context of a possible prosecution under s 7. In principle, however, there appears to be nothing to prevent either the prosecution or defence having reference to other materials. The SFO and DPP Joint Prosecution Guidance also recognises that departure from the MOJ final guidance does not raise a presumption of inadequacy of procedures.

MOJ final guidance on 'procedures', not guidance on 'adequate procedures': the central problem of 'adequacy'

6.25 Section 9 does not appear to require the publication of guidance about the adequacy of anti-bribery procedures for the purposes of the s 7(2) 'adequate procedures' defence. There is no reference in s 9 to that defence, merely to the offence. The MOJ draft guidance did not provide any detailed discussion of what procedures ought to be put in place so as to constitute an 'adequate' anti-bribery compliance programme for the purposes of the defence.

6.26 The language of the MOJ final guidance is more directive than the draft. The approach adopted is to discuss the types of procedures which could be put in place under each of the six Principles. The MOJ final guidance uses the phrase 'suggested procedures' and the commentary uses words and phrases such as 'policies are likely to include' and 'should be designed'. The Case Studies seek to provide practical illustrations of the application of the Principles to particular scenarios. Although more directive than the draft guidance, it is clear that the MOJ final guidance is flexible and outcome-focused rather than prescriptive. The Introduction to the MOJ final guidance states at para 4:

> 'The guidance is designed to be of general application and is formulated around six guiding principles, each followed by commentary and examples. The guidance is not prescriptive and is not a one-size-fits-all document. The question of whether an organisation had adequate procedures in place to prevent bribery in the context of a particular prosecution is a matter that can only be resolved by the courts taking into account the particular facts and circumstances of the case. The onus will remain on the organisation, in any case where it seeks to rely on the defence, to prove that it had adequate procedures in place to prevent bribery. However, departures from the suggested procedures contained within the guidance will not of itself give rise to a presumption that an organisation does not have adequate procedures'.

6.27 It is essential therefore that commercial organisations understand that the MOJ final guidance does not create any 'safe harbours' by way of lists of steps to be taken that can simply be ticked off to ensure that they have 'adequate procedures' to provide a defence to s 7. Ultimately, the establishment of an anti-bribery compliance programme will be an exercise in legal and business judgement. Even with a tailored anti-bribery compliance programme, there can be no certainty that it will be effective to prevent bribery on behalf of the commercial organisation. The MOJ final guidance goes so far as to recognise that no anti-bribery compliance programme will be capable of preventing bribery at all times (para 11). Likewise there can be no certainty that, should such bribery nonetheless occur on behalf of a commercial organisation so that, prima facie, a s 7 offence has been committed, its procedures will be found to have been 'adequate' for the purposes of the defence.

Procedures, policies or both?

6.28 Section 7(2) talks of 'adequate procedures', not 'adequate' policies. The idea of an active anti-bribery compliance programme rather than merely passive policies is one that is seen in other guidance. The US Federal Sentencing Guidelines Manual talks generally of a 'compliance and ethics program' [sic] and 'procedures' rather than just of 'standards' or 'policies'. The Introduction to Transparency International's 'Business Principles for Countering Bribery: TI Six Steps Process' explains that 'it is not enough for an enterprise to rely on a no-bribes policy—effective anti-bribery performance depends on an effective implementation programme as well as rhetorical commitment'. The MOJ final guidance itself states that anti-bribery policies alone will 'not achieve [their objective] unless they are properly implemented'.

6.29 This focus on procedures rather than policies alone increases the burden on commercial organisations. The MOJ final guidance makes it clear that the rolling out of the policies through training of the organisation's employees, the provision of advice and/or whistleblowing lines and the ongoing monitoring, review and updating of the policies and procedures could well be important elements of an anti-bribery compliance programme, at least in larger organisations. By implication, these elements may well be expected in an anti-bribery compliance programme that is 'adequate' and resources will be required to implement them. In a large commercial organisation, with many employees spread across the globe, it is possible that dedicated compliance personnel charged full time with these various tasks will be required. There is also a risk that the MOJ final guidance will lead to the adoption of overly comprehensive processes by some organisations.

6.30 There is also the possibility, particularly in industries with known bribery risks, of an organisation which has been subject to enforcement action putting an anti-bribery compliance programme in place which is significantly more thorough than those of its competitors. There is an understandable risk that this sets an unrealistically high expectation of what is 'adequate' in a particular business sector. Competitors may feel the need to put in place procedures which meet this benchmark for fear of their anti-bribery compliance programmes being labelled 'inadequate'. This may not be necessary, but an organisation which is significantly 'out of step with the herd' in a sector should be prepared to justify its position.

6.31 The MOJ final guidance and other resources often refer to 'policies' or 'procedures' almost interchangeably. Whilst the two concepts are not easily de-coupled and the one is derived from the other, it is important to appreciate that s 7(2) itself refers to 'procedures' and it is the adequacy of the given organisation's procedures that matters when determining whether a defence is made out, as opposed to the 'adequacy' of its policies. The MOJ final guidance makes it clear that its text encompasses policies as well as practical procedures. An overall anti-bribery compliance programme will almost inevitably consist of both policies and procedures. So where is the boundary between the two? Generally speaking, 'policies' are the commercial organisation's written statements as to what is and is not acceptable conduct. For example, a policy might contain a general statement of zero-tolerance of bribery or, at a finer level of detail, a statement that no corporate hospitality over a certain threshold value should be given. In turn 'procedures' are the practical mechanisms by which the policies are given effect. For example in a larger organisation, at a high level, procedures are the monitoring systems used to check the anti-bribery policy has been respected such as internal audit, down through the due diligence procedures on prospective business partners to, at a finer level of detail, the process by which any required senior management approval for proposed corporate hospitality above a threshold is sought, given and recorded. This distinction is described in the discussion of Principle 1 at paras 1.1 and 1.6.

The application of the MOJ final guidance by multi-national groups

6.32 One particular issue faced by multi-national groups of companies is the extent to which the Bribery Act 2010 dictates the standards to be applied in their anti-bribery compliance programme across the world. It has been said by many commentators that the Bribery Act 2010 is the toughest anti-bribery law in the world. Multi-national businesses, whether headquartered in the UK or elsewhere, will be subject to the Bribery Act 2010 in respect of those parts of their operations that are carried on by entities either incorporated in part of the UK (and thus subject to all four offences) or which are incorporated outside the UK but which carry on a business in part of the UK (and thus subject to the s 7 offence). Other parts of their global businesses will be carried on by entities which are not subject to the Bribery Act 2010. Should multi-national groups of companies which are exposed to the Act somewhere within their groups now ensure that their anti-bribery compliance programmes are Bribery Act 2010 compliant? Or does it make sense for those groups to develop a specific programme applicable just to the parts of those groups that are clearly covered by the Act, resulting in two different anti-bribery compliance programmes, one which is less rigorous for those parts of groups which are not subject to the Act?

6.33 In favour of applying the standards implicit in the Bribery Act 2010 across a whole group's anti-bribery compliance programme is the fact that this provides a consistent and practical approach. It minimises the risks arising from the fact that the exact reach of the Act across a multi-national group cannot be definitively identified in advance, due to the uncertainty of the jurisdictional reach of the Act and the fact that the exposure of a group is likely to change over time as its business evolves. It also minimises the practical difficulties of a risk of confusion as to which policy applies in any given circumstances and reduces the compliance burden. There may well be increasing international harmonisation of anti-bribery legislation in years to come, such that standards implicit in the Bribery Act 2010 may in due course apply more widely in any event.

6.34 Set against these considerations is the fact that the Bribery Act 2010 does not have automatic global reach across an entire multi-national group. The legal standards applicable to subsidiaries in other parts of the world may be compliant with international treaty obligations such as the OECD Treaty. The fact that UK law goes further might be argued not to lead to the imposition of procedures which would be expensive and time-consuming to implement across a whole group as opposed to those parts of the group which are obviously directly affected. Anecdotal evidence from businesses suggests, however, that the practical difficulties faced by adopting a twin-track approach mean that the Bribery Act 2010 is becoming the default standard for anti-bribery compliance programmes in many multi-national businesses.

The application of the MOJ final guidance by SMEs

6.35 The inherent uncertainty created by the scope of the 'adequate procedures' defence and the lack of any checklists in the MOJ final guidance will be of particular concern to those businesses, particularly small and medium enterprises ('SMEs')[1], which have not previously had an anti-bribery compliance programme and which are faced with designing one for the first time.

[1] Defined in the EU as businesses with less than 250 employees and turnover of €50m or less or a balance sheet of €43m or less (Article 2 of the Annex of Recommendation 2003/361/EC).

6.36 The MOJ draft guidance provided limited material focused on SMEs. However, alongside the MOJ final guidance, the MOJ published a short Quick Start Guide, intended to assist small businesses in particular. The Quick Start Guide summarises the six Principles and emphasises the proportionate, risk-based approach so that an SME facing 'minimal bribery risks will require relatively minimal procedures to mitigate those risks'. The Quick Start Guide addresses a series of basic questions, drawing distinctions between larger and smaller businesses. For example, a distinction is drawn between how a large organisation might disseminate policies and how it might be done in a 'micro-business'. The Quick Start Guide aims to allay fears that the Bribery Act 2010 creates uncertainty and burdens for SMEs in particular. It answers questions such as 'Do I need to employ consultants or lawyers . . . ?' and 'Can I provide hospitality . . . ?' and provides practical commentary on how to assess risk or carry out due diligence without engaging in sophisticated or costly techniques. The MOJ final guidance itself recognises that 'the application of the principles is likely to suggest procedures [for SMEs] that are different to those that may be right for a large multinational organisation'. Most of the Case Studies in Appendix A to the MOJ final guidance are specific to SMEs.

6.37 Other resources, such as the 'Business Anti-Corruption Portal'[1] are specifically targeted at SMEs. Transparency International has published an 'SME Edition' of its 'Business Principles', along with an 'SME Edition' of the accompanying guidance document. These documents provide some more focused discussion of the particular challenges faced by SMEs in establishing an effective anti-bribery compliance programme and provide a useful additional source of guidance.

[1] www.business-anti-corruption.com.

6.38 Despite efforts to simplify the entire process of establishing 'adequate procedures' for SMEs, they may face particular issues. This can be due to their smaller size and their more informal and entrepreneurial culture. SMEs are also not necessarily domestic focused with lower risks—some SMEs trade alongside their larger cousins in higher risk jurisdictions or sectors or through third party agents. Finally, although the Quick Start Guide and other resources might suggest that with some common sense SMEs may not need to do too much, their the customers or clients may be larger commercial organisations. Given that more extensive procedures are likely to be expected of such larger organisations, it is possible that those larger organisations may require an SME which performs services on their behalf (and thus may be their 'associated person') to have a more extensive anti-bribery compliance programme than that which the SME would otherwise consider appropriate for its own circumstances.

Other sources of guidance on 'adequate procedures'

6.39 As noted above, the MOJ final guidance does not address the central question of 'adequacy'. Transparency International has sought to provide its own guidance on adequate procedures[1]. It provides commentary on the features of what it regards as an adequate anti-bribery compliance programme and provides a series of checklists. At nearly 100 pages long, it is perhaps of greater interest to larger commercial organisations, although an SME edition is proposed for the future.

[1] At www.transparency.org.uk/working-with-companies/adequate-procedures.

D   COMMENTARY ON THE SIX PRINCIPLES

6.40 The detailed design and implementation of an anti-bribery compliance programme is outside the scope of this work. Resources other than the MOJ final guidance in the form of precedents, sector-specific codes, and guidance publications from governmental and international agencies and non-governmental organisations discuss, to varying extents, the process by which a programme can be designed. For example, Transparency International's 'Six Step Process' provides a useful guide to the process of design and implementation of an anti-bribery compliance programme, as do the checklists provided in its publications on adequate procedures referred to above. What follows is a practical discussion of the six Principles set out in the MOJ final guidance.

Is it all just 'common sense'?

6.41 The Secretary of State said in Parliament on 15 February 2011, during the course of the Ministry of Justice's extended consideration of the consultation responses, that:

> 'I hope to put out very clear guidance for businesses of all sizes to make that clear and to save them from the fears that are sometimes aroused by the compliance industry-the consultants and lawyers who will, of course, try to persuade companies that millions of pounds must be spent on new systems that, in my opinion, no honest firm will require to comply with the Act'[1].

This theme is picked up in the Foreword to the MOJ final guidance: 'combating the risks of bribery is largely about common sense, not burdensome procedures'. As the Quick Start Guide and other similar resources make clear, for many SMEs this may be correct. However, for any business of appreciable size and even for SMEs operating in high risk countries or industries or through agents[2], their size and/or risk profile may dictate that their procedures will need to be much more than just common sense.

[1] 523 HC Official Report (6th series) col 793, 15 February 2011.
[2] As is recognised in Principle 1, para 1.2.

E   PRINCIPLE 1: PROPORTIONATE PROCEDURES

6.42

> 'A commercial organisation's procedures to prevent bribery by persons associated with it are proportionate to the bribery risks it faces and to the nature, scale and complexity of the commercial organisation's activities. They are also clear, practical, accessible, effectively implemented and enforced'.

Proportionality

6.43 Proportionality was not itself one of the six Principles in the MOJ draft guidance, although the concept ran through that document. However, in the MOJ final guidance it was expressly incorporated in the first Principle. A proportionate approach is also suggested by other resources. Each commercial organisation should adapt its anti-bribery compliance programme to reflect the risk profile its activities present in a proportionate way. Proportionality is therefore strongly reliant on Principle 3 (risk assessment). A risk-based and proportionate approach is likely to introduce procedures for a domestic SME or even a large company with a primarily UK-focus which are less complex than those that would be 'adequate' for a multi-national business with operations in higher risk jurisdictions and higher risk business sectors.

Procedures

6.44 Other than recognising the need for proportionality, this Principle focuses on 'procedures', and it refers to a wide range of important topics. While some of these topics may themselves be addressed in the subject of other Principles (such as 'due diligence'), the MOJ final guidance as a whole has little to say about others of them in practice. Given its focus on procedures, Principle 1 is perhaps the most wide-reaching of all the Principles.

Documentation of the policies

6.45 Principle 1 makes reference to both the policies and procedures that make up the anti-bribery compliance programme, recognising the distinction referred to at para **6.31**. However, the MOJ final guidance does not provide a model set of policies. It provides an indicative and non-exhaustive list of elements that organisations may wish to cover in its policies. These are a commitment to bribery prevention (tying in with Principle 2 of 'top-level commitment'), the organisation's general approach to mitigation of specific bribery risks and an overview of its implementation of the policy. Some more detail of possible topics covered by policies is found in Principle 5, para 5.3, which suggests that there should be policies on areas such as decision making, financial control, hospitality and promotional expenditure, facilitation payments, training, charitable and political donations and penalties for breach of the rules and articulation of management responsibility at different levels. There is, however, little commentary on the way in which these topics will be dealt with in the policy.

6.46 In a larger organisation the documentation may go beyond the policies alone: policy documents which record specific practical 'do's and don'ts' for employees and separate procedures documentation, which set out all of the detailed elements that go together with the policy to make up the anti-bribery compliance programme. The policy documents should, no doubt, be widely publicised and available and will form an important part of the communication and training suggested under Principle 5 (communication (and training)). The procedures document, however, will include matters which are mostly relevant to those charged with responsibility for the anti-bribery compliance programme, such as the roll-out plan for the programme, expectations of monitoring and review milestones and other procedural matters which are of little interest to the majority of employees and managers in the organisation. It may also make sense for there to be gathered together in one document or suite of documents all the elements, both policies and procedures, which make up the programme. In a smaller organisation with simpler procedures, the documentation may be less extensive and one short document may be capable of recording the majority of the overall policies and procedures.

6.47 As for the detailed content of policy and procedures documents, this will reflect the outcome of the risk assessment and the design of the overall anti-bribery compliance programme. However, it is likely that they will include at least general statements of a zero-tolerance approach to bribery and guidance on obvious risk areas such as the use of corporate hospitality and promotional expenditure and gift giving. Examples of these basic kinds of policy documents can be found in the Annexes to the SME edition of Transparency International's 'Business Principles for Countering Bribery'.

6.48 Transparency International suggests nine clear and simple principles for SMEs:

'1   We will carry out our business fairly, honestly and openly;
2   We will not make bribes, nor will we condone the offering of bribes on our behalf, so as to gain a business advantage;

3   We will not accept bribes, nor will we agree to them being accepted on our behalf in order to influence business;

4   We will avoid doing business with others who do not accept our values and who may harm our reputation;

5   We will set out our processes for avoiding direct or indirect bribery, and keeping to and supporting our values;

6   We will keep clear and updated records;

7   We will make sure that everyone in our business and our business partners know our Principles;

8   We will regularly review and update our Programme and processes as needed; and

9   We will keep to these Principles even when it becomes difficult.'

Such statements of values or mission statements are not an unknown concept to a commercial organisation, even SMEs. Beyond this statement of broad principles, Transparency International does not propose much more detail even for the obvious risk areas such as gifts and entertainment (see Annex B of the 'SME Edition').

6.49 Any policy, even in a larger commercial organisation, will be more effective if it is based on broad and easily understandable principles. Long and detailed policies will be more difficult to understand across an organisation and be less effective. Nevertheless, it is likely that in a larger organisation more extensive policies will be required as they may include details of other elements of the overall procedures, for example: contact details for any advice line and details of whistleblowing arrangements and the consequences of any breach. As noted at para **6.12**, the anti-bribery compliance programme may also form part of a wider code of business conduct or ethics and need to be integrated into that.

The procedures themselves

6.50 At Principle 1, para 1.7, a list of possible procedures to support the policies is given. Again, it is said to be indicative and non-exhaustive. Fourteen topics are included, some of which are cross-references to other Principles, such as 'due diligence'. Others are separate topics which are dealt with in some further detail elsewhere under another Principle, such as whistleblowing (for example in Principle 5, para 5.3). Some are not given any detailed treatment in the MOJ final guidance at all, such as 'financial and commercial controls'. While controls are identified in the Principles as procedures such as bookkeeping, auditing and expenditure approvals, the design of such controls is a topic in its own right and it would be unrealistic to expect the MOJ final guidance to provide definitive advice as to how these routine business processes ought to be adapted to form part of an anti-bribery compliance programme. In the following paragraphs, those procedures suggested under Principle 1, and which are not themselves another Principle, are considered.

Gifts, hospitality and promotional expenditure; charitable and political donations

6.51 As set out in detail in Chapter 5, a review of FCPA cases from the United States reveals that a number result from the provision of corporate hospitality, the giving of gifts and other kinds of promotional expenditure. In the run up to the commencement of the Bribery Act 2010, one of the biggest concerns of businesses was that they did not know what was permitted by way of promotional expenditure, particularly in relation to foreign public officials. The risks under the Act are under ss 1 and 2: ie that promotional expenditure is used as a cover for a bribe such that there is direct evidence of an intention that: (1) the recipient (or someone else) perform a relevant function improperly; or (2) perhaps more concerning for businesses, that the expenditure is regarded outside the commercial organisation as so lavish as to raise an inference of such an intention. Given the wider scope of s 6, there is a risk that promotional expenditure intended simply to 'influence' the foreign public official where the provider of the promotional expenditure was seeking business or a business advantage is an offence.

6.52 Promotional expenditure by commercial organisations is, however, not *per se* unlawful and has for many years formed a normal part of doing business in the UK and around the world. In some parts of the world the giving of gifts, for example, is said to be an essential part of doing business in accordance with local cultural expectations. The Bribery Act 2010 does not have the effect of prohibiting these activities, something which the MOJ final guidance is at pains to emphasise:

— 'no one wants to stop firms getting to know their clients by taking them to events like Wimbledon or the Grand Prix' (Foreword);

— 'for example, an invitation to foreign clients to attend a Six Nations match at Twickenham as part of a public relations exercise designed to cement good relations or enhance knowledge in the organisation's field is extremely unlikely to engage section 1' (para 20);

— 'Bona fide hospitality and promotional, or other business expenditure which seeks to improve the image of a commercial organisation, better to present products and services, or establish cordial relations, is recognised as an established and important part of doing business and it is not the intention of the Act to criminalise such behaviour. The Government does not intend for the Act to prohibit reasonable and proportionate hospitality and promotional or other similar business expenditure intended for these purposes' (para 26);

— 'travel and accommodation costs [may] not even amount to a "financial or other advantage" to the relevant official because it is a cost that would otherwise be borne by the relevant foreign Government' (para 27);

— 'there [must be] a sufficient connection between the advantage and the intention to influence and secure business . . . The more lavish the hospitality or the higher the expenditure . . . then, generally, the greater the inference that it is intended to influence the official to grant business or a business advantage' (para 28); and

— 'it is unlikely, for example, that incidental provision of a routine business courtesy will raise the inference that it was intended to have a direct impact on decision making, particularly where such hospitality is commensurate with the reasonable and proportionate norms of the particular industry . . . ' (para 30).

The Government has, through the MOJ final guidance, sought to provide comfort that the Act has not criminalised activities which were previously thought to be perfectly normal business activities. Even before the Bribery Act 2010, many commercial organisations already had specific policies and procedures designed to regulate the circumstances in which they could undertake such promotional activities so that they might not be perceived in any way as corrupt. In addition, anti-bribery resources such as Transparency International's 'Business Principles for Countering Bribery' had previously focused on these activities as risks and made suggestions on how to control the risks associated with them.

6.53 Principle 1 does not provide any suggestions on the content of the policies or procedures that can be put in place to control the risks of an offence being committed through the inappropriate use of corporate hospitality, gifts or other forms of promotional expenditure. In response to the risks associated with these activities, some commercial organisations have adopted policies that prohibit them outright or beyond a more or less nominal value. Others will wish to continue to use them as part of their way of doing business. Indeed, in some industries such as leisure and entertainment, they form an integral part of the business itself. In commercial organisations which expect to make use of these business tools, policies and procedures designed to reduce the risks ought to be included in the anti-bribery compliance programme. As with any element of a particular anti-bribery compliance programme, the precise approach will be dictated by the circumstances of the commercial organisation. In designing the policies and procedures in this sphere, the comments in the MOJ final guidance about the boundaries of liability ought to be borne in mind.

6.54 Policies in this area often adopt a number of similar elements. Common steps taken to control the risks associated with hospitality and gifts include:

— the specific consideration of this topic as part of the initial risk assessment process. This may include benchmarking the levels of hospitality that appear standard in the same sector;
— drafting and roll-out of a specific hospitality and gifts policy;
— explaining to employees through the terms of the relevant policy, and in training sessions, the risks that the giving of hospitality or gifts creates. One aim of this can be to instil in employees the need, as a first step, to ask themselves a number of questions, such as why they wish to provide the hospitality or gift, how it might be perceived by others and whether the intended recipient is actually prohibited from receiving it in any event;
— seeking to classify hospitality and gifts into categories which can (normally) be given or received without any internal approvals, those which can never be given or received and those which require approval. These are often classified by reference to either value thresholds or type. For example, hospitality or gifts below a certain value, perhaps a nominal one, will be presumed to be approved unless they fall within a category of type of hospitality or gift which can never be given, such as where there is a current tender process under way with the recipi-

ent's employer. For hospitality or gifts of values above the threshold and which are not otherwise always prohibited, a prior approval can be sought. These thresholds may vary by region around the world;

— the use of a register on which outbound and inbound hospitality and gifts are recorded, again perhaps subject to certain value thresholds; and

— the position of 'public official' may be expressly carved out from the policy altogether and special rules applied to hospitality or gifts to them, not least in light of the risks under the FCPA for commercial organisations subject to that US law, but now also because of the even wider provisions of the Bribery Act 2010, s 6.

6.55 Similar considerations apply to the making of charitable or political donations as to the giving of hospitality and gifts. Some commercial organisations will wish to make political donations, while others will prohibit them altogether. In keeping with many organisations' desire to be seen as 'good corporate citizens', they will wish to make charitable donations or carry out sponsorship. The risks associated with these two activities differ.

6.56 In the case of political donations, particularly overseas, the donation may be portrayed by political opponents of the recipient or by competitors of the commercial organisation as a straightforward attempt to buy influence. In addition, s 6 increases the risks where the recipient of the political donation is connected to a foreign public official (which includes someone holding a legislative or administrative position). For example, the making of a donation to the party of a member of a legislature or government may be an offence. In any event, the UK Companies Act 2006 also regulates the making of political donations by companies incorporated under that Act, including by way of shareholder approval.

In the case of charitable donations and sponsorships, one risk is that a simple bribe is obscured as a charitable donation or sponsorship and therefore allowed to go through a system of controls which permits such payments. Another risk is that a donation to a charity for which a senior and influential employee of a customer or potential customer is seeking to raise funds is seen as an attempt to indirectly influence that senior employee.

6.57 Specific policies and procedures put in place to manage the risks associated with political and charitable donations are likely to be similar to those associated with hospitality and gifts. For example, these may seek to focus the employee proposing the donation on why he wishes to make it, whether there is any obvious reason why it should not be made and in keeping a register of donations. However, any such donations by commercial organisations are likely always to require specific approval, possibly from very senior management and this may provide a further check

Facilitation payments

6.58 Facilitation payments are examined in detail in Chapter 5. Unlike the position in the United States under the FCPA, so-called 'facilitation payments' amount to bribes under the Bribery Act 2010 and are thus illegal. No doubt because of the prevalence of requests for facilitation-type payments in many places around the world and the fact that the FCPA permits them (but only in

the circumstances described at Chapter 5), there have been numerous suggestions that English law ought to also permit them, including in the run up to the
publication of the MOJ final guidance. This has been suggested on the basis
that it is impossible to do business in certain parts of the world without making
facilitation payments. These suggestions have been rejected. A facilitation
payment is a bribe.

6.59 The MOJ final guidance discusses these payments at paras 44–47 and
they are further considered in the SFO and DPP Joint Prosecution Guidance on
pp 8 and 9. In addition, the MOJ final guidance points out at para 48,
immediately following the discussion of facilitation payments, that the common law defence of duress may be applicable where a bribe has been paid to
protect life, limb or liberty.

6.60 The practical difficulties presented by the prevalence of requests for such
payments are acknowledged, but no exemption, express or implied, is
provided (nor could it be, otherwise than by primary legislation). It appears
from the SFO and DPP Joint Prosecution Guidance that low-level, one-off
payments made without pre-planning or payments made by someone in a
vulnerable position are unlikely to attract prosecution. Large or repeated
payments or those that are pre-planned are more likely to attract prosecution.
The indications do not alter the basic position that even low-level, one-off
facilitation payments are bribes. The question that therefore arises is whether
an 'adequate' anti-bribery compliance programme can be drafted so as to cater
for the prevalence of requests for such payments in certain places and the
likelihood that such payments may be made from time-to-time by the
commercial organisation's 'associated persons', such as its employees. In
addition, some organisations may wish to make it clear to their employees that
payments to secure, life, limb or liberty are not prohibited. However, it is
perhaps debatable whether any employee truly facing loss of life, limb or
liberty would ever be inhibited from making a requested payment out of fear
of being in breach of his employer's code of conduct.

6.61 Any exemptions to the blanket ban on bribery risk undermining
anti-bribery compliance programmes as they confuse the clarity of the message
and have the potential to be abused. In the context of 'adequate procedures',
were an anti-bribery compliance programme to seek to permit facilitation
payments, this would dilute the zero-tolerance approach to bribery in general
and potentially weaken the programme as a whole. In addition, identifying
what would be a 'permissible' facilitation payment under the relevant anti-
bribery compliance programme may be difficult, not least as 'facilitation
payment' is a term that is rather difficult to pin down. It has a narrow meaning
under the FCPA, but is often used by lay people in a much wider way, for
example, to include small payments made to employees of commercial
organisations or to describe payments of amounts well above a small sum. The
risk that a permission in an anti-bribery compliance programme to make
'facilitation payments' would lead to bribes other than those properly considered facilitation payments is obvious.

6.62 Principle 5, para 5.3 contemplates that a commercial organisation may
have a policy on facilitation payments as that is one of the 'policies on
particular areas' listed. The MOJ final guidance is silent on the possible
content of such a policy. It appears, however, that the SFO and DPP Joint

Prosecution Guidance contemplates that such a policy may actually permit the making of facilitation payments. One of the factors tending against prosecution given on page 9 is 'Where a commercial organisation has a clear and appropriate policy setting out procedures an individual should follow if facilitation payments are requested and these have been correctly followed'. For this question to arise for consideration by a prosecutor, prima facie an offence must have been committed through a facilitation payment having been made in accordance with applicable policy/procedures that permitted facilitation payments, at least in certain circumstances. It appears therefore that the prosecutors recognise a possibility that a commercial organisation might permit such illegal payments.

6.63 This is surprising as it would appear tacitly to permit a commercial organisation to render an illegal payment legal by having a procedure that allows it, as long as that procedure is followed. It may be, however, that the prosecutors are merely recognising that in some operational areas facilitation payments are a way of life and that companies may have policies and procedures which explain to employees what they should do in situations where they are demanded and that the person to whom the request for a payment is made may be in a vulnerable position and have to pay (even if that does not amount to the defence of duress). If the demandee has followed the procedures, which are likely to include immediate reporting to someone more senior, that is unlikely to result in prosecution.

6.64 Even if the SFO and DPP Joint Prosecution Guidance is indeed contemplating procedures that permit the making of facilitation payments in comparatively extreme circumstances, few commercial organisations may wish to have procedures that expressly permit and regulate criminal conduct by its employees. Senior employees are unlikely to wish to be in a position where they are asked to approve, prospectively, the payment of bribes. Further, under the provisions of the Proceeds of Crime Act 2002, the organisation would, once the payment was drawn to its attention by its employee, be likely to have requisite knowledge or suspicion of its possession of a benefit which has resulted from the illegal facilitation payment and it may therefore wish to obtain the statutory consent provided under that Act to insulate it from liability under that Act, thus leading to a self-report to the authorities.

6.65 In light of these risks and practical difficulties, the better view is that zero-tolerance to all bribery within the terms of the Bribery Act 2010 should be maintained in a commercial organisation's anti-bribery compliance programme. If a commercial organisation concludes that its anti-bribery compliance programme should permit facilitation payments, it would risk rendering the whole programme 'inadequate' for the purposes of the defence. It would indicate that the organisation was not in fact fully committed to anti-bribery compliance. It may be the case that in reliance on a narrow reading of the SFO and DPP Joint Prosecution Guidance as set out above, adequate procedures could include provision for payment of facilitation payments, although the risks of legislating for this policy are clear. Anecdotal evidence from large multi-national organisations is that, although there may be some initial difficulties, once the message gets out in a particular overseas market that the organisation does not make facilitation-type payments, the flow of requests for them dwindles and the seekers of such payments move on to organisations with weaker anti-bribery compliance programmes. For businesses facing ongoing pressure to make such payments in a particular market, there may be alternatives to having to choose between withdrawing from the market altogether or capitulating and making the facilitation payment, such as engagement with the local government, through collaboration with other market participants or through diplomatic and/or law enforcement agencies.

Employment issues: employees as 'associated persons'

6.66 Direct and indirect employment is included as a topic for consideration in the procedures listed in Principle 1. Employees are presumed to be 'associated persons' of their employers. Accordingly, the risks posed by actions of employees ought to be within the scope of the commercial organisation's anti-bribery compliance programme. In many ways this is self-evident: a commercial organisation can only act through human agency and accordingly the actions of its employees are the very front line of the programme.

6.67 Specific issues relating to employment that might be relevant to an anti-bribery compliance programme include:

— recruitment. How will the commercial organisation ensure that it recruits people who are likely to act in an ethical manner (see Principle 4: due diligence, para 4.6)? How will the new recruit on joining receive training on the organisations' procedures?
— terms and conditions. Many organisations incorporate the terms of their code of ethics or business conduct into the contracts of employment or ensure that the employee receives the code and signs to acknowledge it;
— disciplinary processes relating to breaches of the commercial organisation's policies. This topic is considered at paras **6.81–6.83**;
— remuneration mechanisms. Rewarding employees by way of bonus or commission on the basis of sales can give an incentive to employees to cut corners and act in an unethical way giving rise to liability both for them, under ss 1 or 6, and for their employer, under s 7. As a counter to this, in addition to other techniques such as training and monitoring, employers sometimes seek to build into performance assessment rewards for ethical behaviour such as reporting requests for bribes or similar concerns;
— the creation of a culture that encourages employees to 'speak up'. This is considered further at paras **6.84–6.86**.

Business relationships with other 'associated persons'

6.68 The fact that a commercial organisation will, prima facie, commit an offence under s 7 as a result of independent acts of bribery by an 'associated person' seeking business for the commercial organisation, demonstrates the high level of risk presented by such relationships. Indeed, the MOJ final guidance is required, as mandated by s 9, to focus on the risks of bribery by 'associated persons'. Principle 1 and other resources therefore identify this as a topic which might well be covered by the anti-bribery compliance programme to mitigate those risks.

Who is an 'associated person'?

6.69 Arguably, the MOJ draft guidance proceeded on the basis of a view of the risk created by 'associated persons' in a way which was inconsistent with the Bribery Act 2010 itself. The scope of the s 8 definition of 'associated person' is considered in Chapter 4. The only test is whether the third party performs 'services for or on behalf of' the commercial organisation. Although the concept of 'associated person' is therefore capable of including such a wide range of situations and relationships, the MOJ draft guidance appeared to suggest that whole classes of third parties outside the direct (or even indirect) control of a commercial organisation might, almost automatically, be expected to fall within the definition in circumstances where it was unclear as to whether such a sweeping generalisation could in fact be made. So, for example the MOJ draft guidance seemed to proceed on the basis that all joint venture entities, joint venture partners, consortia partners, suppliers and all elements of the supply chain were to be considered 'associated persons'. The implication was that a commercial organisation seeking to have 'adequate procedures' would have had to extend those procedures to encompass the activities of these third party business partners.

6.70 This loose wording in the MOJ draft guidance led to increased concerns on the part of commercial organisations that the Act was imposing very wide obligations indeed. It was difficult to see how suppliers of, for example, materials on an arm's length basis with no associated or ancillary provision of services could fall within s 8. Yet read literally, the MOJ draft guidance implied that such a supplier was highly likely to be an 'associated person' and accordingly, in order to have 'adequate procedures', the commercial organisation was obliged to impose a wide ranging anti-bribery programme on such a 'business partner'.

6.71 Happily, the MOJ final guidance has stepped back from such a wide interpretation and focused again on the words used in s 8. Accordingly, paras 38–41 of the MOJ final guidance recognise that suppliers of goods will not, without more, be 'associated persons' and that the parties further down a supply chain are even less likely to be supplying services to the commercial organisation. It also puts the true nature of many joint venture relationships into their proper context by recognising that by virtue of simple participation in a joint venture, a commercial organisation is not automatically responsible, within s 7, for the acts of the joint venture itself or the other parties to the joint venture or the employees or agents of the joint venture of the other parties. The facts of any particular business relationship with a third party, whether supplier, joint venture partner, joint venture entity or any other person or organisation, will determine whether the third party is an 'associated person'. Whilst some broad categorisation can be helpful, it could lead to confusion and imply that the Act's ambit is wider than it really is.

6.72 Paragraph 43 of the MOJ final guidance recognises that the question of the degree of control the commercial organisation has over the person alleged to be an 'associated person' will be relevant. This concept of 'control' is one that also appears in the Transparency International guidance document to the 'Business Principles for Countering Bribery' and is perhaps a more useful way of approaching the question of to whom a commercial organisation ought to seek to extend its anti-bribery compliance programme. For example, Transparency International makes suggestions about how one partner to a joint venture may have 'effective control' over it through being designated the managing partner and notes that it is therefore in a position to implement an effective anti-bribery compliance programme in the joint venture. By contrast, it notes that where a commercial organisation owns a minority stake in a company and does not have control, the commercial organisation can seek to influence the associated company but no more, suggesting in extreme cases it contacts law enforcement agencies and/or withdraws its investment.

6.73 When mentioning 'all other associated persons' as a topic for inclusion in an anti-bribery compliance programme, Principle 1 refers to pre- and post-contract agreements. Adopting a consistent approach towards contract management, establishing a clear procedure to persuade business partners to accept an anti-bribery programme consistent with its own, monitoring compliance with such obligations and formulating a clear strategy for exiting relationships if a bribery incident occurs or there is reasonable suspicion that it has happened, will be important, regardless of the size of the commercial organisation.

6.74 Pre-contractual steps that a commercial organisation can take in respect of 'all other associated persons' include:

— **due diligence**, as explored fully under Principle 4;
— **remuneration policies for third parties** determining how a commercial organisation is prepared to remunerate those acting on its behalf. In particular, a commercial organisation may seek to avoid commission-type remuneration arrangements for business partners. This is because commission arrangements can have the effect of incentivising business partners to engage in bribery in order to win business for the commercial organisation and thus earn their commission;
— **contractual terms,** other than remuneration. Contractual protections of this kind are often built into relationships with business partners. These will vary enormously. In the context of two large multi-national companies, each with developed anti-bribery compliance programmes creating a joint venture, the obligations are likely to be relatively straightforward. In the case where the business partner is a sole trader based overseas, the contractual provisions are likely to be far more extensive. The kinds of contractual terms which could be agreed include express requirements on the business partner:
  • to abide by the commercial organisation's anti-bribery compliance programme;
  • to attend training on the anti-bribery compliance programme as requested by the organisation;
  • to keep appropriate books and records;
  • to permit the commercial organisation to audit both the books and records and the business partner's general compliance with the anti-bribery compliance programme;
  • to assist with any investigation conducted into alleged or suspected bribery;
  • to provide appropriate certifications of compliance, for example annually or before any payment is made; and

- • a right to terminate without notice in certain circumstances including allegations or suspicions of bribery;
- — an **approval process** for new business relationships. This process will vary by size and complexity of the organisation as well as by size and complexity of the new business relationship. For example, the hiring of a small advertising agency for a one-off piece of work is different from the engagement of an agent to represent the commercial organisation overseas in a high risk jurisdiction. The process might involve approval of a more senior line manager all the way through to approval from the Board, perhaps even at a group level with the benefit of in-depth due diligence and legal/compliance advice. However, whatever arrangements are adopted, the selection and engagement of business partners should be identified in training as a key risk and the due diligence and approval process adopted in the organisation should be set out clearly.

6.75 Post-contract procedures could include the implementation of training obligations on the third party as well as a process whereby documentation is monitored throughout the life of any relationship with a business partner, for instance regular audits of contracts could be made to ensure continued compliance. Periodic reviews of business relationships and the documentation underpinning the results of such reviews should be kept, the local market's (where applicable) attitudes and opinions should be monitored for changes, and, where necessary, changes in positions with business partners should be discussed at management or Board level, and job rotation for relationship managers might be considered.

6.76 If a commercial organisation becomes concerned about the ethical standards of its business partner, it ought to be very careful about renewing that relationship. Renewal of a previous relationship should therefore not be overlooked as a potential risk and approval processes for new business partners should also apply to renewal. Principle 1 at para 1.5 recognises that retrospective application of new procedures to existing ongoing relationships with third parties is more difficult, but advocates an approach of doing so over time, allowing for what can be achieved and the level of control of existing relationships. It seems from this that the MOJ does not expect commercial organisations to put themselves in breach of existing contractual obligations.

Financial and commercial controls

6.77 Principle 1 refers to 'adequate bookkeeping, auditing and approval of expenditure' under this topic. These are subjects in their own right and serve business and control purposes that are not specific to an anti-bribery compliance programme. Nonetheless, such everyday controls have an important role to play in such programmes. For example, the approval process by which promotional expenditure is approved could require expenditure over a certain level to be approved by a manager of certain seniority depending on the level of the expenditure. While this serves the unrelated purpose of ensuring control on the costs of the commercial organisation, it can obviously be used to ensure that expensive hospitality is not provided without a senior manager being satisfied that it is for a genuine and proportionate business purpose.

Transparency and disclosure (record keeping)

6.78 Transparency of transactions and disclosure of information are topics mentioned under Principle 1 (proportionate procedures) for consideration. A commercial organisation which requires internal (and in some cases external) transparency and disclosure of information may be better placed to avoid an offence. For example, keeping track of the level of hospitality provided to a particular business contact over a period will allow the organisation to monitor whether there is a risk that it could be alleged that the contact is being corrupted by receipt of excessive entertainment.

6.79 Despite this Principle calling for transparency and disclosure, the Bribery Act 2010 does not create a 'books and records' offence. As noted elsewhere, however, the SFO has used the general offence in the Companies Act of failing to keep adequate accounting records[1] in connection with civil recovery cases with suspected incidents of bribery. The Principles do not expressly suggest any record-keeping procedures as part of an anti-bribery compliance programme. The potential importance of record keeping does feature in other resources, such as those published by Transparency International. The absence of a discrete discussion of record keeping in the Principles is perhaps surprising, because many policies are likely to be needed to be underpinned by record-keeping procedures that make the policy effective. A good example is the keeping of training records, where it will assist the organisation to know which and how many of its staff received anti-bribery training, and how recently.

[1]   Companies Act 2006, s 387 (previously Companies Act 1985, s 221).

Decision making

6.80 This topic gives as examples delegation of authorities, separation of functions and the avoidance of conflicts of interests. These first two concepts are perhaps part of others such as appropriate financial and commercial controls, which have been discussed above. Conflicts of interest are often dealt with in wider codes of conduct so as to avoid the appearance of impropriety.

Enforcement

6.81 Enforcement is an important part of an effective anti-bribery compliance programme. A commercial organisation will risk its programme being seen as 'inadequate' if it is not prepared to take firm action to deal with breaches. It is likely that a programme will, as set out above, have provided contractual protections both in the case of employees and third parties. To aid effective enforcement, the policy (and training given as part of the programme) could spell out the likely serious consequences of breach for employees and also for business partners so that it is clear, internally and externally alike, that breaches of the policy will not be tolerated and employment or third party contractual relationships terminated.

6.82 In addition, in large commercial organisations with particularly high risk exposures, a pre-determined procedure for investigating allegations or suspicions of bribery is sometimes included as part of the anti-bribery compliance programme so as to provide ease and consistency of response. See Chapter 10 for further detail on the approach to whistleblowing and the protections afforded to employees wishing to raise concerns.

6.83 As with all elements of an effective anti-bribery compliance programme, the policy needs to be applied in practice. If an allegation or suspicion of bribery is identified it should be addressed, rather than ignored. If a breach of policy is then confirmed, it will be important that it is treated seriously in accordance with any applicable policy statements and that robust sanctions are applied if merited. To do otherwise would undermine the adequacy of the programme, since weak enforcement may be perceived in the organisation as permitting miscreants (internal or external) to 'get away with it'.

'Speak up'/whistleblowing

6.84 One of the objects of anti-bribery compliance programmes is to create a culture of compliance. As part of that effort, commercial organisations wish to ensure that employees can 'speak up' about concerns without fear of it having an adverse impact on their careers. Such processes are considered in Principle 5 (communication), para 5.3. This can have a number of aspects. One is to encourage employees to voice concerns as part of their everyday role. For example, if an employee has concerns about the level of hospitality being offered to a business contact, they ought to be able to feel that their concern can be raised without fear. Employment policies may be tailored so as to recognise and even reward such behaviour, through performance review including assessments of ethical behaviour.

6.85 However, it is possible that employees may not feel able to raise their concerns in an open manner, particularly where those concerns are about the conduct of a colleague or manager. In some organisations, a general whistle-blowing policy may exist that provides a dedicated anonymous mail box or phone line on which to report concerns, and which expressly recognises the need for employees to report concerns, not just over possible bribery, confidentially and without fear of reprisal. Whistleblowing policies can be expressly linked to anti-bribery compliance, for example, by identifying concerns over possible bribery as an issue that might be raised through the whistleblowing arrangements and by highlighting the existence of such arrangements as part of the anti-bribery training.

6.86 Finally, as a complement to 'speaking up' and whistleblowing, some organisations specify in their policies a route for obtaining internal advice about the implementation of the policy and procedures in particularly difficult or novel circumstances.

Implementation processes

6.87 The Principle recognises that consideration will have to be given in the anti-bribery compliance programme to how it will be implemented, for example, in relation to different projects or parts of an organisation. This is unlikely to appear as part of the formal policies but rather is a concern of those charged with the implementation. It may be appropriate to tailor or focus the implementation of an anti-bribery compliance programme on those areas of the commercial organisation's activities which present the greatest bribery risks. For example, in a manufacturing business the risk of a shop-floor worker engaging in bribery so as to put the commercial organisation at risk of an offence might be assessed to be very low, whereas the risks of the sales staff engaging in such behaviour may be considerably higher, particularly if they are seeking large contracts in countries with known corruption risks for which they stand to earn significant commissions personally. It would be sensible to focus the roll-out of the policy and relevant training on the sales staff rather than provide a single blanket roll-out and training to all staff including those on the shop-floor.

F   PRINCIPLE 2: TOP LEVEL COMMITMENT

6.88

> 'The top-level management of a commercial organisation (be it a board of directors, the owners or any other equivalent body or person) are committed to preventing bribery by persons associated with it. They foster a culture within the organisation in which bribery is never acceptable'.

6.89 As with any important activity undertaken by a commercial organisation, senior leadership and the clear allocation of responsibility is essential. The approach taken by the six Principles and other resources is to look to the most senior management in a commercial organisation both to commit to the anti-bribery compliance programme and to spread the anti-bribery message through the organisation from the top-down. The Principle identifies top-level management commitment as encompassing communication of the policy and an appropriate degree of supervision of developing the programme. Top-level commitment is sometimes referred to as setting the 'tone from the top' and as being the first step in creating a 'culture of compliance' throughout the organisation. For this reason, anti-bribery compliance is often combined with other compliance programmes in larger commercial organisations as part of an attempt to create a culture of ethical business behaviour in all employees from the top down, rather than it being separated into a stand-alone programme.

6.90 Depending on the size of the organisation, mechanisms by which top-level commitment can be demonstrated include the formal adoption of the anti-bribery compliance programme or an anti-bribery statement by the Board, the nomination of an anti-bribery champion on the Board, an introduction by the Chairman or Chief Executive to any published policies, and podcasts from the Chairman or Chief Executive as part of any training materials rolled out to employees. Principle 2 sets out in para 2.3 in some detail examples of what a top-level statement of the commercial organisation's commitment to ethical behaviour might include.

6.91 As for the leadership/supervision element of top-level commitment, para 2.4 of the Principle recognises that this will vary by size of organisation and provides a list of elements that will be encompassed by it. These include the top-level management delegating leadership of the anti-bribery compliance programme to senior managers while retaining responsibility for high profile and critical decision-making as well as providing leadership and visibility in communication of top-level commitment to anti-bribery compliance both internally and externally. Transparency International recognises the likelihood of a project manager being appointed to implement the anti-bribery compliance programme.

6.92 However, Principle 2 might risk confusion. As set out in Principle 2, 'top level management' means the 'board of directors, the owners or any other equivalent body or person' as that is the terminology used in parenthesis. It is true that a clear commitment to an anti-bribery compliance programme from the Board, as the highest organ of a company, is likely to be an important part of making such a programme effective by setting an appropriate culture. However, at least in the case of larger commercial organisations, it is unrealistic to expect 'top-level management' (as defined in the Principle) to necessarily be involved in the detail of matters referred to in other Principles.

6.93 Principle 2 should not be read so as to mean that the Board is necessarily expected to have hands-on involvement in the implementation of an anti-bribery compliance programme, particularly in its application to day-to-day business. While ultimate responsibility for implementation of an anti-bribery compliance programme will rest with the Board and the Board ought to set the 'tone from the top', medium to large businesses are likely to delegate day-to-day responsibility to managers who are not on the Board, not only for implementation of the whole programme itself but also for its application in specific business situations.

G   PRINCIPLE 3: RISK ASSESSMENT

6.94

'The commercial organisation assesses the nature and extent of its exposure to potential **external and internal** risks of bribery on its behalf by persons associated with it. The assessment is **periodic, informed and documented**'.

6.95 The starting point under the six Principles and other resources for the design of an anti-bribery programme is for the commercial organisation to assess its bribery-related risks. This process of risk-assessment is likely to be fundamental to the design of an 'adequate' anti-bribery compliance programme. By identifying the specific risks that are relevant to it, the organisation will be able to tailor its anti-bribery compliance programme to meet those risks and to avoid unnecessarily complex and costly procedures that are inappropriate to its circumstances. While this does not automatically mean that the procedures adopted in response to a risk assessment will be 'adequate', a risk-based approach does allow for greater clarity in considering the range of possible responses to each specific risk and the application of the necessary judgement to decide which of the available procedures to implement.

6.96 Risk assessment is not binary: its outcome is not necessarily either an overall high or low risk. The objective of a risk assessment exercise should be to describe both the overall risk to the commercial organisation and the specific risks an organisation faces. A commercial organisation operating in an overall lower risk environment may nonetheless identify specific risks which are higher and which justify targeted procedures.

6.97 The MOJ final guidance suggests a number of possible risk assessment procedures. First of all, management should have oversight of the risk assessment process and be satisfied that those tasked with such process have the necessary internal authority, resources, skills, knowledge of the business and objectivity to perform the task competently. Reviews of existing policies and procedures, the organisation's history of bribery-type incidents and any complaints or whistleblowing logs and internal audit or investigation reports can all provide useful information. Ultimately, however, there is little substitute for those carrying out the risk assessment engaging with employees working in the business, through interviews, group meetings or focus groups. The output of the risk assessment process should be documented.

6.98 As well as looking at the specific risks relevant to it, a commercial organisation can usefully spend time understanding the different ways in which an offence could be committed by, or affect, it. These include:

— the commercial organisation itself committing a primary bribery offence through the involvement of sufficiently senior management. This is perhaps a particular risk in SMEs where owner-managers or senior managers are more likely to be involved in many practical day-to-day decisions, such as the engagement of agents overseas or the giving of corporate hospitality. Even in larger organisations, operational procedures may be such as to escalate decisions on matters which could amount to an offence to Board-level;

— in a group situation, the actions of a sister company (Company X) of a commercial organisation which is subject to s 7 (Company Y), can lead to liability for Company Y if Company X is performing services for or on behalf of Company Y and, is thus, an 'associated person' of Company Y and it seeks to win business for Y. The scope of the 'associated person' concept in group situations is discussed in Chapter 4. However, examples of where this risk might arise are situations where Company Y's products or services manufactured or provided out of the UK are marketed in an overseas market by its sister Company X, which acts as its agent or distributor in that foreign market. This possibility raises the question of how far a group of companies, some of which are subject to the primary offences, some of which are commercial organisations within s 7 and some of which are not subject directly to the Bribery Act 2010 at all, should go in organising an anti-bribery compliance programme across the group by reference to the expectation of 'adequate procedures' for the purposes of the defence under the Bribery Act 2010 or whether it should seek to focus only on those parts of the group which expose it to risk under the Bribery Act 2010, which is considered above;

— a well-intentioned (but misguided) employee, motivated simply by a desire to obtain business for the commercial organisation, engaging in bribery. Given the scope of the Bribery Act 2010 this could, for example, occur through the extravagant use of corporate hospitality or similar promotional expenditure perhaps in respect of a foreign public official, or through an employee foolishly acceding to a request for a bribe in order to win a contract. The employee believes they are doing the best for their employer, but in reality is creating serious problems both for themselves and for the employer. Risks of this kind are best addressed by creating a culture of ethical behaviour within the organisation and through training;

— an ill-intentioned employee engaging in bribery for personal gain, for example a sales executive who is partly remunerated on a commission-basis and who bribes in order to generate sales for his employer and boost their commission. The risk of conduct of this sort is present in almost every organisation, but the effect of s 7 is now to make the employer, prima facie, liable for the rogue employee. This risk is always difficult to manage but can be addressed both by the creation of a culture of ethical behaviour (including training) and in particular by strong enforcement of policies in the case of identified breaches;

— a business partner who is clearly an 'associated person' for s 7 purposes, such as a consultant or agent, engaging in bribery to win business for the commercial organisation. This risk is one of the major ones faced by businesses under the Bribery Act 2010;

— a more remote 'associated person' engaging in bribery to win business for the commercial organisation. The scope of the concept of 'associated person' under s 7 is discussed at paras **6.69–6.76**, but it is possible for more remote parties than just agents or consultants to be 'associated persons'. In certain circumstances this could include joint ventures, consortia partners and suppliers where there is a risk that they might be performing services for the commercial organisation;

— the commercial organisation receiving a bribe and thus committing an offence under s 2. An example might be an organisation which agrees to do 'a favour' for a competitor on one tender in return for it being given preferential treatment on another. This risk is sometimes overlooked, but it is certainly feasible for a corporation to commit the s 2 offence. It can be addressed by ensuring that the relevant parts of the anti-bribery compliance programme make it clear that the acceptance of anything which might be regarded as an inducement to the organisation to act improperly is prohibited.

— the commercial organisation itself being the victim of bribery, through an employee receiving a bribe from a supplier in return for that employee approving the engagement of that supplier on disadvantageous terms for his employer.

6.99 The MOJ final guidance gives examples of risk factors, both internal and external to the organisation. The external risks are broken down into five categories:

— country risk (ie whether the commercial organisation does business in countries with a reputation for corruption);

— sectoral risk (ie some sectors are known to have greater risks than others);

— transaction risk (ie risks associated with specific kinds of transaction such as charitable or political donations);

— business opportunity risk (ie risks arising from the nature of the opportunity such as high value contracts); and

— business partnership risk (ie risks associated with relationships with business partners).

6.100 In assessing these external risk factors faced by a commercial organisation a number of issues arise, some of which are relevant under a number of the different categories:

— **Country** Does the commercial organisation do business in or through countries with reputations for high levels of corruption? In assessing this it is important that reference is not made just to presumptions about the ethical standards of particular countries or regions. Transparency International publishes a 'Corruption Perceptions Index' which seeks to measure the perceived levels of public sector corruption around the world as well as other resources. These reveal that general presumptions can often be wrong. For example, some countries within the EU are, according to Transparency International, perceived to have appreciably greater levels of public sector corruption than some countries in less developed parts of the world such as the Middle East, Asia and Africa. Transparency International also publishes a 'Bribe Payers Index' which seeks to rank 22 of the world's largest economies by the likelihood of their companies paying bribes abroad and also to rank the likelihood of corruption in business sectors. The World Bank publishes its 'Governance Indicators', which are a further source of objective information about country risk.

— **Sector** Does the commercial organisation have operations in business sectors which have had known corruption problems? The discussion at para 3.5 of Principle 3 gives examples of extractive industries and large-scale infrastructure. Other examples of business sectors with histories of corruption problems (mostly from the US experience of enforcing the FCPA) include: defence, heavy manufacturing, construction and real estate, pharmaceuticals and healthcare, freight forwarding and logistics, and oil and gas support services. As mentioned above, Transparency International's 'Bribe Payers Index' includes rankings of industrial sectors by the likelihood of corruption within that sector and that is a useful further check, as are publicly available resources on trends in anti-bribery enforcement around the world. Commercial organisations with operations in sectors identified as high risk ought to take into account that their anti-bribery compliance programme may need to be more extensive than if they operated only in lower risk sectors.

— **Transaction** Is the commercial organisation involved in transactions which may carry higher risk? The Principle suggests that charitable or political donations, applications for licences or permits and public procurement all carry such higher risk. To this list might be added activities such as extensive use of corporate hospitality/ entertainment/gift giving by the organisation as part of its everyday activities. In some business sectors, such as the leisure and entertainment industry, it is likely that there will be extensive use of such promotional activities. The increased risks of an offence being committed are obvious.

— **Business opportunity** Does the manner in which the commercial organisation carries on its business increase its exposure to bribery problems? This covers a variety of factors, but examples include:

- reliance on external 'associated persons', such as agents, representatives and consultants as an important part of the way in which business is done in many locations;
- use of commission either for employees or external agents as an incentive; and
- does the organisation sell its products 'at the factory gate' at arm's length prices determined by an active market? Or are its products/services routinely or, even occasionally, sold in one-off, large, contracts worth many millions of pounds? The latter is likely to present greater opportunity and temptation to engage in bribery than the former.

— **Business partnership** Is the commercial organisation involved in higher risk relationships? Obvious examples are the use of third parties such as agents and consultants, relationships with foreign public officials or politically exposed persons, as well as other situations where the actions of third parties could lead to consequences for the commercial organisation such as joint ventures or involvement in consortia.

6.101 It is notable that some of the risk factors can aggregate (and perhaps even have a tendency to do so). For example, many oil and gas fields are located in less politically and economically stable parts of the world which rank poorly on the 'Corruption Perceptions Index'. It is often the case that in these parts of the world, companies from developed countries believe that they will find it difficult to do business or they are required by local laws to have a local business partner. They therefore enter business relationships with business partners, such as an agent or local representative or joint venture partner. This business partner is often somebody who has significant connections, commercial or political, in that country. All three risk factors in this example should therefore be assessed as high: this is a high-risk business sector, the operations are in a high-risk country and the commercial organisation has chosen or been required to be in a relationship with a business partner whose actions might lead to liability for the organisation. This combination of factors would point to the company having an extensive anti-bribery compliance programme, designed to meet these particular risks.

6.102 Examples of internal risks given in the Principle include:

(1)   remuneration policies (such as a bonus culture rewarding risk taking or perhaps simply a commission-based system);
(2)   lack of knowledge of the anti-bribery compliance programme;
(3)   lack of awareness on the part of employees as to the bribery risk generated by the organisation's business profile;
(4)   the organisation's remuneration structures; and
(5)   unclear policies on such things as corporate entertainment and gifts.

6.103 External assistance might be sought in carrying out the risk assessment. While this may make sense for some larger organisations, in many cases it may not be appropriate or necessary. Engaging external advisers may be expensive and, in any event, it is those who are involved in the business day-to-day who are likely to have the best understanding of how it operates in detail.

6.104 Finally, given that an 'adequate' anti-bribery compliance programme will involve some form of monitoring and review (see Principle 6) it is likely that risk assessment will be an ongoing process. As the MOJ final guidance states, businesses evolve and external circumstances change. Accordingly, the anti-bribery compliance programme ought to cater for the future assessment of risks either at pre-determined dates or upon the occurrence of certain events, such as the entering of new markets or business sectors: see para **6.108**.

H   PRINCIPLE 4: DUE DILIGENCE

6.105

> 'The commercial organisation applies due diligence procedures, taking a proportionate and risk based approach, in respect of persons who perform or will perform services for or on behalf of the organisation, in order to mitigate identified bribery risks'.

6.106 Due diligence has often been used, certainly by larger organisations, as a general business tool to assist in assessing the risks presented by business opportunities, particularly when entering relationships with unfamiliar counterparties or in new markets. This assists the organisation in identifying business risks presented by the opportunity which may not be immediately obvious. The commentary to Principle 4 recognises this role of due diligence as a part of good corporate governance.

6.107 As an extension of this general use of due diligence by businesses, it is now deemed an important part of an anti-bribery compliance programme specifically. Its significance is described in Principle 4, para 4.1, 'in bribery risk mitigation' as such to justify 'its inclusion as a separate Principle in its own right'. It is given similar prominence in many other resources. By conducting due diligence on potential business partners and markets, a commercial organisation will be better able to assess whether there is anything to suggest that the potential partner might conduct themselves unethically and thus risk liability for the organisation or whether involvement in a particular market carries with it a high risk of corruption in the business environment there. It can then decide whether to enter the relationship or market at all and, if so, whether it wishes to seek to put in place additional protections so as to reduce the risks identified. The Principle emphasises that due diligence should take 'a proportionate and risk based approach'. What is appropriate for any particular situation will vary 'enormously'.

When?

6.108 The obvious times when due diligence will be required are the entering into of new business relationships or new markets. In a comprehensive anti-bribery compliance programme in a larger organisation, it may be the case that specific processes are introduced that require due diligence to be conducted on potential business partners, or at least considered, before the partner can be engaged. In a smaller organisation, due diligence may be undertaken on a more ad hoc basis, although it nonetheless makes sense for the possible need for due diligence to be highlighted within the anti-bribery compliance programme and included within any training materials. The Quick Start Guide seeks to offer comfort to smaller businesses on the question of due diligence in particular.

6.109 *'Adequate procedures' in practice*

Who?

6.109 In keeping with the risk-based approach it is possible to limit due diligence by reference to the risk posed by the particular proposed relationship. It may make sense to first consider whether the relationship is with someone who may be expected to be performing services for or on behalf of the commercial organisation and may therefore be an 'associated person'. If the potential business partner may indeed be an 'associated person', then a consideration of the nature and importance of the potential relationship will help to identify the extent of the due diligence called for. For example, para 4.3 draws a distinction between a low-risk contract for IT services as against a high-risk engagement of a party to act as an intermediary in foreign markets.

How much due diligence?

6.110 Due diligence can take a variety of forms from simple 'desk-top reviews' based on internet searches through to the instruction of specialist external consultants to conduct detailed enquiries. Potentially high value or important relationships, the use of obviously 'associated persons', such as agents, or entry into new markets may require extensive due diligence. By contrast, conducting due diligence on small, routine, every-day relationships with parties who are low risk beyond some simple desk-top searches of the internet may be disproportionate to the risk and value involved. The Quick Start Guide provides a useful discussion of how an SME might approach this issue.

What should the due diligence cover?

6.111 The due diligence should aim to elicit information of practical use to the commercial organisation when deciding whether to take up a business relationship or enter a new market and, if so, what protections it should put in place to mitigate any identified risks. It should therefore cover the reputation of the potential business partner in order to establish whether there have been allegations of unethical behaviour. The programme might also require, as part of that due diligence process or parallel to it, that the commercial organisation seek to satisfy itself as to the anti-bribery processes applied by the potential business partner. Copies of any anti-bribery policies or procedures operated by the potential business partner should be obtained where possible and reviewed. As for market risk, the due diligence should aim to identify the operational risks presented by the legal, political and business landscape, as well as the country's reputation for corruption using such tools as the 'Corruption Perceptions Index'.

I   PRINCIPLE 5: COMMUNICATION (INCLUDING TRAINING)

6.112

'The commercial organisation seeks to ensure that its bribery prevention policies and procedures are embedded and understood throughout the organisation

198

through internal and external communication, including training, that is proportionate to the risks it faces'.

6.113 It is obvious that even the most sophisticated anti-bribery compliance programme will be of no value (and unlikely to be 'adequate') if it makes no provision for its effective implementation through communicating it throughout the organisation and, should the risks and organisational size and structure necessitate it, providing training. The anti-bribery compliance programme will therefore need to specify how it is to be communicated. In an SME, where it will be easier to implement the procedures simply because of the more compact nature of the organisation, the plans for implementation are likely to be less extensive given the smaller numbers of people and the likely simpler nature of the business. In a large organisation, the process of communication will be more complex and require greater planning and is likely to involve some training element.

Documentation

6.114 The documents through which the policy and procedures will be communicated need to reflect the target audience, be written with an appropriate level of detail and with the right tone. What may be appropriate for internal use is likely to differ from the statements that a commercial organisation wishes to make externally to shareholders and business partners; what is appropriate internally for senior managers may not be appropriate for more junior members of staff. The extent of the policies and their content is considered at paras **6.45–6.49**.

Communication/publicity

6.115 As part of the roll-out of any new corporate policy or programme, publicity will be important in the effective implementation of an anti-bribery compliance programme, even in an SME. Depending on the size of the organisation, the anti-bribery compliance programme can be publicised in a variety of ways. Hard copies of important policies can be sent to key categories of staff, presentations can be laid on, to be followed by training as necessary. Those documents will likely be made available on internal internet sites. The organisation may wish to promote its programme externally, if only by including copies of important policies on its website (Transparency International promotes the publication by a commercial organisation of detailed information on the implementation of its anti-bribery compliance programme through its 'Reporting Guidance'). The organisation may also be prepared to provide copies to its potential or existing business partners on request in much the same way that the anti-bribery compliance programme might require the organisation to obtain such policies from third parties as part of its due diligence processes.

Training

6.116 Training may be an important part of implementation, particularly if there are sufficient employees who are likely to face bribery risks in their day-to-day roles. Principle 5 indicates that whether training is required is a matter of proportionality. Training can be delivered in a variety of ways, for example, through e-learning modules, as part of a suite of general compliance training or as bespoke training to different categories of employees or management in accordance with the bribery risks they are likely to face in practice. The training could be prioritised so that those facing higher risks are trained before, and then more often, than those in lower risk areas. In smaller and lower risk commercial organisations, the training may consist of little more than a presentation on the introduction of the new policy, its key features and application to the organisation followed by a general discussion. In larger or higher risk commercial organisations, the training is likely to be more detailed and could include problem scenarios and even multiple-choice questions.

6.117 In setting up the training element of an anti-bribery compliance programme, it will be important to cover both the commercial organisation's existing employees when the programme is rolled out for the first time and subsequent new joiners. New joiners can often be catered for as part of an induction programme which often already contains some element of compliance or business ethics training. In any event, training will be most effective when it is repeated at appropriate intervals: anti-bribery training should therefore not been seen as a one-time obligation to be discharged and then forgotten about. This is not a new concept for commercial organisations. Case law has previously asserted that training, to be effective and implemented fully, needs to be updated regularly and a system established to periodically ensure that training is adequate and, where necessary, that re-training be provided. See for example *Tesco Supermarkets Ltd v Nattrass*[1] and *Croydon London Borough Council v Pinch A Pound (UK) Ltd*[2].

[1]   [1972] AC 153, [1971] 2 All ER 127.
[2]   [2010] EWHC 3283 (Admin), [2010] All ER (D) 162 (Dec).

6.118 Given the risks presented by the acts of business partners who are 'associated persons' for the purposes of s 7, an organisation should consider whether it may be appropriate for those business partners to be required to receive training from the commercial organisation so that it can be satisfied that those parties are aware of the risks and of the expected and acceptable standards of behaviour. While it will be for a commercial organisation to assess whether a particular business partner ought to be trained, business partners who operate in higher risk jurisdictions or sectors, those remunerated on a commission basis and those who are a significant source of business (whether in respect of a few large contracts or many smaller ones) all present examples of higher risks to the commercial organisation which might well justify training being given to the business partner. The possibility of obtaining contractual protections on this front is considered at para **6.74**.

6.119 The content of the training programme will vary by commercial organisation, but might cover a basic overview of the Bribery Act 2010, the risks presented to the organisation (and importantly its employees as individuals) under the Bribery Act 2010 and the policy and procedures that the organisation has to combat these risks. The fact that anti-bribery compliance is not just a problem for the employer can be emphasised; the fact that the individual employee responsible for the act of bribery will be guilty and face imprisonment may be salutary. A focus on examples of difficult topics or situations that might be faced in the particular organisation in the real world will assist in illustrating the line between acceptable and unacceptable behaviour. These difficult areas might include: examples of what is acceptable to provide (if anything) by way of corporate hospitality or gift; the special situation of foreign public officials and the difference between facilitation payments and cases of extortion. Identification of the availability of advice and whistleblowing support could also be given.

Enforcement

6.120 As mentioned at para **6.83**, and at Chapter 10, it is important that allegations or suspicions of bribery are addressed appropriately and any breaches of policy result in the appropriate sanction. This has the effect of reinforcing the ethical culture: to brush allegations or suspicions under the carpet, or to fail to impose appropriate sanctions, will undermine the policy.

J   PRINCIPLE 6: MONITORING AND REVIEW

6.121

'The commercial organisation monitors and reviews procedures designed to prevent bribery by persons associated with it and makes improvements where necessary'.

6.122 This final Principle is an important element of making an anti-bribery compliance programme effective and thus 'adequate'. A system of monitoring and reviewing the operation of the specific procedures that make up the anti-bribery compliance programme serves three purposes:

(1)   it will identify any internal or external developments which may necessitate changes to the programme;

(2)   it will assist in identifying any systemic weaknesses in the procedures themselves; and

(3)   it may also identify instances of non-compliance with the procedures by employees or other 'associated persons'.

The business of the commercial organisation will inevitably evolve over time. New business opportunities will emerge, new products will be developed, new customers won and new markets opened up. This evolution may have the effect of altering the bribery risks faced. External conditions may also alter. An existing country or market may become unstable due to political factors. New anti-bribery resources might become available or the MOJ final guidance might be updated. An incident of bribery in a competitor may receive publicity and be prosecuted (whether in the UK or abroad, eg under the FCPA) which may highlight deficiencies in the commercial organisation's own procedures. The experience gained through the day-to-day operation of the programme can also be an impetus for changes to the anti-bribery compliance programme in order to make it more effective. For example, it might be the case that one part of the programme is generating a disproportionate number of queries to a helpline, which may indicate a lack of clarity in that part of the programme. Other procedures imposed by the programme might be hampering business efficiency unnecessarily. Feedback from employees on the efficacy and ease of operation (or otherwise) of the anti-bribery compliance programme in practice, along with suggestions for improvements, could be encouraged by the written policies.

6.123 How this monitoring is carried out will depend on the nature of the organisation's systems and controls. For example, in the case of financial limits and approvals, systems might be put in place to ensure that an invoice or an expenses claim for a corporate hospitality event is approved for payment by the accounts department. The accounts department could be required to check that the necessary approvals within the requirements of the anti-bribery compliance programme were obtained as well as updating records. In addition to this kind of monitoring, which itself forms part of the front line controls, specific targeted monitoring can be undertaken. If a commercial organisation has an internal audit function, compliance with the anti-bribery compliance programme can sensibly be added to the list of matters they consider when auditing a relevant part of the organisation. This will provide an objective check on the effectiveness of the programme. The Principle also suggests staff surveys, questions and feedback from training can provide another source of monitoring information. Certification of compliance from business unit heads may also feature as reporting mechanism. Two potentially difficult areas are monitoring compliance with the anti-bribery compliance programme by the organisation's overseas offices and by business partners (even more so when they too are overseas). The compliance programme could provide special monitoring arrangements for these situations, for example, by making them the subject of more frequent or more in-depth internal audit visits or requiring 'sign-offs' of compliance with the programme from the head of the overseas office or the business partner at appropriate regular intervals. As for the challenges presented by business partners, a right to monitor their compliance with their own or the commercial organisation's anti-bribery compliance programme, as the case may be, can form part of the suite of contractual protections for the commercial organisations as discussed above. There may well be significant practical difficulties in enforcing such rights and, in the event that monitoring is not permitted to the reasonable satisfaction of the commercial organisation, that may constitute a due-diligence type warning that the relationship with the partner ought to be terminated.

Planning for review

6.124 Thought should be given as to when the anti-bribery compliance programme, no matter how limited or extensive, will be reviewed. In that context, establishing a date on which a review will be performed ought to be included in the procedures themselves. In an SME this may be nothing more than putting a note in a diary for some future date. In a larger organisation this review period might be formally recorded in the procedures documentation and could even be broken down into a rolling plan for review of different elements of the programme over time. In a more comprehensive programme the executives charged with its day-to-day management should also be aware of the possibility of external or internal trigger events which ought to precipitate a review of some or all of the elements of the programme.

Reporting and external review

6.125 Given the responsibilities of the directors, especially of those companies with public share listings, it is likely that the whole Board or the audit committee will want to receive periodic reports on the performance of the organisation's anti-bribery compliance programme from those charged with its supervision day-to-day and from more senior executives who have responsibility for the programme up to an including the Chief Executive. Public companies sometimes include information on their 'corporate social responsibility' or 'business ethics' programmes in their Annual Report as a way of demonstrating their commitment to ethical business conduct, in keeping with the suggestion in Principle 2 (top-level commitment).

6.126 Finally, the discussion of Principle 6 acknowledges that a commercial organisation might want to seek an external, independent review of the effectiveness of the anti-bribery compliance programme. While having some obvious benefits, such an exercise may be expensive and disruptive. It is debatable that this step would ever be required (in the sense of being a necessary part of an 'adequate' anti-bribery compliance programme) except perhaps in the cases of commercial organisations which have experienced problems with bribery in the past and those with a very high risk exposure. The Principle notes at para 6.4 that an external certification does not necessarily mean that the anti-bribery compliance programme is in fact 'adequate' for the purposes of the defence.

K   THE CASE STUDIES

6.127 The MOJ final guidance also provides 11 case studies which are intended to illustrate and complement the Principles. These scenarios are expressly stated not to form part of the guidance required by s 9 and are not intended to set standards, establish any presumption or reflect a minimum baseline or be appropriate for all organisations. The scenarios are all based on possible real-life scenarios and examine the anti-bribery steps that could be taken in response to the specific scenario. The studies are primarily focused on scenarios facing small to medium-sized companies and the international aspects of bribery risks rather than domestic risks. They cover:

(1)   facilitation payments (medium-sized company, overseas);
(2)   proportionate procedures (small to medium-sized company, domestic);
(3)   joint venture (medium-sized company, overseas);
(4)   hospitality and promotional expenditure (a partnership, overseas);
(5)   assessing risks (small company, overseas);
(6)   due diligence of agents (medium to large company, overseas);
(7)   communicating and training (small company, overseas);
(8)   community benefits and charitable donations (company, overseas);
(9)   due diligence of agents (small company, overseas);
(10)   top-level commitment (small to medium-sized company, overseas); and
(11)   proportionate procedures (small company, overseas).

The case studies are of some practical use and provide, particularly for SMEs, useful illustrations of the six Principles. However, they are short and do not provide any critical or quantitative analysis of the issues raised under the scenarios. Therefore, while helpful, they only take the MOJ final guidance a little further.

KEY POINTS FROM CHAPTER 6

6.128 Key points from this chapter are:

- The 'adequate procedures' defence is the only defence available to s 7.
- There are no 'safe harbours'.
- There are no one-size-fits-all 'adequate procedures'.
- Instead, the government has formulated six Principles to guide commercial organisations through the establishment of an anti-bribery compliance programme.
- The first step is for a commercial organisation to conduct a risk assessment to identify its particular exposure to liability under the Bribery Act 2010.
- Using its understanding of the risks it faces, the commercial organisation can then tailor a proportionate anti-bribery compliance programme to its circumstances as best it can.
- There will remain a risk that any anti-bribery compliance programme will, in hindsight, be found to have been 'inadequate' and thus it will not work as a defence to s 7.
- However, the defence only has to be demonstrated on a balance of probabilities rather than beyond reasonable doubt.
- Commercial organisations can put themselves in the best position to obtain the protection of the defence by adopting procedures which are clearly aimed at creating a culture of zero-tolerance of bribery within the organisation.
- Particular risk issues for consideration in the commercial organisation's anti-bribery compliance programme include relationships with third parties who may be 'associated persons', the use of corporate hospitality, gifts and promotional expenditure (especially foreign public officials) as well as the making of political and charitable donations and the prohibition of so-called 'facilitation payments'.

Chapter 7

THE INTERNATIONAL PERSPECTIVE: LESSONS FROM US AUTHORITIES' ENFORCEMENT OF THE FOREIGN CORRUPT PRACTICES ACT

A   INTRODUCTION

7.1 The Bribery Act 2010's broad and largely undefined terms will leave much to the discretion of the prosecutors who will enforce it, most notably the Serious Fraud Office ('SFO'). This uncertainty has generated significant interest and apprehension among both corporates and individuals seeking to comply with the new law. While recent guidance from the UK government provides some insight into the potential interpretation of the Act[1], the Act nonetheless remains a mosaic that is largely unfilled. In order to gain insight into the possible interpretation and enforcement of the Bribery Act, it is helpful to look at the development, interpretation and enforcement of other anti-corruption Acts. In that regard, the United States' three decades of experience enforcing the US Foreign Corrupt Practices Act of 1977 ('FCPA')[2] may well be the most instructive.

[1] See paras **7.39**, **7.41**, **7.44** (discussing the MOJ's final guidance of 30 March 2011 and the SFO's 2009 'Approach of the Serious Fraud Office to Dealing with Overseas Corruption').
[2] Public Law 95-213, 91 Stat 1494 (codified as amended at 15 USC §§ 78m(b)(2)–(5), 78dd-1, 78dd-2, 78dd-3, 78ff(c)).

7.2 Although the FCPA's prohibitions and penalties were amended several times in the first two decades following its 1977 enactment until 1998, the Act was rarely enforced before 1998. Not so today. From 1998 to present, and particularly after 2006, US enforcement of the FCPA has grown exponentially. Nonetheless, there have been few FCPA cases that have been litigated all the way to court decisions, so the body of FCPA 'precedent' consists largely of negotiated dispositions between defendants and US enforcement authorities rather than judicial opinions. It is likely that the unlimited fines and even broader reach of the UK Bribery Act 2010 will similarly encourage defendants to resolve Bribery Act investigations through negotiated dispositions, thereby giving the SFO considerable leverage over the practical application of the Act—provided that UK judges' hostility towards negotiated dispositions does not rein in prosecutors' discretion.

7.3 The US experience under the FCPA provides several lessons regarding the possible enforcement of the Bribery Act 2010. Because there will always be pressure to make corrupt payments and evade anti-corruption laws, enforcement authorities in the US have responded by interpreting the FCPA broadly and increasing enforcement activity over time. US enforcement authorities have interpreted the FCPA's provisions broadly regarding the definitions of statutory terms such as 'foreign official', 'obtain or retain business', and 'anything of value'. Enforcement authorities have likewise applied the FCPA's jurisdictional provisions very broadly to corporates outside the US, and have applied successor liability to corporates that acquire other organisations that have made corrupt payments. Finally, these enforcement authorities (primarily the Department of Justice ('DOJ') and the Securities and Exchange Commission ('SEC')) have coordinated their activities with one another and have also increased their cooperation with international law enforcement partners.

7.4 These developments have combined to create a dramatic increase in FCPA enforcement. For example, in the nine-year period from 1998 through 2006, US authorities brought 89 FCPA-related enforcement actions; in the following four years US authorities brought 222 FCPA-related enforcement actions, an annual rate nearly 4.6 times greater than that from 1998 through 2006[1]. Corporates paid approximately $142 million in criminal and other penalties from 1998 through 2006 to resolve FCPA-related criminal investigations; from 2007 through 2010, corporates paid approximately $3.4 billion to resolve such investigations, an average annual amount of nearly 53 times the average annual amount from 1998 through 2006[2].

[1] See para **7.92**.
[2] See para **7.93**.

7.5 The broad interpretation of the FCPA, coupled with increased enforcement and penalties, has caused great uncertainty and unease among businesses subject to the FCPA. The US government has gradually provided some guidance in the form of advisory opinions and other guidance. This guidance, however, has been of limited value because the advisory opinion process has been rarely used, the government's guidance is narrowly limited to the particular facts of each request, and the government has expressly refused to attach any 'precedential' value to the opinions.

7.6 These trends may well be replicated in the UK. Although the SFO has expressed its intent to exercise carefully its prosecutorial discretion[1], the US example over the past 30-plus years suggests that such restraint may gradually erode, particularly in the face of complex and creative efforts to evade the Act's prohibitions. And enforcement authorities' broad discretion over the interpretation of the Bribery Act will present fertile conditions for increased anti-bribery-related prosecutions and monetary penalties.

[1] See Christopher M Matthews, SFO Director: No 'Safe Harbor' under New UK Bribery Law, MainJustice.com, 20 October 2010 (reporting that SFO Director Richard Alderman 'said the SFO would exercise prosecutorial discretion when deciding whether to probe the [gift or hospitality] payment in question' and that the Director said 'Sensible, proportionate expenditure is perfectly lawful, and remains lawful under the [Bribery Act]'), available at www.mainjustice.com/justanticorruption/2010/10/20/sfo-director-no-safe-harbor-under-new-u-k-bribery-law (last visited 10 January 2011) (subscription required).

7.7 The UK thus may find it a challenge to fashion a system of providing official compliance guidance to corporates while preserving the prerogatives of prosecutors, but such guidance will be sorely needed by corporates subject to the Act: uncertainty regarding the interpretation and enforcement of the law breeds criticisms that compliance is unduly costly, interferes with legitimate business activity, or creates an unlevel playing field for global business.

7.8 This chapter addresses these and other lessons from the FCPA. First, this chapter provides a brief history and summary of the FCPA. Second, this chapter explains the effects of shared enforcement responsibility between multiple enforcement agencies, enforcement policy guidance, and broader guidance as to corporate prosecutions and effective compliance and ethics programs. Finally, this chapter analyses trends in US enforcement authorities' interpretation of the FCPA's substantive provisions and such authorities' enforcement activity. Throughout, this chapter will offer insight as to lessons UK authorities and corporations can draw from the more than 30 years of US experience with the FCPA.

B   HISTORY AND SUMMARY OF THE FCPA

Historical context

7.9 The FCPA was born of several US political developments in the 1970s. The FCPA was a direct result of the investigation resulting from the infamous Watergate burglary in 1972 and the involvement of President Nixon and other officials in his administration with the burglary and resulting cover-up. The Office of the Special Prosecutor empowered to investigate Watergate charged several public companies and executive officers with making illegal US political contributions with corporate funds[1]. In 1974, the SEC concluded that this misuse of public company assets should have been disclosed to investors[2] and undertook to investigate the use of so-called corporate 'slush funds' to effect the illegal contributions[3].

[1]   See Report of the Securities and Exchange Commission on Questionable and Illegal Corporate Payments and Practices, Submitted to the Commission on Banking, Housing and Urban Affairs, 94th Cong, 2d Sess at 2 (Comm Print, May 12, 1976) ('SEC Report').
[2]   US SEC, Corporation Finance Division, Views on Disclosure of Illegal Campaign Contributions, Rel Nos 33-5,466, 34-10,673, 35-18,315, 40-8,265 (8 March 1974), 39 Fed Reg 10,237 (19 March 1974).
[3]   SEC Report at 3–7.

7.10 Through investigations and a voluntary disclosure program, the SEC discovered that such funds were also being used to effect payments to foreign officials[1]. Ultimately, more than $300 million in questionable or outright illegal payments from corporate funds to foreign officials, politicians, and political parties by more than 400 corporates, including 117 in the Fortune 500, were uncovered[2].

[1]   SEC Report at 25–27.
[2]   See HR Rep 95-640, at 4 (1977).

7.11 These disclosures attracted considerable public attention. Particularly notorious were the disclosures concerning Lockheed Aircraft Corporation which, as recently as 1971, had secured the federal government's guarantee of up to $250 million in loans necessary to keep the corporation in business[1]. As a condition of settling the SEC's enforcement action, Lockheed's board appointed a special committee to investigate its use of corrupt payments[2]. The special committee's May 1977 report concluded, among other things, that Lockheed made between $30 and 38 million in questionable payments to foreign officials during the six-year period ending 28 December 1976[3]. The prior disclosure of these payments through congressional hearings and media reports significantly undermined US foreign policy, ultimately resulting in the resignation and criminal conviction of the Japanese prime minister, destabilisation of the Dutch monarchy, and substantial election gains for the Communist Party in Italy[4]. Throughout 1976 and 1977, Congress held hearings and proposed legislation to address the conduct of these public companies.

[1] See Lockheed Bribery: Hearings Before the Senate Committee on Banking, Housing and Urban Affairs, 94th Cong 1 (1975) (statement of Senator William Proxmire).

[2] Report of the Special Review Committee of the Board of Directors of Lockheed Aircraft Corp, at 3–4 (May 16, 1977) (Lockheed Aircraft Corp, Current Report (Form 8-K), Exhibit A (June 3, 1977)).

[3] Report of the Special Review Committee of the Board of Directors of Lockheed Aircraft Corp, at 18, 33, 36 (May 16, 1977) (Lockheed Aircraft Corp, Current Report (Form 8-K), Exhibit A (June 3, 1977)).

[4] See S Hrg 99-766, to Amend and Clarify the Foreign Corrupt Practices Act of 1977: Joint Hearing Before the Subcommittee on International Finance and Monetary Policy and the Subcommittee on Securities of the Senate Commission on Banking, Housing, and Urban Affairs, 99th Cong 20–21 (statement of Senator William Proxmire) (summarising the foreign policy effects of the Lockheed scandal).

1977 enactment

7.12 On 19 December 1977, President Jimmy Carter signed the FCPA into law. The FCPA both amended the Securities Exchange Act of 1934 ('Exchange Act')[1] as to issuers of securities that were required to register their securities or file reports with the SEC ('issuers') and enacted stand-alone legislation as to non-issuer US corporates or persons ('domestic concerns'). The FCPA imposed book-keeping and internal accounting requirements on issuers (collectively, the 'accounting provisions')[2]. The FCPA included two anti-bribery provisions that prohibited such issuers and domestic concerns from making corrupt payments to foreign officials, political parties, or politicians, or to third persons while knowing or 'having reason to know' that such third parties would pass all or part of the payments on to foreign officials, parties, or politicians, for the purpose of causing the official to act, refrain from acting, or influence any act or decision of the foreign government in order to assist in obtaining or retaining business for or with, or directing business to, any person[3].

[1] Public Law 73-290, 48 Stat 881 (codified as amended at 15 USC §§ 78a ff).

[2] FCPA § 102 (amending Exchange Act § 13(b)) (codified at 15 USS § 78m(b)(2)).

[3] FCPA §§ 103(a) (enacting Exchange Act § 30A) (codified as amended at 15 USC § 78dd-1(a)), 104(a) (codified as amended at 15 USC § 78dd-2(a)).

7.13 Soon after its enactment, the FCPA was subject to renewed legislative scrutiny. Less than one year after signing the FCPA into law, President Carter expressed concern that uncertainty about the meaning of the FCPA might discourage lawful exports by US corporates[1]. A 1981 report by the US General

Accounting Office concluded that the FCPA was, in fact, adversely affecting US corporates' business[2]. Yet legislative efforts to amend the FCPA fell short in 1981, 1983, 1985, and 1986[3].

[1] United States Export Policy, Statement by the President, 2 Pub Papers 1631, 1633–34 (Sept 26, 1978).

[2] US General Accountability Office, Report to the Congress of the United States: Impact of Foreign Corrupt Practices Act on US Business, at i (1981) ('GAO Report').

[3] S Rep 100-85, at 44–45 (1987) (summarising prior legislative efforts).

1988 amendments

7.14 On 23 August 1988, Congress made substantial modifications to the FCPA. The modifications, on balance, focused primarily on strengthening US enforcement authorities' power while meeting only some of corporates' concerns. Among the most important changes, the amendments:

— increased the maximum criminal penalties for anti-bribery violations to $2 million for issuers and domestic concerns (the maximum criminal penalty for individuals was increased in 1987 to $250,000 under the Alternative Fines Act[1]);

— expanded the definition of the 'knowledge' required to commit an offence from the original knowing or 'having reason to know' standard to include wilful ignorance[2];

— added an express exception for facilitating or expediting payments for routine government action (the original FCPA had instead excluded ministerial or clerical officials from the definition of foreign officials); and

— added affirmative defences to the anti-bribery provisions for payments expressly permitted by local law and for reasonable, bona fide promotional expenses[3].

Only a few months after the enactment of the 1988 amendments, Congress increased the maximum criminal penalties under the accounting provisions to $2.5 million for issuers and $500,000 and ten years' imprisonment for natural persons[4].

[1] Criminal Fine Improvements Act of 1987, Public Law 100-185, § 6, 101 Stat 1279 (codified at 18 USC § 3571(b)–(d)). The alternative fines provisions do not apply to statutes that expressly opt-out of the Alternative Fines Act, see 18 USC § 3571(e), but the FCPA does not opt-out of these provisions.

[2] See para **7.70** (further discussing the current knowledge requirement).

[3] Omnibus Trade and Competitiveness Act of 1988, Public Law 100-418, Title V, §§ 5001–5003, 102 Stat 1107 (amending Exchange Act §§ 13(b), 30A, 32 and FCPA § 104(a)) (codified as amended at 15 USC §§ 78m(b), 78dd-1, 78dd-2, 78ff).

[4] Insider Trading and Securities Fraud Enforcement Act of 1988, Public Law 100-704, § 4, 102 Stat 4677 (amending Exchange Act § 32(a)).

1990–1995 expansion of the SEC's authority

7.15 Through 1990 legislation commonly known as the Remedies Act, Congress granted the SEC authority to seek greater civil monetary penalties for issuer's violations of the FCPA as part of broader authority to impose civil monetary penalties under the Exchange Act generally, through either civil or administrative proceedings[1]. Congress also expanded the SEC's authority to impose secondary liability on non-issuers, such as an issuer's officers, directors, or agents, for issuers' violations of the Exchange Act. Since the 1934 enactment of the Exchange Act, the SEC had been able to bring a civil action to enjoin potential or actual violations of the Exchange Act or causing such an action[2], including civil actions against control persons even where such control persons did not have knowledge of the conduct by persons under their control[3]. The Remedies Act allowed the SEC to seek civil monetary or injunctive relief for control person violations[4], but did not extend its authority to impose civil monetary penalties for acts that caused a violation of the Exchange Act[5]. In 1995, Congress expanded the SEC's secondary liability authority to include civil monetary penalties and injunctive relief for aiding and abetting violations of the Exchange Act[6]. Together, these grounds for secondary liability provide a powerful incentive to non-issuers, such as officers, directors, or agents of issuers, not to engage in conduct that might violate the Exchange Act.

[1]   Securities Enforcement Remedies and Penny Stock Reform Act of 1990 ('Remedies Act'), Public Law 101-429, § 201,104 Stat 931 (codified at 15 USC § 78u(d)(3)).
[2]   Exchange Act § 21(e) (codified at 15 USC § 78u(e)).
[3]   Exchange Act §§ 20(a), 20(b) (codified at 15 USC §§ 78t(a), 78t(b)).
[4]   Remedies Act § 201 (amending Exchange Act § 21(d)) (codified at 15 USC § 78u(d)).
[5]   Remedies Act § 203 (creating Exchange Act § 21C) (codified at 15 USC § 78u-3); see Exchange Act § 20(b) (codified at 15 USC § 78t(b)).
[6]   Private Securities Litigation Reform Act of 1995, Public Law 104-67, § 104(2), 109 Stat 737 (enacting as amended Exchange Act § 20(e)) (codified as amended at 15 USC § 78t(e)).

1998 amendments implementing the OECD Convention and the increase in penalties for issuers under Sarbanes-Oxley

7.16 Ever since the enactment of the FCPA, the uneven playing field facing US corporates prompted calls for the US to secure an international anti-corruption agreement with the goal of holding foreign corporates to the same standards[1]. Eventually, the Organisation for Economic Cooperation and Development ('OECD') adopted the Convention on Combating Bribery of Foreign Public Officials in International Business Transactions ('Anti-Bribery Convention' or 'Convention'), which entered into force in February 1999, more than 20 years after the FCPA's enactment[2]. In order to implement the Convention, the United States had to amend the FCPA, which it did on 10 November 1998.

[1]   See eg Omnibus Trade and Competitiveness Act of 1988 § 5003(d), GAO Report at 45–46.
[2]   OECD, OECD Anti-Bribery Convention: Entry into Force of the Convention, www.oecd.org/document/12/0,3343,en_2649_34855_2057484_1_1_1_1,00.html (last visited 10 January 2011).

7.17 The 1998 amendments effected substantial changes to the FCPA, including:

—   adding a new anti-bribery provision applicable to 'other persons', such as non-issuer foreign corporates and persons, who act in furtherance of an FCPA violation 'while in the territory of the United States';

— extending the anti-bribery provisions to prohibit corrupt payments for the purpose of 'securing any improper advantage' to assist in obtaining or retaining business; and

— adding alternative, nationality-based jurisdiction over US issuers and domestic concerns for conduct outside of the United States.

7.18 The most recent amendments to the FCPA occurred in 2002, when the Sarbanes-Oxley Act dramatically increased the maximum criminal penalties for violations of the accounting provisions to $25 million for issuers and $5 million and 20 years' imprisonment for natural persons[1].

[1] Sarbanes-Oxley Act of 2002, Public Law 107-204, § 1106, 116 Stat 745 (amending Exchange Act § 32(a)) (codified at 15 USC § 78ff(a)).

Lessons from the history and development of the FCPA

7.19 The FCPA and the UK Bribery Act 2010 are similar in that they are both the result of significant political upheaval that created the conditions and demand necessary for more effective anti-corruption legislation; the controversy over corrupt payments by BAE Systems to obtain or retain foreign business may have been the equivalent of Watergate for UK anti-corruption legislation.

7.20 Based on the US experience with the evolution of the FCPA since 1977, there are several lessons that might apply to the UK Bribery Act. First, a country that gets out ahead of other countries' anti-enforcement efforts must decide how it will address the inevitable competitive disadvantage imposed on businesses subject to its laws: either it will under-enforce its own laws, or it will work to raise the level of enforcement in other countries. After more than 20 years of appearing to under-enforce its own anti-corruption legislation, the US finally secured an international anti-corruption agreement and has exponentially increased enforcement following that agreement's entry into force[1]. With the Bribery Act 2010 in effect, some in the UK may argue for limited enforcement so that corporates doing business in the UK are not at a competitive disadvantage relative to other corporates. This pressure may, however, be mitigated because of the efforts of the OECD in recent years to encourage all of its member states to enforce their anti-corruption laws.

[1] See paras **7.92–7.98**.

7.21 Second, Parliament will probably face frequent attempts to amend the Bribery Act 2010, principally to soften its impact on corporates doing business in the UK. The outcome of such attempts, however, is far from predictable, as the 1988 amendments arguably increased the FCPA's effect on businesses, even though the momentum for amendments began as a pro-business effort[1].

[1] See paras **7.13–7.15**.

7.22 Finally, the Bribery Act 2010 will be significantly affected by developments in related areas of law, particularly laws relating to publicly-traded companies. The changes described above to the broader US securities laws have had a profound effect on the enforcement of the FCPA by the SEC, and changes in related UK laws will likely also affect enforcement of the Bribery Act.

C   SHARED ANTI-CORRUPTION ENFORCEMENT RESPONSIBILITIES

Allocation of enforcement responsibility across multiple agencies

7.23 Both the FCPA and the Bribery Act 2010 spread enforcement authority across multiple agencies. While the shared FCPA enforcement responsibility in the US initially faced criticism that it could lead to inconsistent interpretations, competing or duplicative enforcement efforts, and wasted resources, the scheme has nonetheless continued. This is because both of the enforcement agencies involved—the DOJ and the SEC—have separate but important interests underlying their jurisdiction, have adopted policies to divide enforcement responsibility, have coordinated their enforcement efforts, and have taken steps to avoid divergent interpretations of the law.

7.24 The Bribery Act 2010 divides enforcement responsibility between the Crown Prosecution Service, the SFO, and the Revenue and Customs Office[1]. The SFO is likely to have the most prominent role, as it will serve as the lead agency regarding the corporate offence of failing to prevent foreign bribery[2]. In the US, the DOJ and the SEC share enforcement authority over the FCPA. The SEC enforces the US securities laws and its primary role is to protect investors, but it has only civil and administrative enforcement authority[3]. The SEC does not have criminal enforcement authority. The DOJ, among other things, has exclusive criminal enforcement authority for the federal government and has civil enforcement authority in certain contexts[4].

[1]   Bribery Act 2010, s 10.
[2]   SFO, Approach of the Serious Fraud Office to Dealing with Overseas Corruption, at 1 (July 21, 2009).
[3]   The SEC is an independent federal agency created in 1934 to protect investors, promote confidence in US markets, and to administer federal securities legislation such as the Exchange Act. The SEC may bring civil lawsuits or conduct administrative proceedings to accomplish these ends. Because the SEC is an independent agency, the President's ability to remove SEC commissioners is limited to removal for 'cause', such as inefficiency, neglect of duty, or malfeasance in office.
[4]   The DOJ was established in 1870 and is an executive department charged with responsibility for all federal criminal prosecutions and all civil litigation in which the US is a party. The US Attorney General is in charge of the DOJ and is subject to the President's ultimate constitutional authority to execute the laws and set federal law enforcement policies and priorities.

7.25 The division of responsibility between the SEC and the DOJ over the FCPA is as follows. The SEC has civil and administrative jurisdiction over issuers, which gives the SEC jurisdiction to enforce the anti-bribery provisions applicable to issuers (including any officer, director, employee, or agent of an issuer, or a stockholder acting on the issuer's behalf)[1] and to enforce the accounting provisions in the FCPA (which apply only to issuers)[2]. The DOJ has criminal enforcement authority over the FCPA[3] and civil enforcement authority of the anti-bribery provisions applicable to non-issuers[4]. While the DOJ therefore has both criminal and civil enforcement authority regarding the FCPA, it is the DOJ's criminal enforcement authority that gives it most of its power and influence regarding the FCPA.

1   Exchange Act § 30A(a) (codified at 15 USC § 78dd-1(a)).
2   As noted above, these provisions are amendments to the Exchange Act. Exchange Act §§
    13(b)(2)–(6), 30A, and 32 (codified at 15 USC §§ 78m(b)(2)-(6), 78dd-1, 78ff).
3   An Act to Establish the Department of Justice, ch 150, 16 Stat 162 (1870) (codified as
    amended at 28 USC §§ 501 ff); see US DOJ, Layperson's Guide to the FCPA, www.justice.go
    v/criminal/fraud/FCPA/docs/lay-persons-guide.pdf (last visited 10 January 2011).
4   FCPA §§ 104(a), 104A (codified at 15 USC §§ 78dd-2, 78dd-3).

7.26 The sharing of enforcement responsibility for the anti-bribery provisions between the DOJ and the SEC has not been without controversy. Initially, the business community feared that the agencies would adopt divergent interpretations of the law, further complicating the challenge of complying with the FCPA[1]. In practice, however, the DOJ and the SEC have taken steps—largely successful—to cooperate with each other and coordinate their FCPA enforcement actions[2]. When the DOJ's criminal enforcement authority overlaps with the SEC's civil enforcement authority, the agencies frequently coordinate their independent, parallel investigations[3]. The DOJ and the SEC strive to present a unified enforcement front by frequently acknowledging each other's assistance, resolving FCPA enforcement actions concurrently, and coordinating their civil and criminal sanctions. The SEC further strives to create a unified enforcement standard for the business community by giving deference to DOJ Opinion Procedure Releases[4].

1   GAO Report at 1, 43 (1981).
2   Mike Koehler, The Foreign Corrupt Practices Act in the Ultimate Year of Its Decade of
    Resurgence (2010) 43 Ind L Rev 389, 385–87.
3   US SEC, Enforcement Manual, at 110 (January 13, 2010) (noting that 'parallel civil and
    criminal proceedings are not uncommon' and encouraging SEC staff to 'work cooperatively
    with criminal authorities, to share information, and to coordinate their investigations with
    parallel criminal investigations when appropriate'); US Attorneys' Manual § 9-47.110 (noting
    that '[c]lose coordination of [FCPA] investigation and prosecutions with the Department
    of State, the [SEC] and other interested agencies is essential). The United States Supreme Court
    has approved parallel criminal and civil investigations, so long as the government does not act
    in bad faith by bringing a civil or criminal action purely to advance the other. *United States
    v Kordel* 397 US 1, 11–13 (1970).
4   US SEC, Statement of Comm'n Policy Concerning Section 30A of the Securities Exchange Act
    of 1934, Release No 34-18,255 (Nov 12, 1981), 46 Fed Reg 56,692 (Nov 18, 1981).

7.27 The DOJ and SEC have also taken important steps to centralise FCPA enforcement efforts internally within each of the two agencies. For example, the DOJ has largely consolidated its FCPA prosecutions within its Criminal Division in Washington, DC, in contrast to much of the Department's other criminal enforcement, which is handled regionally among the 93 US Attorney's Offices across the country. The DOJ requires express approval by its Criminal Division, run by a presidentially-appointed Assistant Attorney General, to initiate any FCPA investigation or prosecution and delegates to the Criminal Division's Fraud Section the responsibility for such investigations or prosecutions[1]. The DOJ expressly cites the need for international investigations and the potential impact of such investigations on foreign officials, which may require the DOJ to coordinate its efforts with the US Department of State and other agencies, as compelling reasons for centralised enforcement[2]. Similarly, in 2010, the SEC established a nationwide FCPA unit within its Enforcement Division to facilitate more proactive investigations, including more 'sweeps and sector-wide investigations, alone and with other regulatory counterparts both here and abroad'[3]. This centralisation within both the DOJ and the SEC promotes intra-agency consistency across anti-bribery prosecutions and facilitates the inter-agency and international coordination necessary to conduct effective multinational bribery investigations.

[1]   US Attorneys' Manual § 9-47.000.
[2]   US Attorneys' Manual § 9-47.110.
[3]   US SEC, Speech by SEC Staff: Remarks at News Conference Announcing New SEC Leaders in Enforcement Division (Jan 13, 2010), available at www.sec.gov/news/speech/2010/spch 011310newsconf.htm (last visited 10 January 2011).

7.28 As explained above, the UK Bribery Act also divides enforcement responsibility between several enforcement agencies: the Crown Prosecution Service; the SFO; and the Revenue and Customs Office[1]. Unlike the US, which divides enforcement authority between an executive branch agency (the DOJ) that reports to the President and an 'independent' regulatory agency (the SEC) whose commissioners serve for fixed terms, the Directors of all three UK agencies are civil servants who report to the UK Attorney-General[2]. The UK Attorney-General serves as the government Minister responsible for prosecution and has authority to issue guidance for prosecutors in all three agencies to ensure consistency in the UK's law enforcement practices[3]. For example, the Directors are already subject to a common policy on corporate prosecutions, which includes an overview of the bases for, and limitations on, corporate criminal liability under UK law and discusses the evidentiary and policy considerations relevant to a corporate charging decision[4]. And just as the US enforcement agencies have taken steps to consolidate enforcement efforts internally, the UK's SFO announced in July 2009 the creation of a specialised Anti-Corruption Domain within its office[5].

[1]   Bribery Act 2010, s 10.
[2]   See generally Attorney General's Office, Protocol Between the Attorney General and the Prosecuting Departments (July 2009).
[3]   See Attorney General's Office, Protocol Between the Attorney General and the Prosecuting Departments (July 2009).
[4]   See, eg, The Crown Prosecution Service, Legal Guidance: Guidance on Corporate Prosecutions (21 April 2010), available at www.cps.gov.uk/legal/a_to_c/corporate_prosecutions/#a01 (last visited 10 January 2011).
[5]   SFO, Approach of the Serious Fraud Office to Dealing with Overseas Corruption, at 1 (July 21, 2009).

Specific prosecutorial guidance on enforcement policies

7.29 One of the most significant criticisms of the FCPA is that it is a broadly-worded statute that gives corporates and individuals little guidance regarding what is permissible in real-world business situations. As an effort to address this, the DOJ has an opinion procedure release process that gives requestors guidance as to whether the DOJ would take enforcement action regarding particular factual scenarios. As described below, the procedure has been infrequently used. Thus, while it has given valuable guidance regarding some aspects of the FCPA, it does not provide the kind of routine guidance that its proponents may have expected.

7.30 The original FCPA did not require enforcement authorities to issue guidelines on anti-bribery enforcement policies. Indeed, some enforcement officials initially objected to requests that they do so on the grounds that such guidance would amount to a 'roadmap for fraud' or 'guidelines for corporations who want to bribe foreign officials'[1]. President Jimmy Carter, however, expressly directed the DOJ to provide such guidance so that businesses did not forego legitimate export opportunities 'because of uncertainty about the application of the statute'[2]. The DOJ responded by stating broad anti-bribery enforcement priorities in November 1979 and adopting an FCPA Review Procedure in March 1980[3].

[1]   See William C Georges, The Foreign Corrupt Practices Act Review Procedure: A Quest for Clarity, 57 Cornell International LJ 57, 68 (1981) ('roadmap for fraud'); GAO Report at 43–44 (1981) (quoting the Director of the SEC's Enforcement Division as saying 'We do not have guidelines for rapists, muggers and embezzlers, and I do not think we need guidelines for corporations who want to bribe foreign officials').

[2]   See para **7.13** fn 1.

[3]   US DOJ, Establishment of the Foreign Corrupt Practices Act Review Procedure, 45 Fed Reg 20,800 (Mar 31, 1980); see William C Georges, The Foreign Corrupt Practices Act Review Procedure: A Quest for Clarity, 57 Cornell International LJ 57, 68–69 (1981).

7.31 The Review Procedure initially adopted by the DOJ was not embraced by the business community. Under the procedure, an issuer or a domestic concern was required to submit detailed information about a proposed transaction and the DOJ would provide, endeavoring to respond within 30 days, a statement of the DOJ's 'present enforcement intention' with regard to facts of the specific transaction[1]. The DOJ disavowed any precedential value beyond the facts and parties addressed in the opinion[2], and the act of requesting an FCPA opinion carried substantial risks for the requestor:

—   the DOJ reserved the right to disclose the identity of the requestor, the 'general nature and circumstances' of the intended conduct, and the action taken by the DOJ, thereby risking unwanted public attention;

—   the DOJ would not issue advice based on hypothetical fact patterns;

—   only limited protections were available to protect from disclosure any confidential business information submitted with the request;

—   information of sufficient detail might not be readily available from foreign agents;

—   the business decision would likely have to be made before DOJ provided its advice; and

—   the fact of submitting a request could expose the requestor's other operations to authorities' scrutiny[3].

Accordingly, for the 12 years that this Review Procedure was in place (1980–1992), the DOJ released only 22 opinions, each limited to the particular facts of the transaction at issue[4].

[1]   US DOJ, Establishment of the Foreign Corrupt Practices Act Review Procedure, 45 Fed Reg 20,800 (Mar 31, 1980).

[2]   US DOJ, Establishment of the Foreign Corrupt Practices Act Review Procedure, 45 Fed Reg 20,800 (Mar 31, 1980).

[3]   GAO Report at 43 (1981); William C Georges, The Foreign Corrupt Practices Act Review Procedure: A Quest for Clarity, 57 Cornell International LJ 57, 77–86 (1981).

[4]   See US DOJ, Review Procedure Releases, www.justice.gov/criminal/fraud/FCPA/review/ (last visited 10 January 2011).

7.32 The SEC refused to participate in the Review Procedure program, generating concern that SEC and DOJ interpretations of the anti-bribery provisions would diverge, thereby compounding the challenges of complying with the law[1]. Nonetheless, the SEC did adopt a policy of declining to take enforcement action with respect to conduct for which an issuer obtained 'no action' relief in an advisory opinion from the DOJ[2].

[1] See GAO Report at 43–44 (1981) (discussing the SEC's position).
[2] US SEC, Statement of Comm'n Policy Concerning Section 30A of the Securities Exchange Act of 1934, Release No 34-18,255 (Nov 12, 1981), 46 Fed Reg 56,692 (Nov 18, 1981) (permanent extension of prior policy); US SEC, Statement of Comm'n Policy Concerning Section 30A of the Securities Exchange Act of 1934, Release No 34-17,099 (Aug 28, 1980), 45 Fed Reg 59,001 (Sept 5, 1980) (announcement of prior policy).

7.33 In part because of the criticism and shortcoming of the Review Procedure, Congress directed the DOJ to create a new process. When Congress amended the FCPA in 1988, it added express statutory provisions regarding the promulgation of the DOJ's enforcement policy and the establishment of a new FCPA opinion procedure. Regarding the DOJ's enforcement policy, Congress required the Attorney General to consult with the SEC and other interested agencies and to seek public comment regarding whether further clarification of the FCPA would improve compliance, but Congress left the decision whether to issue such guidelines to the Attorney General[1]. Congress mandated, however, a new FCPA advisory opinion process by which persons subject to the FCPA's anti-bribery provisions could obtain an opinion stating whether prospective conduct conformed with the DOJ's enforcement policy[2]. Congress directed that, to the 'maximum extent practicable,' the Attorney General provide guidance to small businesses unable to obtain specialised counsel on both the new opinion process and 'general explanations of compliance responsibilities and of potential liabilities' under the anti-bribery provisions[3].

[1] Omnibus Trade and Competitiveness Act of 1988, Public Law 100-418, § 5003, 102 Stat 1415 (codified at 15 USC §§ 78dd-1(d), 78dd-2(e)).
[2] Omnibus Trade and Competitiveness Act of 1988, Public Law 100-418, § 5003, 102 Stat 1415 (codified at 15 USC §§ 78dd-1(e), 78dd-2(f)).
[3] Omnibus Trade and Competitiveness Act of 1988, Public Law 100-418, § 5003, 102 Stat 1415 (codified at 15 USC §§ 78dd-1(e)(4), 78dd-2(f)(4)).

7.34 In the 1988 amendments, Congress also mandated specific aspects of the DOJ's new opinion process in response to some of the criticisms of the Review Procedure. Congress required the Attorney General to issue his or her opinion within 30 days and granted persons who act on the opinion a presumption—in either a criminal or civil enforcement action—that their conduct did not violate the anti-bribery provisions, unless there was a deficiency in the information the person submitted to DOJ[1]. The 1988 amendments also expressly exempted from public disclosure any documents or other material 'provided to, received by, or prepared in' the DOJ in connection with a request for an advisory FCPA opinion[2].

[1] Omnibus Trade and Competitiveness Act of 1988, Public Law 100-418, § 5003, 102 Stat 1415 (codified at 15 USC §§ 78dd-1(e), 78dd-2(f)).
[2] Omnibus Trade and Competitiveness Act of 1988, Public Law 100-418, § 5003, 102 Stat 1415 (codified at 15 USC §§ 78dd-1(e)(2), 78dd-2(f)(2)).

7.35 After considerable delay, in 1992 the DOJ adopted a new FCPA Opinion Procedure consistent with Congress's direction[1]. The DOJ has also issued a brochure, commonly known as the Lay-Person's Guide, providing small businesses who cannot obtain specialised counsel a general explanation of the FCPA's anti-bribery provisions and FCPA compliance obligations[2]. The Attorney General has not issued FCPA enforcement guidelines intended for a broader audience, but a brief overview of the DOJ's interpretation of the FCPA is publicly available in the Criminal Resource Manual that is provided to federal prosecutors[3].

[1] US DOJ, Antibribery Provisions of the Foreign Corrupt Practices Act, 57 Fed Reg 39,598 (Sept 1, 1992) (codified at 28 CFR, Part 80).
[2] US DOJ, Layperson's Guide to the FCPA, www.justice.gov/criminal/fraud/FCPA/docs/lay-pers ons-guide.pdf (last visited 10 January 2011).
[3] See US DOJ, Criminal Resource Manual § 1018 ('Prohibited Foreign Corrupt Practices').

7.36 The DOJ's new Opinion Procedure remains as infrequently used as its predecessor was. A sign of how little value the business community placed in even the revised procedures was that the proposed Opinion Procedure received only one public comment during the administrative notice and comment period[1]. That comment's suggestion that the DOJ give precedential weight to prior FCPA opinions was rejected[2]. Despite the stronger protection from disclosure granted to any documents and materials submitted to the DOJ, the DOJ retained the right to disclose the name of the requestor, the general nature and circumstances of the proposed conduct, and the action taken by the DOJ in response[3]. Additionally, the DOJ reserved the right to identify the foreign country in which the proposed conduct would take place[4]. From 1993 through 2010, only 33 FCPA opinions have been released under the new procedures[5].

[1] 57 Fed Reg at 39,599.
[2] 57 Fed Reg at 39,599.
[3] 28 CFR § 80.13.
[4] 28 CFR § 80.13.
[5] See US DOJ, Opinion Procedure Releases, www.justice.gov/criminal/fraud/FCPA/opinion/ (last visited 10 January 2011).

7.37 References to prior FCPA opinions on related issues in recent FCPA opinions[1] and a recent instance of referring to a prior opinion release as precedent[2] have both attracted attention in the compliance community, starved for precedents given the dearth of FCPA enforcement actions or prosecutions that have been contested in open court. But both developments are largely academic because the DOJ continues to state that its advisory opinions do not have precedential value[3]. In the US experience under both advisory opinion regimes, the narrowness of the programs and the potential collateral reputational and legal consequences facing requestors have discouraged businesses from seeking guidance on a more routine basis.

[1] See Opinion Procedure Releases 10-02 (July 16, 2010) & 10-03 (Sept 1, 2010).
[2] Opinion Procedure Release 08-02 (June 13, 2008) (citing Opinion Procedure Release 01-01 (May 24, 2001)).
[3] 28 CFR §§ 80.1-16 (2010) (stating that DOJ Opinion Releases only create a 'rebuttable presumption' should the DOJ decide to later bring action based on the disclosed conduct and that the FCPA Opinion 'will not bind or obligate any agency other than the Department of Justice').

7.38 In the UK, the SFO has indicated a willingness to engage in a more liberal guidance practice than have US enforcement agencies. In December 2010, SFO Director Richard Alderman stressed that it would be 'misguided solely to concentrate on investigations and prosecutions' at the expense of prevention, education, and understanding 'the context of the work we do'[1]. Mr Alderman explained the SFO's current practice in detail regarding the 'adequate procedures' defence to the offence of failure to prevent bribery:

'Lots of corporates come to talk to us and talk through their [compliance] procedures with us. They know that we are not going to give them some form of certificate that their procedures are adequate for the purposes of the [Bribery] Act and that they have a complete defence in the future. That is not what it is about at all. What we do is to talk through what the corporate is doing and to offer any views that we have about whether or not there are areas that need to be developed further'[2].

The SFO Director has also recently emphasised the benefit of 'direct dialogue . . . not just at the level of general theory, but at the level of what is really happening in the business and what are the real risks in that business worldwide,' and he stated that such discussions 'are totally confidential'[3].

[1] SFO, Speech by Richard Alderman, Director, Ninth Corporate Accountability Conference (Dec 9, 2010).
[2] SFO, Speech by Richard Alderman, Director, Ninth Corporate Accountability Conference (Dec 9, 2010).
[3] SFO, Speech by Richard Alderman, Director, Association of the British Pharmaceutical Industry Legal Day (Oct 4, 2010).

7.39 Prior to the passage of the Bribery Act, the SFO had announced its willingness to provide guidance on the specific issue of successor liability for corrupt pre-acquisition acts of the acquired corporate that are discovered during pre-acquisition due diligence[1]. The SFO indicated that it would consider taking no enforcement action if the acquirer's proposed remedial actions occur; however, the SFO might conduct a criminal investigation if the corruption discovered in due diligence was 'long lasting and systemic'[2]. The SFO also expressed its appreciation for the facts that issues in an acquisition are likely to be confidential and to have a considerable effect on the price paid and that the requestor will need to conclude its discussions with the SFO before the deal is made[3].

[1] SFO, Approach of the Serious Fraud Office to Dealing with Overseas Corruption, at paras 17–18 (July 21, 2009).
[2] SFO, Approach of the Serious Fraud Office to Dealing with Overseas Corruption at para 19.
[3] SFO, Approach of the Serious Fraud Office to Dealing with Overseas Corruption at para 20.

7.40 Hopefully, the result of the SFO's intended advisory opinion practices will be that persons subject to the Bribery Act 2010 will consider seeking guidance from the SFO to be a more worthwhile exercise than submitting a request for a DOJ FCPA opinion, with redounding benefits to the ability of persons to comply with the law of the UK to prevent corrupt practices.

D   LESSONS FROM BROADER GUIDANCE AS TO CORPORATE PROSECUTIONS AND EFFECTIVE COMPLIANCE PROGRAMS

7.41 Clear guidance on what is an 'effective' or 'adequate' compliance program is critical to compliance program design and implementation. The Ministry of Justice's final guidance, discussed in Chapter 6, helpfully provides a baseline on what UK enforcement agencies will expect from an institutional compliance program[1]. Given the parallels between the Bribery Act and the FCPA, US enforcement guidelines can provide additional insight into what will constitute an effective Bribery Act compliance program.

[1]   See Chapter 6.

Compliance program guidance in the United States

7.42 Compliance program guidance exists in several forms. The most obvious resources are the internal prosecution principles and enforcement guidelines created by the DOJ and the SEC. Although non-binding, these documents provide corporates with a general overview of the government's 'carrot and stick' approach to enforcement. Another useful resource are the United States Sentencing Guidelines ('USSG') applicable to business organisations, which provide an advisory sentencing recommendation to US sentencing judges and include what factors to consider when deciding whether a corporate defendant's compliance program is sufficiently 'effective' to warrant a mitigated sentence. Enforcement actions themselves also provide insight into government enforcement priorities, as deferred prosecution agreements ('DPAs') and non-prosecution agreements ('NPAs') typically highlight conduct that mitigates or increases FCPA-related sanctions and often impose minimum components of an effective compliance program. While these sources are not binding on prosecutors or enforcement agencies, the principles they promote can supplement the MOJ final guidance and help organisations refine and improve their compliance efforts under the Bribery Act.

Generally applicable DOJ Prosecution Principles for business organisations

7.43 The DOJ's Principles of Federal Prosecution of Business Organisations ('Prosecution Principles') are guidelines that US prosecutors use to determine whether to prosecute corporations for criminal offences, including FCPA violations. The Prosecution Principles outline nine factors prosecutors will consider before pressing charges against an organisation, including:

—   Special Policy Concerns: prosecutors consider the potential harm each offence could cause to the public[1];

—   Pervasiveness of Wrongdoing: prosecutors distinguish between violations caused by an individual bad actor and violations stemming from complicit or participating management[2];

—   Corporate History: prosecutors are more likely to seek increased fines or impose harsher penalties on repeat offenders because a history of prior FCPA violations implies that the organisation either failed to implement an effective compliance program or consciously disregarded the FCPA[3];

— Cooperation and Disclosure: corporates facing FCPA-related charges can receive reduced fines and avoid prosecution by providing relevant facts to prosecutors and disclosing potential FCPA violations prior to government inquiry[4];

— Corporate Compliance Programs: prosecutors can offer remediation credit to corporates that had effective compliance programs in place at the time of the violation. Compliance plans, therefore, can benefit corporates by reducing both the consequences of a FCPA violation and the chances of an FCPA violation occurring[5];

— Restitution and Remediation: the DOJ rewards corporations that are willing to take responsibility for FCPA violations by paying restitution (disgorging illicit profits and paying penalties) or implementing remedial reforms (such as improving compliance programs or disciplining wrongdoers)[6];

— Collateral Consequences: the DOJ makes efforts to avoid punishing FCPA offenders at the expense of the general public, the business community, and innocent employees. Consequently, the DOJ often seeks to deter and punish FCPA offenders without the disastrous ripple-effects of a corporate conviction[7];

— Adequacy of Prosecuting Individual Bad Actors: according to the DOJ, '[w]here the facts and law allow, the Justice Department will pursue individuals responsible for illegal conduct just as vigorously as we pursue corporations'[8]. When the DOJ can identify the specific parties responsible for a FCPA violation, the DOJ will consider whether the prosecution of individual wrongdoers is sufficient to address the wrongdoing and to deter others[9]; and

— Civil/Regulatory Alternatives: as discussed above, the DOJ does its best to avoid the collateral consequences of corporate prosecution and conviction. When appropriate, the DOJ will consider whether regulatory or civil authorities (such as the SEC) will impose sanctions sufficient to deter, punish, and promote the rehabilitation of FCPA offenders[10].

[1] Prosecution Principles at 9-28.300(A)(1) and at 9-28.400.
[2] Prosecution Principles at 9-28.500(A).
[3] Prosecution Principles at 9.28-600(B).
[4] Prosecution Principles at 9.28-700(A).
[5] Prosecution Principles at 9.28-800.
[6] Prosecution Principles at 9.28-900.
[7] Prosecution Principles at 9-28.200(B).
[8] US DOJ, Press Release, Pharmaceutical Company Lawyer Charged with Obstruction and Making False Statements (Nov 9, 2010), available at www.justice.gov/opa/pr/2010/November/10-civ-1266.html (last visited 10 January 2011).
[9] Prosecution Principles at 9-28.300(A).
[10] Prosecution Principles at 9-28.1100(B).

7.44 The MOJ final guidance bears several similarities to the Prosecution Principles. Both documents encourage organisations to conduct thorough due diligence and to develop effective internal controls. Both documents also emphasise the importance of preventative monitoring. Both forms of guidance are also specifically non-binding and intentionally general, giving authorities considerable flexibility under each.

Generally applicable SEC guidance

7.45 As discussed above, the SEC shares FCPA enforcement authority with the DOJ. The SEC operates under a separate set of guidelines from the DOJ.

Through its 2001 'Seaboard Report,' the SEC offered guidance on the criteria it considers while determining when, and to what degree, it rewards organisations with mitigation credit during an FCPA enforcement action[1]. The Seaboard report listed 13 categories of criteria which, in essence, fall into the following general categories:

— the nature and seriousness of the offence, calculated in part based on the nature of the misconduct, how the misconduct occurred, where in the organisation the misconduct occurred, how long the misconduct occurred, and the level of harm the misconduct inflicted upon investors;
— pre-existing efforts to self-police for misconduct, including an organisation's efforts to implement an effective compliance program and whether it fostered an appropriate anti-corruption culture;
— how the misconduct was identified and the investigative-efforts employed by the organisation to review the nature, extent, origins, and consequences of the misconduct;
— whether an organisation self-reported the misconduct and the extent to which the organisation disclosed the misconduct to the public and appropriate regulatory agencies;
— remedial efforts taken to prevent future misconduct, including efforts to modify and improve internal controls, efforts to discipline parties responsible for the misconduct, and efforts made to compensate those adversely affected by the misconduct; and
— the level of cooperation the organisation provides during any subsequent government or regulatory investigation[2].

[1] US SEC, Report of Investigation Pursuant to Section 21(a) of the Securities Exchange Act of 1934 and Commission Statement on the Relationship of Cooperation to Agency Enforcement Decisions, Exchange Act Release No 44969 (Oct 23, 2001) ('Seaboard Report').
[2] US SEC, Report of Investigation Pursuant to Section 21(a) of the Securities Exchange Act of 1934 and Commission Statement on the Relationship of Cooperation to Agency Enforcement Decisions, Exchange Act Release No 44969 (Oct 23, 2001).

7.46 In January 2010, the SEC supplemented its Seaboard Report with an updated Enforcement Manual[1]. This Enforcement Manual emphasised the importance of cooperating with SEC investigations by outlining how organisations that violate or allegedly violate provisions of the FCPA could obtain proffer, cooperation, deferred prosecution, or non-prosecution agreements. In particular, the SEC Enforcement Manual suggests that an organisation's ability to obtain favourable agreements will be significantly affected by, among other things, whether the organisation self-reports the violation and cooperates with the government's investigation.

[1] US SEC, Enforcement Manual (2010), available at www.sec.gov/divisions/enforce/enforcementmanual.pdf (last visited 10 January 2011).

Specific guidance from the US Sentencing Commission regarding effective compliance programs

7.47 The United States Sentencing Commission promulgates advisory sentencing guidelines that US courts consider when sentencing any defendant, including corporations. The sentencing guidelines applicable to business organisations suggest that courts mitigate the fines imposed on organisations that have 'effective' compliance and ethics programs and provide specific guidance on the content of an effective program. Whether or not a corporate has an effective compliance program is one of several factors that can mitigate a corporation's recommended fine by as much as 95%, while the same factors can justify as much as double the recommended fine for corporations who fail to follow the Commission's guidance[1]. The greatest culpability reductions go to organisations that report offences to the appropriate government authorities, fully cooperate with any resulting investigation, and clearly demonstrate recognition of, and firmly accept responsibility for, their criminal conduct[2].

[1] US Sentencing Guidelines Manual § 8C2.6.
[2] US Sentencing Guidelines Manual § 8C2.5(g).

7.48 As recently amended in November 2010, the Sentencing Commission's guidance is that an 'effective' compliance and ethics program includes:

— establishing standards and procedures to prevent and detect criminal conduct;

— the organisation's governing authority exercising 'reasonable oversight' regarding the program's implementation and effectiveness, with specific high-level individuals assigned overall responsibility for the program and others assigned day-to-day responsibility;

— excluding from compliance responsibility individuals who have engaged in illegal or questionable activities;

— conducting effective training programs and sharing information with members of the governing authority, high-level personnel, employees, and, as appropriate, the organisation's agents;

— taking reasonable steps to monitor and audit the compliance and ethics program, including implementing systems through which employees and agents can report potential violations or ask questions;

— promoting and enforcing the program throughout the organisation; and

— after any criminal conduct is detected, taking reasonable steps to respond appropriately to the conduct and to prevent further similar conduct, potentially including the engagement of outside professional advisers[1].

[1] US Sentencing Guidelines Manual § 8B2.1(b) & cmt 6.

Specific guidance on effective compliance programs from deferred prosecution and non-prosecution agreements

7.49 The DOJ often resolves FCPA investigations against corporations through either a deferred prosecution agreement ('DPA'), under which charges are filed but held in abeyance pending the corporate's compliance for a term of years, or an non-prosecution agreement ('NPA'), which is similar to a DPA except that no formal charges are filed. These DPAs and NPAs often include large financial penalties and promises by the corporation to take certain remedial steps. Despite the fact that DPAs and NPAs do not create any binding precedent, these agreements provide insight into what US enforcement authorities consider to be the minimum components of an effective compliance program. For example, in November 2010 the DOJ entered into a series of DPAs in which corporates were expressly given credit for proactively hiring outside professional advisers, indicating enforcement authorities' acknowledgment of the US Sentencing Guidelines' encouragement of such practices[1].

[1]   See, eg, Deferred Prosecution Agreement para 5(i)(ix), *United States v Panalpina World Transport (Holding) Ltd*, 4:10-cr-769 (SD Tex, Nov 4, 2010).

7.50 In addition to generally tracking the components of an effective compliance and ethics program recommended by the US Sentencing Commission, consistent terms across recent DPAs and NPAs required that the corporate's compliance program, at minimum, also include:

—   'appropriate' due diligence requirements pertaining to the retention and oversight of agents and business partners;
—   standard anti-corruption representations and warranties, audit rights, and termination rights in agreements with agents or business partners;
—   periodic testing and evaluation of the program;
—   a system of financial and accounting procedures, including a system of internal accounting controls, designed to ensure the maintenance of 'fair and accurate' books, records, and accounts;
—   promulgation of compliance standards specifically targeting compliance with the FCPA, other applicable anti-corruption laws, and the corporate's code of conduct that apply—'where necessary and appropriate'—to all parties acting on the corporate's behalf in non-US jurisdictions;
—   direct reporting authority from persons responsible for the implementation and oversight of the program to the governing authority (usually the Board of Directors) or a committee thereof; and
—   annual certifications of compliance with the training requirements by all persons receiving training[1].

Although more onerous than the guidance provided by the Sentencing Commission, these common DPA or NPA requirements are generally applied consistently and can reasonably be inferred to reflect current US enforcement authorities' expectations for effective compliance programs.

[1]   See, eg, Deferred Prosecution Agreement, Attachment C: Corporate Compliance Program, *United States v Daimler AG* 1:10-cr-00063 (DDC, Mar 24, 2010).

Lessons from US enforcement guidance

7.51 Under the US experience, the extensive guidance provided above continues to present challenges for business organisations. The most obvious challenge is the guidance's mercurial nature. The Prosecution Principles, the Seaboard Report, and the SEC Enforcement Manual are non-binding and do not constitute an exhaustive list of factors US enforcement agencies may consider when deciding whether to initiate an enforcement action. Identifying trends within the constant flow of DPA and NPA agreements requires both an expansive understanding of past agreements and the diligent monitoring of new agreements that becomes cost-prohibitive for small corporates. The non-binding, extra-judicial nature of these agreements and the DOJ's advisory opinions further muddies the waters for well-meaning business organisations[1]. Corporates seeking to comply with the Bribery Act 2010 must anticipate similar challenges, and are wise to view the prosecutorial guidelines released by the SFO and the Public Prosecutions Office as merely the foundations of their compliance efforts.

[1]   NPAs are not filed with any court and, as such, are not subject to judicial scrutiny. A study conducted by the US Government Accountability Office suggests that, although DPAs must be filed in court, judges are 'generally not involved' in their formation. US Government Accountability Office, Corporate Crime: DOJ Has Taken Steps to Better Track Its Use of Deferred and Non-Prosecution Agreements, But Should Evaluate Effectiveness, at 25 (2009), available at www.gao.gov/new.items/d10110.pdf (last visited 10 January 2011).

7.52 Additionally, the language of DOJ and SEC guidance tends to be just as vague as the FCPA itself. The vague terms of the FCPA, as discussed above, create a broad and flexible enforcement vehicle for US prosecutors. When faced with the staggering penalties associated with a FCPA violation, most organisations agree to harsh, semi-predictable settlement terms in lieu of disputing the meaning of key definitions in court. To this end, the vague enforcement guidance offered by the DOJ and the SEC is effective in the sense that it encourages cautious corporates to adopt broad, stringent compliance programs. The uncertainty regarding the interpretation and enforcement of the FCPA has, however, prompted some criticism that compliance is unduly costly, interferes with legitimate business activity, or creates an unlevel playing field for those subject to the FCPA.

7.53 The UK has an opportunity to learn from the US experience with the guidance summarised above. Even US guidance, which is currently more battle-tested than the recent MOJ final guidance, lacks the specificity and consistent application needed to assuage corporate concerns. Parliament can anticipate that it will face a demand for clearer anti-corruption standards for business organisations, and may face pressure to require an opinion procedure release system that clarifies how the Bribery Act 2010 will be implemented in specific circumstances. Business organisations and members of the legal community, for their part, should view SFO guidance as a starting point rather than the finish line for their compliance efforts.

E   LESSONS FROM US ENFORCEMENT TRENDS

7.54 Criminal statutes that prosecutors frequently employ in so-called 'white collar' prosecutions in the US, such as statutes proscribing conspiracies to commit a criminal offence, conspiracies to defraud the United States, mail and wire fraud, and money laundering, have resulted in numerous criminal trials and, as a result, decisions by US courts—from 'district' or trial courts, and up through circuit courts of appeal to the Supreme Court of the United States—seeking to resolve positions contested through the adversarial process. This body of case law has helped both to define the general meaning of the statutes themselves and to explain the statutes' application to particular facts and circumstances.

7.55 Not so the FCPA. Until 1998, the FCPA was rarely enforced and even more rarely subject to litigation that would give courts the benefit of hearing truly adversarial positions on disputed issues. In this context, the vast majority of 'precedent' is negotiated dispositions between defendants and US enforcement authorities. A handful of individuals and corporates have opted to go to trial and put the government to its burden of proof, but the last FCPA-related acquittal on all charges occurred in 1990[1]. Accordingly, the number of aspects of the FCPA on which US courts have opined remains but a very small percentage of those that a corporate or person subject to the FCPA must navigate in order to comply with the law. Additionally, the DOJ has provided sporadic interpretive guidance through FCPA advisory opinions, although these are subject to the limitations described above and the DOJ expressly deprives such opinions of any precedential value[2].

[1] *United States v Harris Corpn* 3:90-cr-00456 (ND Cal, 1991).
[2] See paras **7.33–7.37**.

7.56 US enforcement authorities' interpretation of the FCPA faces few challenges in the absence of meaningful opportunities for courts to resolve disputed FCPA issues and in the shadow of such substantial potential penalties. It is likely that the SFO will also have considerable leverage over the practical application of the Bribery Act for similar reasons—provided that UK judges' hostility towards negotiated dispositions has little real impact on the terms of negotiated dispositions or Parliament gives prosecutors more express authority to plea bargain. Although the SFO has expressed its intent to exercise discretion in how broadly it interprets the Bribery Act[1], the US example for the past 30-plus years suggests that such restraint may gradually erode in order to overcome complex and creative efforts to evade the Act's prohibitions. Enforcement authorities' leverage over the meaning of the Bribery Act will present fertile conditions for more enforcement actions and increased monetary penalties, should there be an increase in enforcement activity.

[1] See Christopher M Matthews, SFO Director: No 'Safe Harbor' under New UK Bribery Law, MainJustice.com, Oct 20, 2010 (reporting that SFO Director Richard Alderman 'said the SFO would exercise prosecutorial discretion when deciding whether to probe the [gift or hospitality] payment in question' and that the Director said 'Sensible, proportionate expenditure is perfectly lawful, and remains lawful under the [Bribery Act]'), available at www.mainjustice.c om/justanticorruption/2010/10/20/sfo-director-no-safe-harbor-under-new-u-k-bribery-law (last visited 10 January 2011) (subscription required).

Lesson 1: There will always be pressure to make corrupt payments

7.57 The political context that led to the passage of the FCPA was, as discussed above[1], the disclosure of 400 US public companies' use of slush funds to make over $300 million in corrupt payments. Although the brazen use of cash[2]—sometimes in briefcases[3]—still occurs, corporates and individuals subject to the FCPA have employed complex and creative schemes to avoid liability for making corrupt payments to obtain or retain business. Although, of course, only those schemes that have failed have come to public attention, illustrative examples of such (unsuccessful) means employed to avoid detection include:

— the creative use of internal accounting techniques, such as transfers between subsidiaries or departments designed to obscure the use to which the funds will be put[4];
— the use of undisclosed side letters or unwritten agreements[5];
— taking a 'hands-off' approach to the conduct of joint ventures between foreign subsidiaries and foreign government instrumentalities[6];
— the engagement of a subcontractor or joint venture partner in which foreign officials have a beneficial interest[7];
— making contributions to a charity run by a foreign official who, in another capacity, has influence over hospitals' procurement decisions[8];
— agreeing to extra-contractual payments to consultants or third parties[9];
— paying tuition for foreign officials' family members[10]; and
— the use of independent customs agents[11].

Many of these methods are not illegal in and of themselves; only when they are employed as a means to indirectly or directly effect a corrupt payment do they fall foul of the FCPA.

[1] See paras **7.9–7.11**.

[2] See, eg, Plea Agreement, Ex 1 (Statement of Facts) para 2, *United States v SSI Int'l Far East, Ltd* 1:06-cr-00398 (D Or, Oct 10, 2006).

[3] See Ben Conery, Bribe Scheme Key in Jefferson Corruption Trial, Wash Times (July 31, 2009) (describing video surveillance of $100,000 in cash handed over in a briefcase). On August 5, 2009, former US Congressman William J Jefferson was acquitted at trial of the substantive FCPA bribery charges, but was convicted of conspiracy to solicit bribes, deprive citizens of honest services, and violate the FCPA's anti-bribery provisions. Jury Verdict, *United States v Jefferson* 1:07-cr-00209 (ED Va, Aug 5, 2009).

[4] See, eg, Deferred Prosecution Agreement, Attachment A (Statement of Facts) at 2, *United States v Daimler AG*, 1:10-cr-00063 (DDC Mar 24, 2010).

[5] See, eg, Deferred Prosecution Agreement, Attachment A (Statement of Facts) at 61–62, *United States v Daimler AG* 1:10-cr-00063 (DDC, Mar 24, 2010; Complaint paras 19, 40, *SEC v General Electric Co* 1:10-cv-01258 (DDC, July 27, 2010).

[6] See, eg, Complaint paras 14–15, *SEC v RAE Systems Inc* 1:10-cv-02093 (DDC, Dec 10, 2010).

[7] See, eg, Deferred Prosecution Agreement, Attachment A (Statement of Facts) at 36-44, *United States v Daimler AG* 1:10-cr-00063 (DDC, Mar 24, 2010).

[8] See, eg, Complaint paras 1, 6, 13, *SEC v Schering-Plough Corpn* No 1:04-cv-00945 (DDC, June 10, 2004).

[9] See, eg, Complaint para 14, *SEC v Wurzel* 1:09-cv-01005 (DDC, May 29, 2009).

[10] See, eg, Plea Agreement, Ex 1 (Statement of Facts) para 17, *United States v Control Components, Inc* 8:09-cr-00162 (CD Ca, July 24, 2009); Indictment para 21, *United States v Carson* No 8:09-cr-00077 (CD Cal, Apr 8, 2009).

[11] Deferred Prosecution Agreement, Attachment B (Statement of Facts) para 4, *United States v Panalpina World Transport (Holding) Ltd* No 4:10-cr-769 (SD Tex, Nov 4, 2010); Deferred Prosecution Agreement, App B (Statement of Facts) paras 58–59, *United States v Pride Int'l Inc* 4:10-cr-766 (SD Tex, Nov 4, 2010).

7.58 US enforcement authorities have responded to these evasive efforts in two ways:

(1) they have aggressively interpreted the FCPA to expand the scope of prohibited conduct and their own jurisdiction; and

(2) they have increased both enforcement activity and the severity of the consequences for violators.

Corporates and persons subject to the UK Bribery Act 2010 can be expected to be no less creative in attempting to avoid its application, and, to maintain the effectiveness of the Bribery Act, UK authorities may respond to such efforts as have their US counterparts.

Lesson 2: Enforcement authorities interpret anti-bribery laws broadly

7.59 The US experience has been that enforcement agencies will interpret the scope of the law and their jurisdiction broadly and will build support for such interpretations through negotiated dispositions of FCPA investigations. As noted above, for corporate defendants facing a DOJ investigation, this means typically either a DPA or NPA. In some instances, however, a corporate or its subsidiaries will be required to plead guilty to a criminal offence, often under the framework of a negotiated plea agreement. SEC investigations are typically resolved through agreed final judgments in civil proceedings. For natural person defendants, the negotiated disposition available for a DOJ investigation is more commonly an agreement to plead guilty to a violation and, for an SEC investigation, an agreed final judgment in a civil proceeding.

7.60 Although such negotiated dispositions—whose interpretations of the FCPA could be considered 'prosecutorial common law'[1]—certainly indicate how the enforcement agencies interpret the FCPA, the results are by no means an authoritative, binding interpretation for any US court and, as such, are at best guideposts to understanding US agencies' desired scope of the law rather than what the law actually means. Even though a US court must approve plea agreements and deferred prosecution agreements[2], US courts have rarely challenged negotiated dispositions to FCPA investigations, and both parties before a court considering such a disposition share an interest in securing the settlement's approval. Accordingly, US enforcement agency expectations provide the practical interpretation of the law for defendants seeking to resolve an FCPA investigation and mitigate the substantial maximum penalties that attach to FCPA violations.

[1]   See Bruce A Green & Fred C Zacharias, Prosecutorial Neutrality, 2004 Wis L Rev 837, 898 (2004) (discussing how prosecutors' offices develop uniform ways of handling specific types of cases).

[2]   Fed R Crim P 11.

7.61 The following examples demonstrate US enforcement authorities' broad interpretation of the FCPA and their success at engraining their interpretation into negotiated dispositions.

Definition of 'foreign officials'

7.62 The FCPA defines foreign officials, in part, to include officers or employees of foreign governments or foreign government departments or agencies and persons 'acting in an official capacity for or on behalf of' a government, department, or agency[1]. Whether a person is an officer or employee of, or acting in an official capacity for or on behalf of, a foreign government, department, or agency, will rarely be controversial. But the FCPA also defines 'foreign officials' to include officers or employees of foreign government 'instrumentalities' and persons acting in an official capacity for or on behalf of such instrumentalities[2].

[1]   Exchange Act § 30A(f)(1)(A), FCPA §§ 104(h)(2)(A), 104A(f)(2)(A) (codified as amended at 15 USC §§ 78dd-1(f)(1)(A), 78dd-2(h)(2)(A), 78dd-3(f)(2)(A)).
[2]   Exchange Act § 30A(f)(1)(A), FCPA §§ 104(h)(2)(A), 104A(f)(2)(A) (codified as amended at 15 USC §§ 78dd-1(f)(1)(A), 78dd-2(h)(2)(A), 78dd-3(f)(2)(A)). Foreign officials are also defined as officers or employees of public international organisations, such as the World Bank or the United Nations, or persons acting in an official capacity for or on behalf of such organisations: Exchange Act § 30A(f)(1)(B), FCPA §§ 104(h)(2)(B), 104A(f)(2)(B) (codified at 15 USC §§ 78dd-1(f)(1)(B), 78dd-2(h)(2)(B), 78dd-3(f)(2)(B)).

7.63 The FCPA does not define an 'instrumentality' of a foreign government, but other US laws have defined the term in the context of instrumentalities of the US federal or regional governments. For example, in 1976 Congress enacted the Foreign Sovereign Immunities Act ('FSIA')[1]. The FSIA defined an 'agency or instrumentality' of a foreign government as 'an organ of a foreign state or political subdivision thereof, or a majority of whose shares or other ownership interest is owned by a foreign state or political subdivision thereof'[2]. Since 1957, the US Internal Revenue Service has applied a six-part test to determine whether an organisation is an 'instrumentality' of a state or local government and, therefore, exempt from certain federal withholdings from employees' wages:

(1) [W]hether it is used for a governmental purpose and performs a governmental function; (2) whether performance of its function is on behalf of one or more states or political subdivisions; (3) whether there are any private interests involved, or whether the states or political subdivisions involved have the powers and interests of an owner; (4) whether control and supervision of the organisation is vested in public authority or authorities; (5) if express or implied statutory or other authority is necessary for the creation and/or use of such an instrumentality, and whether such authority exists; and (6) the degree of financial autonomy and the source of its operating expenses'[3].

[1]   Public Law 94-583, 90 Stat 2891.
[2]   Public Law 94-583 at § 4, 90 Stat 2891 (codified at 28 USC § 1603(b)(2)).
[3]   IRS Rev Rul 57-128, 1957-1 CB 311.

7.64 The US DOJ, however, has not provided explicit guidance on the meaning of 'instrumentality'. Its FCPA advisory opinions on the subject to date leave much unanswered. In 2010, the DOJ advised that it would not take enforcement action regarding a requestor's retention of a consultant who currently had contracts to act on behalf of the foreign government on other matters because the consultant would not be acting on behalf of the foreign government for the purposes of consulting the requestor[1]. The requestor, among other things, had obtained a local law opinion that the consultant could represent both the foreign government and the requestor at the same time[2]. The DOJ previously, however, had advised that other persons were foreign officials despite local law opinions—including one by the foreign government itself—that the foreign person was not a government officer or employee[3].

[1]   Opinion Procedure Release 10-03 (Sept 1, 2010).
[2]   Opinion Procedure Release 10-03 (Sept 1, 2010).

³   See Opinion Procedure Releases 08-01 (Jan 15, 2008), 94-01 (May 13, 1994).

7.65 In negotiated settlements, the DOJ has taken the position that an unspecified level of foreign government ownership or foreign government control establishes that an organisation is a foreign government instrumentality. As a result, instrumentalities that have been the subject of FCPA dispositions have included state-owned or -controlled airlines[1], hospitals[2], oil companies[3], railways[4], and telecommunications companies[5], even in instances where persons who are foreign officials—rather than the foreign government itself—control the alleged instrumentality[6] or the foreign government owns less than 50% of the instrumentality's shares[7]. Given US enforcement agencies' broad interpretation of 'instrumentality', any involvement, however attenuated, of a foreign official with a business opportunity greatly increases the compliance risk under the FCPA.

[1]   See, eg, Complaint para 2, *SEC v Con-Way Inc* 1:08-cv-01478 (DDC, Aug 27, 2008).
[2]   See, eg, Deferred Prosecution Agreement, Attachment A (Statement of Facts) paras 9–10, *United States v AGA Medical Corpn* 0:08-cr-00172 (D Minn, June 3, 2008).
[3]   See, eg, Plea Agreement, Ex 1, para 5, *United States v Baker Hughes Services International, Inc* 4:07-cr-00129 (SD Tex, Apr 11, 2007).
[4]   See, eg, Non-Prosecution Agreement, Westinghouse Air Brake Technologies Corporation ('WABTEC'), App A (Statement of Facts) paras 3–4, available at www.justice.gov/criminal/fra ud/FCPA/cases/docs/02-08-08wabtec-agree.pdf (last visited 10 January 2011).
[5]   See, eg, Complaint paras 8–9, *SEC v Veraz Networks, Inc* 5:10-cv-02849 (ND Cal, June 29, 2010); Factual Agreement at 1, *United States v Perez* 1:09-cr-20347 (SD Fla, Apr 27, 2009); Factual Agreement at 1, *United States v Diaz* 1:09-cr-20346 (SD Fla, May 18, 2009); Non-Prosecution Agreement, Lucent Technologies Inc, App A (Statement of Facts) paras 1–2, available at www.justice.gov/criminal/fraud/FCPA/cases/docs/11-14-07lucent-agree.pdf (last visited 10 January 2011).
[6]   See, eg, Plea Agreement, Ex 1 (Statement of Facts) para 12, *United States v Baker Hughes Services Int'l, Inc*4:07-cr-00129 (SD Tex, Apr 11, 2007).
[7]   See, eg, Plea Agreement, Ex 3 (Statement of Facts) para 14, *United States v Kellogg Brown & Root LLC* 4:09-cr-00071 (SD Tex, Feb 11, 2009).

Directly or indirectly assisting in obtaining or retaining business

7.66 The FCPA prohibits corrupt payments made 'in order to assist . . . in obtaining or retaining business for or with, or directing business to, any person'[1]. US enforcement authorities have broadly interpreted this 'business nexus' requirement to include payments made in order to:

—   avoid shakedowns through unfounded foreign tax audits or false charges of mislabeling products[2];
—   support the repeal or amendment of laws limiting foreign investments or relating to land development[3];
—   alter design specifications to favour a bidder for government contracts[4];
—   obtain discounted utility and service pricing[5];
—   obtain or expedite official permits, licenses, certifications, or reports[6];
—   expedite or avoid customs inspections or duties[7];
—   reduce or avoid taxes[8];
—   excuse the need for an environmental impact study[9];
—   amend an administrative decree[10]; or

— obtain favourable treatment by foreign courts[11].

[1] Exchange Act § 30A(a), FCPA §§ 104(a), 104A(a) (codified as amended at 15 USC §§ 78dd-1(a), 78dd-2(a), 78dd-3(a)).

[2] See, eg, Non-Prosecution Agreement, Alliance One Int'l Inc, App A (Statement of Facts) para 13, available at www.justice.gov/criminal/fraud/FCPA/cases/docs/08-06-10alliance-one-n pa.pdf (last visited 10 January 2011); Complaint paras 6–7, *SEC v The Dow Chemical Co* No 1:07-cv-00336 (DDC, Feb 12, 2007); Complaint paras 18–21, 28–29, *SEC v KPMG Siddharta Siddharta & Harsono* 4:01-cv-03105 (SD Tex, Sept 11, 2001).

[3] See, eg, Complaint para 9, *SEC v BellSouth Corpn* 1:02-cv-00113 (ND Ga, Jan 15, 2002); Plea Agreement at 2–3, *United States v Halford* 4:01-cr-00221 (WD Mo, Aug 3, 2001).

[4] See, eg, Plea Agreement, Ex 1 (Statement of Facts) para 12, *United States v Control Components, Inc* No 8:09-cr-00162 (CD Ca, July 24, 2009); Complaint para 10, *SEC v ITT Corpn* 1:09-cv-00272 (DDC, Feb 11, 2009).

[5] See, eg, Statement of Offense para 28, *United States v Latin Node, Inc* 1:09-cr-20239 (SD Fla, Apr 3, 2009).

[6] See, eg, Complaint para 4, *SEC v Delta & Pine Land Co* 1:07-cv-01352 (DDC, July 25, 2007); Complaint para 11, *SEC v Dow Chem Co* 1:07-cv-00336 (DDC, Feb 12, 2007).

[7] See, eg, Deferred Prosecution Agreement, Attachment B (Statement of Facts) para 4, *United States v Panalpina World Transport (Holding) Ltd* No 4:10-cr-769 (SD Tex, Nov 4, 2010); Plea Agreement, Ex 4 (Statement of Facts) para 26, *United States v Vetco Gray Controls Inc* 4:07-cr-00004 (SD Tex, Feb 6, 2007).

[8] See, eg, Cease & Desist Order at 2, In the Matter of Bristow Group Inc, SEC Admin Proceeding File No 3-12833 (Sept 26, 2007), available at www.sec.gov/litigation/admin /2007 /34-5633.pdf (last visited 10 January 2011); Complaint paras 21–26, *SEC v Triton Energy Corpn* 1:97-cv-00401 (DDC, Feb 27, 1997).

[9] See Opinion Procedure Release 98-01 (Feb 23, 1998) (advising that such payments could be the basis for an enforcement action).

[10] Deferred Prosecution Agreement, App A (Statement of Facts) paras 4, 7, *United States v Monsanto Co* 1:05-cr-00008 (DDC, Jan 6, 2005).

[11] Deferred Prosecution Agreement, Attachment A (Statement of Facts) para 40, *United States v Willbros Group, Inc* 4:08-cr-0287 (SD Tex, May 14, 2008).

7.67 This 'business nexus' requirement is one of the rare FCPA provisions that have been the subject of a US judicial opinion. Two individual defendants argued, unsuccessfully, at trial that the government failed to establish the business nexus element of an FCPA violation because the payments at issue—to Haitian officials to reduce customs duties and sales taxes on rice—were not payments made strictly to obtain or retain business in Haiti[1]. The court, however, agreed with the government's broad interpretation of the business nexus requirement and held that the FCPA proscribed conduct that either directly or indirectly had an effect that would assist with obtaining or retaining business[2]. Such payments to reduce duties and taxes indirectly assisted the defendant's corporation in obtaining or retaining business, the court held, because they reduced the cost to the corporate of doing business in Haiti[3].

[1] *United States v Kay* 359 F 3d 738, 755–56 (5th Cir, 2004).
[2] *United States v Kay* 359 F 3d 738.
[3] *United States v Kay* 359 F 3d 738 at 756.

7.68 Under US enforcement authorities' broad interpretation of the business nexus requirement, and the courts' apparent endorsement of this interpretation, any activity that has a positive effect on a corporate's business in a foreign country—provided that it is also related to a corrupt payment—can form the basis of an FCPA prosecution.

Payment of 'anything of value'

7.69 The FCPA prohibits the corrupt payment of anything of value to obtain or retain business—there is no *de minimus* exception for trivial payments or the payment of items of nominal value. For example, FCPA liability has resulted from payments of flowers for a foreign official's wife[1], bottles of wine[2], and less than several hundred US dollars[3]. Nor is it required that the thing of value be provided directly to the foreign official. For example, in addition to the aforementioned flowers, given to the foreign official's wife, the SEC resolved an enforcement action against Schering-Plough in 2004 for its contributions to a charitable Polish healthcare foundation headed by a foreign official responsible for procurement decisions at Polish hospitals, even though the payments were not made directly to the official[4].

[1] Complaint para 13, *SEC v Veraz Networks, Inc* 5:10-cv-02849 (ND Cal, June 29, 2010).
[2] Complaint para 23, *SEC v UTStarcom, Inc* 3:09-cv-06094 (ND Cal, Dec 31, 2009).
[3] See, eg, Non-Prosecution Agreement, Paradigm BV, App A (Statement of Facts) para 9, available at www.justice.gov/criminal/fraud/FCPA/cases/docs/09-21-07paradigm-agree.pdf (last visited 10 January 2011); Complaint para 16, *SEC v Avery Dennison Corpn* No 1:09-cv-5493 (CD Cal, July 28, 2009); Complaint para 12, *SEC v The Dow Chemical Co* 1:07-cv-00336 (DDC, Feb 12, 2007).
[4] Complaint paras 6-7, *SEC v Schering-Plough Corpn* No 1:04-cv-00945 (DDC, June 10, 2004).

Sufficient 'knowledge' that payments to third parties will be passed on to a prohibited recipient

7.70 When enacted in 1977, the FCPA prohibited corrupt payments to third parties if the payor knew or had 'reason to know' that all or part of the payment would be passed on to a foreign official, foreign political party or party official, or candidate for foreign office[1]. This standard was criticised for permitting the prosecution of a person who was merely negligent in ascertaining the third party's conduct, even though the DOJ's policy was not to prosecute anyone for negligent FCPA violations[2]. In 1988, Congress amended the level of 'knowledge' required to target more clearly corporates that took a 'head-in-the-sand' approach to compliance, also known as 'willful blindness'[3]. After the 1988 amendments, a person has culpable knowledge of an FCPA violation when:

'1   [S]uch person is aware that [the third party] is engaging in such conduct, that such circumstance exists, or that such result is substantially certain to occur;' or

'2   [S]uch person has a firm belief that such circumstance exists or that such result is substantially certain to occur'[4].

And in the context of a person's knowledge of the existence of a particular circumstance, 'such knowledge is established if a person is aware of a high probability of the existence of such circumstance, unless the person actually believes that such circumstance does not exist'[5].

[1] See FCPA §§ 103(a), 104(a), 91 Stat 1494 (as enacted).
[2] S Rep 99-486, at 25 (1986) (citing S 430, to Amend and Clarify the Foreign Corrupt Practices Act of 1977: Joint Hearing Before the Subcomm. on Int'l Finance and Monetary Policy and the Subcomm on Securities of the S Comm on Banking, Housing, and Urban Affairs, 99th Cong, 2d Sess, at 70 (Statement of John C Keeney, Deputy Assistant Attorney General)).
[3] See HR Rep 100-576, at 920 (1988) (Conf Rep).

⁴ Exchange Act § 30A(f)(2), FCPA §§ 104(h)(3), 104A(f)(3) (codified as amended at 15 USC §§ 78dd-1(f)(2), 78dd-2(h)(3), 78dd-3 (f)(3)).
⁵ Exchange Act § 30A(f)(2), FCPA §§ 104(h)(3), 104A(f)(3) (codified as amended at 15 USC §§ 78dd-1(f)(2), 78dd-2(h)(3), 78dd-3 (f)(3)).

7.71 Unsurprisingly, US enforcement authorities have interpreted broadly the amended knowledge requirement, particularly as to corporates or individuals who, the government alleges, were aware of a 'high probability' that all or part of a payment to a third party would be passed on to a prohibited recipient. For example, evidence of a 'high probability' of such third party diversion has included structuring commission payments into smaller amounts and instructing staff regarding how to avoid raising 'too many questions' about the payments[1], continued payments beyond the expiration of a consulting agreement that were for services not needed to perform the project[2], and even, in an FCPA-related disposition, failing to implement controls that would have alerted the corporate to a 'high probability' of third parties' improper use of payments[3].

[1] Non-Prosecution Agreement, Alliance One Int'l Inc, App A (Statement of Facts) para 45, available at www.justice.gov/criminal/fraud/FCPA/cases/docs/08-06-10alliance-one-npa.pdf (last checked 30 December 2010).
[2] Complaint para 14, *SEC v Wurzel* 1:09-cv-01005 (DDC, May 29, 2009).
[3] Plea Agreement, App B (Statement of Offense) paras 26, 31, 44, *United States v BAE Systems plc* 1:10-cr-00035 (DDC, Mar 1, 2010) (BAE Systems pleaded guilty to a false statement offence under 18 USC § 1001 rather than an FCPA violation, but the DOJ includes the BAE Systems plea agreement as an FCPA-related disposition, see www.justice.gov/criminal/fraud/FCPA/cases/bae-systems.html (last visited 10 January 2011)).

7.72 In 2009, a defendant who chose to go to trial on, among other charges, an alleged conspiracy to violate the anti-bribery provisions, requested a narrower definition of knowledge for the court's instructions to the jury. The court, however, adopted the US government's interpretation of the knowledge requirement and instructed the jury that an example of 'knowledge' of a third party's corrupt payments is where a 'person suspects the fact [and] realised its high probability, but refrained from obtaining the final confirmation because he wanted to be able to deny knowledge'[1]. The jury convicted the defendant, of the conspiracy and other offences, after which the foreman was quoted as saying, 'We thought he knew and definitely should have known'[2].

[1] Jury Instructions at 27, *United States v Bourke* No 1:05-cr-00518-2, Second Superseding Indictment (SDNY, July 8, 2009), available at Richard L Cassin, Back to Bourke, The FCPA Blog (July 19, 2009), www.FCPAblog.com/blog/2009/7/20/back-to-bourke.html (last visited 10 January 2011). The defendant appealed the validity of these instructions to the US Court of Appeals for the Second Circuit. See Notice of Appeal, *United States v Bourke* 1:05-cr-00518-2 (SDNY, Nov 10, 2009).
[2] See Mark Hamblett, Entrepreneur Is Found Guilty of Conspiracy in Azerbaijan, NY Law J, July 13, 2009.

Successor liability for pre-merger conduct

7.73 Perhaps a corollary to the fact that willful blindness is a sufficient level of knowledge to violate the FCPA's anti-bribery provisions, US enforcement authorities' position is that successor liability for an acquired corporate's pre-acquisition or -merger FCPA violations may attach to the acquiring corporate, particularly if the acquiring corporate fails to conduct due diligence and take whatever remedial steps are reasonably necessary to ensure that the post-acquisition cash flows are not the fruits of pre-acquisition corrupt payments. US enforcement authorities also believe that purchasers of corporates who were not subject to the FCPA pre-acquisition can incur FCPA liability if future cash flows are the fruits of prior acts that would have violated the FCPA, had they been done by the purchaser.

7.74 In 2010, the DOJ secured a negotiated disposition whereby a successor corporation admitted to liability for the acts of its corporate predecessors, as opposed to prior instances where the DOJ had penalised the target. Alliance One International, Inc was formed by the 2005 merger of Dimon, Inc and Standard Commercial Corporation, both of whom allegedly violated the FCPA prior to the merger[1]. Although the DOJ entered into a non-prosecution agreement with Alliance One due to Alliance One's voluntary disclosure, subsequent internal investigation, cooperation with US authorities, and lack of post-merger violations, Alliance One still 'admit[ted], accept[ed], and acknowledge[d] successor corporate responsibility for the conduct of its corporate predecessors,' agreed to adopt enhanced internal accounting controls, and agreed to retain—at its own expense—a compliance monitor for a three-year term[2]. Additionally, Alliance One disgorged $10 million of ill-gotten gains to the SEC, and two Alliance One subsidiaries and a former executive pleaded guilty to FCPA violations, paid $9.45 million in criminal fines, and the executive was sentenced to three years' probation[3].

[1]   See generally Non-Prosecution Agreement, Alliance One Int'l, Inc, App A (Statement of Facts), available at www.justice.gov/criminal/fraud/FCPA/cases/docs/08-06-10alliance-one-npa.pdf (last visited 10 January 2011).
[2]   See Non-Prosecution Agreement, Alliance One Int'l, Inc, Apps B and C.
[3]   Plea Agreement, *United States v Alliance One Int'l AG* 4:10-cr-00017 (WD Va, Aug 6, 2010); Complaint, *SEC v Alliance One Int'l, Inc* 1:10-cv-01319 (DDC, Aug 6, 2010); Plea Agreement, *United States v Alliance One Tobacco OSH, LLC* 4:10-cr-00016 (WD Va, Aug 6, 2010); Complaint, *SEC v Elkin* 1:10-cv-00661 (DDC, Apr 28, 2010); Plea Agreement, *United States v Elkin* 4:10-cr-00015 (WD Va, 2010).

7.75 Prior to this 2010 disposition, DOJ advisory opinions had presumed the potential for successor liability and highlighted significant steps taken by requestors to secure no-action relief. In Opinion Procedure Release 04-01, the requesting party had discovered actual FCPA violations by a US acquisition target, including violations by US officers and employees of the target[1]. The DOJ promised to take no enforcement action against the requestor for pre-acquisition conduct, but only after the requestor and the target had conducted extensive, global investigations and the requestor agreed to continue to disclose the results of the investigations to the DOJ and SEC, discipline the employees and officers involved in the misconduct, and extend its compliance program and internal accounting controls to the target[2]. Presumably, these steps are the minimum efforts that US enforcement authorities expect of successor corporates whose predecessors have violated the FCPA.

[1]   Opinion Procedure Release 04-01 (Jan 6, 2004).
[2]   Opinion Procedure Release 04-01 (Jan 6, 2004).

7.76 In Opinion Procedure Release 08-02, the DOJ declined to take enforcement action for a contemplated—and ultimately unsuccessful—acquisition of a corporate that may have committed FCPA or other anti-bribery violations pre-acquisition, although the basis for US FCPA jurisdiction over the target pre-acquisition was not evident from the face of the advisory opinion. The DOJ declined to take enforcement action, however, only because the bidder agreed to undertake an immediate risk assessment, conduct thorough, expedited post-acquisition due diligence that local law did not permit it to conduct pre-acquisition, take remedial steps as necessary, and report periodically to the DOJ[1]. The DOJ reserved the right to take enforcement action against the acquired entity or its personnel (presumably if US jurisdiction had somehow been triggered), a reservation that likely lessened the potential value of the acquisition to the bidding corporate.

In light of such broad successor liability, FCPA due diligence is a critical component of any merger or acquisition due diligence by any entity potentially subject to the FCPA.

[1]   Opinion Procedure Release 08-02 (June 13, 2008).

Other persons 'causing' an act to occur in the US

7.77 In 1998, consistent with its obligations under the OECD's Convention on Combating Bribery of Foreign Public Officials in International Business Transactions, the US expanded the FCPA to exercise territorial jurisdiction over corporates and persons not otherwise subject to the FCPA who, 'while in the territory of the United States,' do any corrupt act in furtherance of a payment to assist with obtaining or retaining business[1]. US enforcement authorities currently interpret this provision, however, to apply to any foreign organisation or natural person who 'causes' an act to occur in the US, regardless of whether such organisation or person is actually in US territory when they cause the act to occur[2].

[1]   International Anti-Bribery and Fair Competition Act of 1998, Public Law 105-366, § 4, 112 Stat 3302 (enacting FCPA § 104A) (codified at 15 USC § 78dd-3(a)).
[2]   US Attorneys' Manual, Criminal Resource Manual § 1018; US DOJ, Layperson's Guide to the FCPA, at www.justice.gov/criminal/fraud/FCPA/docs/lay-persons-guide.pdf (last visited 10 January 2011).

7.78 The questionable legal basis for this reading of the 1998 amendments underscores the aggressiveness of US enforcement authorities' position. This broad interpretation is remarkable given that both houses of the US Congress interpreted the 1998 amendments to apply only when the organisation or natural person was 'physically present' in the US[1], and the unanimity of this legislative history could hardly have surprised US enforcement authorities because it tracked verbatim the DOJ's own 'proposed' legislative history that was submitted to Congress in support of the amendments[2]. And a June 2010 decision by the Supreme Court of the United States reinvigorated the statutory presumption against extraterritorial application of US laws absent a clear indication of congressional intent for such application, at least in the context of securities fraud laws, thereby casting serious doubt on the extraterritorial application of a provision of the FCPA in which Congress expressly tied liability to acts done 'while in the territory of the United States'[3].

[1]   HR Rep 105-802, at 22 (1998); S Rep 105-277, at 6 (1998).
[2]   See US DOJ, Proposed Legislative History, available at www.justice.gov/criminal/fraud/FCPA/docs/leghistory.pdf (last visited 10 January 2011).

[3] *Morrison v Nat'l Australia Bank Ltd* 130 S Ct 2869, 2879-81, 2883 (2010); FCPA § 104A(a) (codified at 15 USC § 78dd-3(a)).

7.79 Regardless, US enforcement authorities have applied, and continue to apply, the 1998 amendments to conduct that caused an act to occur in the US in furtherance of a corrupt payment. Most notably, several recent negotiated dispositions involve foreign subsidiaries of US corporates pleading guilty to FCPA violations for conduct such as causing a proposed budget to be sent from the US to China[1], causing an invoice to be sent by the US parent to the foreign government customer[2], causing a wire transfer from a bank in US territory[3], asking a US parent company to review and approve a wire transfer[4], sending a memorandum to a US parent company's offices regarding 'special' and 'black' payments to foreign officials[5], and causing affiliated US entities to perform acts in US territory in furtherance of the corrupt payment[6]. Until a defendant is willing to risk a criminal conviction in order to put this issue before a US court, US enforcement authorities will likely continue to apply the FCPA to foreign corporates and persons, who would otherwise not be subject to the FCPA, merely because they cause an act to occur in US territory.

[1] See, eg, Plea Agreement, Ex 2 (Statement of Facts) paras 5, 10, *United States v DPC (Tianjin) Co Ltd* 2:05-cr-00482 (DDC, May 20, 2005).
[2] See, eg, Plea Agreement, Ex 1 (Statement of Facts) paras 25, 35, *United States v Alliance One Int'l AG* 4:10-cr-00017 (DDC, Aug 6, 2010).
[3] See, eg, Information paras 48, 50, 73, *United States v Alcatel-Lucent France, SA* 1:10-cr-20906 (SD Fla, Dec 27, 2010). A criminal 'information' is similar to an indictment in that it sets forth the government's allegations, but, unlike an indictment, an information is not returned by a grand jury. Accordingly, informations are the charging documents on which negotiated pleas or deferred prosecutions are based.
[4] Plea Agreement, Ex 1 (Statement of Facts) at paras 2, 17, *United States v SSI Int'l Far East, Ltd* 1:06-cr-00398 (D Or, Oct 10, 2006).
[5] Plea Agreement, Ex 1 (Statement of Facts) para 9, *United States v Alliance One Tobacco OSH, LLC* 4:10-cr-00016 (WD Va, Aug 6, 2010).
[6] Plea Agreement, Ex 4 (Statement of Facts) para 9, *United States v Vetco Gray UK Ltd* No 4:07-cr-00004-2 (SD Tex, Feb 6, 2007).

7.80 It should be noted, however, that many of the examples of foreign subsidiaries' pleading guilty are part of global resolutions between the corporate parent and US enforcement authorities, whereby the corporate parent either avoids pleading guilty or pleads guilty to a non-bribery offence. If US authorities had not been not willing to agree to guilty pleas to bribery-related offences by the foreign subsidiaries, they might have instead required guilty pleas to bribery offences by corporate parents.

Broad application of the SEC's disgorgement remedy

7.81 In 1990, Congress expressly granted the SEC the power, among other things, to enter administrative orders requiring the disgorgement of ill-gotten gains, with pre-judgment interest, for violations of the Exchange Act[1]. Since its enactment in 1934, the Exchange Act had granted US courts the authority to enforce any liabilities or duties arising under the Act[2]. Yet, although the FCPA's anti-bribery and accounting provisions applicable to issuers are part of the Exchange Act, it was not until 2004 that the SEC first reached a negotiated settlement of an FCPA investigation that required disgorgement of ill-gotten gains and prejudgment interest, in that case totalling more than $5.9 million[3].

1   Securities Enforcement Remedies and Penny Stock Reform Act of 1990 (popularly known as the 'Remedies Act'), Public Law 101-429, § 202, 104 Stat 931 (enacting Exchange Act § 21B(e)) (codified at 15 USC § 78u-2(e)).
2   Exchange Act § 27 (codified as amended at 15 USC § 78aa).
3   Complaint at 10, *SEC v ABB Ltd* 1:04-cv-01141 (DDC, July 6, 2004).

7.82 Since 2004, disgorgement and prejudgment interest have become the norm, rather than the exception. For example, in 2010 the SEC recovered over $487 million in disgorgement and prejudgment interest from 16 corporates in FCPA-related investigations, up from nearly $200 million from four corporates in 2009. The SEC has also recovered disgorgement or prejudgment interest of substantial amounts in notable cases, foremost among them the $350 million disgorged by Siemens AG in 2008, the $177 million disgorged by KBR in 2009, and the $125 million disgorged by Snamprogetti Netherlands in 2010.

7.83 Although the SEC had the statutory authority to seek disgorgement and prejudgment interest for nearly 15 years prior to its first use of the remedy, this is an example of an enforcement agency identifying rarely-used powers, at least in the context of anti-corruption enforcement, to further increase the scope of penalties applicable to violators. UK authorities may, if they have not already, identify authorities beyond the Bribery Act 2010 itself that will enhance their ability to punish and deter corrupt payments.

Secondary liability for non-issuers under the Exchange Act for control persons, aiding and abetting, and causing a violation

7.84 Another 're-discovered' basis for SEC enforcement authority in FCPA-related dispositions is control person liability under section 20(a) of the Exchange Act[1]. Section 20(a) has been part of the Exchange Act since its 1934 enactment, but was first used in an FCPA-related disposition in 2009 against corporate executives who, although they had no direct involvement in FCPA violations committed by other corporate personnel, were in a position of supervisory authority and failed to require personnel to make and keep books and records in reasonable detail or to devise and maintain a system of internal accounting controls to provide reasonable assurances that the registration of the corporate's products sold from a Brazilian subsidiary was adequately monitored[2]. The SEC did not allege that the executives had any knowledge of the underlying accounting provision violations; such knowledge is not a requirement for section 20(a) control person liability. As with the disgorgement remedy disclosed above, section 20(a) had granted the SEC authority to impose control person liability well before the recent increase in FCPA enforcement activity, but only recently has the SEC sought to assign secondary liability in the context of an FCPA disposition.

1   Exchange Act § 20(a) (codified as amended at 15 USC § 78t(a)).
2   Complaint paras 66–69, *SEC v Nature's Sunshine Products, Inc* 2:09-cv-00672 (D Utah, July 31, 2009).

7.85 The Exchange Act also permits the SEC to impose aiding and abetting liability against non-issuers, such as corporate officers, directors, or agents[1].

For example, in 2007 the SEC had imposed aiding and abetting liability on a corporate's Chairman and CEO under section 20(e) of the Exchange Act for his corporate's accounting provisions violations, in addition to his own direct liability under the same provisions[2]. The Exchange Act further grants the SEC authority to seek injunctive relief against non-issuers through an administrative proceeding, under section 21C, for causing an issuer to violate the Exchange Act[3]. The SEC's ability to impose secondary liability on non-issuers such as an issuer's officers, directors, and agents of an issuer under theories of control person liability, aiding and abetting liability, and causation liability demonstrates how far US enforcement authorities can reach to enforce the FCPA.

[1] Exchange Act § 20(e) (codified as amended at 15 USC § 78t(e)).
[2] Complaint para 34, *SEC v Fu* 1:07-cv-01735 (DDC, Sept 27, 2007).
[3] Exchange Act §§ 20(b), 21C (codified at 15 USC §§ 78t(b), 78u-3).

Evisceration of available defences or exceptions

7.86 The US experience with the viability of two defences and one exception to FCPA anti-bribery liability is that enforcement authorities will seek to limit their availability until they have little visible significance.

7.87 The anti-bribery provisions provide an affirmative defence for payments that are 'lawful under the written laws and regulations' of a foreign country[1]. In 2008, a US court agreed with prosecutors that this defence was only available when local law permitted the corrupt payment, not when local law proscribed the corrupt payment but absolved those who subsequently disclosed the payment to authorities of criminal liability[2]. Thus limited, this defence will only be available in the unlikely instance of a foreign country expressly allowing the bribery of its officials to obtain or retain business[3].

[1] Exchange Act § 30A(c)(1), FCPA §§ 104(c)(1), 104A(c)(1) (codified at 15 USC §§ 78dd-1(c)(1), 78dd-2(c)(1), 78dd-3(c)(1)).
[2] Opinion & Order, *United States v Bourke* 1:05-cr-00518-2 (SDNY, Oct 21, 2008).
[3] In debating the 1988 amendments that included this affirmative defence, it was reported that a 1977 study relating to the enactment of the FCPA found that no country permits such payments. S Hrg 99-766, at 21 (1986) (Statement of Senator William Proxmire). Reportedly, a 1988 Department of State survey confirmed that no foreign state had since enacted such legislation. Statement of Peter B Clark, Deputy Chief of the Fraud Section, Criminal Division, Department of Justice (Apr 20, 1995) (as reported in Don Zarin, Doing Business under the Foreign Corrupt Practices Act § 5:3 n 24 (2010)).

7.88 The other affirmative defence to an anti-bribery violation applies to reasonable and bona fide promotional expenses directly related to 'the promotion, demonstration, or explanation of products or services' or 'the execution or performance of a contract with a foreign government or agency thereof'[1]. US enforcement authorities have strictly construed this defence. For example, per diems for foreign officials who already have their expenses reimbursed[2], first-class airfare[3], travel arrangements for foreign officials' family members[4], sightseeing or leisure side trips[5], and bogus itinerary items[6] have all been the basis for penalties under the FCPA.

[1] Exchange Act § 30A(c)(2), FCPA §§ 104(c)(2), 104A(c)(2) (codified at 15 USC §§ 78dd-1(c)(2), 78dd-2(c)(2), 78dd-3(c)(2)).

[2] See, eg, Complaint paras 18–19, *United States v Metcalf & Eddy International, Inc* No 1:99-cv-12566 (D Mass,Dec 14, 1999).

[3] See, eg, Complaint para 20, *United States v Metcalf & Eddy International, Inc*, 1:99-cv-12566 (D Mass Dec 14, 1999).

[4] See, eg, Complaint para 19, *United States v Metcalf & Eddy International, Inc*, 1:99-cv-12566 (D Mass Dec 14, 1999).

[5] See, eg, Non-Prosecution Agreement, Lucent Technologies Inc, App A (Statement of Facts) para 13, available at www.justice.gov/criminal/fraud/FCPA/cases/docs/11-14-07lucent-agree.p df (last visited 10 January 2011).

[6] Non-Prosecution Agreement, Lucent Technologies Inc, App A (Statement of Facts) at para 9 (factory inspections where no factories existed).

7.89 Finally, the anti-bribery provisions provide an exception for so-called 'facilitating or expediting' payments, 'the purpose of which is to expedite or to secure the performance of a routine governmental action . . . '[1]. Under the FCPA, 'routine governmental action' includes actions 'ordinarily and commonly performed by a foreign official', such as securing permission to conduct business and utility service, but does not include any action relating to obtaining or retaining business with or from a foreign official[2]. US enforcement authorities have, however, entered into negotiated settlements involving conduct that appears to have been a facilitating payment, such as payments to expedite the customs process[3], and have even prosecuted a corporation for payments to collect monies due to the corporation from the foreign government in relation to completed business[4]. Coupled with the fact that many other countries—including the UK—do not permit facilitating payments, such a narrow interpretation of the already-limited facilitation payments exception largely removes its usefulness.

[1] Exchange Act § 30A(b), FCPA §§ 104(b), 104A(b) (codified at 15 USC §§ 78dd-1(b), 78dd-2(b), 78dd-3(b)).

[2] Exchange Act § 30A(f)(3), FCPA §§ 104(h)(4), 104A(f)(4) (codified at 15 USC §§ 78dd-1(f)(3), 78dd-2(h)(4), 78dd-3(f)(4)).

[3] Mike Koehler, The Payments . . . Would Not Constitute Facilitation Payments for Routine Governmental Actions Within the Meaning of the FCPA, FCPA Professor Blog, November 10, 2010, http://FCPAprofessor.blogspot.com/2010/11/payments-would-not-constitute.html (last visited 10 January 2011); Complaint, *SEC v Con-Way Inc* 1:08-cv-01478 (DDC, Aug 27, 2008).

[4] Plea Agreement, Ex B (Stipulated Facts) paras 4–7, *United States v Vitusa Corpn* No 2:94-cr-00253 (DNJ, Apr 13, 1994).

7.90 Criticism of the defences' and exception's limited applicability might be less well founded if the defences and the exception played a significant role in the DOJ's internal determination whether to investigate or prosecute an alleged corrupt payment. But the data and factual circumstances about such decisions are not visible to corporates seeking to comply with the FCPA, and such assertions—absent transparent data and specific examples from the DOJ—are insufficient bases on which a corporate could proceed with any confidence that a defence or the exception would apply.

Lesson 3: Enforcement authorities will increase enforcement activity over time

7.91 Hand-in-hand with US enforcement authorities' ever-broadening interpretation of the FCPA has been the exponential increase in enforcement activity since 2005, including the number of enforcement actions brought, the amount of monetary penalties imposed, and the number of natural persons charged with criminal violations of the FCPA.

Enforcement statistics[1]

7.92 Since the FCPA was last amended in 1998, there has been an exponential increase in both the number of enforcement actions[2] and the amount of criminal fines and other monetary penalties imposed to resolve FCPA investigations. Since 1998, the number of FCPA-related enforcement actions has increased from the 2000 low of three to a high of 66 in 2009, followed closely by 61 in 2010. In the nine-year period from 1998 through 2006, US authorities brought 89 FCPA-related enforcement actions; from 2007 through 2010, US authorities brought 222 FCPA-related enforcement actions, an annual rate nearly 4.6 times greater than that from 1998 through 2006:

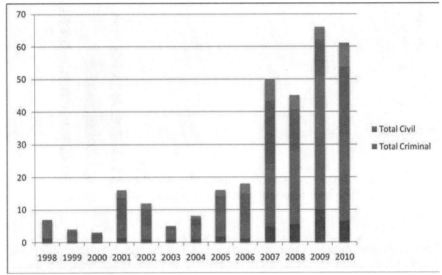

---

[1] The statistics herein for dispositions before and including 30 September 2010 are taken from the Response of the United States, Questions Concerning Phase 3, OECD Working Group on Bribery, App B (updated through Sept 30, 2010), available at www.justice.gov/criminal/fraud/FCPA/docs/response3-appx-b.pdf (last visited 10 January 2011). Data for the remainder of 2010 was based on publicly available information as at 10 January 2011.

[2] The US defined a criminal enforcement action as each person charged with a criminal offence and a civil enforcement action represents the aggregation of each person charged with a civil violation plus each person charged with an administrative violation.

7.93 Since 1998, the US government has also recovered ever-increasing monetary penalties under the FCPA. Part of this increase could be due to increases in the statutory maximum fines[1]. From 1998 to 2004, the total monetary penalties imposed in dispositions with corporations never exceeded $36 million a year and often was below $1 million a year. Then penalties on corporations rose to $48 million in 2005, passed $120 million in 2007, shot to nearly $900 million in 2008, and reached $1.75 billion in 2010. Put another way, corporates paid approximately $142 million in criminal and other penalties from 1998 through 2006 to resolve FCPA-related criminal investigations; from 2007 through 2010 corporates paid approximately $3.4 billion to resolve such investigations, an average annual amount of nearly 53 times the average annual amount from 1998 through 2006.

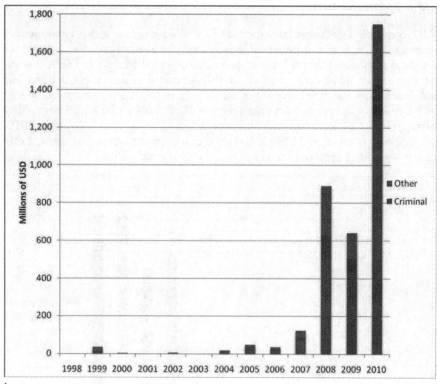

¹ See paras **7.9–7.22**.

7.94 Although outliers skewed the data in 2008 (Siemens: $800 million) and 2009 (KBR: $579 million), 2010 saw three FCPA-related prosecutions resolved for between $330 and 400 million (BAE Systems (false statements), Technip, and Snamprogetti Netherlands) and another three resolved for between $80 and 185 million (Daimler, Panalpina, and Alcatel-Lucent).

7.95 Additionally, US enforcement authorities have taken the position that sending culpable individuals to prison is necessary for the FCPA to have a meaningful deterrent effect. Since 1998, the number of individuals prosecuted for FCPA violations has increased, although these numbers are skewed by the indictment of the 22 sting operation defendants in December 2009:

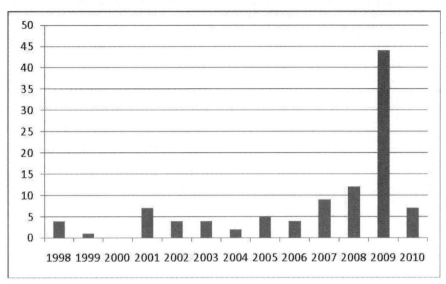

Enforcement methods

7.96 Additionally, the DOJ and SEC now have the resources to conduct industry-wide sweeps once they discover potential FCPA violations by a particular corporate or in a particular geographic region. For example, in February 2007 three wholly-owned subsidiaries of Vetco Gray, Inc pleaded guilty to violating the anti-bribery provisions of the FCPA by employing 'the services of a major international freight forwarding and customs clearing company' to make at least 378 corrupt payments to the Nigerian customs officials[1]. Vetco Gray itself obtained a deferred prosecution agreement, in part, because it had cooperated and agreed to continue cooperating with the DOJ by identifying, among other parties, the consultants, contractors, and subcontractors related to the FCPA violations[2]. This likely marked the beginning of the 'first FCPA-related sweep of a particular industrial sector', according to the SEC, which in November 2010 resulted in seven additional international corporates and their subsidiaries concluding negotiated settlements with the DOJ and SEC[3]. The SEC and the DOJ adopted this proactive tactic to combat what they described as the 'widespread corruption in the oil services industry'[4]. While this was the first such sweep, the SEC vowed that its 'FCPA Unit will continue to focus on industry-wide sweeps, and no industry is immune from investigation'[5]. In 2010, media reports and public financial disclosures suggested that the pharmaceutical industry is currently under DOJ and SEC collective scrutiny for potential FCPA violations[6].

[1] The three subsidiaries were Vetco Gray Controls, Inc, Vetco Gray Controls Ltd, and Vetco Gray UK Ltd. See US DOJ, Press Release, Three Vetco Int'l Ltd. Subsidiaries Plead Guilty to Foreign Bribery and Agree to Pay $26 Million in Criminal Fines (6 February 2007), available at www.justice.gov/opa/pr/2007/February/07_crm_075.html (last visited 10 January 2011).

[2] See Deferred Prosecution Agreement at paras 3–4, *United States v Aibel Group Ltd* 4:07-cr-00005 (SD Tex, Feb 6, 2007).

[3] US SEC, Press Release, SEC Charges Seven Oil Services and Friend Forwarding Companies for Widespread Bribery of Customs Officials (Nov 4, 2010), available at www.sec.gov/news/press/2010/2010-214.htm (last visited 10 January 2011).

⁴ US SEC, Press Release, SEC Charges Seven Oil Services and Friend Forwarding Companies for Widespread Bribery of Customs Officials (Nov 4, 2010), available at www.sec.gov/news/press /2010/2010-214.htm (last visited 10 January 2011).
⁵ US SEC, Press Release, SEC Charges Seven Oil Services and Friend Forwarding Companies for Widespread Bribery of Customs Officials (Nov 4, 2010), available at www.sec.gov/news/press /2010/2010-214.htm (last visited 10 January 2011).
⁶ See, eg, Stephanie Kirchgaessner, US Probes Corruption in Big Pharma, (2010) Financial Times, 12 August.

7.97 After years of encouraging voluntary disclosures of FCPA investigations, in 2009 the DOJ employed more traditional law enforcement tactics by executing a large-scale FCPA sting operation. In December 2009, the DOJ indicted 22 individuals from 16 corporates who believed that they would have the business opportunity to sell equipment to the Gabonese military if they made corrupt payments to third parties while believing that the payments would benefit Gabonese officials[1]. The operation was the first large-scale use of undercover law enforcement techniques to target violations of the FCPA.

¹ US DOJ, Press Release, Twenty-Two Executives and Employees of Military and Law Enforcement Products Companies Charged with Foreign Bribery Scheme (Jan 19, 2010), available at www.justice.gov/opa/pr/2010/January/10-crm-048.html (last visited 10 January 2011).

7.98 And on 3 November 2010, the SEC proposed rules to implement an expanded securities law whistleblower program established by the Dodd-Frank Wall Street Reform and Consumer Protection Act ('Dodd-Frank Act')[1]. The Dodd-Frank Act expanded the program from its prior focus on insider trading offences to include any securities law violation, which would include violations by issuers of both the FCPA's anti-bribery and accounting provisions[2]. Under the proposed rules, whistleblowers who provide accurate, original information that leads to a SEC enforcement action or a DOJ criminal disposition can collect between 10% and 30% of any resulting disgorgement, prejudgment interest, and civil or criminal fines or monetary penalties that exceed $1,000,000. The proposed rules have already generated much public comment, and the SEC has until April 2011 to promulgate a final version of the rules[3].

¹ Dodd-Frank Act, Public Law 111-203, § 922, 124 Stat 1841 (2010) (enacting Exchange Act § 21F).
² Dodd-Frank Act, Public Law 111-203, § 922, 124 Stat 1841 (2010) (enacting Exchange Act § 21F).
³ The Dodd-Frank Act gives the SEC no more than 270 days after the Act's date of enactment—21 July 2010—to implement the regulations, which gives the SEC no later than Sunday 17 April 2010, to do so. Dodd-Frank Act § 924.

The rise of corporate monitors

7.99 A common feature of deferred prosecution agreements after the 2002 enactment of Sarbanes-Oxley was the requirement that corporates engage, at their own expense, an outside compliance monitor for a certain term of years. Over time, the DOJ established a policy to formalise the selection of monitors and to set expectations for resolving disputes between a corporate and the monitor about required compliance steps[1]. The SEC has also occasionally required corporates to engage compliance consultants, who serve the same function as monitors and sometimes are the same person, as part of the negotiated resolution of its investigations. Although the DOJ and SEC do not impose a corporate monitor in every negotiated FCPA disposition[2], monitors remain an important tool in US enforcement agencies' compliance arsenal.

[1] Memorandum from Craig S Morford for Heads of Department Components and US Attorneys (Mar 7, 2008), available at www.justice.gov/dag/morford-useofmonitorsmemo-03072008.pdf (last visited 10 January 2011), supplemented by Memorandum from Gary G Grindler, Acting Deputy Attorney General for Heads of Department Components and US Attorneys (May 25, 2010), available at www.justice.gov/dag/dag-memo-guidance-monitors.html (last visited 10 January 2011).

[2] See, eg, Deferred Prosecution Agreement, Attachment D, *United States v Panalpina World Transport (Holding) Ltd* No 4:10-cr-769 (SD Tex, Nov 4, 2010) (requiring only compliance self-reporting).

7.100 Some corporates proactively engage a compliance monitor during the course of cooperating with US authorities, and others have independently hired chief compliance officers or tasked general counsels with compliance responsibility. Such practices complement the recently-amended United States Sentencing Guidelines that entered into effect on 1 November 2010, which reward entities for employing internal compliance monitors as a part of their anti-corruption efforts with mitigated penalties[1].

[1] USS G § 8B2.1, cmt 6 (noting that companies can receive remediation credit for hiring 'outside professional advisor[s] to ensure adequate assessment and implementation' of effective compliance programs).

Overall lessons for UK enforcement

7.101 Based on the US experience described above, UK authorities will likely need to broadly interpret and apply the Bribery Act 2010 in order to detect, punish, and deter increasingly sophisticated attempts at evasion. The text of the Bribery Act is likely to provide the SFO with much fodder for broad interpretation. Its ability to do so, however, might be limited if early rumblings against negotiated criminal settlements by UK judges result in altering or preventing such settlements and Parliament does not step in to provide the SFO with the necessary authority[1].

[1] See, eg, Jane Croft, BAE Fined £500,000 in Tanzania Probe, (2010) Financial Times, 20 December (reporting the sentencing judge's misgivings about the negotiated plea process but eventual acceptance of the plea).

KEY POINTS FROM CHAPTER 7

7.102 The key lessons from the US experience under the FCPA are:

*   The ever-present incentives and pressures to pay bribes will cause many persons to attempt to evade the acts' prohibitions, and enforcement authorities will respond by broadly interpreting the substance of such acts and their jurisdiction to enforce such acts.

- If UK judges eventually reduce their hostility to negotiated criminal settlements of anti-corruption investigations, the SFO will have considerable leverage over the practical meaning and implementation of the Bribery Act through prosecutorial common law.
- Given the breadth of the Bribery Act and its potential impact on business with UK operations, it will likely generate frequent attempts at legislative modification or amendment, with unpredictable results.
- Shared enforcement responsibility requires clear communication both among responsible enforcement agencies and between enforcement agencies and persons subject to their authority.
- Effective guidance will be difficult for UK authorities to promulgate; even the most detailed guidance will likely leave unanswered questions.

Chapter 8

THE PROSECUTING AUTHORITIES

A   THE SERIOUS FRAUD OFFICE

8.1 The Serious Fraud Office ('SFO') is currently the lead agency in England, Wales and Northern Ireland in prosecuting cases of domestic and overseas corruption. The Bribery Act 2010 creates a new regime and the SFO is poised to become the principal enforcer of that regime, particularly with regard to the conduct of companies. Its declared aim in exercising its prosecutorial powers is to generate a cultural change in business so that bribery is no longer seen as a necessary or acceptable practice.

Culture change at the SFO

8.2 As part of the research for this book an interview was held with Richard Alderman, Director of the Serious Fraud Office ('SFO') in December 2010. What emerged with clarity from that exchange is the proactive approach of the SFO to its task of enforcing the Bribery Act 2010.

8.3 The SFO has the twin aims of education and prevention in addition to its more traditional role as enforcement agency. As the Director saw it, 'the SFO has to be out there talking to business and advisers in the UK and internationally about how they build up an anti-corruption culture. A dialogue has begun with a number of large FTSE companies (together with major corporates based in other jurisdictions) with the regulator taking heed of concerns expressed about enforcement of the new Act'. In particular the SFO is cognisant of company concerns about over-zealous prosecutors. Mr Alderman went on to say:

> 'I want to be at pains to say we will be behaving in a proportionate manner and that we are focussing on the development of an anti-corruption culture. I want to save the SFO's time and resource for the real corruption cases—those companies that will not subscribe to the culture. Those are the corporations, UK or foreign, that we will be after . . . The SFO is becoming a prevention focussed authority as well as educative, it is no longer just the traditional investigation/prosecution model. If you look at successful regulatory models I think we should be heading for the Hong Kong and Singapore models which are very successful and are world leaders. There is a culture change progress . . . There is a different culture developing in the SFO as well—the traditional law enforcement culture needs commercial sensitivity and awareness of the needs of business as well as the fact that business is very varied. We are focusing on trying to make sure staff have commercial awareness. We have also developed excellent links with a range of

non-governmental organisations and international institutions who talk to us about the very real damage that is done to societies by corruption and the impact on the citizens of those societies'.

8.4 The SFO is seeking to warn and educate about the aspects of corporate culture which may fall foul of the Act. To that end the Serious Fraud Office has produced joint guidance with the Director of Public Prosecutions which was published on 29 March 2011. The SFO Guidance is to be read in tandem with the MOJ final guidance which was published on 30 March 2011. These two documents will be key to the approach of the SFO to its enforcement role.

8.5 The SFO will revisit its guidance on self-reporting published in July 2009, which is discussed below, following the issue of the MOJ final guidance. Part of that review will involve reflecting upon the comments of companies on the current system and including some of their suggested changes.

8.6 The SFO's dialogue with companies extends to listening to their concerns about the difficulties where demands for a bribe are made in corrupt jurisdictions. Companies are asking for the SFO's help in resisting the demands. For example, the SFO has been approached by a company being subjected to increasing demands at the border of a country to which it is exporting its goods. The SFO encouraged the company to talk to other companies (including competitors based in other jurisdictions). As a result of this, there was a process of discussion with the country concerned. This process had an impact and reduced the demand for bribes. One of the difficulties identified by companies is that often those individuals seeking the bribes are not paid by their governments and their income is dependent on receiving bribes. Mr Alderman commented:

> 'The SFO has no magic wand but because of the wide range of our international contacts we can raise the issues with the national government and others. This can be very influential if carried out sensitively and constructively. We all need to play a stronger part therefore in curbing the demand side to prevent ethical UK players being at a competitive disadvantage in a number of countries'.

8.7 The Director's view was that the new proposed Economic Crime Agency ('ECA') should have the potential to be a significant body in this area because it will have a more comprehensive range of tools to tackle the problems of bribery.

SFO Guidance on Corporate Prosecutions

8.8 The Guidance on Corporate Prosecutions sets out the common approach to be taken by the Director of Public Prosecutions, the Director of the SFO and the Director of the Revenue and Customs Prosecution Office in relation to corporate offences other than manslaughter. It was agreed in conjunction with the Attorney-General and outlines in detail additional public interest factors for and against the prosecution of corporate offenders which are additional to the 'public interest' factors set out in the Code for Crown Prosecutors.

8.9 Paragraph 30 onwards sets out those additional 'public interest' factors. The evidence in a case must, of course, provide a realistic prospect of conviction before the prosecutor turns to the 'public interest' test. The more serious a case is, the more likely it will be in the public interest to pursue a prosecution. Markers of seriousness include the value of any gain or loss, the risk of harm to the public, to unidentified victims and shareholders, employees and creditors and to the stability and integrity of financial markets and international trade. The impact of offending in other countries, not just the UK, will be taken into account.

8.10 The list of additional factors in favour of prosecution in the Guidance is not exhaustive and includes:

— where there is a history of similar conduct (including prior criminal, civil and regulatory enforcement actions against the company);
— where the conduct alleged is part of the established business practices of the company;
— where the offence was committed at a time when the company had an ineffective corporate compliance programme;
— where the company had previously been subject to warning, sanctions or criminal charges and had nonetheless failed to take adequate action to prevent future unlawful conduct or had continued to engage in the conduct;
— failure to report wrongdoing within a reasonable time of the offending coming to light;
— failure to report properly and fully the true extent of the wrongdoing.

8.11 The Guidance gives the following as additional public interest factors against prosecution:

— a genuinely proactive approach adopted by the corporate management team when the offending is brought to their notice, involving self-reporting and remedial actions, including the compensation of victims. In applying this factor the prosecutor needs to establish whether sufficient information about the company in its entirety has been supplied in order to assess whether the company has been proactively compliant. This will include making witnesses available and disclosure of the details of any internal investigation;
— a lack of history of similar conduct including prior criminal, civil and regulatory enforcement actions against the company: contact will be made with other regulators to ascertain whether investigations are being conducted in relation to the due diligence of the company;
— the existence of a genuinely proactive and effective corporate compliance programme;
— the availability of civil or regulatory remedies that are likely to be effective and more proportionate. This may include Civil Recovery Orders or Serious Crime Prevention Orders. The prosecutor must ensure the totality of the offending is identified;
— the offending represents isolated actions by individuals, for example by a rogue director;
— the offending is not recent in nature and the company in its current form is effectively a different body to that which committed the offence, for example it has been taken over by another company, it no longer operates in the relevant market, culpable individuals have left or been dismissed, or corporate structures have been changed in such a way as to make re-offending impossible;

— the fact that a conviction will have adverse consequences for the company under European law because it will exclude it from tendering for public contracts within the European Union (article 45 of Directive 2004/18/EC). However, prosecutors should bear in mind that a decision not to prosecute because the Directive is engaged will tend to undermine its deterrent effect;

— the company is in the process of being wound up.

8.12 The Guidance goes on expressly to remind prosecutors of the UK's commitment to abide by article 5 of the OECD Convention, namely that investigation and prosecution of bribery by a foreign public official shall not be influenced by considerations of national economic interest, the potential effect upon relations with another state or the identity of the natural and legal persons involved. Prosecutors are reminded to consider the commercial consequences of a conviction under European law to ensure any outcome is proportionate.

8.13 One of the issues which remains to be resolved is whether the SFO should take into account the commercial consequences of a decision to prosecute a company. Is the regulator ready to precipitate what the Director of the SFO termed an '*Arthur Andersen scenario*', effectively preventing a company from participating in procurement and thus destroying its ability to function? Arthur Andersen was prosecuted in the USA for obstructing the course of justice in relation to an investigation into its role as the auditor to Enron, which had collapsed in a vast scandal in 2001. Ultimately, the Supreme Court in the USA overturned the conviction, but by then Arthur Andersen had lost the majority of its customers and had shut down. Is it any function of a regulator to have regard to the consequences for employment with its inevitable impact upon families? It is understood that this impact on Arthur Andersen was one of the reasons why the US developed deferred prosecution agreements, so that in future cases this impact could be avoided. The Director's view is that he would have reservations about taking action if the wrongdoing were below board level:

'If a company is genuinely rotten, however, or there is such serious offending such that the public would not understand the justification for not pursuing them the SFO would prosecute'.

He would also have to consider in any event what action (if any) to take at the individual level.

The SFO's corruption indicators

8.14 What is of note is that the current corruption indicators published on the SFO's website are reflective of the guidance on corporate prosecutions, suggesting that a consistent approach is being taken to determining whether or not to pursue a prosecution against a corporate generally and a corporate involved in bribery. The SFO's non-exhaustive list of 'corruption indicators' is there to assist employees of companies to detect questionable practices. These 19 indicators give a good insight into what the SFO will consider to be evidence of corrupt practices in any investigation it undertakes. Examples selected from the list include: abnormal cash payments; pressure exerted for urgent payment; abnormal commission percentages; private meetings with contractors hoping to tender for contracts; lavish gifts being received; agreeing unfavourable contracts; an unexplained preference for certain contractors during tendering; avoidance of independent checks; missing documents or records; company procedures not being followed, and the payment of, or making funds available for, high value expenses or school fees.

The Prosecutor's discretion

8.15 The power of the Director of the SFO to investigate a suspected offence is conferred by statute under the Criminal Justice Act 1987, s 1(2). Although he is required to discharge his functions under the superintendence of the Attorney-General, any decision he makes as to investigation or prosecution is for him to reach independently.

8.16 The most recent judicial examination of the scope of discretion of the Director of the SFO to instigate and pursue an investigation into corruption is that of Moses LJ in *R (on the application of Corner House Research and the Campaign Against the Arms Trade) v Director of the Serious Fraud Office and BAE Systems plc*[1]:

'He described the discretion whether to investigate as even more open-ended than the decision to prosecute . . . The process by which decisions to prosecute are taken is well-known; there are two stages: the evidential stage and, if passed, the public interest stage . . . The Code lists a wide range of public interest factors in favour and against prosecution . . . It is true that the question whether a prosecution is in the public interest will usually be decided after the prosecutor has collated all the information necessary to reach a conclusion as to whether the evidence is sufficient to found a successful prosecution. The Code (at 5.1) does not envisage any need to consider the public interest if the evidence is insufficient. But a prosecutor is entitled to conclude an investigation well before all potential evidence is gathered, for example when he foresees that the process will be so long and costly as not to be worth the candle. Moreover, there is a danger in placing the evidential and public interest issues in too confined a pair of compartments. An investigation which raises public interest issues may well be required to pass a more stringent evidential test than one in which no public interest issue arises. The instant case is an example of the overlap: once it is accepted that a prosecution would seriously damage commercial and diplomatic relations with Saudi Arabia, it would be folly to pursue a prosecution without a rigorous analysis of its prospect of success.

We must start, therefore, by accepting, at least as a generality, that the Director's discretion is of sufficient width to entitle him to take into account risk to life and to national security in deciding whether to continue an investigation. For example, the need to protect the safety, or even the life of an informant may lead to a decision to discontinue a prosecution. Article 2 of the ECHR requires the Director and a government in a democratic society to protect and safeguard the lives of its citizens . . .

Independence is fundamental to the proper exercise of the Director's powers. Those authorities on which the Director relied to establish the width of his discretion support that proposition. One of the very bases for affording a prosecutor so wide an ambit of judgment is the recognition of his independence (see the references by Lord Bingham CJ to the independence of the Director of Public Prosecutions, answerable to the Attorney-General and to no one else and to the independent judgment of Treasury Counsel in *R v DPP Ex p Manning* [2001] 1 QB 330 at § 23). The Director of the SFO is answerable to no one. By the 1987 Act, Parliament has conferred on him alone the power to reach an independent, professional judgment, subject only to the superintendence of the

Attorney-General. Whatever superintendence may mean, it does not permit the Attorney-General to exert pressure on the Director, let alone make a decision in relation to an investigation which the Director wishes to pursue'.

[1]   [2008] EWHC 714 (Admin), [2009] AC 756, [2008] 4 All ER 927.

8.17 The House of Lords allowed the Director's appeal against the decision of the Divisional Court and Lord Bingham of Cornhill made the following observations[1]:

'32 Of course, and this again is uncontroversial, the discretions conferred on the Director are not unfettered. He must seek to exercise his powers so as to promote the statutory purpose for which he is given them. He must direct himself correctly in law. He must act lawfully. He must do his best to exercise an objective judgment on the relevant material available to him. He must exercise his powers in good faith, uninfluenced by any ulterior motive, predilection or prejudice. In the present case, the claimants have not sought to impugn the Director's good faith and honesty in any way.

33 The first duty of the Director is, in appropriate cases, to investigate and prosecute. The Director and his colleagues performed that duty'.

[1]   [2008] UKHL 60.

8.18 The SFO, like the Financial Services Authority and the Office of Fair Trading, is what can be described as a 'selective prosecutor,' in that it has a range of options available to it in considering how to dispose of a case. The obligation incumbent on a selective prosecutor is set out in *R v IRC, ex p Mead*[1], namely to consider each case fairly on its merits and dispassionately to see whether the criteria for prosecution are met. The decision to prosecute must be taken in good faith in order to meet the prosecuting agencies' proper objective. A 'selective prosecutor's' decisions will not be overturned unless they can be shown to be *Wednesbury* unreasonable or taken in bad faith.

[1]   [1993] 1 All ER 772, [1992] STC 484.

8.19 In each instance careful consideration will be given to whether the case is suitable for a criminal, regulatory or civil route. Doubtless, recent judicial comment will form part of that consideration. Of note were the sentencing remarks of Thomas LJ in *R v Innospec Ltd*[1], who gave a clear warning that conduct which is criminal in nature should not be dealt with by the civil route merely because a corporate entity is involved:

'However there is a more important general principle. Those who commit such serious crimes as corruption of senior foreign government officials must not be viewed or treated in any different way to other criminals. It will therefore rarely be appropriate for criminal conduct by a company to be dealt with by means of a civil recovery order; the criminal courts can take account of cooperation and the provision of evidence against others by reducing the fine otherwise payable. It is of the greatest public interest that the serious criminality of any, including companies, who engage in the corruption of foreign governments, is made patent for all to see by the imposition of criminal and not civil sanctions. It would be inconsistent with basic principles of justice for the criminality of corporations to be glossed over by a civil as opposed to a criminal sanction. There may, of course, be a place for a civil order, for example, as a means of compensation in addition to a fine'.

[1]   [2010] Crim LR 665.

8.20 This echoes the views of the Lord Chief Justice as expressed in *R v McQuoid*[1], an appeal against sentence in the first insider dealing case prosecuted by the FSA (para 9):

'We therefore emphasise that this kind of conduct does not merely contravene regulatory mechanisms. If there ever was a feeling that insider dealing was a matter to be covered by regulation, that impression should be rapidly dissipated. The message must be clear: when it is done deliberately, insider dealing is a species of fraud; it is cheating. Prosecution in open and public court will often, and perhaps much more so now than in the past, be appropriate. Although those who perpetrate the offence may hope, if caught, to escape with regulatory proceedings, they can have no legitimate expectation of avoiding prosecution and sentence'.

[1] [2009] EWCA Crim 1301, [2009] 4 All ER 388, [2010] 1 Cr App Rep (S) 269 (430).

When will the SFO prosecute?

8.21 Guidance entitled 'The Approach of the Serious Fraud Office to dealing with cases of Overseas Corruption' has also been published to which corporations seeking to ensure compliance with the Act regarding the offence of failing to prevent bribery should have regard. Paragraph 22 of that Guidance repeats the central aim of promoting a 'modern corporate culture' and states that the SFO wishes to encourage the development of such a culture in its dealings with business, reserving prosecution for those who will not participate. In determining whether it is in the public interest to prosecute, the SFO will look for evidence of procedures designed to reduce risk and encourage a 'non-bribery culture' within the business. Examples of this include a clear anti-corruption policy which is supported by those in senior positions, a code of ethics, principles that apply regardless of local law or culture, individual accountability, a policy on gifts, hospitality and facilitation payments, a helpline for employees to report concerns, appropriate and consistent disciplinary procedures and remedial action if corruption has previously arisen.

Joint Prosecution Guidance of the Director of the Serious Fraud Office and the Director of Public Prosecutions

8.22 The press release of 30 March 2011 which issued the Joint Guidance stated that its purpose is to enable prosecutors to adopt a consistent approach to decision making across the whole range of bribery cases. It aims to set out clearly the issues a prosecutor must consider before seeking the personal consent of either the Director of Public Prosecutions or the Director of the SFO to prosecute a corporation or an individual. It endeavours to make decisions to prosecute more open and transparent. The Joint Guidance is not exhaustive and is intended to give a steer to prosecutors considering a wide range of circumstances and levels of culpability which may arise any particular case.

The Joint Guidance is subject to the standard Code for Crown Prosecutors and should also be read in conjunction with the Guidance on Corporate Prosecutions discussed at para **8.8**. The introduction to the Guidance states 'The Act is not intended to penalise ethically run companies that encounter an isolated incident of bribery'. The scope of the Act is set out to embrace primarily commercial bribery, but the Guidance goes on to make it clear that it will cover non-commercial bribery, for example attempts to influence decisions by local authorities, regulatory bodies or elected representatives on matters such as planning consent, school admission procedures and driving tests.

Under the Code for Crown Prosecutors it is clear that a prosecutor must first consider the evidential test. A case must not proceed, no matter how serious or sensitive, if the evidential threshold is not met. In determining this limb of the test, prosecutors are directed by the Guidance to consider both the direct evidence there may be of actual intention to bribe, or knowledge or belief of the same, as well as whether the relevant state of mind can be inferred from the circumstances, including the value of the advantage sought or obtained. Prosecutors are reminded to draft separate counts to cover actual knowledge or inferred knowledge to avoid duplicity and to make it clear if these counts are charged in the alternative.

If the evidence is sufficient, the prosecutor will proceed to consider the public interest element of the test, which is expressly stated as not being merely a matter of adding up the factors for or against prosecution in any given case, but a full evaluation of all the evidence. The full list of factors is set out in the Code for Crown Prosecutors and the Guidance draws attention to some of particular relevance in the context of bribery offences as follows:

'Factors tending in favour of prosecution:

— A conviction for bribery is likely to attract a significant sentence (Code 4.16a);
— Offences will often be premeditated and may include an element of corruption of the person bribed (Code 4.16e and k);
— Offences may be committed in order to facilitate more serious offending (Code 4.16i);
— Those involved in bribery may be in positions of authority or trust and take advantage of that position (Code 4.16n).

Factors tending against prosecution:
The factors tending against prosecution may include cases where:

— The court is likely to impose only a nominal penalty (Code 4.17a);
— The harm can be described as minor and was the result of a single incident (Code 4.17e);
— There has been a genuinely proactive approach involving self-reporting and remedial action (additional factor (a) in the Guidance on Corporate Prosecutions).'

In addressing s 6 (bribery of foreign public officials), the guidance states that 'prevention of bribery of foreign public officials is a significant policy aspect of the Act'. When considering the public interest stage, the factors tending in favour of or against prosecution referred to in respect of 'active bribery' (s 1) are likely to be relevant. 'A prosecution will usually take place unless the prosecutor is sure that there are public interest factors tending against prosecution which outweigh those tending in favour'. Further, the guidance states that:

'Bribery of foreign public officials may also be prosecuted, in appropriate cases, under section 1, making use of the extended extra-territorial jurisdiction. This may be the case, for example, if it is difficult to prove that the person bribed is a foreign public official. It should be noted, however, that under section 1 it will be necessary to prove the improper performance element'.

The guidance then goes on to specifically deal with facilitation payments and with hospitality and promotional expenses. The guidance identifies the factors in favour or against prosecution in relation to facilitation payments. For a detailed discussion of these payments and hospitality, see Chapter 5.

In dealing with s 7 (the failure of commercial organisations to prevent bribery) the guidance states that this offence:

' . . . does not replace or remove direct corporate liability for bribery. If it can be proved that someone representing the corporate 'directing mind' bribes or receives a bribe or encourages or assists someone else to do so then it may be appropriate to charge the organisation with a section 1 or 6 offence in the alternative or in addition to any offence under section 7 (or a section 2 offence if the offence relates to being bribed)'.

In dealing with the defence of adequate procedures the guidance states that prosecutors must, at the evidential test stage, consider this defence as it will be highly relevant to a consideration of a realistic prospect of conviction and:

'Prosecutors must look carefully at all the circumstances in which the alleged bribe occurred including the adequacy of any anti-bribery procedures. A single instance of bribery does not necessarily mean that an organisation's procedures are inadequate. For example, the actions of an agent or an employee may be wilfully contrary to very robust corporate contractual requirements, instructions or guidance'.

Practicalities

8.23 The SFO keeps a register of all overseas corruption allegations. It discusses the allocation of each case with the City of London police. The working assumption is that the police, with special funding for this task, would look at the role of individuals and that if it is a corporation it will be dealt with by the SFO.

The SFO's powers under the Criminal Justice Act 1987, s 2

8.24 The SFO's primary investigation powers are contained in the Criminal Justice Act 1987 ('CJA 1987'). Under the CJA 1987, s 2, the SFO has statutory powers to search property and to compel persons to answer questions and produce documents. It gives the Director or a designated member of staff the power to require a person or entity to provide information for the purpose of an investigation. This takes the form of interviewing people, requiring them to produce material or searching premises.

8.25 The SFO may only use this power if the Director finds reasonable grounds to suspect an offence has been committed involving serious or complex fraud or bribery (corruption). The CJA 1987 places restrictions on the extent to which answers given by a defendant in response to questions pursuant to a notice under the CJA 1987, s 2 may be used in evidence against that defendant:

'(8) A statement by a person in response to a requirement imposed by virtue of this section may only be used in evidence against him—

(a)   on a prosecution for an offence under subsection (14) below; or
(b)   on a prosecution for some other offence where in giving evidence he makes a statement inconsistent with it.

(8AA) However, the statement may not be used against that person by virtue of paragraph (b) of subsection (8) unless evidence relating to it is adduced, or a question relating to it is asked, by or on behalf of that person in the proceedings arising out of the prosecution'.

B   THE CROWN PROSECUTION SERVICE

8.26 Under the Bribery Act 2010, s 10 the CPS and the Director of Revenue and Customs Prosecutions ('RCPO') are also named prosecution agencies. The CPS Central Fraud Group ('CFG') was formed by the merger of the former Fraud Prosecution Service (the serious fraud arm of the CPS) and the Revenue and Customs Prosecutions Office fiscal (tax and duties) fraud divisions. The Group is headed by David Green QC and has three divisions as follows:

—   Fraud North which has offices in Manchester and York. The York office was formerly the Fraud Prosecution Service Northern Office. Fraud North deals with both fiscal and non-fiscal cases. At the date of publication the head of this division was Elizabeth Bailey;
—   Fiscal Fraud South, headed by Matthew Wagstaff and based in London;
—   Non-Fiscal Fraud South, the former Fraud Prosecution Service, in London. This division is headed by Malcolm McHaffie and covers the southern half of England and Wales including the City of London (fraud and corruption) and Metropolitan Police SCD6 (fraud, corruption, money laundering, e-crime, and Olympic team). The division also deals with all HMRC investigated cases relating to the brokering of weapons, military and nuclear goods;
—   in addition to this the CFG is supported by a specialist restraint and asset recovery unit within the CPS known as the Proceeds of Crime Unit ('POCU') headed by Jeremy Rawlins which sits within the CPS Organised Crime Division (headed by Alun Milford). POCU deals with all restraint and enforcement work on behalf of CFG.

8.27 The CFG defines fiscal fraud as tax fraud such as VAT, MTIC, alcohols, fuel oils, tobacco frauds, and non-fiscal fraud as all other frauds, such as those which formerly fell within the remit of the Fraud Prosecution Service. It encompasses HMRC investigated arms dealing and sanctions cases.

8.28 Cases are referred to the CFG by investigators or internally within the CPS. Police and HMRC are the main referrers but a range of other investigators also refer cases to it, including local authorities, the Ministry of Defence and the Financial Services Authority. The CFG's non-fiscal cases largely involve alleged offending in a corporate context, although the view of the CFG is that it is generally more practical and effective to prosecute individuals rather than companies. At the date of publication the CFG had approximately 25 'live' corruption cases which include corruption in both the domestic and foreign arenas.

When will the CFG prosecute?

8.29 The CFG accepts cases which meet the following referral criteria:

(1)   all work flowing from HMRC investigations including tax and duty fraud and arms brokering and export control (weapons and military goods and technology);

(2)   all other fraud cases accepted on the criteria set out below. Suitable cases for the CFG will be cases of alleged fraud which are considered to be serious, complex and/or highly sensitive. The CFG has regard to the following indicators in determining whether a case falls within its remit:

—   a provable actual or intended loss of £1 million;

—   corruption and bribery cases with a particular focus on public bodies and officials;

—   cases where local concern makes it appropriate that the case should be seen to be reviewed impartially;

—   substantial and significant fraud on government departments;

—   frauds on the governments of other countries;

—   cases in which, because of widespread public concern, the CFG may be expected to perform a co-ordinating and standard-setting role;

—   difficult cases requiring specialised knowledge involving, for example, Stock Exchange practices, regulatory bodies, complex banking issues, shipping law, onshore and offshore trusts and computer misuse in perpetrating the fraud;

—   complex and high value 'boiler room' and 'Ponzi' frauds;

—   significant and complex cases of money laundering providing the laundering has occurred in connection with fraudulent activity.

8.30 The CFG estimates its top ten fiscal cases exceed £5bn in value. Its top ten non-fiscal cases exceed £1bn. It has recently prosecuted a number of 'boiler room', 'Ponzi' and other high yield investment frauds that affect thousands of victims, as well other fraudulent conduct which affects large numbers of people.

8.31 The CFG will shape its approach to prosecution using the joint guidance from the SFO and DPP against a recognition that the CFG considers bribery to be a serious offence which there is an inherent public interest in prosecuting.

8.32 The CFG's current corruption case load includes bribes paid to foreign officials to 'save' tax, hospitality aimed at contract managers, cash and other services supplied to bank managers, cash and gifts to foreign politicians to induce contracts, bribes to those involved in awarding money from development funds, surcharging commodities contracts and sporting corruption.

The will to prosecute and the budget to do so

8.33 Offences under the Bribery Act 2010 will be expensive to investigate and to prosecute. The prosecution agencies are required by the Treasury to make 25% savings over the next four years. Matching the will to prosecute with the financial ability to do so will prove to be a difficult balancing act for the SFO and the CPS. It is reasonable for a selective prosecutor such as the SFO to have regard to its finite (or limited) resources in deciding which cases to prosecute and which cases to deal with by way of civil or regulatory penalty.

The Overseas Anti-Corruption Unit (OACU)

8.34 On 22 June 2006 Tony Blair announced new measures to tackle international corruption, identified as one of the priorities at the Gleneagles G8 summit. The Overseas Anti-Corruption Unit of the City of London Police, which works with the SFO and Metropolitan Police, was established shortly thereafter. The unit consists of a Detective Superintendent, a Detective Inspector, two Detective Sergeants and eight Detective Constables—all experienced officers from the City of London Police Economic Crime Department.

8.35 Additionally the unit works closely with the SFO and the CFG, who in order to meet the demands of investigating overseas corruption have formed a small team working under the Deputy Director. This team is responsible for maintaining the register of all allegations of bribery or corruption of overseas officials by British persons and companies. The SFO have the responsibility for assessing each allegation and if an investigation is merited, allocating cases to the investigative agency best suited to deal with it.

OACU reporting line

8.36 The reporting line is a 24/7 confidential answerphone service, which allows the caller to report their suspicions either openly or anonymously. The number is + (44) 020 7601 6969; email: OACU@cityoflondon.police.uk.

C   MUTUAL LEGAL ASSISTANCE

8.37 Where a suspected bribery offence has an overseas element, it may well be necessary to seek evidence from abroad. The relevant domestic legislation which covers mutual legal assistance ('MLA') is the Crime (International Co-operation) Act 2003 ('CICA 2003'). The authority to request assistance abroad comes from CICA 2003. All letters of request issued by a designated prosecuting authority (which includes the SFO, CPS and RCPO) must therefore comply with the terms of CICA 2003.

8.38 Useful practical guidance on the operation of CICA is contained in the Home Office MLA Guidelines for the UK (8th edition), issued on 1 April 2010[1] and the CPS Guidance on MLA—Letters of Request[2].

[1]   www.homeoffice.gov.uk/publications/police/operational-policing/MLA-guidelines-8th-edition ?view=Binary.
[2]   www.cps.gov.uk/legal/l_to_o/obtaining_evidence_and_information_from_ abroad/mutual_leg al_assistance_(mla)_-_letters_of_request/#a02.

8.39 The introduction to the Home Office Guidelines states (in part):

'[MLA] is the formal way in which countries request and provide assistance in obtaining evidence located in one country to assist in criminal investigations or proceedings in another country. Due to the increasingly global nature of crime MLA is critical to criminal proceedings and ensuring justice for victims of crime. The UK is committed to assisting investigative, prosecuting and judicial authorities in combating international crime and is able to provide a wide range of MLA.

Types of MLA that can be provided
There is a wide range of MLA that can be provided by the UK conditional on the correct criteria being met. The type of MLA available include: service of procedural documents, witness evidence, banking and telecommunications data, search and seizure, temporary transfer of prisoners and interception of telecommunications. Please refer to Section 3 of this guide for information about each of the different types of MLA.

Countries which the UK can assist
The UK can assist any country or territory in the world, whether or not that country is able to assist the UK. The UK can provide most forms of legal assistance without bilateral or international agreements. Please see Annex A for a list of the international agreements that the UK is party to. Where a treaty or Convention imposes specific conditions or procedures on the provision or requesting of MLA the UK expects such conditions or procedures to be adhered to.

Reciprocity
The UK does not require reciprocity but would expect assistance from countries which are parties to relevant bilateral or international agreements with the UK. The UK would also expect reciprocity from countries to which we give assistance without a treaty or international agreement'.

D   SELF REPORTING

To report or not to report?

8.40 The SFO has sought to promote the self-reporting regime for corporations where bribery is detected, on the basis that it may allow a company to receive a civil rather than criminal penalty where the company engages fully with the regulator. This may also enable the company to lessen any adverse publicity. This is a good example of the SFO's role as a 'selective prosecutor'. It is a very useful alternative to what may be a prolonged and very expensive criminal investigation and prosecution, particularly in times of such limited financial resources. The SFO will have to consider carefully in each case whether a prosecution is called for in the public interest, but provided it exercises its discretion in accordance with the principles set out in *Mead* (above) then its decisions will not be impugned by the courts. The purported benefits for corporations in self-reporting are outlined on the SFO's website as follows:

'—   we will consider the full range of options for dealing with your case, including criminal and civil alternatives;
—   coming forward to discuss your concerns with us will be treated sensitively;
—   you can discuss with us about the possibility of conducting an internal investigation in a discreet way (to lessen the impact on your business);
—   there may be greater opportunities to secure evidence that will result in a successful outcome for both us and your company against fraud or corruption'.

The SFO website then links an observer to the guidance on corporate prosecutions discussed at para **8.8**.

8.41 In July 2009 the SFO issued further guidance, entitled the *Approach of the SFO to dealing with overseas corruption*, with a section focusing on self reporting. This again stresses that 'the benefit to the corporate (in appropriate cases) will be the prospect of a civil rather than criminal outcome as well as the opportunity to manage, with us, the issues and the public proactively'. The guidance goes on to state that one benefit of a negotiated civil settlement which may be open to a company which self-reports is that the automatic debarment provisions under article 45 of the EU Public Sector Procurement Directive 2004 will not apply.

8.42 Once a report has been made the SFO will seek to establish whether the corporate is genuinely committed to an anti-bribery culture. In so doing it will have regard to the following factors:

— the extent of the co-operation the company will provide in carrying out any further investigation the SFO deems necessary;
— what the approach of the corporate would be to remedial measures at the end of any investigation such as restitution through civil recovery, re-training of staff, taking appropriate disciplinary action against individuals where necessary and external monitoring of the company to demonstrate culture change;
— whether the corporate has insight into the fact that any resolution must be transparent and satisfy the public interest. This will frequently involve a joint public statement agreed between the company and the SFO;
— whether or not the company is seeking the assistance of the SFO in reaching a global settlement and in so doing will be seeking to involve the SFO with other regulators and criminal agencies abroad.

8.43 Although no guarantee of a civil outcome can be given by the SFO, where a company meets the criteria set out above its declared aim is to pursue a civil remedy. The caveat to this principle concerns where Directors of a company have engaged in corrupt practices personally and benefited from them. In those circumstances the SFO is likely to commence its own criminal investigation. It would, however, be seeking cooperation from the company by way of plea negotiation under the Attorney-General's Guidelines, discussed at para **8.55**.

8.44 When considering whether to prosecute individuals a company will be given no guarantees by the SFO as to how it will choose to proceed. The guidance states the SFO will assess the position of each individual on its merits, having particular regard to the following factors:

— the level of involvement of the individual concerned; were they actively engaged in corruption or was it a failure of oversight on their part?
— what action has the company taken?
— did the individual enjoy financial benefit and is he or she still doing so?
— if the individuals are professional people, should the SFO be contacting their regulatory body?
— should the SFO be considering a Director's Disqualification Order?
— should the SFO be considering a Serious Crime Prevention Order?

8.45 It should be noted that self-reporting does not relieve a corporate or a professional adviser of his or her obligation to make reports where a legal duty arises either within the UK or any other jurisdiction. Subject to this caveat, any discussions held with the SFO will be confidential and will be treated as information gathered under its powers under the CJA 1987 and so can be used in accordance with the Bribery Act 2010.

8.46 If an investigation is deemed to be necessary by the SFO it will be carried out at the expense of the corporate by its professional advisers. This is a marked change of approach: at one time the involvement of the corporate in such a way could have opened a company to accusations of perverting the course of justice. The SFO will expect to discuss the results of the investigation with the company and to be updated throughout. If the SFO is satisfied with the results of an investigation, a matter on which the guidance is silent, it will turn its mind to settlement of the case. The five key limbs of any settlement will be:

— restitution by way of civil recovery of the amount of unlawful property, interest and the SFO's costs;
— in some cases monitoring by an independent body nominated by the company and agreed by the SFO. The scope of the monitoring will be agreed with the SFO and will be proportionate to the issues raised;
— a program of culture change agreed with the SFO;
— discussion about the role of key individuals;
— a public statement agreed between the corporate and the SFO for public transparency.

8.47 Specific advice is given regarding the situation where one company merges with or acquires another and during due diligence on the takeover discovers the company to be acquired has a corruption issue. Where the acquiring company is committed to a modern ethical corporate culture and undertakes to carry out any remedial work necessary on its acquisition, the SFO will take no action providing the promised remedial work occurs.

8.48 What is clear is that the costs of the investigation, as well as any remedial work, will be borne by the company. Whilst the SFO undertakes to keep investigation costs proportionate, this must be of concern to a corporate. However, the financial burden of self-reporting must be weighed in the balance against a decision not to self-report and the consequences which will follow if detection of corruption comes from a source external to the company.

8.49 The SFO makes it clear that if a company does not self-report and information is obtained through a whistleblower or a statutory report such as a Suspicious Activity Report, its approach will be to assume that the organisation which is the subject of the investigation has *chosen* not to self-report. The prospects of a criminal prosecution and confiscation will be greatly enhanced in these cases, including the prospect of money-laundering charges.

8.50 The case of *Mabey and Johnson*[1], described as a 'landmark outcome' by the Director of the SFO and promoted as a model of self-reporting, should be considered by any company determining whether to use the self-reporting route. On 7 August 2009, the company pleaded guilty at Southwark Crown Court to conspiring to corrupt officials in Ghana and Jamaica between 1993 and 2001 and breaching the United Nations sanctions against Iraq. Mabey used agents to represent it in foreign countries, who were paid a commission. Despite the company having policies on hospitality as well as business ethics the evidence in the case demonstrated that bribes were authorised at director level. The company self-reported following allegations made in civil proceedings against former employees and agents. Mabey commenced an internal investigation the results of which were shared with the

SFO waiving privilege in that respect. This approach was expressly commended by the SFO as a model of proper cooperation and credit was given in court for this approach. Such waiver of privilege is now expected by the SFO as a hallmark of companies which are considered to be cooperating fully. Such cooperation was late in the day, however, as Mabey had not been frank in its reply to the Volcker investigation into the breaching of sanctions against Iraq or in responding to the SFO's notice to produce documents.

Sentence was determined on 25 September 2009, the company was fined £750,000 for each of the two corruption offences and £2m for breaching the Iraq sanctions. A confiscation order of £1.1m was made in respect of the corruption offences and £618,484 to the UN Iraq development fund. Monies were also repaid to Ghana and Jamaica.

[1]   Unreported.

8.51 What is of note is that self-reporting in this case did not result in a civil outcome for the company. Any corporation considering self-reporting will doubtless pay heed to this outcome when considering making such a disclosure. Once the criminal route is engaged the mandatory debarment provisions under EU procurement rules bite, as does the confiscation regime.

8.52 In *AMEC plc*[1], however, the company self-reported and the SFO elected to pursue a civil recovery route having determined that the company had failed to keep accurate records as required by the Companies Act 1985, s 221[2]. An order was made for almost £5m following the company's disclosure that it had received irregular payments in respect of a project in which it was a shareholder. The *AMEC* case followed the civil recovery order obtained against Balfour Beatty plc in October 2008, the first of its kind[3]. Balfour Beatty self-reported, following the discovery of irregular payments to a subsidiary in Egypt. The company paid a £2.25m settlement plus a contribution to the SFO's costs. Key factors in the SFO's decision to pursue a civil route appear to be the speed and openness with which the report was made, full cooperation and a willingness to take steps to reduce the risk such irregularities would recur.

[1]   Unreported.
[2]   Now the Companies Act 2006.
[3]   Unreported.

Practicalities

8.53 If a company elects to self-report it must bear the following in mind:

—   *the timing of reporting*: a corporate will only want to report once its advisers or an internal investigation reveal a real problem that requires remedial action. The SFO policy permits a company to approach it at an early stage to get an indication of how the SFO will deal with the problem;

—   *the effect of reporting*: if a company elects to use the self-reporting regime it must consider the global effect, as the SFO states that it would expect to be notified at the same time as the Department of Justice in the USA (providing it has jurisdictional reach over the corruption);

— *to whom should a report be made?* Corporates wishing to discuss self reporting should contact the SFO direct. Guidance on who to contact is on the SFO's website at www.sfo.gov.uk/media/133724/approach-of-t he-sfo-to-dealing-with-overseas-corruption-v3.pdf.

A leniency regime?

8.54 There will be no leniency regime equivalent to that at the Office of Fair Trading in respect of cartel conduct on offer at the SFO. The purported benefits for a corporate which self-reports and delivers other companies are similar to those discussed above. The SFO will seek to pursue a civil recovery route or could use a SOCPA agreement (discussed in detail at paras **8.60–8.79**).

E   PLEA NEGOTIATION

Plea bargaining in the UK

8.55 In corruption cases, as in other types of corporate crime, businesses facing the prospect of criminal charges will be concerned chiefly with commercial considerations and in particular the need to ensure the viability of the company and to minimise reputational damage. For this reason, the way in which a settlement can be reached with the relevant authorities is of particular interest to businesses. Individuals too, will often be anxious to explore settlement, as will be prosecutors, who will be keen to avoid the uncertainty and cost of a criminal investigation and a jury trial. The UK lacks a formalised system of plea bargaining such as exists, for example, in the US. However, elements of 'plea negotiation' have long existed in the UK.

8.56 For instance, prosecutors have always had the power to accept pleas to a lesser offence if they consider that it is in the public interest to do so (subject to the constraints of the Code for Crown Prosecutors and the Attorney-General's Guidelines on the Acceptance of Pleas and the Prosecutor's Role in the Sentencing Exercise, as revised 1 December 2009).

8.57 In addition, it has long been the practice of the courts to recognise the benefit to the criminal justice system which result from a defendant entering a timely guilty plea by reducing the sentence imposed. In 2000 this was formalised by statute (the Powers of Criminal Courts Sentencing Act, s 152 since incorporated into the Criminal Justice Act 2003, ss 144 and 174) and guidance has also been issued by Sentencing Guidelines Council (revised in July 2007) to which the court is required to have regard. As the Council states:

'A reduction in sentence is appropriate because a guilty plea avoids the need for a trial (thus enabling other cases to be disposed of more expeditiously), shortens the gap between charge and sentence, saves considerable cost, and, in the case of an early plea, saves victims and witnesses from the concern about having to give evidence'.

8.58 Since the case of *R v Goodyear*[1], defendants have also been able to obtain from a judge an 'advance indication as to sentence'. The aim of *Goodyear* was to put on a more formal basis the longstanding and informal indications which would frequently be given privately, in the judge's chambers. Guidelines have been laid down which are set out in the practice direction relating to pleas of guilty in the Crown Court *Practice Direction (criminal proceedings: consolidation)*[2].

1   [2005] EWCA Crim 888, [2005] 3 All ER 117[2005] 1 WLR 2532.
2   [2002] 1 WLR 2870, para IV.45.29–IV.45.33 (as inserted by *Practice Direction (criminal proceedings: substituted and additional provisions)* [2009] 1 WLR 1396).

8.59 However, the most conspicuous (and often the most powerful) means of negotiating pleas is by offering assistance to the prosecution. This important aspect is considered immediately below. Also considered below are the Attorney-General's Guidelines on Plea Discussions in cases of Serious or Complex Fraud, which build on the pre-existing elements summarised above and provide the framework for discussing pleas with the prosecuting authorities.

Plea agreements under SOCPA

General principles

8.60 It has long been the practice of the courts to recognise the benefit to the criminal justice system which result from a defendant entering a timely guilty plea by reducing the sentence imposed. But the real prize for the investigating and prosecuting authorities is not only a guilty plea, but an offer by the defendant to cooperate and give evidence against other offenders. This speeds up the trial process and increases the impact of prosecutions on wider criminal networks by drawing in major players and generating mistrust within criminal gangs[1]. The common law acknowledged this and defendants who provided assistance could expect a reduction in their sentence[2]. As the Court of Appeal observed in *R v P; R v Blackburn*[3], whilst there has never been, and never will be, much enthusiasm about a process by which criminals receive lower sentences than they otherwise deserve because they have informed on or given evidence against others, this is a longstanding and pragmatic convention.

1   Government's White Paper, 'One Step Ahead; a 21st Century Strategy to Defeat Organised Crime' (CM 6167), March 2004.
2   *Re A and B* [1999] 1 Cr App Rep (S) 52 in which the Court of Appeal reviewed the existing law on sentencing discounts for accomplices who gave evidence against co-accused.
3   [2007] EWCA Crim 2290, [2008] 2 All ER 684, [2008] 2 Cr App Rep (S) 16.

8.61 Historically, the arrangements which led to defendants 'turning Queen's Evidence' were informal and often private. Consequently, they were vulnerable to suggestions of 'double dealing' and, even if not in any way shady, sometimes were perceived as such. Sections 71–75 of the Serious and Organised Crime and Police Act 2005 ('SOCPA 2005') which came into force on 1 April 2006, created a statutory framework which formalised these arrangements. The framework is intended to avoid some of the problems to which the previous arrangements could sometimes give rise and to encourage the use of Queen's Evidence by introducing a transparent system of binding co-operation agreements between the prosecution and defence.

8.62 Of principal relevance to the topic of plea negotiation are ss 71–73, which deal the following:

— agreements not to prosecute a person (an immunity notice under s 71);

— agreements not to use certain evidence (a 'restricted use' undertaking under s 72);

— agreements which set out in writing the terms under which a person who, with a view to obtaining a reduced sentence, is willing to assist an investigation or prosecution (s 73).

A prosecutor may be asked by an investigator or by the legal representatives of an offender to consider making an agreement under SOCPA 2005.

8.63 Section 75B of the SOCPA 2005[1] provides for the Attorney-General to issue guidance to prosecutors as to the use of their powers under ss 71–75. As at 1 February 2011, no such guidance had been issued. The CPS has, however, issued guidance, which was published on 14 January 2011: 'Queen's Evidence—Immunities, Undertakings and Agreements under the Serious organised Crime and Police Act 2005'. In its Guidance, the CPS lists ten factors which are likely to be relevant when considering whether to make a formal agreement with an offender who is willing to assist the prosecution. In essence, the CPS will be concerned to assess the strength of the prosecution case with and without the information from the witness/accomplice, whether that person is able and willing to provide reliable evidence and whether he or she is likely to be a credible witness. In practice, this guidance also informs the SFO's approach.

[1] As inserted by the Coroners and Justice Act 2009, s 113.

8.64 The CPS is not enthusiastic about agreements under SOCPA 2005, ss 71–75 being used to deprive the prosecution authorities of an opportunity to recover the proceeds of unlawful conduct through civil recovery proceedings under the Proceeds of Crime Act 2002 ('POCA 2002'), Pt 5. If criminals were routinely allowed to keep the profits of their criminal activities in return for cooperation, public confidence in the criminal justice system would be likely to be damaged. For these reasons, it is only in very exceptional circumstances that the prosecuting authorities will consider it justifiable and in the public interest to agree that any agreement should apply to Part 5 proceedings. Rarely, if ever, will it be appropriate to agree that the prosecutor will not ask the court to proceed to consider confiscation under POCA 2002, s 6[1]. Such an agreement could not in any event bind the court which, under POCA 2002, s 6(3)(b), must proceed if it considers it appropriate to do so.

[1] See the CPS Guidance 'Queen's Evidence—Immunities, Undertakings and Agreements under the Serious Organised Crime and Police Act 2005', published 14 January 2011.

8.65 Although not a statutory requirement, the prosecuting authorities will expect offenders who wish to benefit from a written agreement to fully admit their criminality. This is especially so where it is envisaged that the assisting offender will give evidence in court, rather than simply provide assistance by way of intelligence. The process of admitting other criminality is often called 'cleansing'. As to the importance of 'cleansing' see *R v P; R v Blackburn*[1] and the CPS Guidance 'Queen's Evidence—Immunities, Undertakings and Agreements under the Serious Organised Crime and Police Act 2005', published 14 January 2011. Defendants who do not take part in full cleansing cannot expect to receive the fullest discount available[2].

¹   [2007] EWCA Crim 2290, [2008] 2 All ER 684, [2008] 2 Cr App Rep (S) 16.
²   *R v D* [2010] EWCA Crim 1485 at para 13.

Immunity notices

8.66 In exceptional cases, prosecutors may consider offering immunity from prosecution to a defendant. The CPS Guidance makes it clear that, as a general rule, an accomplice should be prosecuted, whether or not he or she is to be called as a witness, and this should be the first option considered by investigators and prosecutors. Only where it is clearly in the public interest to depart from this position should consideration be given to entering into some form of agreement not to prosecute. It is submitted that, in reality, it will be extremely rare for a full immunity notice (or for that matter, a restricted use undertaking) to be granted without a requirement to give evidence, if court proceedings follow.

8.67 The criteria to be considered by the prosecutor in determining whether it is appropriate to grant immunity to a witness is the same as was set out by the then Attorney-General, Sir Michael Havers QC, in 1981. In response to questions in the House of Commons (prompted in part by the revelation that Anthony Blunt had been granted immunity from prosecution) the Attorney-General made a statement explaining his current practice in the following terms[1]:

> 'Immunity from prosecution can only be granted by the Attorney-General or the Director of Public Prosecution because it is only with them there lies the power to stop any prosecution. Each application made to either the Director of Public Prosecutions or myself is treated separately on its merits, and it is not possible to set out any comprehensive set of rules.
> The criteria which we apply include:
> whether in the interests of justice it is of more value to have a suspected person as a witness for the Crown than as a possible defendant;
> whether in the interests of public safety or security the obtaining of information about the extent and nature of criminal activities is of greater importance than the possible conviction of an individual;
> whether it is very unlikely that any information could be obtained without an offer of immunity and whether it is also very unlikely that any prosecution could be launched against a person to whom immunity is offered'.

¹   12 HC Official Report (6th series) col 12, 9 November 1981.

8.68 Reflecting previous practice, only a prosecutor can give an immunity notice (not the investigators)[1] and the Attorney-General should be consulted before any decision is made.

¹   *R v Turner (BJ)* (1975) 61 Cr App Rep 67 at 80, CA.

8.69 Immunity notices can only be granted in respect of offences which have already been committed. No immunity notice can be granted which authorises or purports to authorise the commission of future offending[1].

¹   *R (on the application of Pretty) v DPP (Secretary of State for the Home Dept intervening)* [2001] UKHL 61, [2002] 1 AC 800, [2002] 1 All ER 1.

8.70 Immunity notices must be in writing[1]. Where a person is given an immunity notice, no proceedings for the offence specifically described in the notice may be brought against that person except in circumstances specified in the notice[2]. The ability to make the giving of an immunity notice subject to specific conditions distinguishes the new statutory scheme from previous arrangements in which immunity, once granted, was absolute. Under s 71(3) an immunity notice ceases to have effect if the person to whom it relates fails to comply with any condition specified in the notice. Where this occurs, a formal notice of revocation should be issued to avoid any uncertainty.

[1]   SOCPA 2005, s 71(1).
[2]   SOCPA 2005, s 71(2).

8.71 It is good practice for both the prosecution and the offender to draft the agreement fully and with as much precision as possible. The agreement will usually be disclosed to co-defendants and is likely to provide fertile ground for cross-examination. To ensure transparency and to prevent the suggestion that something shady or underhand has been agreed, the agreement should spell out clearly the assistance with the offender it willing to give, how it is to be provided and what benefit the offender is getting.

8.72 In his sentencing remarks in *R v BAE Systems plc*[1] Bean J was highly critical of the decision of the SFO to grant immunity in what he termed a 'loosely' drafted plea agreement. He stated (at para 5):

'It is relatively common for a prosecuting authority to agree not to prosecute a defendant in respect of specified crimes which are admitted and listed in the agreement: this is done for example where a defendant is an informer who will give important evidence against co-defendants. But I am surprised to find a prosecutor granting a blanket indemnity for all offences committed in the past whether disclosed or otherwise. The Department of Justice did not do so in this case: it agreed not to prosecute for past offences which had been disclosed to it.'

[1]   (21 December 2010), unreported, Southwark Crown Court.

Restricted use undertakings

8.73 Section 72 of SOCPA 2005 allows a prosecutor to offer a person an undertaking that information of a specified description will not be used in criminal or confiscation proceedings or proceedings for civil recovery under POCA 2002, Pt 5.

8.74 The undertaking will be in writing. Where such an undertaking is given it allows, in effect, a person to waive the privilege against self-incrimination without risk of prosecution on the basis of that evidence alone. As with immunity notices, a restricted use undertaking may be made subject to conditions, breach of which may lead to the revocation of the undertaking[1].

[1]   SOCPA 2005, s 72(4).

8.75 A restricted use undertaking is, in effect, a form of immunity from prosecution. The relevant CPS guidance makes it clear that the criteria to be considered by a prosecutor in determining whether it is appropriate to grant a restricted use undertaking are the same as those which are considered in deciding whether to grant full immunity (which are summarised at paras **8.66–8.72**). The distinction between the two is that a restricted use undertaking does not prevent a witness from being prosecuted where other evidence which justifies a prosecution is, or becomes, available. The relevant CPS guidance states that 'other evidence' may include evidence from another source obtained directly or indirectly as a result of information given in reliance on a restricted use undertaking. This, as the CPS acknowledges, could only be justified in exceptional circumstances where the interests of justice clearly call for it and a prosecution based solely on evidence obtained as a result of what the suspect said in response to a restricted use undertaking is likely to amount to an abuse of process.

Agreements for a reduction in sentence under SOCPA 2005, s 73

8.76 Section 73 of SOCPA 2005 deals with those cooperating defendants who have not benefited from an immunity from prosecution or a restricted use undertaking but who have, nonetheless, assisted or offered to assist in the investigation or prosecution of others.

8.77 A defendant who has, pursuant to a written agreement made with a specified prosecutor, assisted or offered to assist the investigator or prosecutor is eligible to receive a reduction in sentence provided he has entered a guilty plea[1]. It is not necessary that a defendant should have pleaded guilty before an agreement under s 73 is signed. Sentencing reductions are only available in a Crown Court, although a defendant who pleads guilty in the magistrates' court may still avail himself of s 73 if committed to the Crown Court for sentence. Guidance on this aspect of the statutory scheme has been provided by the Court of Appeal in *R v P; R v Blackburn*[2] and *R v H; R v D; R v Chaudhury*[3].

[1] SOCPA 2005, s 73(1).
[2] [2008] 2 Cr App Rep (S) 5.
[3] [2009] EWCA Crim 2485, [2010] 2 Cr App Rep (S) 18.

8.78 The sentencing judge will require a report setting out the quantity and quality of the assistance given, the results arising from it (eg arrests or prosecutions directly attributable to the defendant's information), the willingness of the defendant to give evidence and an assessment of the risks that the defendant and his family face as a result of his cooperation. This report will normally be prepared by the senior investigating officer, but will be approved by the prosecutor.

8.79 The reduction in sentence is not mandatory. Rather, s 73(2) provides that, in determining what sentence to pass on the defendant, the court 'may' take into account the extent and nature of the assistance given or offered. In practice, sentencing discounts where assistance has been offered or given are well established. The approach to be taken in cases involving agreements under s 73 was explained in *R v P; R v Blackburn*[1] and is considered further in Chapter 9.

[1] [2007] EWCA Crim 2290, [2008] 2 All ER 684, [2008] 2 Cr App Rep (S) 16.

The Attorney-General's Guidelines on Plea Discussions

The plea agreement procedure

8.80 The Attorney-General's Guidelines on Plea Discussions in cases of Serious or Complex Fraud ('the Guidelines')[1] built on the pre-existing elements summarised above. The Guidelines have their origins in the final Report of the Fraud Review, published in July 2006[2], which recommended that a framework be devised governing plea bargaining in fraud cases. The Guidelines set out the process by which a prosecutor may discuss allegations of serious or complex fraud with a person whom he is prosecuting or expecting to prosecute, or with that person's legal representative. Fraud is defined as including any financial, fiscal or commercial misconduct or corruption which is contrary to the criminal law. Fraud may be serious or complex if at least two of a number of factors specified in the Guidelines are present (eg that the amount of money obtained or attempted to be obtained is alleged to amount to at least £500,000, or that there is a significant international dimension etc).

[1] Issued on 18 March 2009.
[2] www.afmdni.gov.uk/pubs/FCI/fraudreview_finalreport.pdf.

8.81 It must be appreciated that the Guidelines do not, and do not purport to, introduce a 'plea bargaining' regime. Pursuant to the Guidelines, the purpose of plea discussions is simply to narrow the issues in the case with a view to reaching a just outcome at the earliest possible time, including the possibility of reaching an agreement about acceptable pleas of guilty and preparing a joint submission as to sentence. In reality, it is hard to envisage any formal 'plea bargaining' regime being introduced in the absence of primary legislation which carries with it the support of the judiciary. Recent cases (considered at paras **8.95–8.104**) have shown that the judiciary is not prepared in any way to 'rubber stamp' plea agreements and is determined to preserve its unfettered discretion to deal with a guilty plea in accordance with the facts and the overall interests of justice.

8.82 The Guidelines are intended to be evolutionary, rather than revolutionary (references in brackets below are to the relevant paragraphs of the Guidelines):

— the Guidelines are not intended to prevent or discourage existing practices of informal plea bargaining (A8);

— the Guidelines do not affect the existing practice of '*Goodyear* indications' (A8);

— the Guidelines do not affect the procedures in place under SOCPA 2005, ss 71–75 for giving assistance to the authorities (D6);

— they complement and do not detract from or replace the Attorney-General's Guidelines on the Acceptance of Pleas and the prosecutors' role in the sentencing exercise or any other relevant guidance (eg The Victim's Charter).

8.83 The most significant developments introduced by the Guidelines are:

— they permit plea discussions to take place prior to charge and prior to the investigation being completed (A7). It is to be noted that legal aid is, in principle, available for such discussions: see the Criminal Defence Service (General) (No 2) (Amendment) Regulations 2009[1]; and

— where agreement is reached as to pleas, the parties are required to discuss the appropriate sentence with a view to presenting a joint written submission to the court (D9).

[1] SI 2009/1853.

8.84 Under the Guidelines, the prosecutor may initiate plea discussions with any person who is being prosecuted, or investigated with a view to prosecution, in connection with a serious or complex fraud and who is being legally represented. The prosecutor and the investigating officer must be satisfied that the suspect's criminality is known, although it is acknowledged that the investigation may not be complete.

8.85 Where agreement is reached, it must be reduced to writing and will include a list of charges, a statement of facts and a declaration, signed by the defendant personally, to the effect that he or she accepts the stated facts and admits he or she is guilty of the agreed charges. In addition, in the event of agreement, the parties should discuss the appropriate sentence with a view to presenting a joint written submission to the court. This document should list the aggravating and mitigating features arising from the agreed facts, set out any personal mitigation available to the defendant, and refer to any relevant sentencing guidelines or authorities. In the light of all of these factors, it should make submissions as to the applicable sentencing range in the relevant guideline. The prosecutor must ensure that the submissions are realistic, taking full account of all relevant material and considerations.

The Plea Discussions Guidelines have been endorsed by the judiciary in *Practice Direction (criminal proceedings: consolidation)*[1].

[1] [2002] 1 WLR 2870, para IV.45.18–28.

8.86 There is little scope to negotiate on confiscation, although some flexibility is afforded to the prosecution. Paragraph D11 of the Guidelines states:

'Fraud is an acquisitive crime and the expectation in a fraud case should be that a confiscation order will be sought by the prosecutor reflecting the full benefit to the defendant. However, in doing so it is open to the prosecutor to take a realistic view of the likely approach of the court to the determination of any points in dispute (such as the interest of a third party in any property)'.

8.87 Experience suggests that suspects are very concerned about the prospect of confiscation proceedings and the consequences of any such proceedings on their family. However, POCA 2002, s 6 imposes on the court a mandatory requirement to consider making a confiscation order (where the pre-conditions are met) and it can proceed on its own motion even if no application is made by the prosecution. Once the court has calculated a defendant's benefit, it has no discretion to mitigate the effects of the confiscation regime. In essence, a basis of plea cannot usurp the court's powers under POCA 2002. The powers of the court to make a confiscation order are considered in Chapter 9.

8.88 There is scope, however, to agree the facts, and any agreement on the facts is likely to provide some restriction on the sum which the court determines is the defendant's benefit for the purposes of confiscation proceedings. As a general rule, the court will be bound by the facts contained in the plea agreement at any subsequent confiscation proceedings. However, the court is not required to accept an agreement reached between the parties in respect of confiscation which is not grounded on any of the facts of the case or is wholly unrealistic on the facts of the case.

8.89 Once a concluded and signed plea agreement has been reached, then the defendant will be brought before the court. It is vital for those involved in this process to bear in mind the following points:

— the court may accept the plea agreement but reject the joint submission as to sentence;

— the court may reject the plea agreement, in the same way that a court can reject a basis of plea in any case:

> 'the prosecution should not lend itself to any agreement whereby a case is presented on an unreal and untrue set of facts concerning the offence to which the plea is to be tendered'[1].

[1] *R v Beswick* [1996] 1 Cr App Rep 427, [1996] 1 Cr App Rep (S) 343, CA; see also *R v Tolera* [1999] 1 Cr App Rep 29, [1999] 1 Cr App Rep (S) 25, CA and *R v Underwood* [2004] EWCA Crim 2256, [2005] 1 Cr App Rep 178, [2005] 1 Cr App Rep (S) 478.

Limitations on plea agreements

8.90 Defendants should appreciate that the agreements under the Guidelines are subject to two important limitations:

— the defendant does not achieve complete certainty. Any agreement reached between the parties is not in any way binding on the court dealing with the defendant: 'Where a plea agreement is reached, it remains entirely a matter for the court to decide how to deal with the case' (A9); and

— there are important limitations on the confidentiality of the process. At first blush, the Guidelines provide some comfort on confidentiality to a suspect who wishes to engage in this process. Paragraph C6 requires the prosecution to give an undertaking to the effect that the fact that the defendant has taken part in plea discussions and the information he is provided will be treated as confidential. In addition, para C8 sets out that 'In relation to the use of information, the prosecutor will indicate that he or she intends to undertake not to rely upon the fact that the defendant has taken part in the plea discussions, or any information provided by the defendant in the course of the discussions, as evidence in any prosecution of that defendant for the offences under investigation, should the discussions fail'. However, this protection is qualified in a way which may make the process unattractive to a potential defendant.

8.91 Paragraph C6 states: 'The undertaking will make it clear that the law in relation to the disclosure of unused material may require the prosecutor to provide information about the plea discussions to another defendant in criminal proceedings'. Where a suspect engages in the plea negotiation process, the formal minutes of their meetings and correspondence will constitute 'prosecution material' under the Criminal Procedure and Investigations Act 1996 ('CPIA 1996'), as will any other information provided by him on a less formal basis (prosecution material is material of any kind which is obtained in the course of a criminal investigation and which may be relevant to the investigation). Information given to the prosecutor may be disclosable to other defendants (including co-defendants) as unused material in accordance with the CPIA 1996's disclosure regime. This is not limited to any signed plea agreement. If the material undermines the prosecution's case or assists that of a co-defendant, it will be disclosed in accordance with the CPIA 1996. It is not unusual in cases of this nature for there to be co-defendants, nor for them to be blaming one another, so such disclosure may be a very real risk for a suspect engaging in plea discussions.

8.92 Furthermore, save in exceptional circumstances, in accordance with para C8, the prosecutor is not prevented from:

(1)   relying upon any evidence obtained from enquiries made as a result of the provision of information by the defendant;

(2)   relying upon information provided by the defendant as evidence against him or her in any prosecution for an offence other than the fraud which is the subject of the plea discussion and any offence which is consequent upon it, such as money laundering; and

(3)   relying upon information provided by the defendant in a prosecution of any other person for any offence (so far as the rules of evidence allow). Moreover, in accordance with para C9, the prosecutor must not surrender the ability to rely upon a concluded and signed plea agreement as evidence against the defendant.

F   THE APPROACH OF THE SFO TO PLEA NEGOTIATION

8.93 The SFO has been an enthusiastic advocate of plea negotiation in corruption pleas. The SFO's guidance 'Approach to Dealing with Overseas Corruption' (see para **8.41**) emphasises its willingness to enter into plea negotiations in accordance with the Attorney-General's Guidelines and, where the offender has self-referred, to agree a civil settlement and thereby avoid criminal proceedings altogether.

8.94 As noted at paras **8.50–8.52**, the SFO has enjoyed some initial success in arriving at negotiated plea agreements:

—   in October 2008, Balfour Beatty agreed to a civil settlement of £2.25m for 'books and records' offences after the SFO elected to use its civil recovery powers under POCA 2002, Pt 5 instead of prosecuting. In its press release, the SFO states 'the use of these powers should be seen as an important example of how the SFO will use the new tools at its disposal to enhance the criminal justice process';

—   in July 2009 Mabey & Johnson pleaded guilty to ten counts of violating sanctions and was sentenced to a fine of £6.6m. Whilst the Mabey & Johnson investigation largely pre-dated the Attorney-General's Guidelines, it is the first case in substance to have followed the new procedures;

— in October 2009, following an internal investigation into the receipt of irregular payments, Amec plc agreed to pay a civil recovery order of almost £5m having self-referred to the SFO and admitted failures to keep accurate records as required by the Companies Act 1985, s 221;
— in October 2010, Julian Messent, the former CEO of reinsurance broker PWS Holdings, entered into a plea agreement with the SFO, in accordance with the Attorney-General's Guidelines, which was approved by Southwark Crown Court. He was jailed for 21 months, after pleading guilty to paying £1.2m in bribes to Costa Rican state officials between 1999 and 2002.

8.95 The conduct of the prosecuting authorities in making plea agreements has come under the scrutiny of the courts in a number of recent cases. In all these cases, the court restated the cardinal principle that sentence is a matter for the judiciary and is not a matter to be negotiated under the plea agreement or a matter to be jointly advocated before the court.

R v Whittle

8.96 In *R v Whittle*[1] the defendants pleaded guilty to a cartel offence under the Enterprise Act 2002, s 188, and received sentences of three years' imprisonment (Whittle and Allison) and 30 months' imprisonment in the case of Brammer. Each individual was disqualified from acting as a director of a limited company. The defendants entered into plea agreements with the US authorities, part of which included entering pleas to offences in the UK and not seeking a sentence less than that stated in the agreement. The appeal was allowed and the sentences were reduced to the periods agreed in the plea agreement. The court indicated that had it heard argument that sentences should have been reduced below those agreed with the US, it may have been minded to do so. The court expressed its doubts as to the propriety of a US prosecutor seeking to inhibit the way defence counsel represented their clients before a UK court.

[1]   [2008] EWCA Crim 2560, (2008) Times, 27 November.

R v Innospec Ltd

8.97 *R v Innospec Ltd*[1] was the first case where a 'global settlement' had been sought by the SFO in respect of concurrent criminal proceedings in the UK and the US and it raised the important issue of the legality of the process by which agreement with the defendant was reached, as well as the proper scope of the settlement.

[1]   [2010] Crim LR 665.

8.98 Innospec Ltd is a UK subsidiary of a US NASDAQ listed company (Innospec Inc). Both entities were implicated in systemic and large-scale corruption in Indonesia and Iraq and were keen to settle. The problem was that the fines and other penalties which could properly be imposed in the US and UK would exceed by many times what Innospec was able to pay (around $40 million) and the SFO and the DOJ agreed that, in light of

Innospec's full admission and cooperation, they should not seek to impose a penalty which would drive the company out of business. In March 2010, Innospec entered into a global settlement with the SFO and various regulatory agencies in the US whereby it was agreed that the SFO would seek a penalty of no more than $12.7 million. In effect, the $40 million pot was divided equally between the SFO, DOJ and the SEC. It was also agreed that the $12.7m SFO share would be divided between a $6.7m fine or confiscation to be imposed in the Crown Court, with the balance being the subject of a civil settlement.

8.99 It was on this basis that Innospec Ltd pleaded guilty to conspiracy to corrupt contrary to the Criminal Law Act 1977, s 1. The plea was limited to the company's activities in Indonesia. Innopec Ltd admitted it had conspired with its directors and others to make corrupt payments to public officials of the Government of Indonesia to secure contracts from the Government of Indonesia for the supply of Tetraethyl lead (TEL).

8.100 The sentencing judge, Thomas LJ, considered that $12.7m was wholly inadequate as a fine to reflect the criminality displayed by Innospec Ltd. Moreover, he was highly critical of the scope and content of the agreement reached by the SFO which, on one reading, suggested a penalty had in fact been agreed. The sums suggested had not been the subject of judicial determination in either the UK or the US (save that inherent in the Federal District Court's approval of the relevant plea agreement). Nor was the division agreed one which, on the facts of the case, accorded with principles. He concluded that the Director had no power to enter into the arrangements made and that no such arrangements should be made again. The court commented that as in *R v Whittle*[1], it was placed in a position where it had little alternative but to agree to the suggested financial penalties if it was to avoid injustice. However, the court warned that the circumstances of Innospec were unique and that it would not consider its powers restricted by future agreements.

[1]   [2008] EWCA Crim 2560, [2010] Crim LR 665.

8.101 Thomas LJ observed at para 27 of the sentencing remarks:

'The Practice Direction reflects the constitutional principle that, save in minor matters such as motoring offences, the imposition of a sentence is a matter for the judiciary. Principles of transparent and open justice require a court sitting in public itself first to determine by a hearing in open court the extent of the criminal conduct on which the offender has entered the plea and then, on the basis of its determination as to the conduct, the appropriate sentence. It is in the public interest, particularly in relation to the crime of corruption, that although, in accordance with the Practice Direction, there may be discussion and agreement as to the basis of plea, a court must rigorously scrutinise in open court in the interests of transparency and good governance the basis of that plea and to see whether it reflects the public interest'.

8.102 As noted at para **8.19**, *R v Innospec* may also signal some limitations upon the SFO's strategy of seeking civil settlements instead of pursuing criminal prosecutions. Thomas LJ stated that the only room for a civil recovery order in serious corruption cases was as a means of compensation, in addition to a punishment.

R v Dougall

8.103 In *R v Dougall*[1] the Court of Appeal addressed the issue of the benefit to be given to defendants who cooperated fully with the authorities under SOCPA 2005, s 73, agreements. The court was addressed on the need for white-collar defendants to have some guidance as to likely sentence if they cooperated to the extent of Mr Dougall and invited to give some certainty.

1   [2010] EWCA Crim 1048, [2010] Crim LR 661, 174 CL&J 365.

8.104 Robert Dougall, a mid-level executive with DePuy International, cooperated with the SFO in its investigation of DePuy's corruption in Greece, pleading guilty and signing an agreement in accordance with SOCPA 2005, s 73 and with the Attorney-General's Guidelines on plea discussions. Under the terms of the agreement, Mr Dougall provided a witness statement setting out an account of his activities and others involved in the corruption. He further agreed to provide full cooperation to any foreign competent judicial authority investigating the affairs of the businesses involved and their employees, and in particular agreed to assist the US Department of Justice and the SEC. In exchange, the SFO, in effect, agreed to invite the court to impose a suspended sentence of imprisonment. The Lord Chief Justice, giving the judgment of the court, heavily criticised this approach (an approach which prosecuting counsel conceded, in argument, had gone further than appropriate). The Lord Chief Justice endorsed the observations of Thomas LJ in *Innospec* and added the following comments at paras 19 and 20:

> 'In this jurisdiction a plea agreement or bargain between the prosecution and the defence in which they agree what the sentence should be, or present what is in effect an agreed package for the court's acquiescence is contrary to principle. That applies to cases of this kind, as it does to others. No such agreement is envisaged in the "Guidelines on Plea Discussions" issued by the Attorney-General. These guidelines, which are said to have governed the plea agreement with which this case is concerned, are framed in unequivocal language'.

Plea bargaining—the future?

8.105 Undeterred by the recent judgments of the courts, the view of Richard Alderman is that the plea negotiation regime must continue to be road tested. The SFO will learn from the comments made by the judges. The most difficult problems here arise in cases where there are international aspects and the corporate concerned is seeking an agreement at the same time with the authorities in the other country. Our system has not yet developed the tools needed to achieve what appears to the SFO to be a legitimate aim while at the same time enjoying judicial and public confidence. This is a big challenge. One of the possible solutions is earlier judicial involvement. Another is deferred prosecution agreements. The SFO would welcome changes here. *Dougall* and *Innospec* were, in his view, unusual cases and he points to *R v Messent*[1] as a successful example of a plea bargain. However the recent comments in the *BAE* case surely cannot give the SFO much comfort that its pursuit of court approval of a plea bargain is becoming an easier route.

1   [2011] EWCA Crim 644, [2011] All ER (D) 22 (Mar). The defendant was sentenced to 21 months' imprisonment after admitting making or authorising corrupt payments of almost

$2m to Costa Rican officials in the state insurance company. He was ordered to pay an additional £100,000 compensation to the Republic of Costa Rica. He had entered into a plea agreement with the SFO under the Attorney-General's Guidelines and was sentenced in accordance with that agreement.

8.106 The SFO is aware that the key for multinational corporations is a worldwide deal giving certainty pre-charge. The Director points out that at the moment a corporate has options in concurrent UK/USA prosecutions because of double jeopardy. A corporate can reach certainty with the US and then argue double jeopardy in the UK out on the basis of double jeopardy. This is not something that Richard Alderman wishes to see. He is looking for co-ordinated global settlements where each country's criminal judicial system deals with the part of the offending that is relevant to that jurisdiction. This system has not yet been worked out by the courts and the SFO is looking for further judicial guidance. The SFO is also looking for further guidance from the courts on how the real victims in other countries of offences committed by corporates within the jurisdiction of our courts can receive compensation, even though they are not victims in the sense of victims of fraud, who can be compensated through asset forfeiture legislation.

8.107 What would be of assistance to the SFO is guidance on corporate penalties, as at present there is none—undermining the rule of law and legal certainty. The SFO await guidelines from the Sentencing Guidelines Council indicating what the discount is on self-reporting. This is something that will doubtless be of interest to defendants when considering the self-reporting route.

8.108 It appears that the SFO's stratagems of encouraging self-reporting, pursuing civil agreements and negotiating global settlements have been given only limited support by the courts of the UK to date. Business can derive little certainty from the guidance given by the regulator in cases where systemic corruption has occurred. Court judgments do, however, make it clear that considerable mitigation can be drawn from full cooperation with the regulator, although what sentence is to be imposed remains a matter solely for the judiciary.

Alternative proposals

8.109 The SFO has made it plain that it would like to add the power of a 'deferred prosecution' to its armoury. This tool is available to the Department of Justice ('DOJ') in the USA as part of its criminal justice system. In the USA, a deferred prosecution agreement effectively gives a corporation a period of probation, during which time charges are held in abeyance, so that the company can put its house in order and cooperate with the DOJ. The agreements made in the USA are very detailed and ordinarily include a substantial fine. It is different from a plea agreement, as if the company complies with the DoOJ's requests then no charges are brought.

8.110 By way of an example, the DOJ entered into a deferred prosecution agreement with UBS which contained the following terms (DOJ press release, 18 February 2009):

'As part of the deferred prosecution agreement and in an unprecedented move, UBS, based on an order by the Swiss Financial Markets Supervisory Authority (FINMA), has agreed to immediately provide the United States government with the identities of, and account information for, certain United States customers of UBS's cross-border business. Under the deferred prosecution agreement, UBS has also agreed to expeditiously exit the business of providing banking services to United States clients with undeclared accounts. As part of the deferred prosecution agreement, UBS has further agreed to pay $780 million in fines, penalties, interest and restitution. Earlier today, the agreement was accepted in Ft Lauderdale, Fla. by US District Judge James I. Cohn'.

It is of note that the agreement was approved by the court in the USA. The difficulty faced by the SFO is that it has no statutory powers to enter into such an arrangement. A Crown Court would have no power to 'sanction' any agreement entered into by the parties as no charges would have been brought against the company.

8.111 The Director of the SFO acknowledged the difficulties faced by the SFO in seeking to introduce such an arrangement without statutory authority in an interview with The Independent[1]:

'Mr Alderman says: "It's very different [in the US] because it is part of the criminal justice system and it wouldn't be so over here. But I wouldn't want to send out the wrong signals. This is not going soft on people. In fact, the experience of America is rather the reverse and it's a way of being really tough on people. When you look at the settlements in respect of Siemens and UBS, the sums of money involved are really very considerable"'.

[1]   5 March 2009.

8.112 The SFO has no power to impose a fine as such, but it is assumed that a major part of a deferred prosecution agreement would be the acceptance by the corporation of a substantial penalty (whether civil or criminal), including reparation and costs.

8.113 The Crown Court in the *Innospec* case (Thomas LJ sitting as a first instance judge) gave the SFO a very clear warning against exceeding its powers by seeking to make arrangements without any statutory authority[1]. It would be far more satisfactory if the power to enter into a deferred prosecution agreement was the product of legislation by parliament, rather than simply emerging as a result of a decision by a prosecuting authority to introduce such a scheme.

[1]   [2010] Crim LR 665 at paras 26–28.

8.114 It would be sensible for a statutory framework to include a requirement for any such agreement to be approved by the High Court. The Crown Court would not have any jurisdiction over the case, as under the intended scheme no criminal charges would have been brought against the company. Judicial oversight of the process and judicial determination of the amount of a criminal penalty are essential to provide public confidence.

KEY POINTS FROM CHAPTER 8

8.115 Key points from this chapter are:

- the SFO is actively promoting the development of an 'anti-corruption culture', both in the UK and abroad;
- the SFO, as a selective prosecutor, is keen to promote a culture of 'self-reporting' by corporations. There is a tension between settling for an alternative civil penalty and the public interest in pursuing cases where there is evidence of criminal conduct. A 'selective prosecutor' should have the ability to take regulatory or civil action rather than bring criminal proceedings, provided that its discretion is exercised in accordance with the principles in the case of *R v IRC, ex p Mead*[1];
- the SFO wants to be able to defer a prosecution in certain circumstances, thus enabling a corporation to put its house in order and demonstrate compliance with the law. A 'deferred prosecution' ought to have a statutory basis, which includes requiring the approval of a court for any final settlement;
- the Mutual Legal Assistance regime is of considerable importance in respect of bribery investigations and prosecutions;
- the SFO is keen to pursue 'plea bargaining' where it feels it is appropriate to do so. The current state of the law substantially inhibits 'plea bargaining'. Plea agreements under SOCPA 2005 only govern cases where an accused person is willing to assist and investigation or prosecution. The Attorney-General's Guidelines on plea discussion in serious or complex fraud provide a useful framework for negotiating pleas but provide limited protection for an accused person, as any concluded and signed plea agreement may be used in evidence against him and 'plea discussions' may become discloseable unused material under the CPIA. Further, the courts have stated repeatedly that sentence is a matter for the judiciary and that they will not 'rubber stamp' any plea agreements reached between the parties. Any formal system of plea bargaining, as exists for example in the US, will require primary legislation.

[1] [1993] 1 All ER 772, [1992] STC 484.

Chapter 9

PENALTIES AND REMEDIES

9.1 This chapter considers the consequences that may flow from a business's involvement in corruption. In addition to dealing with the criminal penalties and reputational damage which businesses may suffer, this chapter explores the quasi-criminal and civil remedies which are open to prosecutors, regulators and victims of bribery. The chapter is structured in the following way:

— Sentencing;
— Liability for money laundering offences;
— Confiscation;
— Civil recovery under POCA 2002;
— Civil remedies;
— Reputational damage;
— Extradition;
— Key points from Chapter 9.

A   SENTENCING

Relevant provisions under the Bribery Act 2010

9.2 The relevant sentencing provisions are contained in the Bribery Act 2010, s 11. In summary, for an individual, the maximum penalty for offences under s 1 (bribing another), s 2 (being bribed) and s 6 (bribery of a foreign public official) is:

— on conviction on indictment, 10 years' imprisonment, or a fine, or both;
— on summary conviction in England and Wales, 12 months' imprisonment, or a fine, or both[1];
— on summary conviction in Northern Ireland, six months' imprisonment, or a fine, or both.

[1]   Where an offence is committed before the Criminal Justice Act 2003, s 154 comes into force, the magistrates' court docs not have the power to impose imprisonment for more than six months in respect of any one offence. As at the date of publication, s 154 is not yet in force.

9.3 It should be noted that the 'consent and connivance' provisions contained within s 14 do not create a separate offence. Consequently, if a senior officer is judged to have consented to or connived in the commission of a bribery offence by a body corporate, he will be guilty of the bribery offence and will be subject to the sentencing provisions above.

9.4 For any other person, the maximum penalty for offences under ss 1, 2 or 6 is, on conviction on indictment, an unlimited fine and, on summary conviction, a fine up to the statutory maximum (presently £5,000). The maximum penalty for a relevant commercial organisation for an offence under s 7, namely failing to prevent bribery (an offence which can only be tried on indictment) is an unlimited fine.

9.5 The maximum penalty of ten years' imprisonment is an increase on the seven-year maximum penalty which is available to the courts under the Bribery Act 2010's predecessors, namely the Public and Corrupt Practices Act 1889 and the Prevention of Corruption Act 1906 (as supplemented by the Prevention of Corruption Act 1916). This increase implements the recommendation of the Law Commission, which was concerned:

> 'that there is currently a significant "perverse incentive" to charge fraud instead of bribery in the most serious cases, because the maximum penalty (10 years' imprisonment) is higher'[1].

[1]   Reforming Bribery (Law Com No 313) at 3.127.

Sentencing principles

9.6 The starting point for the court will be the Criminal Justice Act 2003, ss 142 and 143. Section 142 sets out the purpose of sentencing, namely, the punishment of offenders, the reduction of crime (including its reduction by deterrence), the reform and rehabilitation of offenders, the protection of the public and the making of reparation by offenders to persons affected by their offences. Section 143 requires the court, when considering how serious the offence before it is, to take into account the defendant's culpability in committing the offence and any harm which the offence caused, was intended to cause or might foreseeably have caused. These principles apply to a corporate defendant as well as individuals.

9.7 In addition, the court is required to give credit for a guilty plea. The arrangements for calculating discounts for a guilty plea have been formalised by statute[1] and the definitive guidelines, 'Reduction in Sentence for a Guilty Plea' issued by the Sentencing Guideline Council[2]. The level of the reduction is gauged on a sliding scale ranging from a recommended one third (where the guilty plea was entered at the first reasonable opportunity in relation to the offence for which sentence is being imposed), reducing to a recommended one quarter (where a trial date has been set) and to a recommended one tenth (for a guilty plea entered at the 'door of the court' or after the trial has begun).

[1]   First by the Powers of Criminal Courts (Sentencing) Act 2000, s 152 and subsequently by the Criminal Justice Act 2003, ss 144 and 174.
[2]   Revised July 2007.

9.8 As regards the appropriate reduction for assistance provided by a defendant, the court will act in accordance with well-established principles, summarised by the Court of Appeal in *R v P; R v Blackburn*[1]. Any discount for the guilty plea is separate from and additional to the appropriate reduction for assistance provided by the defendant[2]. Particular value should be attached to those cases where the defendant provides evidence in the form of a witness statement or is prepared to give evidence at any subsequent trial. The court will also have regard to the nature and extent of the personal risks to, and potential consequences faced by, the defendant and members of his family. Assisting offender agreements, made pursuant to the Serious Organised Crime and Police Act 2005 ('(SOCPA'), s 73 (considered in Chapter 8) requires the defendant to reveal the whole of his previous criminal activities (this is known as 'cleansing'). This is likely to mean that he will admit and plead guilty to offences which would never otherwise have been attributed to him and may indeed have been unknown to the relevant authorities. In order for the process to work as intended, sentencing for offences which fall into this category should usually be approached with these realities in mind and, so far as s 73 agreements are concerned, should normally lead to the imposition of concurrent sentences. It is only in the most exceptional case that the appropriate level of reduction would exceed three quarters of the total sentence which would otherwise be passed. The normal level is a reduction of somewhere between one half and two thirds of a sentence. Defendants who do not take part in full 'cleansing' cannot expect to receive the fullest discount available[3].

1   [2007] EWCA Crim 2290, [2008] 2 All ER 684, [2008] 2 Cr App Rep (S) 16, in particular paras 37–41.
2   *R v Wood* [1992] 1 Cr App Rep (S) 347.
3   *R v D* [2010] EWCA 1485 at para 13.

Suspended sentences

9.9 In *R v Dougall*[1] the Lord Chief Justice gave guidance to sentencing courts on the circumstances in which a defendant, who had entered into an assisting offender agreement under SOCPA 2005, s 73 and had pleaded guilty to corruption, was likely to receive a suspended sentence of imprisonment:

> 'Where the appropriate sentence for a defendant whose level of criminality, and features of mitigation, combined with a guilty plea and full co-operation with the authorities investigating a major crime involving fraud or corruption, with all the consequent burdens of complying with his part of the SOCPA agreement, would be 12 months' imprisonment or less, the argument that the sentence should be suspended is very powerful. This result will normally follow'.

1   [2010] EWCA Crim 1048, [2010] Crim LR 661, 174 CL&J 365.

Aggravating and mitigating features generally

9.10 In view of the fact that the maximum penalty has been increased to ten years' imprisonment, the sentencing decisions under the old law are of limited relevance to cases under the Bribery Act 2010. Nonetheless, they provide a helpful indication of the factors that the courts are likely to regard as 'aggravating' and 'mitigating' in the context of corruption cases. For a review of many of the decisions of the Court of Appeal (Criminal Division) under the old law, see Chapter 3, and also section B9 1.3 of the *Current Sentencing Practice*[1]. The sentences recently imposed on the former directors of Mabey & Johnson for providing €420,000 of kickbacks to the Iraqi Government of Saddam Hussein indicate that where a senior manager or director has been convicted of bribery, the starting point is likely to be a custodial sentence. On

23 February 2011, following conviction after trial, Richard Forsyth, former managing director, was sentenced to 21 months' imprisonment and David Mabey, former sales director, to 8 months' imprisonment. Richard Gledhill, former sales manager (who had pleaded guilty and given evidence for the prosecution) was sentenced to 8 months' imprisonment suspended for two years[2]. In passing sentence, HHJ Rivlin QC stated 'When a director of a major company plays even a small part, he can expect to receive a custodial sentence'.

[1] Looseleaf, by David A Thomas QC.
[2] Mabey & Johnson Ltd had earlier pleaded guilty (in September 2009) to breaching UN sanctions in relation to Iraq and to corruption offences in relation to Ghana and Jamaica and was sentenced to a fine of £6.6 million.

9.11 The CPS has published a sentencing manual as an aid to guide Crown Prosecutors in the use of their discretion in making decisions. The section on bribery, produced in February 2008, deals only with the position at common law but lists some of the aggravating and mitigating features that the CPS considers are likely to be relevant to corruption cases[1].

[1] www.cps.gov.uk/legal/s_to_u/sentencing_manual/bribery_(common_law).

9.12 As at the date of publication, the Sentencing Council has not published guidance for bribery cases. In the absence of bespoke guidance, the Sentencing Council's definitive guidelines 'Sentencing for fraud—statutory offences'[1] are a useful starting point in establishing the relevant general principles. There is a substantial overlap between fraud and bribery. When a financial gain is made 'corruptly', it may amount to fraud, or bribery, or both, depending on the circumstances. An example given by the Law Commission in which both offences may be committed is where P pays R a secret commission to accept P's bid for a contract, when it would have been in R's employer's financial interests that someone else be awarded the contract. In this example, R's employer is the victim of fraud, but the payment in exchange for the favour is also bribery. In addition, comparison may usefully be made with the general guidance on sentencing given by the Court of Appeal in *R v Whittle*[2] which concerned hard core cartel activity contrary to the Enterprise Act 2000, s 188 (albeit the maximum sentence for such an offence is just five years' imprisonment).

[1] Published October 2009.
[2] [2008] EWCA Crim 2560 at para 34.

9.13 Having regard to the sentencing decisions under the old law and the material referred to above, it is suggested that the following are likely to be regarded by the courts as aggravating factors:

— corruption of foreign government ministers or officials;
— conduct sustained over a lengthy period;
— high level of planning and sophistication;
— large number of individuals acting together in pursuance of the corrupt enterprise;
— large sums involved;
— high level of profit;
— breach of a position of authority or trust, such as by an employee, director or trustee;

— where the individual defendant is high up the corporate hierarchy and/or an organiser, planner or prime mover in the corrupt enterprise;
— where the defendant's conduct was contrary to guidelines laid down in a company compliance manual;
— vulnerable victim.

9.14 Factors which the court will consider to be mitigating and which are most likely to be present in corruption cases are:

— the defendant self-reported;
— guilty plea;
— complete and unprompted disclosure of the extent of the corruption;
— cooperation (and in particular, entering into an assisting offender agreement under SOCPA 2005);
— where the defendant has played a minor or peripheral role in the corruption;
— voluntary restitution;
— personal factors such as illness, disability, family difficulties, etc.

Sentencing corporate defendants

9.15 The general principles above will apply equally to corporate defendants. However, in the case of corporate defendants, the means of the defendant will be particularly relevant. Pursuant to the Criminal Justice Act 2003, s 164, the court must take into account the financial circumstances of the defendant.

9.16 In the absence of specific guidance in the context of corruption, the decisions in *R v F Howe & Son (Engineers) Ltd*[1] and *R v Balfour Beatty Rail Infrastructure Services Ltd*[2] provide some assistance. Whilst both cases concern a very different type of corporate misconduct (serious offences contrary to the Health and Safety at Work etc Act 1974) it is submitted that they give some indication of the approach that the courts will take when setting the level of fine for corporate defendants.

[1]   [1999] 2 Cr App Rep (S) 37.
[2]   [2006] EWCA Crim 1586, [2007] 1 Cr App Rep (S) 370.

9.17 In *R v F Howe & Son (Engineers) Ltd*, the Court of Appeal stated that particular aggravating features included: (1) a failure to heed warnings; and (2) where the defendant had deliberately profited financially. Other matters relevant to sentence included: the extent of the breaches (for example, whether it was an isolated incident or continued over a period) and, importantly, the defendant's resources and the effect of the fine on its business. Particular mitigating features included: (1) prompt admission of responsibility and a timely guilty plea; (2) steps to remedy the deficiencies; and (3) a good record. The court observed that it was impossible to lay down any tariff or say that the fine should bear any specific relationship to the turnover or net profit of the defendant, but stated:

> 'The objective of prosecutions for health and safety offences in the work place is to achieve a safe environment for those who work there and for other members of the public who may be affected. A fine needs to be large enough to bring that

message home where the defendant is a company, not only to those who manage it but also to its shareholders"[1].

[1] [1999] 2 All ER 249, [1999] 2 Cr App Rep (S) 37 at 43–44.

9.18 Regarding the financial information to be provided by the corporate defendant, the court stated:

'Difficulty is sometimes found in obtaining timely and accurate information about a corporate defendant's means. The starting point is its annual accounts. If a defendant company wishes to make any submission to the court about its ability to pay a fine it should supply copies of its accounts and any other financial information on which it intends to rely in good time before the hearing both to the court and to the prosecution. This will give the prosecution the opportunity to assist the court should the court wish it. Usually, accounts need to be considered with some care to avoid reaching a superficial or perhaps erroneous conclusion. Where accounts or other financial information are deliberately not supplied the court will be entitled to conclude that the company is in a position to pay any financial penalty it is minded to impose"[1].

[1] [1999] 2 Cr App Rep (S) 37 at 44.

9.19 In *R v Balfour Beatty Rail Infrastructure Ltd* (the prosecution that followed the Hatfield Rail Crash) the Lord Chief Justice stated:

'Section 3 of [the HSWA 1974] requires positive steps to be taken by all concerned in the operation of the business of a company to ensure that the company's activities involve the minimum risk, both to employees and to third parties. Knowledge that breach of this duty can result in a fine of sufficient size to impact on the shareholders will provide a powerful incentive for management to comply with this duty. This is not to say that the fine must always be large enough to affect dividends or share price. But the fine must always be large enough to reflect both the degree of fault and the consequences so as to raise appropriate concern on the part of the shareholders at what has occurred. Such an approach will satisfy the requirement that the sentence should act as a deterrent. It will also satisfy the requirement, which will be rightly reflect by public opinion, that a company should be punished for culpable failure to pay due regard for safety and, for the consequences of that failure"[1].

[1] [2006] EWCA Crim 1586, [2007] 1 Cr App Rep (S) 370 at para 42.

9.20 The aggravating and mitigating features listed at paras **9.13–9.14** will be as relevant to the sentencing of corporate defendants as they are to individuals. In addition, it is suggested that the following factors are likely to be regarded by the courts as aggravating features[1]:

— a history of similar conduct (including prior criminal, civil or regulatory enforcement action against the company for corruption);
— the conduct alleged is part of the established business practice of the company;
— the offence was committed at a time when the company had an ineffective compliance programme;
— the company had previously been subject to warnings.

[1] Cf 'Guidance on Corporate Prosecutions,' issued by the DPP, SFO and RCPO and 'Bribery Act 2010: Joint Prosecution Guidance of the Director of the SFO and the DPP' (published 30 March 2011), which lists similar factors as being relevant to the decision whether or not

to prosecute a company.

9.21 In addition to the mitigating factors identified at para **9.14**, it is suggested that the following factors are likely to mitigate the sentence of a corporate defendant for corruption[1]:

— a proactive approach by the corporate management team when the offending is brought to their notice, including, for example, self-reporting, remedial actions and the compensation of victims;

— the existence of a genuinely proactive and effective corporate compliance programme;

— the offending represents isolated actions by rogue employees;

— the offending is not recent in nature and the company in its current form is effectively a different body to that which committed the offence;

— the fact that a conviction will exclude it from tendering for public contracts.

[1] Cf the types of public interest factors which militate against prosecution, listed in 'Guidance on Corporate Prosecutions,' issued by DPP, SFO and RCPO and in 'Bribery Act 2010: Joint Prosecution Guidance of the Director of the SFO and the DPP' (published 30 March 2011).

Corporate corruption of foreign government officials

9.22 The decision of Thomas LJ in *R v Innospec Ltd*[1] indicates that courts take a very serious view of corruption of foreign officials. Companies found guilty of such conduct can expect very substantial fines. Whist this is a first instance decision, it is a decision of an experienced Court of Appeal judge and, moreover, was implicitly approved by the LCJ at para 7 of his judgment in *R v Dougall*[2]. The relevance of this decision to 'plea bargaining' is considered at para **8.103**. As regards sentencing, Thomas LJ stated[3]:

— sentences in cases of corruption of foreign government officials or foreign government ministers must be effective, proportionate and dissuasive in the sense of having a deterrent element;

— corruption of foreign government officials is at the top end of serious corporate offending both in terms of culpability and harm;

— the courts have a duty to impose penalties appropriate to the serious level of criminality that are characteristic of this offence. For example, one of its many effects is to distort competition; the level of fines in cartel cases is now very substantial and measured in tens of millions. Corruption is much more serious in terms both of culpability and harm caused;

— there is no reason to differentiate the financial penalties imposed for corruption between the US and England and Wales. Indeed there is every reason for states to adopt a uniform approach to financial penalties for corruption of foreign government officials so that the penalties in each country do not discriminate either favourably or unfavourably against a company in a particular state. If the penalties in one state are lower than in another, businesses in the state with lower penalties will not be deterred so effectively from engaging in corruption in foreign states, whilst businesses in states where the penalties are higher may complain that they are disadvantaged in foreign states;

— the fines should be quite separate from, and in addition to, depriving the corporate defendant of the benefits it had obtained through its criminality.

1 [2010] Crim LR 665.
2 [2010] EWCA Crim 1048.
3 At paras 30–32.

Costs

9.23 The relevant provisions for the making of orders for costs in criminal proceedings, whether in favour of the prosecution or the defendant, are contained in the Prosecution of Offences Act 1985, the Access to Justice Act 1999, the Lord Chief Justice's Practice Direction (costs: criminal proceedings)[1] and the Costs in Criminal Case (General) Regulations 1986[2].

1 [2004] 2 All ER 1070, CA.
2 SI 1986/1335.

9.24 As regards prosecution costs, generally speaking where any person is convicted of an offence, the court may make such order as to costs to be paid by the accused as the court considers is just and reasonable. Where a defendant is in a position to pay the whole of the prosecution costs, the court made clear in *R v F Howe & Son (Engineers) Ltd* that, in addition to the fine, there was no reason in principle for the court not to make an order accordingly. The court must, however, have regarded to the totality of the sentence. In *R v Associated Octel Co Ltd*[1] and *R v Northallerton Magistrates' Court, ex p Dove*[2] the Court of Appeal gave guidance on what costs may be claimed and the approach the courts should take.

1 [1997] 1 Cr App Rep (S) 435, [1997] Crim LR 144, CA.
2 [2001] 1 Cr App Rep (S) 137.

9.25 As regards defence costs, in the event of a prosecution not being proceeded with, or in the event of an acquittal, the court may make an order in favour of the defendant for a payment to be made out of central funds, pursuant to the Prosecution of Offences Act 1985, s 16 (this is known as a defendant's costs order). It should be for such an amount as the court considers reasonably sufficient to compensate the defendant for any expenses properly incurred by him in the proceedings. A defendant's costs order should normally be made unless there are positive reasons for not doing so. Thus, for example, where the defendant's own conduct has brought suspicion on himself and has misled the prosecution into thinking that the case was stronger than it was, the defendant can be left to pay his own costs. In the case of a partial acquittal the court may make a part order[1].

1 Practice Direction (costs: criminal proceedings) [2004] 2 All ER 1070, CA.

Compensation

9.26 The courts also have the power to make compensation orders against convicted persons, 'for any personal injury, loss or damage from that offence or any other offence which is taken into consideration by the court in determining sentence'[1]. The question is whether the loss 'can fairly be said to result from the offence'[2]. The level of compensation will be an amount that the court considers 'appropriate' having considered the evidence and any representations put before it by the prosecution and the defence and having regard to the means of the defendant. Third parties (including victims) do not have locus standi to make representations on any compensation order.

[1]   Powers of Criminal Courts (Sentencing) Act 2000, s 130(1).
[2]   *Rowlston v Kenny* (1982) 4 Cr App Rep (S) 85, CA; *R v Vivian* [1979] 1 All ER 48, [1979] 1 WLR 291, CA.

9.27 Compensation may be ordered having regard to assets which are lawful and nothing to do with the proceeds of crime. The purpose of such an order is to compensate the loser[1].

[1]   *R v Copley* (1979) 1 Cr App Rep (S) 55, CA.

9.28 Criminal courts are unenthusiastic about the making of compensation orders in fraud and orruption cases. Compensation in such cases is generally complicated and controversial. The Court of Appeal has held that no order for compensation should be made unless the sum claimed has either been agreed or proved and the criminal courts are discouraged from conducting complicated investigations which are more appropriately dealt with in the civil courts (see para **9.56**ff for civil remedies available to victims of bribery):

> 'It has been stressed in this court more than once recently that the machinery of a compensation order . . . is intended for clear and simple cases . . . In a great majority of cases the appropriate court to deal with the issues raised by matters of this kind is in the appropriate civil proceedings. A compensation order made by the court can be extremely beneficial as long as it is confined to simple, straightforward cases and generally where no great amount is at stake'[1].

[1]   *R v Kneeshaw* [1975] QB 57, [1974] 1 All ER 896, CA; see also *R v Bewick* [2007] 1 EWCA Crim 3297, [2008] 2 Cr App Rep (S) 31.

B   LIABILITY FOR MONEY LAUNDERING OFFENCES

The principal money laundering offences

9.29 The money laundering offences created by the Proceeds of Crime Act 2002 ('POCA 2002') are of broad application. They cover, in essence, the possession of or dealing with any benefit from any predicate criminal conduct, whether that conduct took place in the UK or overseas[1]. It follows that they capture those who deal with the proceeds of corruption. Significantly, the SFO has recently telegraphed its intention to use the money laundering provisions to tackle corruption. On 3 March 2011, at a conference organised by Transparency International Belgium and the Belgian Ministry of Foreign Affairs on overseas corruption, the Director of the SFO stated:

> 'Speaking for the SFO, we have tended to concentrate on corruption offences by themselves. What we have been doing recently though and I certainly see this developing much more in the future, is to make the important link between corruption and money laundering. We are starting to do this in cases. I expect to

285

see far more of this work in future. I expect us to follow the money against a range of individuals and organisations so that all of those involved in corruption and the laundering of corrupt monies are dealt with by prosecution or through some other way. It seems to me that there is a very great deal of potential in this area. There will be some very important messages that we can stress.'

[1]   The potential for money laundering where the conduct producing the property took place overseas is subject to the foreign legality exclusion. As to conduct which is exempt from this exclusion see the Proceeds of Crime Act 2002 (Money Laundering: Exceptions to Overseas Conduct Defence) Order 2006, SI 2006/1070.

9.30 Section 327 of POCA 2002 provides that a person commits an offence if he conceals, disguises, converts or transfers criminal property or removes criminal property from the UK. POCA 2002, s 328 provides that a person commits an offence if he enters into or becomes concerned in an arrangement, which he knows, or suspects facilitates (by whatever means) the acquisition, retention, use or control of criminal property by or on behalf of another person[1]. Section 329 provides that a person commits an offence if he acquires, uses or has in his possession criminal property. Together these offences are known as the principal money laundering offences. The emphasis in these offences is on the property, not the predicate offender. Section 340 provides that property is criminal property if:

—   it constitutes a person's benefit from criminal conduct or it represents such benefit (in whole or in part and whether directly or indirectly); and
—   the alleged offender (namely, the person dealing with the property) knows or suspects that it constitutes or represents such benefit.

The meaning of suspicion was considered by the Court of Appeal in *R v Da Silva* where Longmore LJ said:

'It seems to us that the essential element in the word "suspect" and its affiliates, in this context, is that the defendant must think that there is a possibility, which is more than fanciful, that the relevant facts exist. A vague feeling of unease would not suffice. But the statute does not require the suspicion to be "clear" or "firmly grounded and targeted on specific facts", or "based upon reasonable grounds"'[1].

[1]   Unlike the offences in ss 327 and 329, there are two mental elements in the offence under s 328, one with regard to the property itself and the other in relation to the knowledge or suspicion that the relevant arrangement will facilitate.
[1]   [2006] EWCA Crim 1654, [2006] 4 All ER 900; see also *K Ltd v National Westminster Bank plc (Revenue and Customs Prosecution Office and Serious Organised Crime Agency intervening)* [2006] EWCA Civ 1039, [2006] 4 All ER 907; *Shah v HSBC Private Bank (UK) Ltd* [2010] EWCA Civ 31, [2010] 3 All ER 477.

9.31 A person guilty of one of the principal money laundering offences will be liable, on conviction on indictment, to imprisonment for a term not exceeding 14 years.

9.32 The mere act of giving a bribe does not, of itself, constitute an offence under POCA 2002, s 328[1]. In order for an offence under s 328 to be committed, the arrangement into which the defendant enters, or in which he becomes involved, must be one which facilitates the acquisition, retention, use or control by another of property which has already become criminal property before the arrangement takes place. However, businesses need to be aware that once a bribe has been paid, the bribe itself, and any benefit received as a result of the bribe, may constitute criminal property. This will include the benefit of any contract obtained by corruption, including any payments made under that contract, profits and revenues generated by the contract and share dividends payable from those profits. Thus officers or employees who are involved in the making of payments linked to corrupt contracts may be exposed to criminal liability for money laundering under ss 327–329 even though they may not be complicit in the corrupt arrangement itself. In the event that the knowledge or suspicion is held by an individual who can be identified as the company's directing mind and will, then the company will also be exposed to the risk of criminal liability[2].

1   *R v Abida Shaheen Amir; R v Urfan Akhtar* [2011] EWCA Crim 146; *Kensington International Ltd v Republic of Congo* [2008] EWCA Civ 1128, [2008] 1 WLR 1144 per Moore-Bick LJ: 'A person who gives a bribe may know that it will constitute criminal property in the hands of the recipient, but that does not make him guilty of entering into an arrangement which facilitates the acquisition of what is already criminal property'..

2   In accordance with the doctine of identification, see *Tesco Supermarkets Ltd v Nattrass* [1972] AC 153,[1971] 2 All ER 127, HL and *AG's Reference (No 2 of 1999)* [2000] QB 796, [2000] 3 All ER 182, CA.

9.33 Officers and employees who are concerned that they may be dealing with the proceeds of corruption will need to make an authorised disclosure under s 338 seeking 'appropriate consent' from the Serious and Organised Crime Agency (SOCA) to go ahead with the transaction (in accordance with the POCA 2002, s 335). Under ss 327(2)(a), 328(2)(a), 329(2)(a) a person does not commit a principal money laundering offence if he makes an 'authorised disclosure'. The 'consent provisions' under POCA 2002 have two purposes. First, they offer law enforcement agencies an opportunity to gather intelligence or intervene in advance of potentially suspicious activity taking place. Second, they give those who, in the course of their business, need to complete a transaction which they know or suspect constitutes one of the three money laundering offences, the means of obtaining the authorisation necessary to complete the transaction[1]. Whilst the consent regime in effect provides immunity in relation to the principal money laundering offences, it does not provide protection against criminal liability for any predicate corruption offence.

1   Home Office Circular 029/2008 (drawn up in consultation with ACPO, SOCA, CPS, HMRC and RCPO) which provides guidance on the operation of the consent regime; see also the Explanatory Notes to POCA 2002.

Reporting suspected money laundering

9.34 Section 330 of POCA 2002 imposes a duty on those in the 'regulated sector'[1] to report suspected money laundering as soon as is practicable. The duty is triggered when a person 'knows or suspects or has reasonable grounds for knowing or suspecting, that another person is engaged in money laundering' and where such knowledge or suspicion came to him in the course of his business. This duty is quite separate from the requirement on businesses (their officers and employees) to make an authorised disclosure seeking consent in order to avoid criminal liability for the principal money laundering offences. The penalty for failing to disclose under POCA 2002, s 330 is, on conviction on indictment, imprisonment for a maximum of five years, or a fine, or both[1]. On summary conviction the maximum penalty is a term of imprisonment not exceeding six months, or a fine of £5,000, or both[2].

1 As defined in POCA 2002, Sch 9. It includes, for example, financial institutions, estate agents, casino operators, tax advisors, accountants, auditors, legal services providers in respect of financial or real property transactions.
1 POCA 2002, s 334(2)(b).
2 POCA 2002, s 334(2)(a).

9.35 Businesses in the regulated sector, for example, financial institutions, accountants and auditors, need to be alert to the requirement to report their client if they become suspicious that it has paid bribes and received some benefit as a result, or received bribes or otherwise dealt with the proceeds of corruption. The Court of Appeal has underlined the absolute obligation to observe scrupulously the terms of s 330 and indicated that a failure to do so will almost inevitably result in a custodial sentence[1].

1 *R v Griffiths and Pattison* [2006] EWCA Crim 2155, [2007] 1 Cr App Rep (S) 581.

C CONFISCATION

9.36 The regime under POCA 2002 under which the proceeds of crime are confiscated comes into play only where a defendant has been convicted. This is in contrast to the provisions for civil recovery under POCA 2002, Pt 5 (which are considered at para **9.48**ff). There are three legitimate aims of confiscation: punishment, deterrence and the reduction in profits available to fund further criminal enterprises[1]. The ability to confiscate the proceeds of crime is an important and powerful law enforcement tool. In recent years the number of orders and the sums confiscated have steadily risen. Confiscation orders can have a particularly punitive effect in relation to bribery offences and can lead to the financial ruin of the defendant company.

1 *R v Benjafield; R v Rezvi* [2003] 1 AC 1099, HL.

General principles

9.37 The relevant provisions governing the confiscation of the proceeds of crime are contained in POCA 2002, Pt 2. The regime applies to offences committed after 24 March 2003.

9.38 In *R v May*[1] (the first of a trilogy of important appeals relating to the confiscation of criminal assets[2]) the House of Lords emphasised the broad principles which should be followed by the courts when exercising their powers to make confiscation orders under POCA 2002, Pt 2. Subsequently, on 28 May 2009, the CPS issued guidance for prosecutors on the discretion to instigate confiscation proceedings, which conveniently summarises much of the recent case law. There can be no substitute for direct reference to the relevant statutory provisions and to the judgments of the House of Lords in *May, Jennings* and *Green* and the subsequent Court of Appeal cases.

1 [2008] UKHL 28, [2008] 1 AC 1028, [2008] 4 All ER 113.
2 The two other appeals are *Jennings v Crown Prosecution Service* [2008] UKHL 29, [2008] 1 AC 1046, [2008] 4 All ER 113 and *R v Green* [2008] UKHL 30, [2008] 1 AC 1053, [2008]

4 All ER 119.

9.39 As the House of Lords stated in the trilogy of appeals, the starting point must be an appreciation that the legislation is intended to deprive defendants of the benefit they have gained from relevant criminal conduct, whether or not they have retained such benefit, within the limits of their available means. It does not provide for confiscation in the sense understood by schoolchildren and others, but nor does it operate by way of fine. The rationale of the confiscation regime is to deprive the defendant of what he has gained or its equivalent and not to operate by way of a fine. The benefit gained is the total value of the property or advantage obtained, not the defendant's net profit after deduction of expenses or any amounts payable to co-conspirators.

9.40 As the proliferation of decisions of the Court of Appeal and the House of Lords demonstrates, the statutory framework which governs the making of confiscation orders is far from straightforward. A detailed consideration of the framework is beyond the scope of this work[1]. The key requirements which must be met before a confiscation order is made are set out in POCA 2002, s 6. In summary:

— the defendant must be convicted of an offence;
— the prosecution must ask the court to embark on confiscation proceedings or the court must believe it is appropriate for it to do so;
— the court must decide whether the defendant has a criminal lifestyle;
— if the court decides that the defendant has a criminal lifestyle, the court must determine whether he has benefited from his 'general criminal conduct'. The court calculates the benefit from 'general criminal conduct' using certain 'assumptions' set out in POCA 2002;
— if the court decides that the defendant does not have a criminal lifestyle, the court must decide whether he has benefited from his 'particular criminal conduct';
— if the court decides that the defendant has benefited from either his general or particular criminal conduct, then it must determine the recoverable amount (which is an amount equal to the defendant's benefit from the conduct concerned);
— the court must then make a confiscation order in the sum of the recoverable amount, unless the court believes that there may be civil proceedings taken by the victim of the order or the defendant is able to show that the available amount is in fact less, in which case the confiscation order will be in the available amount.

Significantly, the requirements under s 6 are mandatory. Where the conditions in POCA 2002, s 6(2) and (3) are met, the court has no discretion not to make the confiscation order if it concludes that the defendant has benefited from his criminal conduct.

[1] For a full exposition, the reader is referred to Mitchell, Taylor & Talbot *Confiscation and the Proceeds of Crime*, Ch V.

9.41 In determining whether the defendant has obtained property or a pecuniary advantage and, if so, the value of any property or advantage so obtained, the court should (subject to any relevant statutory definition) apply ordinary common law principles to the facts as found. The exercise of this jurisdiction involves no departure from familiar rules governing entitlement and ownership[1].

[1]   *R v May* [2008] UKHL 28, [2008] 1 AC 1028, [2008] 4 All ER 113.

Calculating the benefit of corruption

9.42 The legislation is intended to deprive defendants of the benefit they have gained from relevant criminal conduct. Since the powers of confiscation were first introduced, the consistent decision of the courts has been that the statutory language does not allow the expression 'benefit' to be limited to the net profit or gain, or the retained profit or gain, of the defendant. The jurisdiction to make confiscation orders is not restitutionary. It follows that not infrequently the amount of money confiscated will exceed the profit made by the criminal from his offence[1]. Indeed, in general benefit cases, where the lifestyle provisions apply, it is often the case, and perfectly proper, for a confiscation order to be 'massively greater' than a defendant's benefit from particular offending[2].

[1]   *R v Smith (David Cadman)* [2001] UKHL 68, [2002] 1 All ER 366,[2002] 1 WLR 54 ; *R v May* [2008] UKHL 28, [2008] 1 AC 1028, [2008] 4 All ER 113; *R v Shabir* [2009] 1 Cr App Rep (S) 84.
[2]   *R v Shabir* per Hughes LJ at para 27.

9.43 Businesses must be aware that the effect of this regime on defendants (corporate and individual) who have been convicted of corruption is likely to be particularly punitive. For example, where a business has paid a bribe in order to win a contract, prosecutors are likely to argue that the 'benefit' of that criminal conduct is the entire value of the underlying contract rather than either the amount of the bribe or the net profit. This may well have a devastating effect on the business's ability to trade and, because of the mandatory nature of POCA 2002, s 6, the court has little discretion in the matter.

9.44 In *R v Innospec Ltd* Thomas LJ had little hesitation in stating that the benefits were not merely profits derived from the contracts obtained by corruption but the very contracts themselves. Innospec had paid an estimated $8m to senior government officials as bribes to secure contracts worth $160m. Whilst his observations on this issue were obiter, Thomas LJ considered that the benefit to Innospec might therefore have been as high as $160m[1]. A similar approach was taken by the courts in *R v Uberoi*[2] in the context of an insider dealing prosecution brought by the FSA. His Honour Judge Tester at first instance determined that the benefit obtained by the first defendant, who had been convicted of buying and selling shares on the basis of inside information, was the full value of the shares purchased (£288,050.05) and not his net profit from the transactions (approximately £110,000). The Joint Committee on the Draft Bribery Bill provided a particularly dramatic illustration of how the regime might operate in the context of bribery: 'Take for example an individual who makes a buyout offer worth £15m to a company's sharehold-ers, and who pays a bribe of £50,000 to a Chief Executive to secure his endorsement of the buyout. That individual risks losing the entire value of the company and its assets if he acquires it due to the bribe succeeding. In other words, the penalty for paying a bribe of £50,000 could be as high as £15m'[3].

[1]   *R v Innospec Ltd* [2010] Crim LR 665, Southwark Crown Court. In the unusual circumstances of the case, which was governed by the Criminal Justice Act 1988 (the predecessor to POCA) the court was not required to make a confiscation order.

[2]   7 July 2010, (unreported).

[3]   Joint Committee Report on the Draft Bribery Bill First Report, para 186.

Avoiding confiscation proceedings

9.45 The desire to avoid confiscation proceedings through cooperation is often a powerful incentive for some offenders. However, rarely will it be appropriate to agree that the prosecutor will not ask the court to proceed to consider confiscation under POCA 2002, s 6 as part of a plea agreement[1]. Such an agreement could not, in any event, bind the court which, under POCA 2002, s 6(3)(b), must proceed if it considers it appropriate to do so.

[1]   See: CPS Legal Guidance 'Queen's Evidence—Immunities, Undertakings and Agreements under the Serious Organised Crime and Police Act 2005' (published 14 January 2011) and also the Attorney-General's Guidelines on Plea Discussions in Cases of Serious or Complex Fraud, para D9.

9.46 A basis of plea agreed between the prosecution and defence may have the effect (intended or otherwise) of limiting the confiscation order which can properly be sought[1]. However, the court does not have to accept any matters that are agreed between the parties. POCA 2002 requires the trial judge to undertake his own enquiry and not to 'rubber stamp' an agreement between the parties not related to the facts of the case[2].

[1]   *R v Lunnon* [2004] EWCA Crim 1125, [2005] 1 Cr App Rep (S) 111, [2004] Crim LR 678.

[2]   *R v Atkinson* (1992) 14 Cr App Rep (S) 182, [1992] Crim LR 749, CA; *Telli v Revenue and Customs Prosecution Office* [2007] EWCA Civ 1385, [2008] 3 All ER 405, [2008] 2 Cr App Rep (S) 278.

9.47 In the event that the prosecution invokes the confiscation regime, depending on the circumstances, it may be open to the defendant to submit to the court they are oppressive and an abuse of the court's process and should therefore be stayed. The jurisdiction to stay confiscation proceedings is of limited scope[1]. It will only be exercised 'with considerable caution' and is ordinarily confined to cases of 'true oppression'[2]. It is not sufficient to establish that the effect of a confiscation order would be to extract from a defendant a sum greater than his profit from the crime, since confiscation orders are not intended to be restitutionary measures. Examples of when the courts may be minded to intervene to stay confiscation proceedings as an abuse of process are[3]:

—   where the prosecution has reneged on an earlier agreement not to proceed;

—   in a simple benefit case, where the defendant has voluntarily paid full compensation to the victims or is ready, willing and able to do so, and has not profited from his crime[4];

—   where the prosecution's only purpose in pursuing confiscation proceedings is to inflict an additional financial penalty on the defendant. The confiscation jurisdiction should not operate as a fine[5];

—   where there is an enormous disparity between the amount of the defendant's elicit gain and that of the confiscation order. Such a disparity will not constitute oppression in every case. In particular, in general benefit cases, where the lifestyle provisions apply, it may be perfectly proper for a confiscation order to be 'massively greater' than a defendant's benefit from particular offending[6]. Any injustice perceived by the court can, in any event, be overcome by the court declining to apply the lifestyle presumptions.

The unintended consequence of the inflexible and fairly draconian nature of the confiscation regime is that it operates as a substantial disincentive to companies to come forward and self-report incidents of suspected bribery.

[1]   *R v Nelson; R v Pathak; R v Paulet* [2009] EWCA Crim 1573, [2010] 4 All ER 666, [2010] 2 WLR 788; *R v Lowe* [2009] 2 Cr App Rep (S) 81; *R v Wilkinson* [2009] EWCA Crim 2733, [2009] All ER (D) 121 (Dec).

[2]   *R v Shabir* [2008] EWCA Crim 1809, [2009] 1 Cr App Rep (S) 497.

[3]   See also CPS Guidance to prosecutors issued on 28 May 2009 'Guidance for prosecutors on the discretion to instigate confiscation proceedings', which acknowledges that, in some of these examples, it would be inappropriate to invoke the confiscation regime.

[4]   *R v Morgan* [2009] 1 Cr App Rep (S) 60.

[5]   *R v May* [20008] UKHL 28, [2008] 1 AC 1028, [2008] 4 All ER 97.

[6]   *R v Shabir* per Hughes LJ at para 27.

D   CIVIL RECOVERY UNDER POCA 2002

The relevant provisions

9.48 Part 5 of POCA 2002 provides a regime through which the relevant authorities can recover, in civil proceedings, property which is or represents property which has been obtained through unlawful conduct. From April 2008, the powers to recover property through a civil recovery order have been conferred on the Serious Fraud Office, SOCA and the Director of Public Prosecutions.

9.49 The civil recovery regime is quite distinct from confiscation proceedings under POCA 2002, Pt 2 (considered at para **9.36**ff). The purpose of the regime is to recover the property itself. Proceedings are brought in the High Court (or in Scotland, the Court of Session) under the Civil Procedure Rules 1998 ('CPR 1998'), Pt 8. The key features of the civil recovery regime are:

—   the property itself is the target;

—   the derivation of the property is in issue, not the conduct of the defendant/respondent. There is no need for a finding of misconduct nor for there to be a previous conviction;

—   the court may make a civil recovery order on the basis of the civil standard of proof (ie balance of probabilities) rather than the criminal standard of proof[1];

—   the relevant authority must prove on the balance of probabilities that the property was obtained by, or in return for, a particular kind or one of a number of kinds of unlawful conduct. The authority should identify the matters alleged to constitute unlawful conduct in sufficient detail to enable the court not to decide whether a particular crime had been committed by a particular individual, but to decide whether the conduct so described was unlawful under the criminal law in the UK[2];

— civil recovery proceedings may be brought against any person who the relevant authority thinks holds recoverable property[3]. Recoverable property is defined as property obtained through unlawful conduct[4];

— unlawful conduct includes conduct that occurs in a country outside the UK and is unlawful under the criminal law of that country and if it occurred in a part of the UK would be unlawful under the criminal law of that[5]. This enables property obtained through unlawful conduct abroad to be recovered;

— a person obtains property through unlawful conduct (whether his own conduct or another) if he obtains property by or in return for the conduct[6].

1   POCA 2002, s 241(3).
2   *Director of the Assets Recovery Agency v Green* [2005] EWHC 3168 (Admin); *Director of the Assets Recovery Agency v Kean* [2007] EWHC 112 (Admin).
3   POCA 2002, s 243(1).
4   POCA 2002, s 304(1).
5   POCA 2002, s 241.
6   POCA 2002, s 242(1).

The Attorney-General's Guidance on civil recovery

9.50 The Attorney-General issued guidance to prosecuting bodies on their asset recovery powers under POCA 2002 on 5 November 2009 which states, at para 1:

'The reduction of crime is in general best secured by means of criminal investigations and criminal proceedings. However, the non-conviction based asset recovery powers available under the Act can also make an important contribution to the reduction of crime where (i) it is not feasible to secure a conviction, (ii) a conviction is obtained but a confiscation order is not made, or (iii) a relevant authority is of the view that the public interest will be better served by using those powers rather than by seeking a criminal disposal'.

9.51 The Guidance emphasises, at para 4, the importance of retaining public confidence in the criminal justice system as a whole:

'In particular, care must be taken not to allow an individual or body corporate to avoid a criminal investigation and prosecution by consenting to the making of a civil recovery order, in circumstances where a criminal disposal would be justified under the overriding principle that the reduction of crime is generally best served by that route, and in accordance with the public interest factors in the relevant prosecutors' Code'.

The Guidance goes on to provide, for illustrative purposes only, a non-exhaustive list of circumstances in which use of the non-conviction based powers might be appropriate because it is not feasible to secure a conviction.

Civil recovery powers and agreements under the Serious Organised Crime and Police Act 2005, ss 71–75

9.52 The desire to avoid confiscation or civil recovery proceedings through cooperation is often a powerful incentive for some offenders. However, the CPS discourages the use of agreements under the Serious Organised Crime and Police Act 2005 ('SOCPA 2005'), ss 71–75 to deprive the prosecution authorities of an opportunity to recover the proceeds of unlawful conduct through civil recovery proceedings under POCA 2002, Pt 5. If criminals were routinely allowed to keep the profits of their criminal activities in return for co-operation, public confidence in the criminal justice system would be likely to be damaged. For these reasons, it is only in very exceptional circumstances that the prosecuting authorities will consider it justifiable and in the public interest to agree that any agreement should apply to Part 5 proceedings[1].

[1] See CPS legal guidance, 'Queen's Evidence—Immunities, Undertakings and Agreements under the Serious Organised Crime and Police Act 2005' (published 14 January 2011).

The use of civil recovery powers as an alternative to prosecution

9.53 The SFO has been enthusiastic about its use of civil recovery powers to tackle corruption. In October 2008, the SFO elected not to purse a criminal prosecution against Balfour Beatty, and instead used its civil recovery powers leading to an agreed order of £2.25m and the introduction of external monitoring for an agreed period. In its press release, the SFO stated 'the use of these powers should be seen as an important example of how the SFO will use the new tools at its disposal to enhance the criminal justice process'. A year later, Amec plc agreed to pay a civil recovery order of almost £5m, having self-referred to the SFO. Both cases were said to relate to irregular payments but the unlawful conduct was characterised not as corruption but as 'books and records' offences, namely failures to comply with certain accounting requirements under the Companies Act 1985.

9.54 Civil settlements under POCA 2002, Pt 5 hold a number of attractions for businesses. As noted above, historically, businesses have had little reason to self-report since there was little scope to 'plea bargain' and the inflexible and fairly draconian nature of the confiscation regime operated as a substantial disincentive. In contrast, a civil recovery order provides the business with certainty, permits the recovery of property obtained by unlawful conduct without a criminal prosecution and does not require proof (or any admission) that a company or individual has committed any offence of bribery (with the attendant reputational damage). Civil settlements under POCA 2002, Pt 5 also hold attractions for law enforcement. They avoid the costs and risks associated with long criminal prosecutions and are likely to lead to an increased willingness by businesses to self-report[1].

[1] The SFO's published guidance 'Approach to dealing with overseas corruption' emphasises the possibility of a civil 'deal' as a potential benefit of self-reporting. See Chapter 8.

9.55 In so far as the *Balfour Beatty* and *Amec* cases signalled an important change in strategy by the SFO, then it may be short lived. In *R v Innospec Ltd*[1],

Thomas LJ indicated that the only room for a civil recovery order in serious corruption cases was as a means of compensation in addition to a punishment. He stated, at para 38:

> 'Those who commit such serious crimes as corruption of senior foreign government officials must not be viewed or treated in any different way to other criminals. It will therefore rarely be appropriate for criminal conduct by a company to be dealt with by means of a civil recovery order; the criminal courts can take account of cooperation and the provision of evidence against others by reducing the fine otherwise payable. It is of the greatest public interest that the serious criminality of any, including companies, who engage in the corruption of foreign governments, is made patent for all to see by the imposition of criminal and not civil sanctions. It would be inconsistent with basic principles of justice for the criminality of corporations to be glossed over by a civil as opposed to a criminal sanction'.

There may still, however, be scope to agree a civil recovery order where the SFO is persuaded that it is not feasible to obtain a conviction and/or where the defendant is not 'at fault'. The civil recovery proceedings brought against MW Kellogg is one such example. In February 2011, M W Kellogg Ltd agreed to pay just over £7 million, in settlement of civil recovery proceedings issued by the SFO under POCA 2002, Pt 5. The £7 million represented share dividends payable from profits and revenues generated by contracts obtained by bribery and corruption undertaken by MW Kellogg's parent company and others. Significantly, the SFO acknowledged that MW Kellogg had not taken any part in the criminal activity which had generated the funds. The Director of the SFO restated his enthusiasm for the use of civil recovery powers. He stated

> 'The SFO will continue to encourage companies to engage with us over issues of bribery and corruption in the expectation of being treated fairly. In cases such as this a prosecution is not appropriate. Our goal is to prevent bribery and corruption or remove any of the benefits generated by such activities. This case demonstrates the range of tools we are prepared to use'.

[1]   [2010] Crim LR 665.

E   CIVIL REMEDIES

9.56 Criminal law is, broadly speaking, focused on punishment of an offender rather than restitution of proceeds of crime to the victim. Therefore, a victim of bribery may need to look to civil remedies to recover losses resulting from acts of bribery[1]. The case law in this area is focused on recovery of a bribe by a principal from his agent or fiduciary and/or the payer of the bribe. As these areas fall outside the ambit of the Bribery Act 2010 itself, they are considered only briefly below[2].

[1]   Although see paras **9.26–9.28** for discussion of compensation and paras **9.48–9.55** for a discussion of civil recovery under POCA 2002, Pt 5.
[2]   See *Bowstead and Reynolds on Agency* (19th edn) for further discussion of the relevant concepts.

9.57 Bribery occurs most often when there is a business relationship involving contractual obligations and a principal is represented by an agent who owes that principal a fiduciary duty. Acceptance of, or agreement to receive, a bribe is in itself a breach of fiduciary duty[1]. A bribe may be defined as follows:

'[i]f a gift be made to a confidential agent with the view of inducing the agent to act in favour of the donor in relation to transactions between the donor and the agent's principal and that gift is secret as between the donor and the agent—that is to say, without the knowledge and consent of the principal—then the gift is a bribe in the view of the law'[2].

Where there is no corrupt purpose to the payment, it is more appropriately referred to as a secret commission[3].

1   *Shipway v Broadwood* [1899] 1 QB 369 at 373, CA.
2   *Hovenden & Sons v Millhoff* (1900) 83 LT 41 at 43, per Romer LJ.
3   *Bowstead and Reynolds on Agency* (19th edn), § 6-085.

9.58 As a result of the bribe, a principal may pay substantially more than he would have otherwise paid or he may be deprived of a bargain[1]. A principal has a number of avenues he can pursue where a bribe has been paid to an agent or fiduciary. An action may lie in restitution; a claim may arise under the tort of deceit; or the principal may have a contractual remedy[2]. The principal will also be justified in summarily dismissing the agent or fiduciary[3]. Until recently, it was thought that a proprietary claim could be made against the agent or fiduciary as trustee of the bribe. However, as at the time of writing, recent case law has closed off this potential avenue with respect to bribery cases[4].

1   *Dubai Aluminium Co Ltd v Salaam (Livingstone, third parties)* [2002] UKHL 48, [2003] 2 AC 366, [2003] 2 All ER (Comm) 451; *Mahesan S/O Thambiah v Malaysia Government Officers' Co-operative Housing Society Ltd* [1979] AC 374, [1978] 2 All ER 405, PC.
2   It should be noted that the remedies in equity and tort are alternative rather than cumulative and the claimant should elect which remedy to pursue before judgment is entered on one cause of action or the other (*Mahesan*).
3   *Bulfield v Fournier* (1895) 11 TLR 282
4   See further para **9.62**.

Restitution

9.59 If a bribe has been paid and is in money, an action in restitution will lie against an agent or fiduciary[1]. Such an action will be a personal action for an account and will lie regardless of whether any relevant contract with the third party briber is affirmed or rescinded[2]. The briber is also liable jointly and severally[3].

1   *Mahesan S/O Thambiah v Malaysia Government Officers' Co-operative Housing Society Ltd* [1979] AC 374, [1978] 2 All ER 405, PC.
2   *Logicrose Ltd v Southend United Football Club Ltd* [1988] 1 WLR 1256 at 1263.
3   *Mahesan.*

Tort

9.60 The fiduciary or agent and the briber are jointly and severally liable in fraud or deceit for loss suffered. However, the fiduciary or agent cannot recover the full sum against both; a judgment satisfied in part against one operates pro tanto against the other[1]. An action in deceit will be attractive where the loss suffered is greater than the amount of the bribe; where the bribe has decreased in value; or where a bribe has not yet been paid to an agent or fiduciary.

1   *Mahesan S/O Thambiah v Malaysia Government Officers' Co-operative Housing Society Ltd* [1979] AC 374; *Fyffes Group Ltd v Templeman* [2000] 2 Lloyd's Rep 643, [2000] 25 LS Gaz R 40.

Contract

9.61 Where an agent or fiduciary has acted dishonestly and thereby without authority, the contract between the principal and third party briber is likely to be void[1]. In other cases, the contract will be voidable at the option of the principal[2]. Where the principal has recovered the bribe, but rescinds the contract, he is entitled to keep the bribe and need not give credit for it in the rescission[3].

1   *Bowstead and Reynolds on Agency* (19th edn) § 6-087.
2   *Taylor v Walker* [1958] 1 Lloyd's Rep 490.
3   *Logicrose Ltd v Southend United Football Club* [1988] 1 WLR 1256, 132 Sol Jo 1591.

A proprietary remedy?

9.62 Until recently, it was considered that where a bribe had been paid to an agent or fiduciary, it would be regarded as the property of the principal and held on trust by the fiduciary for the principal. The principal would therefore be able to recover the additional value of property, where, for example, it had been invested[1]. However, according to recent case law, this will only be the case where the agent or fiduciary has assumed pre-existing fiduciary duties to the property (eg where a profit is made directly from property owned by the company)[2]. It is not enough for the imposition of a constructive trust that the profit derives, in a broad sense, from a fiduciary's misuse, in breach of fiduciary duty, of the company's property or his position as fiduciary (as in bribery cases). In cases where there is no pre-existing assumption of fiduciary duty, the claimant's remedy will be limited to the claims set out in the preceding paragraphs.

1   *A-G for Hong Kong v Reid* [1994] 1 AC 324, [1994] 1 All ER 1, PC.
2   *Sinclair Investments (UK) Ltd v Versailles Trade Finance Ltd (in administration)* [2010] EWHC 1614 (Ch), [2010] All ER (D) 10 (Jul). See in particular [80]. Approved by the Court of Appeal in *Sinclair Investments (UK) Ltd v Versailles Trade Finance Ltd (in administration)* [2011] EWCA Civ 347. See in particular [88]–[92].

Interim relief

9.63 As to the forms of interim relief available to a claimant who has made or wishes to make a civil claim, these include:

—   requests for pre-action disclosures[1];
—   search and seizure orders[2];
—   bankers book orders[3];
—   an injunction under the Senior Courts Act 1981, s 37 for preservation of evidence;

—   issuing a Letter of Request to the judicial authorities of a foreign country;

—   witness summonses[4];

—   freezing orders[5].

[1]   Note that pre-action disclosure can be obtained against third parties under the principles established in *Norwich Pharmacal Co v Customs and Excise Comrs* [1974] AC 133, [1973] 2 All ER 943, HL.

[2]   Under CPR 1998, Pt 25.

[3]   Under the Bankers' Book Evidence Act 1879, s 7.

[4]   Under CPR 1998, r 34.2.

[5]   Under CPR 1998, Pt 25.

F   REPUTATIONAL DAMAGE AND OTHER CONSEQUENCES OF CONVICTION

9.64 The risk of reputational damage arising from conviction under the Bribery Act 2010 is self-evident. However, there are a number of other possible consequences of conviction that merit further examination. These include debarment from bidding in public procurement contracts; regulatory attention from the FSA; disqualification of directors; and the imposition of serious crime prevention orders and financial reporting orders by the court. These consequences may in themselves lead to further reputational and indeed, financial, damage to an individual or company convicted of a Bribery Act 2010 offence. It will be extremely important that companies and individual directors are made aware of these potential risks when they are given advice regarding Bribery Act 2010 compliance.

Press notices

9.65 Whilst there is no statutory 'name and shame' sanction akin to the 'publicity order' introduced under the Corporate Manslaughter and Corporate Homicide Act 2007 (for offences of corporate manslaughter), businesses should appreciate that criminal proceedings, including the sentencing hearing at which the prosecution will 'open the facts', take place in public. There is little scope to curtail the reporting of these proceedings. Furthermore, it is not possible to agree with the prosecution an 'approved' press notice in an attempt to control publicity. Such attempts were deprecated in *R v Innospec Ltd*[1] by Thomas LJ, who stated:

> 'There was at some stage a suggestion that a press notice in a form approved could be used by Innospec. This is not a practice which should be adopted in England and Wales. Publicity orders are very different as they are made under the direction of the court to ensure that in appropriate cases the conviction of the company is properly publicised. It would be inconceivable for a prosecutor to approve a press statement to be made by a person convicted of burglary or rape; companies who are guilty of corruption should be treated no differently to others who commit serious crimes'.

[1]   [2010] Crim LR 665; record of judgment 26 March 2010 (Southwark Crown Court).

Debarment—public contracts

9.66 Regulation 23(1) of the Public Contracts Regulations 2006[1] provides that a contracting authority shall treat as ineligible and shall not select an economic operator if the contracting authority has actual knowledge that the economic operator or its directors or any other person who has powers of representation, decision or control of the economic operator has been convicted of bribery[2]. Regulation 23(2) provides that a contracting authority may disregard the prohibition if it is satisfied that there are 'overriding requirements in the general interest which justify doing so in relation to that economic operator'. Because corporate convictions do not become spent, a conviction for bribery is likely to result in a company's permanent exclusion from bidding on public procurement contracts. Under the legislation as it currently stands, it is therefore technically possible that a company convicted of the strict liability offence of failing to prevent bribery under the Bribery Act 2010, s 7, could be permanently excluded from bidding in public procurement contracts.

[1] SI 2006/5, implementing article 45 of the Public Procurement Directive (Directive (EC) 2004/18).
[2] A similar provision is contained in the Utilities Contracts Regulations 2006, reg 26(1).

9.67 The government's Joint Committee Report on the Draft Bribery Bill[1] noted problems with perpetual debarment, such as the fact that neither the seriousness of the offence, nor mitigating factors can be taken into account; the danger of businesses which survive on procurement work collapsing overnight; the lack of scope for 'self-cleaning' under the Regulations; and the fact that companies would be disinclined to self-report bribery. The report went on to note that the government should:

'[t]ake action at a European level to prevent companies being automatically and perpetually debarred following a conviction, while exploring shorter-term measures to prevent disproportionate penalties being imposed in the meantime. The government must ensure that the UK reaches a position where debarment is discretionary, if self-reporting is to work effectively in practice'[2].

[1] Published on 28 July 2009.
[2] See §§ 188–192.

9.68 The government stated in its response to the Joint Committee Report[1]:

'[b]ribery is a serious offence and the government considers it important that we work with our European partners to identify good practice in the application of exclusion procedures. We are considering whether a conviction for the proposed new corporate offence of failure to prevent bribery would trigger the conditions for automatic debarment'[2].

[1] Dated November 2009.
[2] See § 29.

9.69 Although the MOJ final guidance does not cover the question of debarment, Kenneth Clarke dealt with this issue in his 30 March 2011 written statement to the House of Commons regarding the Bribery Act[1] in which he stated:

'[t]he Government have also decided that a conviction of a commercial organisation under section 7 of the Act in respect of a failure to prevent bribery will attract discretionary rather than mandatory exclusion from public procurement under the UK's implementation of the EU Procurement Directive (Directive 2004/18). The relevant regulations will be amended to reflect this'.

[1]   Daily Hansard, Written Ministerial Statement, col 21 WS (30 March 2011).

9.70 The timetable for amendment of the regulations is not currently clear. However, prior to amendment of the regulations, the only ways for a company to avoid automatic debarment will be to self report and to reach a purely civil settlement with the SFO, or to negotiate a plea bargain for offences which do not constitute bribery/corruption (eg books and records offences)[1].

[1]   However, see paras **9.53–9.55**as to the viability of this approach.

9.71 It was expected that the MOJ final guidance would deal with the issue of procurement, but in fact it was silent on the subject.

Regulatory proceedings

9.72 A conviction for bribery could also have regulatory consequences for FSA-regulated firms or individuals. One of the FSA's four statutory objectives is the reduction of financial crime.

9.73 The FSA is likely to view breaches by a firm of the Bribery Act 2010 as evidence of a deficiency in a firm's systems and controls and may seek to bring regulatory proceedings for breaches of the FSA's Senior Management Arrangements Systems and Controls Handbook. Additionally a firm may be found not to be fit and proper[1] and/or to have breached the FSA's Principles for Businesses (PRIN). In particular:

—   principle 1, which requires firms to conduct business with integrity;
—   principle 2, which requires firms to conduct their business with due skill, care and diligence; and
—   principle 3, which requires firms to take reasonable care to organise and control their affairs responsibly and effectively, with adequate risk-management systems[2].

In relation to such failures, a public sanction or financial penalty might be imposed. In serious cases, the firm's authorisation may be withdrawn.

[1]   Threshold condition 5. See the Financial Services and Markets Act 2000, s 41, Sch 6.
[2]   See PRIN 2.1.

9.74 The FSA can also take enforcement action against approved persons for failure to comply with its Statements of Principle for Approved Persons or for not being a fit and proper person to perform functions in relation to a firm's regulated activities[1]. Enforcement action against individuals may include a public statement; financial penalty; prohibition or withdrawal of FSA approval.

[1]   Financial Services and Markets Act 2000, s 61(1).

9.75 The FSA has indicated that in the coming years it will paying more attention to the systems and controls firms have in place to prevent bribery and corruption. A vision of the future was provided by the enforcement action brought against Aon. The FSA fined Aon £5.35m in January 2009 for failing to take reasonable care to establish and maintain effective systems and controls to counter the risks of bribery and corruption associated with making payments to overseas businesses and individuals. Aon was found to be in breach of principle 3 of FSMA 2000[1]. In a press release following the case Margaret Cole, the FSA's Director of Enforcement, stated:

'The involvement of UK financial institutions in corrupt or potentially corrupt practices undermines the integrity of the UK financial services sector . . . The FSA has an important role to play in the steps being taken by the UK to combat overseas bribery and corruption. We have worked closely with other law enforcement agencies in this case and will continue to take robust action focussed on firms' systems and controls in this area'.

[1] Final Notice re Aon Limited dated 6 January 2009: www.fsa.giv.uk/pubs/final/aon.pdf.

9.76 The FSA's interest in this area is unlikely to wane. The failures of Aon led to the FSA conducting a thematic review of anti-bribery and corruption in the commercial insurance broker industry, the results of which were published in May 2010. The FSA identified a number of common concerns and, whilst noting that there had been progress in the last year, concluded in the following terms:

'We have concluded that broker firms have approached higher risks business involving third parties far too informally and many firms are still not operating at acceptable standards . . . At present, we judge the serous weaknesses identified in some broker firms' systems and controls mean there is a significant risk of illicit payments or inducement being made to, or on behalf of, third parties to win business. We also believe that many firms are not currently in a position to demonstrate adequate procedures to prevent bribery—a defence to the Bribery Act 2010's new criminal offence of "failing to prevent bribery"'.

9.77 Given the potential consequences of enforcement action, FSA regulated firms should be advised of the dangers of conviction under the Bribery Act 2010 from a regulatory standpoint. However, it is of course possible that FSA action might be taken alongside or even in the absence of criminal proceedings under the Bribery Act 2010. The potential consequences of enforcement action are likely to increase firms' internal impetus to have adequate policies and procedures in place to prevent bribery.

Directors' disqualification

9.78 Any conviction of a director under the Bribery Act 2010 may lead to company director disqualification proceedings[1]. Such proceedings can result in an individual being prohibited from acting as a director or shadow director of any UK company for up to 15 years[2]. It is therefore extremely important that directors of companies are aware of the directors' disqualification legislation when they are given Bribery Act 2010 compliance advice.

[1] The Company Directors Disqualification Act 1986, s 2(1) provides:

'the court may make a disqualification order against a person where he is convicted of an indictable offence (whether on indictment or summarily) in connection with the promotion, formation, management, liquidation or striking off of a company, with the receivership of a company's property or with his being an administrative receiver of a company'.

²   Company Directors Disqualification Act 1986, s 3.

Serious crime prevention orders

9.79 Serious crime prevention orders ('SCPOs') were introduced as a new type of civil order under the Serious Crime Act 2007 ('SCA 2007'). An SCPO can be imposed following conviction for a bribery offence under the Bribery Act 2010, ss 1, 2 and 6 or 'following a decision that, applying the Code for Crown Prosecutors, the evidence available does not provide a realistic prospect of a conviction or a prosecution would not be in the public interest, for reasons other than the availability of an SCPO'[1]. They can be made against individuals or businesses and can contain onerous provisions in relation to financial, property or business dealings, including types of contractual agreements that can be entered into, use of premises by businesses and employment of staff[2]. SCPOs therefore represent significant additional restrictions on an individual or business on whom they are imposed. The legislation in this area is detailed and they key provisions are summarised below.

[1]   Crown Prosecution Service Legal Guidance on SCPOs, para 18.3.
[2]   See further paras **9.90–9.94**.

Process

9.80 An SCPO can only be made on the application of the DPP, the Director of Revenue and Customs Prosecutions, or the Director of the SFO[1]. SCPOs can be imposed by the High Court or Crown Court and contain such prohibitions, restrictions, requirements or other terms as the court considers appropriate for the purpose of protecting the public by preventing, restricting or disrupting involvement by the person concerned in serious crime[2]. Prohibitions, restrictions and requirements can also be placed on bodies corporate, partnerships, and unincorporated associates[3].

[1]   SCA 2007, s 8.
[2]   SCA 2007, ss 1, 19.
[3]   SCA 2007, ss 30–32.

The High Court's jurisdiction

9.81 The High Court may make an SCPO if:

—   it is satisfied that a person has been involved in serious crime (in England and Wales or elsewhere); and
—   it has reasonable grounds to believe that the order would protect the public by preventing, restricting or disrupting involvement by the person in serious crime in England and Wales[1].

When considering such an order, the court is concerned with future risk. There must be a real or significant risk that the defendant will commit a further serious offence[2].

[1]   SCA 2007, s 1(1).
[2]   *R v Hancox* [2010] EWCA Crim 102, [2010] 4 All ER 537, [2010] 1 WLR 1434 at [9].

9.82 A person is treated as 'involved in serious crime' if, in England and Wales or outside England and Wales[1]:

— he has committed a serious offence (a serious offence includes the new bribery offences under the Bribery Act 2010, ss 1, 2 and 6)[2]; or
— he has facilitated[3] the commission by another person of a serious offence; or
— he has conducted himself in a way that was likely to facilitate the commission by himself or another person of a serious offence (whether or not such an offence was committed)[4].

[1] A serious offence in a country outside England and Wales means an offence under the law of a county outside England and Wales which would be an offence under the law of England and Wales if committed in or as regards England and Wales; and would be a serious offence if committed in England and Wales (SCA 2007, s 2(5)).
[2] SCA 2007, Sch 1, Pt 1.
[3] In relation to facilitation, the court must ignore any act that the respondent can show is reasonable in the circumstances and, subject to that exception, it must also ignore his intentions, or any other aspect of his mental state at the time the offence was committed (SCA 2007, s 4(2)).
[4] SCA 2007, s 2(1), (4).

9.83 On an application by a third party, the High Court must give the third party an opportunity to make representations in proceedings before it about the making of the SCPO if it considers that the decision would be likely to have a significant adverse effect on that person[1].

[1] SCA 2007, s 9(1).

9.84 On application, the High Court may discharge or vary an SCPO[1]. It may only vary an SCPO if it has reasonable grounds to believe that the terms of the order as varied would protect the public by preventing, restricting or disrupting involvement, by the person who is the subject of the order, in serious crime in England and Wales[2]. Such an application may be made by:

— the relevant applicant authority[3];
— the person who is the subject of the order (provided the court considers there has been a change of circumstances affecting the order)[4]; and
— any other person (provided the person is significantly adversely affected by the order and, in relation to variation, the application is not for the purpose of making the order more onerous on the person who is the subject of it)[5] and either:
  (i)   in earlier proceedings in relation to the order, the person made a s 9 application and was given an opportunity to make representations, or made an application otherwise than under that section, and there has been a change of circumstances affecting the order; or
  (ii) the person has not made an application in earlier proceedings and it was reasonable in all the circumstances for the person not to have done so[6].

On an application by a third party, the High Court must give the third party an opportunity to make representations in proceedings before it about the variation or discharge of the SCPO (or a decision not to vary or discharge it) if it considers that the decision would be likely to have a significant adverse effect on that person[7].

1   SCA 2007, ss 17(1), 18(1)(a).
2   SCA 2007, s 17(1).
3   SCA 2007, ss 17(3)(a), 18(2)(a). An application for variation may include an extension of the period during which the order, or any provision of it, is in force (subject to relevant time limits) (SCA 2007, s 17(8)).
4   SCA 2007, ss 17(3)(b)(i), (4), 18(2)(b)(i), (3).
5   SCA 2007, ss 17(3)(b)(ii), (5)(a), (5)(c), 18(2)(b)(ii), (4)(a).
6   SCA 2007, ss 17(5)(b), (6), (7), 18(4)(b), (5), (6).
7   SCA 2007, s 9(2), (3).

9.85 An appeal may be made to the Court of Appeal in relation to a decision of the High Court to make an SCPO; to vary, or not to vary such an order; or to discharge or not to discharge such an order[1]. An appeal can be made by any person who was given an opportunity to make representations in the proceedings or any other person entitled to bring an appeal by virtue of the Senior Courts Act 1981, s 16[2]. Appeals to the Supreme Court (Civil Division) are governed by the Administration of Justice Act 1960.

1   An order to discharge an order cannot be made by the Crown Court.
2   SCA 2007, s 23. See also s 9(5).

The Crown Court's jurisdiction

9.86 Where a person has been convicted of a serious offence in England and Wales before a Crown Court; or before a magistrates' court, having been committed to the Crown Court to be dealt with, the Crown Court may, in addition to dealing with the person in relation to the offence, make an SCPO[1]. It may only do so if it has reasonable grounds to believe that the order would protect the public by preventing, restricting or disrupting involvement by the person in serious crime in England and Wales[2]. An SCPO may only be made in addition to a sentence imposed in respect of the offence concerned; or in addition to discharging the person conditionally[3].

1   SCA 2007, s 19(1).
2   SCA 2007, s 19(2).
3   SCA 2007, s 19(7).

9.87 The Crown Court's powers to vary an order are more limited than the High Court's and the Crown Court does not have power to discharge an SCPO. The SCA 2007 provides that where a person has been convicted of a serious offence in England and Wales before a Crown Court; or before a magistrates' court, having been committed to the Crown Court to be dealt with, the Crown Court may, in addition to dealing with the person in relation to the offence, vary an SCPO[1]. It may only do so if it has reasonable grounds to believe that the order would protect the public by preventing, restricting or disrupting involvement by the person in serious crime in England and Wales[2]. A variation to an SCPO may only be made in addition to a sentence imposed in respect of the offence concerned; or in addition to discharging the person conditionally[3]. A variation may include an extension of the period during which the order, or any provision of it, is in force (subject to original time limits)[4].

1   SCA 2007, s 20(1), (2). It may also vary a SCPO on breach, as to which see para **9.99**.

2   SCA 2007, s 20(2).
3   SCA 2007, s 20(6).
4   SCA 2007, s 20(7).

9.88 On an application by a third party, the Crown Court must give the person an opportunity to make representations in proceedings before it arising by virtue of ss 19, 20 or 21[1] if it considers that the making or variation of the SCPO concerned (or a decision not to vary it) would be likely to have a significant adverse effect on that person[2].

1   As to which see paras **9.87**, **9.88** and **9.99**.
2   SCA 2007, s 9(4).

9.89 An appeal against a decision of the Crown Court made in relation to an SCPO may be made to the Court of Appeal by the person who is subject of the order; or the relevant applicant authority[1]. An appeal may also be made to the Court of Appeal in relation to a decision of the Crown Court to make an SCPO or to vary, or not to vary such an order by any person who was given an opportunity to make representations in the SCPO proceedings[2]. Both types of appeal require either leave of the Court of Appeal or a certificate from the judge whose decision is appealed, certifying that the decision is fit for appeal[3]. Appeal lies from any appeal decision of the Court of Appeal (Criminal Division) to the Supreme Court at the instance of any person who was a party to the proceedings before the Court of Appeal[4]. Such an appeal can only be made with the leave either of the Court of Appeal or the Supreme Court and such leave must not be granted unless the Court of Appeal certifies that the decision involves a point of law of general public importance and the Court of Appeal or the Supreme Court considers that the point is one that ought to be considered by the Supreme Court[5].

1   SCA 2007, s 24(1).
2   SCA 2007, s 24(2).
3   SCA 2007, s 24(3), (4).
4   SCA 2007, s 24(6).
5   SCA 2007, s 24(7), (8).

Content of an SCPO

9.90 Section 5 of the SCA 2007 contains non-exhaustive examples of prohibitions, restrictions or requirements that may be imposed by SCPOs. In relation to individuals, these include prohibitions, restrictions or requirements in relation to:

—   an individual's financial, property or business dealings or holdings;
—   an individual's working arrangements;
—   the means by which an individual communicates or associates with others, or the persons with whom he communicates or associates;
—   the premises to which an individual has access;
—   the use of any premises or item by an individual; and
—   an individual's travel (within the UK and between the UK and other places)[1].

1   SCA 2007, s 5(3).

9.91 In relation to bodies corporate, partnerships and unincorporated associations, SCPOs may include prohibitions, restrictions or requirements in relation to:

— financial, property or business dealings or holdings;
— the types of agreement to which such persons may be party;
— the provision of goods or services by such persons;
— the premises to which such persons have access;
— the use of any premises or item by such persons; and
— the employment of staff by such persons[1].

Both individuals and other bodies can be required to answer questions, provide specified information or produce documents as specified in the SCPO[2].

1   SCA 2007, s 5(4).
2   SCA 2007, s 5(5).

9.92 In *Hancox*[1], the Court of Appeal indicated that the SCPO's interference with the defendant's freedom of action must be justified by the benefit that it created. The provisions of the order should therefore be commensurate with the risk of involvement by the defendant in serious crime[2]. Further, Hughes LJ indicated that much of *R v Boness*[3] would be applicable including the test of proportionality; the emphasis on the order being practicable and enforceable; the test of precision and certainty; and the fact that the order is preventative not punitive.

1   [2010] 1 WLR 1434.
2   Per Hughes LJ at [10].
3   [2005] EWCA Crim 2395, [2006] 1 Cr App Rep (S) 690, 169 JP 621.

9.93 An SCPO may not require a person to:

— answer questions or provide information orally[1];
— answer privileged questions[2], provide privileged information[3] or produce a privileged document[4];
— produce excluded material as defined by the Police and Criminal Evidence Act 1984, s 11[5];
— disclose any information or produce any document in respect of which he owes an obligation of confidence by virtue of carrying on a banking business unless the person to whom the obligation of confidence is owed consents to the disclosure or production or the order contains a requirement to disclose information or produce documents of this kind or to disclose specified information of this kind or produce specified documents of this kind[6];
— answer any question, provide any information or produce any document if the disclosure concerned is prohibited under any other enactment[7].

1   SOCPA 2005, s 11.
2   A question which the person would be entitled to refuse to answer on grounds of legal professional privilege in High Court proceedings (SOCPA 2005, s 12(2)).
3   Information which the person would be entitled to refuse to provide on the grounds of legal professional privilege in High Court proceedings (SOCPA 2005, s 12(3)).
4   A document which the person would be entitled to refuse to produce on grounds of legal professional privilege in such proceedings (SOCPA 2005, s 12(4), 12(1)).
5   SOCPA 2005, s 13(1).

⁶ SOCPA 2005, s 13(2)–(4).
⁷ SOCPA 2005, s 14.

9.94 An SCPO against a company, partnership or unincorporated association may authorise a law enforcement agency to enter into arrangements with a person or description of persons specified in the order to perform monitoring services[1]. Monitoring services is defined as analysing some or all information received in accordance with an SCPO; reporting to a law enforcement officer as to whether, on the basis of the information and any other information analysed for this purpose, the subject of the order appears to be complying with the order or any part of it and related services[2].Such a person is known as an authorised monitor[3].

[1] SCA 2007, s 39(1).
[2] SCA 2007, s 39(10).
[3] SCA 2007, s 29(2). See s 39 for further provisions.

Safeguards

9.95 The subject of an SCPO will only be bound by it or a variation of it if he is represented at the proceedings at which the order or variation is made or a notice setting out the terms of the order or variation has been served on him[1]. Further, SCPOs may not be made against individuals under the age of 18[2].

[1] SOCPA 2005, s 10(1).
[2] SCA 2007, s 6.

9.96 As to duration, an SCPO may not be in force for more than five years[1]. It must specify when it is to come into force and when it is to cease to be in force[2]. Commencement can therefore be delayed, eg to start upon a defendant's release from prison. The order may provide for different provisions to come into force or cease to be in force at different times[3]. However, the five-year period starts with the coming into force of the first provision[4].

[1] SCA 2007, s 16(2). However, the fact that an order or provision of an order ceases to be in force does not prevent the court from making a new order to the same or similar effect (SCA 2007, s 16(5)). A new order may be made in anticipation of an earlier order or provision ceasing to be in force (SCA 2007, s 16(6)). These powers are limited to the High Court (the Crown Court's jurisdiction being limited by SCA 2007, ss 18–21).
[2] SCA 2007, s 16(1).
[3] SCA 2007, s 16(3).
[4] SCA 2007, s 16(4).

9.97 A person who complies with a requirement imposed by an SCPO to answer questions, provide information or produce documents does not breach any obligation of confidence or any other restriction on making the disclosure concerned (however imposed)[1].

[1] SCA 2007, s 38(1).

Standard of proof

9.98 Proceedings in the High Court and Crown Court (under ss 19, 20 or 21) are civil proceedings and the standard of proof is the civil standard[1]. However given the engagement of the European Convention on Human Rights, article 8, the civil standard of proof is likely to be affected by such considerations[2]. Part 77 of the Civil Procedure Rules 1998[3] deals with applications in the High Court for or relating to SCPOs. Part 50 of the Criminal Procedure Rules ('civil behaviour orders after verdict or finding') applies to SCPOs by virtue of r 50.1.

[1] SCA 2007, ss 35, 36(1), (2). In relation to criminal proceedings, the court is therefore not restricted to considering evidence that would have been admissible in the criminal proceedings in which the person concerned was convicted and the court may adjourn any proceedings in relation to an SCPO even after sentencing the person concerned (SCA 2007, s 36(3)).
[2] See *R (on the application of N) v Mental Health Review Tribunal (Northern Region)* [2005] EWCA Civ 1605, [2006] QB 468 and *Chief Constable of Merseyside Police v Harrison (Secretary of State for the Home Department intervening)* [2006] EWHC 1106 (Admin), [2007] QB 79, [2006] WLR 171.
[3] SI 1998/3132.

Failure to comply

9.99 A person who, without reasonable excuse, fails to comply with an SCPO commits an offence and is liable to a term not exceeding 12 months' imprisonment and/or to a fine not exceeding the statutory maximum on summary conviction or a term not exceeding five years' imprisonment and/or to a fine on conviction on indictment[1]. The court before which the person is convicted of the s 25 offence may make an order for the forfeiture of anything in the person's possession at the time of the offence, which the court considers to have been involved in the offence[2]. On conviction, the Crown Court may also vary the SCPO if it has reasonable grounds to believe that the terms of the order as varied would protect the public by preventing, restricting or disrupting involvement by the person in serious crime in England and Wales[3]. A company, partnership or relevant body[4] may be wound up if convicted of a s 25 offence[5].

[1] SCA 2007, s 25(1), (2). In such proceedings, a copy of the original order or any variation of it and oral evidence of these things is admissible as evidence of the order or variation having been made and of its contents (SCA 2007, s 25(4)).
[2] SCA 2007, s 26(1). Provided that before making an order, the court gives an opportunity to make representations to any person who claims to be the owner of the thing or to otherwise have an interest in it (SCA 2007, s 26(2)).
[3] SCA 2007, s 21.
[4] Defined as a building society, an incorporated friendly society, an industrial and provident society, a limited liability partnership or such other description of person specified by order of the Secretary of State (SCA 2007, s 27(12)).
[5] SCA 2007, s 27.

9.100–9.101 A statement made by a person in response to a requirement imposed by an SCPO may not be used in evidence against him in criminal proceedings unless:

— the criminal proceedings relate to an offence under s 25; or
— in relation to another offence, the person who made the statement gives evidence in the proceedings during the course of which the person makes a statement that is inconsistent with the statement made in response to the requirement imposed by the order and evidence relating to the statement made is adduced or a question about it is asked by the

person or on his behalf[1].

1   SCA 2007, s 15.

Financial reporting orders

9.102 Following a conviction for bribery under the Bribery Act 2010, ss 1, 2 or 6, in addition to sentencing or otherwise dealing with the person, the court may make a financial reporting order[1]. A financial reporting order can require a defendant to submit detailed financial information to the court and as such imposes additional burdens on a defendant convicted of a Bribery Act 2010 offence.

1   SOCPA 2005, s 76(1). It will be open to the court to make an order either at the time of sentence or when 'otherwise dealing with' the defendant at a hearing (eg in relation to confiscation). 'Otherwise dealing with' includes dealing with a defendant for the purposes of quantification of a defence costs order (*R v Adams (Terrance)* [2008] EWCA Crim 914, [2008] 4 All ER 574, [2009] 1 WLR 310).

9.103 A court may make a financial reporting order provided it is satisfied that the risk of the person committing another offence listed in SOCPA 2005, s 76(3) is sufficiently high to justify the making of the order[1]. An order made in the magistrates' court can be for a maximum of five years and one made in other courts for a maximum of 15 years[2].

1   It is suggested that the test of this should be a 'real and not fanciful' risk in line with *R v Mansfield Justices, ex p Sharkey* [1985] QB 613, [1985] 1 All ER 193 (in the context of bail).
2   SOCPA 2005, s 76(6), (7). If a person is sentenced to life imprisonment the order may extend to 20 years.

9.104 The court in *R v Wright*[1] said that in theory, a financial reporting order could be made in the case of a defendant sentenced to a long custodial sentence, particularly a career 'master' criminal who could use persons outside prison to manipulate his assets. However, the court emphasised that such an order should not be made for the purpose of facilitating the enforcement of a confiscation order. Judges should give careful consideration to whether such an order would achieve anything where there are alternative powers available which would have the same effect. There is a right to appeal against a financial reporting order[2]. The order will be treated as a sentence under the Criminal Appeal Act 1968.

1   [2009] 2 Cr App Rep (S) 45, CA.
2   *R v Adams (Terrance)* [2008] EWCA Crim 914, [2008] 4 All ER 574, [2009] 1 WLR 310.

Content of financial reporting orders

9.105 For the duration of the financial reporting order, the person must make a report. The order must:

—   state to whom the report must be made[1];
—   specify the intervals at which reports must be submitted[2];
—   specify the number of days after the end of each period by which the report must be received[3];

— set out the particulars of the financial affairs required and the manner in which they must be reported[4];
— include details of any documents required[5].

1   SOCPA 2005, s 79(6).
2   SOCPA 2005, s 79(2).
3   SOCPA 2005, s 79(5).
4   SOCPA 2005, s 79(3).
5   SOCPA 2005, s 79(4).

9.106 A financial reporting order may include requirements to submit details of income, assets and expenditure. It might include, eg, a requirement to submit copies of all bank statements, credit card accounts or other documentation detailing financial transactions, including tax returns and business accounts[1]. The White Paper that dealt with financial reporting orders[2] acknowledged that such requirements 'would inevitably impose a considerable burden on the released prisoner but one which is fully compatible with the normal goal of probation to encourage those released to turn away from crime'. As article 8 of the European Convention on Human Rights is likely to be engaged by such requirements, orders should be proportionate with regard to the person and his past and future offending.

1   See CPS Legal Guidance on Financial Reporting Orders.
2   Step Ahead: A 21st Century Strategy to Defeat Organised Crime (CM 6167, Mar 2004).

Failure to comply

9.107 A person who without reasonable excuse includes false or misleading information in a report, or otherwise fails to comply with any requirement set out in SOCPA 2005, s 79, will be guilty of an offence and liable on summary conviction to imprisonment for a term not exceeding 51 weeks, or a fine not exceeding level 5 on the standard scale, or to both[1].

1   SOCPA 2005, s 79(10).

Variation/revocation

9.108 Either the person in respect of whom the order has been made or the person to whom the report must be made can apply to the court for variation or revocation of the order[1]. Application is to the court that made the order unless it was made on appeal, in which case the application must be made to the court that originally sentenced the person[2]. If the court was a magistrates' court, the application may be made to any magistrates' court acting in the same local justice area[3]. SOCPA 2005 does not set down criteria which might support such an application, or what should be considered by the court in deciding whether to grant such an application. However, the Protection from Harassment Act 1977 has a similarly phrased variation provision[4]. The court in *Shaw v DPP*[5] made it clear that there must be a good reason in the form of some change of circumstances to justify the variation of an order. The same principle is likely to apply to orders under SOCPA 2005[6].

1   SOCPA 2005, s 80(1).
2   SOCPA 2005, s 80(2), (3).
3   SOCPA 2005, s 80(4).

4   Protection from Harassment Act 1977, s 5(4).
5   [2005] EWHC 1215 (Admin), [2005] All ER (D) 93 (Apr).
6   See CPS Legal Guidance on Financial Reporting Orders.

Disclosure

9.109 The person to whom the report must be made may disclose a report[1] to anyone he reasonably believes may be able to assist with checking the accuracy of the report or any other report made pursuant to the same order or in order to check the true position[2]. Anyone else can disclose information to the person specified in the order to receive the reports, or to anyone to whom that person has disclosed the report for the same reasons[3].

1   Defined as including any of the report's contents, any document included with the report or any contents of such a document (SOCPA 2005, s 81(8)).
2   SOCPA 2005, s 81(1), (2), (4).
3   SOCPA 2005, s 81(3).

9.110 The person to whom the report is made may also disclose a report for the purposes of:

—   preventing, detecting, investigating or prosecuting criminal offences in the UK or abroad; or
—   preventing, detecting or investigating conduct for which non-criminal penalties are provided under UK law of the laws of any other country[1].

1   SOCPA 2005, s 81(5). This will allow for disclosure for civil confiscation etc.

9.111 Disclosure under SOCPA 2005, s 81 will not breach any obligation of confidence owed by the person making the disclosure or any other restriction on the disclosure of information. However, disclosure of personal data in contravention of any provisions of the Data Protection Act 1998 is not authorised by the section[1].

1   SOCPA 2005, s 81(6).

G   EXTRADITION

9.112 In certain situations, persons outside the UK may be accused of offences under the Bribery Act 2010[1]. In these circumstances, the UK authorities may seek their extradition to the UK for trial or punishment[2]. This type of extradition is known as 'import extradition'. The procedure for requests for extradition to the UK is governed by the Extradition Act 2003, Pt 3, in relation to category 1 territories (ie member states of the EU) and the royal prerogative and various treaty provisions in relation to category 2 territories (states outside the EU)[3].

1   See Chapter 4.
2   Extradition should not be granted to secure the return for questioning of those who are suspected of committing crimes (*Re Ismail* [1999] 1 AC 320, 326).
3   For the definition of category 1 and category 2 territory, see paras **9.113** and **9.124**.

Extradition from category 1 territories

What is a category 1 territory?

9.113 Part 1 of the Extradition Act 2003 relates to extradition to those EU countries operating the European Arrest Warrant (the EAW). At the time of writing, the following are category 1 territories: Austria, Belgium, Bulgaria, Cyprus, Czech Republic, Denmark, Estonia, Finland, France, Germany, Gibraltar, Greece, Hungary, Ireland, Italy, Latvia, Lithuania, Luxembourg, Malta, the Netherlands, Poland, Portugal, Romania, Slovakia, Slovenia, Spain and Sweden[1].

[1]   SIs 2003/3333; 2004/1898; 2005/365; 2005/2036; 2006/3451 and 2007/2238.

Extradition offences

9.114 The UK may seek extradition of a defendant from a category 1 territory in respect of an 'extradition offence' as defined in the Extradition Act 2003, s 148. Extradition requests may be made where:

—   a person has not been convicted and sentenced;
—   a person has been convicted and sentenced and is 'at large'.

9.115 Where a person has not been convicted and sentenced, the Bribery Act 2010, s 1, 2 and 6 offences fall within the definition of an extradition offence set out in the Extradition Act 2003, s 148(1) and (2). Where a person has been convicted and sentenced, the Bribery Act 2010, s 1, 2 and 6 offences will constitute an extradition offence where a sentence of imprisonment or another form of detention for a term of four months or greater has been imposed in relation to the conduct[1].

[1]   Extradition Act 2003, s 148(4), (5).

The extradition process

9.116 In order to begin the extradition process, a Part 3 warrant (otherwise known as an EAW) must be obtained from an appropriate judge[1]. Part 3 warrants will usually be drafted by a prosecuting lawyer[2]. The Extradition Act 2003 provides that the Part 3 warrant must contain the following provisions[3]:

—   in relation to persons accused of offences: a statement that the person in respect of whom the warrant is issued is accused in the UK of the commission of an extradition offence specified in the warrant, and the warrant is issued with a view to his arrest and extradition to the UK for the purpose of being prosecuted for the office[4];
—   in relation to persons convicted of an extradition offence: a statement that the person in respect of whom the warrant is issued has been convicted of an extradition offence specified in the warrant by a court in the UK, and the warrant is issued with a view to his arrest and extradition to the UK for the purpose of being sentenced for the offence or of serving a sentence of imprisonment or another form of detention imposed in respect of the offence[5]; and
—   a certificate certifying:

      (i)   that the conduct constituting the extradition offence specified in the warrant falls within the European framework list[6];

      (ii)   whether the offence is an extra-territorial offence;

      (iii)   what is the maximum punishment that may be imposed on conviction of the offence or (if the person has been sentenced for the offence) what sentence has been imposed[7].

[1]   Extradition Act 2003, s 142(1). Appropriate judge is defined in s 149 as in England and Wales, a district judge (magistrates' courts), a justice of the peace or a judge entitled to exercise the jurisdiction of the Crown Court.

[2]   The Part 3 warrant template is available on the CPS website at www.cps.gov.uk/legal/d_to_g /extradition/annex_b.

[3]   Extradition Act 2003, s 142(3).

[4]   Extradition Act 2003, s 142(4).

[5]   Extradition Act 2003, s 142(5).

[6]   The list of conduct set out in the Extradition Act 2003, Sch 2 as amended (Extradition Act 2003, s 215) including an attempt, conspiracy or incitement to carry out conduct falling with the list, or aiding, abetting, counselling or procuring the carrying out of conduct falling within the list (Extradition Act 2003, s 142(7)). The list includes corruption (Sch 2, para 7).

[7]   Extradition Act 2003, s 142(6).

9.117 An appropriate judge may issue a Part 3 warrant provided a constable or appropriate person[1] applies to the judge for a Part 3 warrant; and provided that[2]:

—   there are reasonable grounds for believing that the person has committed an extradition offence, and a domestic warrant[3] has been issued in respect of the person[4]; or

—   there are reasonable grounds for believing that the person is unlawfully at large after conviction of an extradition offence by a court in the UK, and either a domestic warrant has been issued in respect of the person or the person may be lawfully arrested without a warrant[5].

[1]   A person of a description specified in an order made by the Secretary of State for the purposes of s 142 (s 142(9)). See SI 2003/3335 and SI 2005/1127.

[2]   Extradition Act 2003, s 142(1).

[3]   A warrant for the arrest or apprehension of a person which, in England and Wales, is issued under the Criminal Justice Act 1967, s 72; the Bail Act 1976, s 7; or the Magistrates' Courts Act 1980, s 1 (Extradition Act 2003, s 142(8), (8A)).

[4]   Extradition Act 2003, s 142(2).

[5]   Extradition Act 2003, s 142(2A).

Specialty protection for defendants

9.118 The rule of specialty is the principle that if a state agrees to extradite a person, the requesting state can only conduct proceedings against that person for offences in respect of which he was extradited. A defendant extradited to the UK from a category 1 territory pursuant to a Part 3 warrant may therefore only be tried in respect of an offence committed before his extradition if:

—   it is one specified in the Extradition Act 2003, s 146; or

—   the person has been given an opportunity to leave the UK but has not done so before the end of the permitted period[1]; or

—   he has left the UK before the end of the permitted period and has returned again[2].

1   45 days starting with the day on which the person arrives in the UK (Extradition Act 2003, s 146(5)).
2   Extradition Act 2003, s 146(1), (2), (4).

9.119 The relevant offences specified in the Extradition Act 2003, s 146 are:

—   the offence in respect of which the person is extradited;
—   an offence disclosed by the information provided to the category 1 territory in respect of that offence;
—   an extradition offence in respect of which consent to the person being dealt with is given on behalf of the territory in response to a request made by the appropriate judge;
—   an offence which is not punishable with imprisonment or another form of detention;
—   an offence in respect of which the person will not be detained in connection with his trial, sentence or appeal;
—   an offence in respect of which the person waives the right that he would have not to be dealt with for the offence[1].

1   Extradition Act 2003, s 146(3).

Breach of specialty rights—principles

9.120 A defendant who believes that his trial will breach his specialty rights may invoke a variety of remedies including applying to quash counts on the indictment or applying to have the case stayed as an abuse of process. The onus is on the defendant to show that his trial or sentence breaches the rule of specialty[1]. The restrictions on offences for which an extradited person may be tried do not justify any other departure from the normal rules of procedure; there is therefore no bar on the prosecution obtaining and adducing additional evidence not used in the extradition to support charges that comply with the specialty rule[2]. Further, the rule of specialty does not prevent the defendant from being tried in civil proceedings[3].

1   *R v Corrigan* [1931] 1 KB 527, 22 Cr App Rep 106.
2   *R v Aubrey-Fletcher, ex p Ross-Munro* [1968] 1 QB 620, [1968] 1 All ER 99, DC.
3   *Pooley v Whetham* (1880) 15 Ch D 435, CA.

9.121 It is worth noting that any offence for which a defendant is indicted should be specifically mentioned in the warrant. In *R v Seddon*[1], the defendant had been convicted for failing to answer bail. The defendant had pleaded guilty to blackmail, but then absconded and failed to appear at his sentencing hearing. The arrest warrant did not make any allegation of a bail offence save for the words 'for failing to answer bail'. The Court of Appeal held that it was clear that s 146(3)(b) did not extend to allowing the defendant to be dealt with for the bail offence, as that was wholly extraneous to and additional to the blackmail offence, and had received merely a passing mention in the warrant. As the warrant did not seek surrender for failing to surrender to bail and since s 146(3)(b) did not extend to the inclusion of that offence, the conviction was without jurisdiction and was quashed. The court noted that the best course was to include reference to the bail offence specifically as one of the extradition offences for which surrender was sought.

¹   [2009] EWCA Crim 483, [2009] 1 WLR 2342, [2009] 2 Cr App Rep 143.

9.122 Where a defendant has consented to his extradition in the category 1 state, the Extradition Act 2003, s 147 applies¹. This provides that the defendant's right to specialty protection under the Extradition Act 2003, s 146(2) *will not* apply if²:

—   under the law of the category 1 territory from which the defendant has been extradited, the effect of the person's consent is to waive his right to specialty protection under s 146(2) and such consent has not been revoked in accordance with that law (if permitted to do so)³; or

—   under the law of the category 1 territory, the effect of the person's consent is not to waive his right under s 146(2); the person has expressly waived his right under s 146(2) in accordance with that law; the person has not revoked his consent in accordance with that law (if permitted to do so); and the person has not revoked the waiver of his right under s 146(2) in accordance with that law (if permitted to do so)⁴.

¹   Extradition Act 2003, s 147(1).
²   Extradition Act 2003, s 147(2).
³   Extradition Act 2003, s 147(3).
⁴   Extradition Act 2003, s 147(4).

Service of sentence in category 1 territory

9.123 If a Part 3 warrant is issued in respect of a person and the certificate contained in the warrant certifies that a sentence has been imposed, an undertaking may be given on behalf of the category 1 territory that the person will be required to serve the sentence in the territory. In such a situation, the person may not be extradited to the UK¹. In such a case, so far as the UK is concerned, the punishment for the offence must be treated as remitted but the person's conviction for the offence must be treated as a conviction for all other purposes².

¹   Extradition Act 2003, s 145(1).
²   Extradition Act 2003, s 145(2).

Extradition from category 2 territories

What is a category 2 territory?

9.124 Category 2 territories are those designated for the purposes of the Extradition Act 2003, Pt 2, by order¹. At the time of writing, the following are category 2 territories: Albania, Algeria, Andorra, Antigua and Barbuda, Argentina, Armenia, Australia, Azerbaijan, The Bahamas, Bangladesh, Barbados, Belize, Bolivia, Bosnia and Herzegovina, Botswana, Brazil, Brunei, Canada, Chile, Colombia, Cook Islands, Croatia, Cuba, Dominica, Ecuador, El Salvador, Fiji, The Gambia, Georgia, Ghana, Grenada, Guatemala, Guyana, Hong Kong Special Administrative Region, Haiti, Iceland, India, Iraq, Israel, Jamaica, Kenya, Kiribati, Lesotho, Liberia, Libya, Liechtenstein, Macedonia

(FYR), Malawi, Malaysia, Maldives, Mauritius, Mexico, Moldova, Monaco, Montenegro, Nauru, New Zealand, Nicaragua, Nigeria, Norway, Panama, Papua New Guinea, Paraguay, Peru, Russian Federation, Saint Christopher and Nevis, Saint Lucia, Saint Vincent and the Grenadines, San Marino, Serbia, Seychelles, Sierra Leone, Singapore, Solomon Islands, South Africa, Sri Lanka, Swaziland, Switzerland, Tanzania, Thailand, Tonga, Trinidad and Tobago, Turkey, Tuvalu, Uganda, Ukraine, the United Arab Emirates, the United States of America, Uruguay, Vanuatu, Western Samoa, Zambia and Zimbabwe[2].

[1] Extradition Act 2003, s 69(1).
[2] SIs 2003/3334; 2004/1898; 2005/365; 2005/2036; 2006/3451; 2007/2238; 2008/1589; 2010/861.

Relevant law

9.125 The content of the extradition request is not governed by the provisions of the Extradition Act 2003 but by relevant treaty provisions[1]. The request is made pursuant to the royal prerogative. Most extradition arrangements allow for the provisional arrest of a defendant prior to a formal extradition request. Dependant on the relevant extradition arrangements, the extradition request may need to contain:

— where a person has not been convicted: a first instance warrant setting out in full all charges for which extradition is sought, or a bench warrant. In the case of a bench warrant, the usual practice is to invite the issuing judge to endorse it attaching a copy of the indictment to which it relates;

— where a person has been convicted: the original, or a certified copy, of the memorandum of conviction and if sentenced, the sentence;

— identification material, eg full names, photograph, fingerprints, physical description, details of aliases, date and place of birth, passport details, present whereabouts if known, details of the defendant's entry into the country concerned;

— statement of law in relation to the offences, including any relevant limitation periods;

— depending upon the country to which the request is being sent it will also contain one of the following:

    (i)   a summary of the facts of the offence (this will be prepared by the prosecutor or investigating police officer); or

    (ii)   a sworn 'hearsay' statement setting out in detail the evidence of each witness (this will usually be from the investigating officer or prosecutor); or

    (iii) sworn depositions from each witness required to disclose a prima facie case against the defendant[2].

[1] See, for example article 8(2) of the Extradition Treaty concluded in 2003 between the UK and the USA (Cm 5821). For relevant treaties, see www.cps.gov.uk/legal/d_to_g/extradition/annex _c_-_extradition_with_territories_outside_the_european_union_/
[2] CPS Legal Guidance on Extradition [4.5].

Specialty protection

9.126 Where the defendant is extradited to the UK from a Commonwealth country[1], British overseas territory, or the Hong Kong SAR, the Extradition Act 2003, s 150 provides that the person may be dealt with in the UK for an offence committed before his extradition provided that the protected period[2] has ended and the offence is:

— the offence in respect of which the person is extradited;
— a lesser offence[3] disclosed by the information provided to the category 2 territory in respect of that offence; or
— an offence in respect of which consent to the person being dealt with is given by or on behalf of the relevant authority[4].

[1] See paras **9.120–9.121** for relevant case law regarding specialty protection.
[2] Defined as 45 days starting with the first day after the person's extradition to the UK on which the person is given an opportunity to leave the UK (Extradition Act 2003, s 150(7)).
[3] An offence is a lesser offence in relation to another offence if the maximum punishment for it is less severe than the maximum punishment for the other offence (Extradition Act 2003, s 150(4)).
[4] Extradition Act 2003, s 150(1), (2), (3) and (6). Relevant authority is defined as the government of a Commonwealth country, the person administering the British overseas territory and the government of the Hong Kong SAR as applicable (Extradition Act 2003, s 150(5)).

Specialty protection for other persons[1]

9.127 Where a person is extradited to the UK from a territory that is neither a category 1 territory, nor one falling within the Extradition Act 2003, s 150, s 151A of the 2003 Act applies. Section151A provides that the person may be dealt with[2] in the UK for an offence committed before his extradition provided that:

— the offence is:
  (i) the offence in respect of which the person is extradited; or
  (ii) an offence disclosed by the information provided to the territory in respect of that offence; or
  (iii) an offence in respect of which consent to the person being dealt with is given by or on behalf of the territory[3]; or
— the person has returned to the territory from which the person was extradited[4]; or
— the person has been given an opportunity to leave the UK[5].

[1] See paras **9.120–9.121** for relevant case law regarding specialty protection.
[2] Extradition Act 2003, s 151A(5) provides that a person is dealt with in the UK for an offence if they are tried in the UK for it or detained with a view to trial in the UK for it.
[3] Extradition Act 2003, s 151A(2), (3) and (4).
[4] Extradition Act 2003, s 151A(4)(a).
[5] Extradition Act 2003, s 151A(4)(b).

Undertakings

Extradition of serving prisoners to the UK

9.128 Where a person is serving a prison sentence in a territory, the UK may still request extradition of that person in exchange for suitable undertakings by the Secretary of State[1] under the Extradition Act 2003, s 153A. Section 153A is applicable if:

— a person is accused in the UK of the commission of an offence or has been convicted of an offence by or before a court in the UK;

— a Part 3 warrant is issued in respect of the person or the Secretary of State makes a request for extradition of the person;

— the person is serving a sentence of imprisonment or another form of detention in a territory;

— the person's extradition to the UK from the territory in pursuance of the warrant or request is made subject to the condition that an undertaking is given by or on behalf of the UK with regard to the person's treatment in the UK or return to the territory (or both)[2].

[1] Extradition Act 2003, s 153A(2) provides that the Secretary of State may give an undertaking to a person acting on behalf of the territory with regard to the treatment in the UK of the person and/or the return of the person to the territory. With respect to a person accused in the UK of the commission of an offence, the terms which may be included by the Secretary of State include that the person be kept in custody until the conclusion of proceedings and/or that the person be returned to the territory to serve the remainder of the sentence on the conclusion of the proceedings (Extradition Act 2003, s 153A(3)). With respect to a person convicted of an offence by or before a court in the UK, the terms which may be included are that the person be returned to the territory to serve the remainder of the sentence after the person would otherwise be released from detention pursuant to the sentence imposed in the UK (Extradition Act 2003, s 153A(4)). See s 153B for guidance on the situation where an undertaking is given under s 153A(2), the person is returned to the territory pursuant to the undertaking and the person returns to the UK.
[2] Extradition Act 2003, s 153A(1).

Return to territory to serve sentence

9.129 If, when a person is extradited to the UK, his extradition is made subject to an undertaking by or on behalf of the UK as to the person's return to the territory[1], he must be returned as soon as reasonably practicable after any sentence is imposed and any other proceedings in respect of the offence are concluded[2]. If this obligation is not complied with, the person may apply to the court that imposed his sentence to expedite return to the territory and the court must order return by such date as is specified in the order unless reasonable cause is shown for the delay[3].

[1] Extradition Act 2003, s 153C(2) and (3) provide that the Secretary of State may give such an undertaking, the terms of which may include terms that if the person is convicted of the offence and a sentence of imprisonment or another form of detention is imposed in respect of it, the person is to be returned to the territory to serve the sentence.
[2] Extradition Act 2003, s 153C(1), (4).
[3] Extradition Act 2003, s 153C(7), (8).

9.130 The Extradition Act 2003, s 153D provides that nothing in s 153A or s 153C of the Act requires the return of a person to a territory in a case in which the Secretary of State is not satisfied that the return is compatible with Convention rights within the meaning of the Human Rights Act 1998 or with the UK's obligations under the Refugee Convention[1].

[1] The Refugee Convention is defined as the Convention relating to the Status of Refugees done at Geneva on 28 July 1951 and the Protocol to the Convention' (Extradition Act 2003, s 153D(3)).

Other general provisions

Grant of bail where undertaking given to requested state

9.131 Where extradition to the UK is subject to an undertaking given by the Secretary of State that the defendant will be kept in custody until the conclusion of proceedings against him in the UK, a court, judge or justice of the peace may only grant bail to the defendant if they consider that there are exceptional circumstances that justify it[1].

[1] Extradition Act 2003, s 154.

Outstanding convictions and remission of punishment

9.132 Where:

— a person is extradited to the UK from a territory;
— before his extradition he has been convicted of an offence in the UK;
— he has not been extradited in respect of that offence

the sentence for the offence must be treated as served by the person's conviction for the offence and must be treated as a conviction for all other purposes[1].

[1] Extradition Act 2003, s 152.

Return of persons acquitted or not tried

9.133 In the situation where a person has been accused in the UK for the commission of an offence and has been extradited to the UK, the Secretary of State must arrange for him to be sent back, free of charge and with as little delay as possible to the territory from which he was extradited, where:

— proceedings against the person for the offence are not begun before the period of six months starting with the day on which the person arrives in the UK; and the person asks the Secretary of State to return him to the territory from which he was extradited within three months of the end of the six-month period; or
— at his trial for the offence the person is acquitted or discharged[1] and within three months of his acquittal or discharge the person asks the Secretary of State to return him to the territory from which he was extradited[2].

[1] In England and Wales, under the Powers of Criminal Courts (Sentencing) Act 2000, s 12(3) (Extradition Act 2003, s 153(4)).
[2] Extradition Act 2003, s 153(1), (2), (3) and (5).

Abuse of process

9.134 Where a defendant is returned to the UK for trial other than through regular extradition procedures then, if there has been bad faith on the part of the UK authorities or a deliberate flouting of domestic or international law, the criminal proceedings against him are liable to be stayed as an abuse of process[1].

[1]   *R v Horseferry Road Magistrates' Court, ex p Bennett* [1994] 1 AC 42, [1993] 3 WLR 90, HL.

KEY POINTS FROM CHAPTER 9

9.135 The key points in this chapter are summarised below:

- Under the Bribery Act 2010, the maximum sentence of imprisonment for bribery and corruption has been increased from 7 years to 10 years. The maximum penalty for a relevant commercial organisation for an offence under s 7 (failing to prevent bribery) is an unlimited fine.
- The courts take a very serious view of corruption of foreign officials. The approach taken by Thomas LJ in *R v Innospec Ltd* signals a significant increase in penalties for businesses involved in overseas corruption, which may be comparable to those imposed in the US;
- Businesses need to be aware that once a bribe has been paid, the bribe itself and any benefit received as a result of the bribe may constitute criminal property. This will include the benefit of any contract obtained by corruption. Businesses (their officers and employees) involved in dealing with the proceeds of corruption may therefore be exposed to liability for money laundering even though they are not complicit in the corrupt arrangement itself. In such circumstances, consideration will need to be given to making an authorised disclosure to SOCA seeking consent to deal with the money;
- Businesses need to be aware that the effect of the confiscation regime on defendants who have been convicted of bribery is likely to be particularly punitive. The benefit of corruption (which is liable to confiscation) is not merely the bribe monies or the net profits derived from the contract obtained by corruption and may encompass the entire value of the contract. There is little scope for the prosecution to agree not to pursue confiscation proceedings as part of a plea agreement and the court has no discretion not to make the order if it concludes that the defendant has benefited from his criminal conduct;
- There may be scope to agree a civil settlement with the SFO, under POCA 2002, Pt 5, which permits the recovery of property obtained by unlawful conduct without a criminal prosecution and does not require proof (or any admission) that a company or individuals has committed any offence of bribery. However, whilst the SFO has shown an enthusiasm to enter into such agreements, this approach has been deprecated by Thomas LJ in *R v Innospec*;

- Businesses wishing to recover a bribe or other losses resulting from acts of bribery will have remedies against their agent and/or the briber in restitution, tort or contract. It would appear that proprietary remedies are no longer available in light of the recent decision in *Sinclair Investments v Versailles*;
- In advising on Bribery Act 2010 compliance, it is important to highlight not only the dangers of reputational damage but other potentially serious consequences, which may lead to further reputational and/or financial damage to a business, such as debarment from bidding in public contracts; regulatory attention from the FSA; disqualification of directors and imposition of SCPOs and financial reporting orders;
- It is important to keep an eye on process when advising those extradited from abroad. Failure on the part of the prosecuting authorities to follow the proper procedures (including a breach of specialty rights) will enable a defendant to apply to quash counts on the indictment or to stay the proceedings as an abuse of process.

Chapter 10

OTHER FIELDS

A   EMPLOYMENT AND WHISTLEBLOWING

10.1 Employers will be keen to ensure that the framework of rules and policies governing their employment relationships prohibits or at least dissuades their employees from committing offences under the Bribery Act 2010 or allows such conduct to be identified and stamped out. At the very least, employers will want to ensure that they are able to make out the statutory defence. This section will deal with:

— implied terms and duties;
— express terms, duties and policies;
— whistleblowing.

Implied terms and duties

10.2 There are two possible sources from which an implied obligation upon employees not to commit acts of corruption, or to inform the employer of corruption by themselves and others, may be derived. The first is the duty of fidelity, the employees' implied contractual duty to render good and faithful service to their employer. The second is the fiduciary obligation imposed upon particular employees (or in particular circumstances) to act in the employer's best interests, even if this involves placing the employer's interests above their own.

10.3 In this context, the two forms of obligation will often produce the same result. However, they are conceptually distinct and it is an error to elide the two. The duty of fidelity is implied as a matter of contract, whilst a fiduciary obligation is imposed as a matter of equity by virtue of relationship. The genesis and nature of the fiduciary obligations of an employee were addressed in detail by Elias J in *Nottingham University v Fishel*[1] at paras 80–98. At paras 90 and 91, he said:

> '[90] . . . [T]he essence of the employment relationship is not typically fiduciary at all. Its purpose is not to place an employee in a position where he is obliged to pursue his employer's interests at the expense of his own. The relationship is a contractual one and the powers imposed upon the employee are conferred by the employer himself. The employee's freedom of action is regulated by the contract, the scope of his powers is determined by the terms (express or implied) of the contract, and as a consequence the employer can exercise (or at least he can place himself in a position where he has the opportunity to exercise) considerable control over the employee's decision-making powers.

[91] This is not to say that fiduciary duties cannot arise out of the employment relationship itself. But they arise not as a result of the mere fact that there is an employment relationship. Rather they result from the fact that within a particular contractual relationship there are specific contractual obligations which the employee has undertaken which have placed him in a situation where equity imposes these rigorous duties in addition to the contractual obligations'.

¹ [2000] ICR 1462, [2000] IRLR 471, QBD.

10.4 As a result, questions of fiduciary duties are most likely to be relevant to senior managerial employees. Some very senior employees may also hold a dual role of statutory directors of the company, and will owe the company fiduciary duties in that capacity.

10.5 Nonetheless, there is unlikely to be much doubt that any employee accepting or offering a bribe without the knowledge of their employer would be in breach of the duty of fidelity. Employees are under a duty to behave honestly¹. In addition, there will be a fiduciary obligation on all employees, irrespective of seniority, not to accept a bribe. In *Nottingham University v Fishel²* Elias J said:

'. . . circumstances may arise in the context of an employment relationship, or arising out of it, which, when they occur, will place the employee in the position of a fiduciary. . . . Thus every employee is subject to the principle that he should not accept a bribe and he will have to account for it (and possibly any profits derived from it) to his employer. Again, as Fletcher-Moulton LJ observed in *Coomber v Coomber* [1911] 1 Ch 723 at 728, even an errand boy is obliged to bring back my change, and is in fiduciary relations with me. But his fiduciary obligations are limited and arise out of the particular circumstances, namely that he is put in a position where he is obliged to account to me for the change he has received. In that case the obligation arises out of the employment relationship but it is not inherent in the nature of the relationship itself'.

¹ *Tesco Stores Ltd v Pook* [2003] EWHC 823 (Ch), [2004] IRLR 618.
² [2000] ICR 1462, [2000] IRLR 471 at para 86.

10.6 Generally speaking, an employee is under no contractual obligation to report to his employer his own misconduct¹ nor to report a fellow employee's misconduct or breach of contract. However, such a duty may arise from the contract or terms of employment of the particular employee, particularly where the employee has managerial responsibility for the wrongdoer. For example, in *Sybron Corpn v Rochem Ltd²* there was a hierarchical system of management, in which a Mr Roques was responsible for a particular sector of the business and was required to make monthly reports as to the state of the business in that sector. He was found to have been in breach of an obligation to disclose the misconduct of some of his subordinates, even though doing so would have exposed his own wrongdoing as a co-conspirator. A similar approach is likely to be taken where a non-managerial employee has particular responsibility for overseeing a particular area, so that those employed in a finance department to check and process expenses claims are likely to be under an obligation to report corrupt payments.

¹ *Bell v Lever Bros Ltd* [1932] AC 161, 101 LJKB 129, HL.
² [1984] Ch 112, [1983] 2 All ER 707, CA.

10.7 In other cases, such a duty may be constructed out of more general provisions contained within a contract of employment. In *Swain v West (Butchers) Ltd*[1], the general manager's contract included a clause which required that 'during the continuance of the agreement the general manager shall devote all his time to the business of the company and do all in his power to promote, extend and develop the interests of the company'. He became aware of misconduct by his superior, the managing director, which he did not disclose to his employer. As a result, he was found to be in breach of his contract, as it was 'his duty if he knew of acts which were not in the interests of the company to report them to the board. He did not do so'. However, there are limits. In *Lonmar Global Risks Ltd (formerly SBJ Global Risks Ltd) v West*[2], Hickinbottom J found that a contractual term requiring an employee to 'use his best endeavours to promote the general interests and welfare of the company . . . ' was a 'general clause which, certainly without more, could not require the law to impose wide-ranging duties to report wrongdoing and conduct that might be contrary to the interests' of the employer.

1 [1936] 3 All ER 261, 80 Sol Jo 973, CA.
2 [2010] EWHC 2878 (QB), [2010] All ER (D) 118 (Nov).

10.8 Employees will only be under a fiduciary obligation positively to act in the best interests of the employer by disclosing such misconduct if they are in a fiduciary role. However, whilst the courts will impose such fiduciary duties upon employees, it will not be done lightly[1], and only with caution[2]. Whether the employee is in such a position will depend upon the particular duties imposed on the employee under the contract and, according to Elias J in *Nottingham University v Fishel*[3], 'whether he has placed himself in a position where he must act solely in the best interests of his employer'. In *Tesco Stores Ltd v Pook*[4], Peter Smith J found that a senior employee, who was just below board level, was under a duty to disclose corruption by himself and others. In *Lonmar Global Risks Ltd (formerly SBJ Global Risks Ltd) v West*[5], two senior salesmen who did not have managerial responsibility for those whose behaviour they did not disclose (nor, indeed, any others) were found not to have been in a fiduciary position, even though one of them was an executive (but not a statutory) director.

1 *Helmet Integrated Systems Ltd v Tunnard* [2006] EWCA Civ 1735, [2007] FSR 437, [2007] IRLR 126 at para 36.
2 *ABK Ltd v Foxwell* [2002] EWHC 9 (Ch), [2002] All ER (D) 103 (Jan) at para 73.
3 [2000] ICR 1462, [2000] IRLR 471, QBD.
4 [2003] EWHC 823 (Ch), [2004] IRLR 618.
5 [2010] EWHC 2878 (QB), [2010] All ER (D) 118 (Nov).

10.9 Finally, there is an implied term of trust and confidence in any contract of employment, pursuant to which the employer shall not:

' . . . without reasonable and proper cause, conduct itself in a manner calculated and likely to destroy or seriously damage the relationship of confidence and trust between employer and employee'[1].

In *Malik*, the bank was found to have been in breach of this term by conducting its affairs in a fraudulent manner, causing loss to the innocent employees who, though uninvolved in the fraud, were stigmatised as a result of their employment at the bank. Presumably the same could be said where business is carried out in a corrupt manner.

[1] *Malik v BCCI SA (in liq)* [1998] AC 20, [1997] 3 All ER 1, HL; although note that later
   authorities have clarified that the formulation should refer to ' . . . calculated or likely
   . . .'.

Express terms, duties and policies

10.10 Most employers will doubtless seek to deal with matters by express provision, rather than by relying upon the implied duties. Not only will that avoid the pitfalls and uncertainties inherent upon relying only on the implied terms, but express steps will need to be taken if the statutory defence is to be made out. In addition, clarity as to the standards of behaviour expected and the consequences of failing to meet those standards will be important to avoid successful challenges to any disciplinary action taken by the employer.

10.11 Employers may consider including express terms forbidding bribery offences and requiring the disclosure of information about the corruption of others in the contracts of senior employees or those working in high risk sectors or areas. This is easily done in the case of new employees or, where existing contracts contain unilateral variation clauses, employers may be entitled to introduce such terms through the variation provisions. In the absence of such a power to vary contracts unilaterally, it will be necessary to seek the agreement of the employee to the variation.

10.12 Ultimately, in the face of a (perhaps unlikely) refusal to consent to such changes, the employer could terminate the contract on notice whilst offering to re-engage on terms including the bribery provisions. However, whilst possible, this would have to be done in accordance with the manifold requirements of the law regarding unfair dismissal and collective redundancies. The detail of those requirements falls outside the scope of this book, and the more so because a satisfactory result will usually be achievable by adopting appropriate and specific anti-bribery policies instead of (or, in the case of new employees, as well as) express contractual provisions.

10.13 Most employers operating in the UK will already have written disciplinary policies. As discussed in Chapter 6, these may need to be amended to deal expressly with corruption issues. For example, accepting or offering bribes, failing to report corruption or penalising those who do report it could be added to the list of examples of gross misconduct commonly contained in such policies. Similarly, many employers will already have an existing policy regarding whistleblowers. Again, it may be helpful to make specific reference to bribery issues in these policies. Whistleblowers are discussed further at para **10.24**.

10.14 Such policies will usually be non-contractual, so that the employer will be entitled to make changes to them without obtaining agreement. Occasionally disciplinary policies are contractual documents, so that any substantial revision will require agreement (and usually collective agreement via collective bargaining) unless they contain provision for unilateral variation.

10.15 However, even in such circumstances, it should be possible to introduce an express instruction, either individually or by way of an announcement and/or a specific anti-bribery policy, requiring employees not to engage in corruption and to report any corruption of which they become aware. Whether or not there are any relevant implied contractual or fiduciary duties, employees are under a contractual obligation to carry out the reasonable instructions of their employer. If such an instruction is given, any subsequent failure to comply with the lawful instruction will amount to a breach of the duty of fidelity. Where the instruction is deliberately flouted, the breach will be fundamental, entitling the employer to dismiss the employee summarily[1]. It will be easier to demonstrate that the instruction has been deliberately flouted where the importance has been emphasised as part of Principle 2: with a top level commitment to preventing bribery and fostering a culture in which bribery is never acceptable.

[1]   *Laws v London Chronicle (Indicator Newspapers) Ltd* [1959] 2 All ER 285, [1959] 1 WLR 698, CA.

10.16 In addition to giving an employer the right to dismiss summarily as a matter of contract law, this would also strengthen the employer's position in relation to a claim for unfair dismissal. For example, a former employee may say that it was unreasonable to dismiss for making a facilitation payment when he or she thought it was acceptable or common practice. Likewise, it could be suggested that it was unreasonable to dismiss for failing to report corruption when the obligation to do so and/or the consequences of failing to comply had not been made clear. A specific, well publicised and enforced anti-bribery policy could avoid such arguments, as well as being a key element of any statutory defence.

10.17 As discussed in Chapter 6, the statutory defence will not be made out simply by the adoption of such policies in a document left gathering dust on a shelf. Principle 5 requires that the anti-bribery policies are effectively implemented in fact and embedded throughout the employer's organisation. Parallels may be drawn with the defence to (civil) discrimination claims now found in the Equality Act 2010, s 109(4), whereby an employer may avoid vicarious liability for the discriminatory acts of an employee if it has 'taken all reasonable steps to prevent' the employee from carrying out such acts of discrimination. Employment tribunals considering the equivalent defence under the Race Relations Act 1976 would consider what positive steps had been taken to promulgate and implement the policy amongst lower level managerial and supervisory staff—those groups being key to the effectiveness of the policy in practice. In *Colley v British Road Services Ltd*[1], the tribunal described the employer's equal opportunities policy as being 'excellent'. However, the defence failed as they had taken no steps to put the policy into practice. In contrast, in *Al-Azzawi v Haringey Council (Haringey Design Partnership Directorate of Technical & Environmental Services)*[2], the EAT allowed Haringey's appeal and found that it had taken all reasonable steps to prevent incidents of racial abuse committed by X. Not only did it have policies in place, but:

> 'those policies were not just for show; employees were (when breach was provable) disciplined under them; employees were sent on relevant courses and [X] had been sent on a course less than a year before the incident'.

The EAT also found that the tribunal had erred, when reaching the opposite conclusion, by relying upon the fact that whilst disciplinary proceedings had been taken against X as a result of the incident, a charge involving gross misconduct had been dropped and the penalty eventually imposed on X had been, in the view of the tribunal, derisory. In refusing leave to appeal from that decision Mummery LJ said[3]:

> '[18] In my judgment, it is possible in some cases to conclude that an act which is committed, and the way with which it is dealt, throws light on how reasonable and effective the steps are that are taken by the council to prevent the commission of the act. But, in this case, the employment tribunal were not relying upon that to cast any doubt on the validity of the preventive steps which the council had taken. [19] I would agree with the Employment Appeal Tribunal that, having found that the council were not simply paying lip service to the policies that had been put in place, it was not a legitimate conclusion for the employment tribunal to reject the defence under section 32(3). The Employment Appeal Tribunal were not in error of law by saying that events taking place after the act of discrimination are irrelevant in this case. They may be relevant in another case, but, in my view, they were not relevant in this case because they did not in any way affect the validity of the preventive steps'.

For example, failing to investigate a particular incident or to impose the sanction provided for in the policy may not, in itself, deprive the employer of this defence to a discrimination claim. However, if such failures were commonplace, it would seriously undermine the proposition that the policy was genuinely being implemented.

[1]   ET Case No 4890/94.
[2]   (EAT/158/00), [2001] All ER (D) 11 (Dec).
[3]   [2002] EWCA Civ 862.

10.18 One further lesson that may be drawn from the discrimination law cases is this. In *Canniffe v East Riding of Yorkshire Council*[1] the EAT rejected a suggestion that an employer would make out the statutory defence where it had failed to take an otherwise reasonable step that would not in fact have prevented the discrimination in question. Burton P said that the proper approach was:

> '(1) to identify whether the respondent took any steps at all to prevent the employee, for where it is vicariously liable, from doing the act or acts complained of in the course of his employment;
> (2) having identified what steps, if any, they took to consider whether there were any further acts, that they could have taken, which were reasonably practicable. The question as to whether the doing of any such acts would in fact have been successful in preventing the acts of discrimination in question may be worth addressing, and may be interesting to address, but are not determinative either way. On the one hand, the employer, if he takes steps which are reasonably practicable, will not be inculpated if those steps are not successful; indeed, the matter would not be before the court if the steps had been successful, and so the whole availability of the defence suggests the necessity that someone will have committed the act of discrimination, notwithstanding the taking of reasonable steps; but on the other hand, the employer will not be exculpated if it has not taken reasonable steps simply because if he had taken those reasonable steps they would not have led anywhere or achieved anything or in fact prevented anything from occurring'.

[1]   [2000] IRLR 555.

10.19 Although this is authority for the proposition that the likely efficacy of a step is not determinative, it does not mean that it is to be ignored. At para 61 of *Croft v Royal Mail Group plc*[1], the Court of Appeal said that:

> 'consideration of the likely effect, or lack of effect, of any action it is submitted the employers should have taken is not the sole criterion by which that action is to be judged in this context. In considering whether an action is reasonably practicable, within the meaning of the subsection, it is however permissible to take into account the extent of the difference, if any, which the action is likely to make. The concept of reasonable practicability is well-known to the law and it does entitle the employer in this context to consider whether the time, effort and expense of the suggested measures are disproportionate to the result likely to be achieved. In considering what steps are reasonable in the circumstances, it is legitimate to consider the effect they are likely to have'.

[1]   [2003] EWCA Civ 1045, [2003] ICR 1425, [2003] IRLR 592.

10.20 It remains to be seen whether a similar approach will be taken in relation to the adequate measures defence. Of course, it could not sensibly be a requirement of the adequate measures defence that they were in fact adequate to prevent the acts of bribery in question, as this would limit the availability of the defence to circumstances in which no offence had been committed so that no defence was required. However, as discussed in Chapter 6, the stringency of the test in its application will be one of the keenest fought issues under the new law.

10.21 Finally, a few points should be made in relation to the detection and investigation of corruption. In many cases, the employer will rely upon information from other employees, and the position of whistleblowers is considered at para **10.24**. However, other investigations will also be required, whether or not prompted by such a disclosure. There will be no obligation to caution the employee or remind him or her of any rights against self incrimination. Materials (such as statements and reports) produced in the course of such an investigation could be seized by prosecuting authorities should they become aware of them and may, in certain circumstances[1], be admissible as evidence against the employer in the course of any prosecution. However, in practical terms, the benefits from carrying out a proper investigation (which in itself will assist the employer to make out the statutory defence) is likely to outweigh any tactical advantage from structuring any investigation as an exercise in obtaining legal advice (so as to benefit from legal professional privilege) or, worse, failing properly to investigate.

[1]   The details of which are outside the scope of this work, but note the Criminal Justice Act 2003, s 114.

10.22 Furthermore, there are a number of potential constraints upon employers carrying out such investigations, which could be ameliorated by appropriate provisions in anti-bribery or other policies or contracts of employment. It is to be emphasised that such investigations will be carried out by the employer in the capacity of employer. One key source of information will be emails and other communications to and from employees. Subject to their nature, monitoring such communications will be subject to the Regulation of Investigatory Powers Act 2000 and/or the Telecommunications (Lawful Business Practice) (Interception of Communications) Regulations 2000[1]. Subject to various conditions, reg 3(1)(iii) entitles employers to intercept communications for the purpose of preventing or detecting crime. One such condition, imposed by reg 3(2)(c), is that the 'system controller has made all reasonable efforts to inform every person who may use the telecommunication system in question that communications transmitted by means thereof may be intercepted'. These reasonable efforts could include notifying employees that their communications may be intercepted for these purposes in any IT and communications policy in addition to any specific anti-bribery policy. Provided monitoring is carried out in accordance with the relevant legislation and following such notification, there should be no violation of the European Convention on Human Rights, article 8 right to privacy. Prior to the enactment of the relevant legislative provisions, the European Court of Human Rights had found that monitoring telephone calls made from work was a violation of article 8 rights where no such notification had been given[2].

1   SI 2000/2699.
2   *Halford v United Kingdom (Application 20605/92)* (1997) 24 EHRR 523, [1997] IRLR 471 and *Copland v United Kingdom (Application 62617/00)*[2007] IP & T 600, (2007) Times, 24 April.

10.23 In addition, information obtained through these investigations is likely to be covered by the Data Protection Act 1998 ('DPA 1998'), so that any processing of the information will need to be carried out without violating the data protection principles set out in the DPA 1998, Sch 1. Processing data in order to prevent, detect and prove corruption is very likely to fall within the 'legitimate interests' condition set out in the DPA 1998, Sch 2, para 6 (at least one of which must be met if the processing of data is to be in accordance with the first data protection principle), although it would be preferable if employees had given consent to the processing of data so as to fall within the consent condition at Sch 2, para 1. However, it is noteworthy that the Information Commissioner's Employment Practices Code states that:

> '3.4.1 Senior management should normally authorise any covert monitoring. They should satisfy themselves that there are grounds for suspecting criminal activity or equivalent malpractice and that notifying individuals about the monitoring would prejudice its prevention or detection.
> Key points and possible actions
> •   Covert monitoring should not normally be considered. It will be rare for covert monitoring of workers to be justified. It should therefore only be used in exceptional circumstances.
> 3.4.2 Ensure that any covert monitoring is strictly targeted at obtaining evidence within a set timeframe and that the covert monitoring does not continue after the investigation is complete.
> Key points and possible actions
> •   Deploy covert monitoring only as part of a specific investigation and cease once the investigation has been completed'.

Whistleblowing

10.24 Corruption is, by its very nature, likely to be hidden. It is widely acknowledged that whistleblowing will play a key role in uncovering such behaviour. Transparency International, in its Bribery Act Adequate Procedures: Guidance on good practice procedures for corporate anti-bribery programmes, states:

'to be effective [an anti-bribery programme] should rely on employees and others to raise concerns and violations as early as possible. To this end, the company should provide secure and accessible channels through which employees and others should feel able to raise concerns and report violations ("whistleblowing") in confidence and without risk of reprisal'.

10.25 Many employers already have whistleblowing policies to enable concerns to be raised and support to be given to those raising concerns. Much guidance is available as to the nature and content of such policies, including the British Standards Institute's publicly available specification 1998 Whistleblowing Arrangements Code of Practice and the International Chamber of Commerce Guidelines on Whistleblowing. It will, of course, be necessary always to modify any standard form where this is appropriate to take account of the particular concerns that may arise in an anti-bribery context in any particular area or sector.

10.26 In addition to internal policies, whistleblowers have had some statutory protection in the UK, following the coming into force of the Public Interest Disclosure Act 1998 ('PIDA 1998'). PIDA 1998 was prompted by a series of disasters and financial scandals in the UK in the 1980s and 1990s. It was introduced as a private member's Bill with strong support from the government. Although introduced as a piece of employment legislation, and described by the Fairness at Work White Paper[1] as providing one of the key new rights for individuals, it has always been recognised as a valuable tool to promote good governance and transparency in organisations. It received broad support from the Confederation of British Industry, the Institute of Directors and all key professional groups.

[1] (May 1998) Cm 3968.

10.27 The basic approach of PIDA 1998 is to give some whistleblowers (namely workers who make particular 'protected disclosures') protection from reprisals by their employers. This approach has subsequently been taken in, for example, the Council of Europe's Civil Law Convention on Corruption, article 9 of which requires the parties to the Convention to:

'provide in its internal law for appropriate protection against any unjustified sanction for employees who have reasonable grounds to suspect corruption and who report in good faith their suspicion to responsible persons or authorities'.

10.28 This protective approach was also seen in Resolution 1729 (2001) and Recommendation 1916 (2010) on the Protection of Whistleblowers adopted by the Parliamentary Assembly of the Council of Europe on 29 April 2010. The Report[1] in which the Draft Resolution appeared had itself described PIDA 1998 in glowing terms. However, despite some detailed references to the development of whistleblower legislation in the USA, there was no reference to the whistleblower bounty programmes found in some US legislation, such as the Dodd–Frank Wall Street Reform and Consumer Protection Act. These programmes provide for whistleblowers to obtain a percentage (typically 10–30%) of fines and penalties imposed on wrongdoers in certain circumstances. Two employees of a large pharmaceutical company shared a $45,000,000 payment in 2010. However, there appears to be no legislative enthusiasm for such bounty programmes in the UK or EU. In fact, some PIDA 1998 protection is conditional upon the disclosure not being made for reasons of personal gain.

¹   Document 12006 of 2009.

10.29 PIDA 1998 operates by giving workers the right to complain to employment tribunals where they have been dismissed or subjected to another detriment because they have made a 'protected disclosure'. The relevant provisions of PIDA 1998 are incorporated into the Employment Rights Act 1996, Pt IVA ('ERA 1996'). Furthermore, any agreement (including an agreement to refrain from instituting or continuing proceedings under the ERA 1996 or for breach of contract) is void in so far as it purports to prevent the worker making a protected disclosure¹. It follows that a confidentiality clause in a contract of employment will not prohibit the making of a protected disclosure.

¹   ERA 1996, s 43J.

10.30 The protection is given to employees (ie those employed under a contract of employment for the purposes of the ERA 1996, s 230(1)) and other workers (ie those employed under another form of contract whereby they undertake to do or perform personally any work for the other party to the contract who is not a client or customer of any profession or business undertaking carried on by the individual, for the purposes of the ERA 1996, s 230(3)). In addition, worker is given an extended meaning by the ERA 1996, ss 43K and 43KA, so that it extends, for example, to contract workers and various office holders.

10.31 To attract protection, a disclosure must be a 'protected disclosure' within the meaning of the ERA 1996, s 43A. A protected disclosure is a 'qualifying disclosure' made by a worker in accordance with ERA 1996, Pt IVA.

10.32 A qualifying disclosure is defined by the ERA 1996, s 43B as being the 'disclosure of information which, in the reasonable belief of the worker making the disclosure, tends to show one or more' of the matters specified therein, including that '(a) a criminal offence has been committed, is being committed or is likely to be committed; . . . or (f) that information tending to show [this] has been, or is likely to be deliberately concealed'. It is immaterial whether the matter to which the information relates occurred, occurs or would occur in the UK or elsewhere, or whether the applicable law is that of the UK or some other country¹.

¹   ERA 1996, s 43B(2).

10.33 However, the disclosure will not be a qualifying disclosure if:

—   the person making it thereby commits a criminal offence¹; or
—   the information is covered by legal professional privilege, having been disclosed to the person making the disclosure in the course of obtaining legal advice².

¹   ERA 1996, s 43B(3).

2   ERA 1996, s 43B(4).

10.34 The reference to a 'disclosure of information' is intended to be broadly construed. Information is still disclosed for these purposes even if it is given to a person who already has the information[1]. However, there must be a disclosure (and not just a threat to disclose). A disclosure also requires more than just an allegation of wrongdoing. In *Geduld v Cavendish Munro Professional Risks Management Ltd*[2], Slade J said that:

> '[24] . . . the ordinary meaning of giving "information" is conveying facts. In the course of the hearing before us, a hypothetical was advanced regarding communicating information about the state of a hospital. Communicating "information" would be "The wards have not been cleaned for the past two weeks. Yesterday, sharps were left lying around". Contrasted with that would be a statement that "You are not complying with Health and Safety requirements". In our view this would be an allegation not information.'

1   ERA 1996, s 43L.
2   [2010] ICR 325, [2010] IRLR 38, EAT.

10.35 Where information has been provided, it will be a qualifying disclosure if, in the reasonable belief of the worker, the information tends to show one of the relevant matters set out in s 43B, such as that a criminal offence has been committed. Provided the individual does hold such a belief at the time of making the disclosure, it does not matter if the information is in fact incorrect[1] or that no such offence is in fact being committed[2].

1   *Darnton v University of Surrey* [2003] ICR 615, [2003] IRLR 133, EAT.
2   *Babula v Waltham Forest College* [2007] EWCA Civ 174, [2007] ICR 1026, [2007] IRLR 346, overruling *Kraus v Penna plc* [2004] IRLR 260, EAT on this point.

10.36 Nor need the offence have been committed by the employer (or another employee of the employer) of the worker making the disclosure[1]. Therefore, if an employee of Slog Co makes a disclosure about the corruption of Sweep Ltd, the employee will still fall within the protection of these provisions. In *Elstone v BP plc*[2] it was held that protection will extend to a disclosure of information made by the employee when he was not employed by the employer who dismisses or subjects the worker to a detriment. In this case BP were held to have acted unlawfully in refusing to offer Mr Elstone further freelance work (and thereby subjecting him to a detriment) as a result of a disclosure he had made whilst working for his previous employer. The courts have emphasised that the legislation is to be construed purposively to protect whistleblowing workers[3].

1   *Hibbins v Hesters Way Neighbourhood Project* [2009] 1 All ER 949, [2009] ICR 319, EAT.
2   (UKEAT/141/09), [2010] ICR 879, [2010] IRLR 558.
3   *Stolt Offshore Ltd v Miklaszewicz* [2002] IRLR 344, 2002 SC 232 and *Woodward v Abbey National plc* [2006] EWCA Civ 822, [2006] 4 All ER 1209, [2006] ICR 1436.

10.37 Even if the disclosure is of the appropriate type, it will only attract protection if it is made in the proper manner, as required by the ERA 1996. Broadly speaking, the ERA 1996 usually requires the worker to seek to resolve matters internally by raising it with his or her employer in the first instance. Only if this has failed, or, exceptionally, is unrealistic, is the worker entitled to make the disclosure externally. However, a disclosure will only attract protection if it is made in good faith. The purpose of the legislation is not to allow people to advance personal grudges, but to protect those who make certain disclosures of information in the public interest. Therefore, if a disclosure is made because of a personal grudge it will not be protected under the legislation, even if information disclosed is true and would otherwise qualify for protection[1].

[1]   *Street v Derbyshire Unemployed Workers' Centre* [2004] EWCA Civ 964, [2004] 4 All ER 839, [2005] ICR 97.

10.38 Provided it is made in good faith, a qualifying disclosure is protected if it is made in the following circumstances:

—   to the employer[1]; where the employer's own policies provide for disclosures to be made in a particular manner, a worker who makes a disclosure in accordance with that procedure is treated as having made the disclosure to the employer[2];
—   where the worker reasonably believes that the matter relates solely or mainly to someone other than his employer, to that person[3];
—   to a legal adviser whilst obtaining legal advice[4];
—   to a Minister of the Crown or member of the Scottish Executive, where the worker's employer is appointed under an enactment, ie employees of government agencies or quangos[5];
—   to a person prescribed by the Secretary of State, where the worker reasonably believes that they are the relevant person for such disclosures and that the information and any allegation are substantially true[6]; so, for example, disclosures about fraud and corruption in local government and the NHS are to be made to the Audit Commission; the relevant watchdogs and regulators are listed in the Schedule to the Public Interest Disclosure (Prescribed Persons) Order 1999[7].

[1]   ERA 1996, s 43C(1)(a).
[2]   ERA 1996, s 43C(2).
[3]   ERA 1996, s 43C(1)(b).
[4]   ERA 1996, s 43D.
[5]   ERA 1996, s 43E.
[6]   ERA 1996, s 43F.
[7]   SI 1999/1549.

10.39 A qualifying disclosure will also be protected if made to another person, provided the conditions set out in the ERA 1996, s 43G are satisfied. Those conditions are that:

—   the disclosure must be made in good faith;
—   the worker must reasonably believe that information disclosed and any allegation are substantially true;
—   the disclosure is not made for the purposes of personal gain;
—   (a) at the time of the disclosure the worker reasonably believes he will be subjected to a detriment by his employer if he makes the disclosure to his employer or to a prescribed person; or (b) where there is no prescribed person, the worker reasonably believes that it is likely that evidence will be destroyed if he makes a disclosure to his employer; or (c) he has previously made a disclosure of substantially the same matter to his employer or to a prescribed person[1];

— it is reasonable for the worker to make that disclosure; whether or not it is reasonable will depend in particular upon (a) the identify of the person to whom the disclosure is made; (b) the seriousness of the matter disclosed; (c) whether the matter is continuing or likely to recur; (d) any breach of confidentiality; (e) any action taken or which might reasonably have been expected to have been taken as a result of any previous disclosure to the employer or prescribed person; and (f) whether the worker had made a previous disclosure in accordance with a procedure authorised by the employer, ie in accordance with the internal whistleblowing policy[2].

[1] ERA 1996, s 43G(2).
[2] ERA 1996, s 43G(3).

10.40 Finally, there are provisions for disclosures in exceptionally serious cases. These allow for a qualifying disclosure to be protected if made to another person, provided the conditions set out in s 43H are satisfied. Those conditions are that:

— the disclosure must be made in good faith;
— the worker must reasonably believe that information disclosed and any allegation are substantially true;
— the disclosure is not made for the purposes of personal gain;
— the disclosure is of a matter that is of an exceptionally serious nature; and
— it is reasonable for the worker to make that disclosure; whether or not it is reasonable will depend in particular upon the identity of the person to whom the disclosure is made.

10.41 Workers have a right not to be subjected to a detriment by their employers on the ground that they have made a protected disclosure[1]. The right is enforced by complaint to an employment tribunal, which may make a declaration and an award of compensation[2]. The power to make an award of compensation is not subject to a financial cap.

[1] ERA 1996, s 47B(1).
[2] ERA 1996, ss 48 and 49.

10.42 Where the worker is an employee, and the detriment consists of dismissal, the remedy is by way of a claim for unfair dismissal. An employee is deemed to have been unfairly dismissed if the only or principal reason for the dismissal (or selection for redundancy) of the employee is that he made a protected disclosure[1]. There is no qualifying period for such an unfair dismissal claim, and again no cap on any compensatory award.

[1] ERA 1996, ss 103A, 105(6A).

10.43 Note that these provisions only protect against detriment or dismissal because of the act of disclosure. They do not protect the workers who use improper means to investigate their suspicions, such as unauthorised hacking into the employer's computer system, and are disciplined for that behaviour alone[1].

[1] *Bolton School v Evans* [2006] EWCA Civ 1653, [2007] IRLR 140.

10.44 Since 6 April 2010, the Secretary to an employment tribunal may, if s/he considers it appropriate, send a copy of the claim or part of it, to the prescribed regulator:

— where a claim or part of a claim has been accepted by an employment tribunal; and

— the claim alleges that the claimant has made a protected disclosure as defined by the ERA 1996, s 43A; and

— the claimant has consented to the referral (the ET1 claim form now contains a tick box for the claimant to give consent).

B   THE DEFENCE AND EXTRACTIVE INDUSTRIES

10.45 It is neither necessary nor perhaps desirable to compile a league table for the purposes of this chapter of those industries most susceptible to issues relating to bribery and corruption. However, the extractive[1] and defence industries, because of their relationship with national security and infrastructure, merit special consideration. In addition the vast sums of money involved in the procurement of goods and services within their geographic areas of operation tend to make them, and those that operate within them, extremely vulnerable to corruption and allegations of financial impropriety. Whether domestically or internationally, extraction and defence involve the participation of national governments, nationally recognised institutions and private sector firms (perhaps intrinsically wed to the other two) with considerable public profiles.

[1]   Perhaps more commonly thought of as the extraction industry but to include all activities to do with the mining and deployment of oil, gas and minerals.

10.46 The Al Yamanah defence contracts between the Kingdom of Saudi Arabia, British Aerospace and the UK in the 1980s give some insight into, in the context of defence, how significant even the implication of corruption can be in terms of public interest and perception. Extraction equally has its big stories: scandal involving billions of dollars and the building of dams in Lesotho is but one example. The potential for impropriety on the part of institutions and individuals involved with those cases seems to be defined by the scale of commitment, investment, industrial advancement and, perhaps above all, profit to be derived. As this chapter will seek to explain, accepted practices within both industries leave their participants heavily exposed to allegations of corruption both corporately and individually.

10.47 The fact that, in relation to the Al Yamanah defence contracts, the UK government of the day positively intervened, on public interest grounds, to prevent a prosecution for criminal offences that appeared to be otherwise justified only serves to illustrate what is at stake in terms of international relations and, one might imagine, future business. The Al Yamanah defence contracts still represent the biggest export arms deal that the UK has ever entered into amounting to in the region of £30 billion even at 1986 prices.

10.48 The extraction industry requires vast investment, which in turn can generate vast profit. Conversely the vast profits generated have a habit of not reaching, in terms of wealth creation, the lives of citizens, particularly in developing nations. On 15 July 2010 in the United States Senate, Senator Dick

Lugar was speaking in support of the Cardin Lugar amendment (transparency in the extraction industries) to the Dodd-Frank Wall Street Reform and Consumer Protection Act. He said:

> 'History shows that oil, gas reserves, and minerals frequently can be a bane, not a blessing, for poor countries, leading to corruption, wasteful spending, military adventurism, and instability. Too often, oil money intended for a nation's poor ends up lining the pockets of the rich or is squandered on showcase projects instead of productive investments. A classic case is Nigeria, the eighth largest oil exporter. Despite $ 1/2 trillion in revenues since the 1960s, poverty has increased, corruption is rife, and violence roils the oil-rich Niger Delta'.

Plainly the Senator was principally referring to the distribution of oil revenue rather than specifically to procurement corruption in the country concerned, but if the statistics he quotes and consequences he refers to are a reflection of the atmosphere within which revenues from the extraction industry are deployed (in aftermath of external investment) his comments are just as relevant to the way in which goods and services are procured in these industries in the first instance.

10.49 The purpose of this chapter is to highlight the potential for market abuse whilst at the same time discussing what appears to be tolerated within the context of these particular industries at present.

10.50 It is not the substantive contracts that will attract the greatest scrutiny in terms of impropriety, because invariably the details of them are likely to be more readily in the public domain. It is the role of third party intermediaries, fixers and lobbyists and the sub-deals, the collateral arrangements that orbit like moons around the main contractual subject matter that will attract attention.

10.51 Third party involvement is rife and can pass entirely unscrutinised. The sub-deals would not exist without the substantive contract but may operate entirely independently of it. They are sometimes referred to as 'offsets' in the defence industry and 'social and barter payments' in the extraction industry. It is this framework that will inform those called upon to advise the participants as to their potential vulnerabilities. Whether or not the Bribery Act 2010 will have an impact, particularly with regard to the offence of bribing a foreign official in the context of these sub-deals, remains to be seen.

10.52 In the extraction industry, the issue of transparency is a topic of major significance going forward into the next decade. For a variety of reasons, perhaps the relationship between extraction revenue and continuing poverty in the Niger Delta being an example, global initiative in relation to increased integrity in the extraction industry is gathering momentum. The Bribery Act 2010 may well represent the high point of the UK government's resolve in that regard.

10.53 Worldwide, the efforts of Extractive Industries Transparency Initiative ('EITI') probably represent the gold standard of what the extraction industry could achieve through compliance both by nation states and corporate players. Progress has been steady over the last eight years and needs to, at the very least, keep its momentum. As at the end of 2010 the only developed industrial nation in the world which had signed up to the initiative, and thus recorded as compliant, was Norway.

10.54 The UK government, despite providing financial support (and being a formal 'supporter' of the process) for EITI through the Department of Overseas Development, cites low oil and resource revenues as a reason for not becoming involved to any greater extent. The election in March 2011 of former Westminster MP Clare Short to the Chair of the EITI International Board in at the International EITI conference in Paris may provide new domestic impetus for the UK taking its involvement further. An avalanche of developing nations, perhaps with a view to improving their overall image in the extraction sector, have voluntarily taken part.

10.55 Meanwhile the United States, as of July 2010, has in existence article 1504 of the Dodd-Frank Wall Street Reform and Consumer Protection Act, also known as the Cardin Luger amendment. This provides for unilateral transparency on the part of USA corporates with regard to dealings with the USA and foreign governments in the extractive industry. The format of that disclosure is currently under consideration, with considerable lobbying by the industry as to the form, detail and contact that the disclosure is to take.

10.56 In the defence industry, in April 2010, Transparency International UK published a paper (the expertise of which has been substantially drawn on for this chapter) on defence offsets called 'Addressing the Risks of Corruption and Raising Transparency'. The defence industry does not have an EITI equivalent; neither does there appear to be any initiative in that regard.

10.57 In the context of extraction or defence, transparency means establishing greater public knowledge of the terms and components of an extraction or defence contract to include not only the subject matter of the contract itself but also the nature and extent of the 'offsets' and 'social and barter payments' that may exist alongside the contract itself. The information should also include how those sub-deals are to be delivered and who, within a contracting nation, is to be responsible for that delivery. As will be seen, there are a myriad ways in which the main 'deal' can be enhanced by an importing nation by parallel contractual commitments by the supplying nation or company in an area perhaps completely unrelated to the subject matter of the main contract. What is even more compromising is the lack of governance and accountability in relation to these sub-deals. There is rarely any basis upon which delivery of 'offset' commitment is actually verified.

10.58 Increased transparency in terms of contractual dealing will, it might be supposed, filter down to improve the culture of corporate and individual behaviour and thus lead to less obvious means of corporate impropriety, although how the cards will fall remains to be seen. It has always been and will remain impossible to control a rogue individual, but broader and more transparent access to the terms of a contract as a whole is, it is said, likely to make impropriety more difficult.

Jurisdiction and scope of the Bribery Act 2010

10.59 The nature of the defence and extraction industries make activity abroad highly likely for a broad range of individuals and institutions. The Bribery Act 2010 has a similarly broad reach. Jurisdiction is discussed in Chapter 4.

10.60 The offences of giving and receiving bribes and bribing foreign public officials will apply to UK companies, partnerships, citizens and individuals ordinarily resident in the UK regardless of where the relevant act occurs. This equally applies to any other commercial organisation that carries on business or part of their business in the UK.

10.61 The offence under the Bribery Act 2010, s 6 is committed if a person bribes a foreign public official intending the bribe to influence the foreign public official in his official capacity. The person offering the bribe must also intend to obtain or retain business, or an advantage in the conduct of business and the act is not permitted by the local written law. The s 6 offence does not require the intention that the foreign public official will perform his functions improperly, nor do they require that the payment should be made 'corruptly'—indeed that term is not to be found within the Bribery Act 2010. The offence is committed if a financial or other advantage is offered, or given or promised to a foreign public official where it is not legitimately due pursuant to the written law applicable to the official abroad. For instance, if the written law applicable to the foreign public official permits or requires him to accept an advantage then the financial or other advantage will be regarded as 'legitimately due'.

10.62 By virtue of the Bribery Act 2010, s 12(2), however, activity undertaken outside the UK by a company or individual will be deemed to be have been committed in the UK if it amounts to an offence under ss 1, 2 or 6 of the Act and if the relevant body, individual or corporate, has a 'close connection' with the UK. Sections 12(2)(c) and 12(4) define 'close connection' as:

— a British citizen;
— a British overseas territories citizen;
— a British National (Overseas);
— a British Overseas citizen;
— a person who under the British Nationality Act 1981 was a British subject;
— a British protected person within the meaning of that Act;
— an individual ordinarily resident in the UK;
— a body incorporated under the law of any part of the UK;
— a Scottish partnership.

10.63 On the basis that whatever a company puts in place to prevent bribery taking place, it may yet still happen, alternative corporate structures for UK companies involved in international dealings might be considered so as not to be caught by the above definition.

10.64 For example a UK company being represented by a company incorporated in France and staffed by foreign nationals would not be caught by this definition. It is not unusual, particularly for extraction companies, to have wholly-owned subsidiaries operating in (and incorporated in) a country where extraction or processing is being undertaken. The fact that the company incorporated abroad is a wholly-owned subsidiary of the UK corporate may not bring the former within the ambit of s 12 if its activities have fallen foul of the Act. Those companies can equally expect to have a number of local employees, for appropriate reasons, involved in negotiating and procuring locally for the subsidiary and, in turn the UK company. Thus both individuals and subsidiaries at the front line of negotiation, and therefore at highest risk of acting in breach of the legislation, stand a chance of operating outside the scope of an offence under s 12.

10.65 However, the same UK company (and a foreign company carrying on business in the UK) would or could be at risk of an offence under s 7 of the Act, bribing a foreign official, if it fails to have adequate procedures in place to prevent a bribe being passed by an associated person or company performing services for the UK company elsewhere.

10.66 Section 7 is particularly important with regard to negotiation, procurement and performance of contracts abroad, especially in remote undeveloped parts of the world. Section 7(3) specifically removes the application of s 12(2)(c) and 12(4) from consideration. Thus the determining factor for liability of the relevant commercial organisation (as to which see s 5(a)) under s 7 is not whether the person or corporate committing a substantive offence under ss 1 or 6 of the Act has a 'close connection with the UK' pursuant to s 12, but is he/she/it an 'associated person'. Thus s 7 creates a strict liability offence for commercial organisations where a person associated with the commercial organisation bribes another person (where the associated person commits an offence under ss 1 or 6) intending to obtain or retain either business or an advantage in the conduct of business, save where the commercial organisation can prove that it had in place adequate procedures designed to prevent bribery.

10.67 It is to be noted that the offence under s 6 does not require improper performance on the part of the person being bribed. Bribing relates simply to whether the official concerned is entitled to receive the payment made and is not measured against how he or she proposes to discharge any obligation; not being entitled (by way of local written law) to receive the payment in the first place is enough.

10.68 Section 8 determines who (or what) an 'associated person' is for the purposes of s 7. The definition is as broad as it could be. It is a person who performs services for or on behalf of the UK company. The capacity in which the person performs those services does not matter; the 'person' who performs those services can be an employee, agent, or subsidiary.

10.69 Subsidiary as a concept may be problematic, as there are a number of investment structures available for companies which may or may not fall within the description 'subsidiary'. How these arrangements will inform a court examining the relationship between a corrupt entity and a defendant company remains to be seen.

10.70 The significance of this new broad definition will be better understood against the background of the case of BAE Systems plc[1]. In the aftermath of the case, BAE Systems ('the Company') was at pains to stress that that the case concerned activity which took place over a decade prior to the sentencing date; since then it had systematically enhanced its compliance policies and processes with a view to ensuring that it is as widely recognised for responsible conduct as it is for high quality services and advanced technologies[1]. That assertion is gladly repeated to put what occurred in its proper historical context.

[1]   *R v BAE Systems plc* (21 December 2010, unreported).

¹   See press release, 21 December 2010.

10.71 The case involved the Company pleading guilty in the magistrates' court to an offence under the Companies Act 1985, s 221. The Company was then committed to the Crown Court for sentence. The offence itself and the basis for the Company's guilt had been agreed by reference to a 'settlement agreement' between the Company and the SFO before the matter even reached court, and was the subject of considerable debate before the sentencing judge in the Crown Court and adverse comment in the judge's sentencing remarks. The SFO's press release following the conclusion of the case made no reference to that adverse comment.

10.72 The settlement agreement included the proposition that £30m would be paid to the government of Tanzania in a matter to be agreed by the SFO. Further, the Company and the SFO agreed and that 'there shall be no further prosecutions of any member of the BAE Systems Group for any conduct preceding 5th February 2010'. This latter undertaking by the SFO was to include, as the judge observed, conduct that it (the SFO) either knew of or, perhaps more surprisingly, did not know of¹. 'Conduct' did not attract its own definition and so one can only guess at the degree of immunity that has been agreed by the SFO in relation to members of the BAE Systems Group.

¹   It is perhaps interesting to note that in parallel with the SFO's prosecution of BAE Systems plc, the United States Department of Justice took a similar line but only agreed not to prosecute for past offences that had been disclosed to it at the time the agreement was reached. Conversely, the SFO agreed not to prosecute offences prior to the relevant date, whether it was aware of them or not.

10.73 In any event, the basis of plea for the offence was, in terms, that;

In September 1999 a new contract for the sale of a radar system to the government of Tanzania was agreed with British Aerospace Defence Systems Ltd at a price of £39.97m.

From the outset of negotiations Siemens Plessey Electronic Systems Ltd (originally negotiating the sale) had retained the services of a named third-party marketing adviser to assist with negotiations and the sale process. The Company acquired Siemens Plessey in spring 1998 and also engaged the same named third party as a marketing adviser. From October 1999 there was a written agreement between two other companies controlled by BAE plc and two companies controlled by the named third party whereby the latter two companies were to receive a total of 31% of the radar system contract sale price.

Once the contract had been signed, payments of approximately £12.4 million were made to the named third party's companies. BAE plc chose to make those payments from another company controlled by it and registered in the British Virgin Islands. The payments were recorded in the Company's accounting records as payments for the provision of technical services by the named third party.

Although it was not alleged that the Company was party to an agreement to corrupt, it was agreed that there was a high probability that part of the £12.4m would be used in the negotiation process to favour British Aerospace Defence Systems Ltd.

The payments were not subjected to proper or adequate scrutiny or review and the Company maintained inadequate information to determine the value for money offered by the named third party and entities controlled by him. The failure to record the services accurately (ie to refer to them as 'for technical services') was the result of a deliberate decision by one or more officers of British Aerospace Defence Systems Ltd. This default was described in the basis of plea as 'inexcusable'.

It was not known at the Company who was responsible for creating the relevant inaccurate accounting records (which, on the SFO's case should have been referred to as 'provision of public relations and marketing services') but it was known by the Company that such inaccurate accounting records were in existence and it failed to scrutinise them adequately to ensure that they were reasonably accurate and permitted them to remain uncorrected. Thus the company was guilty of failing to keeping accounting records 'sufficient to show and explain the transactions of the company' contrary to the Companies Act 1985, s 221.

10.74 The purpose of setting out the above is not to criticise BAE Systems plc or indeed the SFO. No doubt there were any number of legitimate public policy reasons for reaching an agreement to bring vastly expensive criminal investigations and litigation to a conclusion. The complex criminal law that pre-dated the Bribery Act 2010 was almost certainly a factor in agreeing that an accounting offence would meet what was perceived by the parties to be the justice of the case. The fact that the SFO could not prove or demonstrate what happened to the £12.4m paid to the named third party would also have presented some evidential problems.

It does, however, serve as a useful example of how the Bribery Act 2010, in replacing the old law, might operate if, as an illustration only, the matters complained of occurred after the commencement of the Bribery Act 2010.

10.75 As has been pointed out, by the time the case came to court it was not possible to establish precisely what the named third party had done with the money that was paid to him[1]. Neither was it possible, it would seem, to infer from the evidence that the named third party had actually behaved inappropriately. It is suggested that this position may not be the same in every case. There may be circumstances in which a bribe offence under the Bribery Act 2010, s 1 or payment to a foreign official (s 6) may be inferred by the surrounding evidence but it would not be straightforward.

[1] The judge did describe the notion that the third party was simply 'a well paid lobbyist' as 'naive in the extreme'.

10.76 However, if it could be proved by direct evidence or inferred that, at the very least, the named third party had, transferred money to a public official of Tanzania in circumstances whereby that official was not entitled to receive payment as a result of local written law, the matter would be different under the new law:

— the named third party and/or the companies to which payment was actually made was/were plainly 'associated persons' for the purposes of s 7;

— it might not have been difficult to establish that an offence under the Bribery Act 2010, s 6 had been committed by reference to an intention to obtain or retain either business or an advantage in the conduct of business; the company admitted as part of its basis of plea that there was a 'high probability that part of the £12.4 million would be used in the negotiation process to favour British Aerospace Defence Systems Ltd'.

10.77 As the judge found, the company were concealing from the auditors and the public the fact that they were making payments to the named third party, 97% of it via off-shore companies. The company intended that the named third party should have free rein to make such payments to such people as he thought fit in order to secure the radar contract for the company, but it did not want to know the details.

Lord Nelson's famous application of a telescope to his blind eye at the battle of Copenhagen in 1801 would not avail the company. If an offence under either s 1 or 6 of the Bribery Act 2010 was complete, the burden of establishing that it had 'adequate procedures' to prevent bribery would befall the company.

10.78 Although, of course, the case set out above did not address this issue, it was accepted in the basis of plea that the company did not subject payments made to the named third party to scrutiny or review. Moreover, it maintained inadequate information to determine the value for money offered by the named third party and entities controlled by him. One might imagine therefore, that it be extremely difficult, if not impossible, for the Company to discharge the burden of proof that it had any, let alone adequate, procedures in place to prevent bribery taking place.

Thus it may be that the Bribery Act 2010 improves the ability of enforcement agencies to deal with events occurring largely abroad.

10.79 As to the resolution that had been reached with BAE Systems plc, Richard Alderman, Director of the SFO addressed a Corporate Investigations Seminar (long before the matter came to court but after agreement had been reached) on 16 February 2010 and had this to say:

'I do not think that I could conclude this speech at this particular time without offering a few thoughts on the very recent BAE outcome. This has rightly given rise to much interest and much discussion. People feel very passionately about these issues and rightly so. This is not the end of the process because BAE will be standing trial before the Crown Court on the issue relating to Tanzania and will be pleading guilty. As in any other guilty plea, counsel will be explaining the facts to the judge and counsel for the company will enter a plea in mitigation. I am sure that there will be much interest in the hearing.
Let me though just offer you a few thoughts about what has happened.
First, this was very much a team effort by the Department of Justice in the US and the SFO in order to produce a global settlement. We worked very hard with the DOJ over a period of many months over this. The overall settlement of some £286 million was achieved as a result of the joint efforts of the DOJ and the SFO. The SFO could not have achieved this without the DOJ and the DOJ have acknowledged publicly and privately that they could not have achieved this result without the involvement of the SFO. The first lesson is therefore that the DOJ and the SFO work very well together.
The second lesson is that global settlements can be achieved. This is the first time that we have been able to achieve anything of this nature. In doing so we had to

address very many legal issues about the US system, the UK system and how those systems relate to each other. Nevertheless, innovative solutions can be found to these problems as a result of the skill and ingenuity of the many excellent people in DOJ and the SFO.

The last lesson is a simple one. If we think we are right, we do not give up. There are many who thought that the SFO investigation would come to nothing either because we were unable to find evidence or because of a lack of will and commitment on the part of the SFO to continuing with such a high profile case. Those who said that were wrong. Clearly there were moments when I had anxious thoughts about the investigation but I continued to take the view that what we were doing was right. This means that both I and the SFO will continue to pursue cases when we think it right to do so but that we are always open to appropriate solutions. I believe that what happened in BAE has demonstrated that'.

10.80–10.81 As to the future, in the same speech, Mr Alderman also addressed the issue of enforcement in terms that some might find surprising. Dealing with the SFO's approach to what was then the Bribery Bill, he said:

'Let me put this in context. You will all know that there are very good commercial opportunities in countries where governance, security and corruption are systemic issues. These countries have a very low score on the rating scales published by various organisations. Doing business in these countries presents very different issues to doing business in more developed countries. But the future may well lie in doing business with those countries.

For me, there are certain guiding principles here:

- I do not want the SFO to be seen in any way as an obstacle to legitimate and ethical corporate activity;
- I also believe very strongly that if our ethical corporates go and do business in these countries, then the overall standard in that country ought to improve to the benefit of ordinary members of society in those countries;
- A number of these countries will be applying for financial assistance from global institutions. Increasingly, that aid is tied to real change on governance. The SFO has been asked on occasions to help with this by going to countries and doing reviews. We are also frequently asked for our views on these countries generally by international institutions. There can be a real incentive to countries to improve if they need international aid;
- While we cannot compromise overall ethical standards, there needs to be considerable sensitivity as to how those standards play out in those jurisdictions.

And so, what does this mean? Let me give you an example. I was approached by the Board of a corporate that is involved in one of these countries. They had a 100% subsidiary. This was becoming very profitable and so they received an approach from the government. They were told that if they wanted to continue to do business in the country then they would need to transfer a 51% interest in the subsidiary to the family of the president. That gave rise to all sorts of worries for them for obvious reasons. One of these was whether or not the SFO would take the view that payment in this way was a bribe. They were concerned we might investigate and prosecute. I assured them that I would have no intention of doing that whatsoever. I said I recognised the very great difficulty of the moral and ethical position that they were in. This was something they would have to resolve. What I could do though was to give them comfort that whatever they did, we would be sensitive to the circumstances here and would not seek to take any action, even if technically the transfer of the interest in the subsidiary constituted a bribe. They found that very helpful'.

10.82 It is not easy to see how the scenario described would not involve an offence of bribing a foreign official in one form or another unless of course the fiction was also to include a local law designed specifically to allow for the sham transfer. However, even if there were some basis upon which one might argue that an offence under the Bribery Act 2010 had not been committed, it is difficult to see how the sort of arrangement being discussed would not be in breach of the spirit of the legislation. It is not therefore possible to predict how enforcement will unfold: only time will tell. Even alongside other public pronouncements that the SFO have given on these issues, it is not obvious how this approach could be consistent with a policy of zero-tolerance in relation to bribery and corruption.

10.83 The Bribery Act 2010 represents something new and far-reaching in the armoury of enforcement agencies against international corruption, particularly in the defence and extractive industries. The extent to which it is used remains to be seen.

Defence offsets

10.84 As has already been observed, whilst the extraction industry has the EITI, there is no equivalent in the defence industry. As explained below, the nature of offset practice renders the sector particularly vulnerable to corruption and bribery. All of the observations made about the scope of the Bribery Act 2010 in relation to activity abroad apply. The purpose of this section is to illustrate how it is that defence offsets in particular are tolerated but how they also render participants, particularly in terms of supplying companies, vulnerable to strict liability offences under the Bribery Act 2010, s 7.

10.85 Offsets are defined by the World Trade Organisation's Agreement on Government Procurement as:

> 'measures used to encourage local government or improve the balance of payments accounts by means of domestic content, licensing of technology, investment requirements, counter-trade or similar requirements'.

10.86 An offset works on the basis that an importing country (purchasing equipment and/or services from a supplier) demand an offset package along with it. The offset package will usually involve the provision of socio-economic and/or technological advantage to the importing country, but may have little or nothing to do with the subject matter of the contract.

10.87 Conversely the supplier of the equipment and/or services will also become obliged to fulfil the offset obligations but, in order to reduce the costs of so doing can, and often do, engage the services of other individuals and organisations to complete the offset programme. Third parties thus become involved as brokers, consultants and providers.

10.88 Within the importing country offsets can be used to develop economic policy, but the growth generated by them risks being regarded as unsustainable and therefore contrary to long-term economic advantage. Once the offset provider withdraws, its obligations being regarded as complete, the advantages created by the original offset package may not be capable of being maintained. The principal difficulty in the context of corruption and bribery, however, is that offset arrangements can be more lucrative than similar competitive activities within the importing country, as they may involve significant subsidy by the offset provider and/or importing country. Meanwhile, the offset provider is likely to want its obligations discharged as quickly as possible, encouraging as much sub-contracting locally as allows for an early departure from the commitment. The attraction of such contracts is obvious and the potential for corruption on both sides equally so.

10.89 Offsets can also be deployed by an importing country to facilitate the supply of capital intensive industry to its infrastructure. Developing countries may well struggle, in the normal course of business, to attract investment in industry, which is capital-intensive and requires high levels of technology. If the opportunity to enhance such investment through an offset to a defence contract presents itself, but is not taken, the opportunity may otherwise only rarely present itself.

10.90 However, this sort of investment is highly prone to corruption because capital-intensive investment is less likely to be detected than labour-intensive projects. If they involve infrastructure, they tend to be 'long lasting, technical, difficult to comprehend and, in the absence of specialist knowledge, have a limited number of actors who can be party to them'[1]. It is further thought that if this type of project is undertaken as part of an offset rather than substantive procurement procedure, it will fall under the radar of such anti-corruption elements as exist in large-scale public contracting initiatives. This is particularly so when there are a number of different agencies involved in the process which may make it more difficult to follow negotiations, particularly as offset agreements tend to be made away from the main contractual event (although financially still highly significant) on a discretionary basis with 'little commitment to management evaluation, audit, or completion'[2].

[1]   Transparency International Report April 2010 Defence Offsets 'Addressing the Risks of Corruption and Raising Transparency' p 16, para 2.
[2]   Transparency International Report April 2010 p 16, para 3.

10.91 Despite the role which offsets play in international defence contracts, they are in fact prohibited under the World Trade Organisation's Agreement on Government Procurement. There are, however, exceptions to the prohibition. Developing countries signing up to the agreement can negotiate offsets in the qualification phase of tendering as long as they are not considered as part of the award criteria. In addition, a government can assert a need to protect security interests and thus exclude its procurement processes (and therefore offsets) from the scope of the agreement[1].

[1]   Agreement on Government Procurement, articles XVI and XXIII.

10.92 The European Union also has a framework of regulation in relation to offsets. As with the WTO Agreement on Government Procurement, the starting point is that they are prohibited[1] but there are exemptions. Whilst the EU regulations are more specifically targeted at anti-competitive behaviour within the single market, they increase, perhaps collaterally, transparency and therefore reduce the risk of corruption.

[1]   EU Directives 2004/17/EC and 2004/18/EC.

10.93 Pursuant to Article 346 of the Treaty for the Functioning on the European Union 2008[1]:

'any Member State may take such measures as it considers necessary for the protection of the essential interests of its security which are connected with the production of or trade in arms, munitions and war material; such measures shall not adversely affect the conditions of competition in the internal market regarding products which are not intended for specifically military purposes'.

1   Formerly known as Article 296 under the previous legislation.

10.94 Directive 2009/81/EC is intended to secure respect of the basis provisions of the treaty in the specific field of defence and sensitive security procurement with the overriding principle that 'contracting authorities/entities shall treat economic operators equally and in a non-discriminatory manner and shall act in a transparent way.' Thus, subject to Article 346, a Member State or entity may not require a tenderer to:

—   purchase goods or services from economic operators located in a specific member state;
—   award sub-contracts to operators located in a specific member state;
—   make investments in a specific member state;
—   generate value on the territory of a specific member state.

10.95 The EU does not therefore favour offsets which provide for a 'civil' offset obligation; this would be an offset obligation which does not involve military equipment or services. They are considered to be anti-competitive in relation to other potential suppliers of the offset subject matter and difficult to justify on the basis of national security. Neither does the EU regard the offset as being appropriately part of the award criteria.

10.96 This is not the work in which to analyse the apparatus of this issue in detail but it is up to the member state concerned to prove that it is necessary to contract the offset to protect its necessary security interests. In the event of a dispute on the issue, the matter can be referred to the European Court of Justice for resolution. The EU regulatory framework in relation to offsets appears to have some teeth. An example at the time of writing is one in relation to Greece. Under IP/10/1558 Greece is likely to be referred to the European Court of Justice in relation to a tendering process that it launched in 2009. The Greek government sought tenders for the supply of six submarine battery kits worth a total of £22m. The call for tenders required 35% of the material used for the batteries to be produced in Greece, this offset being justified on the basis of national security interests.

10.97 The EU's current position is that Greece, as a member state, cannot deviate from standard public procurement rules on a discretionary basis with procuring military equipment. Thus far, say the Commission, Greece has failed to justify this offset in terms of danger to its national security interests, therefore rendering the requirement to use Greek companies discriminatory as regards other potential suppliers.

10.98 Presumably the Greek government will seek to justify this offset, at least in part, on the basis that the internal workings of their submarines are relevant to national security but why that should affect the supply of materials for the purpose of the manufacture of the battery sets concerned is not immediately apparent.

10.99 Thus it is that the existing regulatory framework within the EU, albeit focusing on anti-competitive breaches of free market principles, forces transparency and the need for justification. Whilst not specifically alleging that offsets are corrupt or that they should be equated with bribery, they can be correctly characterised as in a grey area, which needs to be very carefully monitored and open to public scrutiny.

Extractive industry

10.100 The purpose of this section on the extractive industry is to focus on current developments rather than go through an analysis of the Bribery Act 2010 specifically. In reality the references herein to the BAE Systems plc case, concluded in December 2010, could just as easily have been a case relating to an extractive industry contract as defence. The observations about the jurisdiction and reach of the Bribery Act 2010 similarly apply.

10.101 Unlike the defence industry, the extractive industry has a global unifying organisation which aims to increase transparency in the extractive industry and thereby root out bribery and corruption. No doubt the scale of the revenues being generated in developing nations sitting alongside the poverty that those revenues have passed by provided some incentive. The fact that so many developing or under-developed nations are rich in mineral resources but seem unable to convert the potential wealth into increased standards of living for their people, has led to the development of the concept of the 'resource curse'. In short, issues of corruption and poor governance seem to be created by the existence of the natural resources.

10.102 To illustrate the point, nearly $30 billion flowed illicitly out of oil-rich Nigeria in 2009, according to calculations provided exclusively to Reuters by Global Financial Integrity ('GFI'), an advocacy group that monitors the market. That sum is part of a much wider stream of illicit money being channelled from resource-rich countries in the developing world to banks and tax havens elsewhere. In a report in 2010, GFI estimated that Africa alone lost $854 billion in illicit flows from 1970 to 2008.

10.103 The Extractive Industries Transparency Initiative ('EITI') was announced by former British Prime Minister Tony Blair in 2002 at the World Summit for Sustainable Development in Johannesburg. It came about partly because of a relationship between BP and the government of Angola, whereby the former came under pressure to explain its dealings with the latter and, eventually, did so. The government of Angola was not particularly impressed by the disclosure and as a consequence BP made it clear that unilateral disclosure in circumstances such as those was highly undesirable. Thus it was that EITI was announced in 2002, entered a pilot phase in January 2003 and today has its home in Helsinki. The former Westminster MP Clare Short was proposed as its new Chair and elected in March 2011.

10.104 'Social and barter payments' are the first cousins of defence offsets. A key challenge for EITI is that these payments would not generally be reflected in government receipts since they were often paid to third parties and so could complicate the reconciliation process, thus compromising transparency in a way that the EITI is trying to avoid. The concerns they raise are similar to those set out in relation to defence offsets.

10.105 EITI has at its core the following principles which must be applied by states which have achieved audited validation:

(1)   regular publication of all material oil, gas and mining payments by companies to governments ('payments') and all material revenues received by governments from oil, gas and mining companies ('revenues') to a wide audience in a publicly accessible, comprehensive and comprehensible manner;

(2)   where such audits do not already exist, payments and revenues are the subject of a credible, independent audit, applying international auditing standards;

(3)   payments and revenues are reconciled by a credible, independent administrator, applying international auditing standards and with publication of the administrator's opinion regarding that reconciliation including discrepancies, should any be identified;

(4)   this approach is extended to all companies, including state-owned enterprises;

(5)   civil society is actively engaged as a participant in the design, monitoring and evaluation of this process and contributes towards public debate;

(6)   a public, financially sustainable work plan for all the above is developed by the host government, with assistance from the international institutions where required, including measurable targets, a timetable for implementation, and an assessment of potential capacity constraints.

10.106 The process of validation requires a country to register as a 'candidate', having met certain bench-mark criteria, and then to move through the process of validation when, if successful, it will then be regarded as 'compliant'. The process between candidacy and compliance is extensive and has at its core a system of transparency and audit of payments to governments alongside publicity and review. A candidate nation has two years to complete the process but can apply for an extension. Validation can only be awarded after a report by an independent validator and approval by the EITI International Board.

10.107 Only Norway, of the European industrial nations, is a candidate. So far only Azerbaijan, Liberia, Ghana, Mongolia and Timor-Leste are compliant and have been awarded validation; 27 developing nations are currently engaged in the process as candidates. Conversely, the UK government is not a candidate but joins a list of almost all European industrial nations and the United States of America as a 'supporter'. Whilst the UK government has in the past justified no longer being resource rich enough to justify the process, the United States position is more complicated as to which see para **10.110**.

10.108 Angola has shown no interest. The increased relationship between Angola and China is causing some to be concerned, as China does not appear to regard governance as a pre-requisite for economic involvement largely because China champions non-interference in its own domestic political affairs. It has to be said, however, that the worst excesses of corruption in the Angolan extractive industry took place whilst the west and western companies were investing in that troubled country and before China began expanding its trading influence in Africa. China has expressed its support for the EITI in several international fora, notably supporting the UN General Assembly Resolution, which emphasises that transparency should be promoted by all member states, and the G20 Pittsburgh declaration that supported participation in the EITI. It also has a form of internal guidelines for extraction companies on the reporting of activities. Chinese companies have reported under the EITI framework in countries such as Gabon, Kazakhstan, Mongolia and Nigeria but it is clear from public statements that the EITI is encouraging increased Chinese involvement, especially as China's unparalleled economic expansion has made it the second largest world commodities consumer.

10.109 Meanwhile, the EITI encourages companies involved in the extractive industry to become supporters so that both sides of a negotiated contract are approaching the issues on a level playing field. Nearly 50 of the world's largest oil, gas and mining companies support and participate in the EITI process and are encouraged to complete an international level self-assessment form which, if brief (a grand total of five questions are asked), requires a commitment to a clear public statement endorsing the EITI principles and criteria and the identification of an individual within the corporate structure responsible for the lead in communicating the company's policy and dealing with relevant issues. Most, if not all, of the big names in oil and gas are on the list of supporters and most have completed a self-assessment form.

The Cardin Luger amendment to the Dodd-Frank Act and beyond

10.110 If the UK government can justify non-candidacy of the EITI on the basis of not being resourse-rich enough to take part in the process, it is difficult to see how the United States, as a vast commodity consumer and producer, could take the same line. As has already been pointed out, the USA is a supporter of the EITI and not a candidate and not therefore compliant; it is, however, one of a limited number of governments that provides details of its extractive contracts in full.

10.111 Much to the horror of its domestic extractive industry, however, and unilaterally in comparison to the international community not otherwise members of the EITI, section 1504 of the Dodd-Frank Wall Street Reform and Consumer Protection Act was inserted by way of amendment on the sponsorship of Senators Cardin and Luger. Right at the end of a torrent of financial services reforms (the Act runs to 848 pages and has 1506 sections) is to be found section 1504, added by way of amendment in July 2010. Following definitions and a preamble, the substance of the section is as follows:

'(2) Disclosure.—
(A) Information required—Not later than 270 days after the date of enactment of the Dodd-Frank Wall Street Reform and Consumer Protection Act, the Commission shall issue final rules that require each resource extraction issuer to include in an annual report of the resource extraction issuer information relating to any payment made by the resource extraction issuer, a subsidiary of the resource extraction issuer, or an entity under the control of the resource extraction issuer to a foreign government or the Federal Government for the purpose of the commercial development of oil, natural gas, or minerals, including—
(i) the type and total amount of such payments made for each project of the resource extraction issuer relating to the commercial development of oil, natural gas, or minerals; and
(ii) the type and total amount of such payments made to each government project of the resource extraction issuer relating to the commercial devel-

opment of oil, natural gas, or minerals; and
(iii)   the type and total amount of such payments made to each government'.

10.112 What is particularly interesting about this amendment is that on one basis it outstrips the EITI by some measure, in that it is the extractive industry companies that have to provide details of all payments they make in the course of their relevant extraction activities (widely defined). As a company supporter of the EITI, no such requirement exists over and above domestic accounting legislation. Howls of derision have followed and the phrase 'level playing field' or rather the opposite, has been deployed by the extraction giants with considerable enthusiasm. It goes without saying that the United States extractive industry is vast and contains some of the biggest names in world extraction.

10.113 Having lost the battle against the amendment being passed at all, all lobbying energy is now being expended by the extraction giants in the consultation process that will lead to the issue of the disclosure rules in the early summer of 2011. What regulations are introduced in that regard remains to be seen.

10.114 Meanwhile the EU launched a consultation on financial reporting on a country-by-country basis by multinational companies, contributions to which were due by 9 January 2011. The aim is to gather stakeholders' views on financial reporting on a country-by-country basis by multinational companies. Country-by-country reporting is a concept that would require multinational companies to disclose financial information on their operations in third countries in their annual financial statements.

10.115 The similarity between this consultation process and the Cardin Luger amendment is not difficult to spot, perhaps to the relief of corporate extractive America. If a similar plan is adopted, at least the playing field will be level between the supplying companies even if the challenges facing the developing resource-rich countries that need to contract with them still seem very considerable indeed.

C   CONSTRUCTION

Introduction

10.116 In 2006 the Chartered Institute of Building ('CIOB') undertook a survey on corruption within the UK construction industry. That survey found that 43% of respondents considered corruption to be common within the UK construction industry and that 41% of respondents had been offered a bribe on at least one occasion. The practice of providing non-cash incentives was considered to be prevalent, with gifts ranging from pens to all-expenses-paid holidays. Respondents felt that the point where an innocent gift became a bribe was not clear, particularly in the field of corporate entertainment, where a respondent described one situation where a free holiday was disguised as a 'site visit'. It is doubtful whether that dividing line has become any clearer with the introduction of the Bribery Act 2010.

10.117 The CIOB's survey respondents overwhelmingly considered that the government was not doing enough to combat corruption. The 2006 CIOB survey echoed the findings of a survey in the previous year undertaken by Transparency International; the earlier survey estimated that the cost of corruption in the UK could be as much as £3.75 billion each year.

10.118 The Bribe Payers' Index, produced by Transparency International in 2008, ranked the construction industry as the one in which firms were most likely to bribe public officials and to use contributions to politicians and political parties to achieve undue influence on government polices, laws or regulations.

Against that background, it is clear that the construction industry is likely to be the focus of intense scrutiny by the prosecuting authorities once the Bribery Act 2010 is in force.

10.119 Already, in 2008, Balfour Beatty paid £2.25m to settle allegations of 'payment irregularities' on a scheme in Egypt as part of a civil recovery order. In 2009 Mabey & Johnson was fined £6.6m after pleading guilty to bribing officials in Jamaica and Ghana. In the same year Amec agreed to pay a £5m fine for 'irregular payments' on a project in South Korea. Three of the recent SFO investigations concern the construction industry[1], including an investigation into Alstom in France and Switzerland; the sector needs to take the Bribery Act 2010 and its penalties very seriously, and needs to address the causes and culture of bribery with some of the remedies set out below.

[1] In the most recent case, the allegations were that inside information was being offered to companies bidding for contracts in high-value engineering projects. Some of the defendants were employed by the companies responsible for the procurement of these projects and are alleged to have passed confidential information to others, who then offered to provide it to companies bidding for the contracts in return for a percentage of the contract value. The aggregate value of the five contracts in question was £66m and the charges related to periods between 1 January 2001 and 31 August 2009 (SFO Press Release, 22 September 2010).

10.120 The construction industry is a sector which has a number of significant risk factors, factors which will become even more risky once the Bribery Act 2010 is in force. For example, unsurprisingly, large projects will often involve multiple parties with multiple contractual arrangements, operating in different countries and jurisdictions with heavy use of agents and other professionals together with extensive interaction between private corporations on the one hand and governments and public sector organisations on the other. Each of those different components provides a layer of supervisory and regulatory risk which, given the strict liability regime provided in s 7, will place a significant burden on an employer to ensure it has in place adequate procedures which will satisfy the statutory defence to the corporate offence

The causes

10.121 Why then is the construction industry a particularly high risk sector? The answer lies in a number of areas: a 2010 PriceWaterhouseCoopers survey of 226 construction companies in 43 countries found that almost a third of respondents think that 'a belief that competitors are paying bribes in order to win contracts' was a reason for bribery occurring. Further, the nature of many construction projects is that they are one-offs, large-scale and involve very significant amounts of money, which means the stakes are high and the rewards great for the successful tenderer.

10.122 The motivation can vary from a voluntary decision, for instance a deliberate act to gain a competitive advantage, to levelling the playing field as everyone is offering a bribe in order to secure some advantage (or to retain business), to facilitation payments, which might sometimes be viewed, in the extreme, as situations more akin to extortion.

10.123 The nature of a construction project lends itself to corruption: the number of people involved; the one-off nature of many projects and the sizeable sums involved each make it more difficult for a company to keep control of its employees, agents and partners down the chain. The nature of many construction projects, which may involve a large number of cross-border transactions of one kind or another, also makes it difficult to prevent and detect bribery. There are a number of factors which militate towards bribery as detailed below:

— contractual structure: there are often a large number of separate parties linked into a complex contractual structure. For example, the owner of the project will contract with a main contractor who in turn will sub-contract work to various specialist companies who themselves in turn will sub-contract. There will also be suppliers of labour, equipment and materials. Each will have a contractual relationship with the person immediately above and below in the chain and, depending on the type and form of contracts used, a relationship with those higher up the chain too. Each contractual relationship provides an opportunity for bribery—to get the contract, for excess payment, for expeditious payment, for certifying defective work, for certifying excessive work, certifying extensions of time and so on;

— skill diversity: many different trades, skills and professions are employed within the industry. This leads to differing expectations and standards of oversight, monitoring and integrity and different professional codes of conduct and responsibilities;

— project phases: projects normally have different phases each with its own management team, each with its own degree of control and monitoring. In addition, projects are often complex (at least logistically), and it can be complicated to untangle or distinguish the relationships between those involved, and particularly the responsibility of one party to another, and for what. As the project shifts from one phase to the next, the need to make a handover can be a temptation to certify work even if incomplete or defective. Defective work can be hidden as the project progresses as work is covered and hidden by later components of the build;

— magnitude: construction projects can be massive in terms of scale and expense, which engenders a greater ability to hide corrupt payments. Further, it can be difficult to make like-for-like cost comparisons as there is such a variety of project in terms of type, size and location. There is little transparency in construction where commercial confidentiality takes precedence;

— government involvement: the sheer scale of involvement of governments and other public authorities around the world in construction projects is immense. That brings with it the involvement of government and public officials whose power to commission projects, grant licences and permissions is equally immense. The potential for bribery is axiomatic.

10.124 What has been industry 'standard practice', or the fact that a competitor is engaged in a particular practice, is not a defence to the corporate offence under the Bribery Act 2010. What in the past might have been usual custom and practice may now be an unacceptable corporate risk. Even where foreign practice means that payments and gifts to foreign officials are permitted under local laws, it is essential that those local laws are written down: mere tolerance towards 'gifts' on the part of foreign public officials will not constitute a valid defence under the Bribery Act 2010.

10.125 The Bribery Act 2010 catches not only the actions of employees and those directly involved with the company, but also 'associated persons' which could include an agent, a joint venture party, a professional engaged to assist a tender or a substantive project. Local agents and intermediaries add further to the chain of risks which UK companies face when attempting to ensure that all elements of the winning and execution of a contract are free from bribery, or conduct which may amount to bribery within the scope of the Bribery Act 2010.

10.126 Projects are often undertaken in emerging and high-growth markets in which government payments and bribes may be more prevalent, encouraged and/or tolerated. The territorial scope of the Bribery Act 2010 is such that the conduct of employees and agents anywhere in the world may render a company liable under the Bribery Act 2010, s 7, since the offence is committed irrespective of where the acts or omissions which form part of the offence take place.

Solutions

10.127 What then are companies working in the construction industry to do so as to best protect themselves from prosecution?

As explained in Chapter 4, companies and their officers are vulnerable to prosecution under the Bribery Act 2010, s 7 for failing to prevent bribery. This is a strict liability offence. There is one defence: that of showing that the company had in place 'adequate procedures' to prevent bribery. 'Adequate procedures' is dealt with in detail in Chapter 6. Further guidance on gifts, hospitality, political and charitable donations and facilitation payments can be found in Chapter 5.

10.128 In brief, there are a number of principal areas which companies should review now:

— review and amend where necessary existing internal policies dealing with charitable giving; giving and receiving corporate hospitality and gifts; accounting, finance and procurement; lobbying and political contributions; keep records of hospitality given and received;

—   prepare and disseminate specific anti-bribery policies and introduce 'adequate procedures';

—   determine who is being dealt with from the board to the people 'on the ground' (supply chain management). Identify where money changes hands and, if this is through an intermediary, undertake due diligence checks to ensure that the process and the people are adhering to the company's policies;

—   undertake adequate due diligence on joint venture partners: check their codes of conduct, and those of any other intermediaries or professionals involved in procurement;

—   train staff, compliance officers, senior corporate officers and ensure that the board has adequate information to enable it to assess the risks facing the company globally and in respect of specific projects;

—   institute whistleblowing, investigation and self-reporting procedures for suspected breaches (whistleblowing is discussed at para **10.24**);

—   prepare and disseminate disciplinary procedures, remedies and punishments (employment issues are discussed at para **10.2**).

Internal policies

10.129 The SFO has stated that it will be looking at a number of factors when considering whether companies' anti-bribery procedures are adequate. There must be a clear statement of anti-corruption culture emanating from board level and disseminated and maintained through all levels of management to front-line staff.

10.130 A code of ethics and a transparent auditing trail will be essential for all potentially high-risk work. Accountability, a system of reporting and investigation and disciplinary process are all likely to be necessary to protect a company from the actions of 'associated persons' throughout the procurement and production phases of projects.

10.131 Companies which have no written policies on the giving and receiving of gifts and hospitality will be vulnerable to criticism, and potentially prosecution in the event that conduct which forms part of an offence is discovered. A policy on political and charitable giving is likely to be important and, in the absence of any official guidance from the government, the recommendations made by the SFO should clearly be complied with so far as possible.

10.132 Such policies need to be kept up-to-date and need to be in place across all group companies wherever they are based. It may also be necessary to amend or adjust those policies to take account of local laws where necessary. English law may not be applicable to group companies outside the UK, albeit that the provisions of the Bribery Act 2010 have global reach.

Auditing, training and risk management

10.133 Large companies may consider it worthwhile to appoint anti-bribery compliance officers who can manage and co-ordinate the finance, accounting and procurement procedures; establish the credentials of third party suppliers and vendors so as to ensure that those third parties also have in place adequate procedures and training for their staff so as to avoid activities which could be caught by the Bribery Act 2010, and, in the event that illegal activity is discovered thereafter, to ensure that the statutory defence is available to the company.

10.134 Small and medium-sized enterprises ('SMEs') face a number of challenges with regard to the Bribery Act 2010. On the one hand, they may be less likely to be involved in the larger-value and geographically-diverse projects which may engender behaviour prohibited by the Bribery Act. On the other, the costs of ensuring that they have adequate procedures in place, and their ability to undertake due-diligence on joint venture or sub-contracting parties may be prohibitive. There is no exemption or lenience given to SMEs under the Bribery Act 2010 and it is to be hoped that the implementation of the Act will take account of the increased burden on smaller companies to ensure that they have adequate procedures in place.

10.135 It should be remembered that what is an adequate procedure will vary depending on the size and complexity of the business and the work under-taken, which perhaps will provide some solace at least for SMEs faced with this further necessary administrative and cultural process.

10.136 All companies will need to incorporate the provisions of the Bribery Act 2010 into their compliance and risk assessment and monitoring regimes. Once the systems are in place and running it will probably be best practice to audit the procedures to ensure that they are fit for purpose, working and being put into practice by staff and all 'associated persons'.

PACS *(Project Anti-Corruption Systems)*

10.137 It is likely that prosecutors, when deciding whether to charge an individual or company with criminal offences under the Bribery Act 2010, and juries, when making factual decisions during a trial for a Bribery Act offence, will look to specific guidance and measures produced to assist the construction industry and assess the adequacy of any step taken to prevent bribery. As explained in Chapter 6, there is no 'one size fits all' adequate procedures package and measures will have to be sector specific. Both Transparency International ('TI') and Global Infrastructure Anti-Corruption Centre ('GIACC') have produced reports and guidance on preventing corruption in construction projects.

10.138 The TI reports and business tools are contained in separate documents to assist project owners, project funders, construction and engineering companies and consulting engineers all of whom face different problems and pressures. TI-UK and GIAAC have produced joint publications including an Anti-Corruption Training Manual designed specifically for the infrastructure, construction and engineering sectors. They have also produced the PACS Standards and PACS Templates which are explored below.

10.139 In outline the 12 PACS Standards (reproduced from the PACS Standard 1 Package) are:

(1)   Independent assessment: an independent assessor should be appointed whose duty is, for the duration of the project, to monitor and assess the project for corruption and make appropriate reports. In the case of a

large and complex project, an independent assessor may be appointed specifically for that project. For smaller projects, an independent assessor may be appointed to monitor a number of projects.

(2)   Transparency: the government or project owner should disclose project information to the public on a website on a regular basis and in an easily accessible and comprehensible form.

(3)   Procurement: the project owner should implement fair and transparent procurement procedures which do not provide an improper benefit or advantage to any individual or organisation.

(4)   Pre-contract disclosure: at tender stage, the project owner and each tenderer for a major contract should provide each other with relevant information which could reveal a risk of corruption (for example in relation to their principal shareholders, officers, financial status, agents, joint venture partners, major sub-contractors, criminal convictions and debarment). Each major contractor should do the same with each tenderer for its major sub-contracts.

(5)   Project anti-corruption commitments: the project owner and each major project participant should provide anti-corruption contractual commitments which expressly cover the main types of corruption, and which oblige them to implement anti-corruption measures. Remedies should be specified in the event of breach of these commitments.

(6)   Funder anti-corruption commitments: the project owner and each project funder (equity investor, bank or guarantor) should provide anti-corruption contractual commitments to each other which expressly cover the main types of corruption, and which oblige them to implement anti-corruption measures. Remedies should be specified in the event of breach of these commitments.

(7)   Government anti-corruption commitments: relevant government departments should take steps to minimise extortion by their officers in the issuing of permits, licences and approvals. They should appoint a senior officer to whom complaints of bribery and extortion can be made, and should publicise a list of fees and time-scales which apply to government procedures.

(8)   Raising awareness: major project participants should raise awareness among their staff of the damage and risks of corruption by:
—   posting up anti-corruption rules at all project and site offices;
—   providing anti-corruption training for relevant staff;
—   implementing a gifts and hospitality policy.

(9)   Compliance: major project participants should appoint a compliance manager who will take all reasonable steps to ensure compliance by the company and its management and staff with their anti-corruption commitments.

(10)   Audit: financial audits should be carried out to ensure as far as possible that all payments by the project owner have been properly made to legitimate organisations for legitimate services. Technical audits should be carried out to ensure as far as possible that the project design, specification and construction are in accordance with good technical practice and provide value for money. Auditors should be aware of the risk that any deficiencies they identify may be caused by corruption, and should make appropriate reports.

(11)   Reporting: safe and effective systems should be established by which corruption on the project can be reported by the public, by project staff, and by the independent assessor.

(12)   Enforcement: enforcement measures for breach of anti-corruption commitments should include civil enforcement (eg disqualification from tender, termination of contracts, damages and dismissal from employment). The risk of criminal enforcement (eg fines and imprisonment) should be highlighted.

10.140 Each PACS Standard is explored in much more detail within the guidance produced by TI-UK and GIACC and gives clear assistance for use when drafting policies and procedures. The Templates themselves provide further additional (and valuable) assistance. For example, Template 8 is a 40-page training manual. That itself contains worked examples of bribery and corruption at every stage of a project, enabling proactive training in order to work through actual instances of bribery.

Other issues

Procurement

10.141 Under the EU Public Sector and Utilities Procurement Directives, implemented in the UK by the Public Contracts Regulations 2006[1] and the Utilities Contracts Regulations 2006[2], public authorities must exclude from public contracts a company, its directors or 'any other person who has powers of representation, decision or control' over the company that has been convicted of (amongst other things) a corruption offence.

[1]   SI 2006/5.
[2]   SI 2006/6.

10.142 This mandatory exclusion is therefore likely to apply to any conviction under the Bribery Act 2010, ss 1, 2 or 6. A conviction under s 7—the failure of a commercial organisation to prevent bribery—may not be covered by the regulations, though there is plainly a significant risk that it too would apply, with the result that a company convicted of 'failing to prevent' bribery could be permanently excluded from government contracts across the whole EU.

Senior officers

10.143 It should be noted that the 'adequate procedures' defence available to a company prosecuted under s 7 does not apply to a senior officer of the company. Accordingly, any director who commits any act of bribery will have committed a criminal offence himself, as well as on behalf of the company.

D   THE BRIBERY ACT AND SPORT

10.144

'I think a serious effort should be made to educate and warn players—particularly before tours to the sub-continent—of the dangers posed by sports betting and gamblers. Most young professional cricket players have little experience of the hard realities of commerce and the gambling world. They are easy prey"[1].

[1] Witness statement of Hansie Cronje, former South African cricket captain, to the King Commission, 15 June 2000, para 69.

Introduction

10.145 Bribery is rumoured to be rife in sport, with allegations surrounding various aspects of the industry. In 2010 alone, there were high profile allegations against three Pakistani cricketers and a UK-based businessman, a world-ranked snooker player was arrested and questioned over allegations of match-fixing, and FIFA was the subject of an undercover newspaper report which alleged that members of its Executive Committee encouraged bribes when being lobbied for their vote over the destination of the 2018 and 2022 football World Cups (in the end two members of the Committee were suspended from all football-related activities, with one member having been found to be in breach of Rule 11 of FIFA's Code of Ethics, which is the Rule concerning bribery[1]). The Pakistani cricketers were committed to the Crown Court for trial in 2011, to answer charges brought under the Prevention of Corruption Act, and the Gambling Act (the trial had not been heard at the time of publication). Two further snooker players were questioned by police in 2009 over their knowledge of irregular betting patterns surrounding a match which they had contested, and in 2010 the three-time world snooker champion John Higgins was videoed by the News of the World apparently agreeing to deliberately lose frames in exchange for a sum of money (he was later cleared of this allegation).

[1] The member has stated his intention to appeal the finding.

10.146 Reaching further back into history, the award of the 2002 Winter Olympic Games to Salt Lake City created the largest scandal in the International Olympic Committee's history, with allegations of bribery resulting in the expulsion from the Committee of numerous members. And in 2000, the former South African cricket captain Hansie Cronje admitted taking money from businessmen in exchange for agreeing to influence the outcome of international cricket matches (Cronje later gave frank evidence to the Commission convened to examine the allegations, chaired by a South African judge, Justice King).

10.147 All of these allegations demonstrate how the sports industry provides a potentially fertile breeding ground for bribery. Two key features of the industry that create scope for suspicion are:

— bidding processes for the right to stage high-profile international sporting events; and
— the gambling activity that is parasitic upon most top-level sport.

10.148 The Bribery Act 2010 has potentially far-reaching ramifications as it arms UK prosecutors with wider powers, and enables them to look more closely at factual scenarios that may previously have been beyond their jurisdiction (most sport is competitively structured so as to incorporate both a domestic and an international arena, with the international arena usually involving the pinnacle of competition). For example, in 2000 the England cricket team were unwittingly embroiled in a Test Match in South Africa that had been 'fixed' (the 5th Test at Centurion Park). The consequence of the fix was that various legitimate gamblers in the UK would have attempted to forecast a result that was in fact impure. Despite this effect the UK authorities had no jurisdiction to enquire into matters, but under the new Act they would have such jurisdiction.

Football/bidding processes

10.149 In 2010, England bid for the right to stage the 2018 World Cup. What this meant in practice was that the Football Association ('the FA') submitted its bid to FIFA, of which it is a member. The FA had established 'England 2018' to submit its bid and run its candidacy. England 2018 is a private limited company, and would therefore be classified as a 'relevant commercial organisation' for the purpose of the Bribery Act 2010, s 7.

10.150 The vote of the FIFA Executive Committee determined the winning bid. In the autumn of 2009, England 2018 created headlines when it distributed £230 Mulberry handbags to the wives of each member of the FIFA Executive Committee. While there is no suggestion that the gifts were at that time improper in a criminal sense, they would potentially be caught by the Bribery Act 2010 (s 1(4) stating that the bribe does not have to be given to the person who is to perform the relevant activity).

10.151 As a result of the succeeding furore, one member of the FIFA Executive Committee returned the handbag, complaining of the 'untold embarrassment' and subsequent slur on his integrity that had been created by the gift. In his letter returning the handbag, the committee member also set out the background context of his trip to the UK. He had travelled with several fellow football administrators (and of course his wife). The committee member wrote:

> 'It was never my intention to place the burden of my accompanying officials on the shoulders of the Football Association and therefore, I paid for our air travel and was prepared to do the same for the accommodation and meals. After several refusals on the part of your FA official to allow me to pay for my accommodation and that of my accompanying officials I reluctantly conceded. In addition, and despite being offered a number of social courtesies, my team and I only acquiesced to a birthday dinner for my wife'.

10.152 England 2018 was extending corporate hospitality to the committee member (and his wife). It is clear from the committee member's letter that they paid for his accommodation and that of his accompanying officials, made other offers which were refused, and paid for a birthday dinner for his wife. In a letter on behalf of the then government (published in anticipation of the awaited statutory guidance), the government minister Lord Tunnicliffe stated that 'lavish' corporate hospitality would be caught by the Bribery Act 2010, but that it would be left to prosecutors to differentiate between legitimate and illegitimate hospitality[1]. The MOJ final guidance to the Act—published in March 2011—did not make matters much clearer. It stated, at para 20:

> ' . . . an invitation to foreign clients to attend a Six Nations Match at Twickenham as part of a public relations exercise to cement good relations or

enhance knowledge in the organisation's field is extremely unlikely to engage section 1 as there is unlikely to be evidence of an intention to induce improper performance of a relevant function'.

On the one hand, the trip could be said to be enhancing knowledge of the England 2018 bid. But on the other hand, if the hospitality were sufficiently lavish, it could be put forward as evidence of an attempt to induce the improper performance of the Committee member's function (his exercise of his vote).

[1] www.justice.gov.uk/publications/docs/letter-lord-henley-corporate-hospitality.pdf   'Bribery Bill, letter of Lord Tunnicliffe, 14 January 2010.

10.153 It is unclear how prosecutors will exercise the discretion apparently provided to them. If the facts of the visit were to occur again, would the prosecutors investigate the nature of the accommodation which was enjoyed by the committee member and his travelling party? Would they investigate the specifics of the birthday meal which England 2018 hosted for his wife? Its location, content, and value? The situation lacks certainty (for further guidance on corporate hospitality and gifts see Chapter 5).

10.154 In the hypothetical world of a prosecution, England 2018 would be forced to rely upon the corporate defence of having in place adequate procedures to prevent illegitimate activity (under s 7(2)).

10.155 It is likely that England 2018's procedures were those that they were asked to adopt by FIFA. Section 11 of the FIFA Code of Ethics contains five lines on the subject of bribery, with the Code being expanded upon by Chapter 11 of the further 'Rules of Conduct'. This is because FIFA requests that each Member Association, and its bidding entity, undertake to be bound by its Rules of Conduct as part of its bid registration, requesting that it:

> 'expressly agrees to be bound by, and to comply with, the FIFA Code of Ethics in its applicable form and the provisions, procedures, terms, rules and requirements outlined in this Bid Registration'[1].

[1] FIFA Bid Registration document: Chapter 11, Rules of Conduct, General Principles.

10.156 Chapter 11 of the Rules of Conduct is vague. Individuals are told, under a paragraph entitled 'ethical behaviour', to 'conduct any activities in relation to the bidding process in accordance with basic ethical principles such as integrity, responsibility, trustworthiness and fairness', and to refrain 'from attempting to influence members of the FIFA Executive Committee or any other FIFA officials, in particular by offering benefits for specific behaviour'. Such broad guidance sits uncomfortably with the best practice guidance previously published by organisations such as the Organisation for Economic Cooperation and Development (OECD)[1] and Transparency International[2] and with the six principles set out in the MOJ final guidance.

[1] Good Practice Guidance on Internal Controls, Ethics, and Compliance, at para 12 (OECD, 18 February 2010).
[2] Business Principles for Countering Bribery' (Transparency International) at 5.5.

10.157 With regard to the Mulberry handbags, the section of the rules concerning gifts states:

'Gifts

The Member Association and the Bid Committee shall refrain, and shall ensure that each entity or individual associated or affiliated with it shall refrain, from providing to FIFA or to any representative of FIFA, to any member of the FIFA Executive Committee, the FIFA Inspection Group, FIFA consultants, or any of their respective relatives, companion, guests or nominees

(i)   any monetary gifts;

(ii)   any kind of personal advantage that could give even the impression of exerting influence, or conflict of interest, either directly or indirectly, in connection with the Bidding Process, such as at the beginning of a collaboration, whether with private persons, a company or any authorities, except for occasional gifts that are generally regarded as having symbolic or incidental value and that exclude any influence on a decision in relation to the Bidding Process; and

(iii)   any benefit, opportunity, promise, remuneration or service to any of such individuals, in connection with the Bidding Process[1].

[1]   FIFA Bid Registration document: Chapter 11, Rules of Conduct, 'Gifts'.

10.158 The Guidance therefore warned bidding committees to refrain from providing to any member of the FIFA Executive Committee, or any of their respective relatives, companions, guests or nominees 'any benefit, opportunity, promise, remuneration or service to any of such individuals, in connection with the Bidding Process'[1]. It would seem arguable that paying for accommodation, and the provision of a birthday meal, are 'benefits' (see also Chapter 5).

[1]   FIFA Bid Registration document: Chapter 11, Rules of Conduct, 'Gifts' (iii).

10.159 It would therefore seem to be arguable that England 2018 was in breach of the very guidance it had adopted. In fairness it must be pointed out that the allegations surrounding the bidding process suggested that such activity was considered standard practice by most bidding entities.

10.160 In the event the England 2018 bid was unsuccessful and the FIFA Executive Committee awarded the 2018 World Cup to Russia (and the 2022 World Cup to Qatar). Prior to the decision, an undercover piece of reporting by the Sunday Times newspaper had resulted in two members of the Executive Committee being excluded from the vote, and suspended from all football-related activities, by FIFA's Ethics Committee. The Committee confirmed that one member (banned from all football related activities for three years) had been found to be in breach of Rule 11 of the FIFA Code of Ethics. Rule 11 states:

'1 Officials may not accept bribes; in other words, any gifts or other advantages that are offered, promised or sent to them to incite breach of duty or dishonest conduct for the benefit of a third party shall be refused.

2 Officials are forbidden from bribing third parties or from urging or inciting others to do so in order to gain an advantage for themselves or third parties'[1].

[1]   FIFA Code of Ethics (2009 edn), rule 11.

10.161 Had the Sunday Times' undercover operation been genuine, under the Bribery Act 2010 the UK authorities would have been entitled to commence an investigation. This is because:

— the offer of inducements in return for the Executive Committee members' votes would fall under s 1 (offences of bribing another person);

— the motivation for the offer was to induce the improper performance of a relevant function (the voting for the World Cup would arguably be a function of a 'public nature' for the purpose of s 3(2)(a), given that both the bid itself and the tournament would be partially funded by government money, and the World Cup itself involves FIFA extracting legislative guarantees from the relevant host government, in exchange for the bidding association being granted the right to bid);

— the Executive Committee members would be expected to discharge this function in good faith, and s 3(1)(b) of the Act would therefore be engaged (by virtue of s 3(3));

— under s 3(6), a function is a relevant function or activity even if it: (a) has no connection with the UK, and (b) is performed in a country or territory outside the UK. The vote actually took place in Switzerland, at FIFA's main headquarters;

— while the undercover meetings took place outside of the UK, s 12 specifically brings the activity back within the province of the UK authorities;

— the analysis becomes strained because the journalists were of course reporters working undercover (in fact posing as individuals acting on behalf of the United States' bid). Whatever their identity, they would have to satisfy the s 12(4) requirements of having the necessary 'close connection' with the UK. Seen as UK reporters, it would seem likely they might satisfy the criteria. Seen as individuals acting on behalf of the US bid, they might not. The question would turn on an application of the s 12(4) criteria.

Cricket/match fixing

10.162 Cricket is surrounded by allegations of corruption, usually involving accusations of match fixing, so called 'spot-fixing', and the influence of bookmakers.

10.163 In 2000, the distinguished South African international cricket captain, Hansie Cronje, was accused of accepting money to influence the outcome of international cricket matches. The accusations resulted in the King Commission, an inquiry chaired by a South African judge of the same name. During evidence to the inquiry, Mr Cronje admitted that he had been introduced in South Africa to a London-based businessman, who had given him money and asked him to ensure that the South African team lost a match in the triangular series in which it was competing:

> 'At the beginning of February I travelled with the team to the Beverley Hills Intercontinental Hotel at Umhlanga. We were due to play the fourth one day international in the series against Zimbabwe in Durban on the second of February. Hamid was at the hotel when we stopped. He introduced me to a man known only to me as Sanjay, who he said was from London. I was not told he was a bookmaker and was not told he was a punter.
> They indicated that Sanjay wanted me to supply them with information but did not specify what information. They also said I could make a lot of money if we would

lose a match. I said I was not prepared to do it unless we were assured of a place in the final of the triangular series. I was spinning them along as I do not think I had any real intention of throwing a match. Sanjay handed me a cell phone box containing US dollars in case I changed my mind.

I did not count the money, which was kept in a filing cabinet at home together with my prize money from the World Cup, the Kenya tour, and left over subsistence allowances. It was subsequently counted (not by me) on 11 April, when I confessed to receiving it, and I was told that it was about US10,000 but may have been US15,000'[1].

[1]   Witness statement of Hansie Cronje to the King Commission, 15 June 2000, paras 36–38.

10.164 Mr Cronje reflected upon his actions elsewhere in his evidence to the Commission:

'It was not initially my intention to throw any games or to fix results. Driven by greed and stupidity, and the lure of easy money, I thought that I could feed Sanjay information and keep the money without having to do anything to influence matches. In fact there was no manipulation of games or results in South Africa, and I supplied no information in respect of the matches in South Africa.

I realize now that the purpose of the payment was to "hook" me for the Indian tour. As set out below, on the Indian tour in February and March 2000. I was increasingly pushed to manipulate results, and found that I had got into something from which it was very difficult to get out'[1].

[1]   Witness statement of Hansie Cronje to the King Commission, 15 June 2000, paras 41–42.

10.165 The matter was dealt with by the King Commission and the South African (and international) cricketing authorities. It was also investigated by the New Delhi police.

10.166 Under the new statutory regime, it is likely that UK prosecutors would have commenced an investigation of their own, given that a major subject of Mr Cronje's evidence was the money received by him from the London-based businessman. In his report, Mr Justice King summarised the individual's status in the following way:

'Sanjay (as he is referred to in this report) is an Indian national, resident in the United Kingdom and is either a bookmaker engaged in betting on cricket matches or a gambler thereon, or possibly both'[1].

[1]   Commission of Inquiry into Cricket Match-Fixing, Interim Report (11 August 2000), Mr Justice King, at para 186.

10.167 If the same facts were to recur then the Bribery Act 2010 would allow the UK authorities to conduct their own investigation (and, if appropriate, prosecution), because:

—   under s 12 of the Act, an offence can be committed under s 1 even if no act or omission which forms part of an offence takes place in the UK;
—   under s 12(2), the matter can still be prosecuted if the person involved in the act has a 'close connection' with the UK;
—   'close connection' is then defined in s 12(4), to include 'an individual ordinarily resident in the United Kingdom';
—   where such conditions are met 'proceedings for the offence may be taken at any place in the United Kingdom' (s 12(3)(b)).

10.168 It is arguable whether the act of influencing the outcome of a cricket match in South Africa is a 'relevant function or activity' for the purpose of s 3. The likely position is that such an international match is a function of a 'public nature', bringing it within s 3(2)(a), because the public can (and were) betting on its outcome. It is also arguable that Mr Cronje was performing an activity 'in the course of a person's employment' (s 3(2)(c)) because he was contracted to the South African cricket board in his role as an international player and captain. Finally, he was of course expected to perform his activity in good faith, thereby engaging s 3(3), and 'Condition A' of that section.

10.169 The set of facts in the Cronje affair demonstrates the far-reaching nature of the Bribery Act 2010. Whereas in 2000 the UK authorities would have had no jurisdiction (the offence being committed in South Africa), the new Act extends their reach.

10.170 Various previous allegations would now be within the purview of the Act: for example the former New Zealand cricket captain Stephen Fleming spoke in his autobiography about how he was approached during the 1999 World Cup while staying in a Leicester hotel, and offered £300,000 to become involved in a gambling syndicate. Chris Lewis, the England all-rounder, then made similar allegations (suggesting that while in England he had been offered £300,000 to help ensure a Test match defeat against New Zealand). More recently, in 2010 two county championship players were questioned over allegations of 'spot-fixing'.

10.171 In September 2010 a piece of undercover reporting by the News of the World led to it accusing three Pakistani international cricketers (Salman Butt, Mohammad Asif, and Mohammad Amir) of being involved in so-called 'spot-fixing'; in this case, agreeing to bowl 'no-balls' to order. The match under scrutiny was the 4th Test at Lords, between Pakistan and England, and the News of the World alleged it had filmed a UK-based businessman accepting money in exchange for agreeing to arrange for the no-balls to be delivered.

10.172 The News of the World's allegations created jurisdictional questions. In January 2011, the International Cricket Council (ICC) convened an Anti-Corruption Panel, chaired by Michael Beloff QC, to hear charges brought under its Anti-Corruption Code for players. Unlike the South African response to the Cronje affair, the six-day hearing in Doha was conducted behind closed doors, relating to charges brought under section 2 of the Code.

10.173 Section 2 of the Code also deals with matters that, in a hypothetical world, would come under the auspices of the Bribery Act 2010 if the necessary link with the UK was present. For example, section 2.1 states that offences are committed in the following circumstances:

'2.1 Corruption:
2.1.1 Fixing or contriving in any way or otherwise influencing improperly, or being a party to any effort to fix or contrive in any way or otherwise influence improperly, the result, progress, conduct or any other aspect of any International Match or ICC Event.
2.1.2 Seeking, accepting, offering or agreeing to accept any bribe or other Reward to fix or to contrive in any way or otherwise to influence improperly the result, progress, conduct or any other aspect of any International Match or ICC Event.
2.1.3 Failing, for Reward, to perform to one's abilities in an International Match.

2.1.4 Soliciting, inducing, enticing, instructing, persuading, encouraging or facilitating any Player or Player Support Personnel to breach any of the foregoing provisions of this Article 2.1'.

10.174 Further, at section 2.4.1, it is a breach of the Code to be found to be:

'providing or receiving any gift, payment or other benefit (whether of a monetary value or otherwise) in circumstances that the Player or Player Support Personnel might reasonably have expected could bring him/her or the sport of cricket into disrepute'.

10.175 The Anti-Corruption Panel found that Mr Butt had failed to disclose an approach that he should deliberately bat out a maiden over, and that Mr Asif and Mr Amir had agreed to bowl and did bowl deliberate no balls in the Test (and that Mr Butt was a party to the bowling of the no balls). The offences were identified as being breaches of section 2.1.1 of the Code. Sanctions of between five and ten years' ineligibility were imposed. While the Tribunal Chair, Mr Beloff QC, recommended that his full judgment be published, the ICC have not done so in light of the decision of the Crown Prosecution Service, announced on 4 February 2011, to charge the players with the offences of conspiracy to accept corrupt payments and conspiracy to cheat. The ICC were apparently concerned that publication of the judgment could place it in breach of the Contempt of Court Act 1981. The ICC therefore announced on its website that out of an 'abundance of caution', it would offer time limited access to the judgment on a 'read-only' basis. This facility was only accessible to website users outside of England and Wales.

10.176 Were future touring players to be accused of breaches flowing from a similar set of facts to those investigated as a result of the Lords Test, the Bribery Act 2010 would come into play. This is because:

— an offence would potentially have been committed under s 2 of the Act (offences relating to being bribed). Under s 2(2), it is an offence if an individual 'requests, agrees to receive or accepts a financial or other advantage intending that, in consequence, a relevant function or activity should be performed improperly (whether by R or another person)';

— the allegations would come within the scope of the Act, as a result of the alleged acts taking place in the UK (for example, the Test match involving the Pakistani cricketers was played at Lords);

— as with the Cronje affair, it is arguable whether the act of influencing the outcome of a cricket match would be a 'relevant function or activity' for the purpose of s 3. The likely position is that such an international match is a function of a 'public nature', bringing it within s 3(2)(a), because the public can bet on its outcome. It is also arguable that international cricketers are performing an activity 'in the course of a person's employment' because they are usually contracted to their national cricketing board;

— finally, international cricketers are expected to perform the activity 'in good faith', for the purpose of s 3(3) of the Act.

Snooker and gambling activity

10.177 Snooker has also been the subject of bribery allegations. In 2010, the three-time world champion John Higgins and his manager were filmed at a meeting in Kiev, apparently arranging to lose frames of snooker in exchange for €300,000. The World Professional Billiards and Snooker Association (WPBSA) Board subsequently brought disciplinary proceedings.

10.178 With regard to Mr Higgins, the WPBSA withdrew the charges that specifically related to bribery before the disciplinary hearing, having accepted his explanation of events:

'Mr Higgins found himself in that meeting having only just beforehand been warned by Mr Mooney that there was a possibility (nothing more) that the subject of throwing frames might arise as part of the overall business discussions that were about to commence. Without any opportunity for mature reflection Mr Higgins, who is by nature someone who seeks to avoid confrontation or unpleasantness, decided to play along with the discussion when the topic did indeed arise. He also found the atmosphere in the meeting somewhat intimidating. His focus was entirely on bringing the meeting to an end as soon as possible and getting on a plane home. He would never throw, and had no intention at that meeting of throwing any frame of snooker for reward'[1].

[1] WPBSA Disciplinary Hearing Board, Decision of Mr Ian Mill QC, Summary of Decision for Publication, p 2.

10.179 With regard to his manager, the specific charges relating to bribery were also withdrawn by the WPBSA. The outstanding charges were admitted (of intentionally giving the impression to others that he was agreeing to act in breach of Betting Rules, and of failing to disclose to the WPBSA full details of the approach received).

10.180 In determining the appropriate sanction for the charges admitted, the Disciplinary Board made and published a number of findings. It noted that at the meeting in Kiev, the manager:

'continued to represent himself as able and willing to participate in, and to procure, corrupt frame throwing. Thereafter, he neither reported the events which had occurred to the Association, nor encouraged or advised Mr Higgins to do so'[1].

The manager's evidence to the hearing was that he did not intend to put any corrupt agreement into effect[2]. However, he accepted that:

'in continuing that engagement and by the words spoken by him on 8 April 2010 he had led Mr D'Sousa to believe that the throwing of frames was something that could be achieved'.

[1] WPBSA Disciplinary Hearing Board, Decision of Mr Ian Mill QC, Summary of Decision for Publication, p 3.
[2] WPBSA Disciplinary Hearing Board, Decision of Mr Ian Mill QC, Summary of Decision for Publication, p 3.

10.181 Were the same facts to recur, UK prosecutors would be entitled to investigate whether an offence had been committed under the Bribery Act 2010. This is because:

— under s 2(2) of the Act, it is an offence if a person 'requests, agrees to receive or accepts a financial or other advantage intending that, in consequence, a relevant function or activity should be performed improperly (whether by R or another person)';

— the activity under discussion would arguably be a 'relevant function or activity' for the purpose of s 3(2)(a) of the Act in that it is a function of a public nature (given that public bets can be placed on the outcome of the frames/matches), but also because it is an activity connected with a business for the purpose of s 3(2)(b). The manager was representing his business (World Series Snooker) at the meeting in Kiev[1] (and stated that it was World Series matches which were under discussion).

[1] WPBSA Disciplinary Hearing Board, Decision of Mr Ian Mill QC, Summary of Decision for Publication, p 3.

10.182 In response to this and other allegations, in late 2010 World Snooker and the WPBSA established an 'Integrity Unit', effectively a body to which snooker professionals can 'report approaches or leave information relating to any integrity issues'[1].

[1] www.worldsnooker.com/page/IntegrityUnit.

Conclusion

10.183 Various sports carry with them a heightened risk of bribery, because of the unique conditions which prevail. Gambling activity is the most striking of these unique conditions, while bidding processes for major tournaments are arguably analogous to large-scale tender processes.

10.184 Because of the international structure of much top-level sport, jurisdictional difficulties have previously fettered prosecuting bodies, and matters have often been left to regulatory bodies. The Bribery Act 2010 creates the potential for international allegations to be investigated by the UK authorities in a more far-reaching manner than was previously possible.

10.185 In light of this combination of circumstances, and the content of the MOJ final guidance, sporting organisations and companies working in the sporting industry must:

— conduct proper risk assessments which address the problem areas that will be well-known to their given industry;

— as part of that assessment, identify where and how all individuals who could be categorised as 'associated persons', for the purpose of the Bribery Act 2010, s 8, are operating;

— examine their procedures and ensure that they are sufficiently robust to deal with the risks that are highlighted (see Chapter 6 for further detail on the adequate procedures defence).

10.186 Finally, with regard to sportsmen and women themselves, it must be appreciated that under the Bribery Act 2010, a criminal investigation is now more likely to precede any regulatory proceedings, should they be alleged to engage in improper conduct.

APPENDIX 1

BRIBERY ACT 2010

2010 CHAPTER 23

An Act to make provision about offences relating to bribery; and for connected purposes.

[8th April 2010]

BE IT ENACTED by the Queen's most Excellent Majesty, by and with the advice and consent of the Lords Spiritual and Temporal, and Commons, in this present Parliament assembled, and by the authority of the same, as follows:—

General bribery offences

APP.1

1 Offences of bribing another person

   (1)   A person ('P') is guilty of an offence if either of the following cases applies.

   (2)   Case 1 is where—

      (a)   P offers, promises or gives a financial or other advantage to another person, and

      (b)   P intends the advantage—

         (i)   to induce a person to perform improperly a relevant function or activity, or

         (ii)   to reward a person for the improper performance of such a function or activity.

   (3)   Case 2 is where—

      (a)   P offers, promises or gives a financial or other advantage to another person, and

      (b)   P knows or believes that the acceptance of the advantage would itself constitute the improper performance of a relevant function or activity.

   (4)   In case 1 it does not matter whether the person to whom the advantage is offered, promised or given is the same person as the person who is to perform, or has performed, the function or activity concerned.

   (5)   In cases 1 and 2 it does not matter whether the advantage is offered, promised or given by P directly or through a third party.

APP.2

2 Offences relating to being bribed

   (1)   A person ('R') is guilty of an offence if any of the following cases applies.

   (2)   Case 3 is where R requests, agrees to receive or accepts a financial or other advantage intending that, in consequence, a relevant function or activity should be performed improperly (whether by R or another person).

   (3)   Case 4 is where—

(a) R requests, agrees to receive or accepts a financial or other advantage, and

(b) the request, agreement or acceptance itself constitutes the improper performance by R of a relevant function or activity.

(4) Case 5 is where R requests, agrees to receive or accepts a financial or other advantage as a reward for the improper performance (whether by R or another person) of a relevant function or activity.

(5) Case 6 is where, in anticipation of or in consequence of R requesting, agreeing to receive or accepting a financial or other advantage, a relevant function or activity is performed improperly—

(a) by R, or

(b) by another person at R's request or with R's assent or acquiescence.

(6) In cases 3 to 6 it does not matter—

(a) whether R requests, agrees to receive or accepts (or is to request, agree to receive or accept) the advantage directly or through a third party,

(b) whether the advantage is (or is to be) for the benefit of R or another person.

(7) In cases 4 to 6 it does not matter whether R knows or believes that the performance of the function or activity is improper.

(8) In case 6, where a person other than R is performing the function or activity, it also does not matter whether that person knows or believes that the performance of the function or activity is improper.

APP.3

3 Function or activity to which bribe relates

(1) For the purposes of this Act a function or activity is a relevant function or activity if—

(a) it falls within subsection (2), and

(b) meets one or more of conditions A to C.

(2) The following functions and activities fall within this subsection—

(a) any function of a public nature,

(b) any activity connected with a business,

(c) any activity performed in the course of a person's employment,

(d) any activity performed by or on behalf of a body of persons (whether corporate or unincorporate).

(3) Condition A is that a person performing the function or activity is expected to perform it in good faith.

(4) Condition B is that a person performing the function or activity is expected to perform it impartially.

(5) Condition C is that a person performing the function or activity is in a position of trust by virtue of performing it.

(6) A function or activity is a relevant function or activity even if it—

(a) has no connection with the United Kingdom, and

(b) is performed in a country or territory outside the United Kingdom.

(7) In this section 'business' includes trade or profession.

APP.4

4 Improper performance to which bribe relates

(1) For the purposes of this Act a relevant function or activity—

(a) is performed improperly if it is performed in breach of a relevant expectation, and

(b)   is to be treated as being performed improperly if there is a failure to perform the function or activity and that failure is itself a breach of a relevant expectation.

(2)   In subsection (1) 'relevant expectation'—

(a)   in relation to a function or activity which meets condition A or B, means the expectation mentioned in the condition concerned, and

(b)   in relation to a function or activity which meets condition C, means any expectation as to the manner in which, or the reasons for which, the function or activity will be performed that arises from the position of trust mentioned in that condition.

(3)   Anything that a person does (or omits to do) arising from or in connection with that person's past performance of a relevant function or activity is to be treated for the purposes of this Act as being done (or omitted) by that person in the performance of that function or activity.

APP.5

5   Expectation test

(1)   For the purposes of sections 3 and 4, the test of what is expected is a test of what a reasonable person in the United Kingdom would expect in relation to the performance of the type of function or activity concerned.

(2)   In deciding what such a person would expect in relation to the performance of a function or activity where the performance is not subject to the law of any part of the United Kingdom, any local custom or practice is to be disregarded unless it is permitted or required by the written law applicable to the country or territory concerned.

(3)   In subsection (2) 'written law' means law contained in—

(a)   any written constitution, or provision made by or under legislation, applicable to the country or territory concerned, or

(b)   any judicial decision which is so applicable and is evidenced in published written sources.

Bribery of foreign public officials

APP.6

6   Bribery of foreign public officials

(1)   A person ('P') who bribes a foreign public official ('F') is guilty of an offence if P's intention is to influence F in F's capacity as a foreign public official.

(2)   P must also intend to obtain or retain—

(a)   business, or

(b)   an advantage in the conduct of business.

(3)   P bribes F if, and only if—

(a)   directly or through a third party, P offers, promises or gives any financial or other advantage—

(i)   to F, or

(ii)   to another person at F's request or with F's assent or acquiescence, and

(b)   F is neither permitted nor required by the written law applicable to F to be influenced in F's capacity as a foreign public official by the offer, promise or gift.

(4)   References in this section to influencing F in F's capacity as a foreign public official mean influencing F in the performance of F's functions as such an official, which includes—

    (a)   any omission to exercise those functions, and

    (b)   any use of F's position as such an official, even if not within F's authority.

(5)   'Foreign public official' means an individual who—

    (a)   holds a legislative, administrative or judicial position of any kind, whether appointed or elected, of a country or territory outside the United Kingdom (or any subdivision of such a country or territory),

    (b)   exercises a public function—

        (i)   for or on behalf of a country or territory outside the United Kingdom (or any subdivision of such a country or territory), or

        (ii)   for any public agency or public enterprise of that country or territory (or subdivision), or

    (c)   is an official or agent of a public international organisation.

(6)   'Public international organisation' means an organisation whose members are any of the following—

    (a)   countries or territories,

    (b)   governments of countries or territories,

    (c)   other public international organisations,

    (d)   a mixture of any of the above.

(7)   For the purposes of subsection (3)(b), the written law applicable to F is—

    (a)   where the performance of the functions of F which P intends to influence would be subject to the law of any part of the United Kingdom, the law of that part of the United Kingdom,

    (b)   where paragraph (a) does not apply and F is an official or agent of a public international organisation, the applicable written rules of that organisation,

    (c)   where paragraphs (a) and (b) do not apply, the law of the country or territory in relation to which F is a foreign public official so far as that law is contained in—

        (i)   any written constitution, or provision made by or under legislation, applicable to the country or territory concerned, or

        (ii)   any judicial decision which is so applicable and is evidenced in published written sources.

(8)   For the purposes of this section, a trade or profession is a business.

Failure of commercial organisations to prevent bribery

APP.7

7 Failure of commercial organisations to prevent bribery

(1)   A relevant commercial organisation ('C') is guilty of an offence under this section if a person ('A') associated with C bribes another person intending—

    (a)   to obtain or retain business for C, or

    (b)   to obtain or retain an advantage in the conduct of business for C.

(2)   But it is a defence for C to prove that C had in place adequate procedures designed to prevent persons associated with C from undertaking such conduct.

(3)   For the purposes of this section, A bribes another person if, and only if, A—

    (a)   is, or would be, guilty of an offence under section 1 or 6 (whether or not A has been prosecuted for such an offence), or

(b)   would be guilty of such an offence if section 12(2)(c) and (4) were omitted.

(4)   See section 8 for the meaning of a person associated with C and see section 9 for a duty on the Secretary of State to publish guidance.

(5)   In this section—

'partnership' means—

    (a)   a partnership within the Partnership Act 1890, or

    (b)   a limited partnership registered under the Limited Partnerships Act 1907,

or a firm or entity of a similar character formed under the law of a country or territory outside the United Kingdom,

'relevant commercial organisation' means—

    (a)   a body which is incorporated under the law of any part of the United Kingdom and which carries on a business (whether there or elsewhere),

    (b)   any other body corporate (wherever incorporated) which carries on a business, or part of a business, in any part of the United Kingdom,

    (c)   a partnership which is formed under the law of any part of the United Kingdom and which carries on a business (whether there or elsewhere), or

    (d)   any other partnership (wherever formed) which carries on a business, or part of a business, in any part of the United Kingdom,

and, for the purposes of this section, a trade or profession is a business.

APP.8

8 Meaning of associated person

(1)   For the purposes of section 7, a person ('A') is associated with C if (disregarding any bribe under consideration) A is a person who performs services for or on behalf of C.

(2)   The capacity in which A performs services for or on behalf of C does not matter.

(3)   Accordingly A may (for example) be C's employee, agent or subsidiary.

(4)   Whether or not A is a person who performs services for or on behalf of C is to be determined by reference to all the relevant circumstances and not merely by reference to the nature of the relationship between A and C.

(5)   But if A is an employee of C, it is to be presumed unless the contrary is shown that A is a person who performs services for or on behalf of C.

APP.9

9 Guidance about commercial organisations preventing bribery

(1)   The Secretary of State must publish guidance about procedures that relevant commercial organisations can put in place to prevent persons associated with them from bribing as mentioned in section 7(1).

(2)   The Secretary of State may, from time to time, publish revisions to guidance under this section or revised guidance.

(3)   The Secretary of State must consult the Scottish Ministers before publishing anything under this section.

(4)   Publication under this section is to be in such manner as the Secretary of State considers appropriate.

(5)   Expressions used in this section have the same meaning as in section 7.

Prosecution and penalties

APP.10

10 Consent to prosecution

(1)   No proceedings for an offence under this Act may be instituted in England and Wales except by or with the consent of—

(a)   the Director of Public Prosecutions,

(b)   the Director of the Serious Fraud Office, or

(c)   the Director of Revenue and Customs Prosecutions.

(2)   No proceedings for an offence under this Act may be instituted in Northern Ireland except by or with the consent of—

(a)   the Director of Public Prosecutions for Northern Ireland, or

(b)   the Director of the Serious Fraud Office.

(3)   No proceedings for an offence under this Act may be instituted in England and Wales or Northern Ireland by a person—

(a)   who is acting—

(i)   under the direction or instruction of the Director of Public Prosecutions, the Director of the Serious Fraud Office or the Director of Revenue and Customs Prosecutions, or

(ii)   on behalf of such a Director, or

(b)   to whom such a function has been assigned by such a Director,

except with the consent of the Director concerned to the institution of the proceedings.

(4)   The Director of Public Prosecutions, the Director of the Serious Fraud Office and the Director of Revenue and Customs Prosecutions must exercise personally any function under subsection (1), (2) or (3) of giving consent.

(5)   The only exception is if—

(a)   the Director concerned is unavailable, and

(b)   there is another person who is designated in writing by the Director acting personally as the person who is authorised to exercise any such function when the Director is unavailable.

(6)   In that case, the other person may exercise the function but must do so personally.

(7)   Subsections (4) to (6) apply instead of any other provisions which would otherwise have enabled any function of the Director of Public Prosecutions, the Director of the Serious Fraud Office or the Director of Revenue and Customs Prosecutions under subsection (1), (2) or (3) of giving consent to be exercised by a person other than the Director concerned.

(8)   No proceedings for an offence under this Act may be instituted in Northern Ireland by virtue of section 36 of the Justice (Northern Ireland) Act 2002 (delegation of the functions of the Director of Public Prosecutions for Northern Ireland to persons other than the Deputy Director) except with the consent of the Director of Public Prosecutions for Northern Ireland to the institution of the proceedings.

(9)   The Director of Public Prosecutions for Northern Ireland must exercise personally any function under subsection (2) or (8) of giving consent unless the function is exercised personally by the Deputy Director of Public Prosecutions for Northern Ireland by virtue of section 30(4) or (7) of the Act of 2002 (powers of Deputy Director to exercise functions of Director).

(10)   Subsection (9) applies instead of section 36 of the Act of 2002 in relation to the functions of the Director of Public Prosecutions for Northern Ireland and the Deputy Director of Public Prosecutions for Northern Ireland under, or (as the case may be) by virtue of, subsections (2) and (8) above of giving consent.

APP.11

11 Penalties

(1) An individual guilty of an offence under section 1, 2 or 6 is liable—

    (a)   on summary conviction, to imprisonment for a term not exceeding 12 months, or to a fine not exceeding the statutory maximum, or to both,

    (b)   on conviction on indictment, to imprisonment for a term not exceeding 10 years, or to a fine, or to both.

(2) Any other person guilty of an offence under section 1, 2 or 6 is liable—

    (a)   on summary conviction, to a fine not exceeding the statutory maximum,

    (b)   on conviction on indictment, to a fine.

(3) A person guilty of an offence under section 7 is liable on conviction on indictment to a fine.

(4) The reference in subsection (1)(a) to 12 months is to be read—

    (a)   in its application to England and Wales in relation to an offence committed before the commencement of section 154(1) of the Criminal Justice Act 2003, and

    (b)   in its application to Northern Ireland,

as a reference to 6 months.

Other provisions about offences

APP.12

12 Offences under this Act: territorial application

(1) An offence is committed under section 1, 2 or 6 in England and Wales, Scotland or Northern Ireland if any act or omission which forms part of the offence takes place in that part of the United Kingdom.

(2) Subsection (3) applies if—

    (a)   no act or omission which forms part of an offence under section 1, 2 or 6 takes place in the United Kingdom,

    (b)   a person's acts or omissions done or made outside the United Kingdom would form part of such an offence if done or made in the United Kingdom, and

    (c)   that person has a close connection with the United Kingdom.

(3) In such a case—

    (a)   the acts or omissions form part of the offence referred to in subsection (2)(a), and

    (b)   proceedings for the offence may be taken at any place in the United Kingdom.

(4) For the purposes of subsection (2)(c) a person has a close connection with the United Kingdom if, and only if, the person was one of the following at the time the acts or omissions concerned were done or made—

    (a)   a British citizen,

    (b)   a British overseas territories citizen,

    (c)   a British National (Overseas),

    (d)   a British Overseas citizen,

    (e)   a person who under the British Nationality Act 1981 was a British subject,

    (f)   a British protected person within the meaning of that Act,

    (g)   an individual ordinarily resident in the United Kingdom,

    (h)   a body incorporated under the law of any part of the United Kingdom,

    (i)   a Scottish partnership.

(5) An offence is committed under section 7 irrespective of whether the acts or omissions which form part of the offence take place in the United Kingdom or elsewhere.

(6) Where no act or omission which forms part of an offence under section 7 takes place in the United Kingdom, proceedings for the offence may be taken at any place in the United Kingdom.

(7) Subsection (8) applies if, by virtue of this section, proceedings for an offence are to be taken in Scotland against a person.

(8) Such proceedings may be taken—

    (a)   in any sheriff court district in which the person is apprehended or in custody, or

    (b)   in such sheriff court district as the Lord Advocate may determine.

(9) In subsection (8) 'sheriff court district' is to be read in accordance with section 307(1) of the Criminal Procedure (Scotland) Act 1995.

APP.13

13 Defence for certain bribery offences etc

(1) It is a defence for a person charged with a relevant bribery offence to prove that the person's conduct was necessary for—

    (a)   the proper exercise of any function of an intelligence service, or

    (b)   the proper exercise of any function of the armed forces when engaged on active service.

(2) The head of each intelligence service must ensure that the service has in place arrangements designed to ensure that any conduct of a member of the service which would otherwise be a relevant bribery offence is necessary for a purpose falling within subsection (1)(a).

(3) The Defence Council must ensure that the armed forces have in place arrangements designed to ensure that any conduct of—

    (a)   a member of the armed forces who is engaged on active service, or

    (b)   a civilian subject to service discipline when working in support of any person falling within paragraph (a),

which would otherwise be a relevant bribery offence is necessary for a purpose falling within subsection (1)(b).

(4) The arrangements which are in place by virtue of subsection (2) or (3) must be arrangements which the Secretary of State considers to be satisfactory.

(5) For the purposes of this section, the circumstances in which a person's conduct is necessary for a purpose falling within subsection (1)(a) or (b) are to be treated as including any circumstances in which the person's conduct—

    (a)   would otherwise be an offence under section 2, and

    (b)   involves conduct by another person which, but for subsection (1)(a) or (b), would be an offence under section 1.

(6) In this section—

'active service' means service in—

    (a)   an action or operation against an enemy,

    (b)   an operation outside the British Islands for the protection of life or property, or

    (c)   the military occupation of a foreign country or territory,

'armed forces' means Her Majesty's forces (within the meaning of the Armed Forces Act 2006),

'civilian subject to service discipline' and 'enemy' have the same meaning as in the Act of 2006,

'GCHQ' has the meaning given by section 3(3) of the Intelligence Services Act 1994,
'head' means—

- (a) in relation to the Security Service, the Director General of the Security Service,
- (b) in relation to the Secret Intelligence Service, the Chief of the Secret Intelligence Service, and
- (c) in relation to GCHQ, the Director of GCHQ,

'intelligence service' means the Security Service, the Secret Intelligence Service or GCHQ,
'relevant bribery offence' means—

- (a) an offence under section 1 which would not also be an offence under section 6,
- (b) an offence under section 2,
- (c) an offence committed by aiding, abetting, counselling or procuring the commission of an offence falling within paragraph (a) or (b),
- (d) an offence of attempting or conspiring to commit, or of inciting the commission of, an offence falling within paragraph (a) or (b), or
- (e) an offence under Part 2 of the Serious Crime Act 2007 (encouraging or assisting crime) in relation to an offence falling within paragraph (a) or (b).

APP.14

14 Offences under sections 1, 2 and 6 by bodies corporate etc

(1) This section applies if an offence under section 1, 2 or 6 is committed by a body corporate or a Scottish partnership.

(2) If the offence is proved to have been committed with the consent or connivance of—

- (a) a senior officer of the body corporate or Scottish partnership, or
- (b) a person purporting to act in such a capacity,

the senior officer or person (as well as the body corporate or partnership) is guilty of the offence and liable to be proceeded against and punished accordingly.

(3) But subsection (2) does not apply, in the case of an offence which is committed under section 1, 2 or 6 by virtue of section 12(2) to (4), to a senior officer or person purporting to act in such a capacity unless the senior officer or person has a close connection with the United Kingdom (within the meaning given by section 12(4)).

(4) In this section—
'director', in relation to a body corporate whose affairs are managed by its members, means a member of the body corporate,
'senior officer' means—

- (a) in relation to a body corporate, a director, manager, secretary or other similar officer of the body corporate, and
- (b) in relation to a Scottish partnership, a partner in the partnership.

APP.15

15 Offences under section 7 by partnerships

(1) Proceedings for an offence under section 7 alleged to have been committed by a partnership must be brought in the name of the partnership (and not in that of any of the partners).

(2) For the purposes of such proceedings—

(a)   rules of court relating to the service of documents have effect as if the partnership were a body corporate, and

(b)   the following provisions apply as they apply in relation to a body corporate—

(i)   section 33 of the Criminal Justice Act 1925 and Schedule 3 to the Magistrates' Courts Act 1980,

(ii)   section 18 of the Criminal Justice Act (Northern Ireland) 1945 (c 15 (NI)) and Schedule 4 to the Magistrates' Courts (Northern Ireland) Order 1981 (SI 1981/1675 (NI 26)),

(iii)   section 70 of the Criminal Procedure (Scotland) Act 1995.

(3)   A fine imposed on the partnership on its conviction for an offence under section 7 is to be paid out of the partnership assets.

(4)   In this section 'partnership' has the same meaning as in section 7.

Supplementary and final provisions

APP.16

16 Application to Crown

This Act applies to individuals in the public service of the Crown as it applies to other individuals.

APP.17

17 Consequential provision

(1)   The following common law offences are abolished—

(a)   the offences under the law of England and Wales and Northern Ireland of bribery and embracery,

(b)   the offences under the law of Scotland of bribery and accepting a bribe.

(2)   Schedule 1 (which contains consequential amendments) has effect.

(3)   Schedule 2 (which contains repeals and revocations) has effect.

(4)   The relevant national authority may by order make such supplementary, incidental or consequential provision as the relevant national authority considers appropriate for the purposes of this Act or in consequence of this Act.

(5)   The power to make an order under this section—

(a)   is exercisable by statutory instrument,

(b)   includes power to make transitional, transitory or saving provision,

(c)   may, in particular, be exercised by amending, repealing, revoking or otherwise modifying any provision made by or under an enactment (including any Act passed in the same Session as this Act).

(6)   Subject to subsection (7), a statutory instrument containing an order of the Secretary of State under this section may not be made unless a draft of the instrument has been laid before, and approved by a resolution of, each House of Parliament.

(7)   A statutory instrument containing an order of the Secretary of State under this section which does not amend or repeal a provision of a public general Act or of devolved legislation is subject to annulment in pursuance of a resolution of either House of Parliament.

(8)   Subject to subsection (9), a statutory instrument containing an order of the Scottish Ministers under this section may not be made unless a draft of the instrument has been laid before, and approved by a resolution of, the Scottish Parliament.

(9)   A statutory instrument containing an order of the Scottish Ministers under this section which does not amend or repeal a provision of an Act of the Scottish

Parliament or of a public general Act is subject to annulment in pursuance of a resolution of the Scottish Parliament.

(10) In this section—

'devolved legislation' means an Act of the Scottish Parliament, a Measure of the National Assembly for Wales or an Act of the Northern Ireland Assembly,

'enactment' includes an Act of the Scottish Parliament and Northern Ireland legislation,

'relevant national authority' means—

(a) in the case of provision which would be within the legislative competence of the Scottish Parliament if it were contained in an Act of that Parliament, the Scottish Ministers, and

(b) in any other case, the Secretary of State.

APP.18

18 Extent

(1) Subject as follows, this Act extends to England and Wales, Scotland and Northern Ireland.

(2) Subject to subsections (3) to (5), any amendment, repeal or revocation made by Schedule 1 or 2 has the same extent as the provision amended, repealed or revoked.

(3) The amendment of, and repeals in, the Armed Forces Act 2006 do not extend to the Channel Islands.

(4) The amendments of the International Criminal Court Act 2001 extend to England and Wales and Northern Ireland only.

(5) Subsection (2) does not apply to the repeal in the Civil Aviation Act 1982.

APP.19

19 Commencement and transitional provision etc

(1) Subject to subsection (2), this Act comes into force on such day as the Secretary of State may by order made by statutory instrument appoint.

(2) Sections 16, 17(4) to (10) and 18, this section (other than subsections (5) to (7)) and section 20 come into force on the day on which this Act is passed.

(3) An order under subsection (1) may—

(a) appoint different days for different purposes,

(b) make such transitional, transitory or saving provision as the Secretary of State considers appropriate in connection with the coming into force of any provision of this Act.

(4) The Secretary of State must consult the Scottish Ministers before making an order under this section in connection with any provision of this Act which would be within the legislative competence of the Scottish Parliament if it were contained in an Act of that Parliament.

(5) This Act does not affect any liability, investigation, legal proceeding or penalty for or in respect of—

(a) a common law offence mentioned in subsection (1) of section 17 which is committed wholly or partly before the coming into force of that subsection in relation to such an offence, or

(b) an offence under the Public Bodies Corrupt Practices Act 1889 or the Prevention of Corruption Act 1906 committed wholly or partly before the coming into force of the repeal of the Act by Schedule 2 to this Act.

(6) For the purposes of subsection (5) an offence is partly committed before a particular time if any act or omission which forms part of the offence takes place before that time.

(7) Subsections (5) and (6) are without prejudice to section 16 of the Interpretation Act 1978 (general savings on repeal).

APP.20

20 Short title
This Act may be cited as the Bribery Act 2010.

SCHEDULE 1
CONSEQUENTIAL AMENDMENTS
Section 17(2)

Ministry of Defence Police Act 1987 (c 4)

APP.21

1

In section 2(3)(ba) of the Ministry of Defence Police Act 1987 (jurisdiction of members of Ministry of Defence Police Force) for 'Prevention of Corruption Acts 1889 to 1916' substitute 'Bribery Act 2010'.

Criminal Justice Act 1987 (c 38)

2

In section 2A of the Criminal Justice Act 1987 (Director of SFO's pre-investigation powers in relation to bribery and corruption: foreign officers etc) for subsections (5) and (6) substitute—
'(5)   This section applies to any conduct—
    (a)   which, as a result of section 3(6) of the Bribery Act 2010, constitutes an offence under section 1 or 2 of that Act under the law of England and Wales or Northern Ireland, or
    (b)   which constitutes an offence under section 6 of that Act under the law of England and Wales or Northern Ireland.'

International Criminal Court Act 2001 (c 17)

3

The International Criminal Court Act 2001 is amended as follows.

4

In section 54(3) (offences in relation to the ICC: England and Wales)—
    (a)   in paragraph (b) for 'or' substitute ', an offence under the Bribery Act 2010 or (as the case may be) an offence', and
    (b)   in paragraph (c) after 'common law' insert 'or (as the case may be) under the Bribery Act 2010'.

5

In section 61(3)(b) (offences in relation to the ICC: Northern Ireland) after 'common law' insert 'or (as the case may be) under the Bribery Act 2010'.

International Criminal Court (Scotland) Act 2001 (asp 13)

6

In section 4(2) of the International Criminal Court (Scotland) Act 2001 (offences in relation to the ICC)—

(a)   in paragraph (b) after 'common law' insert 'or (as the case may be) under the Bribery Act 2010', and

(b)   in paragraph (c) for 'section 1 of the Prevention of Corruption Act 1906 (c 34) or at common law' substitute 'the Bribery Act 2010'.

Serious Organised Crime and Police Act 2005 (c 15)

7

The Serious Organised Crime and Police Act 2005 is amended as follows.

8

In section 61(1) (offences in respect of which investigatory powers apply) for paragraph (h) substitute—

'(h)   any offence under the Bribery Act 2010.'

9

In section 76(3) (financial reporting orders: making) for paragraphs (d) to (f) substitute—

'(da)   an offence under any of the following provisions of the Bribery Act 2010—

section 1 (offences of bribing another person),

section 2 (offences relating to being bribed),

section 6 (bribery of foreign public officials),'.

10

In section 77(3) (financial reporting orders: making in Scotland) after paragraph (b) insert—

'(c)   an offence under section 1, 2 or 6 of the Bribery Act 2010.'

Armed Forces Act 2006 (c 52)

11

In Schedule 2 to the Armed Forces Act 2006 (which lists serious offences the possible commission of which, if suspected, must be referred to a service police force), in paragraph 12, at the end insert—

'(aw) an offence under section 1, 2 or 6 of the Bribery Act 2010.'

Serious Crime Act 2007 (c 27)

12

The Serious Crime Act 2007 is amended as follows.

13

(1)   Section 53 of that Act (certain extra-territorial offences to be prosecuted only by, or with the consent of, the Attorney General or the Advocate General for Northern Ireland) is amended as follows.

(2)   The existing words in that section become the first subsection of the section.

(3)   After that subsection insert—

'(2) Subsection (1) does not apply to an offence under this Part to which section 10 of the Bribery Act 2010 applies by virtue of section 54(1) and (2) below (encouraging or assisting bribery).'

14

(1) Schedule 1 to that Act (list of serious offences) is amended as follows.

(2) For paragraph 9 and the heading before it (corruption and bribery: England and Wales) substitute—

'*Bribery*

9

An offence under any of the following provisions of the Bribery Act 2010—

    (a)   section 1 (offences of bribing another person);

    (b)   section 2 (offences relating to being bribed);

    (c)   section 6 (bribery of foreign public officials).'

(3) For paragraph 25 and the heading before it (corruption and bribery: Northern Ireland) substitute—

'*Bribery*

25

An offence under any of the following provisions of the Bribery Act 2010—

    (a)   section 1 (offences of bribing another person);

    (b)   section 2 (offences relating to being bribed);

    (c)   section 6 (bribery of foreign public officials).'

SCHEDULE 2
REPEALS AND REVOCATIONS

Section 17(3)

APP.22

Short title and chapter	*Extent of repeal or revocation*
Public Bodies Corrupt Practices Act 1889 (c 69)	The whole Act.
Prevention of Corruption Act 1906 (c 34)	The whole Act.
Prevention of Corruption Act 1916 (c 64)	The whole Act.
Criminal Justice Act (Northern Ireland) 1945 (c 15 (NI))	Section 22.
Electoral Law Act (Northern Ireland) 1962 (c 14 (NI))	Section 112(3).
Increase of Fines Act (Northern Ireland) 1967 (c 29 (NI))	Section 1(8)(a) and (b).
Criminal Justice (Miscellaneous Provisions) Act (Northern Ireland) 1968 (c 28 (NI))	In Schedule 2, the entry in the table relating to the Prevention of Corruption Act 1906.
Local Government Act (Northern Ireland) 1972 (c 9 (NI))	In Schedule 8, paragraphs 1 and 3.
Civil Aviation Act 1982 (c 16)	Section 19(1).
Representation of the People Act 1983 (c 2)	In section 165(1), paragraph (b) and the word 'or' immediately before it.

Short title and chapter	*Extent of repeal or revocation*
Housing Associations Act 1985 (c 69)	In Schedule 6, paragraph 1(2).
Criminal Justice Act 1988 (c 33)	Section 47.
Criminal Justice (Evidence etc) (Northern Ireland) Order 1988 (SI 1988/1847 (NI 17))	Article 14.
Enterprise and New Towns (Scotland) Act 1990 (c 35)	In Schedule 1, paragraph 2.
Scotland Act 1998 (c 46)	Section 43.
Anti-terrorism, Crime and Security Act 2001 (c 24)	Sections 108 to 110.
Criminal Justice (Scotland) Act 2003 (asp 7)	Sections 68 and 69.
Government of Wales Act 2006 (c 32)	Section 44.
Armed Forces Act 2006 (c 52)	In Schedule 2, paragraph 12(l) and (m).
Local Government and Public Involvement in Health Act 2007 (c 28)	Section 217(1)(a).
	Section 244(4).
	In Schedule 14, paragraph 1.
Housing and Regeneration Act 2008 (c 17)	In Schedule 1, paragraph 16.

APPENDIX 2

THE BRIBERY ACT 2010: GUIDANCE ABOUT PROCEDURES WHICH
RELEVANT COMMERCIAL ORGANISATIONS CAN PUT INTO
PLACE TO PREVENT PERSONS ASSOCIATED WITH THEM FROM
BRIBING (SECTION 9 OF THE BRIBERY ACT 2010)

FOREWORD

[APP.23]

Bribery blights lives. Its immediate victims include firms that lose out unfairly. The wider victims are government and society, undermined by a weakened rule of law and damaged social and economic development. At stake is the principle of free and fair competition, which stands diminished by each bribe offered or accepted.

Tackling this scourge is a priority for anyone who cares about the future of business, the developing world or international trade. That is why the entry into force of the Bribery Act on 1 July 2011 is an important step forward for both the UK and UK plc. In line with the Act's statutory requirements, I am publishing this guidance to help organisations understand the legislation and deal with the risks of bribery. My aim is that it offers clarity on how the law will operate.

Readers of this document will be aware that the Act creates offences of offering or receiving bribes, bribery of foreign public officials and of failure to prevent a bribe being paid on an organisation's behalf. These are certainly tough rules. But readers should understand too that they are directed at making life difficult for the mavericks responsible for corruption, not unduly burdening the vast majority of decent, law-abiding firms.

I have listened carefully to business representatives to ensure the Act is implemented in a workable way—especially for small firms that have limited resources. And, as I hope this guidance shows, combating the risks of bribery is largely about common sense, not burdensome procedures. The core principle it sets out is proportionality. It also offers case study examples that help illuminate the application of the Act. Rest assured—no one wants to stop firms getting to know their clients by taking them to events like Wimbledon or the Grand Prix. Separately, we are publishing non-statutory 'quick start' guidance. I encourage small businesses to turn to this for a concise introduction to how they can meet the requirements of the law.

Ultimately, the Bribery Act matters for Britain because our existing legislation is out of date. In updating our rules, I say to our international partners that the UK wants to play a leading role in stamping out corruption and supporting trade-led international development. But I would argue too that the Act is directly beneficial for business. That's because it creates clarity and a level playing field, helping to align trading nations around decent standards. It also establishes a statutory defence: organisations which have adequate procedures in place to prevent bribery are in a stronger position if isolated incidents have occurred in spite of their efforts.

Some have asked whether business can afford this legislation—especially at a time of economic recovery. But the choice is a false one. We don't have to decide between tackling corruption and supporting growth. Addressing bribery is good for business because it creates the conditions for free markets to flourish.

Everyone agrees bribery is wrong and that rules need reform. In implementing this Act, we are striking a blow for the rule of law and growth of trade. I commend this guidance to you as a helping hand in doing business competitively and fairly.

Kenneth Clarke

Secretary of State for Justice

March 2011

Introduction

1 The Bribery Act 2010 received Royal Assent on 8 April 2010. A full copy of the Act and its Explanatory Notes can be accessed at: www.opsi.gov.uk/acts/ acts2010/ukpga _20100023_en_1. The Act creates a new offence under section 7 which can be committed by commercial organisations[1] which fail to prevent persons associated with them from committing bribery on their behalf. It is a full defence for an organisation to prove that despite a particular case of bribery it nevertheless had adequate procedures in place to prevent persons associated with it from bribing. Section 9 of the Act requires the Secretary of State to publish guidance about procedures which commercial organisations can put in place to prevent persons associated with them from bribing. This document sets out that guidance.

[1]   See paragraph 35 below on the definition of the phrase 'commercial organisation'.

2 The Act extends to England & Wales, Scotland and Northern Ireland. This guidance is for use in all parts of the United Kingdom. In accordance with section 9(3) of the Act, the Scottish Ministers have been consulted regarding the content of this guidance. The Northern Ireland Assembly has also been consulted.

3 This guidance explains the policy behind section 7 and is intended to help commercial organisations of all sizes and sectors understand what sorts of procedures they can put in place to prevent bribery as mentioned in section 7(1).

4 The guidance is designed to be of general application and is formulated around six guiding principles, each followed by commentary and examples. The guidance is not prescriptive and is not a one-size-fits-all document. The question of whether an organisation had adequate procedures in place to prevent bribery in the context of a particular prosecution is a matter that can only be resolved by the courts taking into account the particular facts and circumstances of the case. The onus will remain on the organisation, in any case where it seeks to rely on the defence, to prove that it had adequate procedures in place to prevent bribery. However, departures from the suggested procedures contained within the guidance will not of itself give rise to a presumption that an organisation does not have adequate procedures.

5 If your organisation is small or medium sized the application of the principles is likely to suggest procedures that are different from those that may be right for a large multinational organisation. The guidance suggests certain procedures, but they may not all be applicable to your circumstances. Sometimes, you may have alternatives in place that are also adequate.

6 As the principles make clear commercial organisations should adopt a risk-based approach to managing bribery risks. Procedures should be proportionate to the risks faced by an organisation. No policies or procedures are capable of detecting and preventing all bribery. A risk-based approach will, however, serve to focus the effort where it is needed and will have most impact. A risk-based approach recognises that the

bribery threat to organisations varies across jurisdictions, business sectors, business partners and transactions.

7   The language used in this guidance reflects its non-prescriptive nature. The six principles are intended to be of general application and are therefore expressed in neutral but affirmative language. The commentary following each of the principles is expressed more broadly.

8   All terms used in this guidance have the same meaning as in the Bribery Act 2010. Any examples of particular types of conduct are provided for illustrative purposes only and do not constitute exhaustive lists of relevant conduct.

Government policy and Section 7 of the Bribery Act

9   Bribery undermines democracy and the rule of law and poses very serious threats to sustained economic progress in developing and emerging economies and to the proper operation of free markets more generally. The Bribery Act 2010 is intended to respond to these threats and to the extremely broad range of ways that bribery can be committed. It does this by providing robust offences, enhanced sentencing powers for the courts (raising the maximum sentence for bribery committed by an individual from 7 to 10 years imprisonment) and wide jurisdictional powers (see paragraphs 15 and 16 on page 9).

10   The Act contains two general offences covering the offering, promising or giving of a bribe (active bribery) and the requesting, agreeing to receive or accepting of a bribe (passive bribery) at sections 1 and 2 respectively. It also sets out two further offences which specifically address commercial bribery. Section 6 of the Act creates an offence relating to bribery of a foreign public official in order to obtain or retain business or an advantage in the conduct of business[2], and section 7 creates a new form of corporate liability for failing to prevent bribery on behalf of a commercial organisation. More detail about the sections 1, 6 and 7 offences is provided under the separate headings below.

[2]   Conduct amounting to bribery of a foreign public official could also be charged under section 1 of the Act. It will be for prosecutors to select the most appropriate charge.

11   The objective of the Act is not to bring the full force of the criminal law to bear upon well run commercial organisations that experience an isolated incident of bribery on their behalf. So in order to achieve an appropriate balance, section 7 provides a full defence. This is in recognition of the fact that no bribery prevention regime will be capable of preventing bribery at all times. However, the defence is also included in order to encourage commercial organisations to put procedures in place to prevent bribery by persons associated with them.

12   The application of bribery prevention procedures by commercial organisations is of significant interest to those investigating bribery and is relevant if an organisation wishes to report an incident of bribery to the prosecution authorities—for example to the Serious Fraud Office (SFO) which operates a policy in England and Wales and Northern Ireland of co-operation with commercial organisations that self-refer incidents of bribery (see 'Approach of the SFO to dealing with overseas corruption' on the SFO website). The commercial organisation's willingness to co-operate with an investigation under the Bribery Act and to make a full disclosure will also be taken into account in any decision as to whether it is appropriate to commence criminal proceedings.

13   In order to be liable under section 7 a commercial organisation must have failed to prevent conduct that would amount to the commission of an offence under sections 1 or 6, but it is irrelevant whether a person has been convicted of such an offence. Where the prosecution cannot prove beyond reasonable doubt that a sections 1 or 6 offence has been committed the section 7 offence will not be triggered.

14   The section 7 offence is in addition to, and does not displace, liability which might arise under sections 1 or 6 of the Act where the commercial organisation itself commits an offence by virtue of the common law 'identification' principle.[3]

[3]   See section 5 and Schedule 1 to the Interpretation Act 1978 which provides that the word

'person' where used in an Act includes bodies corporate and unincorporate. Note also the common law 'identification principle' as defined by cases such as *Tesco Supermarkets v Nattrass* [1972] AC 153 which provides that corporate liability arises only where the offence is committed by a natural person who is the directing mind or will of the organisation.

Jurisdiction

15   Section 12 of the Act provides that the courts will have jurisdiction over the sections 1, 2[4] or 6 offences committed in the UK, but they will also have jurisdiction over offences committed outside the UK where the person committing them has a close connection with the UK by virtue of being a British national or ordinarily resident in the UK, a body incorporated in the UK or a Scottish partnership.

16   However, as regards section 7, the requirement of a close connection with the UK does not apply. Section 7(3) makes clear that a commercial organisation can be liable for conduct amounting to a section 1 or 6 offence on the part of a person who is neither a UK national or resident in the UK, nor a body incorporated or formed in the UK. In addition, section 12(5) provides that it does not matter whether the acts or omissions which form part of the section 7 offence take part in the UK or elsewhere. So, provided the organisation is incorporated or formed in the UK, or that the organisation carries on a business or part of a business in the UK (wherever in the world it may be incorporated or formed) then UK courts will have jurisdiction (see more on this at paragraphs 34 to 36).

4   Although this particular offence is not relevant for the purposes of section 7.

Section 1: Offences of bribing another person

17   Section 1 makes it an offence for a person ('P') to offer, promise or give a financial or other advantage to another person in one of two cases:

- Case 1 applies where P intends the advantage to bring about the improper performance by another person of a relevant function or activity or to reward such improper performance.
- Case 2 applies where P knows or believes that the acceptance of the advantage offered, promised or given in itself constitutes the improper performance of a relevant function or activity.

18   'Improper performance' is defined at sections 3, 4 and 5. In summary, this means performance which amounts to a breach of an expectation that a person will act in good faith, impartially, or in accordance with a position of trust. The offence applies to bribery relating to any function of a public nature, connected with a business, performed in the course of a person's employment or performed on behalf of a company or another body of persons. Therefore, bribery in both the public and private sectors is covered.

19   For the purposes of deciding whether a function or activity has been performed improperly the test of what is expected is a test of what a reasonable person in the UK would expect in relation to the performance of that function or activity. Where the performance of the function or activity is not subject to UK law (for example, it takes place in a country outside UK jurisdiction) then any local custom or practice must be disregarded—unless permitted or required by the written law applicable to that particular country. Written law means any written constitution, provision made by or under legislation applicable to the country concerned or any judicial decision evidenced in published written sources.

20   By way of illustration, in order to proceed with a case under section 1 based on an allegation that hospitality was intended as a bribe, the prosecution would need to show that the hospitality was intended to induce conduct that amounts to a breach of an expectation that a person will act in good faith, impartially, or in accordance with a position of trust. This would be judged by what a reasonable person in the UK thought. So, for example, an invitation to foreign clients to attend a Six Nations match at

Twickenham as part of a public relations exercise designed to cement good relations or enhance knowledge in the organisation's field is extremely unlikely to engage section 1 as there is unlikely to be evidence of an intention to induce improper performance of a relevant function.

Section 6: Bribery of a foreign public official

21 Section 6 creates a standalone offence of bribery of a foreign public official. The offence is committed where a person offers, promises or gives a financial or other advantage to a foreign public official with the intention of influencing the official in the performance of his or her official functions. The person offering, promising or giving the advantage must also intend to obtain or retain business or an advantage in the conduct of business by doing so. However, the offence is not committed where the official is permitted or required by the applicable written law to be influenced by the advantage.

22 A 'foreign public official' includes officials, whether elected or appointed, who hold a legislative, administrative or judicial position of any kind of a country or territory outside the UK. It also includes any person who performs public functions in any branch of the national, local or municipal government of such a country or territory or who exercises a public function for any public agency or public enterprise of such a country or territory, such as professionals working for public health agencies and officers exercising public functions in state-owned enterprises. Foreign public officials can also be an official or agent of a public international organisation, such as the UN or the World Bank.

23 Sections 1 and 6 may capture the same conduct but will do so in different ways. The policy that founds the offence at section 6 is the need to prohibit the influencing of decision making in the context of publicly funded business opportunities by the inducement of personal enrichment of foreign public officials or to others at the official's request, assent or acquiescence. Such activity is very likely to involve conduct which amounts to 'improper performance' of a relevant function or activity to which section 1 applies, but, unlike section 1, section 6 does not require proof of it or an intention to induce it. This is because the exact nature of the functions of persons regarded as foreign public officials is often very difficult to ascertain with any accuracy, and the securing of evidence will often be reliant on the co-operation of the state any such officials serve. To require the prosecution to rely entirely on section 1 would amount to a very significant deficiency in the ability of the legislation to address this particular mischief. That said, it is not the Government's intention to criminalise behaviour where no such mischief occurs, but merely to formulate the offence to take account of the evidential difficulties referred to above. In view of its wide scope, and its role in the new form of corporate liability at section 7, the Government offers the following further explanation of issues arising from the formulation of section 6.

Local law

24 For the purposes of section 6 prosecutors will be required to show not only that an 'advantage' was offered, promised or given to the official or to another person at the official's request, assent or acquiescence, but that the advantage was one that the official was not permitted or required to be influenced by as determined by the written law applicable to the foreign official.

25 In seeking tenders for publicly funded contracts Governments often permit or require those tendering for the contract to offer, in addition to the principal tender, some kind of additional investment in the local economy or benefit to the local community. Such arrangements could in certain circumstances amount to a financial or other 'advantage' to a public official or to another person at the official's request, assent or acquiescence. Where, however, relevant 'written law' permits or requires the official to be influenced by such arrangements they will fall outside the scope of the offence. So, for example, where local planning law permits community investment or requires a foreign public official to minimise the cost of public procurement administration through cost sharing with contractors, a prospective contractor's offer of free training is very unlikely to engage section 6. In circumstances where the additional investment would amount to an advantage to a foreign public official and the local law is silent as to whether the official is permitted or required to be influenced by it, prosecutors will consider the public interest in prosecuting. This will provide an appropriate backstop in circumstances where the evidence suggests that the offer of additional investment is a legitimate part of a tender exercise.

Hospitality, promotional, and other business expenditure

26 Bona fide hospitality and promotional, or other business expenditure which seeks to improve the image of a commercial organisation, better to present products and services, or establish cordial relations, is recognised as an established and important part of doing business and it is not the intention of the Act to criminalise such behaviour. The Government does not intend for the Act to prohibit reasonable and proportionate hospitality and promotional or other similar business expenditure intended for these purposes. It is, however, clear that hospitality and promotional or other similar business expenditure can be employed as bribes.

27 In order to amount to a bribe under section 6 there must be an intention for a financial or other advantage to influence the official in his or her official role and thereby secure business or a business advantage. In this regard, it may be in some circumstances that hospitality or promotional expenditure in the form of travel and accommodation costs does not even amount to 'a financial or other advantage' to the relevant official because it is a cost that would otherwise be borne by the relevant foreign Government rather than the official him or herself.

28 Where the prosecution is able to establish a financial or other advantage has been offered, promised or given, it must then show that there is a sufficient connection between the advantage and the intention to influence and secure business or a business advantage. Where the prosecution cannot prove this to the requisite standard then no offence under section 6 will be committed. There may be direct evidence to support the existence of this connection and such evidence may indeed relate to relatively modest expenditure. In many cases, however, the question as to whether such a connection can be established will depend on the totality of the evidence which takes into account all of the surrounding circumstances. It would include matters such as the type and level of advantage offered, the manner and form in which the advantage is provided, and the level of influence the particular foreign public official has over awarding the business. In this circumstantial context, the more lavish the hospitality or the higher the expenditure in relation to travel, accommodation or other similar business expenditure provided to a foreign public official, then, generally, the greater the inference that it is intended to influence the official to grant business or a business advantage in return.

29 The standards or norms applying in a particular sector may also be relevant here. However, simply providing hospitality or promotional, or other similar business expenditure which is commensurate with such norms is not, of itself, evidence that no bribe was paid if there is other evidence to the contrary; particularly if the norms in question are extravagant.

30 Levels of expenditure will not, therefore, be the only consideration in determining whether a section 6 offence has been committed. But in the absence of any further evidence demonstrating the required connection, it is unlikely, for example, that incidental provision of a routine business courtesy will raise the inference that it was intended to have a direct impact on decision making, particularly where such hospitality is commensurate with the reasonable and proportionate norms for the particular industry; eg the provision of airport to hotel transfer services to facilitate an on-site visit, or dining and tickets to an event.

31 Some further examples might be helpful. The provision by a UK mining company of reasonable travel and accommodation to allow foreign public officials to visit their distant mining operations so that those officials may be satisfied of the high standard and safety of the company's installations and operating systems are circumstances that fall outside the intended scope of the offence. Flights and accommodation to allow foreign public officials to meet with senior executives of a UK commercial organisation in New York as a matter of genuine mutual convenience, and some reasonable hospitality for the individual and his or her partner, such as fine dining and attendance at a baseball match are facts that are, in themselves, unlikely to raise the necessary inferences. However, if the choice of New York as the most convenient venue was in doubt because the organisation's senior executives could easily have seen the official with all the relevant documentation when they had visited the relevant country the previous week then the necessary inference might be raised. Similarly, supplementing information provided to a foreign public official on a commercial organisation's background, track record and expertise in providing private health care with an offer of ordinary travel and lodgings to enable a visit to a hospital run by the commercial organisation is unlikely to engage section 6. On the other hand, the provision by that same commercial organisation of a five-star holiday for the foreign public official which is unrelated to a demonstration of the organisation's services is, all things being equal, far more likely to raise the necessary inference.

32   It may be that, as a result of the introduction of the section 7 offence, commercial organisations will review their policies on hospitality and promotional or other similar business expenditure as part of the selection and implementation of bribery prevention procedures, so as to ensure that they are seen to be acting both competitively and fairly. It is, however, for individual organisations, or business representative bodies, to establish and disseminate appropriate standards for hospitality and promotional or other similar expenditure.

Section 7: Failure of commercial organisations to prevent bribery

33   A commercial organisation will be liable to prosecution if a person associated with it bribes another person intending to obtain or retain business or an advantage in the conduct of business for that organisation. As set out above, the commercial organisation will have a full defence if it can show that despite a particular case of bribery it nevertheless had adequate procedures in place to prevent persons associated with it from bribing. In accordance with established case law, the standard of proof which the commercial organisation would need to discharge in order to prove the defence, in the event it was prosecuted, is the balance of probabilities.

Commercial organisation

34   Only a 'relevant commercial organisation' can commit an offence under section 7 of the Bribery Act. A 'relevant commercial organisation' is defined at section 7(5) as a body or partnership incorporated or formed in the UK irrespective of where it carries on a business, or an incorporated body or partnership which carries on a business or part of a business in the UK irrespective of the place of incorporation or formation. The key concept here is that of an organisation which 'carries on a business'. The courts will be the final arbiter as to whether an organisation 'carries on a business' in the UK taking into account the particular facts in individual cases. However, the following paragraphs set out the Government's intention as regards the application of the phrase.

35   As regards bodies incorporated, or partnerships formed, in the UK, despite the fact that there are many ways in which a body corporate or a partnership can pursue business objectives, the Government expects that whether such a body or partnership can be said to be carrying on a business will be answered by applying a common sense approach. So long as the organisation in question is incorporated (by whatever means), or is a partnership, it does not matter if it pursues primarily charitable or educational aims or purely public functions. It will be caught if it engages in commercial activities, irrespective of the purpose for which profits are made.

36   As regards bodies incorporated, or partnerships formed, outside the United Kingdom, whether such bodies can properly be regarded as carrying on a business or part of a business 'in any part of the United Kingdom' will again be answered by applying a common sense approach. Where there is a particular dispute as to whether a business presence in the United Kingdom satisfies the test in the Act, the final arbiter, in any particular case, will be the courts as set out above. However, the Government anticipates that applying a common sense approach would mean that organisations that do not have a demonstrable business presence in the United Kingdom would not be caught. The Government would not expect, for example, the mere fact that a company's securities have been admitted to the UK Listing Authority's Official List and

therefore admitted to trading on the London Stock Exchange, in itself, to qualify that company as carrying on a business or part of a business in the UK and therefore falling within the definition of a 'relevant commercial organisation' for the purposes of section 7. Likewise, having a UK subsidiary will not, in itself, mean that a parent company is carrying on a business in the UK, since a subsidiary may act independently of its parent or other group companies.

Associated person

37 A commercial organisation is liable under section 7 if a person 'associated' with it bribes another person intending to obtain or retain business or a business advantage for the organisation. A person associated with a commercial organisation is defined at section 8 as a person who 'performs services' for or on behalf of the organisation. This person can be an individual or an incorporated or unincorporated body. Section 8 provides that the capacity in which a person performs services for or on behalf of the organisation does not matter, so employees (who are presumed to be performing services for their employer), agents and subsidiaries are included. Section 8(4), however, makes it clear that the question as to whether a person is performing services for an organisation is to be determined by reference to all the relevant circumstances and not merely by reference to the nature of the relationship between that person and the organisation. The concept of a person who 'performs services for or on behalf of' the organisation is intended to give section 7 broad scope so as to embrace the whole range of persons connected to an organisation who might be capable of committing bribery on the organisation's behalf.

38 This broad scope means that contractors could be 'associated' persons to the extent that they are performing services for or on behalf of a commercial organisation. Also, where a supplier can properly be said to be performing services for a commercial organisation rather than simply acting as the seller of goods, it may also be an 'associated' person.

39 Where a supply chain involves several entities or a project is to be performed by a prime contractor with a series of sub-contractors, an organisation is likely only to exercise control over its relationship with its contractual counterparty. Indeed, the organisation may only know the identity of its contractual counterparty. It is likely that persons who contract with that counterparty will be performing services for the counterparty and not for other persons in the contractual chain. The principal way in which commercial organisations may decide to approach bribery risks which arise as a result of a supply chain is by employing the types of anti-bribery procedures referred to elsewhere in this guidance (eg risk-based due diligence and the use of anti-bribery terms and conditions) in the relationship with their contractual counterparty, and by requesting that counterparty to adopt a similar approach with the next party in the chain.

40 As for joint ventures, these come in many different forms, sometimes operating through a separate legal entity, but at other times through contractual arrangements. In the case of a joint venture operating through a separate legal entity, a bribe paid by the joint venture entity may lead to liability for a member of the joint venture if the joint venture is performing services for the member and the bribe is paid with the intention of benefiting that member. However, the existence of a joint venture entity will not of itself mean that it is 'associated' with any of its members. A bribe paid on behalf of the joint venture entity by one of its employees or agents will therefore not trigger liability for members of the joint venture simply by virtue of them benefiting indirectly from the bribe through their investment in or ownership of the joint venture.

41 The situation will be different where the joint venture is conducted through a contractual arrangement. The degree of control that a participant has over that arrangement is likely to be one of the 'relevant circumstances' that would be taken into account in deciding whether a person who paid a bribe in the conduct of the joint venture business was 'performing services for or on behalf of' a participant in that arrangement. It may be, for example, that an employee of such a participant who has paid a bribe in order to benefit his employer is not to be regarded as a person 'associated' with all the other participants in the joint venture. Ordinarily, the employee of a participant will be presumed to be a person performing services for and on behalf

of his employer. Likewise, an agent engaged by a participant in a contractual joint venture is likely to be regarded as a person associated with that participant in the absence of evidence that the agent is acting on behalf of the contractual joint venture as a whole.

42   Even if it can properly be said that an agent, a subsidiary, or another person acting for a member of a joint venture, was performing services for the organisation, an offence will be committed only if that agent, subsidiary or person intended to obtain or retain business or an advantage in the conduct of business for the organisation. The fact that an organisation benefits indirectly from a bribe is very unlikely, in itself, to amount to proof of the specific intention required by the offence. Without proof of the required intention, liability will not accrue through simple corporate ownership or investment, or through the payment of dividends or provision of loans by a subsidiary to its parent. So, for example, a bribe on behalf of a subsidiary by one of its employees or agents will not automatically involve liability on the part of its parent company, or any other subsidiaries of the parent company, if it cannot be shown the employee or agent intended to obtain or retain business or a business advantage for the parent company or other subsidiaries. This is so even though the parent company or subsidiaries may benefit indirectly from the bribe. By the same token, liability for a parent company could arise where a subsidiary is the 'person' which pays a bribe which it intends will result in the parent company obtaining or retaining business or vice versa.

43   The question of adequacy of bribery prevention procedures will depend in the final analysis on the facts of each case, including matters such as the level of control over the activities of the associated person and the degree of risk that requires mitigation. The scope of the definition at section 8 needs to be appreciated within this context. This point is developed in more detail under the six principles set out on pages 20 to 31.

Facilitation payments

44   Small bribes paid to facilitate routine Government action—otherwise called 'facilitation payments'—could trigger either the section 6 offence or, where there is an intention to induce improper conduct, including where the acceptance of such payments is itself improper, the section 1 offence and therefore potential liability under section 7.

45   As was the case under the old law, the Bribery Act does not (unlike US foreign bribery law) provide any exemption for such payments. The 2009 Recommendation of the Organisation for Economic Co-operation and Development[5] recognises the corrosive effect of facilitation payments and asks adhering countries to discourage companies from making such payments. Exemptions in this context create artificial distinctions that are difficult to enforce, undermine corporate anti-bribery procedures, confuse anti-bribery communication with employees and other associated persons, perpetuate an existing 'culture' of bribery and have the potential to be abused.

[5]   Recommendation of the Council for Further Combating Bribery of Foreign Public Officials in International Business Transactions.

46   The Government does, however, recognise the problems that commercial organisations face in some parts of the world and in certain sectors. The eradication of facilitation payments is recognised at the national and international level as a long term objective that will require economic and social progress and sustained commitment to the rule of law in those parts of the world where the problem is most prevalent. It will also require collaboration between international bodies, governments, the anti-bribery lobby, business representative bodies and sectoral organisations. Businesses themselves also have a role to play and the guidance below offers an indication of how the problem may be addressed through the selection of bribery prevention procedures by commercial organisations.

47   Issues relating to the prosecution of facilitation payments in England and Wales are referred to in the guidance of the Director of the Serious Fraud Office and the Director of Public Prosecutions.[6]

[6]   Bribery Act 2010: Joint Prosecution Guidance of the Director of the Serious Fraud Office and the Director of Public Prosecutions.

Duress

48   It is recognised that there are circumstances in which individuals are left with no alternative but to make payments in order to protect against loss of life, limb or liberty. The common law defence of duress is very likely to be available in such circumstances.

Prosecutorial discretion

49   Whether to prosecute an offence under the Act is a matter for the prosecuting authorities. In deciding whether to proceed, prosecutors must first decide if there is a sufficiency of evidence, and, if so, whether a prosecution is in the public interest. If the evidential test has been met, prosecutors will consider the general public interest in ensuring that bribery is effectively dealt with. The more serious the offence, the more likely it is that a prosecution will be required in the public interest.

50   In cases where hospitality, promotional expenditure or facilitation payments do, on their face, trigger the provisions of the Act prosecutors will consider very carefully what is in the public interest before deciding whether to prosecute. The operation of prosecutorial discretion provides a degree of flexibility which is helpful to ensure the just and fair operation of the Act.

51   Factors that weigh for and against the public interest in prosecuting in England and Wales are referred to in the joint guidance of the Director of the Serious Fraud Office and the Director of Public Prosecutions referred to at paragraph 47.

THE SIX PRINCIPLES

The Government considers that procedures put in place by commercial organisations wishing to prevent bribery being committed on their behalf should be informed by six principles. These are set out below. Commentary and guidance on what procedures the application of the principles may produce accompanies each principle.

These principles are not prescriptive. They are intended to be flexible and outcome focussed, allowing for the huge variety of circumstances that commercial organisations find themselves in. Small organisations will, for example, face different challenges to those faced by large multi-national enterprises. Accordingly, the detail of how organisations might apply these principles, taken as a whole, will vary, but the outcome should always be robust and effective anti-bribery procedures.

As set out in more detail below, bribery prevention procedures should be proportionate to risk. Although commercial organisations with entirely domestic operations may require bribery prevention procedures, we believe that as a general proposition they will face lower risks of bribery on their behalf by associated persons than the risks that operate in foreign markets. In any event procedures put in place to mitigate domestic bribery risks are likely to be similar if not the same as those designed to mitigate those associated with foreign markets.

A series of case studies based on hypothetical scenarios is provided at Appendix A. These are designed to illustrate the application of the principles for small, medium and large organisations.

PRINCIPLE 1 PROPORTIONATE PROCEDURES

A commercial organisation's procedures to prevent bribery by persons associated with it are proportionate to the bribery risks it faces and to the nature, scale and complexity of the commercial organisation's activities. They are also clear, practical, accessible, effectively implemented and enforced.

Commentary

1.1   The term 'procedures' is used in this guidance to embrace both bribery prevention policies and the procedures which implement them. Policies articulate a commercial organisation's anti-bribery stance, show how it will be maintained and help to create an anti-bribery culture. They are therefore a necessary measure in the prevention of bribery, but they will not achieve that objective unless they are properly implemented. Further guidance on implementation is provided through principles 2 to 6.

1.2 Adequate bribery prevention procedures ought to be proportionate to the bribery risks that the organisation faces. An initial assessment of risk across the organisation is therefore a necessary first step. To a certain extent the level of risk will be linked to the size of the organisation and the nature and complexity of its business, but size will not be the only determining factor. Some small organisations can face quite significant risks, and will need more extensive procedures than their counterparts facing limited risks. However, small organisations are unlikely to need procedures that are as extensive as those of a large multi-national organisation. For example, a very small business may be able to rely heavily on periodic oral briefings to communicate its policies while a large one may need to rely on extensive written communication.

1.3 The level of risk that organisations face will also vary with the type and nature of the persons associated with it. For example, a commercial organisation that properly assesses that there is no risk of bribery on the part of one of its associated persons will accordingly require nothing in the way of procedures to prevent bribery in the context of that relationship. By the same token the bribery risks associated with reliance on a third party agent representing a commercial organisation in negotiations with foreign public officials may be assessed as significant and accordingly require much more in the way of procedures to mitigate those risks. Organisations are likely to need to select procedures to cover a broad range of risks but any consideration by a court in an individual case of the adequacy of procedures is likely necessarily to focus on those procedures designed to prevent bribery on the part of the associated person committing the offence in question.

1.4 Bribery prevention procedures may be stand alone or form part of wider guidance, for example on recruitment or on managing a tender process in public procurement. Whatever the chosen model, the procedures should seek to ensure there is a practical and realistic means of achieving the organisation's stated anti-bribery policy objectives across all of the organisation's functions.

1.5 The Government recognises that applying these procedures retrospectively to existing associated persons is more difficult, but this should be done over time, adopting a risk-based approach and with due allowance for what is practicable and the level of control over existing arrangements.

Procedures

1.6 Commercial organisations' bribery prevention policies are likely to include certain common elements. As an indicative and not exhaustive list, an organisation may wish to cover in its policies:

- its commitment to bribery prevention (see Principle 2)
- its general approach to mitigation of specific bribery risks, such as those arising from the conduct of intermediaries and agents, or those associated with hospitality and promotional expenditure, facilitation payments or political and charitable donations or contributions; (see Principle 3 on risk assessment)
- an overview of its strategy to implement its bribery prevention policies.

1.7 The procedures put in place to implement an organisation's bribery prevention policies should be designed to mitigate identified risks as well as to prevent deliberate unethical conduct on the part of associated persons. The following is an indicative and not exhaustive list of the topics that bribery prevention procedures might embrace depending on the particular risks faced:

- The involvement of the organisation's top-level management (see Principle 2).
- Risk assessment procedures (see Principle 3).
- Due diligence of existing or prospective associated persons (see Principle 4).
- The provision of gifts, hospitality and promotional expenditure; charitable and political donations; or demands for facilitation payments.
- Direct and indirect employment, including recruitment, terms and conditions, disciplinary action and remuneration.

- Governance of business relationships with all other associated persons including pre and post contractual agreements.
- Financial and commercial controls such as adequate bookkeeping, auditing and approval of expenditure.
- Transparency of transactions and disclosure of information. Decision making, such as delegation of authority procedures, separation of functions and the avoidance of conflicts of interest.
- Enforcement, detailing discipline processes and sanctions for breaches of the organisation's anti-bribery rules.
- The reporting of bribery including 'speak up' or 'whistle blowing' procedures.
- The detail of the process by which the organisation plans to implement its bribery prevention procedures, for example, how its policy will be applied to individual projects and to different parts of the organisation.
- The communication of the organisation's policies and procedures, and training in their application (see Principle 5).
- The monitoring, review and evaluation of bribery prevention procedures (see Principle 6).

PRINCIPLE 2 TOP-LEVEL COMMITMENT

The top-level management of a commercial organisation (be it a board of directors, the owners or any other equivalent body or person) are committed to preventing bribery by persons associated with it. They foster a culture within the organisation in which bribery is never acceptable.

Commentary

2.1 Those at the top of an organisation are in the best position to foster a culture of integrity where bribery is unacceptable. The purpose of this principle is to encourage the involvement of top-level management in the determination of bribery prevention procedures. It is also to encourage top-level involvement in any key decision making relating to bribery risk where that is appropriate for the organisation's management structure.

Procedures

2.2 Whatever the size, structure or market of a commercial organisation, top- level management commitment to bribery prevention is likely to include (1) communication of the organisation's anti-bribery stance, and (2) an appropriate degree of involvement in developing bribery prevention procedures.

Internal and external communication of the commitment to zero tolerance to bribery

2.3 This could take a variety of forms. A formal statement appropriately communicated can be very effective in establishing an anti-bribery culture within an organisation. Communication might be tailored to different audiences. The statement would probably need to be drawn to people's attention on a periodic basis and could be generally available, for example on an organisation's intranet and/or internet site. Effective formal statements that demonstrate top level commitment are likely to include:

- a commitment to carry out business fairly, honestly and openly
- a commitment to zero tolerance towards bribery
- the consequences of breaching the policy for employees and managers
- for other associated persons the consequences of breaching contractual provisions relating to bribery prevention (this could include a reference to avoiding doing business with others who do not commit to doing business without bribery as a 'best practice' objective)
- articulation of the business benefits of rejecting bribery (reputational, customer and business partner confidence)
- reference to the range of bribery prevention procedures the commercial organisation has or is putting in place, including any protection and procedures for confidential reporting of bribery (whistle-blowing)

- key individuals and departments involved in the development and implementation of the organisation's bribery prevention procedures
- reference to the organisation's involvement in any collective action against bribery in, for example, the same business sector.

Top-level involvement in bribery prevention

2.4 Effective leadership in bribery prevention will take a variety of forms appropriate for and proportionate to the organisation's size, management structure and circumstances. In smaller organisations a proportionate response may require top-level managers to be personally involved in initiating, developing and implementing bribery prevention procedures and bribery critical decision making. In a large multinational organisation the board should be responsible for setting bribery prevention policies, tasking management to design, operate and monitor bribery prevention procedures, and keeping these policies and procedures under regular review. But whatever the appropriate model, top-level engagement is likely to reflect the following elements:

- Selection and training of senior managers to lead anti-bribery work where appropriate.
- Leadership on key measures such as a code of conduct.
- Endorsement of all bribery prevention related publications.
- Leadership in awareness raising and encouraging transparent dialogue throughout the organisation so as to seek to ensure effective dissemination of anti-bribery policies and procedures to employees, subsidiaries, and associated persons, etc.
- Engagement with relevant associated persons and external bodies, such as sectoral organisations and the media, to help articulate the organisation's policies.
- Specific involvement in high profile and critical decision making where appropriate.
- Assurance of risk assessment.
- General oversight of breaches of procedures and the provision of feedback to the board or equivalent, where appropriate, on levels of compliance.

PRINCIPLE 3 RISK ASSESSMENT

The commercial organisation assesses the nature and extent of its exposure to potential external and internal risks of bribery on its behalf by persons associated with it. The assessment is periodic, informed and documented.

Commentary

3.1 For many commercial organisations this principle will manifest itself as part of a more general risk assessment carried out in relation to business objectives. For others, its application may produce a more specific stand alone bribery risk assessment. The purpose of this principle is to promote the adoption of risk assessment procedures that are proportionate to the organisation's size and structure and to the nature, scale and location of its activities. But whatever approach is adopted the fuller the understanding of the bribery risks an organisation faces the more effective its efforts to prevent bribery are likely to be.

3.2 Some aspects of risk assessment involve procedures that fall within the generally accepted meaning of the term 'due diligence'. The role of due diligence as a risk mitigation tool is separately dealt with under Principle 4.

Procedures

3.3 Risk assessment procedures that enable the commercial organisation accurately to identify and prioritise the risks it faces will, whatever its size, activities, customers or markets, usually reflect a few basic characteristics. These are:

- Oversight of the risk assessment by top level management.
- Appropriate resourcing—this should reflect the scale of the organisation's business and the need to identify and prioritise all relevant risks.

- Identification of the internal and external information sources that will enable risk to be assessed and reviewed.
- Due diligence enquiries (see Principle 4).
- Accurate and appropriate documentation of the risk assessment and its conclusions.

3.4 As a commercial organisation's business evolves, so will the bribery risks it faces and hence so should its risk assessment. For example, the risk assessment that applies to a commercial organisation's domestic operations might not apply when it enters a new market in a part of the world in which it has not done business before (see Principle 6 for more on this).

Commonly encountered risks

3.5 Commonly encountered external risks can be categorised into five broad groups—country, sectoral, transaction, business opportunity and business partnership:

- *Country risk:* this is evidenced by perceived high levels of corruption, an absence of effectively implemented anti-bribery legislation and a failure of the foreign government, media, local business community and civil society effectively to promote transparent procurement and investment policies.
- *Sectoral risk:* some sectors are higher risk than others. Higher risk sectors include the extractive industries and the large scale infrastructure sector.
- *Transaction risk:* certain types of transaction give rise to higher risks, for example, charitable or political contributions, licences and permits, and transactions relating to public procurement.
- *Business opportunity risk:* such risks might arise in high value projects or with projects involving many contractors or intermediaries; or with projects which are not apparently undertaken at market prices, or which do not have a clear legitimate objective.
- *Business partnership risk:* certain relationships may involve higher risk, for example, the use of intermediaries in transactions with foreign public officials; consortia or joint venture partners; and relationships with politically exposed persons where the proposed business relationship involves, or is linked to, a prominent public official.

3.6 An assessment of external bribery risks is intended to help decide how those risks can be mitigated by procedures governing the relevant operations or business relationships; but a bribery risk assessment should also examine the extent to which internal structures or procedures may themselves add to the level of risk. Commonly encountered internal factors may include:

- deficiencies in employee training, skills and knowledge
- bonus culture that rewards excessive risk taking
- lack of clarity in the organisation's policies on, and procedures for, hospitality and promotional expenditure, and political or charitable contributions
- lack of clear financial controls
- lack of a clear anti-bribery message from the top-level management.

PRINCIPLE 4 DUE DILIGENCE

The commercial organisation applies due diligence procedures, taking a proportionate and risk based approach, in respect of persons who perform or will perform services for or on behalf of the organisation, in order to mitigate identified bribery risks.

Commentary

4.1 Due diligence is firmly established as an element of corporate good governance and it is envisaged that due diligence related to bribery prevention will often form part of a wider due diligence framework. Due diligence procedures are both a form of bribery risk assessment (see Principle 3) and a means of mitigating a risk. By way of illustration, a commercial organisation may identify risks that as a general proposition attach to doing business in reliance upon local third party intermediaries. Due diligence of specific prospective third party intermediaries could significantly mitigate these risks. The significance of the role of due diligence in bribery risk mitigation justifies its inclusion here as a Principle in its own right.

4.2　The purpose of this Principle is to encourage commercial organisations to put in place due diligence procedures that adequately inform the application of proportionate measures designed to prevent persons associated with them from bribing on their behalf.

Procedures

4.3　As this guidance emphasises throughout, due diligence procedures should be proportionate to the identified risk. They can also be undertaken internally or by external consultants. A person 'associated' with a commercial organisation as set out at section 8 of the Bribery Act includes any person performing services for a commercial organisation. As explained at paragraphs 37 to 43 in the section 'Government Policy and section 7', the scope of this definition is broad and can embrace a wide range of business relationships. But the appropriate level of due diligence to prevent bribery will vary enormously depending on the risks arising from the particular relationship. So, for example, the appropriate level of due diligence required by a commercial organisation when contracting for the performance of information technology services may be low, to reflect low risks of bribery on its behalf. In contrast, an organisation that is selecting an intermediary to assist in establishing a business in foreign markets will typically require a much higher level of due diligence to mitigate the risks of bribery on its behalf.

4.4　Organisations will need to take considerable care in entering into certain business relationships, due to the particular circumstances in which the relationships come into existence. An example is where local law or convention dictates the use of local agents in circumstances where it may be difficult for a commercial organisation to extricate itself from a business relationship once established. The importance of thorough due diligence and risk mitigation prior to any commitment are paramount in such circumstances. Another relationship that carries particularly important due diligence implications is a merger of commercial organisations or an acquisition of one by another.

4.5　'Due diligence' for the purposes of Principle 4 should be conducted using a risk-based approach (as referred to on page 27). For example, in lower risk situations, commercial organisations may decide that there is no need to conduct much in the way of due diligence. In higher risk situations, due diligence may include conducting direct interrogative enquiries, indirect investigations, or general research on proposed associated persons. Appraisal and continued monitoring of recruited or engaged 'associated' persons may also be required, proportionate to the identified risks. Generally, more information is likely to be required from prospective and existing associated persons that are incorporated (eg companies) than from individuals. This is because on a basic level more individuals are likely to be involved in the performance of services by a company and the exact nature of the roles of such individuals or other connected bodies may not be immediately obvious. Accordingly, due diligence may involve direct requests for details on the background, expertise and business experience, of relevant individuals. This information can then be verified through research and the following up of references, etc.

4.6　A commercial organisation's employees are presumed to be persons 'associated' with the organisation for the purposes of the Bribery Act. The organisation may wish, therefore, to incorporate in its recruitment and human resources procedures an appropriate level of due diligence to mitigate the risks of bribery being undertaken by employees which is proportionate to the risk associated with the post in question. Due diligence is unlikely to be needed in relation to lower risk posts.

PRINCIPLE 5 COMMUNICATION (INCLUDING TRAINING)

The commercial organisation seeks to ensure that its bribery prevention policies and procedures are embedded and understood throughout the organisation through internal and external communication, including training, that is proportionate to the risks it faces.

Commentary

5.1 Communication and training deters bribery by associated persons by enhancing awareness and understanding of a commercial organisation's procedures and to the organisation's commitment to their proper application. Making information available assists in more effective monitoring, evaluation and review of bribery prevention procedures. Training provides the knowledge and skills needed to employ the organisation's procedures and deal with any bribery related problems or issues that may arise.

Procedures

Communication

5.2 The content, language and tone of communications for internal consumption may vary from that for external use in response to the different relationship the audience has with the commercial organisation. The nature of communication will vary enormously between commercial organisations in accordance with the different bribery risks faced, the size of the organisation and the scale and nature of its activities.

5.3 Internal communications should convey the 'tone from the top' but are also likely to focus on the implementation of the organisation's policies and procedures and the implications for employees. Such communication includes policies on particular areas such as decision making, financial control, hospitality and promotional expenditure, facilitation payments, training, charitable and political donations and penalties for breach of rules and the articulation of management roles at different levels. Another important aspect of internal communications is the establishment of a secure, confidential and accessible means for internal or external parties to raise concerns about bribery on the part of associated persons, to provide suggestions for improvement of bribery prevention procedures and controls and for requesting advice. These so called 'speak up' procedures can amount to a very helpful management tool for commercial organisations with diverse operations that may be in many countries. If these procedures are to be effective there must be adequate protection for those reporting concerns.

5.4 External communication of bribery prevention policies through a statement or codes of conduct, for example, can reassure existing and prospective associated persons and can act as a deterrent to those intending to bribe on a commercial organisation's behalf. Such communications can include information on bribery prevention procedures and controls, sanctions, results of internal surveys, rules governing recruitment, procurement and tendering. A commercial organisation may consider it proportionate and appropriate to communicate its anti-bribery policies and commitment to them to a wider audience, such as other organisations in its sector and to sectoral organisations that would fall outside the scope of the range of its associated persons, or to the general public.

Training

5.5 Like all procedures training should be proportionate to risk but some training is likely to be effective in firmly establishing an anti-bribery culture whatever the level of risk. Training may take the form of education and awareness raising about the threats posed by bribery in general and in the sector or areas in which the organisation operates in particular, and the various ways it is being addressed.

5.6 General training could be mandatory for new employees or for agents (on a weighted risk basis) as part of an induction process, but it should also be tailored to the specific risks associated with specific posts. Consideration should also be given to tailoring training to the special needs of those involved in any 'speak up' procedures, and higher risk functions such as purchasing, contracting, distribution and marketing, and working in high risk countries. Effective training is continuous, and regularly monitored and evaluated.

5.7 It may be appropriate to require associated persons to undergo training. This will be particularly relevant for high risk associated persons. In any event, organisations may wish to encourage associated persons to adopt bribery prevention training.

5.8 Nowadays there are many different training formats available in addition to the traditional classroom or seminar formats, such as e-learning and other web-based tools. But whatever the format, the training ought to achieve its objective of ensuring that those participating in it develop a firm understanding of what the relevant policies and procedures mean in practice for them.

PRINCIPLE 6 MONITORING AND REVIEW

The commercial organisation monitors and reviews procedures designed to prevent bribery by persons associated with it and makes improvements where necessary.

Commentary

6.1 The bribery risks that a commercial organisation faces may change over time, as may the nature and scale of its activities, so the procedures required to mitigate those risks are also likely to change. Commercial organisations will therefore wish to consider how to monitor and evaluate the effectiveness of their bribery prevention procedures and adapt them where necessary. In addition to regular monitoring, an organisation might want to review its processes in response to other stimuli, for example governmental changes in countries in which they operate, an incident of bribery or negative press reports.

Procedures

6.2 There is a wide range of internal and external review mechanisms which commercial organisations could consider using. Systems set up to deter, detect and investigate bribery, and monitor the ethical quality of transactions, such as internal financial control mechanisms, will help provide insight into the effectiveness of procedures designed to prevent bribery. Staff surveys, questionnaires and feedback from training can also provide an important source of information on effectiveness and a means by which employees and other associated persons can inform continuing improvement of anti-bribery policies.

6.3 Organisations could also consider formal periodic reviews and reports for top-level management. Organisations could also draw on information on other organisations' practices, for example relevant trade bodies or regulators might highlight examples of good or bad practice in their publications.

6.4 In addition, organisations might wish to consider seeking some form of external verification or assurance of the effectiveness of anti-bribery procedures. Some organisations may be able to apply for certified compliance with one of the independently-verified anti-bribery standards maintained by industrial sector associations or multi-lateral bodies. However, such certification may not necessarily mean that a commercial organisation's bribery prevention procedures are 'adequate' for all purposes where an offence under section 7 of the Bribery Act could be charged.

APPENDIX A BRIBERY ACT 2010 CASE STUDIES

Introduction

These case studies (which do not form part of the guidance issued under section 9 of the Act) look at how the application of the six principles might relate to a number of hypothetical scenarios commercial organisations may encounter. The Government believes that this illustrative context can assist commercial organisations in deciding what procedures to prevent persons associated with them from bribing on their behalf might be most suitable to their needs.

These case studies are illustrative. They are intended to complement the guidance. They do not replace or supersede any of the principles. The considerations set out below merely show in some circumstances how the principles can be applied, and should not be seen as standard setting, establishing any presumption, reflecting a minimum baseline of action or being appropriate for all organisations whatever their size. Accordingly, the considerations set out below are not:

- comprehensive of all considerations in all circumstances
- conclusive of adequate procedures
- conclusive of inadequate procedures if not all of the considerations are considered and/or applied.

All but one of these case studies focus on bribery risks associated with foreign markets. This is because bribery risks associated with foreign markets are generally higher than those associated with domestic markets. Accordingly case studies focussing on foreign markets are better suited as vehicles for the illustration of bribery prevention procedures.

CASE STUDY 1 – PRINCIPLE 1 FACILITATION PAYMENTS

A medium sized company ('A') has acquired a new customer in a foreign country ('B') where it operates through its agent company ('C'). Its bribery risk assessment has identified facilitation payments as a significant problem in securing reliable importation into B and transport to its new customer's manufacturing locations. These sometimes take the form of 'inspection fees' required before B's import inspectors will issue a certificate of inspection and thereby facilitate the clearance of goods.

A could consider any or a combination of the following:

- Communication of its policy of non-payment of facilitation payments to C and its staff.
- Seeking advice on the law of B relating to certificates of inspection and fees for these to differentiate between properly payable fees and disguised requests for facilitation payments.
- Building realistic timescales into the planning of the project so that shipping, importation and delivery schedules allow where feasible for resisting and testing demands for facilitation payments.
- Requesting that C train its staff about resisting demands for facilitation payments and the relevant local law and provisions of the Bribery Act 2010.
- Proposing or including as part of any contractual arrangement certain procedures for C and its staff, which may include one or more of the following, if appropriate:
  - questioning of legitimacy of demands
  - requesting receipts and identification details of the official making the demand
  - requests to consult with superior officials
  - trying to avoid paying 'inspection fees' (if not properly due) in cash and directly to an official
  - informing those demanding payments that compliance with the demand may mean that A (and possibly C) will commit an offence under UK law
  - informing those demanding payments that it will be necessary for C to inform the UK embassy of the demand.
- Maintaining close liaison with C so as to keep abreast of any local developments that may provide solutions and encouraging C to develop its own strategies based on local knowledge.
- Use of any UK diplomatic channels or participation in locally active non-governmental organisations, so as to apply pressure on the authorities of B to take action to stop demands for facilitation payments.

CASE STUDY 2 – PRINCIPLE 1 PROPORTIONATE PROCEDURES

A small to medium sized installation company is operating entirely within the United Kingdom domestic market. It relies to varying degrees on independent consultants to facilitate business opportunities and to assist in the preparation of both pre-qualification submissions and formal tenders in seeking new business. Such consultants work on an arms-length-fee-plus-expenses basis. They are engaged by sales staff and selected because of their extensive network of business contacts and the specialist information they have.

The reason for engaging them is to enhance the company's prospects of being included in tender and pre-qualification lists and of being selected as main or sub-contractors. The reliance on consultants and, in particular, difficulties in monitoring expenditure which sometimes involves cash transactions has been identified by the company as a source of medium to high risk of bribery being undertaken on the company's behalf.

In seeking to mitigate these risks the company could consider any or a combination of the following:

- Communication of a policy statement committing it to transparency and zero tolerance of bribery in pursuit of its business objectives. The statement could be communicated to the company's employees, known consultants and external contacts, such as sectoral bodies and local chambers of commerce.
- Firming up its due diligence before engaging consultants. This could include making enquiries through business contacts, local chambers of commerce, business associations, or internet searches and following up any business references and financial statements.
- Considering firming up the terms of the consultants' contracts so that they reflect a commitment to zero tolerance of bribery, set clear criteria for provision of bona fide hospitality on the company's behalf and define in detail the basis of remuneration, including expenses.
- Consider making consultants' contracts subject to periodic review and renewal.
- Drawing up key points guidance on preventing bribery for its sales staff and all other staff involved in bidding for business and when engaging consultants
- Periodically emphasising these policies and procedures at meetings – for example, this might form a standing item on meeting agendas every few months.
- Providing a confidential means for staff and external business contacts to air any suspicions of the use of bribery on the company's behalf.

CASE STUDY 3 – PRINCIPLES 1 AND 6 JOINT VENTURE

A medium sized company ('D') is interested in significant foreign mineral deposits. D proposes to enter into a joint venture with a local mining company ('E'). It is proposed that D and E would have an equal holding in the joint venture company ('DE'). D identifies the necessary interaction between DE and local public officials as a source of significant risks of bribery.

D could consider negotiating for the inclusion of any or a combination of the following bribery prevention procedures into the agreement setting up DE:

- Parity of representation on the board of DE.
- That DE put in place measures designed to ensure compliance with all applicable bribery and corruption laws. These measures might cover such issues as:
    - gifts and hospitality
    - agreed decision making rules
    - procurement
    - engagement of third parties, including due diligence requirements
    - conduct of relations with public officials
    - training for staff in high risk positions

- record keeping and accounting.
- The establishment of an audit committee with at least one representative of each of D and E that has the power to view accounts and certain expenditure and prepare regular reports.
- Binding commitments by D and E to comply with all applicable bribery laws in relation to the operation of DE, with a breach by either D or E being a breach of the agreement between them. Where such a breach is a material breach this could lead to termination or other similarly significant consequences.

CASE STUDY 4 – PRINCIPLES 1 AND 5 HOSPITALITY AND PROMOTIONAL EXPENDITURE

A firm of engineers ('F') maintains a programme of annual events providing entertainment, quality dining and attendance at various sporting occasions, as an expression of appreciation of its long association with its business partners. Private bodies and individuals are happy to meet their own travel and accommodation costs associated with attending these events. The costs of the travel and accommodation of any foreign public officials attending are, however, met by F.

F could consider any or a combination of the following:

- Conducting a bribery risk assessment relating to its dealings with business partners and foreign public officials and in particular the provision of hospitality and promotional expenditure.
- Publication of a policy statement committing it to transparent, proportionate, reasonable and bona fide hospitality and promotional expenditure.
- The issue of internal guidance on procedures that apply to the provision of hospitality and/or promotional expenditure providing:
  - that any procedures are designed to seek to ensure transparency and conformity with any relevant laws and codes applying to F
  - that any procedures are designed to seek to ensure transparency and conformity with the relevant laws and codes applying to foreign public officials
  - that any hospitality should reflect a desire to cement good relations and show appreciation, and that promotional expenditure should seek to improve the image of F as a commercial organisation, to better present its products or services, or establish cordial relations
  - that the recipient should not be given the impression that they are under an obligation to confer any business advantage or that the recipient's independence will be affected
  - criteria to be applied when deciding the appropriate levels of hospitality for both private and public business partners, clients, suppliers and foreign public officials and the type of hospitality that is appropriate in different sets of circumstances
  - that provision of hospitality for public officials be cleared with the relevant public body so that it is clear who and what the hospitality is for
  - for expenditure over certain limits, approval by an appropriately senior level of management may be a relevant consideration
  - accounting (book-keeping, orders, invoices, delivery notes, etc).
- Regular monitoring, review and evaluation of internal procedures and compliance with them.
- Appropriate training and supervision provided to staff.

CASE STUDY 5 – PRINCIPLE 3 ASSESSING RISKS

A small specialist manufacturer is seeking to expand its business in one of several emerging markets, all of which offer comparable opportunities. It has no specialist risk assessment expertise and is unsure how to go about assessing the risks of entering a new market.

The small manufacturer could consider any or a combination of the following:

- Incorporating an assessment of bribery risk into research to identify the optimum market for expansion.
- Seeking advice from UK diplomatic services and government organisations such as UK Trade and Investment.
- Consulting general country assessments undertaken by local chambers of commerce, relevant non-governmental organisations and sectoral organisations.
- Seeking advice from industry representatives.
- Following up any general or specialist advice with further independent research.

CASE STUDY 6 – PRINCIPLE 4 DUE DILIGENCE OF AGENTS

A medium to large sized manufacturer of specialist equipment ('G') has an opportunity to enter an emerging market in a foreign country ('H') by way of a government contract to supply equipment to the state. Local convention requires any foreign commercial organisations to operate through a local agent. G is concerned to appoint a reputable agent and ensure that the risk of bribery being used to develop its business in the market is minimised.

G could consider any or a combination of the following:

- Compiling a suitable questionnaire for potential agents requiring for example, details of ownership if not an individual; CVs and references for those involved in performing the proposed service; details of any directorships held, existing partnerships and third party relationships and any relevant judicial or regulatory findings.
- Having a clear statement of the precise nature of the services offered, costs, commissions, fees and the preferred means of remuneration.
- Undertaking research, including internet searches, of the prospective agents and, if a corporate body, of every person identified as having a degree of control over its affairs.
- Making enquiries with the relevant authorities in H to verify the information received in response to the questionnaire.
- Following up references and clarifying any matters arising from the questionnaire or any other information received with the agents, arranging face to face meetings where appropriate.
- Requesting sight or evidence of any potential agent's own anti-bribery policies and, where a corporate body, reporting procedures and records.
- Being alert to key commercial questions such as:
  - Is the agent really required?
  - Does the agent have the required expertise?
  - Are they interacting with or closely connected to public officials?
  - Is what you are proposing to pay reasonable and commercial?
- Renewing due diligence enquiries on a periodic basis if an agent is appointed.

CASE STUDY 7 – PRINCIPLE 5 COMMUNICATING AND TRAINING

A small UK manufacturer of specialist equipment ('J') has engaged an individual as a local agent and adviser ('K') to assist with winning a contract and developing its business in a foreign country where the risk of bribery is assessed as high.

J could consider any or a combination of the following:

- Making employees of J engaged in bidding for business fully aware of J's anti-bribery statement, code of conduct and, where appropriate, that details of its anti-bribery policies are included in its tender.

- Including suitable contractual terms on bribery prevention measures in the agreement between J and K, for example: requiring K not to offer or pay bribes; giving J the ability to audit K's activities and expenditure; requiring K to report any requests for bribes by officials to J; and, in the event of suspicion arising as to K's activities, giving J the right to terminate the arrangement.
- Making employees of J fully aware of policies and procedures applying to relevant issues such as hospitality and facilitation payments, including all financial control mechanisms, sanctions for any breaches of the rules and instructions on how to report any suspicious conduct.
- Supplementing the information, where appropriate, with specially prepared training to J's staff involved with the foreign country.

CASE STUDY 8 – PRINCIPLE 1, 4 AND 6 COMMUNITY BENEFITS AND CHARITABLE DONATIONS

A company ('L') exports a range of seed products to growers around the globe. Its representative travels to a foreign country ('M') to discuss with a local farming cooperative the possible supply of a new strain of wheat that is resistant to a disease which recently swept the region. In the meeting, the head of the co-operative tells L's representative about the problems which the relative unavailability of antiretroviral drugs cause locally in the face of a high HIV infection rate.

In a subsequent meeting with an official of M to discuss the approval of L's new wheat strain for import, the official suggests that L could pay for the necessary antiretroviral drugs and that this will be a very positive factor in the Government's consideration of the licence to import the new seed strain. In a further meeting, the same official states that L should donate money to a certain charity suggested by the official which, the official assures, will then take the necessary steps to purchase and distribute the drugs. L identifies this as raising potential bribery risks.

L could consider any or a combination of the following:

- Making reasonable efforts to conduct due diligence, including consultation with staff members and any business partners it has in country M in order to satisfy itself that the suggested arrangement is legitimate and in conformity with any relevant laws and codes applying to the foreign public official responsible for approving the product. It could do this by obtaining information on:
  - M's local law on community benefits as part of Government procurement and, if no particular local law, the official status and legitimacy of the suggested arrangement
  - the particular charity in question including its legal status, its reputation in M, and whether it has conducted similar projects, and
  - any connections the charity might have with the foreign official in question, if possible.
- Adopting an internal communication plan designed to ensure that any relationships with charitable organisations are conducted in a transparent and open manner and do not raise any expectation of the award of a contract or licence.
- Adopting company-wide policies and procedures about the selection of charitable projects or initiatives which are informed by appropriate risk assessments.
- Training and support for staff in implementing the relevant policies and procedures of communication which allow issues to be reported and compliance to be monitored.
- If charitable donations made in country M are routinely channelled through government officials or to others at the official's request, a red flag should be raised and L may seek to monitor the way its contributions are ultimately applied, or investigate alternative methods of donation such as official 'off-set' or 'community gain' arrangements with the government of M.

- Evaluation of its policies relating to charitable donations as part of its next periodic review of its anti-bribery procedures.

CASE STUDY 9 – PRINCIPLE 4 DUE DILIGENCE OF AGENTS

A small UK company ('N') relies on agents in country ('P') from which it imports local high quality perishable produce and to which it exports finished goods. The bribery risks it faces arise entirely as a result of its reliance on agents and their relationship with local businessmen and officials. N is offered a new business opportunity in P through a new agent ('Q'). An agreement with Q needs to be concluded quickly.

N could consider any or a combination of the following:

- Conducting due diligence and background checks on Q that are proportionate to the risk before engaging Q; which could include:
    - making enquiries through N's business contacts, local chambers of commerce or business associations, or internet searches
    - seeking business references and a financial statement from Q and reviewing Q's CV to ensure Q has suitable experience.
- Considering how best to structure the relationship with Q, including how Q should be remunerated for its services and how to seek to ensure Q's compliance with relevant laws and codes applying to foreign public officials.
- Making the contract with Q renewable annually or periodically.
- Travelling to P periodically to review the agency situation.

CASE STUDY 10 – PRINCIPLE 2 TOP LEVEL COMMITMENT

A small to medium sized component manufacturer is seeking contracts in markets abroad where there is a risk of bribery. As part of its preparation, a senior manager has devoted some time to participation in the development of a sector wide anti-bribery initiative.

The top level management of the manufacturer could consider any or a combination of the following:

- The making of a clear statement disseminated to its staff and key business partners of its commitment to carry out business fairly, honestly and openly, referencing its key bribery prevention procedures and its involvement in the sectoral initiative.
- Establishing a code of conduct that includes suitable anti-bribery provisions and making it accessible to staff and third parties on its website.
- Considering an internal launch of a code of conduct, with a message of commitment to it from senior management.
- Senior management emphasising among the workforce and other associated persons the importance of understanding and applying the code of conduct and the consequences of breaching the policy or contractual provisions relating to bribery prevention for employees and managers and external associated persons.
- Identifying someone of a suitable level of seniority to be a point-person for queries and issues relating to bribery risks.

CASE STUDY 11 PROPORTIONATE PROCEDURES

A small export company operates through agents in a number of different foreign countries. Having identified bribery risks associated with its reliance on agents it is considering developing proportionate and risk based bribery prevention procedures.

The company could consider any or a combination of the following:

- Using trade fairs and trade publications to communicate periodically its anti-bribery message and, where appropriate, some detail of its policies and procedures.

- Oral or written communication of its bribery prevention intentions to all of its agents.
- Adopting measures designed to address bribery on its behalf by associated persons, such as:
    - requesting relevant information and conducting background searches
    - on the internet against information received
    - making sure references are in order and followed up
    - including anti-bribery commitments in any contract renewal
    - using existing internal arrangements such as periodic staff meetings to raise awareness of 'red flags' as regards agents' conduct, for example evasive answers to straightforward requests for information, overly elaborate payment arrangements involving further third parties, ad hoc or unusual requests for expense reimbursement not properly covered by accounting procedures.
- Making use of any external sources of information (UKTI, sectoral organisations) on bribery risks in particular markets and using the data to inform relationships with particular agents.
- Making sure staff have a confidential means to raise any concerns about bribery.

Index